ROADS AND TRACKWAYS
OF WALES

Roads and Trackways of
·Wales·

Richard Colyer

British Library Cataloguing in
Publication Data

Colyer Richard
     Roads and Trackways of Wales
     1. Roads — Wales — History
     2. Roads, Prehistoric — Wales —
     History
     I. Title
     388.1'09429   HE363.G74W3

ISBN 0 86190 122 3

Printed in the UK by Billings of Worcester
for the publishers Moorland Publishing
Co Ltd, 9-11 Station Street, Ashbourne,
Derbyshire, DE6 1DE England.
Telephone: (0335) 44486

Contents

Preface   7

Introduction   9

1 The Romans in the Mid-West   14

2 Some Medieval and Early Modern
     Roads in Cardiganshire   58

3 Pre-Turnpike Roads in Radnorshire   83

4 The Drovers   112

5 The Turnpike Era   140

Further Reading   183

Glossary of Welsh Words and Terms   186

Index   187

Preface

To date no book dealing exclusively with the history and development of the Welsh road network has appeared in English. The very extensive corpus of local history writing contains frequent references to the road system at various stages of its development, as do several scholarly works concerned with the social and economic history of the Principality. Yet many, if not most of these are not immediately accessible to the general reader unless he has the time and the inclination to wander along the shelves of the public library and to search among innumerable indices. One of the objectives of the present volume has been to disinter some of this material and, by studying in detail an admittedly narrow range of roads of different periods, to provide an introduction to the Welsh road network. And it claims to be little more than an introduction, for in a book of this size it is quite impossible to deal with more than a very modest area of the country. The industrial south and west and the counties of the north-east are largely ignored and I have tended, unashamedly, to concentrate my attention on those parts of Wales which give me most pleasure and which offer the traveller a rich extravaganza of scenic delights.

The roads described are a minute fraction of the thousands of miles of highway, lane and trackway through deep valley and open mountain, linking remote villages or isolated farmsteads, running grandly along riversides, or snaking sinuously through the hills. Some have experienced moments of great drama, others have been immemorially the humble channels of local trade; the haunt of farmer's cart, brewer's dray and pedlar's footfall. Yet all repay close investigation. The farmsteads, churches, wells and houses along a particular roadline — however humble at first glance — can provide the enthusiast with hours of pleasant diversion. A rather plain Victorian farmhouse may turn out to be built on the foundations of a much earlier and grander edifice, which may itself have been preceded by a settlement of medieval date, if not earlier. To the observant traveller prepared to do a little documentary research, a journey along a road can yield valuable insight into the social and economic history of the countryside so that the drudgery of walking the dog or of easing off an ample Sunday lunch can become a mini-voyage of discovery. To schoolchildren, history and geography and the natural environment can be brought thrillingly to life if they are freed temporarily from the classroom and taken for an afternoon's walk along one of the more dramatic mountain roads. I hope, then, that my readers, be they local historians, teachers or students, will be persuaded to arm themselves with OS 1:50,000 maps (or maps of larger scale), liberate themselves from the shackles of their cars and savour the pleasures of Wales on foot. If they take issue with some of the observations and conclusions in the forthcoming chapters then so much the better, since the study of the history of Welsh roads can only benefit from informed debate. I have approached the subject in a fairly conventional manner, beginning with a consideration of elements of the Roman network and working my way through to the turnpike system. However, I have not allowed myself to be altogether limited by considerations of chronology and where an interesting feature from another period occurs, say, alongside a Roman road, I have drawn attention to it. I hasten to point out, too, that I am well aware that the existence of an ancient church or field monument does not necessarily proclaim the antiquity of the road or trackway passing alongside it!

I have avoided footnotes in the text on the grounds that the 'general reader' tends to ignore them while the specialist, in any case, is normally familiar with the literature. Besides, this is an introductory book, compiled in the hope that others, working in detail on a local basis, will enlarge upon it and publish their findings, footnotes and all, in the scholarly journals. Many scholars, local historians and antiquarians will recognise their studies in the forthcoming pages and I apologise to any of these luminaries whose name fails to appear in the bibliography. Any such omission reflects my own incompetence and in no measure detracts from the importance and quality of their work. I must apologise too, to any purists who quibble with my rendering of Welsh place-names. I have been guided by Elwyn Davies' splendid *A Gazetteer of Welsh Place-Names* (Cardiff, 1975) so that any orthographical inexactitudes in the text may be ascribed to my inaccurate reading of that highly authoritative volume. Throughout the book I have adhered to pre-1974 county names on the grounds of both aesthetics and convenience.

I must acknowledge the help and critical advice of numerous friends and colleagues who, at one time or another, have commented on the contents of the forthcoming chapters. I am especially grateful in this regard to Professor D.J. Bowen, Mr D.M. Browne, Dr J.L. Davies, Dr C.S. Briggs, Dr R.A. Dodgshon and Dr M. Haycock, while I owe a particular debt of gratitude to Mr. J.J. Wells who has been responsible for the fine cartographic work throughout the book. To the Librarian and staff of the National Library of Wales I am particularly grateful and to the Vice-Principal of the University College of Wales I extend my thanks for financial assistance towards the cost of fieldwork and photographic materials. Finally, I must thank Mrs P. Mason, Mrs E.D. Thomas and Miss S. Jones who struggled with the desperate and depressing task of translating my handwriting into immaculate typescript. The aerial photographs on pages 28, 31, 43, 45 and 53 appear by courtesy of the University of Cambridge and those on pages 47, 87, 88, 102, 114, 115, 118, 137, 141, 142, 146, 147, 153, 158, 165, 172, 174, 177 and 181 by courtesy of the National Library of Wales. The remaining photographs are by the author.

Richard J. Colyer

Introduction

O happie princely Soyle, my pen is farre to bace,
My bare invention cold, and barraine verses vaine,
When they thy glory should unfold, they do thy Countrie staine.
Thy worth some worthie may, set out in golden lines,
And blaze ye same with colours gay, whose glistring beautie shines.
My boldness was to great, to take the charge in hand,
With wasted wits the braines to beat, to write on such a Land.

Thomas Churchyard
The Worthines of Wales, 1587

To the late Victorians civilisation flowed down the railway lines. Through the enormous expanses of sun-baked India, the massive emptiness of Canada's interior and the fabulous mysteries of Africa, Imperial rolling stock carried bicycles from Birmingham, bibles from east London and billhooks from Sheffield. Young men, too, fresh from comfortable villas in the Home Counties, their faces still pink and hands still soft, travelled hopefully down the iron roads towards unimaginable adventures. The London mandarins shouldering the heavy responsibility for Britain's embarrassingly expansive Empire genuinely believed that these youthful recruits would bring light to the Imperial darkness by promoting stable government, commerce and Christianity. Accordingly they viewed the railways as the great thoroughfares of western civilisation; of laws, of culture, of tiffin and cricket. Accompanied (often with disastrous consequences) by their starched and crinollined memsahibs, the young Victorians carried with them a system of culture and a moral code which had been many generations in the making. Neolithic farmers and their Bronze Age successors, embattled Iron Age tribesmen, lusty Saxon or Scandinavian sea-raiders and stern Normans, all contributed some minute element to the social and cultural makeup of the representative of the *Pax Britannica* who emerged from his train to blink in the harsh sunlight of India. To the native porters, if not to the French *boulevardiers* among whom he had spent his final vacation from Oxford, he was the epitome of civilised values.

It had taken the best part of ten millennia for the British to become an immensely successful Imperial power and throughout those long centuries, like the railways which they later built with such remarkable skill, roads and highways played a fundamental role in the development of the offshore island. Bronze and iron craft skills permeated southern Britain by way of sinuous tracks through the countryside, just as wine and olive oil from the Mediterranean reached the towns and villas of Roman Britain. Like the Dark Age Celtic missionaries landing on the rain-swept coastline of Wales, St Augustine would have had no difficulty in finding some sort of roadway through sixth-century Kent, even if, un-Christianlike, he cursed its poor condition. Pilgrims, pedlars, bards, thieves and civic dignitaries probably followed the same trackways (some of them along remaining stretches of the Roman road system) during the medieval and early modern periods while farmers drove their livestock along 'ways' established generations previously. Inevitably the forging of a 'way' heralded the onset of trade and the influx of external cultural influences. There was virtually no stopping them for, as we see today, only in the most remote and inaccessible regions of the world, like Amazonia and the mountains of western New Guinea, has the concept of external trade failed to develop. In Britain the ultimate expression of the road as a stimulus to trade and economic growth lay in the turnpikes whose steady gradients and 'metalled' surfaces facilitated the ready distribution of the manufactured goods of the early phases of the Industrial Revolution and the more effective movement of agricultural inputs and produce. Equally important, they allowed men to move about relatively rapidly and in comparative safety; the tradesman to his fair or market, the politician to his country weekend and the sporting gentleman to the fox-ridden Shires.

But how did it start? What was the origin of the trackways which already curved through the countryside of Britain by the Neolithic age? The short answer is that we don't really know and archaeologists and prehistorians have been distinctly reluctant to speculate upon this matter. However, where material evidence is non-existent or fragmentary, we must necessarily have recourse to intelligent speculation, in spite of the objections of those who believe that such speculation should never be made in the absence of documentary or, at the very least, artefactual evidence.

We can say with some certainty that with the recession of the third phase of the last glaciation, more or less complete by about 12,000BC, the climate gradually improved and tundra conditions gave way to scrublands of alder and hazel, and dense woodlands of birch and pine. Within this rather bleak environment, Mesolithic man, equipped with a wide range of flint implements, survived by way of hunting animals and gathering berries, roots and other natural products. Paleo-zoologists and archaeologists are now largely unanimous in the belief that hunting was by no means a random and haphazard operation, and that groups of Mesolithic hunters took great care in the selection of their prey so as to ensure that sufficient mature breeding animals survived to maintain stocks. In other words, they behaved in a similar manner to present-day sportsmen who will usually kill off surplus cock pheasants and avoid shooting hen birds in the latter part of the season. It seems, moreover, that our Mesolithic ancestors were able to exercise a considerable degree of control over the movements of their prey by the creation of carefully-planned fire-clearing areas in the forest. Fire clearance had the effect of stimulating new and highly digestible herbage growth to which deer, wild pigs and other grazing and rooting animals were fatally attracted. To the hunter this offered two major advantages. By positioning the cleared area close to his camp he was spared the fatiguing business of carrying his quarry over long distances, and in addition he could now be even more selective as to the animals he killed since he no longer had to wander around the forest on the off-chance of finding the odd animal, but now had an ample supply of game close to hand. Incidentally, fire clearing would have stimulated hazel growth and hence have produced a ready supply of nuts for direct human consumption. It is likely too, that the creation of fire clearings provided opportunities for cooperative hunting ventures — and, no doubt, for friction between neighbouring groups of hunters.

Previously hunting had been merely a matter of following animals along their natural migration routes which, in view of the tendency of herbivores to graze as they move, would have become broad trackways through the forest. Anyone who has driven cattle or sheep over long distances cannot fail to be impressed by their habit of spreading out over a wide area and grabbing a bite of herbage whenever the opportunity arises. Is it possible then, that in these migration routes we see the basis of some of the earliest roadlines, with animal trackways to fire-cleared areas providing further elements in a 'road' network? To the present author at least this model seems quite plausible and it may not be stretching credibility too far to argue that by late Mesolithic times a framework of tracks, maintained by the movements of animals and men, had been established throughout much of Britain.

Although there is a school of thought which holds that the indigenous Mesolithic inhabitants were making tentative beginnings at simple animal husbandry, there can be no doubt that it was the Neolithic farmers who first arrived in these islands around 4,000BC who possessed both the technology and the will to convert large expanses of the natural wildwood into productive farming land. Indeed, recent archaeological discoveries are emphasising the remarkable extent to which Neolithic and Bronze Age communities overcame the limits imposed by the environment. The older archaeology taught us that Neolithic settlement was limited to the higher chalk and limestone uplands where people lived in rather spartan conditions overlooking the dark, impenetrable and potentially hostile forests of the plains. However, developments in archaeological techniques and dating methods, together with a series of dry summers wherein aerial photography has revealed hitherto unidentified sites, has allowed archaeologists to elaborate a very different picture of the prehistoric landscape. With the important *caveat* that there were local and regional variations, we must now see the centuries between 4,000 and 2,000BC as a period of substantial increases in population and social organisation with large tracts of land in both the 'lowland' and 'highland' zones being cleared and intensively farmed. Heavy clayland and light sand, high plain and deep valley bottom, in fact virtually anywhere where the environment was suited to farming, all seem to have been settled at some stage and by 600 500BC farmsteads were widespread in England and Wales on all but the highest and bleakest of hills.

Careful examination of the agricultural technology available at the time (especially by workers at the Butser Ancient Farm Research Project in Hampshire) has established that by the Iron Age, man was quite capable of cultivating most soil types, including the most intractable clays. Even with the prevailing 'primitive' cereal varieties, there seems to have been at least a *potential* for surplus production so that it may no longer be strictly accurate to talk of the landscape of the immediate pre-Roman period as being dominated by 'subsistence' farming. This may apply equally in some upland and marginal areas of Britain, where the remnants of prehistoric arable field systems often survive in a predominantly pastoral landscape originally of Dark Age provenance.

Between the farmsteads and hamlets, perhaps superimposed on tracks already of great antiquity, lines of communication developed so that by the Roman conquest the countryside was already served by a network of 'proto-roads'. This being so, it has become necessary to review the importance of the so-called 'Ridgeways': the 'Jurassic Way', the 'Icknield Way' and the other prehistoric hill-top thoroughfares previously regarded as the major (and by some the sole) lines of communication in pre-Roman Britain. As Christopher Taylor has pointed out, important as these were, they were merely part of a complex pattern of trackways reaching out to virtually every corner of the country.

Knowing of the existence of these trackways is one thing; recognizing them on the ground is quite another matter. Many were transient drift ways between farmsteads and field systems, occasionally highlighted today on aerial photographs, while the more important long distance ways were used by subsequent generations so that all trace of their beginnings is lost. Indeed, it may be that many of our village lanes and even some of our arterial roads had their origins in tracks along which prehistoric men, perhaps trading flint or chert axes, skins or amber, warily picked their way. As with farm hand-tools, many of them evolving their basic structure in the Bronze and Iron Ages and changing only marginally before the Industrial Revolution, the idea of continuity is central to a consideration of the evolution of roads. Once a 'way' became established, its general line would be used over the centuries, though its *actual* course came to vary according to the type of traffic it carried and to locally changing patterns of land occupation and ownership.

In common with the rest of Britain, continuity of use through centuries, if not millennia, is a feature of roads in Wales. The Iron Age tribesman left his well-defended hill fort on the same track used by his medieval descendants and so on down through the ages until its curves and bends were rationalised by the measuring chains and levels of the eighteenth- and nineteenth-century turnpike surveyors. It is this very continuity which makes the precise dating of the origin of a given road so difficult, and this may go some way towards explaining the sparseness of the scholarly literature on the road system for the centuries between the departure of the Romans and the development of turnpiking. For Wales, at least, there are few reliable maps before the seventeenth century, while the early literary sources, though frequently providing a valuable impressionistic view of the countryside, cast little light on the detailed courses of roads. Medieval documents relating to estate boundaries and land settlement are helpful in working out short stretches of a road as it passes through a village or township as are the later estate maps, Enclosure Awards and Tithe Apportionments, used extensively in the present volume. To the meticulous local scholar some of the content of the medieval chapter in this volume will seem highly unsatisfactory in that time limitations and the broad scope of the book have precluded detailed study of the medieval material located in the bowels of the National Library of Wales and other depositories. I can only hope that this deficiency will serve to focus the attention of antiquaries upon the need for further study of the elements of the early road network in Wales.

Place and field names, place-name elements and a strong body of local tradition provide useful clues, if not to the origin, at least to the purpose of a particular road at a given stage of its history. To the contemporary Englishman the pronunciation of Welsh words often presents prodigious difficulties. To his forbears, employed as Enclosure or Tithe commissioners, as estate agents or bailiffs, enunciation of the words was a minor problem compared to the awesome business of committing them to paper. This led inevitably to quite remarkable corruptions, necessitating a cautious approach to, for example, the interpretation of field names on a Tithe Apportionment, many of them bearing little relation to their original meaning. The pioneering work of Melville Richards showed the enormous potential of the study of place names as a means of hanging flesh on the bare bones of documentary and archaeological evidence. As yet he has no true successor.

Aerial photography and a laudable increase in the rate of excavation is at last beginning gradually to lift the veil from the obscurity shrouding our knowledge of the landscape and economy of immediate pre-Roman Wales. Given the nature of the evidence it is perilous to generalise, yet we can state with some confidence that a great deal of the countryside was settled by farmers, their dwellings being constructed of stone, timber, or wattle-and-daub depending upon local availability of materials. Overlooked by the local hill fort — a vital refuge in time of crisis for both men and livestock — the Celtic farmer in the lowlands cultivated permanent arable fields to provide grains and pulses for household consumption and perhaps even for the subsistence of those of his breeding livestock which he chose to maintain over winter. During the summer months he drove his cattle to graze the hills and in so doing probably passed over the remnants of the attempts of his Bronze Age ancestors to establish permanent farmsteads on the uplands. Sadly, their efforts were overwhelmed by a heartbreaking combination of acidic soils and wet climate and the remains of their settlement sites were taken over by later generations of pastoralists.

The constant struggle to farm was made more difficult by the need to be forever on guard against the avaricious attentions of the neighbours across the river or on the other side of the oak coppice and as he applied his hand to the plough or seed basket, our farmer would have ensured that his weapons were never far away. Moreover, he would be called upon to use these same weapons from time to time in the service of his clan chief. Like the Saxons and Scandinavians of a later date then, the Iron Age tribesman was concurrently a farmer and a fighting man, loyal to his chief and subject to the will of a curious pantheon of rather nasty gods. It was against such men that the Imperial legions of Rome were obliged to try their strength as they faced the moist west wind and advanced bravely into the Welsh heartland.

The Romans
in the
Mid-West

I love roads:
The goddesses that dwell
Far along them invisible
Are my favourite gods

Edward Thomas (1878-1917), *Roads*

Beyond the rich plains of England the Romans first encountered the forest and mountain peoples of Wales. Isolated, except in the borderlands, from the influence of the Belgic communities in south-east England, and out of contact with the cross-channel trade so important to cultural developments in that part of Britain, most of the Welsh tribes, in terms of material culture at least, were in a relatively primitive state on the eve of the Roman conquest. Much of Wales lay in what has become termed the 'highland zone'. Here mountain barriers, moorland bogs and rapidly-flowing rivers combined to produce an environment which was a positive godsend to the guerilla fighter, as the Romans were to learn to their cost. Struggling against the rigours of a damp climate, and more often than not, belligerent neighbours, the tribesman wrested a living from the stony, acidic and unrewarding soil. The deeper into the mountains he lived, the greater the likelihood of his farming tools and implements being made of stone and bronze, since in some areas iron tools were even now regarded as a luxury. While he grew a limited quantity of corn for his household and animals our tribesman, in the upland zones at any rate, was essentially a pastoralist living in a small, strongly-defended homestead, an 'open' settlement, or one of the many hill forts some of which continued to be occupied well into the Roman period. From settlements like Tre'r Ceiri in Caernarfonshire, a hill fort densely occupied with huts, the Welsh farmed their lands and mounted sporadic campaigns against the Romans for whom they were to remain a thorn in the flesh for several decades after the initial invasion.

Of the five great Welsh tribes, perhaps the most formidable were the ruddy, curly-haired Silures who held strongholds in the Black Mountains and also occupied one of the few extensive tracts of fertile, easily-workable land in Wales: the coastal plains of Glamorgan and Monmouthshire. To the north, in the hilly terrain of mid-Wales, the powerful and warlike Ordovices held sway, keeping a watchful eye on their neighbours the Gangani who, according to Ptolemy, spent their lives on the remote Llŷn Peninsula. Further north still, in the mineral-rich

14

countryside of Flintshire, lived the Decangli, while the vales of the Tywi and Teifi and the foothills of the Cambrian Mountains were the province of the Demetae.

During the early stages of their campaign to subdue the Welsh, the Romans do not seem to have conceived any grand overall plan, preferring instead to deal with each tribal insurrection as it occurred. They had optimistically believed that morale among the tribes would crumble following the defeat of Caractacus' armies in AD51. Despite this victory and the delivery of Caractacus himself into Roman hands by the treachery of the Queen of the Brigantes, the Ordovices (and to a lesser extent the Silures), continued to offer spirited resistance and vigorously defied Roman attempts to penetrate their territory.

This seems to have steeled Roman resolve and in AD60 Suetonius Paulinus, a seasoned African campaigner, marched against the rebellious Ordovices, taking with him the young Agricola who was to become Governor of Britain twenty years later. Paulinus' main objective was the Druidic stronghold on Anglesey. By wiping out the Druids he believed that he would at one and the same time obliterate a source of material resistance and a cult of great ritual significance. The Romans, as Gibbon tells us, generally adopted a liberal attitude towards the religious observances of their subject peoples. Their own enthusiasm for blood-letting in the interests of entertainment was well developed, yet they found the Druidic practice of using human victims for sacrifice and augury especially repulsive and were unswerving in their determination to destroy the cult. Such edifying thoughts may have passed through the minds of the legionaries as they marched towards the Menai Straits and, like Cromwell's Ironsides approaching a lovely village church, they probably relished the prospect of pulling down the Druids' sacred groves. As they began to cross the Straights in their flat-bottomed boats they were confronted by the blood-chilling sight of Druidic elders pouring terrible curses upon them and, as Tacitus explains '. . . the British army in dense array and lots of black-robed women brandishing torches, their hair dishevelled like Furies'. For a moment it was touch and go, the superstitious Roman troops being terrified by the appalling curses of the formidable Druids. Once they had landed on the Anglesey beaches, though, they recovered their composure and professionalism, and having launched their attack achieved an overwhelming victory. It was now merely a matter of mopping up odd pockets of resistance before establishing firm control over the island.

Before the accession of Flavius Vespasianus to the Imperial throne in AD69, the Romans seem to have lacked the determination to get on with the job and subdue Britain once and for all, their activities being characterized by protracted fighting and stop-go policies. The Flavian period, however, was in marked contrast and after they had rehabilitated those parts of Britain ravaged by the Boudiccan revolt, the military commanders took the decision to grasp the nettle and commit resources to the final conquest and subjugation of the northern island. It was within this political climate that the completion of the conquest of Wales was undertaken in AD74-78 by Julius Frontinus, Governor of Britain and his successor in that post, Julius Agricola. Druidic influence had been destroyed, yet the mountain ranges of Snowdonia and the Berwyns still offered succour to the violently anti-Roman Ordovices. Probably operating from the massive fortress of *Deva* (Chester) or even *Virconium* (Wroxeter) and making full use of the garrison facilities which he had established on the periphery of Ordovician territory, Agricola led a punitive force against the enemy in AD78. He was intent on exacting terrible revenge on the Ordovices who had virtually annihilated a Roman cavalry regiment the previous year. Ordering his men to give no quarter, he exterminated almost the whole tribe and followed up his victory by establishing a series of subsidiary military stations.

Even before Agricola's successes in North Wales, Julius Frontinus had advanced into Silurian country where he founded a system of forts based on *Isca* (Caerleon). This became the headquarters of the Second Legion and for long remained the centre of the Roman south-western command and a point of contact with the civil zone across the River Severn. In contrast to the situation in the uplands which essentially remained 'undeveloped' throughout the Roman period, the vales of Glamorgan and Monmouth offered opportunities for urban and agricultural development and in due course villas and rural estates began to mushroom under the protection of garrisons at Cardiff, Caerleon and elsewhere.

Unlike the Ordovices and the Silures, the Demetae in the south-west may grudgingly have accepted Roman rule, perhaps as a means of gaining protection from harassment by their Silurian neighbours. Certainly there are very few signs of military settlement in Demetian territory (and hence a paucity of Roman roads) while sites like Castell Gogan between the estuaries of the Tywi and Taff, and Coygan near Laugharne suggest, as do other excavated native sites, strong evidence of Romanization. It is important to appreciate, however, that the apparent lack of military fortifications does not necessarily reflect ready acceptance of the conquerors by a timid native tribe and may with equal likelihood be a manifestation of Roman military strategy. The relative sophistication of recently discovered native sites in the lower-lying areas runs counter to Sir Mortimer Wheeler's observation back in the 1930s, that the native peasantry of this part of Wales had little real contact with the Roman world. In particular, excavation of elements of the fine Roman town of *Moridunum* (Carmarthen) with its civic amenities and well-preserved amphitheatre, has revealed beyond doubt the considerable scope and extent of Roman influence in the area. Further excavation will probably show that this remarkable cantonal capital lacked few of the facilities of towns in the civil zone to the east of the Severn.

The map of Roman Wales took on the form of a defensive quadrilateral based on the great legionary fortresses of *Deva* and *Isca* to the east and the auxiliary stations of *Segontium* (Carnarfon) and *Moridunum* to the west. Within this quadrilateral lay a series of forts centred on Caersws and Brecon. Rectangular in shape, the forts of the interior were surrounded by deep ditches and ramparts and contained granaries, workshops, barracks and administrative offices. Granaries (*horrea*) were particularly important since each station was expected to hold a full year's grain supply. Garrisoned by hardy troops and serviced by the interconnecting road system, the forts and fortlets served as a constant reminder of the danger, if not the futility, of flouting the rule of Rome. At the height of the conquest period of the late 70s some 28,000 soldiers were operational in Wales although this number had declined to around 13,500 towards the end of the first century by which time much of the countryside had been subjugated. The evidence provided by inscribed stones and stamped tiles enables us to identify at least some of the units of the Roman army involved in the conquest of Wales. Basically the job was undertaken by two legions, *Legio II Augusta* (operating out of *Isca*) and *Legio XX Valeria Victrix* which succeeded *Legio II Adiutrix* about AD86 and was stationed at *Deva*. Apart from a hundred or so cavalrymen, each legion was made up of 5,300 men, of whom all were Roman citizens and the great majority volunteers. These were the frontline troops; relatively well-paid, highly trained and severely disciplined. They were assisted by auxiliary regiments 500 or 1,000 strong, mostly comprising non-Roman citizens whose reward for 25 years of service (provided they survived it) was a grant of citizenship. From Gaul, Germany, Spain and other outposts of the Empire, these auxiliaries functioned primarily as garrison troops carrying out dreary routine patrol and police duties from the forts and fortlets along the road network. Soldiers in units like *Cohors II Asturum* and *Ala Hispanorum Vettonum* must have rued the day they left the sunny valleys of northern Spain as they cursed the dank atmosphere of Cardiganshire or shivered behind the ramparts of the fort at Brecon Gaer. They would certainly have been envious of the relative security and comfort enjoyed by their legionary colleagues in the massive structures at *Deva* and *Isca*.

In AD75, after 25 years of struggle against the Silures, the Romans began to raise the fine town of *Venta Silurum* (Caerwent) in the hope that as the town evolved the natives would be impressed as much by an example of civilised living as by the military power of their aggressors. To make sure that any necessary lessons in civilised living could be well-enforced, Julius Frontinus built the military headquarters of *Isca* several miles away. The fortress originally contained timber buildings and earth and timber defences, these being replaced with more permanent stone structures in the second century. It must have been a tremendous and awesome sight in its heyday. Twelve hundred years after the place had been abandoned, Thomas Churchyard could still write:

Now I must touch, a matter fit to knowe,
A fort and strength, that stands beyond this towne,
In which you shall behold the noblest showe . . . .

This remarkable edifice was occupied for some 250 years before finally being abandoned when, like other deserted forts, it went steadily into decline. The removal of roofing material and stone for domestic buildings, stimulated by '. . . a principle of avarice', as the eighteenth-century antiquarian Warner put it, set into motion an inevitable process of decay. The inexorable powers of the elements were complemented by the obsessive craving of travellers and antiquaries for mementos of their travels. After happily procuring Roman coins for 6d each at *Venta Silurum* in 1787, the Hon John Byng moved to *Isca* where he wandered around the ruins and poked about among the rubble with his stick. His efforts were well-rewarded. Sitting over his wine that same evening he wrote, 'I thought it behoved me to peep about for something to carry off with me and write about, so I was lucky in stumbling on the fragment of a Roman brick on which some letters are very legible.' Against such odds, the elegantly excavated and preserved fortress remains are with us today, serving as a reminder of the remarkable military and organisational skills of its founders.

In contrast to *Isca*, the majority of the forts, fortlets and practice camps in the Welsh military zone are now recognisable only from aerial photographs or from the remains of grassy banks, terraces and ditches which, with pottery finds or coins, provide tell-tale chronological clues for the specialist. The pattern of occupation — desertion — re-occupation of the sites mentioned in this chapter was often highly complex according to the exigencies of warfare. We find, for example, the early fortlet of Erglodd, near Talybont in Cardiganshire being re-occupied after a period of abandonment, while Caerau, Brecknockshire, was reduced in size following the slimming down of the garrison in Trajan's reign. By the time of Hadrian (AD117-138) this process of garrison reduction, and thus alteration of the extent of fortress defences, had extended to Llandovery and Pumsaint in Carmarthenshire and Llanio and Trawsgoed in Cardiganshire, these latter two having been abandoned for good by AD125.

The visit to Britain of Hadrian himself in AD122 and his decision to build a great wall on the northern frontier of his dominions, was responsible for the abandonment or reduction in scale of some of the forts, whose occupants trudged reluctantly northwards to work on the wall. The re-occupation of southern Scotland and the construction of the Antonine Wall some years later precipitated further abandonment of Welsh forts, although by AD140, several of those remaining had been consolidated, their defences and administrative buildings being remodelled in stone. Owing largely to the absence of readily dateable pottery the subsequent history of most of the Welsh forts is rather shadowy. There seems to have been a dramatic reduction in the Roman military presence in the south after AD160-180 as the Silures and Demetae came to accept the fact of occupation, and by the later third and fourth centuries those forts still in use were apparently functioning as police posts, as opposed to military centres. In this late period the fortification of Caergybi, Holyhead, represents virtually the only major new Roman military work.

As the earthen ramparts and timber towers of the early forts were being thrown up, the locals (or, at least those of them who already regarded guerilla warfare against the Romans as a pointless exercise), naturally became curious about their stern and powerful overlords and it was not long before native settlements began to spring up outside the fortress walls. From these developed the *vici*, which modern excavation is uncovering in association with a number of the more important forts. These *vici*, whose fortunes tended to follow those of the fort, housed local craftsmen and traders along with the usual camp followers, and must have been the nearest thing to a Romanised township that people in the more remote regions would have seen. To them the villas and rural estates of the Vales of Glamorgan and Monmouth and the urban centre at Carmarthen, must have been rather like the city of Oxford to the medieval Cornish peasant; something to be talked of and wondered at, but never to be seen. Though they would have had access to some of the coinage and ceramic work which came with the legions, Romanization would have been very modest indeed. A little more land would have been taken into cultivation to provide for the needs of the forts while they remained occupied and there might even have been local improvements in building technology, but taken overall the Roman presence would have had very little effect on the landscape or way of life of people in the Welsh uplands. They remained for the most part in their farmsteads and maintained only sporadic and casual contact with the Roman money economy.

Military conquest and the subsequent control of a newly-conquered area through a chain of forts and fortlets required, above all, a good system of communications to enable the rapid movement of troops and the provisioning of their barracks. Apart from the numerous personnel who fed and equipped the soldiers, the force landing in south-east England in AD43 comprised 40,000 fighting men and it soon became clear to its commanders that the pre-existing trackways were quite inadequate to provide effectively for the movement of pack animals, ox-carts, cavalry and the whole paraphernalia of an invasion army. So the legions, aided by a grudging army of slaves, set out to build the extraordinary system of roads which were to remain virtually the only *constructed* highways prior to the proliferation of the turnpikes in the eighteenth century. Upwards of 6,000 miles of road were built throughout Britain, most of these being completed in the first hundred years of Roman occupation. Initially the roads were of an exclusively military nature, facilitating the constant patrolling of army units in a country whose inhabitants had not yet accepted the inevitability of Roman domination. By the 50s the Romans had already extracted lead and silver from veins in the Mendips and Derbyshire and as they turned their attention towards the exploitation of other mineral deposits in their newly-acquired territory, road building became a vital component in the economic development as well as the military subjugation of the island. New roads carried iron from the Weald of Kent and the Forest of Dean, tin from Cornwall, gold from Carmarthenshire, copper from Anglesey and Montgomeryshire and lead from central and northern Wales. Moreover, as Britain as a whole became progressively Romanised, these same roads became channels for the distribution of the imported pottery, wines, fine craftwork and other luxury goods demanded by an increasingly civilised population. Concurrently there developed a complex of minor roads, many as yet undiscovered, linking the villas, farms and towns growing up in the lowland civil zone. The civil zone excluded the majority of Wales, yet it is worth emphasizing the point made elsewhere by Christopher Taylor that it was probably the minor road system which drew much of Britain into the Roman Empire and provided the means whereby Imperial thought and policy was able to influence the people in every possible social, economic and political manner.

We have virtually no written records describing the actual *construction* of the Roman roads in Britain so we are obliged to rely entirely on observation and excavation to elucidate the nature of the road surface, the materials used and other matters of technical detail. We do, however, have a very clear picture of how the legions went about the business of deciding on the overall alignment of their roads and how they carried out the necessary surveys before starting construction. The achievements of the *agrimensores*, the trained surveyors responsible for fixing the major road lines, were quite astonishing. Working in hostile environments under constant threat of attack from recalcitrant natives they managed remarkable feats of engineering.

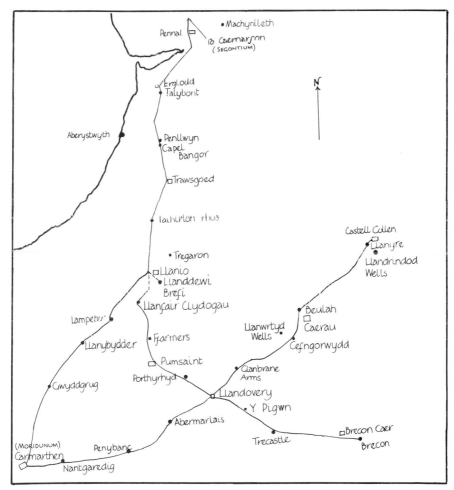

The Roman road network in southern-central and west Wales.

Bearing in mind that his principal objective was to create a road providing the army with an opportunity for rapid movement and relative security from attack, the surveyor's first task was to carry out a general study of the area. This involved gathering local information about pre-existing trackways, the best points for fording rivers and avoiding marshy ground and other aspects of the terrain which would help him to decide where deviations in alignment or major changes in direction were likely to be needed. Having carefully noted this information our surveyor, with his assistants and servants now set out to examine the ground, to assess the difficulties posed by major obstacles, boggy terrain and excessive inclines and finally to decide upon the actual line of the road. Constantly aware of strategic objectives and the fact that the personnel laying out the road would be relatively unskilled, the surveyor sought a road line which could be laid out from point-to-point with lengths as straight as natural conditions and engineering convenience permitted. On the lowland this implied angular changes of direction to avoid natural obstacles, with short zigzag lengths to facilitate ascents of hillsides. In upland country, however, the principle of the angular change of direction was often abandoned in favour of following the contour or of securing a constant gradient, although wherever possible the zigzag method would be used to get to the top of a ridge. Indeed, ridge-top road lines with commanding views were eagerly sought by surveyors and engineers as these provided more secure travelling conditions than the wooded and boggy valley bottoms.

The surveyor's ultimate task was to fix and mark the final position of the road before construction. This was a relatively simple matter involving the use of a set of movable markers — poles or possibly fire baskets — which were visible over considerable distances from adjacent points. In hill and upland country, visibility would frequently have been possible only with hilltop markers, which may explain the frequent changes of direction of Roman roads in this sort of terrain. It is worth remembering too, that since the bulk of the earlier roads in the uplands were used almost exclusively for the package trains and foot patrols of the military, they did not need to be specially sophisticated. Indeed, there is some evidence that less skilled engineers were employed in their construction than was the case with the great lowland roads. Also, in Wales and other 'military' zones of Britain, eventual troop withdrawal gave way to rather less sophisticated civil government than in the lowland and this may partially account for the relative lack of development of the road system.

The quality of Roman roads and the methods of construction varied widely according to local topography and the availability of materials. Though subject to overall supervision, the engineers responsible for specific sections seem to have been left to decide details of construction for themselves so that we find a great deal of variation in material used along the length of any given road. Some were laid out with foundations of large stones surfaced with gravel, others were elaborately paved with slabs and others still were simply tracks with little or no definite plan or surface material, this last category being particularly common among the minor roads in the highland zone. Invariably the Roman engineer sought a firm well-drained base for his road and where this was not available he built embankments (*aggeres*) of large stones or earth often 45-50ft wide and 4-5ft high. Elsewhere the road might be laid between drainage ditches on a foundation of large stones topped with rammed gravel, clay and turf, a central rib-stone and large kerbs lending stability to the structure. The major roads through low-lying country, frequently carried on substantial *aggeres*, varied from 12 to 28ft in width. In broken and mountainous terrain, however, the *aggeres*, if present at all, were usually rather modest affairs and the sophisticated structural techniques employed on the lowland gave way to simple terraced roads of as little as 10ft wide. These, like so many early roads in hill country, are now extremely difficult to trace.

Even more difficult to find, in both hill and lowland, are the points where the road crossed a river or stream. Natural fords seem to have been used wherever possible, often necessitating an alteration in the alignment of the road as it approached the watercourse. Alternatively a ford could be constructed on the original alignment or, in the case of a deep, narrow stream, a culvert built to carry the water under the road. Wide and unfordable rivers were crossed by bridges of timber and stone and the few vestiges suggest that these were often of massive construction with wide embankments or ramps approaching the edge of the water.

Besides the important military and commercial roads with their bridges and milestones and heavy traffic of soldiers, imperial officials and traders, there were the thousands of miles of local trackways serving the purposes of both agriculture and trade. Of recent years aerial photography has revealed surprising numbers of these trackways in many parts of the country from the wet Welsh hills to the chalk lands of the south and from the clay vales of the Shires to the limestone ridges of the south-west. As we have come to know more about the Roman road network in Britain, there has inevitably been a tendency to link known Roman tracks and highways to existing roads, thereby fabricating a complex of routeways which relate in no way whatsoever to the original Roman pattern. There is nothing new in this beguiling temptation to connect existing roads with Roman roadlines and the quest for the detailed course of Roman routes in Wales has not been helped by the obsession of antiquaries over the past three hundred years for this subject. Virtually any trackways looking remotely straight and ancient were often, by prodigious feats of the imagination, conjured into Roman roads and duly recorded in learned articles, most of which need to be read with a highly critical eye. A parish boundary, for example, may follow a 'modern' road in a straight line across country for several miles, but this does not necessarily bespeak a Roman road. It *may* follow a Roman road, but in the final analysis this can only be substantiated by careful study of the relationship of the road to landscape features such as bogs, waterways and the like and by seeking uniquely Roman features including rib and kerb stones and gravel metalling. This implies excavation, of which, for one reason or other, there has been lamentably little in Wales. Thus words like 'may', 'might', 'possibly' and 'probably' will feature with tedious regularity throughout this chapter!

Essentially the Welsh road network evolved from the major military routes between Chester and Caernarfon and those from Caerleon, Cardiff and Brecon connecting with the forts, camps and mining centres of the heartland. The total complex of roads, gradually being elaborated by detailed fieldwork, covers far too large an area for a book of this size and I have chosen to concentrate on the major elements of the road network in southern-central and west Wales, an important military and mining area. The roads considered will include those connecting Carmarthen, Llandovery, Llandrindod Wells and Brecon and the *Sarn Helen*, linking Llandovery with Pennal on the Dyfi Estuary and ultimately with Caernarfon on the Menai Straits.

SARN HELEN

The Flavian auxiliary fort at Pennal on the northern bank of the River Dyfi was a vital link in the chain of military structures between Caernarfon and the Roman establishments in south Wales. Lying in part beneath the buildings of Cefngaer Farm (SN704001), the fort covered rather more than 4.4 acres and is believed to have accommodated a garrison of some 500 men. As much of the original fort is now overlain by Cefngaer Farm (itself of some antiquity) little remains to be seen apart from a few grass-grown banks marking the original earthen ramparts. Even so, the visitor can readily appreciate the strategic importance of the site lying, as it did, at the southern extreme of the great block of the Snowdonia range and at the mouth of the tidal Dyfi. Here, at the junction of land and seaways, this isolated garrison was ideally placed to supervise the *Sarn Helen* road and to keep a close eye on seafarers in Cardigan Bay. Moreover, as with the fortlet at Erglodd further south, it would have been possible, given the high probability of the river having run close to the outer walls in Roman times, to provision the fort by sea if this became necessary.

The early stages of the southerly course taken by the Roman road are as obscure as the origin of the name *Sarn Helen* itself. The existence of place and field names embodying the word *sarn* (causeway) has often been taken as indicative of the presence of a Roman road or trackway although of course, such a causeway (or assumed causeway) may equally be of medieval or even later provenance. While *Sarn* has a clear meaning in English, *Helen* presents difficulties. Most probably *Helen* is a corruption of *Lleng* (legion), hence *Sarn-y-Lleng* (road of the legion) or rather less likely a corruption of *halen* (sea, salt) thereby referring to the relatively close proximity of the road to the coastline of Cardigan Bay. Tradition, nurtured by the writing of Geoffrey of Monmouth and the chroniclers of the Welsh epic *The Mabinogion* links the name of the road with Elen, daughter of a native chieftain married to the Roman Magnus Maximus who, in AD388, marched on Rome with his Welsh allies to lay claim to the Imperial throne. There is strong evidence to support the belief that Magnus (or Macsen Wledig as the Welsh chroniclers preferred to call him) did attempt to grab the crown with the assistance of troops from Wales, only to be defeated at the hands of the Emperor Theodosius. Whether he married a Welsh girl called Elen is another matter, yet it may not be without significance that his name features in the genealogies of a number of Dark Age Welsh princes.

The derivation of the name of the road is likely to remain a tantalising mystery as indeed is the point where it crossed the tidal reaches of the River Dyfi. Tracing

Modern fenceline running along embankments of the Roman fort at Pennal.

The River Dyfi near Furnace; Pennal lies in the far distance

ancient roads in estuarine areas is fraught with problems, not the least being the irritating habit of rivers to change their courses quite substantially over a short span of years. Even in non-tidal areas many rivers exhibit a high rate of channel mobility as indicated by Dr John Lewin's findings that some Welsh rivers annually shift course to the extent of between 0.1 per cent and 5.5 per cent of their areas. This being so, it is virtually certain that any remains of Roman agger in the vicinity of the Dyfi estuary were swept away centuries ago.

The very absence of material has yielded a rich harvest of speculation as to the location of the Roman ford (or even bridge) across the Dyfi. One school of thought favours a crossing point near the present Llugwy Hotel to the south-east of the fort where the river forms a narrow channel with firm ground adjoining it on either bank. Supporters of this view see the southerly course of *Sarn Helen* running either by way of one of the several old trackways across Bwlcheinion towards the Llyfnant Valley, or along the line of the modern A487 as it curves around the edge of the hills towards the village of Furnace. A crossing near the Llugwy Hotel, of course, pre-supposes that the river occupied its present position in Roman times. The second of the more plausible theories proposes that the trackway from the south-western gate of the fort may have been carried by a causeway over the mud-flats to cross the river some distance to the south-west. A few yards below the point where a trackway issues from the present farm buildings, two pre-Flavian glazed-ware vases and a red-ware *mortarium* were discovered several years ago in what some authorities believe to be the remains of a burnt-out building of Roman origin. Although the remnants of the trackway (now a farm lane) peter out in the wet land towards the river it is noteworthy that a continuation would have aligned closely with the medieval motte and bailey on the *south* bank of the Dyfi at Domen Las (SN687969). A medieval site at this location, where the river makes a great curve around the boggy saltings, suggests not only a crossing point but that here at least, the course of the Dyfi has not changed significantly in the last millennium however much it may have changed elsewhere in the estuary. Standing on a rocky eminence amid a bird reserve, the motte commands a tremendous view of the mountains to the north and the sea to the west. From this lonely spot, where heron, teal and mallard abound and the weird cry of the curlew hangs on the wind, it is not difficult to conjure up a vivid image of a solitary Roman patrol heading across the marshes for the river crossing.

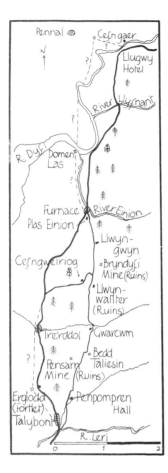

Bryndyfi lead mine remains

Pennal to Talybont

The presumed Roman road from Furnace to Talybont

Before 1976, this suggestion would have seemed rather far-fetched. However, during the dry summer of that year aerial photography identified the turf ramparts of a Roman fortlet on the farm of Erglodd (SN653905) between the villages of Taliesin and Talybont some 8 miles to the south of the fort at Pennal. Located near the significantly-named *Cae maes y palman (palman, palmant* = pavement), the fortlet, whose surface features are no longer visible, occupied an area of some 0.625 acres. Dr J.L. Davies has carefully surveyed this Flavian site and has suggested that it may have formed an important element in the well-established fort-fortlet-fort system of Roman control, particularly as it lies more-or-less equidistant between the forts at Pennal and Penllwyn, near Capel Bangor (SN650806). The fortlet was clearly built to police the Leri river crossing in Talybont and to supervise traffic passing from Pennal to Penllwyn, from which one must conclude that it lay in close proximity to a Roman road. Such a road probably pursued roughly the line of the present A487 and linked with the Dyfi crossing at Domen Las or elsewhere. Following S.J.S. Hughes's discovery that certain objects from Roman sites in west Cardiganshire contain lead from mines in the Talybont area, it seems that the Erglodd fortlet also served as an administrative centre for lead or silver mining activities. Certainly there is strong circumstantial evidence to substantiate a claim for Roman mining in the vicinity of Erglodd and in the woods on the bank to the east of the fortlet. Indeed the name *Erglodd* itself might even be a corruption of *Aurglodd (aur* = gold, *cloddfa* = mine, excavation) thereby hinting at the possibility even of gold mining in the vicinity of this site.

The identification of the Erglodd fortlet proves beyond reasonable doubt that there existed a Roman road (whose detailed course we can now only surmise) linking the Leri crossing at Talybont with Pennal. The question, however, arises as to whether this formed part of the *Sarn Helen* system or whether the latter took what is traditionally believed to be the Roman road running along the country lanes through the hills between Furnace and Talybont. This 'upper' road, was obliged to negotiate several steep-sided valleys, yet it would have possessed the advantage of directness, besides commanding extensive views of the surrounding countryside. It tends, furthermore, to be laid out in short, straight alignments with typically angular changes of alignment at several points. Could there have been two roads? Since the Erglodd fortlet is known to have been abandoned in the mid-second century, and presumably the road with it, is it possible that the 'upper' route was subsequently developed to provide for patrols and to service mining ventures in the hills? All we really know is that this is an old and important road as the early maps indicate, and that apart from a lengthy tradition, there is at present no evidence to prove whether or not it is of Roman origin. The road traverses unspoilt countryside of quiet beauty and I make no apology for describing its course, hoping, as I do so, that people will walk and enjoy it and that some day it will be subjected to more detailed investigation.

Leaving the A487 below the old smeltery in Furnace (SN685952) the road climbs steeply along the western side of the Einion valley to pass behind Plas Einion. Here, where the present road swings eastwards, the old lane is carried straight on, its overgrown course being contained by stone walls on either side until it is crossed by another trackway towards the top of the hill (SN684946). Before long the walls sweep away from the road which is now carried along the outskirts of a patch of woodland on a raised causeway, constructed in all probability when it was used as a coach road in the eighteenth century. At Llwyngwyn (SN683941) our lane is crossed by a modern forestry road beyond which it runs south-westwards between finely-constructed eighteenth-century stone walls to pass the Victorian ruins of the Bryndyfi Lead Mine (SN683934). With extensive remains of the dressing floors, ore bins, crusher house and wheelpit, Bryndyfi is a veritable feast for the industrial archaeologist. As happened so often, the speculators investing in all this high quality masonry failed fully to investigate the potential yield of the underlying lead seams and the enterprise collapsed within two years of the mine's opening in 1881. Workers engaged during the brief life of the mine enjoyed much the same exquisite views as Roman patrolmen fifteen hundred years beforehand. As they watched banks of rain sweeping from the sea through the hillside woodlands of oak, birch and alder, both may have thrilled to the curves of the estuary and to the mysterious and rather menacing Borth Bog, source of a rich corpus of Celtic legend.

After a long, slow ascent from Llwyngwyn the old lane drops down to join the metalled road for Cefngweirog Farm at SN680933. From this junction the logical Roman alignment would have been straight across the fields to the east of the farm in the direction of the Clettwr valley. However, there have been no finds of metalling or causeway in the reseeded fields, so it must be assumed that the older road followed the present one on its course along the slightly higher ground, passing through a larch plantation and eventually aligning with Gwarcwm Farm on the south side of the deep gulch of the River Clettwr (SN674917). Here the two roads diverge, the metalled one being carried across the narrow river by a handsome single-span bridge of nineteenth-century type. The earlier road takes the line of a wet and overgrown trackway running parallel to and below the metalled road and reaching the river some forty yards west of the present bridge where the stone abutments of an old bridge of indeterminate age proclaim a crossing point. Some ten feet away, on the opposite side of the rapidly-flowing Clettwr, the early road continues until it once again picks up the metalled lane past Gwarcwm towards Pensarn Farm (SN669910), passing on the way the remains of a disturbed Early Bronze Age cairn. *Bedd Taliesin*, as the cairn is so-called, is traditionally reckoned to be the last resting place of the sixth century poet, Taliesin. The association of this strangely evocative site with Taliesin provides for an attractive legend, but the story has no basis in fact and the cairn, like several others of similar type in the area may well mark the grave of a Bronze Age chieftain

Victorian bridge over the Clettwr with line of earlier road in foreground

or other man of distinction. Within the precincts of Pensarn Farm, a hundred yards or so below the cairn, travellers will notice the abandoned nineteenth-century chapel languishing among modern farm buildings of the usual unprepossessing type. This originally served the thriving community of miners who struggled to win lead from the Pensarn Mine (SN668912). The remains of the mine workings are visible in the fields to the north-west of the farm, a late nineteenth-century wheelhouse being built into the stone wall of a nearby lane.

Between Pensarn and Talybont, the assumed route is by way of the present minor road past Penpompren Hall and on to the crossing of the River Leri at the site of the bridge carrying the A487 out of the village (SN655892). While there is no doubt that the roads from Pensarn and Erglodd crossed the Leri at this point, there is virtually no field, no place name, no photographic or other evidence to lend substance to the claim that the above road represents the precise Roman line. On the other hand it is difficult to imagine any alternative since, if they had tried to forge even a slightly more direct route, the Roman engineers would inevitably have had to confront the problem of crossing the very steep valley of Cwm Ceulan.

TALYBONT TO PENLLWYN AND TRAWSCOED

In the mid-nineteen seventies, an aerial photographic survey revealed the subterranean remains of one of the largest Roman forts in western Wales. For some time archaeologists had postulated the probable location of a fort guarding the crossing of the River Rheidol, and the discovery of Penllwyn (SN650806) overlooking the river from a west-facing slope behind the village of Capel Bangor, established both the river crossing and the line of *Sarn Helen*. Excavation of the seven acre site, whose remains are barely visible on the ground, suggested that the fort was occupied during the Flavian-Hadrianic period and deliberately demolished when abandoned.

The Roman road linking this fort with the Leri crossing unquestionably takes the line of the present minor road between Talybont and Capel Bangor by way of Penrhyncoch, a road given some prominence on Thomas Kitchin's map of 1752. Known locally as 'The Roman Road', it leaves the A487 some 300yds south of the Leri to run past the Iron Age camp at Llettyllwyd and then to the west of Elgar Farm (where a field called *cae sarn* runs close to the road at SN651862) before running into Penrhyncoch. Apart from the complete lack of evidence of any alternative roadline, it has been carefully laid out to avoid excessive slopes and also offers the most direct and easy route between the two points. South of Penrhyncoch, a village notable for the extreme dullness of its more recent architecture, the road runs through gentle, undulating country of ancient hedgerows and well-maintained farms. As it does so it exhibits several markedly Roman features including a particularly well-engineered gradient near Penyberth (SN646837) and *cae sarn* and *sarnau* name elements at SN647809 and SN647820. The Tithe Apportionment for the township of Parcel Canol mentions on at least six occasions the field name 'Occupation Road', rare in welsh tithe material and probably relating to access of lanes to farms or cottages. It may seem a little far-fetched to suggest that the name reflects a folk memory of Roman associations with the area, but it is nevertheless interesting that these 'Occupation Roads' occur alongside this minor lane as it progresses from Penyberth to the fort at Penllwyn. A straightish alignment south of Penyberth comes to a junction with another old road between Capel Dewi and Bancydarren (SN647830). From this point the Roman course runs along a hedgeline a few yards to the east until it picks up the enclosed lane to Felin-hen on the bank of the little Peithyll stream (SN64827). After zigzagging up the steep slope past the farm buildings the Roman line is apparently continued by way of a green lane (which

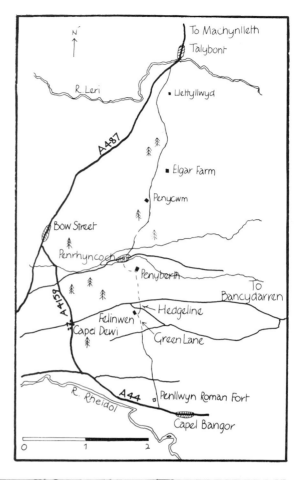

Aerial view of the Roman fort at Penllwyn, Capel Bangor

Green lane on line of assumed Roman course above Felin-hen

may well justify excavation) to rejoin the minor road at SN648823 directly opposite the most northerly 'Occupation Road'.

This part of Cardiganshire is criss-crossed by scores, if not hundreds of miles of trackways of uncertain vintage and it is hardly surprising that other courses for *Sarn Helen* have been postulated. Before the identification of the Penllwyn fort, there was a strong local tradition of a Roman crossing of the Rheidol opposite Pwllcenawon Farm on the south bank of the river (SN640805). This tradition derives from the unearthing, in 1885, of the remains of a 12ft wide 'metalled road' some ten inches below the surface of a field near Cwmwythig Farm to the north-west of what is now known to be the Roman fort. This road fragment, apparently, aligned directly with Pwllcenawon and also with Tynycwm (SN644827) to the north and it was assumed, in the absence of any other evidence, that this alignment represented the original Roman route. Several years before this stretch of roadway had been revealed, a hoard of several thousand third-century Roman coins came to light near an old lane to the south-west of Rhiwarthen-Isaf below Pwllcenawon (SN639795). This was quite sufficient to persuade local antiquaries of the existence of a Roman road whose subsequent course ran through land belonging to Nantybenglog and Penuwch Fawr Farms to arrive at the village of Llanfihangel-y-Creuddyn (SN665760). The latter certainly lies on the route for the major fort at Trawsgoed (SN671727), but it is highly improbable that Roman surveyors would have laid out such an indirect road line as that described above. The discovery of the coin hoard is no evidence in itself as this might represent a random burial made in the turbulent years following Roman withdrawal. Moreover, forty years before these were found, a copper pot containing a further 200 coins was ploughed up at Bwlch (SN608793) almost two miles to the west and well away from any likely road line. Given the location of the newly-discovered Penllwyn fort there can now be no question of the Tynycwm-Pwllcenawon-Penuwch Fawr course representing the line of *Sarn Helen* and the 'metalled' road (of which all traces have long since vanished) remains a mystery.

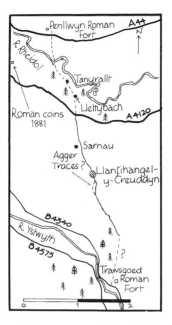

Terraced (Roman?) trackway ascending from
Tanyrallt

Sarn Helen. Penllwyn to Trawsgoed

Movements of the bed of the mature River Rheidol along with agricultural activities over the centuries will have removed any remnants of Roman road material immediately to the south of the fort. A straight continuation of the highway from the north would have extended to a ford across the river several hundred yards above the modern bridge accommodating the minor road to New Cross. Here the Roman surveyor was faced with the problem of negotiating the very steep bank of Rhiw Arthen, which he seems to have solved by taking his road along the base of the hill, roughly corresponding to the track of the Vale of Rheidol light railway. As the railway passes the smallholding of Tanyrallt (SN657789) a terrace ascends towards Llettybach (SN659785) through fine woodlands of oak and beech. Carefully engineered to ensure a steady ascent and to avoid the steepest slope, the narrow terrace rounds the shoulder of the ridge at Llettybach, where a backwards glance offers a splendid view of the incomparable Rheidol Valley. From here its course is difficult to trace through the woodlands, but it almost certainly linked with the old road running from the top of the hill through gentle pastoral country towards Llanfihangel-y-Creuddyn. Half-a-mile or so down this metalled minor road is Sarnau Farm below which, according to the National Monuments Record, aerial photographs reveal slight traces of agger in the fields to the right. They are not, however, visible on the ground. The supposed alignment of these agger remains would have carried the road over the deep gulch of a narrow stream and it is difficult to see why Roman road makers should have preferred this slightly more westerly route to the present line, which crosses the watercourse before it gouges out this awkward channel. At the top of the next hilltop ridge, Llanfihangel-y-Creuddyn comes into view, its fine church dominating the cluster of whitewashed houses. Beyond the village the Roman road can be seen to work its way round the next hillside on the line of an enclosed metalled road with a Roman-type zigzag towards the crest of the hill (SN665755). Another more pronounced zigzag effect occurs after another half-mile where a steep slope runs down to the lovely vale of the Ystwyth (SN670748). From the top of this slope, the fort of Trawsgoed, rather more than a mile distant, would first have come into view, smoke from the chimneys of its timber and wattle-and-daub type garrison buildings rising into the clear air of the wooded vale (SN671727).

Aerial view of the Roman fort at Trawsgoed

Except for the broad bank in the field to the south of the gardens of Trawsgoed House which represents the remains of the rampart, there is little evidence on the ground of the 5.4 acre rectangular fort containing all the services necessary for a garrison of 1,000 men. Aerial photography, however, backed-up by excavation, has highlighted details of the internal structure, the street grid of the *vicus* immediately to the north and the orientation of roads from the four main gates. It seems also that the basic defences of the fort remained of an earth and timber nature from its origins in the late 70s until its apparent abandonment around AD130. Trawsgoed was ideally located to control the crossing of the nearby River Ystwyth, to provide excellent views of the surrounding hilly countryside and to serve as a staging post for patrols operating out of Penllwyn. These patrols would have approached the fort on the *Sarn Helen.* Unfortunately all traces of this road, as it crossed the low-lying vale have been lost, although it presumably ran on a straight alignment from the bottom of the hills to the north.

A thousand years after the Romans left Wales, a local chieftain by the name of Adda Vychan married Dido, daughter of Ieuan Goch ap Gruffydd of Trawsgoed and thereby started the 600-year association between the family of Vaughan and Trawsgoed, only to be broken in 1947 when the running of the estate passed into the control of the Ministry of Agriculture. Like many Welsh gentry families, the Vaughans reached their apogee in the late eighteenth century when they were raised to the peerage as Earls of Lisburne. On the basis that social grandeur necessitated elegant trappings, the third earl pulled down his home in 1795 and built the Regency house forming the eastern wing of the present building. He also proceeded to lay out the fine grounds, planting azaleas, monkey puzzles, wellingtonias, cypresses and all manner of exotic species to complement his parterres, fountains and other delightful contemporary conceits. Sadly the effect was destroyed in 1891 when the sixth earl built an exquisitely vulgar west wing in pseudo-French chateau style. As if this were not enough, the Ministry of Agriculture, whose Agricultural Development and Advisory Service currently occupy the building, has thrown up further extensions in quite scandalously bad taste. Nevertheless, the grounds are worthy of a visit (with the permission of the Ministry) while the ceiling of the library in the Regency house, if somewhat crudely executed, is a charming riot of acanthus leaves and putti.

TRAWSGOED TO CARMARTHEN

From the western gate of the Roman fort lying in the field adjoining the Trawsgoed gardens, a road issued forth and zigzagged down the steep slope towards the River Ystwyth. Now only visible from aerial photographs, this was the southwards continuation of *Sarn Helen*, engineered to align as closely as possible with the fortlet underlying the farm of Taihirion-rhos some 6 miles to the south-west (SN645651). Running through what are now thickets of rhododendron and stands of Douglas Fir, the road seems to have forded the river at a point aligning with a

Trawsgoed House

Sarn Helen. Trawsgoed
to Taihirion-rhos

Ascent of assumed Roman
road from Trawsgoed

field boundary joining the farm lane of Hendre Rhys close to the unsavoury remnants of Trawsgoed railway station (SN665725). From this unkempt and dreary blight in a fine landscape the Roman roadline continues past Hendre Rhys before turning abruptly south and taking the form of a deep track pursuing a steady ascent along field boundaries until it reaches the modern road at the base of the afforested Banc Cwmllechwedd (SN662719). While the road clearly ran towards the piles of stones and enclosure banks which are all that remain of Sarn Ellen Farm (SN656704), its actual course over Banc Cwmllechwedd is obscured by a network of forestry roads. Beyond the ruins of Sarn Ellen though, the Roman line is marked by a continuous series of straight and massive hedgebanks carrying it to the east of Penlan Farm on the old road between Lledrod and Ystrad Meurig (SN655696). Careful inspection of these hedgebanks as they cross pastureland and unreclaimed bog, suggests that they were constructed on a terrace extending in parts between 5ft and 6ft either side of the bank. As this, in all likelihood, comprises the remnants of Roman agger it may merit excavation.

At almost 900ft above sea level, the point of intersection of the Roman and minor roads offers panoramic views of the low, rolling hills to the south where improved pasture alternates with brown, ill-drained wetlands and the poor quality of the older farm and cottage architecture reflects the combined poverty of the agriculture of the last century and the building materials available at that time. A stretch of the Roman road was apparently visible between this point and

Llwynmerchgwilym (SN654685) in the 1930s but a grass mark on the aerial photograph at SN654694 represents the only clue to its course over the next half-mile. Below Llwynmerchgwilym, however, the Roman road briefly follows the modern lane, until at SN653676 the latter turns south-east before rejoining the same alignment a quarter of a mile to the south. The Roman engineers maintained their road on its straight course along a twenty yard wide causeway running almost rush-free through boggy ground for more than a hundred yards. The causeway is discernible on the ground at its northern end and identifiable from aerial photographs at the point where it once again picks up the straight line of the more recent road which carries it over the little Camddwr river.

The aerial photographic record shows clearly the straight continuation, marked on the ground by fieldbanks, of the *Sarn Helen* for the mile or so between the Camddwr to below Taihirion-rhos, the junction with the modern A485. S.R. Meyrick in his *History and Antiquities of the County of Cardigan* of 1808 maintained that stretches of the road were still visible at the time of writing. A hundred and fifty years later local antiquaries excavated several sections to reveal a variety of metalling types ranging from boulders capped with layers of soil and clay to a mixture of clay and stones to a depth of 10 inches resting on a peat base. Today, however, apart from the slightest indication of agger in the field to the east of Taihirion-rhos there is little to highlight the passage of a major Roman road between the river and the fortlet.

Taihirion-rhos is roughly equidistant between Trawsgoed and the important auxiliary fort overlooking the River Teifi near Llanio-isaf Farm several miles due south (SN644564). Tentatively identified with the *Bremia* mentioned in the early eighth century collection of place names known as the *Ravenna Cosmography*, this fort occupied an area of rather more than 3.8 acres and was located on a gravel terrace to the north of the Teifi. Its surface features have been virtually obliterated by centuries of cultivation but excavation has shown that the essentially earthwork and timber complex was founded in the 70s, refurbished in the early second century and abandoned sometime between AD125 and 130. The abandonment of the fort was followed by the decay of its associated *vicus* and also, presumably, of the bathhouse, whose stone and tile remnants a hundred yards south of the fort share with Tomen-y-Mur in Merioneth the distinction of being the only visible remains of such a structure in this part of Wales. *Bremia* apparently, was garrisoned by the Second Cohort of Asturians. Soldiers from the Asturias, an important goldmining district of Spain, would, it has been suggested, have played an important part in the exploitation of the gold workings near Caeo to the south-east. Unfortunately this rather attractive idea ignores the fact that the 'national' characteristics of Roman auxiliary regiments were ephemeral, to say the least, and the Asturians may with equal likelihood have comprised soldiers from other parts of the Empire besides Spain. Consequently we must regard their stationing at *Bremia* as quite incidental. *Bremia* has been known since the seventeenth century and like other similar sites has long been a happy hunting ground for antiquaries, collectors and treasure hunters like Richard Fenton who, in the first decade of the nineteenth century purchased for 1s '. . . a very ancient Pickaxe' at Tomen Llanio not far from the fort. This he 'bore in Triumph to Tregaron' marvelling as he did so at the richness of the surface material around *Bremia*: 'All the fields, every hedge and pile of rubbish pregnant with bricks and tiles of every kind, as likewise cement and pieces of pottery.' The enthusiasm with which he and his fellow antiquaries plundered Roman sites may explain why so little remains today of even the more substantial Roman structures in this part of the Principality.

For the first mile-and-a-half from the point where it joins the A485 below Taihirion-rhos, the course of *Sarn Helen* to *Bremia* roughly follows the modern

Bremia, *the remains of the bath house*

road to the crossroads at Ty'ncelyn to the northeast of which Dr J.L. Davies identified remains of Roman metalling in the early 1970s. South of the crossroads the B4578 takes up the approximate Roman line as it twists and winds through pastureland before adopting a fine, straight alignment directly for *Bremia.* South of the junction with the A485 at SN642572, the Roman road is shown by aerial photographs to run close to the house to the west of the track to Llanio-isaf Farm before heading for a crossing of the broad, shallow River Teifi at SN643559. Traces of the agger were readily visible from the railway bridge close to the farm back in the 1930s and can still just be made out today, in particular where the road crosses the meadow alongside the riverbank. On the opposite side of the Teifi an ancient-looking track climbs the slope on the edge of a strip of woodland and then runs round the contour (its course marked by massive hedgebanks) past Godre'rgarth and Garth Farms (and two fields called *Cae pensarn* at SN645551) to join the modern B4343 which is generally believed to represent the southerly continuation of *Sarn Helen* towards Lampeter. This road takes a gently meandering course through low-lying riverside meadows, the land steadily rising to the east. Such terrain, with few difficult gradients, would have presented the Romans with an ideal opportunity to construct a classically straight road. This they would certainly have done and one can only assume that the fruits of their labours have been obliterated by progressive movements of the Teifi riverbed. Perhaps detailed local fieldwork will eventually reveal remaining stretches of the original on the western side of the B4343.

It is usually maintained that the Roman course for the 25-mile journey through the quiet pastoral landscape between Lampeter and Carmarthen is taken by the present A485. Once again, while there is no question that this road pursues the *overall* Roman line, as evidenced by short straight traverses across the steeper hills, angular realignments and place names, the precise course will be elucidated only by intensive fieldwork. At present it is possible to identify a clear deviation of the Roman from the existing road where it runs from Pencarreg and through the

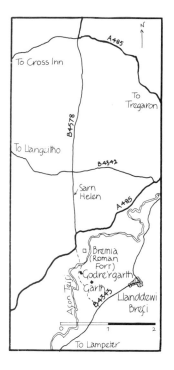

Sarn Helen *before Ty'ncelyn*

Sarn Helen; Taihirion-rhos to Bremia

gloomy little town of Llanybydder to the village of Llanllwni to the southwest. Back in the late nineteenth century a stretch of the original metalled road was uncovered near Neuadd, Pencarreg, a house previously occupied by the vicar of the nearby parish church (SN533451) and also in the gardens of the Old Vicarage a quarter of a mile or so to the south (SN532448). Both these sightings align with a footpath leaving the A485 at SN528444 which itself aligns with a section of the paved road surface revealed in 1820 by drainage operations in fields to the northwest of Capel Aberduar outside Llanybydder (SN525439). The footpath is continued by an old unused lane which, before it reaches Aberduar Farm, turns abruptly to the west (SN528442). The Roman line is maintained for a straight, steep descent past the farm buildings and across the meadows on a slight raised agger of almost 15ft wide, on line with the stretch near the chapel described above. This would have been reached after a short, sharp climb up the south bank of the Einion stream, presumably forded at the point where the agger joins the north bank. Beyond the chapel a continuous hedgeline (now broken by a council estate) originally marked the position of the Roman road as it passed by the base of the hill fort of Penygaer to rejoin the A485 at the Gwrdymawr public house (SN521435). The coincidence of the two roads does not last for long since traces of the Roman surface have been found in Cae dan-yr-efail on Abercwm Farm (SN503407), in Cae Capel, Maesnoni Farm (SN497397) and in three fields belonging to Pensarnhelen, Llanllwni (SN486392) where it seems once again to have joined the modern main road. Rather more than half-a-mile south of here the latter makes a sharp angular turn to negotiate a hillside in a typically Roman manner (SN479385), doing so once again below Gwyddgrug (SN461355) close to a field named *Sarn Elen*. Further fieldwork may cast light on the exact location of the original course of *Sarn Helen* over the final few miles to Carmarthen through Rhydargaeau (with fieldnames *Sarne* and *Sarnebach* at SN438254 and SN438256) and Sarnau village. For the time being, however, drivers through this lovely countryside can rest assured that they are motoring along a road in part at least, familiar to the

Llanybydder; the Roman road towards Aberduar Chapel

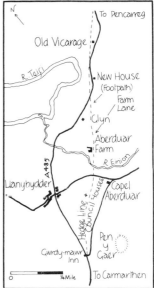

Course of Roman road around Llanybydder

footsoldiers and cavalrymen trudging towards *Moridunum* nineteen hundred years ago.

BREMIA TO LLANDOVERY

The eastern branch of *Sarn Helen* linked *Bremia* with a large fort on the outskirts of modern Llandovery a dozen or so miles to the south east (SN770352). This road parted company with the main *Sarn Helen* to Carmarthen at the village of Llanfair Clydogau where a Victorian bridge carries the present B4343 across Nant Clywedog (SN624511). Just beyond the bridge a narrow minor road climbs steeply out of the Teifi valley, eventually running along a series of very straight alignments through pinewoods and into high, silent and cairn-strewn country. Deep in the forest at SN640493 the remains of a Roman practice camp have been identified while an unfinished practice camp languishes in the open moorland on the left-hand side of the road half-a-mile on towards Llandovery (SN647485). Rectangular or square with rounded corners, practice camps are usually to be found in close proximity to a Roman road and rarely more than a few hours march from an auxiliary fort. The two on this particular road, which, by the way, are the only examples of this earthwork type in West Wales, may be the result of exercises carried out by detachments from *Bremia* or the fort at Pumsaint in the Cothi Valley (SN655405).

The long, straight stretch of road comes to an end beyond the second practice camp and then winds round the side of the hill to a point above the Twrch valley where aerial photographs have suggested a stretch of the original agger. Traces of this can be picked out on the ground as it cuts through the heather to the right of the minor road (SN643472-644476). Roman columns marching this way could now, if they bothered themselves with such things, contemplate the peaks of the Brecon Beacons rising magnificently on the southern horizon before they tackled the steep descent into the Twrch valley. Now a landscape of enclosed pasture, the valley would probably have been heavily wooded in Roman times, and this may well have concentrated the minds of the soldiers on the possibility of ambush as they approached the ford across the little River Twrch before heading for Ffarmers

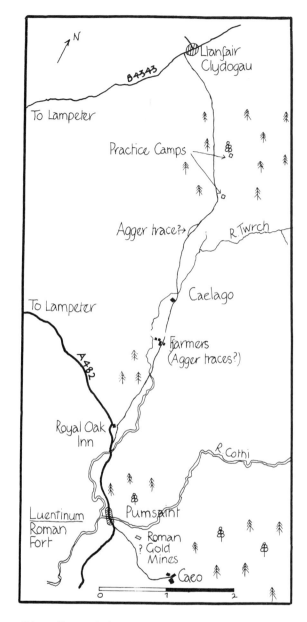

Roman road; Llanfair
Clydogan to Pumsaint

and Pumsaint. On the outskirts of the village of Ffarmers (whose Drovers Arms pub reminds us of the associations of the area with the (cattle trade) there appear to be remnants of agger in the fields to the left of the present road before it once again crosses the Twrch to run due south towards the modern A482 (SN650442).

The new Ordnance Survey map shows the Roman road joining the A482 near the Royal Oak Inn. However, the original Roman line seems to have diverged from the minor road a hundred yards or so to the north of the pub and run along a deep old lane towards Brynmaiog Farm, where it is marked by a hedgebank taking it to a junction with the A482 near a chapel below the pub. The subsequent course of the Roman road to Pumsaint, a mile-and-a-half distant, is unknown although it is probably marked by the A482.

Watching the heavy lorries thunder across the elegant modern stone bridge on

The Twrch Valley

their way to the industrial valleys of South Wales, it is difficult to think of Pumsaint
as an important Roman centre. Yet here, at the confluence of the Cothi and Twrch
rivers, a Roman fort enclosing 4.75 acres was identified in 1972-3. There is little to
see today, but visitors walking to the Dolaucothi Hotel from its adjacent carpark
will pass over the remains of the fort which excavation revealed to have been
founded in the late 70s and subsequently abandoned in the mid-second century.
The fort, tentatively identified with Ptolemy's *Luentinum*, later served to protect
the gold mines at nearby Caeo from which bullion may even have found its way to
the Imperial mint at Rome. A good deal of gold from the mines also came into local
hands if finds in the area are anything to go by. In 1796 numerous gold ornaments
of the second and third century were found near Dolaucothi House thirty years
after a hoard of several thousand copper coins reputedly came to light in the same
vicinity. More recently, 682 *radiates* coins ranging from the time of Decius (AD249-
251) to Carusius (AD291), were uncovered during work on a Forertry Commission
road near Erw-hen (SN676436).

  The Roman emperors enjoyed a monopoly of bullion and no expense (or
sweated labour of slaves) was spared in exploiting to the full the potential of the
gold-bearing pyrites three-quarters of a mile south-east of Pumsaint. Here
depressions in the ground and great gashes in the shaly rock indicate that both
opencast and underground mining were carried out while a series of brilliantly
conceived aqueducts, one of them seven miles long, were cut into the hillside to
carry water for washing the crushed ore and breaking down beds of pyrites. The
remains of water tanks and reservoirs, an underground gallery drained originally
by a large wooden waterwheel, and the 'Carreg Pumsaint', a great block of diorite
apparently used for crushing the ore, may all be seen at this National Trust-owned
site. Later mining has obscured much of the original Roman activity and some
scholars have recently questioned the Roman provenance of sections of the

*The ascent of the Roman
road from Aberbowlan*

aqueduct system. The great oak waterwheel, however, of which parts are now on view in the National Museum in Cardiff, are undoubtedly of Roman origin as indicated by radiocarbon dating. Associated with the gold mines was the Roman bathhouse whose original location was to the south-west of the Pumsaint fort. Containing two hypocausted rooms, the bathhouse was built after the abandonment of the fort thereby suggesting that it was created for the use of mineworkers rather than the military garrison. Judging from coins and other finds, Roman or Romano-British miners were still performing their ablutions here in the late fourth century.

The country road to Caeo village (SN676399) runs through the gold mines and is generally reckoned to represent the original Roman line. Caeo itself is a charming place. Visitors will find little evidence of Roman activity, but they will enjoy the splendid church with its massive tower dominating the surrounding cottages. This part of Wales yields few interesting churchyards, yet here at Caeo we can see headstones whose materials and quality of execution emphasise the prosperity of the minor gentry families living in the area in the past. In a vault near the church lie several of the Johnes family of Dolaucothi who, like so many Welsh county families, contributed much to the affairs of nineteenth-century Wales and to the wider British Empire. Alongside John Johnes, Lieutenant of Carmarthenshire (died 1815) rests James Beck, a young officer who married a daughter of the family before being carried away by dysentery in Jamaica in 1864. Close by moulder the remains of another John Johnes whose career as Recorder of Carmarthen and a county court judge was brought dramatically to a close by a bullet from his deranged butler's gun. The most distinguished of this company was surely Sir James Hills-Johnes, VC, an old India hand who survived numerous Imperial battlefields to become Military Governor of Kabul during the Afghan War of 1879-

Roman gold-mines at Caeo

80. He died, full of honours, in 1918, the closing years of his exciting career having been devoted to county matters and the governorship of the University College of Wales at Aberystwyth. In the latter post his experience at Kabul may have served him well!

From Caeo, a steep climb carries the minor road south-eastwards to the little farm of Aberbowlan on the River Dulais (SN696390). Here the Roman road fords the Dulais and heads across the hills on an alignment for Porthyrhyd (SN710378). Initially proceeding as a deep lane with a typical Roman zigzag on its steepest part, the road eventually becomes a sunken trackway across the open hill with occasional traces of embanking on either side. However, as it once again descends the hill to rejoin the minor road opposite the Drovers Farm in Porthyrhyd, it takes the form of an enclosed lane.

Between Porthyrhyd and Llandovery there are few clues in the literature or from aerial photographs as to the actual course of the Roman road. There is a very strong

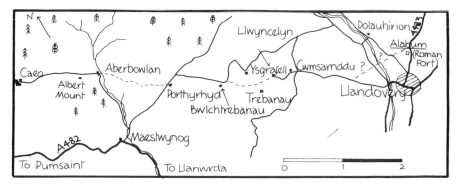

Roman road; Caeo to Llandovery

41

tradition that it ran along the present minor road as far as Bwlchtrebanau (SN722370) and then deviated to cross the tributary of the little Mynys stream at the bottom of a deep valley before running on towards Llwyncelyn (SN727636) and rejoining the minor road to Llandovery at SN742363. Unlike the modern road, curving widely as it does to avoid the steep-sided valley of the Mynys, this course would have offered the advantage of directness. At SN725370, a point beyond Bwlchtrebanau where this curve begins, a gate leads off the road to a narrow unused lane which seems to have been the original access to Trebanau Farm (SN725366). After a few yards this lane turns sharply southwards and deteriorates into a hollow way leading across the fields for the farm. According to local tradition the Roman road followed the early stretch of the farm track before continuing on a straight alignment to descend through the woods and across the valley on the line of the more recent Trebanau Farm lane. Despite the lack of evidence on the ground, this seems probable since, at SN728366 where the farm lane heads north-west for the minor road, an overgrown track, aligned with the lane leaving the same minor road near Bwlchtrebanau, zigzags through woodland towards Llwyncelyn, westwards of which it becomes incorporated in the council-maintained country road to continue past Cwm-sarn-ddu (SN740364) and directly towards the River Tywi on the outskirts of Llandovery. This road has several characteristic features, including a long, straight section on the run into Llandovery, but only tradition and directness can be cited as evidence for its Roman origin. The problem with the final straight stretch is simply that it does not directly align with the fort to the north-east of Llandovery and an alternative crossing of the Tywi opposite Llwyn Howell has been suggested (SN761354). From here the Roman road would have struck out to connect with the Llwyncelyn-Bwlchtrebanau section at an unidentified point. Only intensive fieldwork and excavation in this area is likely to resolve the problem and establish the precise location of the last few miles of the eastern branch of Sarn Helen between Porthyrhyd and Llandovery.

The Llandovery fort was vitally important in the communications and military organisation of Roman Wales. Occupying around 5 acres and providing services for a garrison of 1,000 men, the fort controlled roads running eastwards and westwards for settlements at Brecon and Carmarthen and northwards for the forts of *Bremia* and Castell Collen. In common with several other forts in the area, Llandovery was originally built as an earthwork and timber edifice and after much alteration, rebuilding, and eventual reduction in size, was abandoned in the mid-second century. As usual, only the imagination can serve to remind us of the formidable nature of the original structure, with its wooden towers, barracks and storehouses dominated by the great *principia* whose site is currently occupied by St Mary's Church. Apart from various small finds, including a broken altar and scraps of Samian ware, the remnants of the *vallum* in the field near Llanfair House, and a Roman cemetery at Caefelin to the south-east (SN770347) there remains little by way of a monument to the troops occupying this remote corner of the Empire.

LLANDOVERY TO BRECON GAER

An important road linked Llandovery with the auxiliary fort at Y Gaer, near Brecon. Traces of the early stretches of this road as it heads for the River Brân on a south-easterly alignment for Mynydd Bach Trecastell are shown up on aerial photographs as crop marks in the field immediately below the fort. Also, remains of the original causeway are visible in the eroded river bank and again as a long raised mound running across a sportsfield towards a gate opening on to the A40 opposite the

Aerial view of the Roman marching camps of Y Pigwn

The Roman road from Llandovery to Trecastle

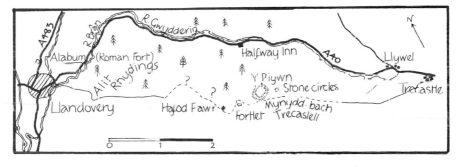

White Swan pub (SN772344). After a second crossing of the Brân the Roman road takes up the line of the pre-1780s turnpike road between Llandovery and Brecon by way of the hills south of the Tywi Valley. Climbing out of Llandovery and past Picton Court, the turnpike makes a wide curve to avoid the steepest part of Allt Rhydings (SN780335). There is no field evidence to indicate any other course, so one must conclude that the turnpike surveyors were following the Roman road at this stage. They certainly did so for some way beyond Allt Rhydings where straight alignments towards Cefntelych eventually give way to a winding stretch of road heading for Hafod Fawr at the base of the mountain (SN814313). Henceforth the road climbs in an almost zigzag fashion to the top of the wastelands of Mynydd Bach Trecastell, passing close to a Roman fortlet at SN821310 and then, at the western end of the ridge, more or less alongside a series of old tile-working mounds to the south of the fine pair of superimposed Roman marching camps of Y Pigwn (SN827313).

At this remote and desolate point over 1,300ft above sea level, detachments of troops originally enclosed an area of more than 37 acres by means of earthworks and ditches, later superimposing a second camp of 23.5 acres. The earthworks of the camps are still traceable on the ground today, the *claviculae* or curved banks defending the openings in the ramparts of the inner camp being easily detected by the keen observer. Marching-camps like these were built during the early phases of the Roman conquest so as to provide an easily-defended temporary camping-site, the ramparts being supplemented by a fence of sharp wooden stakes. An undertaking of this sort must have involved a good deal of hard labour which, in common with that required for the building of practice-camps, would have been far from popular with the soldiers. Troops stationed in Wales no doubt detested the work and cursed it in a variety of languages as they rested in their heavy leather tents behind the earthen ramparts. Unlike the legions in Lower Germany though they stopped short of openly rebelling against the task. Of the latter, Appian wrote '. . . They complained about the hardness of the work and specifically about building ramparts, digging ditches, foraging, collecting timber and firewood and all the other camp tasks that are either necessary or are invented to keep the men busy.' Grumble they might have done, yet here at Y Pigwn on the Brecknockshire-Carmarthenshire border the Roman soldiers left behind an enduring monument to their vigour, discipline and professionalism. Indeed, they left behind a monument which represents one of the few tangible pieces of archaeological evidence for the initial thrust of the campaign to bring the Welsh tribes to heel.

Aerial photographs of the site indicate the original Roman road as a thin line to the south of the old turnpike. It forms a well-engineered terrace running from just above the fortlet (which eventually came to replace the marching camps) to rejoin the turnpike some 500yards eastwards (SN821311-824310). In the mid-eighteenth century 'at a spot called the Heath Cock', approximately a hundred yards inside the Carmarthenshire border, was located a milestone bearing the name of the Gallic

Gateway of Roman fort; Brecon Gaer

Aerial view of the Roman fort at Brecon Gaer

Emperor Postumus (AD258-68). This stone, now lost, was probably sited on the road when it was being repaired by the civil authorities undertaking responsibility for road maintenance after the bulk of the troops had been withdrawn. The turnpike, now a rough track through bleak mountain grasslands until it is taken up by a metalled road to the village, has for long been assumed to follow the overall course of the Roman road to Trecastle. However, excavation by Mrs E. Alcock has identified a road, well-surfaced with chippings of Old Red Sandstone, to the north of the turnpike. This road clearly pre-dates the turnpike, though whether its origins lie in the Roman period or in early mining activities at Y Pigwn is not altogether clear. Equally, the course of the Roman road for most of the remaining 8 miles or so to Y Gaer is rather obscure. While logic suggests a route along the Usk valley, there are neither cartographic nor place-name clues, nor is there any evidence on the ground. Local antiquaries interested in establishing the details of this section of the Roman road should not ignore the traditional belief that it ran, in part at least, along the minor lanes to the north of the Usk, passing through the church near Llwyncyntefin (SN920280) and then to Parc-mawr (SN944300), Trallong (SN965296) and alongside the churchyard at Aberyscir (SN999297). Unquestionably the deserted lane immediately to the west of Aberyscir church, lying as it does in direct alignment with a ford over the Yscir and the west gate of the fort at Y Gaer, represents the initial stretch of the road.

Brecon Gaer, situated magnificently at the confluence of the Rivers Usk and Yscir in what is surely some of the finest countryside in Britain, was one of the largest and most important forts in the Principality. Occupying some 7.8 acres, the earthwork and timber fort was garrisoned sometime between AD75 and 100 by a 500-strong Spanish cavalry regiment. Eventually the earthworks and some of the wooden internal buildings were replaced by stone structures including a commandant's house and granaries, while a substantial *vicus* was later established outside the northern walls. When he excavated the site in the 1920s, Sir Mortimer

45

Roman road?; Y Pigwn to Trecastle

Wheeler was able to identify much of the internal layout. Unhappily the entire area within the ramparts has been ploughed out so that apart from a stretch of the splendid north wall and the remnants of two angle towers, the stone gateways in the east, west and south walls are virtually all that remain immediately visible. The site is worthy of a visit for the gateways alone, their massively-constructed guard-houses reminding us once again of just how formidable these larger Roman forts must have been to the local peasantry.

CARMARTHEN (MORIDUNUM) TO LLANDOVERY

As the Roman armies gradually withdrew from Wales once the fortification process had been completed, a limited degree of autonomy was established under local leaders. Many of these had been successfully cajoled into adopting the habits and way of life of the conquerors and *Moridunum* originally may have developed from a *vicus*, wherein native Demetae had observed and emulated Roman ways. Like *Venta Silurum*, the town was probably constituted as a cantonal capital following Hadrian's visit in AD122 and in any event soon became a highly sophisticated centre. First recognized from the street layout of the modern town, *Moridunum* has been extensively excavated since the 1960s, so that we now know that it occupied a well-defended 32-acre site with the planned layout typical of a Roman town. The wealthier citizens lived in underfloor-heated houses, their larders well stocked with amphorae of wine and olive oil from the Mediterranean and their tables set with fashionable high-quality Gaulish Samian ware. Their less opulent brethren owned flagons, kitchen bowls, dishes and jars made at pottery sites in the central and eastern parts of Britain. Both would have regularly strolled down to the 5,000-seat amphitheatre, cut out of the natural slope outside the east wall. Such a large structure, far in excess of the population of the town, may have served the dual function of being a civic entertainment centre and a meeting-place for natives from the local area. The latter, unlike their countrymen in the remoter hill-country, must inevitably have felt the cultural effect of the Romanized life style emanating

Carmarthen in the early nineteenth century

from this brilliant centre which continued to flourish into the late fourth century
   Visitors to Carmarthen will find an excellent museum, Records Office and
tourist information centre, all providing a great deal of useful material about
Roman *Moridunum* Today's town is dominated by nineteenth-century buildings,
many of them dating from the time when it was a bustling agricultural centre and
an important port for coasting vessels. By 1829 the place boasted no fewer than
eighty-four registered ale houses, many of ancient lineage. Several of these, under
the questionable pretext of making the flesh more tender before slaughter,
maintained the old sport of bull-baiting with dogs, although this came to an abrupt
halt early in the nineteenth century when a spirited bull killed the landlord of the
Boar's Head. This house, The Talbot, The Nag's Head and the Ivy Bush were among
the more notable coaching inns of Carmarthen, whose parlours several of the
town's more famous sons knew well. Richard Steele (1672-1729) died in the house
which later became the Ivy Bush Hotel, while the architect John Nash's earliest
commissions included Carmarthen Gaol (demolished in 1938) and several local
mansions. Another Nash, Richard 'Beau' Nash (1674-1762) was educated in the
town before going up to Jesus College, Oxford and subsequently launching out on
his remarkable career as master of ceremonies and arbiter of taste at Bath.
   The Ivy Bush typified the fine old inns of the coaching age. Standing at the top of
the town with the Vale of Tywi to the rear, it was the epitome of comfort for man

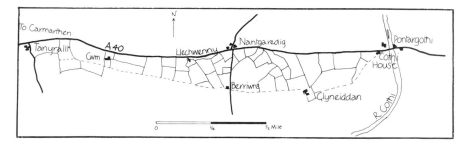

The Roman road from Carmarthen to Pontargothi

and beast. Here, at the meeting place of the 'Upper' and 'Lower' turnpike routes to Milford Haven, travellers could briefly forget the rigours of travel as they watched porters clumping across the cobbled yard with heavy baggage and ostlers rubbing down sweating horses as they cursed the devil-may-care coach drivers. With a bumper of claret in hand and the aroma of succulent roasting beef lending an edge to the appetite, the prospect of the onward journey may have seemed just a little less formidable to the jaded visitor.

For many years it was assumed that the turnpike traveller between Carmarthen and Llandovery more-or-less followed the earlier Roman road currently marked by the A40 highway along the Tywi Valley. More recently, however, the work of Professor G.D.B. Jones, among others, has identified several significant divergences from this general line, the first of these occurring to the north-east of Abergwili railway bridge beyond the crossing of the River Gwili. Here the line of the Roman road drops away from the A40 to be carried on a causeway through pastureland in the direction of Nantgaredig. For a mile or so the course is now lost (presumably owing to the shifting of the bed of the Tywi) only to reappear as a series of continuous hedge boundaries between Tanyrallt Farm (SN478227) and 'The Berriwns', a group of houses below Nantgaredig School. These can be readily viewed from the A40 at Tanyrallt while a little further along the road below Llechwenny, parts of the original agger seem to have been incorporated in the field boundary. Aerial photographs from the 1960s reveal a cropmark at SN492216 which apparently locates the course of the road from the end of the hedgebank series towards 'The Berriwns', in direct alignment with the lane towards Glyneiddan Farm. This shows up on the ground as the slight depression of a hollow way through re-seeded pastureland. A massive hedgebank now takes up the Roman line east of Glyneiddan to the spot where it joins an old lane near Cothi House, several yards to the west of the bridge carrying the A40 over the River Cothi at Pontargothi.

For some miles beyond Pontargothi the details of the Roman route are far from clear. According to most authorities the A40 follows the Roman original as far as Wern Garage (SN535214) whence it runs above the main road on a lane rejoining the latter at Nantarwenllis to the east. Thence straight alignments carry the A40 for 2 miles to Broad Oak, beyond which minor roads are thought to represent the Roman line to the hamlet of Penybanc north of Llandeilo (SN619240). This route, and its subsequent continuation towards Abermarlais Park several miles to the north-east, runs through the beautiful rolling country on the northern side of the Tywi valley and would have certainly provided a more direct approach than the later A40 along the valley bottom. The earlier stretches of the minor road system offer little evidence of Roman activity, despite the discovery many years ago of a milestone of the time of Tacitus (AD275-6). However at SN646255, beyond the crossing of the River Dulais south-east of New Inn, the country lane takes a sharp turn southwards to rejoin the A40, the earlier road being continued by way of a narrow deserted track through woodland to link up with the minor road heading straight for Abermarlais (SN655268). The directness of this section and the commanding views which it offers of the Tywi Valley and the high land above the Dulais support a probable Roman origin, while the broad 20ft-wide causeway at SN663274 undoubtedly represents the remains of the agger. This causeway, to the north-east of the junction of the road for Caledfwlch, was particularly well-preserved in the 1960s, but is now less obvious in consequence of ploughing and re-seeding.

From this point travellers along the present road past Cefnglasfryn in the direction of Abermarlais Park are unquestionably on the course of the Roman road. At Rosehill Cottage (where an eighteenth-century tollhouse indicates that

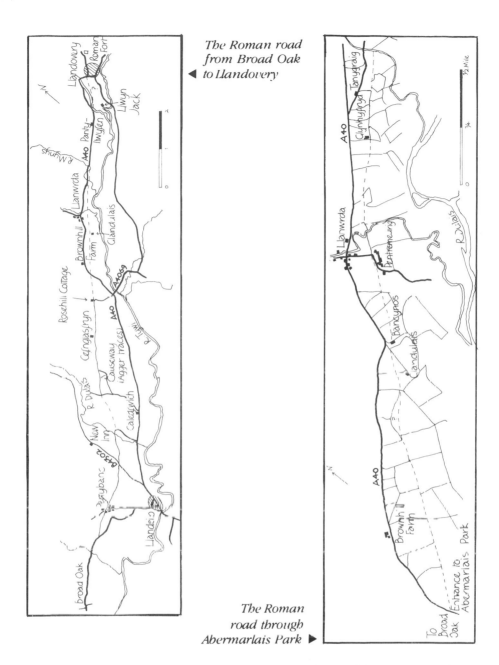

*The Roman road
from Broad Oak
◀ to Llandovery*

*The Roman
road through
Abermarlais Park ▶*

carriages took the same course during the early phases of the turnpike era) the road makes a virtually right-angled turn towards Llangadog. Here, at the original western entrance to Abermarlais, the Roman road continues straight through the park, running for several hundred yards on a raised causeway. It then descends towards a stream, with traces of metalling nearby, before being taken up by a footpath aligning with the eastern gateway of the park opening onto the A40. Sometime before 1851 a gold intaglio ring of Roman make was found close to the spot during drainage operations. Beyond the entrance to the park aerial photography has highlighted a crop mark carrying the Roman road south of the A40 to join a continuous hedgeline (along which is evidence of a causeway) to

Roman road on raised causeway; towards Abermarlais

Bancynos Farm (SN69300-709310). From the south-eastern corner of the farm buildings a long stretch of the original agger heads straight across the fields on a pronounced causeway of between 30ft and 35ft in width eventually joining the lane past Pentremeurig (SN710311-715315). Immediately eastwards of Pentremeurig changes in the Dulais riverbed have removed all traces of the agger. However, it appears once again in a road running below the A40 close to Glynhyfryd (SN722318). A slight causeway on an alignment with the Pentremeurig lane leaves the field directly westwards of Glynhyfryd to join the metalled road, where traces of the causeway may still be identified on either side. Where this road turns north to join the A40, there is the slightest suggestion of a causeway maintaining the easterly progress of the Roman road (SN724319). Significantly this lies on a precise alignment with the field at SN735324 where, in the 1970s, ploughing turned up remains of agger and metalling and thus established the point where the Roman road coincided with the A40 for the final seven miles past Ystrad and into Llandovery. In all probability this was the stretch of road identified by the antiquary Fenton in 1800. 'Its surface [is] so altered', he wrote in a manuscript currently in Cardiff City Library, 'and so intersected with numerous enclosures in every direction that only by snatches can you follow it'. Keen observer as he was Fenton failed to locate the remains of the Roman villa at Llys Brychan near Llangadog, some way to the south of the road. Unearthed in 1961, this late fourth-century structure, with its hypocaust system and walls bedecked with painted plaster, represents the sole example of a villa in this part of Wales and may have been built as the official residence of some Roman or Romano-British dignitary.

The long straight run of the A40 carrying the Roman road past Ystrad House ends at Pantyllwyfen (SN749333), where in the 1870s traces of the road metalling were recorded before being dug out by the tenant of the farm. This implies a straight continuation of the Roman line to cross the Tywi above Llwyn Jack and thence to

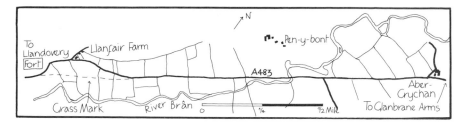

The Roman road from Llandovery to Aber-Crychan

proceed directly north-east to the auxiliary fort on the outskirts of modern Llandovery. The discovery, in 1825, of massive piles of oak in the bed of the Tywi between Blaenos House and Nantyrhogfaen Farm has led to speculation about a crossing further north. This would have involved the road engineers in what seems, superficially at least, to be a rather pointless realignment of their road. On the other hand this stretch of the Tywi may have occupied a rather different course in Roman times such that it was considered a more practical proposition to make a ford (or even a bridge) at the northern location. In all likelihood this will remain a matter for speculation since the meandering of the river over the centuries, coupled with the growth of modern Llandovery, will have removed any material evidence of the Roman road as it ran east of the Tywi for the fort.

LLANDOVERY TO CASTELL COLLEN

The fort at Llandovery played a pivotal rôle in the supervision of the Tywi Valley and of the several smaller valleys adjoining it, besides being an essential component in the chain of communications with the forts of the north, notably that of Castell Collen near Llandrindod Wells (SO056628). The Roman road running towards Castell Collen from Llandovery can be identified on aerial photographs by means of a crop mark in a north-easterly alignment through the grassland immediately below the fort. At SN776356 the crop mark picks up the line of the A483 trunk road which carries the Roman road for the next mile-and-a-half past Aber-Crychan to Tan-y-Parc Restaurant (SN794375). Here the modern and the Roman roads diverge, the former continuing along the edge of the tree-lined hillside, the latter proceeding through the meadows of the Brân Valley. Initially incorporated into a series of hedge boundaries running towards Dolau Brân (SN797381) the Roman alignment was in the direction of the Glanbrane Arms, the old drovers' pub at the head of the valley (SN809396). A dominant feature of the Roman roadline is a massive causeway, some 30-35ft wide, clearly visible in the fields to the north of Dolau Brân and again alongside the river as it heads through the Glanbrane estate (SN803391). The causeway can be traced from Dolau Brân for

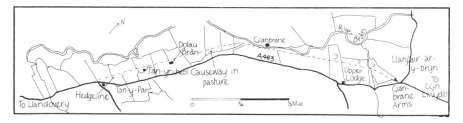

The route of the Roman road through the Glanbrane estate

Roman road towards Caerau

the best part of a mile, although from time to time (for example, at SN801388) it has been eroded by movements in the course of the river. In the field to the north-west of Upper Lodge however, the causeway has been ploughed out and we have only the evidence of aerial photographs and parching in the dry season to show its onward progress (SN807392). The little stream of Nantcwmneuadd has obliterated any evidence on the ground, yet the alignment of the causeway coincides precisely with the minor road running in a north-easterly direction from the Glanbrane Arms on a steady ascent of the slopes of Cefn Llwydlo (SN811396). This road, degenerating into a rough and undriveable track through the Crychan Forest at SN841415, clearly represents the overall course of the Roman route, which, prior to local afforestation, would have offered excellent visibility to all points of the compass. Towards the top of the ridge, at SN849415, lie the remnants of an earthwork whose general appearance and location relative to the chain of Roman fortifications bespeak a possible fortlet, but this has yet to be substantiated by excavation.

Beyond Sarn Cwrtiau (SN872435) the road leaves the forest to join the minor lane past Gellicrugiau, Cefngorwydd and Aberdulais in the general direction of the River Irfon. While it possesses few immediately obvious Roman characteristics, this road certainly follows the general Roman line to the Irfon ford near Glancamddwr (SN920470) whence a northerly alignment heads for the auxiliary fort at Caerau near Beulah. To motor-bound travellers, incidentally, the Glancamddwr ford is impassable at all but the driest times of the year and those wishing to pick up the Roman road north of the river need to make a detour by way of Llangammarch Wells. Pedestrians cross the Irfon on a modern footbridge which, it has to be said, is a rather ill-proportioned piece of work for so charming and elegant a river.

A fine and remarkably straight piece of road (coinciding directly with the Roman line as evidenced by aerial photographs revealing traces of parallel ditching in the adjoining fields) runs through rolling countryside from the Irfon to the Caerau fort some two miles to the north. Standing on a low hill close to the

52

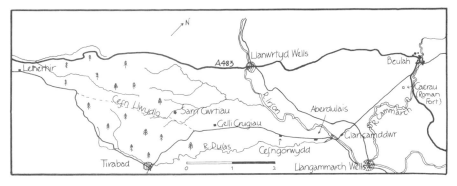

The Roman road across Cefn Llwydlo to Beulah

road and overlooking the river plain, Caerau was an ideal 'half-way house' between Llandovery and Castell Collen. Excavation has uncovered a timber building (possibly the commandant's house) of the Flavian period underlying a later stone granary, its floor supported on small stone pillars. Also, pottery fragments found at the fort and at the adjacent civilian settlement in the fields to the north-east, indicate an occupation period from AD80-140, after which the site seems to have been abandoned. At some time within this period the area of the fort was reduced from 4.2 to a mere 3 acres, suggesting, in common with several other contemporary forts, a possible demotion in status or simply a scaling down

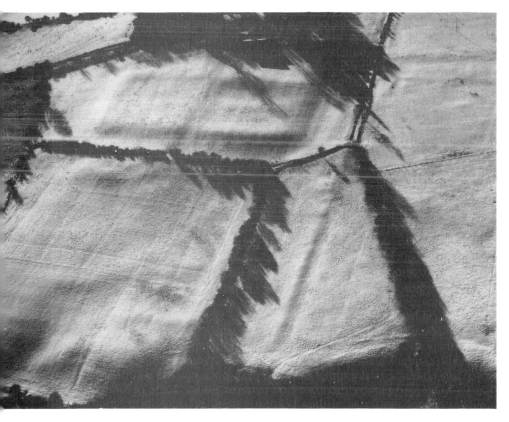

Aerial view of the Roman fort at Caerau

of garrison size. Today farm buildings and a medieval motte occupy the *principia*, and the ramparts of both the original and reduced fort are preserved under the springy turf of the surrounding fields. Outside the north-eastern rampart, where the ground drops away towards the River Cammarch, a ledge may mark the original site of the bathhouse, while the *clavicula* and northern and western earthworks of a large temporary marching camp can be seen to the west of the fort at SN919507.

It used to be thought that the continuation of the Roman road from Caerau followed the modern B4358 as it twisted and wound its way towards Newbridge-on-Wye several miles to the north-east, although it is difficult to see why this should be so since the local terrain would have allowed a more direct course. Indeed there is growing support (and growing evidence) for a totally different roadline independent, for the most part, of the B4358. Marked for part of its route on the new OS 1:10,000 map, this connects Caerau with the farm of Simddelwyd (SN941521) and thence to Glandulas (SN946531) and Sarn Helen Farm (SN970543), in line with the fort at Castell Collen. The straight modern by-road carrying the Roman line past Caerau proceeds northwards to join the A483 at SN922506 and immediately before this intersection traces of the older road may still be made out in the boggy ground to the left. The Roman road then began its north-easterly course, crossing the River Cammarch, ascending through rather wet land and following a series of continuous hedgebanks as far as spot height 253 on the Beulah-Garth road (SN928513). Aerial photographs provide clear evidence for the earlier course, while excavation in the late 1950s (at a point approximately half-a-mile north-east of Caerau) unearthed a road of 18-19ft wide made up of 9in of rammed stone on a bottoming of 7in of red clay. A glance over the roadside hedge at SN928513 reveals the continuation of the road by way of a very pronounced causeway leading directly into an old green lane on the same alignment. This lane peters out after a few hundred yards, the roadline being preserved in the hedgebank series running towards the ford over the Dawffrwd stream beyond which it is carried past Simddelwyd by another deserted green lane of 10-20ft wide. At SN947529, below Glandulas in the delectable Dulas Valley, a causeway in a nearby field identifies a probable north-easterly deviation of the Roman road from the green lane in the direction of Troed-rhiw-dalar. For the next half-mile the original Roman course is less clear although local topography hints at a roadline broadly coincident with the B4358 past the early eighteenth-century Troed-rhiw-dalar Chapel and on as far as Penrhiwdalar (SN956536). Here, in all probability, (and according to local tradition) the road followed the footpath to Esgair-goch (SN967542) and thence to Sarn Helen. It must be emphasized, though, that however logical this course may appear, the unearthing of a few traces of metalling in the fields north of Sarn Helen constitute the only available evidence for Roman road building in the immediate vicinity. The same applies to the final 6 mile stretch running towards a crossing of the River Wye and on to Castell Collen. The orientation of the metalling fragments near Sarn Helen Farm implies an alignment in direct coincidence with the straight run of the B4358 as it heads for the fort. Alternatively, the Roman fortlet at Penmincae (SO006539) on the east bank of the Wye may mark a crossing point on the river in which case the subsequent course would have run north-north-east towards Newbridge-on-Wye before joining the B4358. Beyond the fact that this modern road probably follows the Roman line between SO024587 and SO035610, little more can be said save to suggest that local historians and field workers might care to focus their attention on the problem.

The Castell Collen fort has been much excavated. Immediately before World War I some rather haphazard digging uncovered several fragments of inscribed stones and a set of Castor Ware cups besides establishing the location of the

Roman road on green lane towards Simddelwyd

The Roman road from Beulah to Glandulas

principia and the main walls. Later work in the 1950s directed towards unravelling the history of the fort, located a large extra-mural bathhouse (with provision for bathing in both moist and dry heat), the *praetorium* (commandant's house), *horreum* (granary) and details of timber barrack buildings. Scholars are generally agreed that the fort was originally constructed of turf and timber by Julius Frontinus's troops during the course of the struggle against the Silures in AD75-78. At some time in the mid-second century the defences were revetted with stone, stone gates with projecting semi-circular gate-towers were built, and some of the more important internal buildings were replaced with robust masonry structures. This preceded a period of abandonment followed, in the early third century, by reconstruction and reduction in size so that later in the century, when the defences and gates were once again renovated and the ditches re-cut, the site was occupied by a squarish fort of 3.6 acres capable of accommodating about 500 men. In other words it was now only half the size of the earlier fort, reflecting the changing

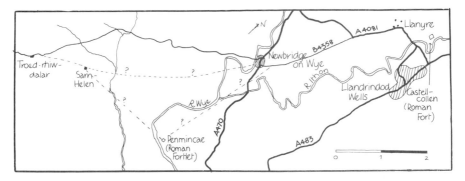

Possible routes of the Roman road to Castell Collen

realities of the political and military situation in Roman Wales since Julius Frontinus's early campaigns.

From the rather dishevelled remnants of Castell Collen (which surely merits further excavation, or at least an attempt to render the remains more immediately comprehensible to the visitor), the spa town of Llandrindod Wells comes into view. Locally celebrated for the curative properties of its waters as early as Restoration times, Llandrindod achieved more widespread recognition when an ambitious entrepreneur by the name of Grosvenor attempted to capitalize on the growing demand for the waters by flatulent and overindulgent country gentlemen and built an elegant hotel in the village during the 1750s. Unhappily this building was officially closed by the local authorities in 1787 on the grounds that the 'entertainment' offered the clientèle amounted to more than a chaste cup of tea and a dry biscuit! Development of the town as a watering-place was limited by poor road access and it was only the arrival of the railway that prompted the building of the hotels, the boating lake, the golf course and all those other facilities which

Remnants of the Roman fort at Castell Collen

Troedrhiwdalar Chapel

contributed to make Llandrindod so fashionable a retreat in the High Victorian era. The medicinal springs no longer attract much interest, yet the town is well worth a visit. It still retains that air of cloying elegance and respectability common to many of Wales' Victorian towns, behind whose bay windows and lace curtains Mr Grosvenor and his raffish friends would have been far from welcome. Indifferent to the ramshackle remnants of an earlier empire just down the road, the Victorian developers of those tall, serviceable houses seem to have built with a confidence that *their* empire and *their* way of life would last for ever.

Some Medieval and Early Modern Roads in Cardiganshire

Like one that on a lonesome road
Doth walk in fear and dread,
And having once turned round walks on,
And turns no more his head;
Because he knows a frightful fiend
Doth close behind him tread.

S.T. Coleridge
The Rime of the Ancient Mariner, 1799

For medieval man long-distance travel was a hazardous affair. The ever-present danger of highway robbery, the miserable condition of the road surfaces and the real possibility of passing unwittingly through a plague-infested area were enough to persuade the prudent to settle their affairs at home before embarking on a lengthy journey. Once Roman Britain had fallen into disarray and the hordes from northern Europe and Scandinavia had imposed their way of life on lowland Britain, there followed a virtually complete collapse in trade which was not to recover until the ninth and tenth centuries. By the sixth century, those communities in Wales that had come to accept the customs and laws of Rome had, by and large, abandoned them and throughout the long centuries between the departure of the Romans and the Norman Conquest the economy was essentially a Celtic one wherein pastoral farming predominated. Nevertheless arable agriculture based on settled farmsteads continued to play a role in the agrarian economy. Analysis of pollen samples indicates fluctuations in the relative significance of corn growing and shows, for example, that arable farming was particularly important in Roman times and again after 1150, though it certainly did not disappear in the intervening period.

As far as the living conditions of the people were concerned, scholars have tended until recently to draw heavily upon the works of medieval chroniclers, notably Giraldus Cambrensis who recorded his impressions of life in Wales in the late twelfth century; 'They do not live in towns, villages or castles, but lead a solitary existence deep in the woods. It is not their habit to build great palaces or vast and towering structures of stone and cement. Instead they content themselves with wattled huts on the edges of the forest, put up with little labour or expense, but strong enough to last a year or so.' Reading this one cannot help feeling that the bulk of the population lived in isolated and rather spartan conditions largely without material comforts. This was certainly so in many cases, yet archaeologists are now beginning to discover that there were occasionally more sophisticated settlements. Indeed, excavation of two of the numerous drystone or rubble-built circular huts in North Wales has revealed paved floors and a simple drainage system. Furthermore, there is growing evidence of continuity of occupation both of Iron Age hill forts and Roman sites well into the early medieval period, so that at a location like *Venta Silurum*, burials in the extra-mural cemetery continued into the ninth century. Giraldus's mention of the 'solitary existence' of the native Welsh has also been called into question on the realisation that there was a tendency towards siting settlements around the old Celtic churches and on the western coastal fringes. In short, we cannot yet make overall generalisations about the pattern of settlement any more than we can be even remotely exact about the size of settlements in the pre-Norman period.

Of one thing, however, we can be sure; the Roman concept of a series of well-defined roads was lost. Wooden bridges gradually rotted and were swept away by winter flood waters; trees fell across metalled highways, drainage channels became blocked and with the abandonment of repair work much of the network decayed, save for short stretches used by local traffic. In other words, throughout the Dark Ages communications became distinctly difficult and movement over long distances must have been tedious in the extreme, above all during the winter months. Even so this is not to imply that roads ceased completely to exist. In upland areas where a considerable proportion of the land on the lower mountain slopes had long been enclosed into hedged or stone-walled fields, there were innumerable local lanes used as access roads by farmers. Again, on the open mountain, unfenced tracks forged by the seasonal movements of livestock provided well-trodden courses for local people to travel in search of bracken and peat and for packhorses to move between farmsteads and hamlets. It has been suggested elsewhere, with reference to Devonshire, that virtually all the farms and their associated trackways on the Ordnance Survey map for that county would have appeared had the map been drawn a thousand years ago. There is good reason to believe that the same would apply to much of the northern and western parts of Wales, particularly as the Laws of Hywel Dda (Hywel the Good) specify in some detail the legal requirements regarding highways and by-ways.

At the time of his death around AD950 Hywel, a close friend of the English King Alfred, was ruler of a substantial part of Wales and he has traditionally been credited with codifying the customs of Wales into a single set of Laws governing virtually every aspect of daily life. The earliest copies of the Laws date from some two hundred and fifty years after Hywel had left the scene and some scholars have questioned the tradition that he and his chieftains were responsible for this massive undertaking. Whether it was Hywel Dda or some later luminary who took on the task, he clearly understood the role of roads and highways in economic development and effective government. Each *tref*, or township, the Laws state, should have a road running across and along it, while every habitation requires two footpaths, one leading to the church and a second to the watering place. Moreover, the same habitation should have a by-road of 7ft in width giving access to the commonland of the *tref* and the *tref* itself should be separated from its neighbour by a meer of 5ft wide. In addition, the large administrative unit, the *cantref*, consisting of 100 *trefs*, was to be delineated by a meer of 9ft wide. According to the Laws, the ruler reserved for himself the punishment of persons committing felonies (such as robbery and the felling of trees) on the King's Highway, which was to be maintained at a width of 12ft.

We find then, in the century before the Norman Conquest, a complex of local roads and trackways between villages and towns which had grown from habitual lines of travel by means of the movements of traders, pilgrims, tax-collectors and ecclesiastical and secular officials. It is important to realise that such roads were rarely 'built'. An occasional causeway over boggy ground might have been constructed, yet as a rule a medieval road represented a right of way along an existing trackway maintained by the passage of generations of men. As such, particularly where they ran through open hill country, these 'roads' would often be of great width since a horseman would always be on the lookout for an unbroken surface to ride on, as would the packhorse trains and strings of panniered horses which provided the principal means for the transport of goods. To this traffic the boggy, unmade surfaces would have offered relatively little obstacle. Even if the great magnate or court official travelling in a heavy covered waggon had cause to complain about the surface of the road, the fact that the extraordinarily mobile Norman and early Angevin kings did not bother to re-forge a definite road system implies that the existing roads were adequate for their purposes. It also suggests that however decayed they may have become, some of the old Roman roads still played a part in local and long-distance communications. This is borne out by the evidence of the celebrated 'Gough' map of 1360, the first to give the general directions of roads, wherein of almost 3,000 miles of road shown, some 40 per cent ran along the lines of recognized Roman roads. In Wales there are plenty of examples of Roman roads persisting in use through the medieval period and for centuries later. We find references in eleventh-century charters relating to properties in south-east Wales indicating that these lay both on local trackways and alongside what we now know to have been the course of Roman roads. Again, the Roman road from Llandovery to Brecon remained in use as a principal highway until the late eighteenth century, while a medieval Bishop of St Davids arranged for produce to be sent from his Brecknockshire farm to his Pembrokeshire palace by way of the Roman road through Carmarthenshire.

In the absence of a fully serviceable road network the movement of large numbers of troops in the more remote parts of Britain could present a field commander with prodigious logistical difficulties. To facilitate military activities in North Wales, Edward I cut a 30-mile highway from Chester to the River Conwy by way of Flint and Rhuddlan in 1277. Apart from the roads forged by the great Cistercian houses, this proved to be one of the few 'constructed' roads of medieval Wales and necessitated the employment of scores of sawyers, masons and charcoal burners. Significantly Edward ordered that the woodland on either side of the road was to be cleared to the width of one bowshot, a principle enshrined in the Statute of Winton of 1285 wherein a clearance of 200ft on each side of the King's Highway was specified.

By the sixteenth century woodland occupied little more than 10 per cent of the total area of Wales, yet in the remote valleys the proportion was considerably higher and in these and the mountainous regions, travel, even on horseback, was very difficult indeed. As he rode through the Principality with Baldwin, Archbishop of Canterbury in 1188, Giraldus Cambrensis experienced at first hand the narrow trackways, treacherous fords and steep mountains which, coupled with the inhospitality of the natives, meant that every mile of the journey carried with it the prospect of some incident or another. Even in the 1780s things were not that much better for, as Walter Davies observed, men and beasts tackled the hills and mountains, ' . . . more by a spirit of daringness than by craft or circumvention'.

Among the fundamental obligations of the medieval landholder to the Crown was that of maintaining the main highways of the land to facilitate the free passage of the king and his subjects. In theory then, the lord of the manor and his tenants were obliged to keep local roads and ways in serviceable condition. In practice because relatively few people benefited directly from road maintenance, this task was tackled with less than tepid enthusiasm. Also, such were the effects of the Black Death and the devastation wrought by the Wars of the Roses in the following century, that manpower availability throughout much of Britain was so reduced that road maintenance became virtually non-existent. As trade began to grow in the sixteenth century an effort to rationalize matters was effected in the concept of 'Statute Labour' whereby every parishioner occupying land was obliged to provide a cart with horses or oxen and two able-bodied men to help with road repairs, non-landholders being expected to work on the roads for four and later six, days each year. Normally carried out under the supervision of a parish-appointed surveyor who knew little about roads and cared less, Statute Labour was extremely unpopular and hopelessly ineffective. By-roads were almost entirely neglected, inter-parish disputes led to the abandonment of whole stretches of highway and in most cases where maintenance was carried out at all it was done in so desultory a manner that little in the way of improvement resulted.

Despite the exhortations of the Council of Wales and the Marches, the secular authorities in the remoter reaches of west Wales paid little attention to enforcing the 'Statute of the Mending of the Highways'. Occasionally, where a large acreage of a parish lay in the hands of a magnate who believed his interests would be served by ensuring adequate road surfaces, some effort was made to improve matters. In general, though, the nature of the lanes and trackways comprising the road network changed little between Roman times and the end of the sixteenth century.

The situation on the estates of the Cistercian abbeys was very different. With a domestic economy based on sheep farming over many thousands of acres and the constant need to provide for the requirements of pilgrims, the Cistercian monks concerned themselves closely with creating adequate communications on their territory and within its vicinity. This chapter will consider some of the roads associated with the abbey of Strata Florida on the edge of the bleak mountains of eastern Cardiganshire (SN746658).

By the end of the sixth century much of Wales had been converted to Christianity by those remarkable Celtic saints whose names are enshrined in church dedications and parish names throughout the Principality. Their early settlements on the coastal fringes of Dyfed, constantly under threat from Viking sea-raiders operating from Ireland or the Isle of Man, became havens of culture and civilization in a turbulent countryside in which the people struggled to exist and the princes engaged in their favourite activity of fighting among themselves. By the twelfth century the energies of the Welsh princes were concentrated on the ultimately unsuccessful attempt to repel Norman encroachment from the east. But even this fearsome threat was not enough completely to stop inter-tribal strife. For the next two hundred years west Wales bore witness to sporadic military activity and neither people nor Church could avoid becoming involved as the fortunes of one prince waxed and another waned and the formidable Anglo-Norman cavalry strove to bring the country to heel.

In 1164 a small group of Cistercian monks from the Abbey of Whitland in Carmarthenshire set out for the remote wastes of central Cardiganshire with the object of building a monastery on land provided for the purpose by Robert Fitz-Stephen, Lord of Pennardd. In accordance with the Cistercian principle of teaching the virtues of a hard life governed by strict rules, the monks had chosen to settle in a barren place, 'far removed from the concourse of men'. Bounded on the west by the peaty morass of Cors Caron and on the east by a great block of inhospitable mountains, they could hardly have selected a less promising locality. Yet, like other Cistercian groups in Wales, the monks of Strata Florida created an agricultural settlement which made a major contribution to the economic development of the area. Initially they occupied a site to the south-east of the present ruins, not far from the old Abbey Farm. However, twenty years after their arrival in Cardiganshire, the great prince Rhys ap Gruffudd granted to the monks large tracts of land stretching virtually from Pumlumon in the east to Aber-arth on the coast of Cardigan Bay. This prompted a shift in the monastery site and heralded the beginning of fifty years of building, the cruciform abbey being completed in the mid-thirteenth century. Constructed of stone brought by sea from Somerset to the little port of Aber-arth, the new abbey of Strata Florida proved to be the largest, if not the grandest, monastic building in medieval west Wales.

As they struggled to build the abbey, the monks concurrently developed their demesne farm, laid out gardens and orchards and directed attention to the more distant outposts of the foundation's lands. At the centre of a large mountain estate with granges throughout Cardiganshire and in the neighbouring counties of Brecknock and Radnor, sheep farming, aided by King John's grant of a licence to export wool, became the mainstay of the monastic economy. The monks' success with sheep did not go unnoticed by the native peasantry and there are indications that by the early thirteenth century sheep began to increase in importance in an agricultural economy wherein animal husbandry had previously been dominated by cattle. Meanwhile, the monks found fish to be readily available in the lakes on the upland granges while weirs constructed in the streams passing through the abbey lands and on the coast at Aber-arth provided further opportunities for fishing. Also, the possession of granges on lower-lying land at Morfa Mawr, Anhuniog and Blaenaeron meant that oats and barley could be grown for consumption by both humans and livestock.

As a market for their surplus produce and that of their tenants and as a source of income from tolls, the monks founded the great fair at nearby Ffair-rhos (SN742680). This proved eminently attractive to visitors, as a visit to the fair could be combined with a pilgrimage to the abbey. To Ffair-rhos on St James Day, the Feast of the Assumption and Holy Rood Day, flocked local farmers, pedlars, pilgrims and the usual gang of ne'er-do-wells along with traders in cattle, sheep and wool. A similar clientèle attended the fair at nearby Ystradmeurig, established under the patronage of the Knights Hospitallers and an important trading centre until the early nineteenth century when the principal fair in this part of Cardiganshire became centred on Pontrhydfendigaid (SN705676).

Strata Florida Abbey;
The great gateway

For almost 200 years Strata Florida Abbey was a major economic and cultural centre, surviving military activity, lightning, fire and the changing fortunes of the medieval economic climate. It was dealt a severe blow during the Glyndŵr rebellion when (and for years later) its precincts housed a royal garrison. Subsequently, bickering between the monks and other Church officials and the break up of the traditional medieval economy resulted in the abbey's falling into decline and the demesne lands being let out to lay tenants. Its fortunes had reached such a low ebb that on the eve of the Dissolution, Strata Florida supported a mere six monks and an abbot, and had a rental income of no more than £150.

In its heyday, though, the abbey was the venue of hundreds of pilgrims, ranging from 'professional' palmers travelling from shrine to shrine motivated by a combination of religious devotion and wanderlust, to the ordinary citizen for whom a pilgrimage provided both a holiday and a means of observing the requirements of the Church. By the late Middle Ages, domestic pilgrimages had become increasingly popular and the papal dispensation that 'twice to St Davids' was equivalent to 'once to Rome' meant that Welsh shrines enjoyed a considerable vogue. Strata Florida was conveniently sited near the meeting place of several ancient tracks with the coastal highway linking the shrine of St David with the holy island of Bardsey, both important centres for pilgrimages. A particular attraction of Strata Florida was a small, much-worn wooden cup, reputed to be a fragment of the True Cross or, according to another tradition, to be that most holy of relics, the cup used at the Eucharist. The cup, escaping the enthusiastic searches of Edward VI's 'anti-relic' commissioners eventually came into the possession of the Powell family of Nanteos near Aberystwyth, and is considered to have been with the monks even before they moved from the earlier abbey site. The cup apparently

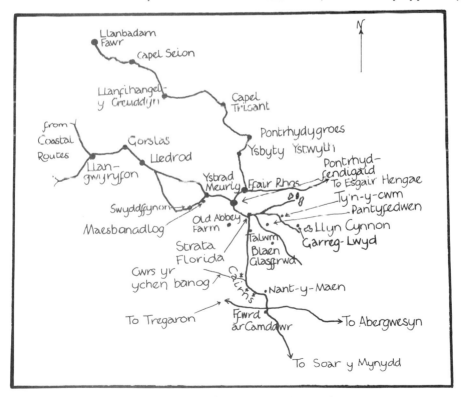

Roads associated with the abbey of Strata Florida, Cardiganshire

possessed miraculous properties and those drinking from it could be cured of all manner of ills. Small wonder, then, that it attracted a multitude of pilgrims to the abbey, particularly in years when plague and pestilence stalked the land.

Towards the end of the pilgrim era, Henry VIII's antiquary John Leland visited Strata Florida and travelled extensively in the surrounding countryside, his horse carrying him through a landscape by now substantially deforested. Since 1280 when the King's Justiciary of West Wales had been ordered to destroy the woodlands, 'where robberies, homicides and other enormities against the King's peace have been wont to be committed', the English kings had striven to reduce forest cover and thus to deny the Welsh a base for guerilla operations. This policy, along with the growing demand for charcoal for lead smelting operations, meant that by the mid-fifteenth century the bulk of the remaining forests on the lowlands of mid-Cardiganshire had yielded to plough and pasture. Readers of Dr Rachel Bromwich's splendid edition, in both English and Welsh, of the works of the great fourteenth-century Cardiganshire poet Dafydd ap Gwilym, might gain a rather different impression. Dafydd's description of his amorous adventures with the local ladies makes frequent reference to forest and woodland where he wandered in pursuit of passion. It is important, however, to differentiate between the term 'forest' in its modern and medieval senses. Within a medieval 'forest' large areas of cleared land used for agricultural purposes were interspersed with groves and blocks of woodland of varying sizes and mix of species.

The mountain sides though, were almost exclusively under rank, open grasslands which, according to Leland, '... be so great that the hunderith part of hitt rottith on the ground and maketh sogges and quikke more by long continuance for lak of eting of hit'. Here the peasants dug peat for their fires, poached the occasional trout and eel and tended their herds during the summer months, living as they did in 'vari poore cottagis for somer dayres for catel'.

The early eighteenth-century maps delineate a roadline from Machynlleth to Ponterwyd across bleak open mountain via Glaspwll, Gwaunbwll, Dolrhuddlan, Bwlch y Styllen and Dinas (SN745007-748808). The young Michael Faraday, with some trepidation, trekked between Ponterwyd and Machynlleth in 1819, describing this trail in his diary as having, '... (1) no roads (2) no houses (3) no people (4) rivers but no bridges (5) plenty of mountains'. Five hundred years previously it would have been little different when groups of pilgrims, preferring this to the longer (if less arduous) coastal route, trudged their way to Ponterwyd to meet like-minded travellers entering Cardiganshire from the east.

The tracing in detail of the routes taken by these medieval pilgrims to Strata Florida and those followed by the monks to their outlying granges is bedevilled by difficulties. Besides the absence of contemporary maps and the scantiness of the printed literature it has to be appreciated that many of the roads and trackways of mid-Cardiganshire had been in use for centuries and it is difficult to differentiate between 'prehistoric', 'dark-age' and 'medieval' roadlines. Nevertheless, the countryside is replete with evocative field and place-names providing valuable clues as to areas with pilgrim or monastic associations. Combined with evidence on the ground, such names, gleaned from the nineteenth-century Tithe Apportionments, enable roadlines to be established with some accuracy and the remainder of this chapter seeks to describe just a few of the many routes leading to and from the abbey of Strata Florida.

PONTERWYD TO STRATA FLORIDA

Pilgrims heading south from Ponterwyd pursued a route which was direct and kept to the higher ground to avoid the rushy morasses of the vales. The available evidence suggests that the medieval road as far as Devils Bridge followed the course of the present A4120 separating the lovely Vale of Rheidol from the grim mountains to the east, and past Ysbyty Cynfyn for the entire length of the journey (SN753791). The word *Yspyty* and its corruptions *Ysbyty*, *Spital* and *Spite* occur frequently in this part of Cardiganshire. Besides the villages of Ysbyty Cynfyn, Ysbyty Ystwyth and Ysbyty Ystrad-meurig, there is a *Spite* and a *Tavernspite* on the line of the Roman Sarn Helen. There are also numerous house and field names of this type on the Cardiganshire coastal road, the course of the major pilgrim route between Bardsey and St Davids. One of these, *Spytty Hâl*, on the site of three demolished cottages at Llanrhystud (SN39698), was located on land granted by Rhys ap Gruffudd to the Knights Hospitallers of St John, who also administered property at Betws Ifan, Betws Leucu and Pontarfynach (Devils Bridge) from their headquarters at Slebech in Pembrokeshire. The derivation of the Welsh *Ysbyty* from the Latin *hospitium* has been questioned by some scholars, but it is not without significance that these name elements occur at strategic points on several established pilgrim routes. In any event, hospitality was a basic duty of all monastic bodies and in the absence of the *hospitia*, where news was exchanged, legends were created and friendships forged, medieval travel would have been a far from pleasant business.

Of recent years scholars have begun to doubt the traditional assumption that Ysbyty Cynfyn itself is of monastic origin. They have, moreover, tended to dismiss the view that the location of the church within a circular enclosure incorporating

Standing stone built into the wall of Ysbyty Cynfyn churchyard

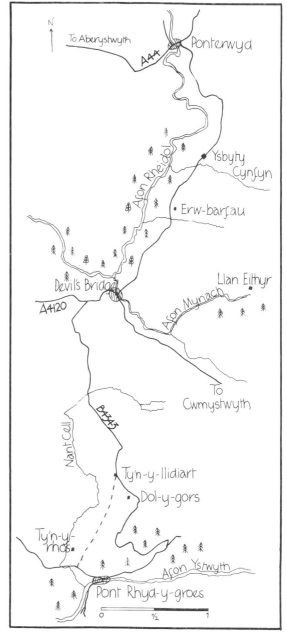

several large standing stones is indicative of continuity of site from pagan times, pointing out that the present shape has its origin in church and churchyard expansion at various times during the nineteenth century. There is no direct evidence to link the Cistercians or Knights Hospitallers with the site, nor, for that matter, with Ysbyty Ystwyth and Ysbyty Ystrad-meurig. Yet the strength of local tradition in this respect cannot be entirely neglected. For example, approximately half-a-mile to the east of the present church lay a chapel of ease, locally believed to have been associated with Strata Florida. It may even have been this site of which Lewis Morris wrote in 1755: '. . . once a year . . . they remain all night in the chapel and try their activities in wrestling, all the benches being removed and the spectators generally young women and old champions who are to see fair play.' Furthermore, at Llaneithyr on the banks of the River Mynach to the south east is *Cae Ffynon Saint* (Field of the saints' spring) traditionally supposed to represent the location of an ancient church. Unfortunately no field evidence remains (SN762772).

Circular cemetery enclosures embracing the older churches are quite common in west Wales and it has been suggested that at least some of these pre-date the church with which they are associated. The place-name element *llan*, commonly found in conjunction with early churches, appears originally to have referred to the enclosure as opposed to the church itself. Evidence for this is provided by those farmsteads and other secular structures which have *llan* in their names and circular enclosures associated with them.

From Ysbyty Cynfyn the pilgrims passed the farm of Erw-barfau (mentioned in a deed of 1590) to arrive at Devils Bridge where the confluence of the Rheidol and Mynach created those remarkable scenic effects that were to move to rapture artists and writers of a later period (SN742770). Of the three bridges over the Mynach gorge only the lowest need concern us as it is usually claimed that this was built for the benefit of pilgrims by the Strata Florida monks in 1087 and provided a convenient crossing place for Giraldus Cambrensis on his oddysey a century later. While Giraldus was travelling through Wales, the monks of Strata Florida would have been busy with their new abbey and it seems rather unlikely that they would have gone to the trouble to build a relatively sophisticated stone bridge at this time in what was, after all, a rather remote spot. It is much more probable that they bridged the Mynach initially with a temporary wooden structure and replaced this with the present one at a later stage in the abbey's history.

Beyond Devils Bridge the pilgrim route pursued the present B4343 towards Pontrhydygroes (*rhyd* = ford; *groes* = cross; *pont* = bridge) as far as the farm of Ty'nyllidiart (SN742746). Here it deviated from the present road winding past Dol-y-gors and Pant-y-craf to take an ancient lane running directly south. Leaving Ty'nyllidiart as a rather marshy enclosed way some six yards wide, the lane runs along a causeway across the hilltop beyond Dol y gors whence it descends for a hundred yards or so as a deep green lane enclosed by high banks surmounted by

The pilgrims' way from Ty'nyllidiart

wych elm trees. Subsequently it follows the line of a deep ditch (created by recent farm drainage work) towards the valley of Nant Gell where it joins a narrow lane opening into the Aberystwyth road approximately one hundred yards to the west of the bridge over the Ystwyth at Pontrhydygroes (SN739728). There may be some significance in the fact that as this lane descends towards Pontrhydygroes it aligns directly with Ysbyty Ystwyth church on the southern side of the Ystwyth valley where, in the fourteenth century, Moelgwyn Fychan is supposed to have granted land to the monks for the building of an *hospitium*.

After crossing the Ystwyth, presumably by way of a wooden bridge, pilgrims and other travellers followed the B4343 through Ysbyty Ystwyth and over rather gloomy countryside towards Ffair-rhôs, passing the farm of *Llwyngwyddel* (Irishman's Grove) on the way (SN741686). This is one of several sites with *Gwyddel* (Irish) or kindred name elements in this part of Wales, many of which may have been associated with Dark Age Irish settlements. We know little of the density of Irish settlement in the fourth, fifth and sixth centuries, yet the presence of ogham inscribed stones throughout south-west Wales and the inclusion of Irish names and traditions in later Welsh genealogies implies that at least some of the Irish raiders who crossed the sea in search of slaves found things sufficiently to their liking to remain permanently. It is even possible that local chieftains offered them land in the hope that this would curtail the blood-letting and rapine accompanying their regular visits to Welsh shores. What is fairly certain from the

Pilgrims' route to Strata Florida

Lôn Nantaches

evidence of inscriptions and place-names is that in the sixth century at least, much of southern Dyfed was Goidelic in character and language. While a great deal can be gained in this connexion from the study of place-names, *Guyddel* calls for an element of caution since some locations may derive their names from those of itinerant Irish harvest labourers of the eighteenth and nineteenth centuries. No such interpretative problems occur with *Llwynguyddel* which appears by name in a Chancery suit of 1532. Anyhow, it is noteworthy that by medieval times the word *Guyddel* had come to be recognized as a term of derision, rather like *Paddy* today, and may have occasioned a wry smile on the part of passing pilgrims.

After Ffair-rhôs, whose local importance as a trading centre was emphasised by its delineation on Speed's and Seller's maps of 1610 and 1695, the road continues for several hundred yards in the direction of Pontrhydfendigaid (Bridge over the Blessed Ford) to Borough Gate. From here to the village, the B4343 follows what is clearly a relatively recent course on a line suggestive of an enclosure road. Medieval travellers approached Pontrhydfendigaid more directly by leaving the existing road and heading south-west for the village school along what, by tradition, represents the course of an old road. Though recent field rationalisation and agricultural activity have removed any evidence on the ground, this road joined what was almost certainly the original approach to the abbey.

In medieval times, the present 'Abbey Road', if in use at all, would have passed through boggy meadowland, difficult to negotiate even during the summer months. It is reasonable to suppose, therefore, that visitors to the abbey and the monks themselves would have sought a drier, and if possible, more direct approach from the north. In all probability this was by way of the old lane running from the village school to the ford over the Teifi immediately to the north of the abbey. *Lôn Nantaches*, the present name of this lane, is apparently a corruption of *Lôn y Fynaches* (Monk's Lane) by which it was known earlier this century. *Lôn Nantaches* leads off the B4343 from a gate adjoining the school and after a few yards of tarmac continues past the remains of an old well as a deep, green lane with banks planted with wych elm, hawthorn and hazel (SN735663). Varying from two to five yards in width it passes through the woods of Coed Penybannau below the Iron Age univallate hill-fort and its adjoining hut circles, and then traverses open fields on a causeway running above some abandoned lead workings towards the nineteenth-century ruins of Bronyberllan (SN746662). Here the abbey first came fully into view and visitors no doubt marvelled at its splendours, the massive limestone walls and finely executed tracery contrasting starkly with the crude

69

vernacular architecture of the surrounding countryside. After a brief pause to stand and stare and perhaps even to offer a prayer of thanks upon the safe completion of their journey, the pilgrims descended along the ancient hedgeline south of Bronyberllan to ford the Teifi at a spot close to the present footbridge leading to the ruins of the abbey.

LLANFIHANGEL-Y-CREUDDYN TO PONTRHYDYGROES

The great church of St Padarn at Llanbadarn Fawr near Aberystwyth, an ancient foundation at the time of the establishment of Strata Florida, was an ecclesiastical centre of importance in medieval times and a port of call for pilgrims and church officials as they travelled through this part of Cardiganshire. From Llanbadarn the route to Strata Florida would have been by way of the Devils Bridge road beyond Capel Seion and thence to Llanfihangel-y-Creuddyn, the meeting place of a complex of deep lanes running through leafy countryside (SN665760).

Leaving this village, medieval travellers ascended the present road past Pen-y-banc, occupying the course of an old upland trail to Capel Trisant, and thus avoided the steep slopes of Banc Cwm Magwr and Banc Nantrhiwgenau (SN717757). To the east of Blaen Cwm Magwr this road meets a number of old lanes, one of which, from Pen Bwlch Crwys to the north, was used by pilgrims working their way to Strata Florida from the Rheidol Valley (SN707765). Beyond the junction a deep narrow lane leads to the farm of Rhyd-y-pererinion (*pererin, pererinion* = pilgrim/s). Thence, instead of continuing down the lane to Mynydd Bach, the pilgrim trail followed a hedge line due south to rejoin the road above Capel Trisant, to pass Fron-goch Pool and on through broken hill country now rendered rather desolate by the remnants of nineteenth-century lead workings. Today's traveller might consider the rather scruffy remains of the many lead mines in the area to be a blight on the scenic beauty of Cardiganshire. It should be remembered, however, that the lead industry contributed significantly to the economy of the county over many centuries and the last vestiges of the mines are as worthy of preservation as any other class of monument. Each year the mines sink further into decay as shafts and leets are filled in and surface material is removed. This is a matter of growing concern to officers of the Royal Commission on Ancient Monuments and National Monuments Record (Wales) whose Aberystwyth headquarters would welcome public interest in the conservation of mines and other remnants of our industial past.

The ruins of Strata Florida from Bronyberllan

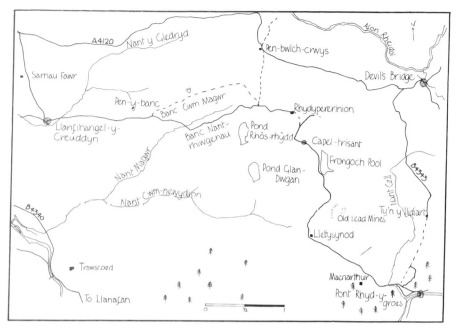

Pilgrims' routes near Devil's Bridge

Beyond the lead workings, past Lletty Synod (which occurs in an indenture of 1571) and the miners' cottages at New Row, the pilgrims' road forded Nant Cell where it left the existing road for the old lane to Pontrhydygroes shared by the route from Devils Bridge. Apart from accommodating pilgrims, the way from Capel Trisant to Pontrhydygroes was of considerable importance to local farmers in the late Middle Ages, as indicated by the frequent mention of the corn mill at *Maenarthur* in fifteenth- and sixteenth-century documents (SN729728).

LLANGWYRYFON TO PONTRHYDFENDIGAID

Travellers leaving the coastal route for St Davids with the intention of visiting Strata Florida had the option of following one of the many ancient trackways winding inland from Llanrhystud and Llanddeiniol towards Llangwyryfon. In respect of Llanddeiniol it is worth noting the location of *Spite* on the A487 to the west of the

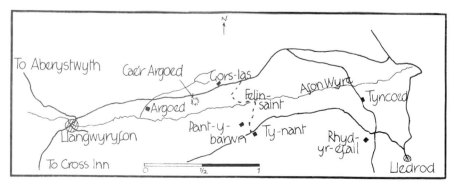

Trackways towards Strata Florida from the west

village and the farm of *Palmon* (= palmer?, pilgrim?) on the banks of Afon Carreg to the east (SN569722).

There is no field or place-name evidence to substantiate it, but a very probable course would have taken pilgrims along the lane from Llanrhystud, skirting the earthwork of Caer Penrhos and across the dry land above Cwm Wyre to Llangwyryfon (SN599708). East of the village the present road meanders past Gors-las before moving away to the north-east and then turning south towards Lledrod. Approximately a hundred yards to the east of Gors-lâs a gate on the right-hand side of the road lies at the end of a raised causeway cutting across the open fields (SN622712). This descends the steep slope of the Wyre Valley to *Felin Saint* (Saints' Mill) and *Rhyd Saint* (Saints' Ford), both of which occur on the Tithe Maps,

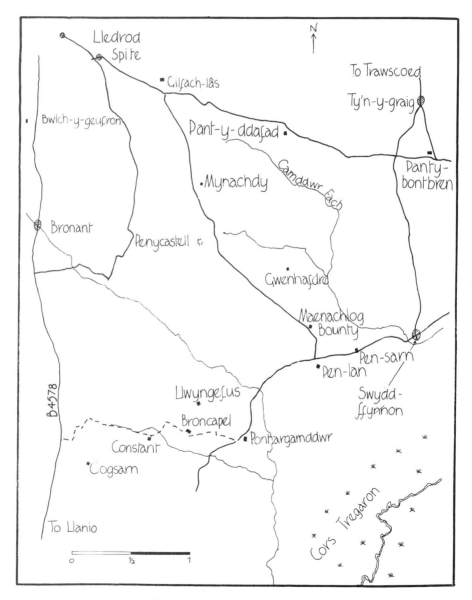

Alternative routes towards Strata Florida from the west

while *Melin Rhyd-y-saint* appears in a legal covenant of 1599 (SN624709). Of the mill, used as a dwelling-house until the early years of the present century, only a pile of debris in the woodlands in the valley bottom now remains. From the ford by the mill a green lane climbs steeply up the side of the valley towards Pantybarwn where it turns abruptly left along a hedge line to meet a gate on the metalled lane leading to Lledrod past Ystafell-wen and Rhiwafallen (SN645703). Since the local mill was of major importance to the community and the lane adjacent to it provided the most direct route between Llangwyryfon and Lledrod, this, like those connecting with other mills in the area, was probably an important trackway in medieval times, while the name 'Saints' Mill' itself is indicative of pilgrim connexions.

An indenture of mid-seventeenth-century date refers to *Tythin yr Artal Mawr*, a farmstead located at the time near Bwlch-y-geufron to the south of Lledrod. *Artal* and its derivatives *Rattal, Ratshole* and *Ratsol* may represent a corruption of *Rhastl* (a rack or crib) or *atal* (to stop or prevent, in the sense of being an impediment). If *atal* is the correct interpretation, it is interesting that this word tends to occur as a place-name element on roadlines where the traveller faced a stretch of boggy ground, a rocky defile or some other obstacle to movement. *Atal* is merely one of many much-corrupted place-names whose deciphering awaits the advent of a Welsh scholar with an interest in historical geography and the stamina to tramp the highways and by-ways of this part of the world.

To the north-east of *Tythin yr Artal Mawr* lies *Spite Cottage* beyond which the pilgrims headed eastwards for Ystrad-meurig along one of two possible routes, the first following the present road past Penlan and across the Roman *Sarn Helen* to enter the village from the north. At Penderlwynwen below Pant-y-bont-bren are

Medieval roadline towards Maesbanadlog

two fields, *Cae dan rhydgaled* (*rhydgaled* = paved ford) and *Cae pwllcleifion* (*cleifion* = invalids), the latter term being of particular significance in view of the association of Ystrad-meurig with the Knights Hospitallers and the tradition that a hospital was maintained at Hafod-y-cleifion near the site of the old Strata Florida railway station (SN712672). While this is some distance from the abbey itself the prevalence of plague and leprosy in the Middle Ages meant that the locating of a quarantine 'hospital' near the junction of several routes to the abbey would have seemed eminently sensible. Here, or perhaps at *Tir-llety y cleifion*, (by the seventeenth century an alternative name for nearby Tre Isaf Farm), sick or invalid pilgrims and other travellers could be 'screened' before being allowed into the abbey.

An alternative route for Ystrad-meurig and Pontrhydfendigaid involved turning south off the previous road beyond Gilfach-las and crossing open common land to pass by the earthwork of Penycastell with its large round motte and counterscarp bank (SN663675). Now served by a metalled road, this course passes through rather melancholy countryside punctuated by clumps of trees representing the sites of abandoned farmsteads, notably Mynachdy Ffynnon Oer with its assoicated wayside spring. Further on, at Gwernhafdre Uchaf, are two fields called *Maenachlog Bounty* (*Maenachlog, Mynachlog* = monastery) below which the road turns left for Swyddffynnon along the lane from Castell Flemish (SN692662). It is widely believed that this lane, in part, lies on the easterly route taken by pilgrims leaving the Roman road of *Sarn Helen* at a point close to Cog-sarn, whence it passed through Constant and Broncapel to join the Castell Flemish-Swyddffynnon road at Pontargamddwr (SN669648). Although the Tithe Map of the area shows a causeway at Constant (SN657649) and a *Ratshole* to the north-east, it is difficult, given the nature of the terrain, to see this as a regularly-used pilgrims' way. However, at Cae Demer, Broncapel, were originally the remains of a chapelry served by the Strata Florida monks who must have approached the place by way of Swyddffynnon, the great bog of Cors Caron preventing the forging of a more direct route.

From the tiny village of Swyddffynnon, today's travellers approach Ystrad-meurig along the metalled road past the remains of the important (and much-fought over) Norman stronghold eventually dismantled by Maelgwyn ap Rhys in 1202 (SN702675). However, at Ty'nybanal, approximately half-a-mile towards Ystrad-meurig an ancient lane leaves the road and skirts the wet land on the northern flank of Cors Caron to run past Maesbanadlog, before joining the B4340 west of Ystrad-meurig Post Office (SN710673). In view of the preponderance of evocative field names in the vicinity it is likely that this lane, varying from 10ft to 30ft in width and enclosed by high banks, originally provided a more direct route to Pontrhydfendigaid and thus to the abbey.

MOUNTAIN WAYS TO THE EAST

Eastwards of the River Teifi much of Cardiganshire is high country of peat-capped plateaux cut by deep, rocky valleys. For much of the year when rain-sodden winds sweep off Cardigan Bay, these lonely uplands comprise an inhospitable environment for both man and beast. Yet, since time out of mind, men have driven their sheep and cattle to the mountain grazings during the brief summer months, the ruins of enclosures and simple *hafod* dwellings bearing silent witness to this practice. Until well into the eighteenth century the transhumance system whereby livestock was transferred for the summer from the lowland *hendre* to the mountain *hafod*, accompanied by the women and older menfolk, remained an important feature of the farming economy. So effective was the *hafod/hendre* system in terms of optimum utilisation of pasture that it was readily adopted by the Cistercian monks on their granges in the heartlands of Wales. The need for the monks and their lay assistants to move readily from the abbey to the upland granges, and for that matter, to the various chapelries on the remoter parts of their property, meant that over the years recognized trackways became established. Many of these trails, followed by countless pack-horse trains throughout the two hundred or so years of Strata Florida's history, probably followed the lines of trackways forged centuries previously. As with so many roads, however, it is virtually impossible to be sure of their origins. In later centuries some of these long-distance cross-country routes came to be used by cattle drovers heading for the English border; later still they became incorporated into the network of Forestry Commission roads.

Singer's map of 1803 shows a road from Ffair-rhôs running to the north of the Teifi Pools and south of the isolated mountain farm of Claerddu (SN793687). This road, known locally as the 'Monks Way', forms part of the ancient route linking Strata Florida with its granges of Nannnerth and Cwmdeuddwr on the River Wye and eventually with the sister foundation of Cwmhir near St Harmon in

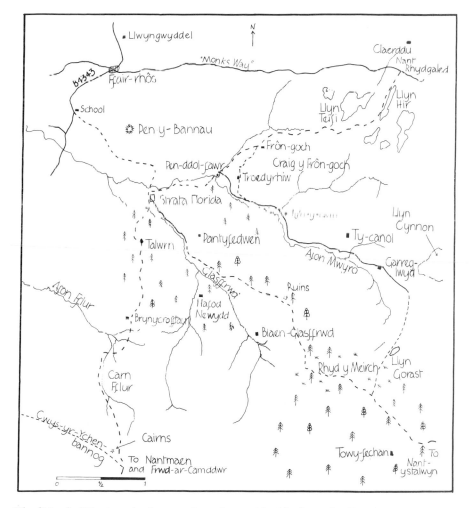

The 'Monks Way' and other tracks to Strata Florida from the East.

75

The 'Monks' Way' fording the Claerwen

Radnorshire. It is possible nowadays to drive along the road to a point just beyond Llyn Hir at 1,400ft above sea level, crossing *Nant Rhydgaled* (Stream of the paved ford) on the way. As they laid their stepping stones in the little stream, the monks probably reflected upon the desolate nature of the terrain which could hardly have been further 'removed from the concourse of men', the rock-strewn countryside silent save for the moaning of the wind. As the modern tarmac comes to an abrupt halt, the 'Monks' Way' deteriorates into a rough track. Recent traffic has changed the nature of the surface, yet careful inspection reveals the remains of clearance cairns and, at points where the road passes over a peaty depression, evidence of the carefully placed flat paving-stones some distance below the present surface. Half-a-mile beyond the ford over the River Claerddu the 'Monk's Way' leaves the track across the great blanket of peat to the south of Claerwen and heads in a north-easterly direction by way of a path across the boggy slopes of Esgair-Hengae (SN805677). Here and there the course of the path seems to be defined by marker stones, although these may be merely incidental. Certainly for most of its course the route is rather difficult to follow, except where it occurs as a sunken way or a terrace around a contour. To the north-east of the ruins of the ancient upland farmstead of Hengae, the 'Monks' Way' fords the River Claerwen before ascending the slope of Esgair Cwynion as a green way into Radnorshire (SN824682). Here again there are occasional suggestions of crude paving where the way crosses a patch of peat on the open hillside. From the brow of Esgair Cwynion the road can be seen as it passes to the south of Llyn Cerrigllwydion Uchaf. It then runs on for several miles to the River Elan ford (SN899719) where it crosses the old Rhayader-Aberystwyth turnpike and negotiates further hills before finally reaching the banks of the River Wye.

The Tithe Map for the parish of Gwnnws marks a road passing through Troedyrhiw and Fron-goch to the north-east of Strata Florida and joining the 'Monks' Way' above Llyn Hir (SN791682). This was the path taken by Leland when he set out from the abbey in the 1530s to view the Teifi Pools and Claerddu River, only to find, 'in no place within sight no woodd but al hilly pastures'. It has changed little; a landscape treeless as far as the eye can see with frost shattered rock, moorland peat and rough pasture being its dominant features. Leaving the abbey, this old road passed Dolau-fflur and then followed the line of the present road to Pen-ddôl Fawr. Here it forded a tributary of the Teifi and ran up the valley to Troedyrhiw, not far from where a medieval long-hut and associated enclosures have been identified (SN764663). Looking westwards from Troedyrhiw the observer cannot fail to be impressed by the numerous ruins of farmsteads dotted about the hillsides. These are likely to have originated as *hafodydd* serving farms in the Teifi Valley east of Pontrhydfendigaid, and provide evidence of the relatively dense occupation of this countryside prior to farm amalgamation and the creation of self-contained upland holdings.

Between Troedyrhiw and Fron-goch, a distance of rather more than half-a-mile, recent agricultural improvements have obscured the course of the road. However, from behind the house at Fron-goch it can be followed round the northern side of Craigyfrongoch along a rough track cleared through the stone-strewn upland pastures. This eventually descends to ford the infant River Teifi before climbing towards Llyn Hir along a hollow way, now only discernible in parts. Leland remarked upon the excellence of the trout and eels of Llyn Hir, Llyn Teifi and the other lakes of the Teifi Pools group, and it seems that the route described, certainly representing the most direct and easily negotiable way between the abbey and the lakes, was that taken by the monks of Strata Florida to their mountain fisheries. There is a local tradition that the monks also took fish from Llyn Cynnon to the south of the Teifi Pools where a medieval complex, including a long-hut linked to the lake by a slabbed trackway under the peat layer, has been reported by the Royal Commission on Ancient Monuments. The Commission suggest that what appears to be a slab-lined store cut into the hillside was used for holding fish before carrying the catch back to the abbey. If this was so, the monks would have reached the remote lake by way of the lane from Ty'n-y-cwm, south-east of Troedyrhiw on the trail to the Teifi Pools (SN771655). This ancient track, running along the vale of the Myro to Garreg-lwyd, passes through a stretch of countryside offering yet another reminder of the relative density of the population of these uplands in former times. The valley bottom and the bracken covered hillsides are dotted with the remnants of houses, farm buildings and livestock enclosures, some abandoned over the last hundred and fifty years during times of agricultural depression and

Enclosed lane on the line of the monks' road near Talwrn

others long before that. Many, connected by a network of trackways, may themselves be of considerable antiquity, while others yet may represent early settlement sites. On the hillside below the ruins of the early nineteenth-century farmstead of Tycanol, for example, are the remains of a single-storey house and several small enclosures. Was this an earlier Tycanol; and if so, when did it originally come into being? What area of land did its occupiers cultivate and what caused them to abandon the site? The problem with questions of this sort is that few of these ruins contain datable artefacts. Also, because there are no *known* surviving farm buildings of Dark Age or medieval construction in Cardiganshire (and a mere handful in the Principality as a whole), it is difficult to decide on the provenance of a ruin unless its architecture proclaims it to be of a recent period. The possibility remains, though, that a ruined farmstead, even of Victorian origin, may mark the location of a settlement with Dark Age and perhaps prehistoric origins. Only a combination of careful and exhaustive local studies by historians and excavation of selected sites by archaeologists will help to give the true picture.

A particularly important route used by the Strata Florida monks was that connecting the abbey with the chapelry of Ystrad-ffin and the grange of Nant-y-bai in Carmarthenshire. From the abbey site the rocky lane behind the adjacent farm fords the Glasffrwd near the present footbridge and climbs through old woodlands of oak and silver birch. At this stage the precise line of the trackway is difficult to follow owing to the cattle tracks running around and across it. However, the approach to the ruins of Talwrn at the edge of the woodland is by way of an enclosed lane lying on the line of the monks' road (SN745649). As it continues southwards beyond the farm, the antiquity of its banks and the diversity of tree species growing upon them, suggest a possible early origin for this road. Passing through a further stretch of woodland into unenclosed countryside beyond the fields south of Talwrn, the banks disappear and the road becomes a hollow way of 4-5ft deep. Here, if one takes the trouble to scrape away the oak, birch and, more lately, coniferous debris of the centuries it appears, in places, to have been paved with small, regular stones set in the underlying clay. Beyond this deciduous woodland the road enters wet open hills and runs through a recent Forestry Commission plantation. Today its course through the young plantation is difficult to identify and the walker's progress is severely hampered by luxuriant growth of rushes and bracken. In the Middle Ages, however, when the track would have been regularly used, the going was no doubt easier and groups of monks would have regularly tramped their way into the gloomy hills of the south, perhaps turning

Brynycrofftau

Medieval hollow way beyond Pantyfedwen

Stones from Strata Florida incorporated into nearby farm buildings

round from time to time to contemplate the fine views over the upper reaches of the Teifi. Rather more than a mile beyond Talwrn the track skirts the ruins of Brynycrofftau (SN744633). Incorporating massive stones, some of them carefully faced, this complex of buildings seems to have been erected without the use of mortar and certainly gives the impression of being of some antiquity. To the south-east of the house are the ruins of what has been identified as a small corn-drying kiln of eighteenth- or nineteenth-century origin with a stone-lined drying chamber and stone-capped flue. This should remind us again that we tend to think of upland Wales as being dominated by an almost exclusively pastoral economy, yet cereals were grown in these hills and valleys in times past. During the Napoleonic Wars, the high price of wheat meant that it was profitable to grow that crop in these ecologically marginal areas while eight hundred years earlier, the need for subsistence led to the cultivation of wheat, barley and oats for human and animal consumption and of flax for making linen. We do not know, and are unlikely ever to know, the relative significance of arable and pastoral farming in the Welsh uplands in medieval times, although it is worth recalling that at the end of the twelfth century climatic conditions were rather more favourable to cereal growing than they are today.

As one looks directly west from Brynycrofftau towards the site of the Old Abbey three miles away, further ruined farmsteads come into view. These scattered holdings, with their tiny enclosed fields carved from the hillside, appear on architectural grounds to be of eighteenth- or nineteenth-century date, but some of them at least, might represent medieval settlement sites. Alternatively they may mark the position of *hafodydd* of indeterminate date or, yet again, the location of eighteenth-century squatters' dwellings. If they are in fact of medieval origin, this particular stretch of countryside would have seemed rather less empty and melancholy to the traveller than it does to us today.

After descending the slopes of Carn Fflur to ford the River Fflur, the road once again begins to climb and after two miles across open mountain it passes to the east of a complex of Bronze Age cairns at 1,776ft above sea level (SN741610). It is likely that these and others of the many cairns in this part of Cardiganshire owe their survival to their having served as markers on routes and trackways. Hundreds, if not thousands, of those cairns in less accessible places have been taken for building material, a practice which, if it continues, will yet further impoverish our already threatened corpus of field monuments. Beyond the cairn complex the road runs southwards to join the line of the ancient earthwork of *Cwys-yr-Ychen Bannog*. The earthwork, visible to the east of the cairns, forms the dividing line between the parishes of Upper and Lower Caron and is believed to have been built by the monks of Strata Florida to define the extent of the land granted them by Rhys ap Gruffudd. The *Cwys* is certainly a boundary marker of some description, but there remains some doubt as to its origins, the most widely held view at present being that it dates from the Dark Ages.

Below the cairns the road is clearly visible on aerial photographs, although rather difficult to follow on the ground as it runs in a south-easterly direction towards Nantymaen (SN762585). The general course, though, was across the slopes of Bryn Cosyn and Esgair Ambor, thereby avoiding the dangerous bogs of Blaen Camddwr. Now and again, especially between the two cairns at the foot of Bryn Cosyn and Esgair Ambor, the road follows a modern fence line and on the descent to Nantymaen it runs alongside the remnants of an earthwork, presumably the southern extension of *Cwys-yr-Ychen Bannog*. At Nantymaen the road is incorporated with the farm lane heading for Ffrwd-ar-Camddwr on the intersection with the older drovers' road between Tregaron and Abergwesyn. From the ruins of Ffrwd-ar-Camddwr, a farm cited in the marriage settlement of James Pryse and

Ellynor Gwynne in 1589, the monks' road continued along the banks of the Camddwr on the long journey south past Soar-y-mynydd to Ystrad-ffin.

Yet another road from the abbey of Strata Florida crosses the mountains in a south-easterly direction to join the Tregaron-Abergwesyn trail at Nantystalwyn, involving a journey of some ten miles. Once again this road is marked on Singer's 1803 map and features prominently on the Tithe Maps of the parish of Caron, while aerial photographs taken in the 1940s, before the Forestry Commission began planting in the area, showed its course very clearly indeed. Needless to say, the roadline is now obscured by the criss-cross of access and service roads following in the wake of afforestation. Nevertheless, for at least half of the exhausting journey to Nantystalwyn the original road can still be followed by the energetic walker. Between the Abbey Farm and Pantyfedwen (both incorporating material from the abbey in their buildings) the road is metalled. A gate at the edge of the forestry opens on to a plethora of tracks, the original road being the one which steadily ascends the planted hillside by way of a rocky lane lined with gorse, heather and whinberry. To the right the lane runs side-by-side with a forestry road with branches leading off to the farms of Hafod Newydd and Blaenglasffrwd, the latter lying close to a cairn cemetery and an early complex of huts and enclosures (SN767633). Passing through ranks of conifers for almost a mile the road runs by the remains of a deserted farmstead to a gate and the open mountain. From this gate it continues to climb alongside the forestry as a shallow green lane which, in common with earlier stages along its length, shows clear signs of having been embanked on its western side in order to ensure a relatively level ascent. After approximately half-a-mile yet another gate carries the road into the forestry and the descent into the marshes around Nant Rhyd-y-meirch (SN779627). Tradition has it that this lonely spot witnessed the passage in 1094 of the troops of Rhys ab Owain and Rhydderch ap Caradog, princes of South Wales, as they journeyed to do battle with the sons of Cadwgan ap Bleddyn, who had been responsible for the murder of their grandfather. A group of platform houses of probable medieval origin and a short length of revetted road leading from this complex into boggy land near the ford have been identified recently on the rocks near Nant Rhyd-y-meirch. From

Continuation of hollow way through forestry towards Rhyd-y-merich

The same route skirting the hillside

Rhyd-y-meirch the road's course is rather obscure, but it is likely to have followed the line of the track flanking the Tywi forest along the banks of Nant Gwineu to its confluence with the Tywi river at the farm of Moel Prisgau (SN806612). It then seems to have extended due south along the rocky Tywi Valley past Nantystalwyn to join the drovers' road between Tregaron and Abergwesyn (SN804569).

Like some of the others described in this chapter, the road to Nantystalwyn was used by cattle and sheep drovers until the development of the railway system in the mid-nineteenth century heralded the beginning of the end of the age-old droving trade. Victorian cattlemen may not have appreciated it, but they and their animals were often travelling along the trackways well-established centuries before the Norman knights landed in England. Continuity of use also applied to many of the farm and settlement sites alongside and in the vicinity of the tracks. Given the choice, the wise farmer will always select well-drained, south-facing land for settlement and cultivation. Such land is normally relatively easy to work and warms up quickly in the spring months thereby triggering off crop growth. The early farmer would soon have learned the vital importance, in terms of getting as high a yield of food as possible from his holding, of selecting an 'early' site and his successors down the years would have had little reason to abandon that site unless forced to do so. True, there would be movement *within* the site as buildings became redundant and the farmer responded to agrarian change, and the area cultivated may also have increased with time. The fact remains, nevertheless, that the original place of settlement may in many cases have remained occupied for centuries. It is significant in this context that Rhys ap Gruffudd's grant to Strata Florida, dated 1184, mentions the farms of Moel Prisgau, Dolfawr, Tref-y-Gwyddel, Mynachty Ffynnon Oer and several others which were still occupied in the early years of the present century. Other sites in the uplands and mountains of Cardiganshire may represent the remains of *hafodydd*, while others still may be squatters' holdings of eighteenth- and nineteenth-century origin. Only when the archaeologists have investigated the ruins will the present-day traveller along the roads of Cardiganshire and of other parts of the north and west of Wales be able to obtain a true idea of the settlement history of the surrounding landscape.

Pre-Turnpike Roads in Radnorshire

These high wild hills and rough uneven ways
Draw out our miles and make them wearisome . . .

William Shakespeare
Richard II

Welsh roads remained largely free of wheeled vehicles before the latter part of the seventeenth century. Occasionally a great magnate trundled through the countryside in an unsprung horse-drawn carriage on a grand, if uncomfortable progress to his mansion, overtaking, perhaps, a local carter, his ox-wagon loaded with goods destined for a country fair. Overall, though, the roads remained the province of the packhorse and mule or the well-shod mare of the parson, squire or man of business. Once they had left the immediate proximity of the village or town most roads were unfenced and tended 'to grow better of themselves' through the combined action of the weather and of travellers turning aside to the surrounding farmland to avoid potholes. It was to the confined roads close to centres of population that most of the legal papers relating to road conditions refer, one such road being in the mind of Sir John Wynn of Gwydir when he penned an *aide-memoire* in 1616; 'Call Petty Sessions and take a mise on the Highways'.

Statute Labour and local enterprise had done little to improve the pitiful surfaces of the roads which had remained with few exceptions in *status quo* since medieval times. This was a serious matter to the authorities because poor communications had the dual effect of limiting the expansion of trade and of impeding the progress of both official and private posts. A primitive postal system for the transmission of the king's mails and those of his more favoured courtiers had existed in Tudor times, but the private individual or merchant had relied on messengers, trusted travellers or drovers to carry gifts, letters and money the length and breadth of the country. Drovers, in particular, played an important part in this traffic. In the spring of 1585 Sir George Chaworth explained to the Countess of Rutland that, '. . . I have done my best to procure you some money to be paid in London, but I could not do so as most of the drovers who were likely to serve you had already gone to London.' A rather anguished letter received by the Anglesey squire, Richard Bulkeley, emphasises the problems for correspondents resulting from drovers' activities being limited to the spring and summer seasons. 'We pray you', wrote Bulkeley's cousin in 1637, 'that our money be paid by November 1st as we cannot return our money [to London] . . . otherwise than by drovers.'

While the importance of the drovers as messengers persisted until well into the eighteenth century, the appointment, by Henry VIII, of Sir Brian Tuke as Master of the Posts was followed, in 1561, by the first line of posts through Wales for which official records are available. Initially this was a temporary affair connecting London with Holyhead which by now had replaced Chester as the main port of embarkation for Ireland. By 1598, however, the Holyhead mail was rendered permanent by an Order in Council confirming the positions of John Ffranceys, Piers Conway, William Prichardes, Rowland ap Roberte and Robert Pepper as postmasters respectively of Chester, Rhuddlan, Conwy, Beaumaris and Holyhead, towns whose commercial and social status was considerably enhanced by being located on a mail route. Much the same applied to Chepstow, Newport, Cardiff, Bridgend, Swansea, Carmarthen and Haverfordwest when the first post to Milford Haven was forged three years later. Inn-keepers now enjoyed a rich harvest of trade, especially when their particular houses were designated as the official posts, when they were paid 1s 8d daily for maintaining a change of horses and ensuring that official letters were safely forwarded to the next post. John Aprice of Holyhead, Richard White of Beaumaris and Nicholas Hookes (famous as the forty-first son of his father and himself the sire of twenty-seven children) were just some of the stalwarts occupying much-sought after positions as postmasters in the late seventeenth century. In addition to keeping at least three horses for the use of King's Messengers, the innkeeper/postmaster enjoyed the monopoly of letting horses to travellers requiring them for an onward journey. This was a useful concession and compensated the postmaster for the fact that the Privy Purse was often less than prompt in paying his salary and expenses. As he was dealing with official, and often secret mail, the postmaster needed to be a man of honesty, tact and discretion and though we find the Brecon postmaster being hauled over the coals in 1672 for tampering with the mail, most of these men carried out their duties diligently and effectively.

Being a charge on the Privy Purse, the posts, officially at least, were used only for Royal mail. But as the seventeenth century progressed, private letters came to be sent along with official mails and as trade grew the need for a public postal service was emphasised. Recognition came in 1635 when a royal proclamation established for 'his Majesties subjects', a postal service from the principal mail routes to the market and shire towns, to be paid for by a fixed level of charges. From now on a letter sent by a man in London to a relative in Wales would be carried by a 'post-boy' (a rather unsatisfactory term for what was usually a mature, if not elderly man) to the most appropriate town on the Holyhead or Milford Haven route. The letter could now either be collected by the addressee, or, if he was particularly affluent, be delivered to his private address on arrangement with the postmaster. Before 1700 letters despatched from North Wales to addresses in the south of the Principality travelled firstly to London on the Chester road and thence to South Wales by way of Bristol and Chepstow. This was a time-consuming and costly process. By 1700, though, a route had been forged between Bristol and Chester passing through Ludlow and Hereford, while a cross-post for mid-Wales through Radnorshire serving the far-flung centres of Tregaron, Aberystwyth and Machynlleth was established at Montgomery under Mrs Elizabeth Davies whose services were rewarded with the not inconsiderable annual sum of £45.

As the 'post-boy' pursued his lonely journey through Radnorshire he would, if not un-nerved by the prospect of highway robbery, have enjoyed the delights of one of Britain's loveliest counties. As Radnorshire continues to offer the modern traveller a multitude of pleasures in terms of scenery, architecture and historical associations, I have chosen to write in this chapter of some of its roads during the immediate pre-turnpike era. Bounded by the rivers Wye and Teme and in the west by the great mass of the Cambrian Mountains, the centre of the county is dominated by Radnor Forest. In medieval times this was an area of unenclosed country reserved for hunting, but its nature has been entirely altered in recent years by teutonic coniferisation. The towns, villages and inter-connecting roads of this thinly-populated pastoral county tended, from the sixteenth to eighteenth centuries, to lie around the Forest which could be approached only on foot or on horseback at that time. Since the mid-fifteenth century when the shattered remnants of Jasper Tudor's Lancastrian army had dispersed through the hills beyond Presteigne after the Battle of Mortimer's Cross, the Radnorshire countryside had become renowned as the haunt of thieves and outlaws and though in the next century Bishop Rowland Lee had mounted a vicious campaign to extirpate them, travel in the county remained a dangerous venture. Even as late as 1720 a lady proposing to travel from Presteigne to London explained in a letter to her daughter that, 'there being such robbery of travellers and carriers that I shall not venture to bring or send a penny of money any other way but what will barely defray the expenses of my journey'.

Around the Forest and in the broken hilly country to the south of the county were numerous tracks and paths connecting the villages and farms. Skirting manorial boundaries, occasionally following prehistoric tracks used since time immemorial, circumventing steep inclines and fording streams and rivulets, these were usually quite adequate to meet the needs of the pastoral economy. A post-boy would occasionally travel from Presteigne, Hay-on-Wye and Knighton into the heartland of the county, or a pedlar carry his backpack to one of the country fairs, yet traffic consisted for the most part of ox-drawn sledges bringing wool, hay or peat from the isolated hill farms. This agricultural traffic might perhaps be accompanied by panniered horses carrying grain from the market of Presteigne to a village mill, or salmon from the Wye to some gentleman's household. Gentlemen, in seventeenth-century Radnorshire, were few and far between if the lament of a Parliamentary Commissioner sent to the county to collect fines from Royalists is anything to go by:

Radnorsheer, poor Radnorsheer,
Never a park and never a deer,
Never a squire of five hundred a year
But Richard Fowler of Abbey Cwmhir.

Shortage of gentlemen and of human beings in general made travelling a very lonely business. Richard Symonds, writing of Charles I's wanderings after his defeat at Naseby, recorded rather disconsolately that when the king and his party set out from Presteigne on September 19th, 1645 and travelled towards Newtown in Montgomeryshire, '. . . except in the first three myle wee saw never a house or church over the mountaynes'.

Though not dealing specifically with Radnorshire, the account of John Taylor (The Water Poet) who rode through Wales on horseback at the age of 74, gives a vivid impression of the frustrations and dangers of travel in Stuart times. Riding from Lampeter to Carmarthen in 1653 he found, 'the way continually hilly, or mountainous and stony, insomuch that I was forced to alight and walke 30 times'. With about four miles to go, darkness descending and little idea of the way, his nerve began to fail and he decided to spend the night in a nearby field of oats, only to sink into a quagmire with his horse! Managing to grope his way back to the road he was fortunate enough to meet a horseman who led him on to Carmarthen and 'good and free entertainment at the home of one Mistris Oakley'. Unable to obtain a tobacco pipe at any price, Taylor was nevertheless impressed by Carmarthen and in particular by the low price of provisions. A happy place it must have been with its numerous taverns, oysters available at one hundred for 1d, a 2½ft salmon for 12½d and beef at 1½d per pound!

The solitary traveller in rural Wales had to deal both with the language problem and, quite often, with rough treatment at the hands of servants and landlords in the taverns along the way. Poor old Taylor was no exception and he was beside himself with rage as he left a Swansea inn where it seems that he was treated in a less than civil manner: 'If my stay in that house that night would save either Mr. Shallow-pate or Mrs. Jullock from hanging . . . I would rather lie and venture all hazards that are incident to hors (sic), man and traveller than to be beholding to such unmannerly mungrils'. As if dangerous roads and poor accommodation were not enough, the

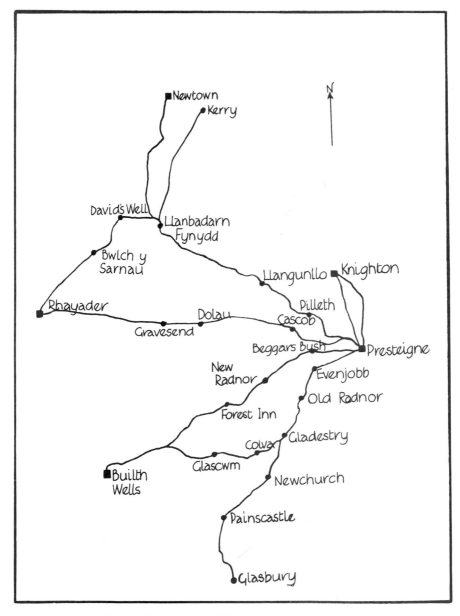

Some Pre-turnpike roads in Radnorshire

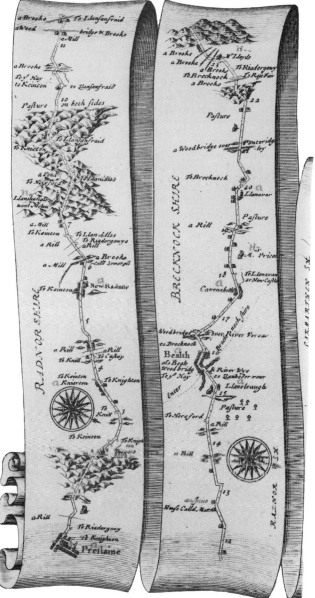

From John Ogilby's
Britannia *of 1676*

traveller also faced the problem of securing provender for his horse, often a difficult matter in a dry summer. When the weary Taylor arrived at Harlech he was mortified to discover that the town was unable to offer grass, hay or oats so that he was obliged to move on to Barmouth where he dined on 'a hen boyld with bacon, as yellow as the cowslip' and his horse on grass cut by two boys who travelled two miles to find it!

So much for the rigours of travel, of which a man making a journey would be aware in advance. However, before Charles II appointed John Ogilby and William Morgan to survey and map the roads of England and Wales, our traveller had to rely upon guides — to a greater or lesser degree extortionate in their demands — his own judgement and an element of luck, in order to find his way through the Welsh countryside. Saxton, Speed and others had produced maps of great beauty and cost, but these usually delineated only townships, villages and the occasional bridge, giving little indication of the direction of roads and trackways. Eventually, after many years works and at a cost of some £7,000, Ogilby published his *Britannia* in 1676, a fine road book in 'strip map' form, replete with information on routes, the local economy and dates of country fairs. Ogilby's work was to revolutionize travel and it was not long before other cartographers began to produce maps, 'delineations' and 'descriptions' of England and Wales. Notable among these were Morden and Taylor who published maps of Wales in 1704 and 1718 respectively while Emmanuel Bowen and Thomas Kitchin's admirable atlas of the kingdom was progressively refined through several editions in the early eighteenth century. This was to remain the best available work before Cary's road books arrived on the scene towards the end of the century. These, and other contemporary sources, together with the Ordnance Survey sheets have been used to define some of the more important pre-turnpike roadlines through Radnorshire.

Following the Acts of Union of 1536 and 1543, New Radnor became the shire town of the newly-created county of Radnorshire. However, it enjoyed this privilege only until after the Civil Wars when the assizes were transferred to Presteigne whose importance in the county was thereby enhanced. As early as 1575 Saxton had been able to write that, 'Prestayn for beauteous buildings is the best in the shire', while a century later Ogilby found a well-built town of four furlongs in extent with the usual markets and fairs, a reputation for excellent malted barley and several good inns including The Antelope, The Swan, The Duke's Arms and The Castle. The Radnorshire Arms, dating from 1616, was traditionally (and wrongly) reputed to have been the home of the regicide John Bradshaw. Presteigne, though, was strongly Royalist in its sympathies and was visited on two occasions by Charles I after the Battle of Naseby. Another distinguished seventeenth century visitor to the town was Henry, Duke of Beaufort who, as Lord President of the Council of the Marches, progressed through Wales in

From Bowen and Kitchin's atlas (early 18th century)

Offa's Dyke near Discoed

1684. As he entered the narrow streets at the head of his entourage, 'The Magistrates in their formalities stood ready to receive his Grace, the streets, windows, trees and tops of the houses abounding with spectators giving shouts, acclamations and expressions of Joy.' Remote Presteigne may have been, yet his Grace's entertainment at the hands of 'the loyall Gentlemen of the County' was far from provincial, and he and his followers had their bumpers charged with 'foreign wine' to supplement the strong local cider.

PRESTEIGNE TO RHAYADER

Presteigne lay at the junction of a number of roads, one of the more important being the highway to Rhayader and across the mountains to the port of Aberystwyth. Designated 'The Great Road' by the early turnpike surveyors, it followed a route into west Wales with origins in the medieval period, if not before. Much of the course of the 'Great Road' was abandoned in 1767 when the Presteigne Turnpike Trustees decided to make a road to Rhayader by way of Beggar's Bush, Kinnerton, New Radnor and Penybont. Previously the line of road lay along the vale of the Lugg, skirting St Mary's Hill and following the present B4356 as far as Rock Bridge where it headed along the lane to Discoed, across Offa's Dyke and past Dyffryn to Cascob at the edge of Radnor Forest (SO239664). Cascob, where wolves roamed until Tudor times, was described by Ogilby as 'an inconsiderable village'. It had, though, enjoyed its moment of glory, for its fine little church was the benefice of Thomas Huett, translator of the Book of Revelations for William Salesbury's Welsh New Testament in 1567. Huett and his fellow Radnorshire clerics may have turned a blind eye to the persistence of pre-Christian beliefs and superstitions among their parishioners, many of whom believed firmly in the efficacy of incantations and invocations, exemplified by the charm currently displayed in the church. Frowned upon by the hierarchy of the Church, such charms were in common use in seventeenth-century pastoral society by people wishing to protect their livestock (and themselves) against 'the evil eye'. The tower of the present church at Cascob is constructed on an artificial mound, originally supposed to have been a Bronze Age barrow. However, like a similar earthwork at Bleddfa Church nearby, the mound is now thought to be the base of an earlier tower probably destroyed at the time of the Glyndwr revolt in the early fifteenth century.

According to Ogilby, Cascob Church lay to the left of the 'Great Road', and its course can be followed along the sunken lane heading westwards in the direction

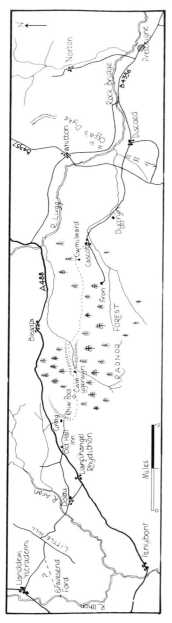

The 'Great road' above Graig Farm

'The Great Road'; Presteigne to Gravesend

*The 'Great road' joining the
Penybont-Knighton turnpike
at the 'Old Hall' Inn*

of Cwmilward some 50yd below the churchyard gate. Beyond the steep ascent to Cwmilward the road reaches the brink of Radnor Forest and its subsequent route over the Forest (not negotiable by motor car) runs along the line of the track passing above Cwmilward towards the farm of Cwmygerwyn (SO191669). Here dwelt the Reverend Samuel Phillips, an eighteenth-century poet of some distinction, who lies at rest in Bleddfa churchyard with others of his family. A man of mordant wit, Phillips delighted in epitaphs and if the following extract of his commemoration of the life of a maiden lady is anything to go by, these were hardly notable as manifestations of Christian charity:

> Scorning and scorn'd, she passed her life away,
> An useless lump of animated clay;
> Now spite and envy rule her frame no more,
> But here it lies — more useless than before.

Ogilby and later cartographers record the passage of the 'Great Road' beyond Cwmygerwyn and Rhiw Pool and its descent from Radnor Forest to Graig. However, such is the spider's web of forestry tracks that tracing the road to Rhiw Pool is very difficult, although further on it can be clearly seen as a raised causeway running alongside the forestry on Graig Hill, eventually being incorporated into a hedged lane as it descends towards Graig Farm (SO173673). From this substantial

Gravesend Ford

The River Lugg

farm the road heads for the Knighton-Penybont turnpike (the present A488) crossing it at the site of the Old Hall Inn directly opposite the mid-nineteenth century Calvinistic Methodist Tanhouse Chapel (SO160674). Leaving the chapel on the right hand side the 'Great Road' follows the deep winding lane through the charming hamlet of Dolau, across the Aran River and over open country above Little Hill, whence it descends towards Llanddewy Ystradenni for almost half-a-mile before turning south-west along an undefined course to Gravesend Ford on the River Ithon (SO106673). While this one-mile stretch of the route is not easy to follow, both Taylor and Kitchin indicate it as crossing the Ithon at 'Grays Inn' or 'Gravesend' along a line past Penlan Farm.

Westwards of Gravesend, the older maps are not particularly helpful with Ogilby mentioning a 'direct road' to Rhayader, and Kitchin and others marking a route

'The Great Road'; Gravesend to Rhyader

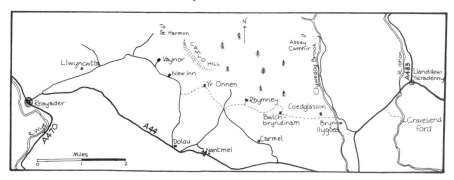

92

Mynachdy

passing above Coedglasson to Rhiwgoch and thence to New Inn and Rhayader. Later maps, such as Cary's (1806) merely show a straight line connecting Gravesend and New Inn. However, by supplementing these sources with a study of the Ordnance Survey 6in maps and with local enquiry, it has been possible to piece together fairly precisely the course of this important pre-turnpike road. Initially, after fording the Ithon, it traversed the boggy land by Rhos Llawdden by way of the lane from the ford to its junction with the present A483. Here the 'Great Road' struck south-east along the A483 for approximately three-quarters of a mile before turning into the Abbey Cwmhir road and on towards Brynllycoed (SO083672). It now left the existing road, forded the River Clywedog and continued along a rough track enclosed by hedges to the south of Coedglasson, a farm located on several of the early maps This track, known locally as 'Muddy Lane' can be traced across Coedglasson towards Bwlchbryndinam, becoming incoporated into the metalled road half-a-mile before the farm (SO062676). Apart from a stretch directly above Coedglasson, the 'Great Road' takes the form of a hedged lane, occasionally rather overgrown, for the whole of its length to Bwlchbryndinam Farm. Passing through the farmyard it crosses Baxter's Bank, skirts the forestry past the ruins of Rhiwgoch and thence across enclosed hill land to Lower Rhymney where it climbs steeply along a metalled lane to the junction of several tracks on the hills above Nantmel (SO041678). Instead of turning south for Cefn Nantmel on the modern road, the 'Great Road' originally proceeded across open hill for Yr Onnen, its course, parts of which may still be traced, being marked by a sunken green lane running alongside the hill. This green lane passed Yr Onnen, along a line apparently represented by the present farm road, while the remainder of the route to Rhayader was along the country lane past Vaynor and Llwyncwtta passing, en route, the New Inn Farm, previously a hostelry important enough to be mentioned on many of the older maps (SO009697).

PRESTEIGNE TO LLANBADARN FYNYDD

At one point on its course the 'Great Road' crossed the ancient route through mid-Wales represented by the A483, upon which lay the village of Llanbadarn Fynydd, itself linked by a direct route to Presteigne. From the outskirts of Presteigne a traveller followed the 'Great Road' as far as Rock Bridge where he forded the Lugg and rode along the river valley, flanked on either side by exquisite meadows with land rising to the north in ancient fields, their lines broken up with gnarled oaks and plantations of larch. This road, currently the B4356, passes through Pilleth whose fourteenth-century church, standing on the slopes of Bryn Glas, witnessed the Battle of Pilleth fought on 22 June 1402 (SO258680). It was here that Owain Glyndwr, guerilla fighter extraordinary, took prisoner Sir Edmund Mortimer after a battle claiming the lives of 1,000 English soldiers. Glyndwr's blood was certainly up. Previously he had sacked Abbey Cwmhir, burned several castles (including New Radnor where he hanged and then beheaded the bulk of the garrison) and he was now ready for an all-out fight. Once Mortimer's Welsh archers had deserted to his adversary's banner there was little doubt as to the outcome of the fight and the English were totally routed on Bryn Glas Hill, their corpses being subject to 'beastly shameless transformation' at the hands of Welsh women as they lay in the field after the battle. Shakespeare, in *Henry IV Part I*, has Pilleth in mind when he has Westmoreland tell the battle-weary king of Mortimer's capture:

A post from Wales loaden with heavy news;
Whose worst was that the noble Mortimer,
Leading the men of Herefordshire to fight
Against the irregular and wild Glendower,
Was by the rude hands of that Welshman taken,
A thousand of his people butchered . . . .

Sir Richard Price, a local landowner, planted a square patch of fir trees on the side of Bryn Glas to commemorate the English dead, but their final resting place is reputed to be marked by the mounds in the river meadows below the road. This, however, would have been marshy ground in the fifteenth century and it is more likely that the unfortunate conscripts were buried where they fell: on the flanks of Bryn Glas Hill.

A mile or so beyond the melancholy field of Pilleth the road passes Mynachdy — 'Monaughty' or 'Monely' on many of the older maps, whose compilers experienced the usual problems with Welsh orthography (SO238686). This fine late sixteenth-century house was built from materials taken from the Abbey Cwmhir grange of Mynachdy which originally lay in the meadows below Griffin Lloyd a mile to the north-west. Seventeenth-century travellers of curious disposition would have learned of the tradition that Mynachdy played host to Glyndwr and his lieutenant Rhys Gethin (the Terrible) on the night before the Battle of Pilleth. They may, or may not have been aware that similar claims have been lodged for Monaughty Poeth in Llanfair Waterdine across the English border.

Beyond Griffin Lloyd the road meanders above the Lugg to Llangynllo, a village, according to one observer, '. . . enhanced by the high average of comeliness among its children and young women'. Crossing the river in the village and again at the junction with the Knucklas road, the route to Llanbadarn passes through oak-wooded country, and into open sheep pasture. For much of its course, the old road tends to follow the B4356 although from time to time re-alignment of the modern road has revealed the original road boundary as a bank in an adjacent field. Passing over Little Hill the old road reaches The Pound and fords the Camddwr before

Old Radnor Church

Old roadline running parallel to the B 4594 above Blaencerde

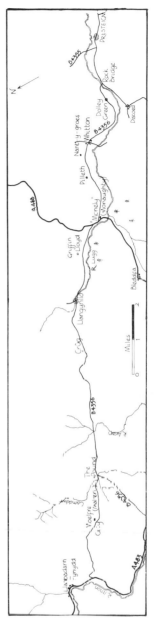

Pre-turnpike route from Presteigne to Llanbadarn Fynydd

deviating from the B4356 to follow a lonely course through open, bracken-infested hill country to the curiously-named Moelfre City, now a single house and an isolated telephone kiosk (SO119754). From this remote spot the same road winds down to Llanbadarn Fynydd, entering the village by Brook Cottage on the course of the modern A483 highway (SO098768).

PRESTEIGNE TO GLASBURY

A much-used roadline connected Presteigne with Newchurch and subsequently with Glasbury on the River Wye to the south-west. Leaving Presteigne on the ancient trackway past Slough and Cold Oak, this road, in the form of a deep lane, ran over the hill to Evenjobb (SO263624). About half-a-mile from the village the traveller crossed Offa's Dyke where he would have enjoyed a fine view of Old Radnor across the cultivated vale of the Summergill. After its descent to Evenjobb the road headed south along the course of the B4357 to pass Hindwell, a pre-Flavian Roman site and home, in the early nineteenth century, of Thomas Hutchinson, Mary Wordsworth's favourite brother. Here, Dorothy Wordsworth first learned to ride, while the poet himself, deeply moved by the glories of the Radnorshire countryside, visited the house in 1810 and 1812. William enjoyed the civilized company of the Hutchinsons and their circle and Dorothy, even if she reckoned the house to be one of the coldest in the land, wrote of Hindwell with great affection. She was particularly fond of the splendid pool in front of the house: 'You could hardly believe it possible for anything but a lake to be so beautiful as the pool before this house. It is perfectly clear and inhabited by multitudes of geese and ducks and two fair swans keep their silent and solitary state apart from all the flutter and gabble of the inferior birds'.

The Wordsworths must have travelled this road many times, their chaise bumping along the lane towards the crossing of the Summergill Brook and the present A44 highway before the steep climb across the side of Old Radnor Hill. The poet would have enjoyed Old Radnor and its pleasantly melancholy churchyard and like other travellers would have pondered on the antiquity of a site where Celtic and Saxon churches had stood centuries before the present Perpendicular building. After viewing the unique Tudor organ case and fine linen-fold chancel screen, he might have wandered down to the remains of King Harold Godwinson's castle mound about 300yd to the south-east of the church. As with Charles I when he travelled this road in the nervous weeks after Naseby, these insubstantial remnants of the Saxon king's dominance of the Marches may have caused the poet to fall prey to thoughts of the transience of kingly existence.

Past Old Radnor the road crossed the Cynon Brook and proceeded through hilly country towards Gladestry, the original following the course of the present B4594 as a green lane enclosed on the field side by a high bank. The earlier road-banks are particularly apparent on the stretch of road a hundred yards or so past Wern Farm (SO239558). Gladestry, bounded on the west and east by Colfa Hill and Hergest Ridge, was the meeting place of several old roads, our particular one continuing along the B4594 towards Newchurch, passing Hengoed and Blaencerde along the way. Here again, road widening has obscured the earlier line although the original road banks can still be seen in the adjacent fields where they run parallel to the modern highway. It was at Blaencerde that Charles I is reputed to have halted and drunk a jug of milk from the hand of a particularly beautiful local woman by the name of Mary Bayliss (SO218519). In 1870 Francis Kilvert met one William Pritchard who claimed to own the very jug from which the king had taken his milk. Moreover, he cited a well-attested tradition that Charles' entourage, riding two by two down the narrow road, extended from Blaencerde to Pontvane, a farm to the south of Newchurch prominently marked on Kitchin's map (SO210502). Past Blaencerde the B4594 descends steeply into Newchurch passing around the ancient churchyard flanked on the south by farm buildings of the fifteenth century. Crossing the River Arrow and turning sharply right at the church, the old road is carried by the present country lane over undulating landscape towards Rhosgoch. On the higher ground above Rhosgoch Common, noted in the eighteenth century for its high quality peat, the B4594 incorporates the Portway, traditionally believed to be of Roman origin. There is little evidence to substantiate this, though the stretch of road is of unquestionable antiquity and in all likelihood first assumed importance in connexion with the medieval stronghold of Painscastle to the southwest. Rhosgoch Mill, south of the village, is currently a farmhouse (SO186475). Until the 1950s though, it had been run as a corn mill by members of the Powell family for over 400 years, and the Miller Powell who was contemporary with Kilvert claimed regularly to have seen fairies dancing on the mill floor. We shall never know how far this supernatural vision resulted from over-indulgence in the cider bottle. The mill, however, remains a magical place and Kilvert's description of '. . . the cosy old picturesque ivy-grown mill house with its tall chimney completely covered with ivy' applies as well today as it would have done two hundred years before Kilvert wrote his admirable diaries.

The old road, still represented by the B4594, enters Painscastle by the Maesllwch Arms, the sole and much modernised survivor of the six drovers' inns

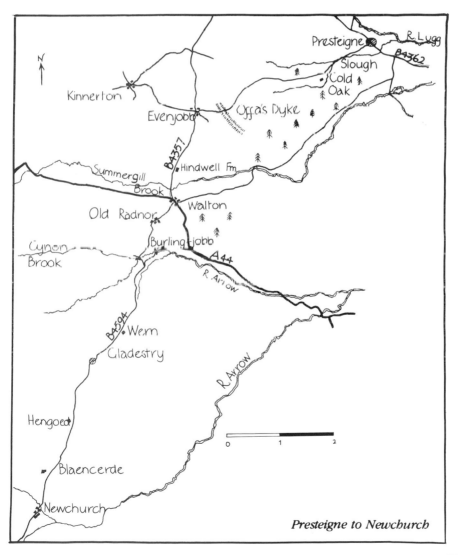

Presteigne to Newchurch

97

boasted by the village in its heyday. After the long and exhausting crossing of the Mynydd Epynt and the hazardous fording of the Wye at Erwood, these inns, with their associated enclosures, offered succour to man and beast before they continued their journey into Herefordshire and the English Midlands. An observer standing on the great mound overlooking the village would have seen the drovers approaching from the west as they urged on their cattle towards Painscastle. By the time Charles I passed through the village the same mound was virtually all that remained of Payne Fitzjohn's motte and bailey and of the castles subsequently built on the site by the rapacious William de Braose and by Henry III, the latter raising a stone building as part of his policy of strengthening the Marcher fortresses (SO166462).

If it was no longer an important centre for the cattle trade, mid-nineteenth-century Painscastle at least achieved some celebrity as the home of one of Wales' most noted eccentrics, the Reverend John Price who lived out much of his life in three bathing-machines serving as study, bedroom and kitchen. Price, a man with an inordinate fondness for the literal interpretation of biblical stories, spent a great deal of his time seeking out vagrants and others, whom he paid 6d per head on condition that they attended his church services. Inside the church the good vicar provided oilstoves for his bemused flock to cook their food on during the sermon. A poor man himself, Price also offered 5s to each pair of vagrants 'living in sin' as a means of persuading them to go through the marriage service. Inevitably this gave rise to skullduggery because the short-sighted unfortunate was unable to distinguish between couples, and many were successfully married several times over! In 1895 Price began to decline in health, and went to stay at Talgarth in neighbouring Brecknockshire where well-meaning friends prevailed upon him to take a bath. The shock of it killed him! He was eighty-five years old and a much-mourned man.

Beyond Painscastle the older road no longer follows the course of the B4594. Instead, it ran south of the village to ford Bach Howey before a steep ascent into the silent open hill country of the Begwns. The traveller could now look back towards the gentle pastoral landscape of Painscastle and westwards to the valley of the Wye, before ascending via a deep lane past Llwynpenderi to the hamlet of Ffynnon Gynydd (SO164413). Here the road turned abruptly left for the River Wye and Glasbury passing the plain little building of Maesyronnen Chapel (SO177411). Built on land bequeathed by one Lewis Lloyd in 1686, Maesyronnen was one of the earliest Nonconformist chapels in Wales and still retains the arrangement and

Maesyronnen Chapel

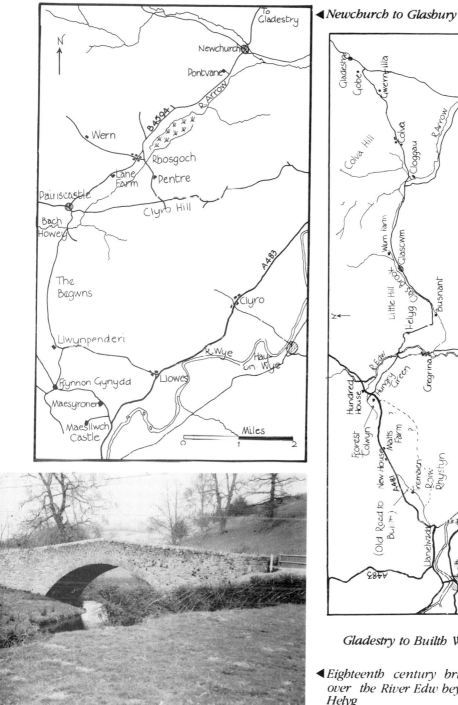

◄ *Newchurch to Glasbury*

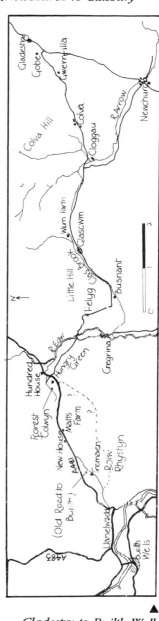

▲
Gladestry to Builth Wells

◄ *Eighteenth century bridge over the River Edw beyond Helyg*

many of the furnishings of the Commonwealth period. Below the chapel, the brief final stretch of the journey to Glasbury pursued the course of the great highway from Hereford to Brecon, the modern A438. The seventeenth-century traveller along this part of the route would have been spared the sight of the Gothic folly of

Maesllwch Castle with its riot of towers, battlements and arrowslits and would have journeyed to Ffynnon Gynydd through heavily wooded countryside. One such traveller was King Charles who rode out from Glasbury through this leafy landscape in August 1645. After dining with Sir Henry Williams at his fine Tudor house of Gwernyfed to the south-west, the king and his followers were conducted by their host over the Glasbury ford, whence they travelled the road over the Begwns for Painscastle, Old Radnor and Presteigne.

GLADESTRY TO BUILTH WELLS

From the quiet village of Gladestry a route struck out westwards for Builth Wells. Taking leave of the B4594 approximately half-a-mile to the south of the village, it passed Gobe and Gwern-illa and went on to Colfa, now little more than a farm and a thirteenth-century church overlooked by Colfa Hill and the great expanse of the Radnor Forest to the north (SO200531). Now an isolated spot, hemmed in by hills and wind-swept sheep pastures, Colfa's well-filled churchyard and the many ruins of farms and houses between here and Glascwm bespeak more populous days. Certainly the seventeenth-century traveller on this route would have found more company along the way than he would today. Colfa parish is mentioned in one of the works of the medieval poet Lewis Glyn Cothi, when he cites the ancient legend that the church was founded by St David himself. There may be little basis to this legend, but it is nonetheless true that a church has stood on the same site since the eighth century.

A mile or so beyond Colfa the now metalled road runs by Cloggau, a farm at the base of Yr Allt whose bracken-covered upper reaches give way to neatly enclosed fields as the hill gently descends to the infant River Arrow (SO187526). The countryside here has a timeless quality. It is a landscape of early enclosure and though fields may be larger, farm buildings more garish, and pastures of less floristic diversity, it has changed relatively little since Stuart times. Cloggau itself was reckoned by Kilvert to be one of the oldest inhabited buildings in the area and the spot moved him to verse:

The Cloggau on her greensward mount
Sat like a queen for ever
With tresses crowned with waving woods
Green throned beside the river.

Crossing the Arrow, the road ascends the treeless side of Glascwm Hill, forming a boundary between the heathery slopes of the hill and the deep valley to the north. The seventeenth-century road line — and, almost certainly, the road line for centuries previously — lays to the right of the present metalled road and can be followed along the flanks of the hill until it enters the village of Glascwm past Wern Farm (SO161535). To the west of Glascwm it takes up the metalled road along the steep-sided Clas Valley towards Busnant, and beyond here, instead of continuing to Cregrina, it turns north and makes its way past Helyg, fording a tributary of the River Edw en route. Half-a-mile distant the old road crossed the same river by a wooden bridge, replaced in the eighteenth century by the present single-span structure. Approximately a hundred yards beyond the bridge it swung to the right to cross Hungry Green for Fforest Colwyn, its original course again pursuing the hedge line several yards to the right of the modern road.

The early maps leave some doubt as to the precise direction of the road for the remainder of the journey to Builth Wells. It certainly crossed Aberedw Hill via the track called *Rhiw Rhystyn*, though whether it climbed the hill from Hungry Green to Fforest Colwyn on the A481 (the Presteigne-Builth Wells turnpike road) is not absolutely clear. However, the well-trodden greensward track through the bracken on top of Aberedw Hill, marking the course of a nineteenth-century drovers' route, probably represents the earlier road line, while the descent of this track from the top of the hill by way of the *Rhiw Rhystyn* towards Llanelwedd definitely does so. The beginning of the descent by a rocky track much-eroded by the rainwater for which it is a natural catchment, presented marvellous views to the seventeenth-century traveller. To the west lay Builth Wells and the mature River Wye meandering magnificently through the enclosed pastures along its banks, while the grey mass of Radnor Forest was visible to the north. Leaving the open hill, the *Rhiw Rhystyn* runs towards Llanelwedd as a sunken lane with a well-marked hedge bank on its western side, until it merges with a lane bounded by hedges of considerable antiquity. An offshoot of this lane heads towards Tremaen Farm and marks the course of the pre-turnpike Prestcigne Builth Wells road (SO069522). The *Rhiw Rhystyn* crosses the present A481 at Crossway Cottage, approximately a hundred yards before the junction of this road with the modern B4567. It then pursues the course of a council-maintained lane to Coed Spoel and is taken up by a hedge line for several hundred yards before rejoining the line of the turnpike for the short journey to Llanelwedd and Builth Wells.

Travellers to Builth Wells in the late seventeenth century found little to divert them as the town was virtually destroyed by fire in 1681 and appeals for funds for rebuilding had met with little success. The remnants of the old town and the new houses that had mushroomed over the next hundred years were described by the antiquary Malkin in 1803 as being in a state of 'dilapidated antiquity', its main streets being 'as fashionless as miserable and as dirty' as anything he had seen. Eventually, though, the town came to enjoy some celebrity as a watering place despite the complaint of one traveller who reckoned that the waters tasted and smelt respectively of sulphur and gunpowder. To sample this malodorous liquid came the gouty, rheumatic and dyspeptic, their journey to Builth being much facilitated by the new turnpike roads of the nineteenth century and James Parry's magnificent six-arched bridge over the Wye, completed in 1779.

The Rhiw Rhystyn

The bridge over the River Wye at Builth Wells, 1815

RHAYADER TO KERRY

By the seventeenth century the market town of Rhayader, with its cattle fairs and associations with the woollen industry was the junction of several roads, one of these heading north for Montgomeryshire through Kerry. After quitting Rhayader on the 'Great Road' the Kerry route joined the present lane to St Harmon at New Inn a mile beyond Llwyncwtta and proceeded north via a series of pitches and dingles to a point above Park Farm where it left the metalled road on what is now a forestry track (SO018719). This can be followed on foot between Pantybrwyn and Cefn-crin forests, passing to the east of Castell y Garn to enter Bwlch-y-Sarnau on the 'Glyndwr Way' (SO029745). From this meeting place of ancient routes, that into Montgomeryshire is shown on the early maps as proceeding north-west across Bailey Hill through enclosed hill country towards David's Well, taking the course of the metalled road skirting Red Lion Hill. Little now remains of David's Well although its reputation as a healing well still persists and many people can remember the days, not so long ago, when the footsore and rheumatic flocked to the spot (SO059786). At David's Well the old road to Llanbadarn Fynydd turns directly south-east towards a junction of several lanes on the flanks of Red Lion Hill approximately a hundred yards past Wain Cottage (SO067779). A metalled and gated track past the ruins of Gwndwm marks the course of the road for a few hundred yards until, for no apparent reason, the tarmac peters out in the middle of the hillside. Here, an observer looking due east can see the original road line running across the open hill until it once again joins a metalled lane leading directly to Llanbadarn Fynydd a mile-and-a-half distant (SO075779).

The maps of Cary (1806) and Coltman (1813) delineate another route going southwards for Llananno from the junction above Wain Cottage. Running through the forestry on Red Lion Hill the road (now a forestry track) passes the charmingly restored Red Lion Inn, standing alone amidst the ranks of conifers, and then heads south-easterly for New Well. Owing to the complex of forestry tracks between the Inn and New Well it is not difficult to get lost and it is important for drivers and walkers wishing to remain on the old road to keep bearing left from the Red Lion on the track skirting the forest and fording the Crychell Brook, as this is the original road line. In the vicinity of the ford over the Crychell lay the village of New Well, complete with its school and cobbler's shop. In the nineteenth century, and presumably in earlier years, the chalybeate spring at New Well enjoyed a local reputation for healing scrofula and was visited regularly by invalids during the

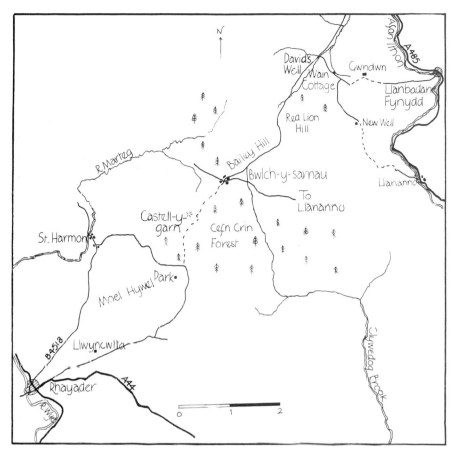

Rhayader to Llanbadarn Fynydd

summer months when the curative powers of the water were at their most efficacious. Now, alas, little remains save the New Well house beyond which the old road originally crossed Yr Allt and entered Llananno down a narrow lane (SO072766).

Returning to Llanbadarn Fynydd we find that the old road into Montgomeryshire follows the modern 'B' road northwards along a tributary of the River Ithon and, after a mile or so, runs into wild, open hill of cotton grass, rushes and bracken. This is elemental country, of cairns and tumuli, curlew and sheep. On a warm day in late spring the views from the road are quite glorious, although a seventeenth-century horseman, travelling in mid-January may have thought otherwise! Driving along this stretch of road one is reminded of Hardy's highway across Egdon Heath: '... the long, laborious road, dry, empty and white. It was quite open to the heath on each side, and bisected that vast dark surface like the parting-line on a head of black hair, diminishing and bending away on the furthest horizon'.

Past the group of tumuli on Garn bryn-llwyd the earlier road continues to follow the B4355 as far as Cider House Farm. Here it turns abruptly east to leave the metalled road and take up the Kerry Hill Ridgeway which runs along a fence line immediately opposite the farm (SO109846). Of great antiquity, the Ridgeway had been used for several centuries by cattle drovers from west Wales as they plodded steadily on towards Herefordshire and the lush grazings of the Midland counties. It is even possible that the Ridgeway was in use as a drove route when the pre-Offan

New Well

boundary dykes, clearly visible at its western end, were constructed (SO115850). By the seventeenth century, the ridgeway road was an important route to Kerry and thence to Newtown and the roads for North Wales. From the early maps it seems that the way to Kerry left the Ridgeway at Radnorshire Gate, past a tumulus on the left and thence by Black Hall and Pentre into the village (SO143862). Most Stuart travellers would not have known it, but sleepy little Kerry witnessed an episode of great drama in 1176 when a row broke out between the Bishop of St Asaph and

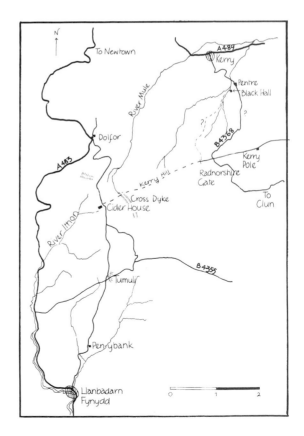

Llanbadarn Fynydd to Kerry

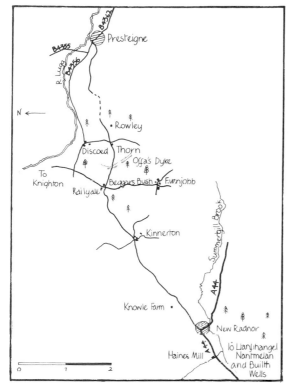

Giraldus Cambrensis, Archdeacon of Brecon, over the consecration of the church, claimed by each to lie in his particular diocese. The dispute seems to have reached epic proportions, leading to each man excommunicating the other. The wily Giraldus finally won the day since, having been first to get possession of the church, he had been able to ring a triplet of bells thereby establishing an act of excommunication in advance of the Bishop!

PRESTEIGNE TO BUILTH WELLS

Turning off Presteigne High Street opposite the Royal Oak pub the pre-turnpike road to Builth Wells climbed steeply through Warden and past Rowley Farm to cross Offa's Dyke before arriving at Beggar's Bush on the junction with Rhos Lane (SO262642). The fugitive Charles I spent an uncomfortable night at Beggar's Bush Farm, a tavern lying within the bounds of the parish of Old Radnor in the 1640s. Sir Henry Slingsby, faithful chronicler of the King's travels and of the tribulations of his entourage, immortalised the now much-modernised house in his diary: 'In our quarter we had little accommodation; but of all ye places we came to ye best was at old Radnor where ye King lay in a poor low chamber and my Ld of Linsey & others by ye kitching fire on hay . . . .' According to local legend the king himself conceived the name 'Beggar's Bush' after his servants and followers had begged the innkeeper for the remains of the single pullet and solitary cheese comprising the royal dinner! Since we know that the young Prince Charles visited Radnorshire and afterwards, as Charles II, was known to his intimates as 'Mr Rowley', the name of Rowley Farm may not be without significance while that king's renowned association with oak trees might be reflected in the naming of the old Royal Oak inn at Presteigne.

105

Beggars Bush

*Earlier roadline alongside
the B 4372 between
Kinnerton and New
Radnor*

For much of the way from Beggar's Bush the old road follows the B4372 to Kinnerton and thence along the flanks of Knowle Hill to New Radnor. However, for several hundred yards on the Kinnerton side of Knowle Farm the original road line appears to the right as a deep green lane overhung by venerable oaks. Soon, after journeying through glorious rolling pastureland, the modern traveller descends to the medieval town of New Radnor where Archbishop Baldwin and Giraldus Cambrensis enjoyed the hospitality of Rhys ap Gruffydd before their peregrinations through Wales. The town was granted borough status by Elizabeth I although, according to John Leland who visited the place in the 1530s, it was in a state of semi-decay by this time: 'New Radnor towne hathe been metely well wallyd and in the walle appere the ruines of iii gates. The buildynge of the towne in some part metely good in most part but rude, many howsys being thakyd. The castle is in ruine . . . .' So ruined was it that very little masonry remained at the time of Prince Charles's visit in 1642. The fate of New Radnor typified that of many of the border castles built by both Welshmen and Normans and of which only the mounds now remain. Half-hearted rebuilding after destruction in times of insurrection and the ravages of heavy artillery during the Civil War meant that the castles were relatively easy to dismantle following the abolition of the Marcher Lordships, whereupon their stonework became available for local domestic buildings. Today the streets of New Radnor are overshadowed by the great castle mound, a place of springy turf and harebells, no longer the malignant symbol of oppression which it must have seemed to the medieval inhabitants.

Our road follows Church Street past the toll house — a reminder that it was eventually turnpiked on the abandonment of the 'Great Road' — to join the A44 which now mercifully by passes the little town. Ogilby's map shows the seventeenth-century road pursuing the course of the A44 across 'a Brooke cal'd Somergil' and past Haines Mill, whose ruins await the arrival of a wealthy restorer (SO203605). Overlooked by a hill to the south with the splendid name of 'The Smatcher', Haines Mill is cited in Letters Patent renewing the charter of New Radnor in 1642. Morris Draper, it appears, had been tenant in 1481. He was succeeded in 1508 by Thomas Davis who held the mill until 1534, when it was let to Anne Griffiths and her son for a term of twenty-one years at an annual rental of thirty shillings.

Skirting the hills to the north of Llanfihangel Nantmelan the road follows the Summergill Brook past Llanfihangel Nantmelan Church, within its ring of ancient yew trees, before leaving the A44 at the Forest Inn tollgate to join the A481 past Llynheulyn, referred to rather dismissively by Ogilby as 'a pond' (SO171585). It now curves its way down to Hundred House, named after the court where trespassers, small debtors and other minor offenders were tried by the Sheriff in medieval times. After it crossed the River Edw, Ogilby shows the road passing 'a House call'd Matts' (Matt's Farm) and then heading for Builth Wells by way of the Wye crossing at Llanelwedd (SO090537). However, Bowen's map of 1726 indicates a road line leaving the A481 a short mile after Matt's Farm and approaching Llanelwedd past Tremaen Farm on the lane joining the *Rhiw Rhystyn*. Apparently the original pre-turnpike road, this can still be followed on foot by turning off the A481 near Hope Chapel beyond New House (SO079530).

Like New Radnor, seventeeth-century Builth must have been dominated by grass-covered banks and mounds, the remains of Edward I's great stone castle. From the time of the first 'motte and bailey' to the final destruction of the Edwardian castle in the sixteenth century, this was the site of much violence, bloodletting and intrigue. William, grandson of Llewelyn ap Iorwerth was publicly hanged, drawn and quartered at the castle following a spell of marital infidelity, while other less distinguished persons met an equally grisly end within its walls. It

The monument to Llewelyn ap Gruffydd

Haines Mill

was to Builth Castle that the great Llewelyn ap Gruffydd came to seek refuge from the English in 1282. Finding the gates closed against him he retreated into the countryside only to meet his death at the hands of a band of English soldiers. The unfortunate prince's body was buried in the grounds of the Cistercian foundation at Abbey Cwmhir, but not before the head had been struck off and sent to London for public exhibition. According to the chronicler Adam of Usk, the English soldiers washed the head in the nearby River Wye which, throughout the day, 'did flow in an unmixed stream of blood'.

PRESTEIGNE TO KNIGHTON

Knighton first came into prominence when the Normans built the nearby fortress of Bryn-y-Castell soon after 1066 (SO290722). Granted to the powerful Mortimer family by Henry III, the town grew rapidly and after receiving its market charter in 1230 it soon became one of the major trading centres of the border country. Once Presteigne had become the administrative 'capital' of Radnorshire upon the transfer of the Great Sessions from New Radnor after the Civil Wars, pre-existing trackways linking the two towns developed into substantial highways.

They were in the late stages of this transition when King Charles passed through Radnorshire on his way to North Wales in September 1645. The king, arriving at Presteigne from Leominster and Weobley, slept for two nights at Lower Heath, the home of one Nicholas Taylor. Legend has it that after leaving the farmhouse and making appropriate farewells to his host, Charles headed westwards along the lane from the Heath until he reached the junction with the New Radnor road, where he

Towards Stonewall Hill

turned north for Stonewall Hill at what has subsequently been named 'Kings Turning'. Afterwards, apparently, he progressed across the meadows alongside the Lugg before fording the river near Brink and riding on past Stapleton Castle for Stonewall Hill and Knighton. This would seem a logical route since the end of Brink Lane, running alongside the river from the medieval bridge in Broad Street, aligns directly with the castle (SO321646). A further tradition avers that the king rode down Broad Street, across the bridge and thence along the lane past Stocking Farm for Stonewall Hill, Llanshay and Knighton (SO315664). Whichever tradition one believes, the Stonewall Hill route was clearly of some importance in the seventeenth century, because by the mid-eighteenth, the Presteigne Turnpike Trust was ordering that the Knighton road be laid out from Lugg Bridge past Stapleton Farm, Stocking, Oxenbrook and Stonewall Hill. Running south from a gate opening to the turnpike road approximately a quarter-of-a-mile before Stocking Farm there appears to be a trackway cutting across the open field to rejoin the road between the cemetery and the sharp turn north for the farm (SO315659). This seems to have crossed the meadows towards Brink and accordingly may mark the line of the original road to Stonewall Hill.

Interestingly, neither Ogilby, Morden nor Bowen indicate the Stonewall Hill road. Their route to Knighton left Presteigne beyond Warden and followed the B4355 to Norton, leaving Boultibrooke ('Fulbrook' in Ogilby) on the right. The present B4355 towards Boultibrooke crosses the Lugg by a bridge constructed in 1932. The earlier road, however, is a lane to the rear of the nearby sawmills, passing over a charming stone bridge of early eighteenth-century design which presumably replaced the wooden structure mentioned by Ogilby (SO309653).

Alternative pre-turnpike routes from Presteigne to Knighton

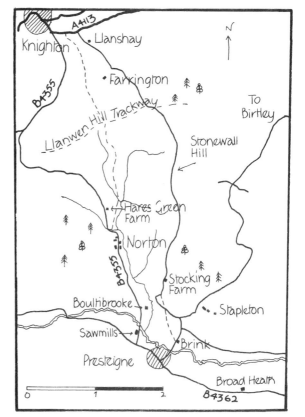

110

Bridge over the River Lugg, carrying the early road from Presteigne to Knighton

North of the sawmills Ogilby's road continued along the B4355 to Norton and then, before reaching Hare's Green Farm, it deviated on to a lane running towards Farrington on the hills to the south of Knighton (SO302674). Today, for the first mile or so, the old lane is metalled, but it eventually deteriorates into a rough track bounded by foxgloves and gorse, the rigours of the ascent being amply compensated for by the splendour of the views to the north and west. Towards the top of the hill Farrington Lane crosses the 'prehistoric' Llanwen Hill trackway before the steady descent to Knighton in the Teme Valley (SO301699).

Like other towns throughout Wales, Knighton was ultimately served by a system of turnpike roads, some of them incorporating pre-existing road lines. The older roads escaping the attention of the turnpike surveyors continued to serve a useful purpose. Maintained, albeit rather poorly, by the local parish, they provided a system of communications of great value to farmer and tradesman alike. It is not generally recognized, moreover, that by the time Queen Victoria came to the throne, only 10 per cent of Britain's highways lay within the turnpike system and once travellers had left the turnpike, their journey took them along roads which had not changed materially for centuries. Like today's drivers along our country lanes they might have been so relieved at getting away from that nineteenth-century juggernaut, the careering mail coach, that for a while at least, the rough and boggy surfaces would have seemed almost tolerable.

Farrington Lane

The
Drovers

Begging politely to be excused on the plea that I was just about to take tea, I asked him in what capacity he had travelled all over England. 'As a drover to be sure', said Mr. Bos, 'and I may say that there are not many in Anglesey better known in England than myself — at any rate I may say that there is not a public house between here and Worcester at which I am not known'.

George Borrow
Wild Wales, 1862

Since he first attempted to exercise control over their feeding and breeding habits, man has needed to master the handling and driving of his livestock. An understanding of the peculiarities of group behaviour among the different types of domestic animals must have been as essential to the pastoralist of the Near East in the sixth millennium BC as was a knowledge of the location of suitable pastures and watering places. The present-day East African herdsman, often forced by climatic conditions to drive his cattle over thousands of miles, is heir to skills shared by the American cowboy, the Alpine shepherd, the long-distance drover in Britain and so on down through the millennia to the earliest livestock farmers in the foothills of Anatolia. In short, the 'art and mystery of droving' is an ancient trade, perhaps as old as the earliest of agricultural tasks, those of shepherding and herding.

In Britain, cattle, sheep and to a lesser degree pigs, have been moved from the highland to the lowland regions for many centuries. Until quite recently environmental and technical factors meant that sheep and cattle were rarely fattened on the hills and there developed a system whereby they were reared on the upland pastures and subsequently finished on the rich grazings and arable fields of the lowlands. Thus, from medieval times, if not before, beasts from the Scottish hills were finished on arable by-products in eastern England, and lean cattle and sheep plodded their way from the northern and western parts of Wales to the fattening pastures of the Midlands and Home Counties. Their common fate was the butcher's pole-axe, administered in the shambles of London and by the early modern period those of other growing towns in lowland England.

This 'export' trade in livestock between Wales and England was of great antiquity. We know that Welsh cattle fed the Roman legions fighting in Gaul, and Dark Age documents provide evidence of an apparently legitimate trade in cattle across Offa's Dyke in the late eighth century. Cattle became the mainstay of the rural economy of much of medieval Wales and the abundant manuscript material of English lay and ecclesiastical estates shows that great magnates regularly

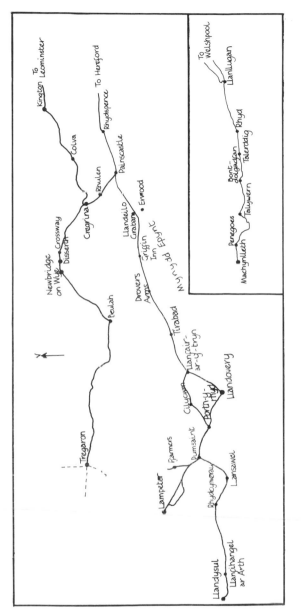

Drovers' roads from central Wales to the English border

sent their agents into the Principality to buy stock. We find also at this time the rapid growth of a mercantile class of Welsh cattle and sheep dealers who drove their animals to the fairs and markets of the English heartland. In 1253 a document relating to the granting of an annual fair at Newent in Gloucestershire mentions, '... the Welshmen who come from the parts of Wales to sell their cattle', while, during the Hundred Years' War (1337-1443), cattle were purchased by the constables of the Welsh castles and taken by drovers to London and the ports of southern England. Many similar examples underline the importance of the livestock trade to the economy of both countries, epitomized by the special protection afforded to drovers by both sides in the Civil War.

Described by the early nineteenth-century commentator Edmund Hyde Hall as

'. . . distinguished persons in the history of this country's economy', the Welsh drovers were a common sight in southern England as they followed their herds along the highways and by-ways, resting at recognized taverns and occasionally holding up at a village smithy while a bullock or pony was re-shod. In an attempt to exclude vagrants and other undesirables from the trade, Tudor and Stuart parliaments had enacted rigorously enforced legislation to regulate the activities of livestock dealers, particularly those involved with cattle. A cattle dealer, for example, had to be a married householder of over thirty and in possession of an annually renewable licence granted by Quarter Sessions. Further statutes imposed severe penalties on cattle stealing and driving livestock on Sundays and others laid down strict rules regarding trading conduct, pre-fair selling and the re-sale of stock within five weeks of the initial purchase.

Despite the frequent references in the contemporary literature to their roguery and dishonesty, based on a few much-publicised eighteenth-century cases of drovers defaulting on credit notes, the droving fraternity was essentially honest and scrupulous and was held in high regard throughout the community. As they were among the few ordinary people in Wales enjoying the opportunity of travelling far beyond their immediate locality, the dealers and their drovers formed an important link with England. Through them the Welsh countryman learned (and often disapproved) of the strange and wonderful happenings east of the border while the English yeoman, quaffing his beer at the roadside tavern, listened spellbound as the old drovers spun the yarns and sagas of their travels. Generally literate and numerate, they carried back to the remote villages and hamlets of the north and west of the Principality news of social, political, cultural and religious developments in England, and in the days before the widespread availability of local news sheets their return must have been eagerly awaited.

From the seventeenth century onwards numerous dealers and drovers were involving themselves in the wider aspects of Welsh life. Some lent financial support to the publication of Welsh language books, others put their knowledge of English to good use and became established as schoolteachers and others participated in local and county government. The pig-drover John Samuel is a typical example. He became a burgess of Carmarthen in 1818 and three of his descendants achieved the distinction of becoming sheriffs of the county. Similarly the father of the artist Thomas Jones of Pencerrig had been sheriff of Radnorshire in 1746 while *his* father had enjoyed a successful career as a drover before meeting his end at the hands of highwaymen. The fine seventeenth-century poet, Edward

Llanybydder Cattle Fair;
late nineteenth century

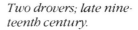
Two drovers; late nine-teenth century.

Morus of Perthi Llwydion regularly drove cattle between North Wales and Essex. Other drovers like William Jones of Trawsfynydd (1770-1837) and the celebrated Dafydd Jones of Caeo (1711-77) became Nonconformists, the latter translating the hymns of Isaac Watts and writing many moving hymns of his own.

When the French wars forced the Bank of England to suspend the redemption of its notes in cash in 1797, numerous local banking houses were established, many of them by individual or groups of drovers. Among those surviving the financial collapse of the 1820s were the Black Sheep Bank at Aberystwyth and the famous Black Ox Bank at Llandovery, established in 1799 by David Jones (1756-1840). Jones was a cattle dealer with the good luck (or good sense) to marry the heiress to a considerable fortune. As he prospered he was created a Justice of the Peace and High Sheriff of Carmarthenshire, at the same time accumulating several substantial properties in the county. Typically, his descendants became firmly established in county society and a member of the family was returned to Parliament in 1868. It says much for the reputation of Jones and his bank that the directors of Lloyd's Bank (which absorbed Jones and Company in 1909) ensured that for some years its Llandovery branch maintained the old Black Ox symbol on its cheques.

These few examples may have given the impression that the drovers were a mild-tempered, bookish, slightly saintly group of men. Nevertheless, physical toughness, courage and stamina were the hallmarks of the typical drover who plied his trade in difficult and often dangerous conditions. Many people learned to their cost that the Welsh drover was not a man to be double-crossed, as the Somerset Quarter Sessions Records for 1657 dramatically reveal. 'William Jenkins with many other Welshmen treated at Thomas Hoddinot's home with Mr. William Knoyle of Sandford to buy a close of grass to put their cattle in and not agreeing they drew their swords and assaulted Mr. Knoyle, Hoddinot, the Tithing man's deputy, his wife and many of them who came to part them using violent language, cudgells and stones'. In 1850 when a Welshman was swindled by a group of Cockneys at Barnet Fair in Hertfordshire he took his revenge in a direct and quite memorable manner. Capturing one of his adversaries with the help of a fellow drover, he tied the unfortunate man over the neck of an unbroken colt and ran the animal four or five miles after which the Englishman was only too glad to purchase his freedom by paying the drover his due!

Tough, clever, articulate and financially astute, the larger drovers and dealers were able to make a good living from their trade. A number of droving families had entered the ranks of the county gentry by the nineteenth century and others had accumulated sufficient capital to be able to lend out money at interest to businessmen and even to local landowners. However, a sizeable proportion of the total volume of trade in livestock was in the hands of smaller men, some of them farmers or tradesmen attempting to supplement their incomes by dealing in livestock as a sideline. These people, most of them without access to capital, tended to operate on credit and were thereby a more risky proposition for farmers with livestock to sell. Sometimes a small operator would promise to pay for his purchased stock after their sale in England. But where the animals failed to sell for a satisfactory price he would be unable to meet his obligations at home with the sad consequence that, '. . . many an honest farmer is duped out of his property in whole or in part'. It was at people of this sort that eighteenth- and nineteenth-century writers levelled their rather astringent criticisms.

In the early fifteenth century the Warwickshire famer John Broome of Baddesley Clinton recorded purchasing oxen of Gruff Hope Wallace from a drove of Welsh cattle on their way to Birmingham. Again, in 1687, the constable's accounts of the Midlands parish of Helmdon contain an entry relating to money being given to, '. . . a poor Welshman who fell sick on his journey driving beasts to London'. These and many other examples testify to the presence of the drovers in villages throughout the Midlands and Home Counties before the coming of the railways. A 'Welsh Road' passed through Staffordshire, Warwickshire and Buckinghamshire; a 'Welsh Way' by-passed Cirencester in Gloucestershire, while 'Welshman's Ponds', 'Welshman's Fields' and various corruptions of Welsh words occur regularly in field and place names. The names of Welsh drovers crop up in farm accounts of the eighteenth century as far apart as Stamford and Brighton, Canterbury and Chipping Sodbury and their own extant account books show that there were few parts of southern and central England east of the Severn estuary which did not echo to the drovers' cry at some time or other.

The cattle and sheep that found their way to England were purchased in large numbers by drovers at the spring and autumn fairs. By the mid-eighteenth century upwards of 30,000 cattle and 'innumerable' sheep annually travelled through Herefordshire to south-east England and in the following century Pembrokeshire alone supplied 25,000 cattle each year to the feeding pastures of Northamptonshire and the neighbouring counties. Cattle droves, often of several hundred head, were assembled at a central point and shod by smiths who moved from fair to fair for the purpose. They then set off on the long journey eastwards, usually taking several days to settle down to a steady two miles per hour. This leisurely pace allowed ample opportunity for wayside grazing and made sure that the drove covered between fifteen and twenty miles each day.

Originally drove routes would have developed by means of a compromise being effected between the quickest and least arduous way between two points and the availability of overnight accommodation and forage at farms or inns with adjoining paddocks. Given the antiquity of the trade, there is reason to suppose

116

that before the development of turnpiking the same long distance routes, forged over open mountain and enclosed lowland, were used by successive generations of drovers down the centuries. The account books of drovers of the eighteenth and nineteenth centuries show clearly that while they strenuously attempted to avoid toll payments, many were quick to take advantage of the more direct access to the Midland counties provided by the turnpikes. By so doing they could reach the point of sale earlier than their competitors travelling along the old drove ways and thus obtain better prices for their stock. The accounts presented below, taken from the papers of Roderick Roderick and David Jonathan, two nineteenth-century drovers from Cardiganshire, illustrate tollgate payments and other aspects of the costs incurred by drovers during this period.

Roderick Accounts (1838)

	s	d		s	d
Lampeter gate		4	Ledbury gate	4	2
Cwmann gate		10	Beer	1	0
Beer at Porthyrhyd	2	0	Allowance at Folly		9
Llanfair-ar-y-bryn gate	5	5	Cash to D.Williams	2	6
Shoes and nails	2	0	Cash to D.Davies		9
Grass at Talgarth	11	6	Hollybush gate	2	10
Beer and lodgings	1	6	Bridge gate	2	10
Allowance	1	0	Tewkesbury gate	2	10
Beer	2	0	Doddington gate	2	10
Grass at Pugh's	16	0	Shoes and nails	1	0
Beer and lodgings	1	6	Lent at Croydon	2	9
Allowance		9	Expense paid	4	0
Keep for mare	4	6	Grass at Staplehurst	4	3
Rhydspence gate	2	9	Staplehurst gate	2	0
Willersley gate	2	9	Cranbrook gate	2	10
Hadmore gate	2	11	Cranbrook grass	8	9
Grass	16	0	Beer and lodgings	2	6
Beer and lodgings	2	9	Hire man	2	9
Shoe the mare	1	0	Beer for man		6
Brockhall gate	2	11	Fair and field	1	4
Shoe and nails	2	0	Fair gate		7
Grass at Hereford	16	0	Grass at Sandway	3	0
Beer and lodgings	2	9	Beer and lodgings		10
Hereford gate	2	11	Gate		7½
Tarrington gate	4	2			
				£8 6 ½	

Drovers' account books, the early maps and the Tithe material, supplemented by place-name clues and local tradition, provide valuable sources for the tracing of drove routes. Many of them have now been incorporated into the present road network, or swallowed up by ever-expanding stands of mountain conifers, yet surviving drovers' roads may be recognized on the ground by various diagnostic features. Hill top tracks, like the Kerry Ridgeway, typify the sunken grass lane created where driven animals were confined to a relatively restricted area. Where there was less confinement, as with the route across Aberedw Hill near Builth Wells, the drovers' ways remain as wide turf tracks rendered bracken-free by the constant treading of driven livestock. Where old roads have been incorporated into modern cultivation systems, crop marks may record their original course. In

first lot May 9th 1843					Do Expence	£ 1 d		
Account Expence the Beast	0	6	1		Lemster gate	0	3	3
Stamp Paper	0	6	1		Josson grass	0	14	0
Randales Toll	0	1	6		Do Logins	0	2	6
Eclwis swrw tavern	0	1	0		6 gates by wurster	0	10	0
Twlfard tavern	0	4	0		wurster grass and login	1	0	6
Do gate	0	0	10		3 gates to Thatford	0	5	2
Do Toll	0	3	4		whilbercastle tavern	0	0	6
Narberth grass	0	3	10		Stratford grass	0	14	2
Do tavern	0	2	10		Do Lodgin	0	2	4
Newcastle	0	12	6		Do gat	0	1	8
men drive the Beast	0	1	3		warwick Hay	1	0	0
Tregaron tavern	1	4	0		Do Lodgin	0	2	6
Do gat	0	1	0		2 gat to the Cock	0	2	8
Maesmynpwrch	1	6	6		Breakfast	0	0	6
Stanfer gate	0	3	0		Cock and Robin	1	1	6
Maserged gates	0	3	3		Hillmorton grass and log	1	1	0
Do Hay and Logins	0	11	0		Letterworth gat	0	1	8
Kingston gates and toll	0	3	4		man mind the Beats	0	1	6
Pembrig gat	0	2	4		showing the mear	0	2	0
£	5	11	7		£	7	6	5

Extract from the accounts of David Jonathan, cattle dealer, 1843

enclosed country where many drovers' roads have evolved into modern highways, extra-wide grass verges are a characteristic feature, while those following farm or estate boundaries, or providing links between fairs, typically become narrow lanes flanked by hedged embankments.

TREGARON TO RHYDSPENCE

Most of the many hundreds of miles of tracks and by-ways in the western counties were used at some time or other by drovers. However, there evolved over the years a relatively limited number of recognized long-distance routes over the rugged terrain of central Wales to the English border. Among these one of the most important was that linking the market town of Tregaron in Cardiganshire with the ford across the River Wye at Erwood in Brecknockshire.

Birthplace of several eminent Nonconformist divines and of that great Radical and man of peace, Henry Richard, Tregaron's development in the eighteenth and nineteenth centuries was closely associated with the cattle and sheep trade and the cottage manufacture of stockings and other woollen commodities. By all accounts the town had little to commend it in the early nineteenth century, being a collection of ill-built houses and thatched cottages dominated by the church on its prominent mound and a wooden bridge spanning the River Berwyn (SN680597). Here it was that many thousands of cattle and sheep converged each year, their drovers bringing welcome trade to the town's three shops and eleven pubs.

The Vestry Book for the parish of Lower Caron, covering the years between 1787 and 1846 makes frequent reference to the maintenance of 'the road across Tygwyn fields' and it seems that once the drovers' animals had been assembled in Pen Pica, the enclosure behind the present Talbot Hotel, they were driven through Tygwyn towards Cwmberwyn, a fine old farm originally the property of the Herbert family. The road to Cwmberwyn and subsequently to Abergwesyn was used both by drovers and by the Tregaron hosiers travelling to South Wales to sell their wares. Both would have appreciated that this road was free of tollgates, which may be another reason for the predominance of Tregaron as a droving centre in the turnpike era.

The drovers' road, now negotiable by car for the whole of its length to Abergwesyn, passes Cwmberwyn (frequently used as an overnight halt by drovers) and Diffwys and runs on towards the isolated ruin of Ffwrd-ar-Camddwr (SN762576). Here it was joined from the north by the ancient monks' road past Moel Prisgau, used by drovers bringing cattle from the fairs of North Cardiganshire. To the south the monks' road continued to the isolated chapel of Soar-y-mynydd, now on the edge of a great block of forestry, but in the last century (and centuries previously) the centre of a mountain sheep walk. Until recently this was one of the most isolated Calvinistic Methodist chapels in Wales and the point of convergence of many tracks used by farmers and others who came on foot or horseback for their weekly devotions (SN785533).

From Nantystalwyn, further along the route from Ffwrd-ar-Camddwr, we notice several deeply sunken tracks leading to the mountain top in the direction of the Drygarn (SN805575). These may represent drove ways used when cattle from Nantystalwyn were driven to the open mountain. Alternatively they may be ways to

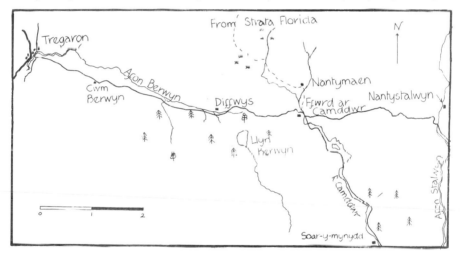

Drovers' road from
Tregaron to Nantystalwyn

Drovers' road from
Tregaron to Abergwesyn

119

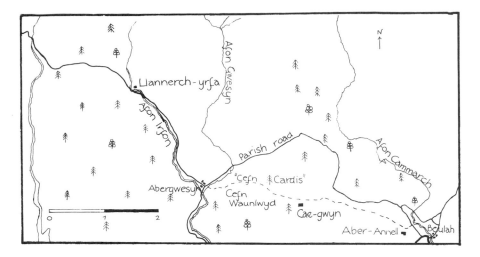

Drovers' road from
Nantystalwyn to Beulah

Cattle shoeing enclosure,
Abergwesyn

the *Rhiw-y-Porthmyn* ('drovers' slope') which, according to the Nanteos estate map of 1819, left the road from Moel Prisgau and crossed the hill for Llannerch-yrfa (SN836556). The main drove road from Tregaron ran past the farm of Llannerch-yrfa, fording the River Irfon no fewer than three times, and on through wild, open country towards the hamlet of Abergwesyn (SN855528). After the long trudge across windswept mountain grasslands, the final approach to Abergwesyn through a lovely vale of oak woodland must have come as a welcome relief, especially on a morning in early autumn when shafts of sunlight through a break in the cloud heightened the golden colour of the bracken and the warm russett of dying leaves. Welcome too would be the refreshment provided at the Grouse Inn (now a farmhouse), the enclosure behind the inn being available for re-shoeing cattle that had lost their original shoes on the rocky track from Tregaron. Onwards from Abergwesyn the present country lane to Beulah does not lie on the drovers' road, they preferring a more direct route across the hills. This crossed the fields in front of the Grouse Inn and forded the River Gwesyn before gently ascending the old hill track known locally as the *Cefn Cardis* (Cardiganshire ridge). In the early 1970s the hedged lane representing the beginning of the *Cefn Cardis* was still visible, but this has now disappeared in the wake of a modern farm road and a nearby bungalow, its course along the flank of the hill being now marked by a graded farm track. For much of its length the *Cefn Cardis* originally ran across open country which may explain why David Jonathan's accounts for 1839 contain a payment of 2s for the hire of an extra 'boy' at Abergwesyn. This local lad presumably helped to drive the herd across the hills until it joined the lane running past Aber-Annell for Beulah (SN915514). This is a lovely lane, varying from five to ten yards in width and enclosed by hedge banks planted with oak, ash and silver birch. Ten years ago the narrow part of the lane towards Aber-Annell itself was fully hedged but, as is so often the case, supposed 'improvements' have led to the removal of the hedge.

As they left Beulah the drovers had the option of several routes to the English border. The first, entering England through Kington, seems to have run across Beulah bridge towards Pencrug before joining what is now the B4358 at Pontardulais to pass through leafy undulating countryside in the direction of Newbridge-on-Wye (SO015585). The ford across the Wye at Newbridge lay to the south of the present bridge, the drove road on the eastern side leaving the river banks to pass under the disused railway bridge and into a lane beside the church. By this time a halt in the journey would be welcome and the bar of the Mid-Wales Inn (now a private art gallery) offered food and beer to the men, the banks of the River Wye providing ample grazing for the livestock. The onward journey carried the drove for several hundred yards in a southerly direction along the course of the A479 trunk road. However by the village school the drovers took the lane for Woodcastle Farm and thence across the fields to ford the River Irfon near the fourteenth-century church at Dyserth (Disserth), with its box pews and three-decker pulpit of the late seventeenth century (SO035584). Since the farmhouse by the churchyard was originally a pub (being licensed as such until 1897) it would have been regularly visited by drovers passing that way. The drove now joined the delightful country lane for Crossway which traverses the old Llandrindod-Builth Wells turnpike (the A483) before striking out across the gorse-covered southern slopes of Gilwern Hill. Subsequently it crossed the Hungry Green for Cregrina on the River Edw, passing the great mound used by John Wesley to preach one of his first outdoor sermons in Wales (SO123527).

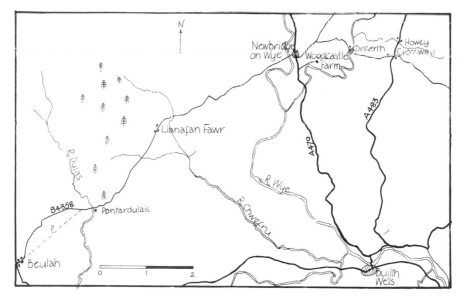

Drovers' road from Beulah to Newbridge-on-Wye

The 'Cefn Cardis' above Aber-Annell

At Cregrina, an important centre for cattle shoeing, the drove trail across Aberedw Hill joined the main route eastwards. Taking the course of an early road described elsewhere in this book, drovers heading for Cregrina ascended Aberedw Hill past Ffynnonau above which, so tradition has it, was a drovers' inn, known variously as *Tafarn Mynydd* or *Tabor Wye* (SO092530). Although none of the cartographic sources marks an early building at this spot, an enclosed

Dyserth Church

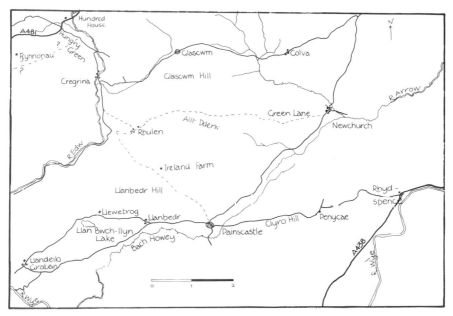

Drovers' roads from Newbridge-on-Wye to Rhydspence

triangular block of land may represent the site of some sort of habitation, the surprisingly fertile nature of the soil in the enclosure being typical of that found on upland sites where cattle have been regularly corralled over many years. From *Tabor Wye* it was but a brief journey across the hill to join Hungry Green and the lane for Cregrina.

Beyond Cregrina was a choice of routes to the border. The first of these, taken by drovers moving into northern Herefordshire, ran along the valley of the Clas Brook

Rhulen Church

The 'Twmpath'

Tafarn Talgarth

Drovers' road across Llanbedr Hill

before joining the road to Glascwm and Colva described in an earlier chapter. Both these villages boasted drovers' inns in the years immediately preceding World War I. The second trail, towards the Wye crossing at Rhydspence, initially involved crossing Llanbedr Hill for Painscastle. Leaving Cregrina, the drove plodded through Rhulen, where a route to Newchurch along the green lane above Bryngwyn headed north east. Thence it went along the side of the hill to the south of the ruins of Ireland Farm and through deserted country before descending to Painscastle along an enclosed way entering the village by the Maesllwch Arms. The tiny hamlet of Rhulen, with its peculiar little church, seems to have lain at the beginning of a series of trackways ascending Llanbedr Hill, many of these still leaving great swathes of greensward through the pernicious bracken (SO138499). Conveniently for the present-day traveller to Painscastle the main drove road has been recently metalled. Driving along this road as it snakes its way over the hill one is still intensely aware of the sense of loneliness and melancholy which the surrounding countryside might have induced in the more sensitive drovers.

Opposite the impressive remains of the Norman castle, a lane leaves Painscastle in the direction of Francis Kilvert's beloved Clyro Hill (SO168462). This lane, leaving Wern Fawr to the south, runs across the top of the hill and then, by way of Penycae and Penyrheol, steadily curls towards Rhydspence, some four miles from Painscastle (SO243473). Kilvert himself spent many hours attempting to locate the sites of the Coldbrook and the Black Ox, two inns reputed to have been used by drovers following this route. The Clyro Tithe Map shows the Coldbrook to have been close to the present Whitehall Cottage, and though there is no reference to the Black Ox there remains a strong local tradition of a drovers' tavern of this name somewhere on Clyro Hill. Rhydspence itself, on the English border in the exquisite vale of the Wye, also had two inns, the one standing today having its origins in the mid-fourteenth century.

TAFARN TALGARTH TO PAINSCASTLE

Drovers converging on Painscastle from the north were probably careful to avoid arriving at the village at the same time as one of the many droves from North Carmarthenshire approaching from the Wye crossing at Erwood. To trace the route followed by the latter we must make our way to the village of Llanfair-ar-y-bryn in the Brân valley to the north-east of Llandovery. Here, at Tafarn Talgarth, (now the

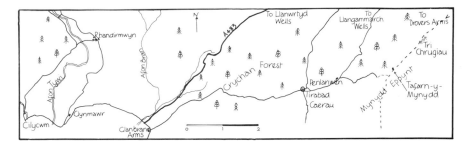

Drovers' road from Talfarn Talgarth (Glanbrane Arms) over Mynydd Epynt

Glanbrane Arms), animals from Cilycwm in the north and from Llandovery itself were prepared for the ascent of the Mynydd Epynt. The route from the inn followed the existing road to Tirabad and provides fine views of the rainswept hills to the west of the Brân valley and of the impressive railway viaduct carrying the line down to Pembrokeshire. The latter may well have been an object of wonder to the last of the drovers. Tirabad is an unprepossessing modern village that has grown up around Llanddulas Farm and would scarcely have been recognizable to drovers of the nineteenth century (SN879414). The old whitewashed church, however, would be familiar to them, though they would have some difficulty in locating the celebrated Cross Inn near Penlanwen, as this is now submerged beneath coniferous forest (SN898419). A second drovers' inn, The Spite, stood on the roadside on the approach to Tirabad. It is widely believed that this hostelry was opened to 'spite' Cross Inn, but it more likely represents the site of an ancient monastic *hospitium* since Tirabad and Ystrad-ffin to the north were part of the property of the monks of Strata Florida. At Penlanwen, approximately a mile beyond Tirabad, the drovers deviated from the lane to Llangammarch Wells to join the Tricrugiau trail at Tafarn-y-Mynydd (now a ruin on the edge of a block of forestry) and to ascend Mynydd Epynt (SN918422).

The great upland tract of the Epynt, in the past a formidable and inhospitable place, is now positively dangerous for the traveller because the Army uses much of the plateau for manoeuvres and target practice. Despite the panoramic views it

The 'Drovers Arms' Mynydd Epynt

offers, the Epynt is a dull, treeless and gloomy place brightened only by sinister red warning flags and enlivened by the occasional rattle of gunfire. Here, even the sheep bear a frightened and hunted look which the author came to share after a nerve-racking (and unsuccessful) attempt to isolate the old drovers' track from the network of military roads. Walkers, therefore, follow the trail at some considerable risk, especially when the red warning flags are hoisted! By the early 1800s the Epynt was a celebrated breeding ground for Brecknockshire cattle and sheep and the drovers, while not having to worry themselves about stray bullets and flying shells, would have had some difficulty in keeping their animals separated from the herds and flocks grazing on the open mountain. On their way to the Drovers Arms to the east they might have purchased stockings and other knitwear from one of the many (now abandoned) sheep farms on the Epynt where weaving and knitting were important means of supplementing a living from the farm. The Drovers Arms itself, approached by today's traveller on the B4519 road between Llangammarch Wells and Upper Chapel, was a notable port of call on the journey to the east (SN986451). Today, one suspects, even the shades of the old drovers would avoid this rather melancholy building, its shored-up windows and corrugated iron roof lending it a distinctly uninviting air.

Eastwards of the inn the military authorities have recently constructed a concrete road linking with the B4520 Builth Wells-Upper Chapel road near the Griffin Inn, a pleasant little pub also well-known to the drovers (SO022433). Between it and the Drovers Arms is open mountain and no clearly identifiable drove trail remains. However, slightly to the north of the Griffin a distinct track, reputed to be that taken by the drovers to the Wye crossing, runs to the south of Pwll-du and across the bleak hillside towards Cwm Gwenddwr Farm. From here it was a matter of driving the animals through more gentle countryside along the lanes linking the farm with Cefn Hirwaun, approximately a mile to the south-east (SO066441). Cefn Hirwaun stands at the head of a steep and circuitous road descending to the peaceful, tree-lined banks of the Wye north of Erwood. Over the centuries thousands, if not millions, of livestock were jostled down here towards the river crossing. A local historian writing two generations ago recalled the condition of the road before the council surfaced it with tarmac: 'The track was ploughed by the hoofs of the cattle in the damp weather, and manured by the cattle as they passed over it. In the dry weather it would be harrowed by the hoofs of the cattle again. No bracken or fern has grown on it since and it is still today a green sward which has not been used since the black cattle went over it'. Known locally as the 'Twmpath' the lane joins the nineteenth-century turnpike road opposite the modern bridge across the Wye, the latter having been constructed slightly to the north of the original ford over the river (SO089438). Below the bridge, on the eastern bank stands *Glanyrafon*, a fine villa whose name in the early years of the present century was *Cafn Twm Bach*. Although the term is rarely used today, the Welsh *cafn* originally referred to a small boat, so the name lends credibility to the tradition that cattle and sheep were ferried across the river at times when high water flooded the ford. Twm Bach (Little Tom), the last of the ferrymen,

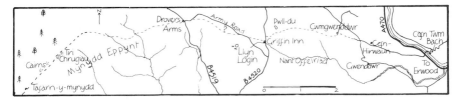

Drovers' road from Mynydd Epynt to Erwood

apparently loaded the animals into a box-like boat which he then winched across the water by means of a heavy chain. Since he ran *Cafn Twm Bach* as an inn, the little man would have relished the prospect of rain so that the drovers obliged to use the ferry would seek consolation in the temptations of his bar parlour. Twm Bach, it seems, died rather romantically when, together with his son, he tried to recover his boat after an accident on the river. The flood proved too much for them and the unfortunate pair were swept away to a watery grave further downstream. This sad event must have taken place before the 1860s when an iron bridge was thrown over the river on the site of the present one.

After safely negotiating the ford or the rigours of Twm Bach's ferry, the drovers could breathe a collective sigh of relief for the most arduous part of the journey was over. Behind them lay the drama of the mountains, the western rains and treacherous fords; ahead was the gentle, easy countryside of England. They pushed on along the eastern bank of the Wye before taking the narrow lane for Llandeilo Graban passing between the medieval church and what is now a deserted farmyard. The next stage took them along the south-eastern flank of Llandeilo Hill towards Llwetrog, leaving Llan-Bwlch-llyn lake to the south (SO120464). After a mile through open moorland beyond Llwetrog, a deep lane carried them past Llanbedr Church and onto the Painscastle road, entering that village to the north of the castle mound.

LAMPETER TO TAFARN TALGARTH

Drovers arriving at Painscastle by the well-trodden route from Tafarn Talgarth normally had with them livestock purchased from the Lampeter area or from further west at one or more of the many country fairs around Newcastle-Emlyn in Carmarthensire. Lampeter, in particular, enjoyed a strong connexion with the livestock trade. The town is mentioned regularly in drovers' account books while references in the Tithe Apportionments to the Drovers' Lane and Drovers' Arms Fields on the banks of the Teifi are further reminders of the importance of the trade to the little town. Several routes between Lampeter and Tafarn Talgarth were available to the drovers and among these one of the most important was that leaving Lampeter by Cwmann and heading for Pumsaint past the Ram, and Lock and Key taverns (SN583473). 'Lock and Key' incidentally, is a common name for old inns close to established drovers' roads and seems to have derived from the inn of the same name in London's Smithfield Market where many Welsh drovers

Glanyrafon (Cafn Twm Bach); the crossing of the River Wye

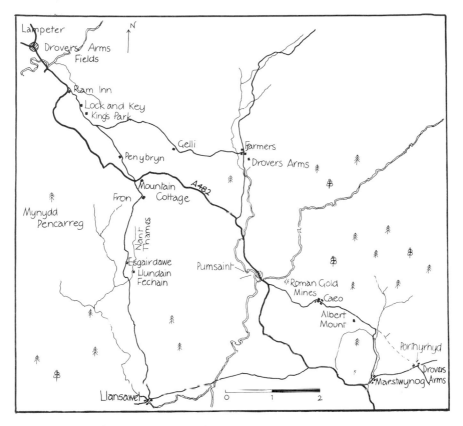

Drovers' roads from Lampeter to Caeo

were accommodated in the early nineteenth century. By the 1850s, when the Smithfield tavern had also become the venue for harp and singing concerts for home-sick Welshmen, it was under the proprietorship of a Mr Robertson who seems to have specialized in executing the wills of drovers unfortunate enough to die before their return to Wales. Among several wills executed by Robertson was that of John Walters of Llan-crwys in Carmarthenshire who died at Hyde in Middlesex in 1859 leaving a modest fortune of some £1,500.

Passing through the Cwmann tollgate the drovers pressed on to Treherbert, and then took the narrow lane past King's Park and Pen-y-bryn to rejoin the Lampeter to Llanwrda turnpike (the present A482) a mile or so later near Mountain Cottage (SN613437). At this spot there was reputedly a shoeing forge although there appear to be no remains of the enclosures normally associated with cattle shoeing forges nor do any of the cartographic sources indicate a smithy in the immediate locality. Entries in several account books recording tollgate payments suggest that at least some of the drovers followed the turnpike road to Pumsaint. On the other hand, those with an eye to reducing over-head costs may well have made use of the old drift road at Brynmanhalog approximately $1\frac{3}{4}$ miles to the south of Cwmann. This lane, having all the characteristics of a drovers' road, leaves the parish road to head towards Fron to the south-east, where it linked with another parish road joining the turnpike *below* the Pentre-Davies tollgate at Pumsaint. It is difficult to trace the lane along the whole of its course past Caer Pencarreg to Fron but it can be picked up between the latter and Esgair Farm.

To the south of Fron, on the outskirts of Esgerdawe, the maps of both Emmanuel

Caeo

Bowen and Thomas Kitchin locate the farm of *Llundain Fechain* (Little London) and the stream of Nant Thames running through it (SN614407). *London* type elements are relatively common in place names adjacent to drove routes. There is, for example, a *Glan Thames* near Talyllychau in Carmarthenshire and a *Llundain Fach* at Brechfa in the same county, while Montgomeryshire boasts a *Little London* near Llandinam and Cardiganshire a *Llundain Fach* near Talsarn. Similarly *Picadilly, Holborn, Victoria* and *Smithfield* names frequently occur in association with drove routes. However, the *Llundain Fechain* near Esgerdawe is of particular interest as this was the first overnight resting-place for Cardiganshire drovers en route to the Epynt crossing. The claim that the drover/hymnologist Dafydd Jones of Caeo settled and named the farm cannot be upheld since an indenture of 1708

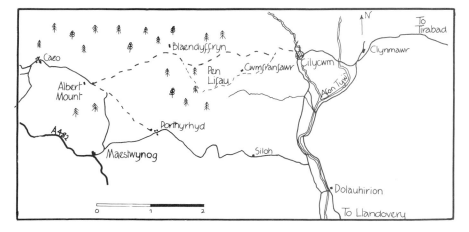

Drovers' routes from Caeo towards Llandovery

(three years before Jones was born) relating to turf cutting on nearby Panaugleision mentions the farm by its present name. Jones, nevertheless, may well have occupied the place at some time or other during his career and if so he would have been acquainted with *Cwm y Gof* (Smith's hollow) on nearby Pwllau Farm where, local lore has it, cattle from Cardiganshire were regularly shod. He would also have been wary, as he took his cattle or sheep down the road to Pumsaint, of animals from the north joining the route by way of the old Roman road from Ffarmers a mile or so above the village, their owners perhaps less than sober after an hour or so in Ffarmers' celebrated *Drovers Arms*.

Making their way from Pumsaint the drovers passed the remains of the Roman gold mines at Ogofau as they trudged the parish road to Caeo. In their company, one day in the early 1850s, walked a nervous young girl, wide-eyed with excitement at the prospect of going to work in London. This was Jane Evans of Ty'nywaun, who, as a commemorative plaque in the vestry of Pumsaint Church tells us, eventually found her way to the Crimea where she joined Florence Nightingale in her efforts to alleviate the sorry lot of the soldiers wounded in that tragic and pointless war.

Caeo was one of the largest cattle trading centres in this part of Wales and great fairs were held on 30 May and 6 October to coincide with the seasonal movements of the drovers to England. As usual, facilities were available for shoeing, either at Gornoethle or in the paddocks behind the church while at Blaendyffryn, a long two miles to the east of the village, the farmer's wife offered both food and ale to drovers as they awaited the shoeing of their animals (SN714403). From Caeo the eastwards route pursued the present parish road to Albert Mount before turning on to one of the several lines and trackways to Blaendyffryn and thence over Pen Llifau and past Cwmfranfawr to Cilycwm (SN753400). The great expanse of Caeo Forest bedevils the tracing of the precise route beyond Blaendyffryn. However, the Cilycwm Tithe Map records *Holborn Fields* alongside the lane from Cwmfranfawr (SN736397). *Holborn* is a name element often associated with a drove route while the *Drovers Arms* in Cilycwm itself, together with the open drain previously used for watering livestock, recalls the presence of the drovers in the village.

The hamlet of Porthyrhyd lay on a second route from Albert Mount to Cilycwm. At Aberbowlan, approximately a quarter of a mile beyond Albert Mount, where the present road deviates towards Maestwynog, drovers en route for Llandovery forded the Dulais stream and followed the old Roman road across the hills to pass by Llynglas and into Porthyrhyd opposite the Drovers' Arms (SN711378). Many drovers, including Roderick Roderick and David Jonathan came this way, the latter in particular being a regular visitor to the Drovers' Arms. In the accounts of both men reference is made to the toll payments at the Dolauhirion gate above Llandovery. This would suggest that these drovers, at least, used the turnpike road between Porthyrhyd and Llandovery and so crossed the Tywi by William Edwards's splendid single-arched Dolauhirion Bridge, completed in 1773. Neither set of accounts indicate payments at the Porthyrhyd gate, and so they probably managed to find some means of getting through the village without dispensing coin to the gate keeper.

Llandovery, considered by Benjamin Malkin to be one of the worst towns in Wales, '. . . its buildings mean, irregular and unconnected; its streets filthy and disgusting', was nevertheless, a flourishing centre for the cattle trade. Here a host of saddlers, carriers, glovers and leather sellers waxed prosperous on the by-products of the trade and relaxed in the the town's numerous taverns so deplored by Vicar Rhys Prichard in the seventeenth century. The denizens of Llandovery were seemingly much addicted to beer which, after the Beer Saloons Act of 1830, could be sold in shops and other places of work as well as at established taverns.

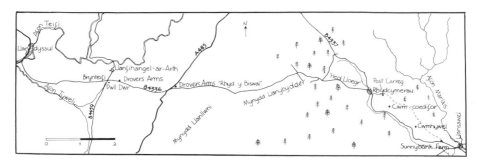

Heol Lloegr ('England road') across Mynydd Llanybydder

The 1830 Act enabled the number of registered beer houses in Llandovery to rise from twenty-one in 1811 to more than fifty in 1840. Visually depressing the town may have been, but it was a beer-drinker's paradise, with each little shop and tavern selling its own peculiar brew and providing the discriminating drinker with the variety of taste so lamentably absent nowadays.

LLANDYSUL TO PORTHYRHYD

Another drove route, connecting the Epynt with south Cardiganshire and North Pembrokeshire, ran from Llandysul in the west towards Porthyrhyd and Cilycwm. Leaving the steep streets of the little town of Llanydsul along the course of the present B4336, this route crossed the B4559 at Bryn Teifi southwards of Llanfihangel-ar-arth where an inn, *Pwll Dwr*, was a frequent port of call (SN458393). Further east, at the junction of the B4336 and A485 (the Llanybydder to Carmarthen turnpike) lay yet another inn, the Drovers' Arms, mentioned by name in the mid-nineteenth-century Tithe Apportionment. From the Drovers' Arms, the last inn for some miles, the route traversed the Mynydd Llanllwni and Mynydd Llanybydder along what is now the road to Rhydeymerau, a journey originally taking the drovers over open mountain. Today's metalled road, known locally along the latter part towards Rhydcymerau as *Heol Lloegr* (England road), passes for much of the way through the northern reaches of the Forest of Brechfa. Rhydcymerau itself offered a cattle shoeing smithy at Efail Fach and the Cart and Horses tavern, a house well-known to the drovers but now reduced to a farm barn (SN578388). Instead of following the line of the B4337, the onward route to Llansawel turned left at the Cart and Horses towards Post Carreg where it joined the drift road above Cwmcoedifor and Cwm Hywel before merging with the B4337 at Sunnybank Farm, half-a-mile to the west of Llansawel (SN612364). Once again there is no ground evidence or references on the early maps, but local people talk of the one-time existence of a shoeing enclosure at *Cwm yr efail bach* on this old road as it passes above Cwmcoedifor (SN588384). As recently as the mid-1880s, however, cattle were certainly shod at Llwyn Felfryn field in Llansawel while both Sunnybank Farm and Rhydyglyn Farm to the south provided overnight accommodation for men and animals. Onwards from Llansawel, the drovers crossed the Cothi above Glanrannell Park and worked their way towards Porthyrhyd along today's road connecting Llansawel and Porthyrhyd by way of Maestwynog.

MACHYNLLETH TO WELSHPOOL

Many of these long-distance drove routes across Wales, last used in the nineteenth

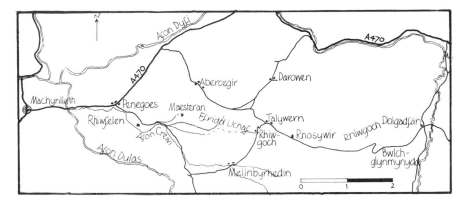

Drovers' road from Machynlleth to Dolgadfan

century, must have been as old as the livestock trade itself. Making his way across windswept hilltops and avoiding where possible the vales of the lowland, the early drover sought a route which reduced to a minimum the number of rivers to be forded and which allowed him an extensive view of the surrounding terrain and ample warning of would-be marauders. By the late eighteenth century, however, when some semblance of law and order had settled on the countryside and the need for security had become less critical, the most direct routes to England were provided by the turnpike system and the more enterprising dealers and drovers abandoned the older routes in favour of the turnpikes as the network developed. Others used both the turnpikes and the old drift roads, as was the case with some of the routes described earlier.

Typical among the larger drovers, David Jonathan and members of his family regularly followed the turnpike between Machynlleth and Shrewsbury with droves of cattle purchased around Dinas Mawddwy and Mallwyd. The Jonathan papers contain references to toll payments at Welshpool and Llanfair Caereinion in Montgomeryshire, while an account of the county in the 1830s draws attention to 'great herds of cattle' being shod in the Wynnstay Fields near the latter town. Alternatively, drovers intending to circumvent the toll bars on the Welshpool to Shrewsbury turnpike crossed the meadowlands to the east of Welshpool before fording the Severn and climbing up to the Welsh Harp Inn on the Long Mountain. Here they joined the Roman road linking Forden and Shrewsbury by way of Westbury. The importance of this route was emphasized in 1853 by witnesses before a Parliamentary Select Committee discussing the establishment of the Montgomeryshire railway, when they pointed out that the great majority of the cattle being driven through Welshpool reached Shrewsbury via the Long Mountain and Westbury.

At the little village of Forden, south of Welshpool, the route across the Long Mountain was joined by an important long-distance trail used for centuries by both cattle drovers from north-west Wales and fish traders from the Dyfi Valley and the villages on the coast of Cardigan Bay. Throughout the droving era Machynlleth was the principal town in this part of the country (SN745006). Served by the port of nearby Derwenlas it was an important centre for the weaving, lead and timber trades besides having featured as an administrative base in the ill-fated Owain Glyndŵr's dreams for an independent Welsh nation. Drovers converging on the town from Gwynedd and north Ceredigion may have known of the Roman auxiliary fort at nearby Pennal, of Cromwell's reputed battle with Royalist supporters on the banks of the Dyfi in 1644 and of Royal House, the old town gaol,

133

Early nineteenth-century Machynlleth

Talywern

where Charles I was reputedly held prisoner. Since the late thirteenth century, when Edward I granted a market and fair charter to the town, Machynlleth had been a venue for generations of drovers. By the 1800s the roads leaving the town had been incorporated into the turnpike system and drovers moving eastwards had no option but to pay tolls on their stock as they made for Penegoes, the first convenient point for leaving the turnpike (SN776006). From Penegoes, birthplace in 1714 of the celebrated landscape painter Richard Wilson, drovers could travel for virtually the whole way to Welshpool without the inconvenience of further tolls. Keeping the valley of the Crewi to the right they journeyed towards Rhiwfelen Farm along the present metalled lane. Approximately a mile beyond the farm, the metalled road curves southwards towards Penybryn, the original roadline continuing as a hedged farm track across Ffridd Uchaf. This, the drovers' trail, eventually meets the Talywern-Melinbyredyn road at the guest house of Rhiwgoch on top of the hill above Talywern (SN825999). After the steep and winding descent to Talywern the drovers and others now joined the old Newtown-Machynlleth road, which steadily ascended through the valley to the pass of Bwlchglynmynydd and then, by way of Dolgadfan Farm, to Bontdolgadfan on the River Twymyn (SN886002).

The replacement of this road by the new turnpike through Cemmaes Road and Llanbrynmair in 1821 effected a minor revolution in local communications. Farmers, previously obliged to carry their lime and manure from the port of Derwenlas along the tortuous upland trackways, now had a graded road and were thus able to replace the packhorse with the cart. Similarly, cottagers making a slender living from flannel weaving could now reach the markets of Welshpool and Newtown with comparative ease, either on foot or by courtesy of some obliging long-distance carter. The flannel industry was vital to the economy of this part of Wales. For centuries the vast majority of farmers carded and spun their wool at home and although several factories with carding engines and spinning-jennies had sprung up by the early nineteenth century, the weaving process remained essentially a cottage industry. A weaving factory built by John Howell at Bontdolgadfan around 1800 supplemented the efforts of the cottage weavers for half a century until competition from the large scale operators in Yorkshire and Lancashire forced it to close, along with many other small factories. The growth of efficient, mechanised factories in the north of England also sounded the death knell for the cottage weavers and the click of the shuttle was finally hushed in hundreds of cottages in west Montgomeryshire. In 1850, flannel to the value of £8,000 was produced by 500 people in the parish of Llanbrynmair alone. By the 1890s this cottage industry had virtually disappeared; like so many other traditional crafts it was destroyed by the Industrial Revolution.

Eighteenth and early nineteenth-century travellers coming down from the Bwlchglynmynydd pass to Bontdolgadfan on the River Twymyn found a busy and dynamic community, most of its members being employed in the weaving trade. Like that famous fictional weaver, Silas Marner, the people in the village and from the countryside around were mainly Methodists. Following the visit in 1739 of Howell Harries of Trefecca, one of the founders of Calvinistic Methodism, a Methodist Society had been formed in the village. In the early days, apparently, the society was beset with difficulties and one of the members, Richard Howell, planted a sprig of holly in a hedgerow, declaring as he did so that God's intercession in the growth of the bush would reflect the future prosperity or otherwise of the Methodist cause. Howell's action indicates a belief in a superstition predating Christianity itself, yet God was clearly on the side of the Methodists, for the sprig became a flourishing bush which was still thriving over a hundred years later. In common with others of their communion in rural Wales, the early Bontdolgadfan Methodists met at each other's homes until the first chapel was built in 1767 on land belonging to Dolgadfan Farm.

After resting at Bontdolgadfan the drovers, by now perhaps in company with groups of weavers on the way to Newtown, pressed on past Werngerhynt on the old road to the south of Newydd Fynyddog across poor, wet country for Talerddig which lay on the 1821 turnpike (SO931001). Even if it was a small village, early nineteenth-century Talerddig boasted a woollen mill, an inn and a thriving Sunday school. Again reflecting a practice common throughout the Welsh countryside, the school was originally held in a Talerddig farmhouse. When this could no longer

Drove road from Talerddig joining the Rhyd y Biswal

Stocking knitter; late nineteenth century

hold the congregation, people crammed themselves into the house for the introductory part of the service before dispersing to their cottages for private Bible study and returning later for a concluding session of hymn-singing and prayers. The very fact that a school room for 247 people built in 1812 proved to be too small, speaks volumes for the enthusiasm with which Welsh country people espoused the Methodist cause.

Walking for a short while along the turnpike road to the south of Talerddig, the drovers and their fellow travellers turned in an easterly direction along the old green road running past Caeauduon and Blaenglanhanog to the hamlet of Rhyd. This road, delineated on the first Ordnance Survey map published in the 1830s, can still be traced for part of its course. After almost two hundred yards out of the village along the turnpike (the present A470) a gate on the left leads to a recently-constructed set of farm buildings from which the old drovers' road runs in an easterly direction across the hills towards Rhyd (SO934998). Initially it takes the form of a somewhat overgrown green lane, varying between fifteen and forty yards in width, in part enclosed by hedgebanks and in part forming a hollow way across the fields. After about a mile the course of the road has been obscured by modern agricultural activities. Towards Rhyd, though, it becomes an overgrown track joining the metalled road for Llanllugan behind the modern telephone kiosk and tiny deserted chapel (SO975005). The latter, ascending Llanllugan Mountain is dignified with the name *Rhyd y Biswal* on the early Ordnance Survey map, a name shared with the track across Mynydd Llanllwni, described earlier in the chapter. The standard Welsh dictionaries translate *Biswal* as 'dung' and it might be argued that 'dung' in relation to a road might merely imply a muddy track. However, since

The Rhyd y Biswal *towards Llanllugan*

the name is associated with known cattle trade routes it seems that, in these two cases, it may derive from the droppings of livestock passing along the road.

The *Rhyd y Biswal* ascends steeply from Rhyd along a recently-metalled course across the windy, treeless moorland of Mynydd yr Hendre. After almost two miles a relatively new road branches south for Adfa, the *Rhyd* continuing past Gwaunmaglau to the Cefn Coch Inn where the drovers left their weaver friends who normally approached Welshpool by Gibbet Hill and Castle Caereinion (SO048028). The drovers are likely to have visited the isolated Cefn Coch Inn and, if one subscribes to the traditional belief that farmers prepared to accommodate cattle and sheep drovers planted pine trees outside their houses, Gwaunmaglau may also have been a port of call. It has to be borne in mind, though, that there remains an equally strong legend that Scots Pine trees were planted by Welsh Jacobite sympathisers as a secret means of identifying 'safe houses' to those of their cause on the run from the authorities.

Beyond Cefn Coch the drovers' route turned south-eastwards along a narrow lane to ford the River Rhiw at Llanllugan before turning left at the crossroads west of Adfa to take the road for Llanwyddelan and New Mills (SO056010). The onward route to the banks of the Severn below Welshpool cannot be made out in detail. Many old lanes wind through the undulating countryside beyond New Mills, eventually converging on Berriew and the Severn Vale. Some of these may have been used by drovers, although the most logical route to Berriew would seem to have been by way of Manafan and the valley of the River Rhiw.

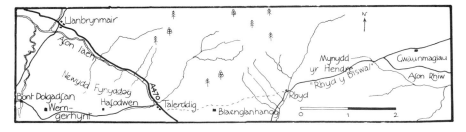

Drovers' road from Dolgadfan towards Welshpool

As the first steam trains chugged into the valleys of east Wales the more perceptive drovers must have realised that the advent of the railway spelt the beginning of the end of long-distance movement of livestock on the hoof. But they had little to fear for some time, since the evolution of the Welsh railway system took place over a long period, with almost fifty years separating the completion of the Llanelli railway in 1839 and that of the Whitland-Crymych branch-line, one of the last lines to be constructed. The great droves continued throughout this period to be taken across the mountains into England, though it seems that once the railhead had reached a convenient point the bigger drovers and dealers were not slow to exploit the new system.

By the mid-1850s Shrewsbury was linked by rail to the major towns of the Midland plain and ten years later, to Machynlleth, Aberystwyth and other towns on the coast of west Wales. The Jonathan family papers show that these dealers responded to the situation by abandoning the old Tregaron Abergwesyn drove route in favour of the turnpike to Shrewsbury and the new railhead. By the sixties even this journey was no longer necessary and from then on 'droving' merely involved assembling animals and driving them to the new station at Aberystwyth. Exploiting the railway facilities meant that henceforth the Welsh livestock dealer would be spared the problem of obtaining forage for his animals on the way to England — a problem made particularly acute in the wake of the Cattle Plague epidemic of 1865-6, when farmers and innkeepers were less willing than before to provide overnight accommodation to drovers of animals of diverse origins. Also, the railway offered benefits in terms of timeliness of marketing and a real reduction in the cost of conveying animals to the fairs of the Midland grazing counties. To take just one example from the Jonathan papers: in the period 1840-9 the average cost per head of taking a drove from west Cardiganshire to Northampton amounted to 12s. By 1865, when the same journey was being undertaken by rail, the cost had declined to 9s 9d.

But the old drover still had his uses. Livestock fairs and markets had by now become concentrated around the railway stations, and yet dealers still needed to employ the skills of the drover to ensure that animals were carefully conveyed to the sidings and loaded into the carriages. Moreover, droving of sheep in particular, continued within Wales until quite recently, and one of the last of the long distance drovers, Dafydd Isaac of Trefenter in Cardiganshire, regularly took flocks of 3-400 sheep on the ninety mile journey from Machynlleth to Brecon Fair in the early years of the present century. Of Dafydd's fellow drovers, those who had prospered at their trade often settled on farms in Wales, others taking holdings in the English Midlands. Indeed, many of the Lewises, Evanses and Williamses currently enjoying a good living as graziers in the Shires owe their prosperity to drover ancestors with the good sense to establish a foothold in these lush pasture lands. These were the fortunate ones and for each of them there must have been dozens who sank without trace into that saddest of nineteenth century social groups, the unskilled labourers.

The men have now gone, but the trade continues. Lean animals from the hills of the Principality arrive in their thousands at the English markets in the spring and autumn months and a driver on any of the major roads into Wales at this time of the year cannot fail to be impressed by the large number of cattle lorries that he meets. As he winds up his car window to shut out the dual horrors of diesel fumes and rock music, he may fall to thinking on the long-dead drovers who once trod the same road to England with their shaggy ponies and lean cattle. In his mind's eye he might see them; smoking noonday pipes under a nearby tree and casting wistful looks down the long and empty road as they exchange ancient yarns in an ancient language.

The Turnpike Era

The route was not along one continuous trust, but here over a bit of turnpike and there over a bit of turnpike, with ever and anon long interregnums of township roads, repaired in the usual primitive style with mud and soft field-stone, that turned up like flitches of bacon.

R. S. Surtees
Mr. Sponge's Sporting Tour, 1852

Regardless of the efforts of a few enlightened landowners to renovate them, most Welsh roads in the eighteenth century remained in a deplorable condition, their maintenance quite beyond the meagre resources of many parishes. The indifference and ineptitude of other parishes was of grave concern to the postal authorities who were often in the habit of applying to the local Quarter Sessions for the imposition of collective fines, these to be appropriated towards the hire of professional road repairers. As late as 1820, for example, long after the establishment of the turnpike system, we find the Post Office writing to the Trustees of the Brecknockshire Turnpike Trust warning them that unless the roads in the county were improved, the Office would apply to the magistrates for a fine to be levied and equally apportioned between the trust and local parishes. Unfortunately efforts of this sort met with little success since the magistracy comprised local landowners and professional people, who were far from enthusiastic about imposing fines which in the main would be met from their own pockets.

Gradually, however, landed proprietors throughout Britain as a whole began to realize that the development of trade and their own social aspirations urgently demanded that measures be taken to improve communications. In 1663, under the first Turnpike Act, the Justices of Hertfordshire, Huntingdonshire and Cambridgeshire had been empowered to raise tolls for the maintenance of the Great North Road from London. This was soon followed by other Acts and after 1700, the powers of erecting barriers and levying tolls were vested in dependent local bodies termed 'Turnpike Trustees'.

The development of turnpiking reflected a growing awareness that the provision of a network of highways was a matter of national as well as local importance. Although there was often lack of co-operation between trusts, cases of corruption at the tollgates and acute financial difficulties, the trusts gradually improved the road system, and turnpikes began to multiply rapidly, embracing some 20,000 miles of road by 1830.

140

To qualify as a Turnpike Trustee, a man had to enjoy a yearly income of £80 from rents, or be the owner of real estate to the value of £2,000. In association with like-minded fellows he would advertise in the local press his intention to establish a turnpike, at the same time inviting interested parties to a meeting to discuss the matter. If they managed to agree among themselves the group would now arrange to subscribe to the cost of securing the passage of the necessary private Act through Parliament. By the time the lawyers, surveyors, clerks and a multitude of others had been paid, this could often amount to more than £500, particularly where the Act was opposed by local vested interests. Having obtained their Act (normally renewable every 21 years) the trustees now addressed themselves to the business of purchasing land, building tollhouses and appointing surveyors and toll collectors, all of which involved borrowing large sums of money. The problem of financing these initial capital developments was a major one for the trustees. Many people who had promised financial support failed to deliver, while the business ability of the trustees themselves often left much to be desired, so that many trusts soon got into difficulty. Indeed, by the mid 1840s, thirteen of the twenty-nine trusts in South Wales were bankrupt, some of them irretrievably so. The situation was not helped by the fact that among those trustees public-spirited enough to attend meetings, local political intrigue often came to the fore, so that gatherings came to be held in an atmosphere of bickering and frustration.

Toll auction notice; 1841

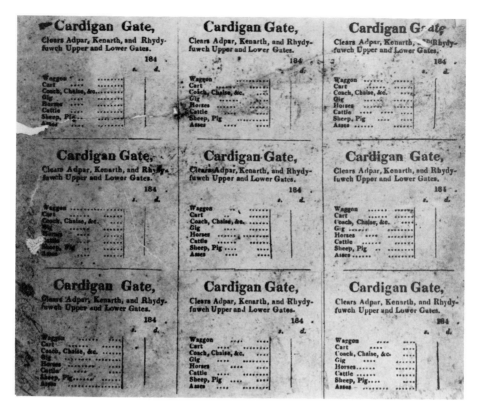

Toll tickets

Nevertheless, once conceived, the project rapidly forged ahead and roads were surveyed and tolls collected. In the earlier years the trustees themselves arranged for the collection of toll money, but as time passed there arose the practice of leasing gates or groups of gates by auction, for periods of up to three years. By so doing the trustees knew their annual income in advance while the lessees, a growing class of professional 'toll farmers', were enabled to pocket any income from tolls in excess of the rent of the gates payable to the trustees. Toll farmers like Richard Morgan, also surveyor of the roads for the Radnorshire Turnpike Trust, were asked to provide security for their lease. If they failed to do so the trustees acted quickly, as in the case of John and Stephen Owens, who rented the Walton and New Radnor gates in 1801. At a meeting of the trustees shortly after the Owens had taken the gates, it was ordered that men be employed 'to turn them out of possession of the tolls and gates and appoint other persons to collect the Tolls, they having neglected to give security for payment of the rent according to their agreement'.

For obvious reasons the toll collectors were an unpopular and often despised group of people, subject to the vilification of some travellers and readily tempted by 'backhanders' from others. Rather like today's traffic wardens, they did an unpopular job in difficult conditions. In the early days their tollhouses by no means approximated to the delightful Georgian and Victorian structures still to be seen today, the originals being flimsy affairs, often of wood and from time to time mounted on wheels. Gradually things improved and more permanent houses were erected, typically of the design recorded in the minutes of the Radnorshire Turnpike Trustees in 1768:

Ordered that Edward Breese build a Turnpike House at the Turnpike Gate at New Radnor, twelve foot in length and ten foot in breadth in the clear within the walls and to erect a chimney at the end and to top the same with brick. To erect a stone wall six foot and an half in height all round the Building and to fix a partition within across the Building and also another partitiion to divide the pantry from the bedchamber and to compleat the whole including glazing, thatching, carriage etc. in a workmanlike manner at the sum of Ten Guineas on or before the twenty second day of October instant.

From houses such as this the tollkeeper operated his gate or bar, the tolls he collected varying from trust to trust according to the extent to which trustees believed a particular conveyance would damage the road surface.

In theory the trustees were supposed to maintain the road surface, but in reality legislation over the years seems to have been designed to make vehicles conform to the requirements of the road rather than to enforce the improvement of the road to facilitate the passage of traffic. On the grounds that they did excessive damage to the road surface (if, in the eighteenth century it could be dignified by such a term) discrimination was particularly severe against narrow-wheeled vehicles. Shortly after the Restoration, wheels of less than 4in wide were prohibited from the roads and from that time onwards the authorities persistently strove to increase wheel width and to reduce the weight of waggons and coaches. This led to surcharges being levied on overweight vehicles while, after 1773, traffic on wheels of more than 16in wide was relieved from toll. It is not surprising that the narrow-wheeled mail coaches, increasingly common after 1780 and exempt from toll, hardly endeared themselves to turnpike trustees the length and breadth of the land. Exempt too were all military horses, waggons and coaches, travellers to and from church or chapel, funeral cortèges, horses going to be shod, livestock moving to water, vagrants with passes and citizens travelling to vote at Parliamentary elections. Similarly exempt were vehicles concerned with the carriage of dung, timber and lime for farming purposes.

To the disgust of the agricultural interest, above all in Wales where large quantities of lime were required to neutralise the acid soils, the lime exemption was discontinued in the first decade of the nineteenth century. Typically, the Brecknockshire Turnpike Trust imposed tolls in 1809 with the concession that a lime cart would pay toll at a gate only once during the day, and thus would be freed from toll if the return journey from the limekiln was completed within a 24-hour period. This meant that the roads were crowded with scores of farmers setting out for the kilns at the break of day in the hope that they could get to the head of the queue, purchase their lime, and be home by midnight. Little wonder that tempers became frayed and fists and knives flashed as they jostled for position. Little wonder too that resentment came to a head with such violence during the Rebecca Riots of the early 1840s when many gates were destroyed, when tollkeepers were assaulted and when the arsonist stalked the countryside. Even before that the appearance of a tollgate or tollbar provoked local rioting, particularly when people believed, with some justification, that the amount of toll collected was usually out of all proportion to the rate of road improvement. Thus, on 10 November 1780, John Lukes of New Radnor was gaoled for attacking the Stanner Gate near Kington with a hedge bill and thirty years later, Charles Lawrence of Llanelwedd was summoned for wilfully breaking the lock on the Builth Wells gate. These men and many others held that tolls were only justified if they were used effectively to improve road surfaces.

The minute books of some trusts reveal that great care was taken in the selection of competent surveyors and clerks who discharged their duties diligently. Others, however, suggest that many surveyors were quite useless, being ignorant of the techniques of road maintenance and, in some cases, not even knowing which roads belonged to the particular trust by which they were employed. In the case of the surveyor to the Carmarthen Trust this was understandable since he was illiterate! His colleague in the Llandeilo and Llandybie Trust was rarely sober, while the clerk to the Main Trust was both sober and cunning enough to abscond to America in 1823 with £650 of trust funds. Hardly the sort of men to inspire public confidence!

Gentlemen, farmers, drovers and others resorted to all manner of ruses to avoid toll payments. These ranged from the use of the dog-drawn (and thus toll-free) cart to the rather ingenious idea, successfully adopted by one man, of constructing a cart to be pushed by a horse thereby circumventing the regulation that tolls be payable on horse-*drawn* vehicles. Others might unhitch an extra horse from their cart and lead it through the gate, and so pay less toll, while farmers were often in the habit of hiding loads of corn beneath a covering of manure or straw, both of which travelled free of toll. Drovers, in particular, would often attempt to pass round a gate, a relatively easy matter when the road traversed unfenced common land. The trusts attempted, usually unsuccessfully, to counter this by cutting long, wide trenches at appropriate points on the roadside to prevent people from leaving the highway. Alternatively, where side roads could be used to avoid a gate, they placed heavy chains across them. This was of questionable legality as was the practice of many toll farmers, keen to maximise their income, of setting up extra gates on fair days. The tenant of the New Radnor gate did this on the occasion of St Luke's Fair in 1771, and, to the credit of the Radnorshire Turnpike Trustees, he was fined fifteen shillings for his trouble.

How far the turnpike trustees put their tolls or gate rents to good use varied enormously. Some trusts improved gradients, forged 'cross roads' and renovated surfaces, while others, less enlightened, were rather more concerned with income than expenditure, so that surfaces tended to remain unimproved. This was gall and wormwood to travellers by coach or post-chaise in the early years of the nineteenth century, as the antiquary Henry Skrine bore witness after a liver-jolting journey through Radnorshire: 'Their turnpike roads may rank among the worst in the kingdom for, notwithstanding the frequency of their tolls and the abundance of good materials in the country, they are generally suffered to languish in a shameful state of neglect for want of a little public spirit'. To the traveller on horseback, poor road surfaces were a minor inconvenience and one would expect criticism to be at its most astringent from those who travelled in some form of wheeled vehicle. Moreover, the nature of the countryside and state of mind of the traveller was bound to influence his attitude towards the condition of the roads. Barber's bitter tirade against the dangers of fords in Wales may not have been entirely unconnected with the fact that he, together with his books, papers and drawings, received a thorough soaking when he forded the upper reaches of the River Loughor. In other words, some of the complaints of contemporary diarists and journalists should be taken with a pinch of salt.

In the eighteenth century commentators had persistently agitated for a system enabling the more rapid and effective exchange of mail. This applied especially to North Wales where, in the 1750s, a package destined for Ireland by way of Holyhead could find a waggon as far as Chester, but no further. Twenty years later traffic capable of safely carrying bulky mails between Shrewsbury and Bangor was limited to a single privately-owned cart travelling twice weekly. The poorly-paid, letter-carrying postboys mounted (often inadequately) on horseback were readily susceptible to bribes and being unarmed were easy prey for wayside vagabonds. So acute, in fact, were the dangers of highway robbery that the Post Office advised its clients who proposed to mail money to cut their banknotes in two and to despatch each half separately. Besides the poor quality of the mail service, the inadequacy of the roads between Wales and England made life difficult for the growing number of Irishmen wishing to come to Britain after the Act of Union. Also, growing numbers of Englishmen, stimulated by the writing of Walpole and Gray and with their senses heightened by the 'Gothick' splendours of Alpine scenery, were keen to explore the romantic scenery of Wales with its druidic associations and picturesque legends.

Regular coach travel through North Wales to Holyhead did not come until 1776 when the enterprising landlord of the White Lion in Chester, showing entrepreneurial spirit typical of the times, started a daily 'flying post chaise' service to Holyhead, charging 2 guineas per passenger. Three years later another innkeeper, Robert Lawrence of the Raven and Bell in Shrewsbury, became the first man to link Holyhead and London by a coach system, thereby siphoning off much of the traffic from Chester and laying the basis to his subsequent fortune. These various developments provided food for thought for John Palmer, a West Country merchant. Protégée of Ralph Allen of Bath, the model for Squire Allworthy in Fielding's *Tom Jones*, Palmer believed he had the answer to the problem of the posts. In 1783 he presented Prime Minister Pitt with a plan for running the mail

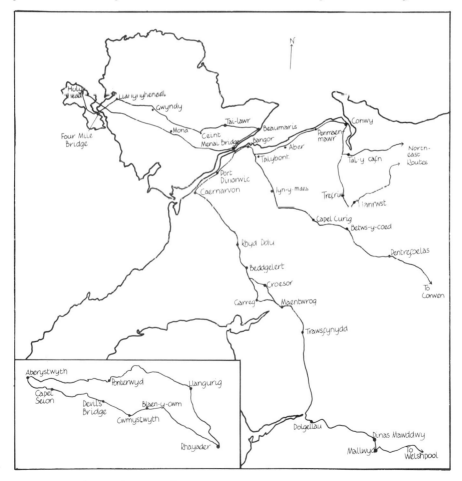

Some turnpike roads in North Wales

system on the basis, not of solitary postboys, but of special coaches running according to strict schedules. These would also carry parcels and a limited number of paying passengers where appropriate. Seeing the obvious benefits of Palmer's proposals, Pitt over-ruled the objections of the conservative Post Office and the stage was set for the glamorous era of the mail coach. So successful was the system, with its carefully scheduled horse changes and well-planned routes supplied with excellently appointed inns, that by 1830 mail coaches nightly covered more than 12,000 miles of road and represented the most efficient system of land transport in the world. Initially they rarely travelled at speeds in excess of 7-8mph and yet they were widely recognized as a major step forward and it was not long before the English mail coach became synonymous with speed and efficiency.

Advances in coach design and the replacement of wooden benches with sprung cushion seats helped considerably, yet the lot of the passenger in the early mail coaches could be less than pleasant, especially before the widespread adoption of Telford and Macadam's methods of road surface improvement. Lurching along on a winter's night, swathed in blankets or straw and peeping nervously at the driver as he pulled at his flask, the traveller may well have wondered whether it was worth travelling at all. His safety was very much dependent upon the reliability and sobriety of the coach drivers, of whom many seem to have taken perverse pleasure in terrifying the wits out of their passengers. Howell Rees, for example, mail coach driver on the Brecon to Llandovery stretch of the turnpike to Haverfordwest, allowed his enthusiasm for keeping to a strict schedule to override any concern for his fellow road users. On one occasion, when Rees had sent a cart from Cardiganshire rolling down the hillside, its red ochre-painted woodwork and gearing smashed to pieces, he responded to the unprintable invective of the carter with a casual wave and the promise of a glass of brandy at their next meeting! In 1827 Thomas Morgan was gaoled for 'furiously driving the Milford and Carmarthen day coach', while Enoch Hughes, a private coach owner, was fined £5 for drunken driving and the use of abusive language as he drove passengers between Shrewsbury and Aberystwyth. Another driver, Edward Jenkins, drunkenly careering along the road to Llandovery, managed to overturn the Gloucester to Carmarthen mail coach outside the town. On this occasion a rather shaken local squire

Rescuing the Gloucester and Aberystwyth Mail Coach from the River Frome

*Coaching advertisement;
1816*

emerged from the coach and administered immediate rough justice by, as the local paper picturesquely put it, 'kicking the coachman's posterior down the road'. After such harrowing escapades passengers were able to enjoy a brief period of respite while the horses were being changed, perhaps ruminating on the remark of a traveller in 1815: 'Once you crawled and were overset gently; now you gallop and are bashed to atoms'

Alongside the mail coaches ran a growing number of conveyances operated by private individuals and by the 1820s villages throughout North Wales, hitherto experiencing little more than the ponderous waggons of local carters, were now regularly visited by gaily-painted stage coaches. Together with the Irish Mail to Holyhead, stage and mail coaches plied between Shrewsbury and Aberystwyth via Welshpool and Newtown, while towns in Merioneth and Llŷn and Denbighshire and Flintshire were provided with coach services linking with these major routes. Also, stage waggon services to deal with heavy freight began to radiate from Chester and Shrewsbury into North Wales, to the great benefit of the wool and flannel trades.

Despite the numerous waggons, mail and stage coaches and the atmosphere of cut-throat competition in the transport business, travel and the despatch of mails remained a very costly affair. To send a letter from Wales to London around 1800 cost more or less twice a labourer's daily wage and it was not until the introduction of the fourpenny and penny posts in 1839 and 1840 that correspondence came within the range of most people's pockets. Expensive though it was, transmission of letters between the major post towns was now very fast and efficient, the journey from London to Holyhead being shortened in stages from forty-eight to twenty-seven hours between 1784 and 1836. As early as 1790 a letter posted in London would arrive in Dublin three days later — Irish sea conditions permitting. The letter would be carried in the mail coach leaving the 'Swan with Two Necks' in Gresham Street, London and be deposited at the 'Eagle and Child' in Holyhead. Irish travellers alighting from the Dublin packet normally proceeded to the 'Eagle and Child' to pick up their coaches for Shrewsbury, London or Chester. These, in the first decade of the nineteenth century, would convey them to their destinations at the following rates:

	Inside	Outside
Royal Mail to London	£6 5s 0d	£3 0s 0d
Royal Mail to Chester	£2 5s 0d	£1 5s 0d
Ancient Briton to London	£4 4s 0d	£2 10s 0d
Ancient Briton to Shrewsbury	£1 15s 0d	£1 5s 0d
Prince of Wales to Shrewsbury	£1 15s 0d	£1 5s 0d

Some nineteenth century milestones

Swift and safe communication with Holyhead was a major objective of the promoters of road improvements in North Wales in the eighteenth and nineteenth centuries. Important too, for local gentlemen with social aspirations, was the need to forge good road links between north-west Wales and the Llŷn Peninsula and the English turnpike system leading to London. By 1752 the road from Shrewsbury to Wrexham had been turnpiked, followed, four years later by the Chester to Conwy route through Rhuddlan, a road line taken by John Taylor ('The Water Poet') on his journey to Beaumaris as far back as 1653. This particular turnpike, however, was soon modified to pass through St Asaph from Holywell thereby avoiding the marshy land around Rhuddlan. 1759 witnessed the opening of yet another turnpike from Chester to reach Conwy by way of Denbigh, Llansannan, Llangernyw and Talycafn, thus linking, like the other roads, with the crossing of the Lavan Sands to Beaumaris and thence to Holyhead.

The problem with these roads, (and one which was to remain until the construction of Telford's remarkable bridges) lay in crossing the River Conwy and subsequently the Menai Straits. The Conwy boasted two ferries, one located at Talycafn and a second lower down the river near Conwy itself. Besides the nuisance of having one's journey interrupted, the crossing of the Conwy was not without its dangers and there are numerous accounts of instances of loss of life and property during the crossing. In the mid-seventeenth century, for example, the ferryboat sank with the loss of all passengers save for one fortunate young woman, who was to live with her memories until the age of 116 and be laid to rest in Llanfairfechan in 1744. In the early nineteenth century the danger may have been less, yet the 'shameful impositions' of the ferrymen who charged half a guinea for the carriage of a gig, '... and after that importune for liquor', remained prejudicial to the blood pressure of the traveller. The Reverend Mr Bingley, who wrote of these 'shameful impositions', was not alone in his condemnation of the ferrymen. Some years previously Richard Fenton and his friends managed to get safely across the river, '... after having our patience tried to the utmost by waiting for above 2 hours at the ferry and experiencing the most unexampled and savage insolence from the ferrymen'. By 1808 the opening of the Capel Curig Road to Bangor and the Menai meant that the ferry could now be avoided, while the completion of Telford's bridge over the Conwy in 1826 freed travellers on the northern route from the inconvenience of the Conwy Ferry. It is worth recording, though, that before the bridge was opened Hugh Evans and five other ferrymen managed to petition successfully for compensation for loss of livelihood.

CONWY TO BEAUMARIS AND MENAI BRIDGE

From Conwy there were several routes to the Menai crossing. One of these was by the old Roman road directly opposite Talycafn, which ran to Aber via Bwlch-y-ddeufan and Bont Newydd (SH787718). Described as 'an exceedingly bad mountainous road' this was previously used by the Parliamentary army during its conquest of Caernarfonshire. In the 1750s the possibility of turnpiking this road was mooted as a means of reducing the length of the journey to the Menai Straits. However, the nature of the terrain made this rather impractical and the Turnpike Acts of 1777 and 1780 took in the road between Talycafn and Conwy, which then headed for Dwygyfylchi and Penmaenmawr through the rocky defile of the Sychnant Pass.

The onward traveller from Conwy, having refreshed himself at one of the many inns of the ancient borough and perhaps, like Henry Skrine, been 'regaled with the strains of a blind harper', said a short prayer, crossed his fingers and advanced on the next stage of his journey to Holyhead — the awesome crossing of

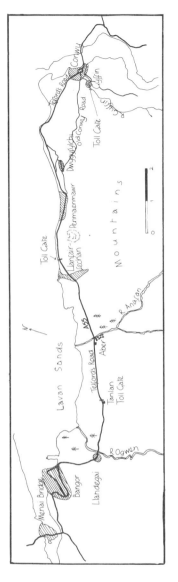

Telford's road across Penmaenmawr, running above the present A55

Turnpike road from Conwy to Menai Bridge

Penmaenmawr. For centuries the short stretch of the journey around Penmaenmawr had struck terror into the hearts of all but the most hardened travellers and as their coaches, gigs or chaises clattered up the Sychnant Pass and along the Old Conwy Road, hearts would begin to beat just a little faster. In 1631 Sir John Braunston had to 'lift his wife over the back of the saddle for her fright', while Dr Johnson was quite terrified by this stage of the journey. Thinking, as ever, of his creature comforts, the doctor was greatly relieved to reach Bangor in safety, only to discover that the accommodation available was limited to '. . . a mean Inn and in a room where the other bed had two men'. In 1762, a Mr Jones, Rector of Llaneilian, riding on horseback with a lady on the saddle behind him, fell with horse and lady down the steepest part of the rock. 'The divine', Pennant tells us, 'with great philosophy, unsaddled the steed and marched off with the trappings, exulting at his preservation'. The fact that his passenger had been killed in the accident seems to have been of little concern to the reverend gentleman.

Originally the crossing of Penmaenmawr was by way of a road running above the present A55. In the 1700s a succession of roads had been built, but none of these seems to have improved greatly upon its forerunners. Consequently travellers continued to peer nervously out of their carriages at the sea pounding the shore far below and to run the risk of rock falls from above due, according to the Reverend John Evans, to, '... the goats, skipping from crag to crag to browse the alpine shrub'. So bad was the road — in 1770 a mere 7ft wide — that the nerves of Irish travellers could stand it no more and the city of Dublin subscribed to the cost of building a breast-high wall on the seaward side. Two years later a Parliamentary grant enabled improvements to be made by the engineer John Sylvester whose efforts sufficed until Telford's restructuring of much of the course of this, and other North Wales roads, several decades later. Henry Skrine was lavish in his praise of Sylvester's work, writing of 'An excellent and almost level road, well protected with walls ... cut for above a mile on the shelf of this mountain and the traveller passes on in the utmost security in spite of the impending horror of the rocks above and the tremendous precipice beat by the roaring billows below'.

Today's motorist on the Old Conwy Road joins the seemingly endless flow of traffic on the A55 as it runs through the long, straggling village of Penmaenmawr towards the notorious rock. Until it reaches a point on the outskirts of the village where a brilliantly-conceived diversion, completed in the 1930s, carries it on a series of arches around the steepest part of Penmaenmawr, the A55 follows roughly the course of Telford's road. Above this diversion, however, a short stretch of Telford's original may be seen, a low wall on the seaward side giving protection for the whole length of the road until it once again merges with the A55 on the outskirts of Llanfairfechan (SH692758).

Since the sixteenth century Holyhead had replaced Chester as the principal point of departure for royal couriers and the Royal Mail to Ireland. The route to Holyhead crossed Anglesey from Beaumaris, the latter being approached from Caernarfonshire by a ferry which had been in existence since the reign of Edward II. Passengers embarked from Aber, a village on the turnpike currently occupied by the line of the present A55 trunk road (SH655727). Like other ferries in North Wales, that to Beaumaris exposed the traveller to a considerable element of danger as it was necessary for passengers and their coaches to traverse the shifting Lavan Sands before reaching the channel where the little boat plied. The danger was such that in 1623 the postmaster of Beaumaris had asked that posts might be fixed in the sands to mark out the track for, '... many times when sudden mistes and foggs do fall the danger is very great upon the sandes so that the Kinges packetts and subjects are like to perish'.

Beaumaris had thrived under the Tudors to become an important port for the receipt and despatch of all manner of merchandise besides developing into a shipbuilding centre of some significance. In earlier times Edward I's fine castle had served as a deterrent to the maurauders and pirates haunting the coastline of this part of Wales. However, by the seventeenth and eighteenth centuries Beaumaris, and the coves and inlets around the Anglesey coast, had become a haven for pirates and smugglers and Revenue cutters frequently fought running battles with those engaged in illegitimate trading in tea, tobacco, rum and other highly-taxed commodities.

In 1718 Beaumaris yielded its position as a post town to Bangor and even if some wealthy travellers continued to use the Lavan Sands crossing, most began to show a preference for the way through Bangor, by this time 'on the great road from London to Holyhead'. After clearing the Penmaenmawr tollgate, this road, turnpiked in the 1760s, ran through Llanfairfechan and Aber to reach Bangor by way of Llandegai, passing en route the Tanlan tollhouse westwards of which the

The Tanlan tollhouse

castle of Penrhyn rose majestically above the surrounding trees.

To the west of Bangor a road branched from the turnpike to the Menai Straits and the Porthaethwy ferry to Anglesey. By the 1780s the ferry was served by an excellent (if overpriced) inn, where travellers could look out over Anglesey as they quaffed their wine and listened to the beguiling strains of the harp. To late-eighteenth-century gentlemen, with an interest in the 'Sublime and Picturesque', this was the perfect way to spend a warm summer's evening. 'I listened', wrote Bingley, 'wrapped in a pleasing melancholy, to the sweetly flowing tones.' Had he arrived on a cattle fair day, Bingley's finer feelings might have been shocked by the sight of huge droves of cattle being swum across the Straits by their drovers. This was a subject which moved Richard Llwyd to verse and numerous travellers to incredulous comments. As one wrote, 'The people tie ropes to the horns of five or six bullocks at once, get into a boat and drag as hard as they can while others on shore beat them cruelly to force them into the water and when they have plunged in, it seems impossible they should not be drowned as their heads often get under the boat's bottom'.

Like other ferries, Porthaethwy was not without its dangers, nor were travellers any less subject to the rapacity and rudeness of the 'rugged Welsh ferrymen' who rarely stood on ceremony. At 2s 6d per wheel, together with 'a liberal remuneration for the ferryman', charges were very high, but at least the ferry was available at all stages of the tide and remained the most effective means of crossing the Menai until the opening of Telford's remarkable bridge in 1826. This wrought-iron masterpiece wherein Telford applied the suspension principle on such a vast scale, was opened on 30 January. The same day the owner of the ferry, Miss Jane Williams, received £26,557 in compensation, a vast sum considering that the bridge itself cost a mere £123,000. The opening, the culmination of eight years work, was a very splendid affair. The London and Chester coaches passed grandly over the bridge at the head of thousands of people; flags were waved, bands played and cannon fired, while the redundant ferrymen looked on, perhaps thinking of the £26,557. At last a safe passage to Anglesey was open to all who could pay the modest tolls: 1d for a pedestrian, 1s for a four-wheeled waggon, 2s 6d for a stage coach and 3s for a post-chaise or private four-wheeled carriage.

ROADS ACROSS ANGLESEY

The establishment of Bangor as a post town heralded the gradual decline of the Lavan Sands crossing and consequently of the original post road. Leaving Beaumaris along what is now the B5109 this road passed the fine set of seventeenth-century almshouses on the Baron Hill estate and ran on through delightful rolling country to a junction with the modern A5025 beyond which it took a narrow lane to the little village of Ceint (SH490750) before following a route to Holyhead taken by later roads as described below.

Robert Morden's 1704 map shows this road as the sole route from the Menai crossing, but later maps such as those of Thomas Taylor (1718) and Thomas Kitchin (1755) indicate the road connecting Porthaethwy and Ceint as the principal highway. This passed Four Crosses and along the lane to Braint before making a right turn for Penmynydd (leaving the almshouses on the left) and thence past Pen-yr-allt for Ceint. As they rode through Penmynydd (SH510745), eighteenth-century travellers might have paused to think of Owain Tudur, grandfather of Henry VII who was born in 1400 and raised in the village, only to meet his end at the hands of the hangman for having the temerity to marry Henry V's widow, Catherine de Valois.

Proceeding into rather featureless country, the traveller now passed through Llangefni and along the course of the present B5109 to Llanynghenedl before turning southwesterly towards Holy Island, to which he gained access across the sands close to Four Mile Bridge (SH280784).

The importance of this line of road in the early eighteenth century is emphasized by the fact that the erection of milestones (long since disappeared) along its length was sponsored by the proprietors of the Dublin packet. William

The 'George' Inn, overlooking the Porthaethwy Ferry and the Menai Bridge; 1844

153

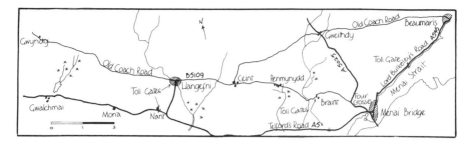

Turnpike roads in southern Anglesey

Morris of Holyhead spoke well of the road's condition or rather, of its condition in parts. Writing from Holyhead to his brother Richard in 1753 he observed, 'We can boast of having four miles of as compleat a road as any in His Majesties Dominions whatever may be the condition of the rest of it to Borth [Porthaethwy]'. His concern with the state of the eastern stretch of the road prompted Morris to combine with other local gentlemen to arrange for it to be turnpiked. An appropriate Act reached the Statute Book in 1765 (being subsequently renewed by Acts of 1775 and 1807) and gates were erected at Braint, Llanynghenedl and Holyhead.

Returning from Holyhead to Bangor in the 1770s, Thomas Pennant drew the attention of his readers to 'the comfortable inn called "Gwindy"'. Gwyndy, located between Trefor and Llynfaes, was a substantial inn which had for many years also served as a post office (SH395794). Unusually for a Welsh inn, most travellers praised its accommodation and its table. Henry Skrine's remarks are typical, '. . . every accommodation was admirably supplied and much enhanced by the attention of our worthy old landlady who had been fixed on the spot for about forty years'. This stalwart matron was probably the wife of Hugh Evans of Gwyndy who regularly carried the mail between the inn and Holyhead from 1745 until the

The ruins of Gwyndy

arrival of the first mail coach in 1785. Thomas Telford himself was mindful of the excellent service provided by Gwyndy and when he completed his new road through Anglesey in the 1820s he recommended that Eliza Jones, widow of the Gwyndy postmaster, receive a pension by way of compensation for lost trade. Today Gwyndy is a gaunt, ivy-clad ruin.

Like many turnpike roads of the time, the Porthaethwy-Holyhead highway served its purpose as long as the traffic loading remained modest. However, following the Act of Union with Ireland in 1800 the road came into heavy use and before long the competence of the turnpike authorities to maintain it in a safe condition was called into question. Finally, in 1819, a Parliamentary Select Committee was set up to investigate the present condition and future rôle of the road and as it collected evidence some horrific stories came to light. Coaches had been overturned, coachmen's legs had been broken and horses had died of exhaustion. An angry Lord Jocelyn explained to the committee that as far as he was concerned travelling along this particular road in a mail coach could not be undertaken without risk to life and limb. Thomas Telford, appointed by the committee to survey the road, had no doubt as to its inadequacies. Citing its narrowness, awkward bends, poor surface and numerous hills he recommended that the existing road be abandoned and replaced by a completely new highway. Subsequent pressure from Irish parliamentarians and others prompted the authorities to adopt Telford's proposals and the construction of a new road across Anglesey, along with the building of the Menai Bridge, was sanctioned by Act of Parliament in 1819. The bulk of the new road, the present A5, was in use by 1822, the project being completed the following year when an embankment was built to carry the highway from the Anglesey mainland to Holy Island and Holyhead. Five gates were positioned: at Stanley (on the end of the causeway to Holyhead), Cae'r Ceiliog, Gwalchmai (on the right of the junction with the road to Bodwina), Nant (on the junction of the road crossing to Llangefni) and Llanfair. Of the handsome octagonal tollhouses controlling these gates, those at Cae'r Ceiliog and Gwalchmai still remain in their original condition, as do the elegant milestones placed at intervals along the highway. Motor-bound travellers along the busy A5, provided their nerves allow their attention to stray momentarily from the traffic stream, will also notice Mona, the fine two-storied house put up by Telford between 1819 and 1821 (SH424750). Built to replace Gwyndy as a post house, Mona remained an important pull-in for stage coaches until the arrival of the railway in 1848. The tradition of hospitality is still maintained by the present owners of the house who provide bed and breakfast for jaded and car-sick travellers en route for Ireland.

Whichever route he took, the earlier traveller's usual destination was Holyhead

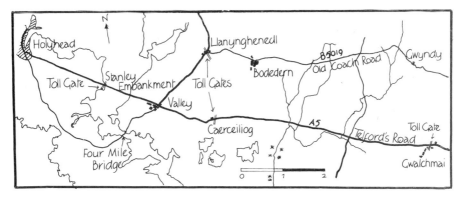

The old coach road and Telford's road to Holyhead

*Milestone on Telford's
road to Holyhead*

Octagonal tollhouse near Holyhead

and the sea passage to Ireland. Few people were impressed with the run across Anglesey which lacked the scenic splendours of Caernarfonshire and failed to kindle the sense of awesome grandeur so dear to the heart of the early nineteenth-century 'man of taste'. George Borrow, blunt as ever, echoed the majority view when he spoke scathingly of Anglesey in general and the landscape around Holyhead in particular: 'The country looked poor and mean — on my right was a field of oats, on my left a Methodist chapel — oats and Methodism! What better symbols of poverty and meanness!'.

Arriving at the rather shabby town of Holyhead the traveller could now look forward to the prospect of a sixty-mile boat journey across the Irish Sea, lasting for six to nine hours depending on the direction and force of the winds. In pre-steam days tides and winds determined times of departure and it was quite usual for passengers to have to kick their heels in the town for several days as they awaited the right conditions. On other occasions they were obliged to wait until the captain was sober enough to set sail or until the boat was filled with sufficient people to make the journey worthwhile. More than once this happened to the unhappy Dean Swift. Advancing in years, deprived of the wit of his friends and stranded among people whose language he did not understand, he sat in a smoky inn early in 1727 and penned the following lines:

Lo, here I sit at holy head,
With muddy ale and mouldy bread;
I'm fastened both by wind and tide,
I see the ships at anchor ride.
All Christian vittals stink of fish,
I'm where my enemyes would wish.
Convict of lies is every sign,
The Inn has not one drop of wine;
The Captain swears the sea's to rough —
(He has not passengers enough)
And thus the Dean is forc'd to stay,
Till others come to help the pay.

Now (presumably) among more convivial company and in a rather happier place, the Dean will derive a crumb of comfort from the knowledge that his name is commemorated in the 'Swift' Service Station on the outskirts of the port of Holyhead!

BEAUMARIS TO MENAI BRIDGE

With the decline in importance of the Lavan Sands crossing, Lord Bulkeley of Baron Hill constructed a fine road from Beaumaris to Porthaethwy and the site of The Menai Bridge. Built in 1804-5 at a cost of £3,000 the road served Bulkeley's own use and the convenience of travellers to Beaumaris. The latter were enabled to enjoy the facilities of, '. . . a house in castellated style for the resort of passengers in case of inclemency of the weather', built by Bulkeley at Garth, half way to Beaumaris (SH575736). By the time the Menai Bridge had opened, the road had deteriorated considerably and since no funds were available for its renovation a Turnpike Act was successfully secured and the Beaumaris-Menai Bridge Turnpike Trust created in 1828. The trustees provided milestones, some of which may still be seen set into the containing wall, and took their tolls at a gate located approximately a hundred yards west of the path from Garth ferry to Llandegdan. This road carried a great deal of traffic, from both the bridge and the ferry, a hackney coach service to Beaumaris being operated by the ferry proprietors. It continued to run until the trust was wound up in 1885.

TURNPIKE ROADS THROUGH CAERNARFONSHIRE

In the late 1770s the attention of travellers was being drawn to a new route from Shrewsbury through Oswestry, Llangollen and Corwen to Llanrwst and thence to Conwy. This was turnpiked in 1777 so that Conwy, by way of its link with Bangor through Penmaenmawr, became part of the great coach road between Holyhead and London, a journey that could be accomplished in three days by 1780.

Until the completion of the highway through Betws-y-coed and Capel Curig in 1804-5, Llanrwst was an important town on the Holyhead road (SH800620). The original turnpike approach left the line of Telford's A5 at Pentrevoelas (SH873514) and took the old road across the Denbighshire moors currently marked by the B5113 and B5427. This was an exhausting journey, initially through enclosed farmland, and then across high open moorland before a steep and (for coaches at least) difficult descent through woodland into Llanrwst itself. Besides being celebrated for the manufacture of fine harps, Llanrwst had long been the principal wool and hide market for North Wales and the town continually thronged with merchants and farmers from the adjoining countryside. The River Conwy, tidal to nearby Trefriw, carried sloops and cutters laden with wool down to the bay and incoming boats supplied the town with the coal, lime and cast iron vital for agricultural and commercial development. Llanrwst's main claim to fame lies in the tradition that Inigo Jones hailed from the area and that he was responsible for building Gwydir Chapel and designing the bridge across the Conwy, completed in 1636. While the attribution is spurious, this splendid structure, described by the chronicler of the Duke of Beaufort's travels through Wales in 1684 as 'a fair new bridge consisting of 3 arches of stone, the middle one being 26 ffoot wide and that on each side 16', has earned the admiration of travellers over the centuries. It

Talycafn Ferry; late nineteenth century

remained the only bridge across the river until the construction of Waterloo Bridge at Betws-y-Coed and the Conwy suspension bridge 200 years later. At the western end of Llanrwst Bridge lies *Tŷ Hwnt i'r Bont* (The house beyond the bridge), a charming, if modest building which, from humble beginnings as a farmhouse, rose to become the local Court of Sessions when the Wynnes of nearby Gwydir Castle held sway in the area.

An important consequence of the construction of the turnpike from Llangollen through Pentrevoelas to Llanrwst was that travellers were now spared the inconvenience of the Conwy or Talycafn ferries, a thought which may have gladdened their hearts as their carriages, post-chaises and gigs lurched across the seventeenth-century bridge and through the Gwydir tollgate. With the Conwy valley on their right and the great block of the Snowdonia massif on their left, they pressed on for Conwy along the course of the present B5106. This was a glorious journey in late summer when, as Bingley put it, '. . . the gay tints of cultivation once more beautified the landscape, for the fields were coloured with the richest hues that ripened corn and green meadows could impart'. Though their reveries may have been rudely disturbed at the Gyffin (Sarnymynech) tollgate (SH778768), such a drive ensured that most travellers who sat down to dinner in Conwy did so in good spirits. Refreshed with mutton chops and porter, they normally set off for Bangor the following morning. Before 1828 their route would have taken them through the Sychnant Pass and the dreaded Penmaenmawr crossing, though this was finally rendered obsolete by Telford's coastal turnpike round Penmaenbach and Penmaenmawr joining the old Bangor turnpike near Llanfairfechan.

BANGOR TO PENTREVOELAS

To late eighteenth and nineteenth century travellers, Snowdonia was a magical place, mysterious, difficult of access and shrouded in the mists of Celtic legend. Its very mention evoked among them a sense of awe similar to that prompted by Timbuctoo or Samarkand to wanderers of a later age. Poets and painters strove in their works to capture something of the 'sublime' qualities of the rugged landscape, while the ordinary genteel traveller, keen to impress his friends with his well-honed sensitivity, struggled manfully to do so in his diaries, letters and sketch-pads. Naturalists too, impressed by the wide variety of habitats — rock faces, moorland, lakes, rapidly-flowing rivers and coastal sand-dunes — flocked to Snowdonia from their rooms in Oxford and rectories in the shires.

The possibility of opening up a road through the mountains of Snowdonia to serve the growing needs of these people and to avoid the circuitous journey to Bangor via Conwy had long been pondered by the postal authorities and the gentry of Caernarfonshire. The most obvious route was from Pentrevoelas, at the end of the turnpike from Llangollen to Betws-y-coed and from there up the Llugwy valley to Capel Curig and along the Nant Ffrancon Pass to Bangor. The earlier stages presented few problems, but the steep inclines and rugged terrain between Capel Curig and the great slate quarries at Bethesda would prove to be a major headache for highway engineers. Apart from two horse paths described by Pennant, no attempt had been made to drive a highway through the Nant Ffrancon Pass until Lord Penrhyn, owner of the Bethesda quarries, took a road up the western side of the valley in 1791-2, extending it to Capel Curig by 1800 (SH720581). Here he built a sixty-roomed inn where horses and carriages were available for hire to travellers. The inn, now Plas-y-Brenin, the Snowdonia recreation centre, offered dried goat as its speciality, a delicacy refused by Bingley when he visited the place, only to dine instead on bacon and eggs and 'dreadfully bad new ale'. Several decades later Penrhyn's inn had become celebrated and the staunch Borrow dined, '. . . in a

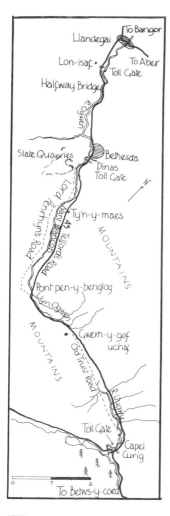

Old Capel Curig Trust road between Pant Cyfyng and Tŷ-hyll

Lord Penrhyn's road and Telford's road to Capel Curig

Llyn Ogwen bridge

Remains of the Capel Curig Trust road beyond Gwernygof Uchaf

grand saloon amidst a great deal of fashionable company, who, probably conceiving from my heated and dusty appearance that I was some poor fellow travelling on foot from motives of economy, surveyed me with looks of the most supercilious disdain, which, however, neither deprived me of my appetite nor operated uncomfortably on my feelings'.

Penrhyn's road to Capel Curig was the first real step towards opening up a new gateway from the east to the Menai Straits. Accordingly when he proposed seeking a Turnpike Act for a road from Llandegai up the eastern side of Nant Ffrancon and on to Capel Curig and Pentrevoelas he found plenty of supporters. The Act was passed in 1802 and six years later the new road was opened amid due celebration. The same year, 1808, the Post Office, acting on Telford's advice, officially adopted this Capel Curig road for the mail coach service to Holyhead with the result that the Llanrwst-Conwy-Bangor highway was relieved of much of its traffic.

The Capel Curig Turnpike Trust road left the Caernarfonshire Trust road from Penmaenmawr at Llandegai and followed the course of the A5 to the River Ogwen where it turned right and ran along the west bank of the river to Pont Twr and the Dinas tollgate. Here it crossed the river and proceeded along the eastern side of the Nant Ffrancon Pass following the A5 as far as Llyn Ogwen, with Lord Penrhyn's older road running roughly parallel to it on the opposite side of the valley (SH650604). Passing over the outflow of the lake by a new bridge and thence along its southern shore, the road deviated from the course of the A5 at the far end of the lake to run past Gwernygof Uchaf and over the moorland to Capel Curig and the Ty'n Lôn tollgate (SH672605-722581). This road, now a rough track overlooked by the massive pile of Tryfan, may still be seen several hundred yards to the south of the main A5 and parallel to it. After rejoining the A5 at Capel Curig, the trust road once again left the later highway at Pont Cyfyng and proceeded south of the River Llugwy on a lovely tree-lined lane, to pass the site of the Roman fort at Caer Llugwy, and to merge again with the A5 opposite the fifteenth-century cottage of Tŷ-hyll outside Betws-y-coed (SH734572-756575). At Pont Cyfyng, incidentally, the remains of Lord Penrhyn's road to the old quarries on Moel Siabod are still visible. Clearing the Betws-y-coed tollgate, those journeying along the trust road passed behind the Waterloo Hotel and along the lane to Pont-yr-Afanc, where they crossed

The Capel Curig Trust road skirting the Fairy Glen

Pont-yr-Afanc

the Conwy and skirted the Fairy Glen along what is now an unmetalled lane enclosed between walls and flanked by tree-lined hills. This romantic stretch of road, with splendid views of the Conwy and Llugwy rivers, rejoined the onward road to Pentrevoelas opposite Dinas Mawr, whence one could travel free of toll until reaching the Capel Curig Trust's final gate at Hendre Isaf, a mile-and-a-half out of Pentrevoelas (SH855512).

Between 1810 and 1811 a Parliamentary Committee investigating the condition

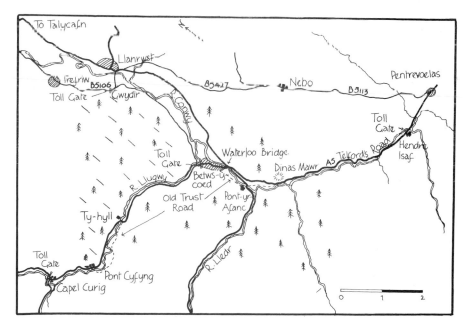

Turnpike roads near Betws-y-coed

of the mail roads received clear evidence that the local turnpike trusts between Bangor and Shrewsbury had neither the finances nor the expertise adequately to maintain a satisfactory road. Telford, as usual, was commissioned to review the situation and his report, published late in 1811, condemned the Capel Curig Trust road's narrowness (in some places no more than 9ft wide) and poor surfaces. Parliament's reaction, after four years of apparent deliberation, was to vote a grant of £20,000 in 1815 and further sums of £30,000 in 1817 and 1818 towards the improvement of the road, thereby creating employment for many people suffering the adverse effects of local land enclosures and the post-Napoleonic War slump. By 1818 the work had begun and a new body, the Shrewsbury-Bangor Ferry Turnpike Trust, was created to supercede existing trusts and was provided with Government funds to maintain the whole Welsh section of the mail road. Thus the Capel Curig Trust came to the end of its seventeen years' life, its relative success compared with other trusts indicated by a positive balance of £251 0s 0d in its favour in 1819. The following extract from the Capel Curig Trust surveyor's accounts typifies the sort of expenditure incurred by a conscientious surveyor employed by a competent group of trustees:

	£	s	d
Jan. 1806 By a dinner provided at Capel Curig for a Turnpike meeting the day so bad nobody attended but myself and surveyor 1	5	0
Feb. 1806 Finger Post at Llandegai 0	7	0
July. 1807 By Printer's bill for Notices to the different parishes to perform Statute work etc..2	3	6
Dec. 1807 Thomas Griffith & Co. for clearing snow..29	5	0
Mar. 1808 Thomas Griffith & Co. for clearing snow in Feb. 6	12	2
July. 1809: By expenses at Capel Curig letting the tolls viz Ale at Auctions, Dinner for Commissioners when only one attended 2	10	0
Feb. 1811 Lewis Hughes a Quarter's expenses and cutting snow and repairing a bridge broke by flood 104	8	6
Nov. 1811 Wm. Edwards Esq., for trespass and gravel for the making of the road 5	0	0
Feb. 1813 Mr. Worthington 4 lamps for Tollhouses 3	2	10
Mar. 1814 My son's expenses in taking 3 journeys along the road to settle with workmen before appointment of new surveyor — out 5 days 3	0	0
July. 1814 Ale at Letting and Dinner Bill 4	19	3
Aug. 1817 Ale at Letting and Dinner Bill 8	10	6
Sep. 1818 Ale at Letting and Dinner Bill 10	10	6
Aug. 1819 Paid Mr. Richard Jones of the House of Commons for his trouble respecting the Holyhead Road Bill......................................1	0	0

Thomas Telford, the son of an Eskdale shepherd, had already become famous with his celebrated Pontcysyllte viaduct over the River Dee, completed in 1805. His remarkable 'Irish Road', 109 miles of it between Shrewsbury and Holyhead, represents an outstanding achievement and established once and for all that road building was now a matter for professionals. Telford's standards were extremely high and he expected the contractors whom he employed to live up to the exacting requirements. John Jones of Bangor had cause to remember this when Telford had him re-make the Llandegai section of the road, his first efforts being considered slipshod by the master. On the other hand, men like John Staphen of Shrewsbury and Thomas Stanton, who had both worked with Telford on the Ellesmere Canal, applied themselves diligently to the task of constructing their sections of the road according to Telford's detailed instructions.

Apart from its narrowness, the old Capel Curig Turnpike Trust road, and, for that matter, its eastern extension through Denbighshire to Shrewsbury, suffered from inadequate foundations so that its gravel surface tended to sink into the underlying soil after a period of heavy rain. Telford therefore insisted that his contractors lay a solid foundation of handset stones before surfacing the road. As far as the overall road line was concerned, his basic strategy was to keep as closely as possible to the old trust road, and while he had encountered few major problems on the Denbighshire stretch through Corwen and Llangollen, the steep gradients of the Caernarfonshire section presented some formidable engineering challenges. This was particularly so in the Nant Ffrancon Pass where the old trust road negotiated a gradient of 1:6 in parts. It is a tribute to Telford's engineering genius that the steepest gradient on his road up the eastern side of the Nant Ffrancon does not exceed 1:22.

Opposite Lôn Isaf, approximately one mile south of Llandegai, Telford's road ran to the River Ogwen where he raised the Halfway Bridge, so called because it lay halfway between the George Hotel, Bangor Ferry and Tyn-y-maes Inn at the head

Waterloo Bridge

of the Nant Ffrancon Pass where the horses were changed on the first stage of the mail to Shrewsbury (SH608690). From Halfway Bridge (dated 1819) a new road was driven through Bethesda and the trust road between Pont Twr and Y Benglog at the western end of Llyn Ogwen, was completely renovated. New tollhouses were erected at Ty'n Twr, overlooking Pont Twr and at Lôn Isaf, while the Dinas gate was discontinued. Beyond Llyn Ogwen, the old road past Gwernygof Uchaf was abandoned in favour of a new line to Capel Curig, as was the Pont Cyfyng to Tŷ-hyll road to the south of the Llugwy. Instead, Telford constructed a new highway to the north of the river which rejoined the renovated Capel Curig Trust road at Tŷ-hyll for Betws-y-coed. Here he built the Waterloo Bridge, a fine example of his use of cast iron, together with a new road along Dinas Mawr connecting the bridge with Rhydlanfair and Pentrevoelas. This completed the great road through Caernarfonshire, which still serves as the principal route to Ireland.

BANGOR TO MAENTWROG

Travellers from Bangor intending to journey through Dolgellau into Cardiganshire and South Wales usually made Caernarfon their first port of call. In 1837 the Caernarfonshire Turnpike Trust built a new road (the present A499) leaving Bangor by Glanadda and passing through Port Dinorwic to the ancient town of Caernarfon. Previously the turnpike ran through Penycwintan and Penrhosgarnedd on the outskirts of Bangor and thence along the periphery of Vaynol Park to the tollgate at Tafarn y Grisiau, near St Mary's church, Port Dinorwic (SH522671). From here it followed the A499 into Caernarfon. Along with the Caernarfon-Llanberis road and several of the roads linking with the Llŷn Peninsula, the original Bangor-Caernarfon turnpike was extensively repaired under the 1810 extension of the Caernarfonshire Turnpike Act. Even before this it had been considered an excellent road, as the Honourable John Byng bore witness in the 1780s. 'In the evening', he wrote, 'we left Caernarfon and rode to Bangor, but not at our usual rate for we went these nine miles in an hour and 20 minutes; owing I suppose to the novelty of a good road'.

The condition of this road, with its tollgates at Vaynol and Pont Seiont, may reflect the fact that Caernarfon lay on an alternative route to Holyhead for travellers from mid-Wales who would cross to Anglesey on the ferry plying between Caernarfon and Newborough. This route, however, never rivalled the one through Beaumaris, and later Bangor. Yet, late eighteenth-century Caernarfon was an important outlet for the export of slate from the mines around Llanberis and for flannels, webs and stockings for which there was a heavy demand in the industrial towns of the north-west. By 1800 it had even become a fashionable resort where assemblies were regularly held and a company of actors from Chester performed three times weekly throughout the summer season. The cheapness of provisions, with salmon at 2d per pound and a pair of soles selling for 6d, may have been one of the factors attracting 'genteel families' to the town, while Lord Uxbridge's recently-completed hot and cold baths may have tempted those with a taste for the exotic.

The turnpike road from Caernarfon to Beddgelert and Maentwrog, constructed in 1801, took the route of the A487 past the ruins of the Roman fort of *Segontium* and through the Glangwna gate to head once again towards the high crags of Snowdonia by way of Llyn Cwellyn where the enthusiast could pick up a guide for the ascent of Snowdonia. South of the lake the road negotiated the River Gwyrfai by a fine bridge of three arches, and a mile further on the Rhyd-Ddu gate keeper exacted his toll before the traveller could press on for Beddgelert past Llyn-y-Gadair and Lion Rock (SH575500).

Rhyd-Ddu, the tollhouse (?)

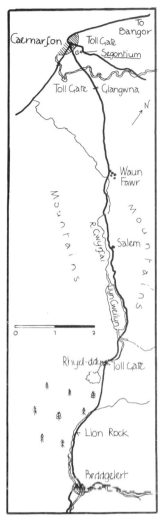

Turnpike road from Caernarfon to Beddgelert

Beddgelert was a much-celebrated port of call for eighteenth-and nineteenth-century tourists who admired both its romantic scenery and the sentimental tale of the dog Gelert, a gift to Prince Llewelyn the Great from his father-in-law, King John. Apparently, they learned, the prince had left the dog to guard his young son while he went out hunting. Returning, Llewelyn found the animal with blood dripping from its jaws and assuming that it had attacked the child, immediately slew it — only to discover that the wretched creature had, in fact, killed a wolf which had attempted to carry off the boy. Overcome with remorse, he buried Gelert with great ceremony and the place thereafter became known as Beddgelert (Gelert's Grave). The story, of course, is apocryphal, having its origins in a tale put about in the 1790s by one David Prichard, landlord of the Royal Goat Inn. In league with the parish clerk, Prichard concocted the tale and built 'Gelert's Grave' in the meadow beside the church, hoping that the romantic 'legend' would persuade travellers to pause at the village and sample the fare offered by the Royal Goat. The growing importance of Beddgelert and of the road passing through it is reflected in its increasingly salubrious inn. In the 1780s and 1790s the local hostelry was barely distinguishable from the rest of the poor houses in the village. Even so, its charges

Beddgelert

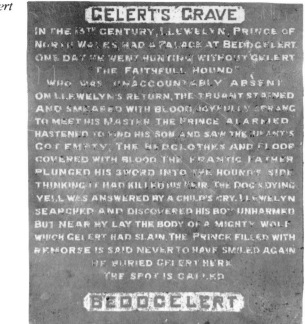

Turnpike routes from Beddgelert

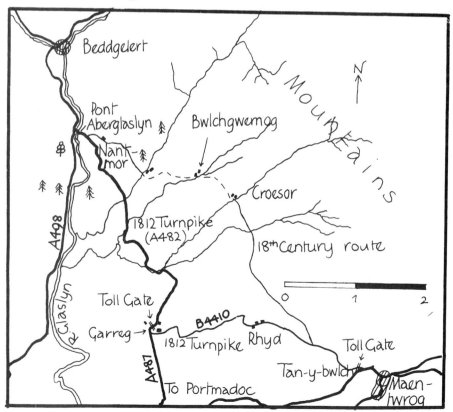

were excessively high, the walls of its rooms full of holes and its fleas unusually voracious. Complaining to one of the servants after a particularly flea-ridden night, Bingley received the splendidly blasé retort that, '. . . if we were to kill one of them ten would come to its burying'. Things were very different by 1810 when a new and comfortable inn was opened, complete with the blind harper, by now virtually *de rigueur* in a Welsh tourist hotel. Three years later we find an enterprising local entrepreneur, who also served as the village schoolmaster, advertising his several services on the new inn door: 'William Lloyd, conductor to Snowdon, Moel Hebog, Dinas Emrys, Llanberis Pass, the lakes, waterfalls etc. etc. Collector of fossils and all natural curiosities in these regions. Dealer in superfine woollen hose, socks, gloves etc.'. Today's Beddgelert attracts tourists in their thousands and apart from the inevitable mushrooming of gift shops selling their tawdry trinkets, the little

The old Croesor road

town, at the confluence of the Glaslyn and Cwelyn rivers has changed little since the early years of the nineteenth century.

Onward travellers to Maentwrog were now obliged to negotiate the rocky defile of the Aberglaslyn Pass, which, until the first decade of the nineteenth century, was a narrow track carried over the tree-lined chasm by Pont Aberglaslyn and able to accommodate horses and foot travellers only (SH595462). Beyond the present bridge, the eighteenth-century traveller deviated from today's road to take a lane

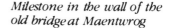

*Milestone in the wall of the
old bridge at Maentwrog*

running towards Bwlchgwernog (SH612452), where, at a "T" junction, the continuation of the old turnpike can be followed on foot in an easterly direction along a rough track through heather and bracken. Rarely more than 10ft wide, this track forges through mountainous country above the hamlet of Croesor before picking up a narrow winding lane to join the later turnpike (the B4410) near Llyn Mair (SH649415). Described by the Reverend John Evans as '. . . eight miles of the worst road in the Principality', this old route was abandoned in 1812 following the opening of the Caernarfonshire Turnpike Trust's new highway round the foot of the mountain. This followed the later A487 as far as the tollgate at Garreg and then turned eastwards to pass through Rhyd to the Tanybwlch gate and on to Maentwrog along the present B4410.

The massively-built stone village of Maentwrog, many of its houses graced with finely-ornamented slate roofs, is at present by-passed on a modern highway across the Vale of Ffestiniog, which, for the onward journey to Dolgellau, more or less follows the earlier turnpike. However, just below the bridge carrying the highway around the outskirts of the village lies an older bridge on a short stretch of the original turnpike road. In the wall of this bridge is set a tall narrow stone on which is roughly engraved, along with other distances, the comforting fact that London lies a mere 226 miles away.

During the early decades of the nineteenth century, the Caernarfonshire Turnpike Trust created a number of other roads. Caernarfon, Tremadoc and Pwllheli were linked by a turnpike system joining with the Porthdinllaen Trust and thereby opening up the remoter regions of the Llŷn Peninsula. The latter trust also joined the Capel Curig Trust by way of a road from Tremadoc to Beddgelert through Nant Gwynant and on to Capel Curig via Penygwryd. Llanrwst and the slate mining centre of Blaenau Ffestiniog, meanwhile, were connected through Dolwyddelan. These and other roads dramatically improved local communications to the benefit of both agriculture and commerce and allowed tourists fascinated by the scenery of North Wales to see more of it in convenience and relative safety.

171

MAENTWROG TO WELSHPOOL

People travelling from Caernarfonshire into mid-Wales had a tough route ahead of them. The turnpike from Maentwrog to Dolgellau made, like many other Merionethshire roads, under the Merioneth Turnpike Act of 1777, was simply appalling. As late as 1834 its condition was being condemned by a correspondent to the *Caernarvonshire and Denbighshire Herald* and even allowing for the hyperbole of the times, his description suggests that the surface was less than ideal: 'In every yard of it there is a rut deep enough for the grave of a child, and to ensure breakdowns the space between is filled up with lumps of stones each as large as cannonballs or Swedish turnips'. If he survived these hazards the traveller passed through Llanelltyd, with its limekilns and ships' chandlers, into Dolgellau, the principal market town of Merionethshire (SH729178).

Dominated by the glowering pile of Cader Idris on one side and the gentler slopes of Foel Faner on the other, Dolgellau lies in a narrow valley at the junction of no fewer than three Roman roads. Today it is a quiet, rather handsome place of massively-built stone houses and crooked streets whose basic layout has changed little since Glyndŵr held the last Welsh Parliament in the town in 1404. Later, Dolgellau became an assize town and an important centre for the manufacture of flannel, which may explain why it was well-served by tollgates in Georgian times. Our traveller, weary and thirsty after his journey from Maentwrog, paid his toll and made a bee-line for the Golden Lion and after jostling with coach passengers awaiting a change of horses, he was able to eat and drink to his fill.

During much of the eighteenth century, individuals travelling for pleasure through this part of the country were few and far between, perhaps no more than a dozen or so annually. By 1800, however, a general improvement in the availability of accommodation, coupled with a growing interest in Wales as a whole fostered by the published descriptions of tourists, encouraged increasing numbers of visitors on foot or on horseback. Some may have been deterred by the tradition, still strong in the late eighteenth century, that the unwary could fall prey to

Tanybwlch Inn and the old bridge at Maentwrog

the *Gwylliaid Cochion Mawddwy*, the red-haired bandits apparently descended from outlaws settling in the countryside between Dolgellau and Dinas Mawddwy after the Wars of the Roses. According to several contemporary observers, travellers often forsook the turnpike road in favour of a hike across the mountains in order to avoid the banditti, while nervous local residents placed scythes in their chimneys to dissuade them from attempting an unorthodox entry!

Stout-hearted tourists, however, pressed on along the turnpike, pausing from time to time to view the large flocks of sheep and cattle on the surrounding mountains or to watch a farmer and his horse as they struggled across a hill face with a sledge laden with peat from the mountain turbaries. Initially their journey from Dolgellau took them through lightly-wooded country, but this soon gave way to a steep climb into rock-strewn mountains before the descent to Dinas Mawddwy

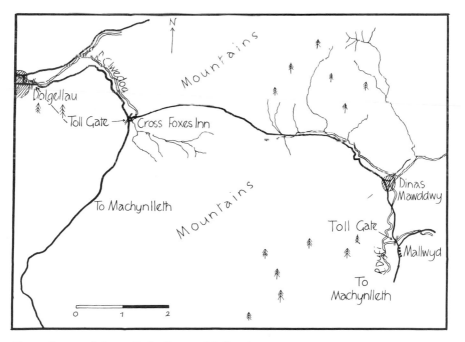

Turnpike road from Dolgellau to Mallwyd

173

through a lovely pass dominated by mixed woodland and rhododendrons (SH859148). Originally a medieval administrative centre of some importance, Dinas Mawddwy was little more than a post-town on the turnpike by the 1780s. Here travellers were confronted by 'a miserable collection of mean houses' occupied principally by lead and stone miners whose intemperant habits were criticized by many a passing reverend gentleman. The English could never quite get the hang of Dinas Mawddwy and they rarely remained in the place for very long. 'Altho' in England I appeared like other men', wrote Mr Hutton in the opening years of the nineteenth century, 'yet at Dinas Mawddwy I stood single. The people eyed me as a phenomenon, with countenances mixed with fear and enquiry. Perhaps they took me for an inspector of Taxes; they could not take me for a window-peeper, for there were scarcely any to peep at and the few I saw were in that shattered state which proved there was no glazier in the place.'

A run-down place indeed! Not so, however, Mallwyd the next port of call where the traveller arrived after a journey of a mile or so (SH863125). Here, at the Cross Foxes Inn (now a private residence), visitors were able to forget the dreariness of Dinas Mawddwy in the company of David Lloyd, keeper of the inn for the first three decades of the nineteenth century. A man of considerable enterprise, Lloyd ran a large farm to supply the inn with fresh produce besides operating a thriving post chaise business between Mallwyd, Machynlleth and Dolgellau. He was also blessed with several tall and comely daughters who gladdened the hearts of the most jaded traveller. The Reverend Mr Warner, a man much given to the pleasures of the table, was entranced by the Cross Foxes. 'Mr. Lloyd', he wrote, 'had provided for us a most substantial meal of mutton chops, bacon and plumb-pye [sic], beans and peas, at which his daughters, two girls of pleasing person, formed manners and good education, did us the honour of attending.' Lloyd and his daughters now slumber in the peaceful churchyard of St Tydecho not far from the resting place of the Reverend John Davies who assisted with the production of the Revised Translation of the Welsh Bible of 1620. The present church dates from the mid-

T. Richardson, Dinas Mawddwy, *1839*

1300s and has many interesting features including a barrow-vaulted sanctuary roof, eighteenth-century tiered pews to the rear of the nave and a seventeenth-century porch over which are suspended two great, mouldering prehistoric animal bones allegedly unearthed in the nearby fields.

The Mallwyd-Welshpool turnpike had its origins in the comprehensive Montgomeryshire Turnpikes Act of 1769 which brought the main routes across the county into one highway system administered by trustees presiding over four turnpike districts. As the powers of the trustees were extended by amendments to the Act over the years, more stretches of highway were taken over and by 1810 there were 260 miles of turnpike road in the county. In spite of the prosperity of the area and the efforts of the trustees, the inadequacy of local road-building materials meant that the standard of surfaces in Montgomeryshire fell below that of much of the rest of North Wales until the widespread adoption of Macadam's methods of surfacing.

Leaving Mallwyd for Welshpool along the course of the present main road, the tourist went through thinly-inhabited countryside to the tollgate at Garthbebio and thence to Cann Office. This was an inn founded in the fourteenth century and by now served as receiving house for letters from a widespread area of the surrounding uplands (SH012108). Apparently the whitewashed tavern was far from salubrious and '. . . the filth within by no means corresponded with the cleanliness without'. To make matters worse the wind was kept out of the broken windows by 'the refuse of the family wardrobe'. The Reverend John Evans, vexed author of these comments, followed his usual practice of protecting himself against nocturnal visitors by fixing his bedroom door to its lintel with two large screws! This certainly deterred intruders although it did little to soften the commotion made by the drunken revellers below who disturbed the old parson's slumbers. Today, though, Cann Office is a fine and well-appointed pub, its ample outhouses and stabling facilities testifying to its important role as a posting-house in those far-off coaching days.

From Cann Office the turnpike progressed to Llanfair Caerneinion and the Milford tollgate and then on to Welshpool, the last significant town before Shrewsbury. Today's motorist, following the turnpike along the main road towards Welshpool will notice that as the hills yield to rolling pasture-land, and the stone walls to straggling hedgerows so does the domestic architecture change with fine half-timbered farmhouses beginning to come into prominence as the English border draws closer. This part of Wales, with its favourable soil and weather conditions and access by land to the rich markets and towns of England has always enjoyed a higher standard of material culture than the hills and vales of the west. Agrarian prosperity, coupled with the fact that this is excellent oak-growing country, laid the basis for the development of the half-timbered house from a simple medieval open-hearthed structure to the sophisticated and often highly ornate buildings of later times.

Welshpool itself has several handsome half-timbered houses dating in the main from the years before the town achieved prominence as an important market for the sale of flannel. Established in 1782, the fortnightly market drew its trade from a wide area and Sunday afternoons witnessed the arrival of packhorse trains and heavily-loaded waggons from all corners of Montgomeryshire, their owners keen to be ready to start trading as early as possible the following morning. Some sellers arrived even earlier, especially those from the countryside around Llanbrynmair, who, '. . . since they were very religious men and having conscientious scruples against Sunday travelling, made the journey on the preceding Saturday'. Cloth buyers from the English border counties and as far north as Cheshire and Lancashire flocked to Welshpool and the little town flourished as never before,

Cann Office

with sales exceeding £65,000 in the peak year of 1816. It was only with the commercial development of Newtown and the establishment there of a flannel market in 1832 that Welshpool's years of boom drew to a close. Thereafter it was Newtown, with its warehouses, commercial offices and elegant public rooms that became, '. . . the principal seat of the flannel manufacturing in the Principality [and] has acquired a appellation of the Leeds of Wales'.

PRESTEIGNE TO ABERYSTWYTH

Not all tourists made North Wales their destination, many preferring the softer contours of the central counties or the coastal resorts of the west, in particular the expanding town of Aberystwyth. Described by Defoe in 1725 as 'a populous but very dirty, black, smoaky place', Aberystwyth had become a bustling commercial centre for ship building, fishing, the lead trade and agriculture by 1800. More importantly for the man in pursuit of pleasure, the town was beginning to enjoy some reputation as a tourist centre with its Assembly Rooms, walks and bathing facilities. To a great extent Aberystwyth's popularity resulted from the successful attempt of a local landowner, Thomas Johnes, to advertise the place. It was he who persuaded Uvedale Price, the authority on the 'Picturesque', to build Castle House (on the site of the splended neo-Gothic extravaganza occupied by the University College of Wales) and to encourage wealthy English gentlemen to brave the roads of mid-Wales in order to visit the little seaside town and enjoy the delights of its hinterland. By 1800 weekly mail coaches were leaving the Gogerddan Arms (later the Lion Royal) for Presteigne or Kington, while the Aberystwyth to Ludlow mail coach would set out from the Talbot Inn at 4.00am for Ludlow, returning to Aberystwyth the same evening.

The principal road into mid-Wales at this time ran into Presteigne and thence along the road (described in an earlier chapter) through Beggars Bush and Kinnerton to New Radnor. It was on this road that Lipscomb met some of the hundreds of Cardiganshire migrant labourers who, 'quitting their native retirement, the peaceful retreat of innocence and penury', trekked east each year to seek employment in the harvest fields of Hereford or Shropshire or even in the Deptford dockyards. Sparing a casual thought for these unfortunates, coach-bound travellers sped through Llanfihangel Nantmelan and Llandegley towards Penybont along what is now the A44 trunk road, the more carefree pedestrian or horseman taking time off to view 'Water-break-its-neck', the waterfall near New Radnor. Even

LLYTHYR.

"At y Cyhoedd yn gyffredinol, ac at ein Cymmydogion yn neillduol.

"NYNI, *John Hughes, David Jones, a John Hugh,* ag ydd yn awr yn gyfyngedig yn ngharchar Caerdydd, gwedi ein heuogfarnu am yr ymosodiad a wnawd ar glwyd ffordd-fawr Pontardulais, ac ar y personau a sefydiwyd i'w hamddiffyn—ac wedi ein dedfrydu i alltudiaeth—a ddymunwn, ac a nawn yn ddifrifol ar ereill i gymmeryd rhybydd oddi-wrthym, ac i ymattal yn eu gweithredoedd gwallgofus, cyn y cwympont i ein con-demniaeth.

" Yr ydym yn euog, ac wedi ein barnu i ddyoddef, pan y mae cannoedd wedi dihengyd —bydded iddynt hwy, a phawb, gymmeryd gofal na byddo iddynt gymmeryd eu har-wain etto i ddifrodi meddiannau gwladwriaethol neu bersonol, a gwrthwynebu gallu y gyfraith, oblegid bydd yn sicr o'u dal gyda dialedd, ac a'u tyn i ddystryw.

"Nid ydym yn awr ond mewn carchar, ond mewn wythnos neu ddwy ni a fyddwn wedi ein trosglwyddo megys anfad-ddynion—i fod yn gaethion i ddyeithriaid mewn gwlad ddyeithr. Rhaid i ni fyned yn mhoreuddydd ein bywyd o'n cartref-leoedd hyfryd, i fyw a llafurio gyda caethion o'r radd waethaf, ac edrych arnom megys lladron.

"Gyfeillion—gymmydogion—pawb—ond yn neillduol dynion ieuainc—cedwch rhag cyfar-fodydd nosol! Gochelwch wneuthur ar gam, ac ofnwch ddychryniadau y barnwr.

" Meddyliwch am beth a raid i ni, a pheth a ddichon i chwi ddyoddef, cyn ag y byddo i chwi wneyd fel y gwnelsom ni.

" Os bydd i chwi fod yn heddychlon, a byw etto fel dynion gonest, trwy fendith Duw gell-wch erfyn llwyddiant; a nyni, ddihirod ysgymunedig a thruenus, a ddichon ddiolch i chwi am drugaredd y goron—oblegid nid ar un telerau ereill ond eich ymddygiad da chwi y dangosir tosturi i ni, neu ereill, pa rai a ddichon gwympo i ein sefyllfa braidd anobeithiol.

(*Arwyddnodwyd*)

"JOHN HUGHES,
"DAVID JONES,
" Marc × JOHN HUGH.

"Carchar Caerdydd, Tachwedd 1taf, 1843.
"Tyst, JOHN B. WOODS, Llywodraethydd."

ISAAC THOMAS, PRINTER, ST. MARY-STREET, CARDIGAN.

A LETTER.

"To the Public generally, and to our Neighbours in particular.

"WE, *John Hughes, David Jones,* and *John Hugh,* now lying in Cardiff gaol, convicted of the attack on Pontardulais turnpike gate, and the police stationed there to protect it—being now sentenced to transportation, beg, and earnestly call on others to take warning by our fate, and to stop in their mad course, before they fall into our condemnation.

" We are guilty, and doomed to suffer, while hundreds have escaped. Let them, and every one, take care not to be deluded again to attack public or private property, and resist the power of the law, for it will overtake them with vengeance, and bring them down to destruction.

" We are only in prison now, but in a week or two shall be banished as rogues—to be slaves to strangers, in a strange land. We must go, in the prime of life, from our dear homes, to live and labour with the worst of villains—looked upon as thieves.

" Friends—neighbours—all—but especially young men—keep from night meetings! Fear to do wrong, and dread the terrors of the judge.

"Think of what we *must*, and you *may suffer*, before you *dare* to do as we have done.

" If you will be peaceable, and live again like honest men, by the blessing of God, you may expect to prosper; and we, poor outcast wretches, may have to thank you for the mercy of the Crown—for on no other terms than your good conduct will any pity be shewn to us, or others, who may fall into our almost hopeless situation.

(*Signed*)

"JOHN HUGHES,
"DAVID JONES,
"The × mark of JOHN HUGH.

"Cardiff Gaol, Nov. 1st, 1843.
" Witness, JOHN B. WOODS, Governor."

'A Letter', from contrite Rebeccaites

for the traveller by coach there was plenty to see, with fine views across pastoral country on either side of the road. Watching the 'innocent' peasantry at work was a diversion dear to the hearts of devotees of the concept of the 'Picturesque' and Lipscomb rhapsodised on the peasant women in Radnorshire 'who are in general very robust and well calculated to endure fatigue' as they ploughed and harrowed the fields alongside the turnpike. Their pleasantness and hospitality too gave pleasure to many tourists, and Benjamin Malkin would quite happily have lingered in Llandegley had it not been for the poor accommodation offered by the local inn. He was nevertheless distressed by the practice here, and elsewhere in Radnorshire, of dancing and the pursuit of other 'sports' in the churchyard and he commented sombrely: 'It is rather singular ... that the association of the place, surrounded by memorials of mortality, should not deaden the impulses of joy in minds in other respects not insensible to the suggestions of vulgar superstition'.

At Penybont, a bustling little place made prosperous by generations of cattle and sheep fairs and John Price's Radnorshire Bank, coaches passed through the tollgate and pulled into the Fleece Inn where horses were changed in preparation for the next stage of the journey. The Fleece, an ancient inn on the banks of the river, was re-built in 1777 only to be replaced in 1814 by the present Severn Arms. Leaving Penybont the turnpike passed through Nantmel, Dolau and Hendre Fach before reaching Rhayader where travellers could hire post chaises at the Red Lion Inn for journeys north and south of the town. In the early years of the nineteenth century the Red Lion was kept by a Mr Evans, to whose civility, hospitality and knowledge of Welsh orthography several tourists paid tribute. Above all, Evans provided a fine table at reasonable prices. Lipscomb praised one particular meal which must have wrought havoc with the digestion of passengers on a mail coach: 'A couple of very fine roasted fowls, a hare, a dish of veal cutlets, a piece of cold roast beef and excellent tarts; for all of which, including about a quart of strong beer per man, we paid only one shilling each'.

Rhayader was virtually encircled by tollgates, and as each of the six roads entering the town was barred, considerable resentment arose on the part of local people and passing travellers. In the 1830s and early 1840s dissatisfaction with the general running of the turnpike system and the frequency of tolls was widespread throughout much of central and south-west Wales, especially among the farming community who had experienced a series of bad harvests combined with low prices for their products. Together with the influence of Chartism, the effects of the New Poor Law and Tithe Commutation, these elements were instrumental in sparking off the Rebecca Riots, wherein a frustrated and embittered rural population vented their wrath on the hated tollgates, regarded by many of them as potent symbols of repression. Though rioting was at its most intense in Cardiganshire and Carmarthenshire, Rhayader was troubled with several outbreaks in 1843. On 2 September, for example, two gates, placed at a point where a lane branched off the road to Aberystwyth beyond the bridge over the Wye, were destroyed and a month later rioters pulled down the Botalog gate further along this road. Attacks on the gates were often very violent and when the Botalog gate was stormed, its keeper, an elderly woman, was virtually blinded by a shot from a powder-loaded gun (SO867747).

The Main and Whitland Trusts in Carmarthenshire were the epicentres of the riots and the majority of their gates and toll houses were either attacked or destroyed in 1843 and 1844 only to be replaced by the authorities and visited by the rioters once more. Eventually, after the intervention of the Yeomanry and a body of Home Office constables the rioting died away; a few ringleaders were transported, others fined and the countryside returned more or less to normality. But it had been more than a storm in a teacup and the Government, recognizing the seriousness of the grievances, set up a Commission of Inquiry under the chairmanship of the distinguished civil servant Thomas Frankland Lewis of Harpton Court in Radnorshire. Concluding that the rioters' only remedy had been to take the law into their own hands, Lewis considered the whole episode to have been 'a very creditable portion of Welsh history'. The final Report of the Commission recommended the consolidation of the South Wales Turnpike Trusts and the establishment of uniform tolls at gates which would be at least seven miles apart. This was enshrined in law at the end of 1844 and County Road Boards were established to manage the roads of South Wales on an equitable basis, and to discharge (with a Government grant of £225,000) the liabilities of the old trusts.

Around 1800, however, these distressing events lay far in the future and most genteel travellers in mail or private coach would rarely concern themselves with the grievances of the countryfolk, even if they noticed their existence. To the majority the peasant was a shadowy figure in the landscape, briefly to be pitied and then conveniently put out of mind. Uppermost in our travellers' minds as they feasted in Rhayader's Red Lion were the rigours of the next stage of their journey: the old coach road to Devil's Bridge and on to Aberystwyth. This was a gruelling course for both man and beast once they crossed the single span bridge over the Wye at Rhayader. Henry Skrine wrote of his state of 'perpetual alarm' as he ascended the rocky road out of the town and subsequently lamented the dreary, treeless expanse of open hill which he traversed 'in mournful silence'. Michael Faraday was hardly less gloomy. 'After a while we got among more mountains and nothing but large concave forms met the eye for a long time. Lively little cattle with myriads of sheep now and then diversified the general monotony and a turf cutter or a peat digger here and there drew the eye for want of a better object'. Other tourists who negotiated the 'dreadful steep pitches and frightful precipices' were relieved to reach the single arch of Blaenycwm bridge, built across the River Ystwyth by Baldwin of Bath in 1783 (SO826755). The blessings of tarmac have made the journey along the old turnpike rather less eventful for the modern traveller. Yet the steep climb from Rhayader by way of Cwmdauddwr is still there and the treeless countryside of peat bog and cotton grass is still capable of inducing the same melancholy as it did in the past. In summer, sheep and horses graze these uplands and the occasional skylark soars joyously towards the sun, but in winter the landscape is deserted save for the ever-watchful carrion crows seeking what pickings they can. Beyond Blaenycwm bridge it was a short run to Cwmystwyth (or Pentrebrunant as it was known to early nineteenth-century travellers) and the Fountain Inn where horses were changed and restorative liquors were available (SO789740).

This was lead mining country and held little appeal for visitors in search of romantic scenery. As one put it: '. . . the dingy and unsightly piles of dross and sifted refuse, with the squalid garb and savage manners of the male and female miners', was hardly a welcome sight. Today's natives are rather more prepossessing although the 'dross' of centuries of lead mining scars the landscape; great banks of shale loom out of the mist to dominate the ruins of early miners' cottages and their associated enclosures while scrub hawthorn bushes represent the remains of once-luxuriant woodland.

The present minor road to Devil's Bridge now marks the continuation of the turnpike and passes close to Pwllpeiran Experimental Husbandry Farm where officers of the Ministry of Agriculture endeavour to follow in the footsteps of Thomas Johnes of nearby 'Hafod' who began improvement of hill land in the locality almost 200 years ago. Collector, scholar, antiquary and farmer, Johnes represented the ideal of the eighteenth-century 'rounded' man. Like so many such men, however, his rather grandiose aspirations outstretched the depth of his pocket and he ended his days in frustration and relative poverty. His activities as a land improver and forester may still be seen in the surrounding countryside, although his marvellous fairy-tale home, to which both Nash and Baldwin contributed, is now reduced to rubble. For the enthusiastic seeker after the

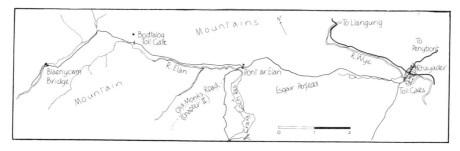

Turnpike road from Rhayader towards Aberystwyth

'picturesque', though, there are still monuments of Johnes's endeavours to be found, including the elegant ice-house to the south of the ruins of the mansion, and the overgrown remnants of his crippled daughter's garden, close to which stands a rather delicately constructed obelisk placed there by the squire to commemorate his friend Francis, 4th Duke of Bedford. A staunch patriot, Johnes celebrated the jubilee of George III by building a stone arch over the turnpike as it passed the outskirts of the Hafod demesne (SO765756). Modern travellers on the turnpike pass beneath the arch as they drive through the coniferous uniformity of the Ystwyth-Myherin Forest and thence to the Hafod Arms at Devil's Bridge, yet another Johnes foundation largely rebuilt by the fourth Duke of Newcastle in the 1840s. For the remainder of the journey to Aberystwyth the turnpike pursued the modern A4120 road above the glorious Rheidol Valley to enter the town at the site of 'Picadilly' tollgate on the junction of this road with the turnpike to Cardigan (SN593798).

Whether real or imagined, the risk to life and limb apparently presented by the old Rhayader to Aberystwyth turnpike seemed great enough to persuade the Aberystwyth Turnpike Trustees to find an alternative route for mail and private coaches. This took the form, in 1812, of a new road from Aberystwyth to Ponterwyd and the base of Pumlumon where it joined the old parish road from Devil's Bridge to Llangurig at the ford over the River Castell. As the latter road was progressively being improved, the Llangurig Turnpike Trust was building a new highway up the valley of the Wye between Rhayader and Llangurig so that by 1829 a complete turnpike link had evolved and the line of the modern A44 trunk road had been laid. Shortly afterwards Kington came to replace Presteigne as the principal 'gateway' to Wales from Herefordshire and a turnpike, with new gates at Walton and Stanner, was established between Kington and New Radnor. Once work on this road had

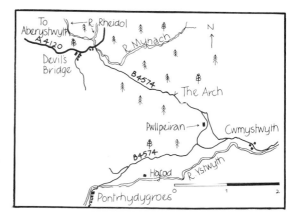

Rhayader-Aberystwyth turnpike near Devil's Bridge

180

The 'Picadilly' tollgate, Aberystwyth (late nineteenth century)

been completed, the Postmaster-General sanctioned a mail coach service between Kington and Aberystwyth, the first coach leaving Kington early in 1835 following a celebration dinner in the Commercial Inn when 'the wines were of a superior vintage and mirth and harmony prevailed till a late hour'. Thus was abandoned the Presteigne-New Radnor route and the old Rhayader-Aberystwyth road in favour of that 'by way of Pont Erwydd and Llangerrig, thereby avoiding those dangerous precipices on the old road, which deterred many visiting a bathing place so improving and healthful.' A traveller by coach could now leave London at 8.00pm and arrive at Aberystwyth at 8.15pm the following day after a journey only slightly more tiring than that experienced by one undertaking the same journey by British Rail in the 1980s.

Until the advent of the railways, the turnpike roads were the major thoroughfares in England and Wales. Following the General Highway Act of 1835, finally abolishing Statute Labour and giving parishes the right to combine into Highway Boards, an Act of 1841 empowered justices to levy rates to relieve the by now impoverished Turnpike Trusts. Effectively this meant the end of the tollgates which gradually disappeared over the next fifty years, the tollhouses being converted to other purposes when the County Councils took over responsibility for the roads in the late 1880s. The last turnpike gate in Britain was removed in 1895 and the turnpike era came to a close after 232 years.

In its later stages, in particular, it had been a stormy era. The conclusion of the Napoleonic Wars had heralded the onset of a lengthy period of agrarian depression bringing with it social unrest and an acceleration in the flow of people from the countryside to the rapidly-growing industrial towns. The old, seemingly immutable, order of the mid-eighteenth century was doomed. Radical demagogues from both Britain and Europe challenged the very structure of rural and market-town society, based essentially on enlightened paternalism. With agriculture giving way to manufacture as the major source of the country's wealth, large numbers of working people gathered in the towns and there developed an undercurrent of protest with an increasingly vocal demand for social, economic and political reform. As Jill and Hodge wandered home from church along the turnpike in the 1840s they were just as likely to be discussing that strange new movement called Chartism as more homely matters like the prospect of the harvest or the price of wool. Others of the congregation, their thoughts on the eternal round of agricultural drudgery which Monday would bring, might have paused for a while to watch the dusty turnpike curving away from the village towards a distant town. At moments like this, perhaps, they came to see the turnpike as a means of liberation, whose course, if they had the courage to take it, would lead them to all manner of delights and prospects.

Roads as yet untrodden can have this unsettling effect on people. No doubt the same sort of feelings arose in the mind of the medieval Welsh peasant as he contemplated the rocky track leading to the next valley, or to his seventeeth-century counterpart as he watched a packhorse train struggle through the mire towards some far-off destination. Few of these people risked the perils of a journey far from home, yet their nineteenth-century descendants had little hesitation about doing so. Demand from the industrial towns of South Wales and the harvest fields of the Midlands tempted thousands of footsore Welshmen and women to trudge down the turnpikes in the hope of securing a job. Many returned later in the year to their little farmsteads while others, seduced by prospects of the New World, left Wales by way of one of the southern ports. Migrations of this sort were at their height in the 1830s and 1840s. Within twenty years, however, the turnpike was no longer the principal means of communication and migrant Welshmen had available a new and remarkably efficient railway system which opened up previously undreamt-of vistas.

Less than a hundred and twenty years later, matters have come full circle. Of those few Welsh railway lines remaining many can only be travelled upon with inconvenience and discomfort, while at least one is positively dangerous. Whether they like it or not, most country people in Wales are now forced to rely on their motor cars for both long and short journeys. In the sense that virtually all the major roads in Wales lie on the course of a turnpike (which itself may represent the line of a much older road), we might be said to have entered the second turnpike age. Like readers of *Punch* in 1856 we must, for the foreseeable future, grin and bear, 'the 'ammer, 'ammer, 'ammer along the 'ard 'igh road'.

182

Further Reading

Most of the manuscript and cartographic material used in the preparation of this book is located in the National Library of Wales, where readers wishing to pursue in further detail the study of the Principality's roads will find a warm welcome and abundant scholarly assistance. Material contained within the files of the Royal Commission for Ancient Monuments (Wales), Queens Road, Aberystwyth, has also been extensively used. For the sake of brevity 'general', historical and historical geography texts have been excluded from the select bibliography below, which contains only those books and articles directly relevant to the contents of particular chapters of the present volume.

Chapter 1

Alcock, L., The defenses and gates of Castell Collen Auxiliary Fort, *Archaeologia Cambrensis,* 1964.

Anon, 'Roman Britain in 1965', *Journal of Roman Studies* 56, 1966

Arber-Cooke, A.T., *Pages from the History of Llandovery,* Llandovery, 1975.

Boon, G.C. and Brewer, R.J. 'Two Central Gaullish Bottles from Pennal, Merioneth and early Roman Movement in Cardigan Bay,' *Bulletin of the Board of Celtic Studies, 29, 1981.*

Bye-Gones, 1885.

Codrington, T., *Roman Roads in Britain,* 2nd edn. London, 1905.

Davies, J.L., *The Roman Period, Ceredigion County History* (Forthcoming).

Davies, J.L., 'A Roman Fortlet at Erglodd, Talybont, Dyfed,' *Bulletin of the Board of Celtic Studies,* 28 (4), 1980.

Davies, R.W., 'Roman Wales and Roman Military Practice Camps,' *Archaelogia Cambrensis,* 117, 1968.

Dilke, O.A.W. *The Roman Land Surveyors, An Introduction to the Agrimensores,* Newton Abbot, 1971.

Evans, J., 'Derwenlas', *Montgomeryshire Collections,* 51, 1949.

Fenton, R., *Tours in Wales, 1804-13,* J. Fisher (ed), London, 1917.

Houlder, C.H., *Wales, an Archaeological Guide,* London, 1974.

Hughes, S., 'The Mines of Talybont; AD70-1800', *Industrial Archaeology,* 16 (3), 1981.

Jones, G.D.B., 'The Roman Camps at Y Pigwn', *Bulletin of the Board of Celtic Studies,* 23, 1970.

Jones, G.D.B., 'Fieldwork and Aerial Photography in Carmarthenshire', *Carmarthenshire Antiquary,* 7, 1971.

Jones, G.D.B., 'The Towy Valley Roman Road', *Carmarthenshire Antiquary,* 8, 1972

Jones, G.D.B. and Thomson, R.W., 'Caerau; A Roman Site in North Breconshire', *Bulletin of the Board of Celtic Studies,* 17, 1958.

Lewin, J., Hughes, D. and Blacknell, C., 'Incidence of River Erosion', *Transactions of the Institute of British Geographers,* 9 (3), 1977

Littler, J., in Barnes, T. and Yates, N. (eds), *Carmarthenshire Studies, Carmarthen, 1974.*

Livens, R.G., 'The Roman Army in Wales', AD120-220', *Welsh History Review,* 7, 1974.

Liversidge, J., *Britain in the Roman Empire,* London, 1973.

Lloyd, J.E., *A History of Carmarthenshire,* Cardiff, 1935.

Lloyd, J.E., *The Story of Ceredigion,* London, 1937.

Lodwick, M. and E., *The Story of Carmarthen,* Carmarthen, 1972.

Malkin, B., *The Scenery, Antiquities and Biography of South Wales,* London, 1804.

Margary, I.D., *Roman Roads in Britain,* London, 1957.

Nash-Williams, V.E., 'The Roman Goldmines at Dolaucothi', *Bulletin of the Board of Celtic Studies,* 14, 1950-2.

Nash-Williams, V.E., *The Roman Frontier in Wales,* Cardiff, 1954 and 1969 eds.

O'Dwyer, S., *The Roman Roads of Cardiganshire and Radnorshire,* Newtown, 1936

O'Dwyer, S., *The Roman Roads of Brecknock and Glamorgan,* Newtown, 1937.

Richmond, I.A., 'Roman Britain in 1957', *Journal of Roman Studies,* 48, 1958.

Richmond, I.A., *Roman Britain,* Penguin Books, 1963.

St. Joseph, J.K. 'Air Reconnaissance in Roman Britain, 1973-6', *Journal of Roman Studies,* 67, 1977.

St. Joseph, J.K. 'Air Reconnaissance in Britain, 1955-7', *Journal of Roman Studies,* 48, 1958.

Taylor, C., *Roads and Tracks in Britain,* London, 1979.

Wilson, R., *A guide to the Roman Remains in Britain,* London, 1975.

Chapter 2
Bromwich, R., *Dafydd ap Gwilym: Poems,* Gomer Press, 1982.
Cunliffe, B., *Iron Age Communities in Britain,* London, 1974.
Davies, D., *Brecknock Historian,* Aberystwth, 1977.
Davies, E., *A Gazetteer of Welsh Place-Names,* Cardiff, 1975.
Davies, W., *Wales in the Early Middle Ages,* Leicester, 1982.
Finberg, H.P.R. (ed) *The Agrarian History of England and Wales, A.D., 43-1042,*
    Cambridge, 1972.
Fraser, M., *West of Offa's Dyke,* London, 1958.
Hawkes, J., *A Guide to Prehistoric and Roman Monuments in England and Wales,* Sphere
    Books, 1973.
Hindle, B., 'The Road Network of Medieval England and Wales', *Journal of Historical
    Geography,* 2, 1975.
Jones, J.E.J., 'Fairs in Cardiganshire', *Cardiganshire Antiquarian Society Transactions,* VII, 1930.
Jones, P., *Welsh Border Country,* London, 1938.

Leland, J., *Itinerary in Wales,* L.T. Smith (ed), London, 1906.
Lewis, W.J., *Leadmining in Wales,* Cardiff, 1967.
Linnard, W., *Welsh Woods and Forests, History and Utlization,* Cardiff, 1982.
Mercer, R. (ed.), *Farming Practice in British Prehistory,* Edinburgh, 1982.
National Library of Wales, *The Crosswood Deeds,* Aberystwth, 1927.
Owen, A., *Ancient Laws and Institutes of Wales,* London, 1841.
Perkins, A., 'Some Maps of Wales and in particular of the counties of Pembrokeshire,
    Cardiganshire and Carmarthenshire,' *Carmarthenshire Antiquary,* 5, 1964.
Pierce, T. Jones, 'Strata Florida Abbey', *Ceredigion,* 1, 1950.
Powell, S.M., 'Pilgrim Routes to Strata Florida', *Cardiganshire Antiquarian Society
    Transactions,* 8, 1931.
Stenton, F.M., The Road System of Medieval England, *Economic History Review,*
    7, 1936.
Thorpe, L. (ed), *Gerald of Wales; the Journey through Wales,* Penguin Books, 1978.
Tomos, D., *Michael Faraday in Wales,* London, 1980.
Turner, E. Horsfall, *Walks and Wanderings in County Cardigan,* e1Bingley, 1901.

Chapter 3
Dineley, T., *An account of the Progress of His Grace, Henry, first Duke of Beaufort through
    Wales in 1684,* C. Baker (ed), London, 1864.
Howse, W., *Radnorshire,* Hereford, 1949.
Kilvert, F., *Diaries,* William Plomer (ed), London.
Kissack, K., *The River Wye,* Lavenham, 1978.
Lewis, M.G., 'The Printed Maps of Breconshire, 1578-1900,' *Brycheiniog,* 16, 1972.
Lewis, M.G., 'The Printed Maps of Cardiganshire, 1578-1900', *Ceredigion,* 2, 1955.
Symonds, R., *Diary of the Marches of the Royal Army during the great Civil War,*
    C.E. Long (ed), Camden Society, 1859.
Taylor, J., *A short Relation of a long journey . . . encompassing the Principality of Wales,*
    London, 1653.
Toynbee, M.R., 'A Royal Journey through Breconshire and Radnorshire in 1645', *Radnorshire
    Society Transactions,* XX, 1950.
Williams, D., *A History of Modern Wales,* London, 1969.

Chapter 4
For reference to the primary and secondary sources used in this chapter and a full
bibliography of the droving trade see: Colyer, R.J., *The Welsh Cattle Drovers,* Cardiff, 1976.
Although many of the roads to which they refer were not connected with the droving trade,
Godwin, F. and Toulson, S., *The Drovers Roads of Wales,* London, 1977, is a useful work,
especially for walkers. Bonser, K.J., *The Drovers,* London 1970, has a chapter on drove roads
from the Welsh border into England.

Chapter 5

Atkin, A., *Journal of a Tour through North Wales*, London, 1797.

Archer, M.S., *The Welsh Post Towns*, Phillimore, 1970.

Archer, M.S., 'The Postal History of Wales with particular reference to Merioneth', *Journal of the Merionethshire Historical and Records Society*, 6, 1971.

Baker, J., *A Picturesque guide through Wales and the Marches*, London, 1795.

Bingley, W., *A Tour round North Wales in 1798*, London, 1800.

Borrow, G., *Wild Wales*, 1963 edn.

Bradley A.G., *Highways and Byways in North Wales*, London, 1898.

Bright, G., A Tour in Central Wales in 1805, *Radnorshire Society Transactions*, 28, 1958.

Byng, J., *The Torrington Diaries*, C. Bruyn Andrews (ed), London, 1936.

Cary, J., *Traveller's Companion*, London, 1806.

Colyer, R.J., 'The Hafod Estate under Thomas Johnes and the Fourth Duke of Newcastle', *Welsh History Review*, 8, 1978.

Davies, H.R., 'The Conway and Menai Ferries', *Bulletin of the Board of Celtic Studies, History and Law Series*, 8, 1948.

Davies, W., *General View of the Agriculture of North Wales*, London, 1810.

Dodd, A.H., The Roads of North Wales, 1750-1850, *Archaeologia Cambrensis*, 5, 1925.

Evans, J., *A Tour through part of North Wales in 1798*, London, 1800.

Fenton, R., *Tours in Wales, 1804-13*, J. Fisher (ed.), London, 1917

Hughes, M., 'Thomas Telford in North Wales, 1815-1830', in D. Moore (ed), *Wales in the Eighteenth Century*, Swansea, 1976.

Hughes, D. and Williams, D., *Holyhead, the Story of a Port*, Denbigh, 1967.

Howell, A., 'Roads, Bridges and Canals of Montgomeryshire', *Montgomeryshire Collections*, 9, 1876.

Howse, W., 'The Turnpike System', *Radnorshire Society Transactions*, 22, 1952.

Hyde-Hall, E., *A Description of Caernarvonshire*, E. Gwynne Jones (ed), Caernarvon, 1952

Jenkins, J.G., *The Welsh Woollen Industry*, Cardiff, 1968

Jones, E. Inglis, *Peacocks in Paradise*, London, 1950.

Jones, R., 'The Post Roads in Anglesey and Caernarvonshire', *Postal History International*, 2, 1873.

Lipscombe, G., *Journey into South Wales*, London, 1802.

Pennant, T., *Tours in Wales* (3 vol), London, 1810.

Pritchard, R., 'The Capel Curig Turnpike Trust', *Caernarvonshire Historical Society Transactions*, 1958.

Pritchard, R., 'The History of the Post Road in Anglesey', *Anglesey Antiquarian Society and Field Club Transactions*, 1954.

Pritchard, R., 'The Beaumaris-Menai Bridge Turnpike Trust', *Anglesey Antiquarian Society and Field Club Transactions*, 1959.

Pritchard, R., 'Denbighshire Road and Turnpike Trusts', *Transactions of the Denbighshire Historical Society*, 12, 1963.

Roscoe, T., *Wanderings and Excursions in North Wales*, London, 1853.

Smith, P., *Houses of the Welsh countryside*, HMSO., 1975.

Tomas, D., *Micheal Faraday in Wales*, London, 1980

Warner, R., *A Second Walk through Wales*, London, 1800.

Williams, D., *The Rebecca Riots*, Cardiff, 1971.

Williams, H., *Stage Coaches in Wales*, Cambridge, 1977.

Williams, R., *The History of Llanbrynmair*, 1889.

Glossary of Welsh words and terms

This brief glossary of some of the more common terms frequently appearing as elements in place-names in rural Wales may be of help to English readers of this book, while those interested in more detail will find Elwyn Davies's *A Gazetteer of Welsh Place-names*, Cardiff, 1975, and Dewi Davies, *Welsh Place-names and their meanings*, Aberystwyth (nd) particularly informative. The former provides an outline of the principles of Welsh pronounciation.

aber: mouth of (a river or stream)
afon: river
allt: hillside or wood
bach: small
banc: mound, bank or hillock
bedd: grave
berth: hedge
blaen: source of river; valley head
bont: bridge
brain: crows
bron: hillside
bryn: hill
buarth: farmyard, enclosure
bwthyn: cottage
cae: field
calch: lime
capel: chapel
carn: cairn; stone-pile
carreg: rock
castell: castle
cefn: ridge
cerrig: stones (as of walls)
craig: rock
cribyn: crest
croes: cross (roads)
crug: mound, cairn, stone-pile
cwm: valley
cwrt: mansion, court
dafad: sheep
dan: under, below
derw: oak
dôl: meadow
du: black
dŵr: water
eglwys: church
eithin: gorse
erw: acre
esgair: mountain ridge
fan: peak
ffelin: mill
ffald: pound; enclosure
ffordd: road
ffos: ditch, brook
ffridd: hill pasture
ffynnon: spring, well
foel: bare hill
fron: hillside
gaer: camp; fort
garth: enclosure
garreg: rock

glan: riverbank
gors: marsh; bog
gwaun: meadow
Gwyddel: Irish
gwyn: white
hafod: summer dwelling
hendre: winter dwelling
heol: road
hir: long
lan: climb; ascent
llan: enclosure; church
llawr: low ground
Lloegr: England
lluest: upland farm
llwyn: grove
llys: mansion
maen: rock
maes: field
mawn: peat
mawr: big
mynydd: mountain
nant: stream
neuadd: mansion, hall
newydd: new
pandy: fulling mill
pant: valley; hollow
parc: park
pentre: village
plas: mansion
pont: bridge
pwll: pond; pool
rhiw: slope; hillside
rhos: moorland
rhyd: ford; stream; brook
saeson, saesneg: English
sarn: paved way; causeway
tal: end
tomen: mound
tre: town
tŷ: house
tyn, tyddyn: cottage, small house
van: peak
vron: hillside
waun: meadow, moor
y: the
ychen: oxen
ynys: island, water meadow
ysgubor: barn
ystrad: valley; wide vale

Index

ab Owain Rhys, 81
Abbey Cwmhir, 75, 93-4, 109
Abbey Farm, Strata Florida, 81
aber, 149, 151
Aber-Annell, Beulah, 121
Aber-arth, 62
Aberbowlan, Caeo, 41, 131
Aber-Crychan, Llandovery, 51
Abercwm, Llanllwni, 36
Aberduar Farm, Llanybydder, 36
Aberdulais, Llangamarch Wells, 52
Abcredw Hill, Builth Wells, 100-1, 117, 122
Aberglaslyn, 170
Abergwesyn, 80, 82, 119-21
Abergwili, 48
Abermarlais, Llanwrda, 48-9
Aberyscir, 45
Aberystwyth, 63, 68, 84, 139, 146-7, 176-81
Aberystwyth, Black Sheep Bank at, 115
Adfa, 138
Agricola, Governor of Britain; 15
Ala Hispanorun Vettonum, 16
Albert Mount, Caeo, 131
Alcock, E., 45
Allen, R., 145
Allt Rhydings, Llandovery; 43
Anhuniog, 62
Antelope Inn, Presteigne, 88
Antonine Wall, the, 17
ap Belddyn, Cadwgan, 81
ap Caradog, Rhydderch, 81
ap Gruffudd, Rhys, 62, 65, 80, 82, 107
ap Gruffydd, Llewelyn, 109
ap Gwilym, Dafydd, 64
ap Iorwerth, Llewelyn, 107
ap Iorwerth, William, 107
ap Rhys, Maelgwyn, 74
ap Roberte, R., 84
Appian, 44
Apprice, J., 84
Aran, River, 92
Arrow, River, 96, 100

Bailey Hill, Bwlch-y-Sarnau, 102
Baldwin, Archbishop of Canterbury, 60, 107
Baldwin of Bath, 179
Banc Cwm Magwr, Llangwyryfon, 70
Banc Nantrhiwgenau, Llangwyryfon, 70
Banc Cwmllechwedd, Trawsgoed, 33
Bancydarren, Aberystwyth, 27
Bancynos, Llanwrda, 50
Bangor, 144, 149-50, 152-4, 158-9, 164, 166
Bardsey Island, 63, 65

Barmouth, 87
Barnet, 116
Baron Hill, Anglesey, 153, 157
Bath, 47
Bayliss, M., 96
Beaufort, Henry Duke of, 88, 158
Beaumaris, Anglesey, 84, 148, 151, 153, 157-8, 161
Bedd Taliesin, Talybont, 26
Beddgelert, 166-7, 169, 171
Bedford, 4th Duke of, 180
Beggar's Bush, Presteigne, 89, 105, 107, 176
Begwns, the, 98, 100
Berriew, 138
Berriwns, the, Nantgaredig, 48
Berwyn, River, 118
Bethesda, 159, 166
Betws Ifan, 65
Betws Leucu, 65
Betws-y-coed, 158-9, 161
Beulah, 120
Bingley, Rev Mr, 149, 152, 159, 169
Black Hall, Kerry, 104
Black Ox Inn, Clyro Hill, 125
Blaenaeron, 62
Blaenau Ffestiniog, 171
Blaencerde, Newchurch, 96
Blaendyffryn, Caeo, 131
Blaenglanhanog, Talerddig, 137
Blaenglasffrwd, Strata Florida, 81
Blaenos House, Llandovery, 51
Blaenycwm Bridge, Cwmystwyth, 179
Bleddfa, 90-1
Boars Head Inn, Carmarthen, 47
Bodwina, Anglesey, 155
Bontdolgadfan, 135-6
Borough Gate, Ffair-rhôs, 69
Borrow, G., 157, 159
Borth Bog, 26
Boultibrooke, Presteigne, 110
Bowen, E., 88, 107, 110, 129-30
Bradshaw, J., 88
Braint, Anglesey, 153-4
Brân, River, 42-3, 51
Braose, William de, 98
Braunston, Sir J., 150
Brechfa, 130, 132
Brecon, 16, 21, 37, 42-3, 84, 99, 139, 146
Brecon Gaer, 17, 42, 45
Breese, E., 143
Bremia, 34-5, 37, 42
Bridgend, 84
Brighton, 116
Brink, Presteigne, 110
Bristol, 84
Broad Oak, Llandeilo, 48

Broad Street, Presteigne, 110
Bromwich, R., 64
Bronberllan, Strata Florida, 69, 70
Broncapel, Strata Florida, 74
Brook Cottage, Llanbadarn Fynydd, 95
Broome, J., 116
Bryn Cosyn, 80
Bryn Glas, Pilleth, 94
Bryn Teifi, Llanfihangel-ar-Arth, 132
Bryn-y-Castell, Knighton, 109
Bryndyfi, Talybont, 25
Bryngwyn, Newchurch, 125
Brynllycoed, Rhayader, 93
Brynmaiog, Pumsaint, 38
Brynmanhalog, Lampeter, 129
Brynycrofftau, Strata Florida, 80
Builth Wells, 100-1, 105, 107, 117, 143
Bulkeley, Lord, 157
Bulkeley, R., 83
Busnant, Glascwm, 100
Bwlch, 29
Bwlch-y-ddeufan, Conwy, 149
Bwlch-y-gcufron, Lledrod, 73
Bwlch-y-Sarnau, 102
Bwlchbryndinam, Rhayader, 93
Bwlchglynmynydd, Talywern, 135
Bwlchgwernog, Croesor, 171
Bwlchtrebanau, Llandovery, 42
Byng, Hon J., 17, 166

Cader Idris, 172
Cacnaduton, Talerddig, 137
Caeo, 34, 39-41, 131
Cae'r Ceilog, Anglesey, 155
Caer Penrhos, Llanrhystud, 72
Caerau, 17, 52-4
Caergybi, Holyhead, 18
Caerleon, 16, 17, 21
Caernarvon, 16, 21, 166, 171
Caersws, 16
Caerwent, 17
Caledfwlch, Llandeilo, 48
Cammarch, River, 54
Camddwr, River, 34, 94
Cann Office, 175
Canterbury, 116
Capel Aberduar, Llanybydder, 36
Capel Bangor, 25, 37
Capel Curig, 149, 159, 161, 163-4, 166, 171
Capel Dewi, Aberystwyth, 27
Capel Seion, Aberystwyth, 70
Capel Trisant, Aberystwyth, 70-1
Caractacus, 15
Cardiff, 16, 21, 40, 50, 84

Carmarthen, 16, 21, 35-7, 42, 46-8, 78, 84-5, 114, 146
Carn Fflur, 80
Caron, 80-1, 118
'Cart and Horses', Rhydcwmerau, 132
Carusius, 39
Cary, J., 88, 102
Cascob, 90
Castell Cogan, 16
Castell Collen, 42, 51, 53-4, 56
Castell Flemish, Swyddffynnon, 74
Castell, River, 180
Castle Inn, Presteigne, 88
'Cefn Cardis', Abergwesyn, 120-1
Cefn Côch Inn, Adfa, 138
Cefn Crin Forest Rhayader, 102
Cefn Hirwaun, Erwood, 127
Cefn Llwydlo, 52
Cefngaer, Pennal, 21
Cefnglasfryn, Llandeilo, 48
Cefngorwydd, Llangamarch Wells, 52
Cefngweiriog, Furnace, 26
Cefntelych, Llandovery, 43
Ceint, Anglesey, 153
Cemmaes Road, 135
Charles I, King, 85, 87-8, 96, 98, 100, 105, 109, 135
Charles II, King, 105
Chaworth, Sir G., 83
Chepstow, 84
Chester, 15-17, 21, 50, 84, 145, 147-9, 151-2, 166
Chipping Sodbury, 116
Church St, New Radnor, 107
Cider House, Llanbadarn Fynydd, 103
Cilycwm, 126, 131-2
Cirencester, 116
Claerddu, Ffair-rhôs, 75
Claerddu, River, 76
Claerwen, River, 76
Clas Brook, 123
Clettwr, River, 26
Cloggau, Colfa, 100
Clyro Hill, 125
Clywedog, River, 93
Coed Penybannau, Pontrhydfendigaid, 69
Coed Spoel, Llanelwedd, 101
Coedglasson, Rhayader, 93
Cog-sarn, 74
Cohors II Asturum, 16, 34
Cold Oak, Presteigne, 96
Coldbrook, Clyro Hill, 125
Colfa, 100
Colfa Hill, 96, 125
Coltman, T., 102
Commercial Inn, Kington, 181
Constant, 74
Conway, P., 84
Conwy, 158-9
Conwy, River, 50, 84, 149, 158, 163
Cors Caron, 61, 74
Corwen, 158, 165
Cothi, River, 37, 39, 48, 132

Coygan, 16
Cranbrook, 117
Cregrina, 100, 121-3, 125
Croesor, 171
Cromwell, O., 133
Cross Foxes Inn, Mallwyd, 174
Cross Inn, Penlanwen, Tirabad, 126
Crossway, Llanelwedd, 101
Crossway, Rhayader, 121
Croydon, 117
Crychan Forest, 52
Crychell Brook, Llananno, 102
Cwelyn, River, 170
Cwm Ceulan, Talybont, 27
Cwm Gwenddwr, Erwood, 127
Cwm Hywel, Rhydcwmerau, 132
Cwm-sarn-ddu, Llandovery, 42
Cwm Wyre, Llanrhystud, 72
Cwmann, Lampeter, 128-9
Cwmberwyn, Tregaron, 119
Cwmcoedifor, Rhydcwmerau, 132
Cwmdeuddwr, 75, 179
Cwmfranfawr, Cilycwm, 131
Cwmilward, Cascob, 91
Cwmwythig, Capel Bangor, 29
Cwmygerwyn, Cascob, 91
Cwmystwyth, 179
Cwys-yr-Ychen-Bannog, 80

David's Well, Bwlch-y-Sarnau, 102
Davies, J.L., 25
Davies, Mrs E., 84
Davies, Rev J., 174
Davies, T., 107
Davies, W., 60
de Valois, C., 153
Dean, Forest of, 18
Decangli, 15
Decius, 39
Deddington, 17
Dee, River, 165
Defoe, D., 176
Demetae, 15-16, 18, 46
Denbigh, 149
Derwenlas, 133, 135
Devil's Bridge, 65, 67, 70, 77, 179
Diffwys, Tregaron, 119
Dinas, 161
Dinas Mawddwy, 133, 173-4
Dinas Mawr, 163, 166
Discoed, 89
Dol-y-gors Pontrhydygroes, 67
Dolau, 92, 178
Dolau Brân, Llandovery, 51
Dolau Fflur, Strata Florida, 77
Dolaucothi Hotel, Pumsaint, 39
Dolaucothi, Johnes family of, 40
Dolfawr, 82
Dolgadfan, Bontdolgadfan, 135-6

Dolgellau, 166, 171-4
Dolwyddelan, 171
Domen Las, Derwenlas, 23, 25
Draper, M., 107
Drovers Arms, Cilycwm, 131
Drovers Arms, Ffarmers, 131
Drovers Arms, Llanfihangel-ar-Arth, 132
Drovers Arms, Mynydd Epynt, 127
Drovers Farm, Porthyrhyd, 41, 131
Druids, 15
Dublin, 147, 151
Duke's Arms, Presteigne, 88
Dulais, River, 41, 48, 50, 131
Dwygyfylchi, 149
Dyffryn, Cascob, 89
Dyfi, River, 22-3, 133, 135
Dyserth, 121

'Eagle and Child' Inn, Holyhead, 148
Edw, River, 100, 121, 147
Edward I, King, 60, 107, 135, 151
Edward II, King, 151
Edwards, W., 131
Efail Fach, Rhydcwmerau, 132
'Egdon Heath', 103
Einion, River, 25, 36
Elan, River, 76
Elen, wife of *M. Maximus*, 22
Elgar Farm, Talybont, 27
Elizabeth I, Queen, 107
Ellesmere, Canal, 165
Erglodd, Talybont, 17, 22, 25, 77
Erw-barfau, Devils Bridge, 67
Erw-hen, Pumsaint, 39
Erwood, 98, 118, 125, 127
Esgair Ambor, 80
Esgair Cwynion, 76
Esgair Farm, Pumsaint, 129
Esgair Hengae, 76
Evans, H., 149, 154
Evans, Jane, 131
Evans, Mr (of Rhayader), 178
Evans, Rev J., 151, 171, 175
Evenjobb, 96

Fairy Glen, Betws-y-coed, 163
Faraday, M., 179
Farrington, Knighton, 111
Felin Saint, Llangwyryfon, 72
Fenton, R., 34, 50
Ffair-rhôs, 62, 69, 75
Ffarmers, 37-8, 131
Ffestiniog, Vale of, 171
Fflur, River, 80
Fforest Colwyn, 100
Ffranceys, J., 84
Ffridd Uchaf, Penegoes, 135
Ffynnon Gynydd, 98, 100
Ffynnonau, Aberedw Hill, 122

Fitzjohn, P., 98
Fitzstephen, Robert, Lord of
  Penardd, 61
Fleece Inn, Penybont, 178
Flint, 50
Foel Faner, Dolgellau, 172
Forden, 133
Forest Inn, Llanfihangel
  Nantmelan, 107
Fountain Inn, Pentrebrunant,
  179
Four Crosses, Anglesey, 153
Four Mile Bridge, Anglesey,
  153
Fowler, R., 85
Fron, Pumsaint, 129
Frongoch, Strata Florida, 70,
  76
Frontinus, Julius, 15-16, 55-6
Furnace, 23, 25
Fychan, Moelgwyn, 68

Gangani, 14
Garn bryn-llwyd, Llanbadarn
  Fynydd, 103
Garreg, 171
Garreg-llwyd, Strata Florida,
  77
Garth, Anglesey, 157
Garthbebio, Welshpool, 175
Gellicrugiau, Llangamarch
  Wells, 52
George III, King, 180
George Hotel, Bangor Ferry,
  165
Gilfach-las, Lledrod, 74
Gilwern Hill, 121
Giraldus Cambrensis, 60,
  67, 105, 107
Gladestry, 96, 100
Glamorgan, Vale of, 18
Glanadda, Caernarvon, 166
Glanbrane Arms, Llanfair-
  ar-y-bryn, 51-2
Glancamddwr, Llangamarch
  Wells, 52
Glanbrane, Llandovery, 51
Glandulus, Newbridge-on-
  Wye, 54
Glanyrafon, Erwood, 127
Glanyrannel Park, Llansawel,
  152
Glasbury, 96, 98-9, 100
Glascwm, 100, 125
Glasffrwd, River, 78
Glaslyn, River, 170
Glaspwll, 64
Gloucester, 146
Glyn Cothi, Lewis, 100
Glyndwr, O., 63, 90, 94,
  133, 172
Glyneiddan, Nantgaredig, 48
Glynhyfryd, Llanwrda, 50
Gobe, Gladestry, 100
Gogerddan Arms,
  Aberystwyth, 176
Golden Lion Inn, Dolgellau,
  172
Gornoethle, Caeo, 131
Gors-las, Lledrod, 72
Graig, Llanfihangel
  Rhydithon, 91

Gravesend Ford, 92
Griffin Inn, Mynydd Epynt,
  127
Griffin Lloyd, Pilleth, 94
Griffiths, A., 107
Grouse Inn, Abergwesyn, 120
Gwalchmai, Anglesey, 155
Gwarcwm, Talybont, 26
Gwaunmaglau, 138
Gwern-illa, Gladestry, 100
Gwernhafdre Uchaf, 74
Gwernyfed, 100
Gwernygof Uchaf, 161, 166
Gwesyn, River, 120
Gwili, River, 48
Gwndwm, Llanbadarn
  Fyn'ydd, 102
Gwnnws, 76
Gwyddgrug, 36
Gwydir Castle, 159
'Gwylliaid Cochion
  Mawddwy', 173
Gwyndy, Anglesey, 154-5
Gwynne, E., 81
Gwyrfai, River, 166
Gyffin, Conwy, 159

Hadrian, 17
Hafod Arms, Devil's
  Bridge, 180
Hafod Fawr, Mynydd Bach
  Trecastell, 43
Hafod Newydd, Strata Florida
  81
Hafod-y-cleifion, Strata
  Florida, 74
Haines Hill, New Radnor, 107
Halfway Bridge, 165, 166
Hare's Green, Presteigne, 111
Harlech, 87
Harold Godwinson, King, 96
Harries, H., of Trefecca, 135
Haverfordwest, 84, 146
Hay-on-Wye, 85
Heath Cock, Mynydd Bach
  Trecastell, 44
Helmdon, 116
Hendre Rhys, Trawsgoed, 33
Hengoed, Newchurch, 96
Henry III, King, 98, 109
Henry V, King, 153
Henry VIII, King, 64, 84, 153
Herbert, family of, 119
Hereford, 84, 99, 117
Hergest Ridge, 96
Hindwell, 96
Hoddinot, T., 115, 116
Holy Island, Anglesey, 153,
  155
Holyhead, Anglesey, 84,
  144-5, 147, 149, 151,
  153-5, 157-8,
  161, 165
Holywell, 149
Hookes, N., 84
Hope Chapel, Llanelwedd,
  107
Howell, J., 135
Howell, R., 135
Huett, T., 89
Hughes, E., 146
Hughes, S.J.S., 25

Hundred House, 107
Hungry Green, 100, 121, 123
Hutchinson, T., 96
Hutton, Mr, 174
Hyde, 129
Hyde Hall, E., 113
Hywel Dda, 59

Ireland, 84, 144, 155, 157
Ireland Farm, Rhulen, 125
Irfon, River, 52, 120
Isaac, D., 139
Ithon, River, 92-3, 103, 120-1
Ivy Bush Inn, Carmarthen, 47

Jenkins, E., 146
Jenkins, W., 115
Jesus College, Oxford, 47
Jocelyn, Lord, 155
John, King, 62, 167
Johnes, T., 176, 179-80
Johnson, S., 150
Jonathan, D., 117, 121, 131
  133, 139
Jones, D. of Caeo, 115, 130-1
Jones, Eliza, 155
Jones, G.D.B., 48
Jones, Inigo, 158
Jones, J., 165
Jones, Rev Mr, 150
Jones, T. of Pencerrig, 114
Jones, W., 115

Kerry, 102, 104
Kerry Ridgeway, 103-4, 117
Kilvert, F., 96-7, 100, 125
King's Park, Lampeter, 129
Kington, 121, 176, 180-1
Kinnerton, 89, 107, 176
Kitchin, T., 27, 88, 92, 96,
  130, 153
Knighton, 85, 109-11
Knights Hospitallers, the,
  62, 65-6, 74
Knowle Farm, New Radnor,
  107
Knowle Hill, Kinnerton, 107
Knoyle, W., 115-16
Knucklas, 94

Lampeter, 35, 85, 117, 128
Lavan Sands, 149, 151, 153,
  157
Lawrence, C., 143
Lee, Bishop R., 85
Leeds, 176
Legio II Adiutrix, 16
Legio II Augusta, 16
Legio XX Valeria Vitrix, 16
Leland, J., 64, 76, 107
Leominster, Hereford, 109
Leri, River, 27
Lewin, J., 23
Lewis, T.F., 178
Lion Rock, 166
Lipscomb, R., 177-8
Llanbwlch-llyn Lake, 128
Llananno, 102-3
Llanbadarn Fawr, 70
Llanbadarn Fynydd, 94-5,
  102-3
Llanbedr, 128

189

Llanbedr Hill, 125
Llanbrynmair, 135, 175
Llanddeiniol, 71
Llanddewi Ystradenni, 92
Llanddulas, Tirabad, 126
Llandegai, 151, 161, 165
Llandegley, 176, 178
Llandeilo Graban, 128
Llandinam, 130
Llandovery, 17, 21, 41-3, 48,
    50-1, 53, 125-6, 131-2, 146
Llandovery, Black Ox Bank
    at, 115
Llandrindod Wells, 21, 51,
    56-7
Llandysul, 132
Llaneithyr, Devil's Bridge, 67
Llaneltyd, 172
Llanelwedd, 101, 107, 143
Llanerch-yrfa, Abergwesyn,
    120
Llanfair, Anglesey, 155
Llanfair-ar-y-Bryn, 117, 125
Llanfair Caereinion, 133,
    138, 175
Llanfair Clydogau, 37
Llanfair Waterdine,
    Hereford, 94
Llanfairfechan, 149, 151, 159
Llanfihangel Nantmelan,
    107, 176
Llanfihangel-y-Creuddyn,
    29, 30, 70
Llangadog, 49
Llangamarch Wells, 52, 126-7
Llangefni, Anglesey, 153
Llangernyw, 149
Llangollen, 158-9, 165
Llangurig, 180-1
Llangwyryfon, 72-3, 77
Llangynllo, 94
Llanio-isaf, 17, 34-5
Llanllugan, 137-8
Llanllwni, 36
Llanrhystud, 65, 72, 77
Llanrwst, 158-9, 171
Llansannan, 149
Llanshay, Knighton, 110
Llanwen Hill, Knighton, 111
Llanwyddelan, 138
Llanybydder, 36
Llanynghenedl, Anglesey,
    153-4
Llechwenny, Nantgaredig, 48
Lledrod, 33, 73
Lletty Synod, Pontrhydygroes,
    71
Llettybach, Capel Bangor, 30
Llettywyd, Talbont, 27
Llewelyn, Prince, 167
Lloyd, D., 174
Lloyd, L., 98
Lloyd, W., 169
Llougwy Hotel, Pennal, 23
Llugwy, River, 161, 163, 166
Llundain Fechain,
    Lampeter, 130
Llwetrog, 128
Llwyd, R., 152
Llwyn Felfryn, Llansawel, 132
Llwyn Jack, Llandovery, 50
Llwyncelyn, Llandovery, 42

Llwyncwtta, Rhayader, 93,
    102
Llwyncyntefin, 45
Llwyngwyddel, Ffair-rhôs,
    68-9
Llwynhowell, Llandovery, 42
Llwynmerchgwilym, 34
Llwynpenderi, 98
Llyfnant, River, 23
Llyn Cerrigllwydion Uchaf, 76
Llyn Cynnon, 77
Llyn Hîr, 76-7
Llyn Mair, 171
Llŷn Peninsula, 14
Llyn-y-Gadair, 166
Llynfaes, Anglesey, 154
Llynheulen, Llanfihangel
    Nantmelan, 107
Llŷs Brychan, Llangadog, 50
'Lock and Key' Inns, 128
Lôn Isaf, 165-6
Lôn Nantaches,
    Pontrhydfendigaid, 69
London, 83-5, 128-9, 145,
    147-8, 152
Loughor, River, 144
Lower Heath, Presteigne, 109
Lower Rhymney, 93
Ludlow, Hereford, 84, 176
Luentinum, 39
Lugg, River, 89, 94, 110
Lukes, J., 143

Macadam, T., 146, 175
Machynlleth, 64, 84, 133,
    135, 139, 174
Maenarthur, Pontrhydygroes,
    77
Maentwrog, 166, 170-2
Maesbanadlog, Ystrad-
    meurig, 74
Maesllwch Arms, Painscastle,
    97, 125
Maesllwch Castle, Glasbury,
    100
Maesnoni, Llanllwni, 36
Maestwynog, 131-2
Maesyronnen Chapel, 98
Magnus Maximus, 22
Malkin, B., 101, 131, 178
Mallwyd, 133, 174-5
Man, Isle of, 61
Manafan, 138
Matt's Farm, Builth Wells, 107
Menai Straits, 15, 21, 151-2,
    161
Mendip Hills, 18
Milford Haven, 48, 84, 146
Moel Prisgau, 82, 119-20
Moel Siabod, 161
Moelfra City, 95
Mona, Anglesey, 155
'Monks' Way', 75-6
Montgomery, 84
Morfa Mawr, 62
Morgan, R., 142
Morgan, T., 146
Morgan, W., 87
Morris, Lewis, 66
Morris, W., 154
Mortimer, family of, 109

Mortimer, Sir E., 94
Mortimer's Cross, battle of,
    85
Morus, E., 115
Mountain Cottage, Lampeter,
    129
Mynach, River, 67
Mynachdy Ffynnon Oer,
    Lledrod, 74, 82
Mynachdy, Pilleth, 94
Mynydd Bach, 70
Mynydd Bach Trecastell, 42-3
Mynydd Epynt, 98, 126-7,
    130, 132
Mynydd Llanllwni, 132, 137
Mynydd Llanybydder, 132
Mynydd yr Hendre, 138
Myro, River, 77

Nag's Head Inn, Carmarthen
    47
Nannerth, 75
Nant, Anglesey, 155
Nant Ffrancon, 159, 161,
    165-6
Nant Gwineu, Strata Florida,
    82
Nant Rhyd-y-meirch, 81
Nant-y-bai, 78
Nanteos, Powell, family of, 63
Nantgaredig, 48
Nantmel, 93, 178
Nantrhydgaled, Teifi Pools,
    76
Nantybenglog, Capel
    Bangor, 29
Nantymaen, 80
Nantyrhogfaen, Llandovery,
    51
Nantystalwyn, 81, 119
Naseby, battle of, 85-6, 96
Nash, J., 47, 179
Nash, R., 47
Neuadd, Pencarreg, 36
New Cross, 30
New Inn, Llandeilo, 48
New Inn, Rhayader, 93, 102
New Mills, 138
New Radnor, 88-9, 94, 107,
    109, 142-4, 176, 180
New Row, Pontrhydygroes,
    71
New Well, Llananno, 102-3
Newborough, Anglesey, 166
Newbridge-on-Wye, 54, 121
Newcastle Emlyn, 128
Newcastle, 4th Duke of, 180
Newchurch, 96
Newent, 113
Newport, 84
Newtown, 85, 135-6, 147, 176
Nightingale, F., 131
Northampton, 139
Norton, 110-11

Offa's Dyke, 96, 105, 112
Ogilby, J., 87-90, 92, 110
Ogwen, River, 161, 165
Old Abbey, Strata Florida,
    61, 81
Old Conwy Road, 150-1

Old Hall Inn, Llanfihangel Rhydithon, 92
Old Radnor, 96, 100, 105
Ordovices, 14-16
Oswestry, 158
Owens, J., 142
Oxenbrook, Presteigne, 110
Oxford, 18

Painscastle, 97-8, 100, 125, 128
Palmer, J., 145-6
Palmon, Llanddeiniol, 72
Panty-y-craf, Pontrhydygroes, 67
Pantybarwn, Lledrod, 73
Pantybontbren, Ystrad-meurig, 73
Pantybrwyn, Rhayader, 102
Pantyfedwen, Strata Florida, 81
Pantyllwyfen, Llandovery, 50, Parc-mawr, 45
Park, Rhayader, 102
Parry, J., 101
Paulinus, Seutonius, 15
Peithyll, Capel Dewi, 27
Pen-ddôl Fawr, Strata Florida, 77
Pen-y-bryn, Lampeter, 129
Pencarreg, 35
Penderllwynwen, Ystrad-meurig, 73
Penegoes, Machynlleth, 135
Penlan, Llanddwcy Ystradenni, 92
Penlan, Lledrod, 33
Penlan, Ystrad-meurig, 73
Penwwlyn, Capel Bangor, 25, 27, 29, 31
Penmaenbach, 159
Penmaenmawr, 149-51, 158-9, 161
Penmllicue, Newbridge on Wye, 54
Penmynydd, Anglesey, 153
Pennal, 21, 25, 133
Pennant, T., 150, 154
Penpompren, Talybont, 27
Penrhyn Castle, 152
Penrhyn, Lord, 159, 161
Penrhyncoch, 27
Pensarn, Talybont, 26-7
Pensarnhelen, Llanllwni, 36
Pentre, Kerry, 104
Pentrebrunant, Cwmystwyth, 179
Pentremeurig, Llanwrda, 50
Pentrevoelas, 158-9, 161, 163, 166
Penybanc, Llandeilo, 48
Penybont, 89, 176, 178
Penybryn, Penegoes, 135
Penycastell, Lledrod, 74
Penygaer, Llanybydder, 36
Penygwryd, 171
Pepper, R., 84
Phillips, Rev S., 91
Pilleth, 94
Plas-y-Brenin, Capel Curig, 159
Ponty Twr, 161

Pont-yr- Afanc, 161
Pontardulais, Beulah, 121
Pontargamddwr, Bronant, 74
Pontcyfyng, 161
Pontcysyllte Viaduct, 165
Ponterwyd, 64, 180
Pontrhydfendigaid, 62, 69, 74, 77
Pontrhydygroes, 67-8, 71
Porthaethwy, Anglesey, 152-3, 157
Porthyrhyd, 41, 117, 131-2
Pontvane, Newchurch, 96
Port Dinorwic, 166
Posthumus, 45
Presteigne, 85, 88-9, 94, 96 100, 105, 109, 176, 180
Price, J., 178
Price, Rev J., 98
Price, Sir R., 94
Price, U., 176
Prichard, D., 167
Prichard, R., 131
Prichard, W., 96
Prichardes, W., 84
Pryse, James, 80
Pumlumon, 62, 180
Pumsaint, 17, 37, 39, 40, 128-9, 131
Pwll-du, Mynydd Epynt, 127
Pwllau Farm, Esgairdawe, Lampeter, 131
Pwllcenawon, Capel Bangor, 29
Pwllheli, 171
Pwllpeiran, Cwymystwyth, 179

Radnor Forest, 85, 89, 91, 100-1
Radnorshire Arms, Presteigne, 88
Radnorshire Gate, Kerry, 104
Ram Inn, Cwmann, Lampeter, 128
Raven and Bell Inn, Shrewsbury, 145
Red Lion Hill, Bwlch-y-Sarnau, 102
Red Lion Inn, Rhayader, 178-9
Rees, H., 146
Rhayader, 88, 92-3, 178-80
Rheidol, River, 29-30, 67, 70, 180
Rhiw Pool, Graig, 91
'Rhiw Rhystyn', Aberedw Hill, 100-1
Rhiw, River, 138
Rhiwarthen-isaf, Capel Bangor, 29
Rhiwfelen, Penegoes, 135
Rhiwgoch, Talywern, 135
Rhos Llawdden, 93
Rhosgoch, Powell family of, 97
Rhosgoch, 96-7
Rhuddlan, Flint, 50, 84, 149
Rhulen, 125
Rhyd, 137, 171
Rhyd Saint, 72
Rhyd-y-Meirch, 82

Rhyd-y-pererinion, Lledrod, 70
Rhydargaeau, 36
Rhydcwmerau, 132
Rhydspence, 117, 125
Rhydyglyn, Llansawel, 132
Richard, H., 118
Robertson, Mr, 129
Rock Bridge, Presteigne, 89, 94
Roderick, R., 117, 131
Rosehill, Llanwrda, 48
Rowley, Presteigne, 105
Royal House, Machynlleth, 133
Royal Goat Inn, Beddgelert, 167
Royal Oak Inn, Ffarmers, 38
Royal Oak Inn, Presteigne, 105
Rutland, Countess of, 83

St Asaph, 104, 149
St David's, 60, 63, 65, 71
St Harmon, 75, 102
St Mary's Hill, Presteigne, 89
Salesbury, W., 89
Samuel J., 114
Sarn Cwrtiau, Llangamarch Wells, 52
Sarn Ellen Farm, Trawsgoed, 33
Sarn Helen, 21-37, 65, 73-4
Sarn Helen Farm, Newbridge-on-Wye, 54
Sarnau, (Cardiganshire), 30
Sarnau, (Carmarthenshire), 36
Saxton, J., 88
Severn, River, 116, 133, 138
Severn Arms Inn, Penybont, 178
Shrewsbury, 133, 139, 144, 146-9, 158, 164-5
Silures, 14, 16, 18, 55
Simdelwyd, Newbridge-on-Wye, 54
Skrine, H., 144, 149, 151, 179
Slebech, 65
Slingsby, Sir H., 105
Slough, Presteigne, 96
'Smatcher', New Radnor, 107
Soar-y-mynydd, 81, 119
Speed, J., 88
'Spite' Inn, Tirabad, 126
Strata Florida, 61, 62, 64, 66-7 70-1, 75, 77-8, 80-2
Stamford, 116
Stanley, Anglesey, 155
Stanner, 180
Stanton, T., 165
Staphen, J., 165
Staplehurst, 117
Stapleton Castle, Presteigne, 110
Steele, R., 47
Stephens, O., 142
Stocking Farm, Presteigne, 110
Stonewall Hill, Presteigne, 110
Summergill, River, 96, 107

Sunnybank, Llansawel, 132
Swan Inn, Presteigne, 88
'Swan with Two Necks' Inn,
    London, 148
Swansea, 84, 96
Swift, J., 157
Swyddffynnon, 74
Sychnant Pass, 149-50, 159
Sylvester, J., 151
Symonds, R., 85

Tabor Wye, Aberedw Hill,
    122-3
Tacitus, 48
Tafarn Talgarth, Cynghordy,
    117, 125, 128
Tafarn-y-Mynydd, Mynydd
    Epynt, 126
Taihirion-rhos, 32, 34
Talbot Hotel, Tregaron, 118
Talbot Inn, Carmarthen, 47
Talerddig, 136-7
Talgarth, 98
Taliesin, 25
Talsarn, 130
Talwrn, Strata Florida, 78, 80
Talybont, 25, 27
Talycafn, 149, 159
Talyllychau, 130
Talywern, 135
Tan-y-parc, Llandovery, 51
Tanlan, 151
Tanybwlch, 177
Tanyrallt, Capel Bangor, 30
Tanyrallt, Nantgaredig, 48
Taylor, C., 19
Taylor, J., 85, 87-8, 149
Taylor, N., 109
Taylor, T., 153
Teifi Pools, 75-7
Teifi, River, 15, 34-5, 69-70,
    74, 77, 80, 128
Telford, T., 146, 149, 151-2,
    158-9, 161, 164-6
Teme, River, 84, 111
Tewkesbury, 117
Theodosius, 22
Tirabad, 126

Tomen Llanio, 34
Trajan, 17
Trallong, 45
Trawsgoed, 17, 29, 31-4
Tre-isaf, Strata Florida, 74
Trebanau, Llandovery, 42
Trecastle, 45
Tref-y-Gwyddel, 82
Trefor, Anglesey, 154
Trefriw, 158
Tregaron, 34, 80, 82, 84,
    118-20
Tremadoc, 171
Tremaen, Llanelwedd, 101,
    107
Troed-rhiw-dalar,
    Newbridge-on-Wye, 54
Troedyrhiw, Strata Florida,
    76-7
Tryfan, 161
Tudor, Jasper, 85
Tudor, O., 153
Twrch, River, 37-9
Twymyn, River, 135
Tycanol, Strata Florida, 78
Tygwyn Fields, Tregaron, 118
Ty'n celyn, Llanio, 35
Ty'n Twr, 166
Ty'n-y-cwm, Strata Florida 77
Ty'n-y-maes Inn, Nant
    Ffrancon Pass, 165
Ty'nbanal, Ystrad-meurig, 74
Ty'nyllidiart, Pontrhydygroes,
    67
Tywi, River, 15, 42, 48, 51,
    82, 131

University College of Wales,
    Aberystwyth, 41
Upper Chapel, 127
Usk, Adam of, 109
Usk, River, 45

Vaynol Park, 166
Vaynor, 93
Venta Silurum, 46, 59
Vespasianus, Flavius, 15
Victoria, Queen, 111

Wain Cottage, Llanbadarn
    Fynydd, 102
Wallace, G., 116
Walters, J., 129
Walton, 142, 180
Warden, Presteigne, 110
Warner, Rev Mr, 174
Waterloo bridge, Betws-y-
    coed, 159, 166
Watts, I., 115
Welshpool, 133, 135, 138,
    147, 175-6
Weobley, Hereford, 109
Wern, Glascwm, 96, 100
Wesley, J., 121
Westbury, 133
Wheeler, Sir M., 45-6
White Lion Inn, Chester, 145
White. R., 84
Whitehall, Clyro Hill, 125
Whitland, 61
Williams, J., Miss, 152
Williams, Sir H., 100
Wilson, R., 135
Woodcastle, Newbridge-
    on-Wye, 121
Wordsworth, D., M. and W.,
    96
Wrexham, 149
Wroxeter, 15
Wye, River, 54, 75-6, 84-5,
    96, 98, 101, 107, 109, 118,
    121, 125, 127-8, 178-9
Wynn, Sir J., 83
Wynne, family of, 159
Wynnstay fields, Llanfair
    Caereinion, 133

Y Pigwn, 43-5
Yr Onnen, Rhayader, 93
Ysbyty Cynfyn, 65, 67
Ysbyty Ystrad-meurig, 33,
    62, 65-6, 73-4
Ysbyty Ystwyth, 65-6, 68
Ystafell-wen, Lledrod, 73
Ystrad-ffin, 78, 81, 126
Ystrad, Llandovery, 50
Ystwyth, River, 30-2, 38, 179

Who's Who in
Early Medieval England

Who's Who in
Early Medieval England
(1066-1272)

being the second volume in the
Who's Who in British History series

CHRISTOPHER TYERMAN

Series Editor:
GEOFFREY TREASURE

SHEPHEARD-WALWYN

First published in 1996 by
Shepheard-Walwyn (Publishers) Ltd
Suite 34, 26 Charing Cross Road, London WC2H 0DH

British Library Cataloguing in Publication Data

Tyerman, Christopher
Who's Who in Early Medieval England (to 1272).
— (Who's Who in British History Series)
I. Title II. Series
942

ISBN 0 85683 091 7 cased
ISBN 0 85683 132 8 limp

Typesetting by Alacrity, Banwell Castle, Weston-super-Mare
Printed in Great Britain by BPC Wheatons Ltd, Exeter

CONTENTS

General Introduction   vii

Preface   x

Introduction   xi

Maps   xix

Genealogical Table   xxi

List of Illustrations & Acknowledgements   xxii

WHO'S WHO IN EARLY MEDIEVAL ENGLAND   1

Select Bibliography   413

Glossary   414

Index   417

For Elizabeth, Edward and Thomas

GENERAL INTRODUCTION

The original volumes in the series *Who's Who in History* were well received by readers who responded favourably to the claim of the late C. R. N. Routh, general editor of the series, that there was a need for a work of reference which should present the latest findings of scholarship in the form of short biographical essays. Published by Basil Blackwell in five volumes, the series covered British history from the earliest times to 1837. It was designed to please several kinds of reader: the 'general reader', the browser who might find it hard to resist the temptation to go from one character to another, and, of course, the student of all ages. Each author sought in his own way to convey more than the bare facts of his subject's life, to place him in the context of his age and to evoke what was distinctive in his character and achievement. At the same time, by using a broadly chronological rather than alphabetical sequence, and by grouping together similar classes of people, each volume provided a portrait of the age. Presenting history in biographical form, it complemented the conventional textbook.

Since the publication of the first volumes of the series in the early sixties, the continuing work of research has brought new facts to light and has led to some important revaluations. In particular the late mediaeval period, a hitherto somewhat neglected field, has been thoroughly studied. There has also been intense controversy about certain aspects of Tudor and Stuart history. There is plainly a need for fuller treatment of the mediaeval period than was allowed for in the original series, in which the late W. O. Hassall's volume covered the years 55 B.C. to 1485 A.D. The time seems also to be ripe for a reassessment of some Tudor and Stuart figures. Meanwhile the continued requests of teachers and students for the series to be reprinted encourages the authors of the new series to think that there will be a warm response to a fuller and more comprehensive *Who's Who* which will eventually include the nineteenth and early twentieth centuries. They are therefore grateful to Shepheard-

Walwyn for the opportunity to present the new, enlarged *Who's Who*.

Following Volume I, devoted to the Roman and Anglo-Saxon period, two further books cover the Middle Ages. The Tudor volume, by the late C. R. Routh, has been extensively revised by Dr. Peter Holmes. Peter Hill and I have revised for re-publication our own volumes on the Stuart and Georgian periods. Between Edward I's conquest of Wales and the Act of Union which joined England and Scotland in 1707, the authors' prime concern has been England, with Scotsmen and Irishmen figuring only if they happened in any way to be prominent in English history. In the eighteenth century Scotsmen come into the picture, in the nineteenth Irishmen, in their own right, as inhabitants of Great Britain. It is hoped that full justice will be done to Scotsmen and Irishmen – and indeed to some early Welshmen – in subsequent volumes devoted to the history of those countries. When the series is complete, we believe that it will provide a comprehensive work of reference which will stand the test of time. Nowadays when so much historical writing is necessarily becoming more technical, more abstract or simply more specialised, when textbooks seem so often to have little room to spare for the men and women who are the life and soul of the past, there is a place for a history of our country which is composed of the lives of those who helped make it what it was, and is. In contributing to this history the authors can be said to have taken heed of the stern warning of Hugh Trevor-Roper's inaugural lecture at Oxford in 1957 against 'the removal of humane studies into a specialisation so remote that they cease to have that lay interest which is their sole ultimate justification'.

The hard-pressed examinee often needs an essay which puts an important life into perspective. From necessarily brief accounts he may learn valuable lessons in proportion, concision and relevance. We hope that he will be tempted to find out more and so have added, wherever possible, the titles of books for further reading. Mindful of his needs, we have not however confined our attention to those who have left their mark on church and state. The man who invented the umbrella, the archbishop who shot a gamekeeper, a successful highwayman and an unsuccessful admiral find their place among the great and good. Nor have we eschewed anecdote or turned a blind eye to folly or foible: it is not the authors' view that history which is instructive cannot also be entertaining.

With the development of a secure and civilised society, the range of characters becomes richer, their achievements more diverse. Besides the soldiers, politicians and churchmen who dominate the mediaeval scene there are merchants, inventors, industrialists; more scholars, lawyers, artists; explorers and colonial pioneers. More is known about more people and the task of selection becomes ever harder. Throughout, whether looking at the mediaeval warrior, the Elizabethan seaman, the Stuart radical or the eighteenth century entrepreneur, the authors have been guided by the criterion of excellence. To record the achievements of those few who have had the chance to excel and who have left a name behind them is not to denigrate the unremarkable or unremarked for whom there was no opportunity to shine or chronicler at hand to describe what they made or did. It is not to deny that a Neville or a Pelham might have died obscure if he had not been born to high estate. It is to offer, for the instruction and inspiration of a generation which has been led too often to believe that individuals count for little in the face of the forces which shape economy and society, the conviction that a country is as remarkable as the individuals of which it is composed. In these pages there will be found examples of heroism, genius and altruism; of self-seeking and squalor. There will be little that is ordinary. It is therefore the hope of the authors that there will be little that is dull.

GEOFFREY TREASURE
Harrow

PREFACE

When younger, I believed it possible to write academically respectable history for a general reader. It has been a suitably humbling experience to try my own hand at it. Whatever the result, it has taken far longer than I, my editor, Geoffrey Treasure, or my publisher, Anthony Werner, hoped or imagined. To them I extend warmest thanks for their patience and encouragement. My intellectual debts will be obvious from the books listed for further reading and to those expert or interested enough to read between the lines. My mistakes as always are my own. I acknowledge the kind permission of Oxford University Press to quote an extract from *The Life of Christina of Markyate*, edited and translated by C. H. Talbot, 1959. There would not have been any book, however slowly written, without the often unconscious help and sustaining vibrancy of my family. My dedication is to those who have for such a long time put up with me, this book and so much more.

C. J. T.
Oxford
January 1996

INTRODUCTION

One of the most beguiling aspects of English history is its apparent continuity. That modern institutions can be traced from ancient origins has proved both the making and the undoing of the study of early England. The monarchy, the treasury, chancery and Exchequer, parliament, the courts of Common Pleas and King's bench, shires, the universities of Oxford and Cambridge: their antiquity and survival have lent a comfortable sense of wholeness with the past; a positive incitement to argue that in continuity lies the uniqueness of the English experience. Such impressions are illusory. In the period covered by this book, the central fact of English political history was dislocation and disruption. The verdict of Hastings was final, indeed a fateful day in William of Malmesbury's phrase. There was no Anglo-Saxon Restoration. However, there was nothing inevitable or providential about this. The consequences distinguished English experience both from the immediate past and from that of neighbouring countries. Twelfth century historians such as William of Malmesbury or story-tellers such as Geoffrey of Monmouth peered into the distant past precisely because of the lack of continuity. This was more than a literary problem. Whereas the kings of France could trace their ancestry and rule back to the tenth century, their title and provenance secured by custom, habit and history, the kings of England owed their position to the accident of war, a bloody and chancy conquest, a rude, drastic and, as it turned out, permanent interruption of English history.

Politically, England was redirected by a new French governing class which, for more than a century, maintained wide and deep links with northern France. Conquering landowners imposed their will through coercion and the visible monuments of military power: castles. Church-life was similarly colonised, the new cathedrals resembling the secular stone towers in proclaiming a new dominant order that owed little or nothing to the Anglo-Saxon past: even the saints buried at Canterbury were weeded out to suit the continental interlopers. The language of government and justice became Latin and French. Even though the numbers of French-born settlers in England cannot have numbered more than a few thousand in a population of a few million, as rulers their impact on certain features of culture and society was profound. At the most basic level of language, the Norman Conquest of 1066 and the Angevin inheritance of 1154 left its marks. Today English-speakers eat beef and pork, not cow and pig: medieval meat-eating was the preserve of the well-to-do, of social superiors who spoke French, not the peasants who herded the animals and spoke English. In justice, as the greatest English medievalist of all, F. W. Maitland, acutely observed, 'almost all our words that have a definite legal import are in a certain sense French words'. The ruled adopted the words of the rulers. They also adopted their names. It was a matter of fashion not demography that from the late eleventh century English parents increasingly used French names for their children. The consciousness of the Norman Conquest as a caesura in English history was recognised in 1272 when a new king, named after the Old English royal saint Edward the Confessor, ascended the throne not as Edward IV, but Edward the First since the Conquest.

Yet Edward's father, Henry III, possibly eccentrically, was devoted to Anglo-Saxon saints (he named his second son Edmund after a ninth century royal martyr). 1066 did not usher in a completely new world; there was exchange, synthesis and continuity linking 1066-1272 with the years before. Twelfth century law books explicitly looked back to the Laws of the Confessor. The economic and social substructure of manor and parish was unaltered even if the vernacular and vocabulary changed from Anglo-Saxon to Latin and French. Contact was confirmed by inter-marriage and bi-lingualism. Many children in the French ruling class had English wet-nurses and nannies. The Norman yoke was maintained by men who had been reared on English nursery rhymes. For the majority of the population, the agrarian workers who lived in various states of legal and economic servitude, the impact of the new aristocracy was limited to harsher exactions. Their language and that of manorial courts and peasant tenures remained English. Beneath the elites who have left records and largely hidden from view, during the two centuries after the Conquest English continued to be spoken, slowly re-emerging as a literary language, famously in the late twelfth century poem *The Owl and the Nightingale*. By the end of Henry III's reign, even some official pronouncements were published in the native vernacular.

Even so, throughout the period, to be *literatus* meant knowing Latin. French, increasingly a learnt, second language for the aristocracy, was a sign of social distinction. Both allowed Englishmen wide, easy and regular access to and participation in European cultural, religious and intellectual developments in philosophy, canon law, education, religious orders, crusading, art, banking and architecture. English responses may have been provincial compared to Paris or Rome, but only in geography was England insular. Just as England attracted foreigners, so Englishmen took their place in a genuinely cosmopolitan Christendom: one of them, Nicholas Brakespeare, even becoming pope.

The landmarks of this period were monuments neither to national vitality nor foreign enslavement, yet, unlike those of pre-Conquest England, they are more accessible to us: Domesday Book, the Exchequer, the martyrdom of Thomas Becket, Richard I's crusade, Magna Carta, the Provisions of Oxford, Simon de Montfort's parliament, the foundation of the universities of Oxford and Cambridge. Each has been etched into the national consciousness in a way that Anglo-Saxon precedents have not. Some recognisable themes of national identity were sketched in this period. But this poses a problem. Such resonance for later observers is frequently wholly at odds with the contemporary reality, a difficulty compounded by the nature of the surviving evidence which tends to be enigmatic, opaque and hardly ever neutral or objective.

The most obvious limitation is that we know almost nothing individually and little collectively about the vast majority of the population. Although by the end of the thirteenth century peasants begin to appear in the political and legal records, there are few if any pieces of direct evidence as to what they thought except through opinions and attitudes ascribed to them by others. Archaeology, manorial accounts and law suits can trace their physical existence, but they have no authentic voice of their own. Inevitably, concentration in this book has been on those whose lives can be traced, but without implying any view of historical causation.

Therefore, those included in this volume are from the ecclesiastical and secular elites. But the pitfalls of evidence remain. Narrative history was written in profusion by monks, canons or secular priests but usually to the sound of grinding axes. Private letters survive usually because they were collected for a purpose other than biographical. History is written by the victors; legal records by the officials of the court. Writing was becoming increasingly important, but nobody wrote without a purpose. Written evidence cannot be taken at face value; but neither can it be ignored or deconstructed in the blender of post-modernism. Evidence is all the historian has to connect with the actuality of the past: there seems little point using it to indulge the present.

If the past, more specifically the distant past, is a world that is lost, a foreign and alien country, the historian can, at least, attempt to observe what contemporaries thought of themselves. Here the evidence is suggestive, not necessarily by its content but by its nature, tone or form. We can see how the fierce corporate loyalty of monastic chroniclers infected their views of the doings of popes and princes. The lives of kings are depicted as morality tales. The preambles to royal documents point to ideologies of monarchic authority. The stories of Arthur hint at a more oligarchic, baronial vision of a world in which king and noble share power. Illustrations in manuscripts reveal vivid social stereotypes, with power clearly delineated and shared between church and state ruling a peasantry by turns drudges, oafs, destitute recipients of charity or rebels. The imagery of devout patronage is matched by those of war and brute force, order with chaos, but the chaos existing within a frame, both artistic and providential. Impersonal typology rather than portraiture predominates.

Images closer to individuals and their assessment of themselves are found in the seals of the great magnates. Commonly they depict themselves as mounted armed knights, a reminder both of the cultural centrality of the martial ethos and chivalry and of the recognition that the basis of the authority of the

English nobility was military conquest. As late as the reign of Edward I, a story went the rounds of the earl Warenne, who, on being asked by what warrant he held his land, produced a rusty sword saying 'this is my warrant! My ancestors came with William the Bastard and conquered their lands with the sword and by the sword I will defend them from anyone intending to seize them'. On one of Simon de Montfort's seals, the earl is shown as a huntsman, riding to hounds. There were few aspects of the lives of medieval nobles more obsessive than hunting which occupied enormous amounts of their time. Hunting was more than a rich man's hobby; it was part of his culture, way of life, and expression of his status, skill and breeding, an assertion of his exclusivity.

The seals and tombs of kings are equally instructive, of what they shared with their magnates and the crucial differences. Royal seals have the king on one side as a knight; on the other he appears robed in majestic state, a hierophant dispensing order and justice under God. In death, too, kings emphasised their quasi-sacral office. Even the grandest of their subjects, such as William Marshal in the Temple Church in London, are por-trayed on their tombs as knights in armour. Yet the earliest sur-viving effigies of kings, those of Henry II and Richard I at Fontevrault Abbey in Anjou, John at Worcester and Henry III in Westminster Abbey, show the king robed like a bishop. The unanointed could not aspire to such status. The king's divinity may have caused political wrangles, but was iconographically unchallenged. At least the propaganda of social hierarchy was consistent.

The years 1066-1272 were formative. Before and after there were English kings; during them there were kings of England whose outlooks were essentially French, Norman then Angevin. Increasingly, the interests of the monarch diverged from those of their more powerful subjects who, by the mid-thirteenth century, had little feeling for France. When Henry III relinquished his claims to his ancestral lands of Normandy and Anjou in 1259, royal policy was reconciled with political reality and the ambi-tions of the barons. By then, too, the political nation had expanded beyond the king's companions and the great lords and churchmen, to include wealthy and assertive burgesses, knights and gentry. Between 1258-65 there emerged the first populist political movement in English history under Simon de Montfort. Thereafter, no government could ignore the non-baronial. Montfort's defeat ensured that leadership of this self-styled community of the realm would remain firmly with the Crown, its agents and law courts in which a Common Law, available to all freemen, was administered by royal justices.

It was a far cry from the violence and insecurity of the generations after the Conquest. Any impression of an ordered progression to a harmonious and united polity is grossly misleading. No royal succession was uncontested until 1272. There were three major civil wars, between 1139-53; 1215-17 and 1263-7. An archbishop of Canterbury and a bishop of Durham were murdered. Kings were excommunicated; church life interrupted by papal interdict. In 1194 and 1213, England was declared a vassal state to, respectively, the Holy Roman Emperor and the pope. By accident the verdict of Hastings was not seriously challenged after 1070, but dynastic stability continued elusive. As late as 1216, another radical change of ruling family — Capetian French for Angevin French — was a distinct possibility.

However, away from politics, this period saw steady change. This was a period of economic growth. The population increased as did the size and diversity of the economy. Agricultural wealth was based on cereals and wool. There were signs by the later thirteenth century of pressure on natural resources and peasant tenancies from the growing number of people. As the economy expanded, the lot of the individual villein may not have improved; it may even have got worse. Some historians have seen the years 1180-1220 as a time of massive inflation, in its own way matching those of the sixteenth century and 1970s. If prices, especially for the government, rose, there is no demonstrable depreciation in wealth. England was prosperous in 1272 and, like 1066, most people had little or no share in it. For those who did, there were more markets and more bankers. The urbanisation seen since the tenth century continued unchecked. In almost every way, 1066 made no effective impact on the basic unit of agrarian organisation, the manor.

Parallel to this were changes in the church and religious life. Investment by lay patrons in the creation and sustenance of

parishes and parish churches may have been given an impetus by
the newly endowed lay aristocracy after 1066. Certainly they
indulged in the expensive fashion of stone churches. The spiritual lives of parishioners remained stubbornly or comfortingly
conservative, but the administration of the clergy and dioceses
were widely overhauled. The aftermath of the papal reform
movement of the late eleventh century led to a greater awareness
and promotion of the differences between the secular clergy and
the laity, a more severe insistence on the spiritual qualities of the
priest being manifest in a privileged status. Fuelling this was the
penetration of canon law and the elaboration of church courts.
Clerical attitudes were informed by the wider study of theology
spreading from Paris to Oxford. The spiritual life of the church
was provided with new models of simplicity in new monastic
orders in the twelfth century and the friars of the thirteenth.
Even so, the number of monks and regular clergy, far greater in
the thirteenth century than the eleventh century, was still a tiny
fraction of the population, their influence hard to judge, but
almost certainly exaggerated by the preponderence of evidence
they themselves provided.

Conflict between church and state, a staple of so much historical writing, is something of a misnomer. Laymen drew no clear
line between the material and the supernatural. Relations of
patrons with churches or monasteries remained close, pruden-
tially so for both parties. The church was part of lay society in a
manner unfamiliar since the sixteenth century. Indeed, one of
the habitual complaints of medieval reformers was that the
church too much followed the grain of secular life. At the highest level, apart from the few spectacular disputes, relations
between bishops and the kings were pragmatic, not heroic.
Rivalries within the church, between bishops, cathedral chapters
and monasteries, were far more virulent than any clash between
church and state. Indeed, there emerged in the thirteenth century
in some clerical circles a view that the main threat to church life
in England came not from the king but the pope.

Ecclesiastical insularity coincided with a growing feeling of
distinctive national identity. 1066 to 1272 witnessed the fracture
and reforging of Englishness. This was not a revival of Anglo-
Saxon independence after foreign subjugation, what could be

called the Ivanhoe theory of English history. Instead, the conquest and rule by foreigners and the interaction between the native and the alien over many generations created a distinct and self-conscious culture and self-image, recognisable alike to peasant and prince. To observe English history without the European context and contribution is to see *Hamlet* without the Danes.

What weight in such developments should be given individuals is hard to tell. The aim here is to place a few of those whose lives can be traced in their surroundings, both masters and victims of circumstance. No doubt there are some who should have been mentioned who are absent. Equally, the choice of others may baffle. The hope is that, from these biographies, an image of the period is revealed that does it justice on its own terms. All periods attract clouds of myth. By studying a few individuals, it is hoped some of this fog may be dispersed. It is impossible to be definitive about the past, especially a period so remote: the sources do not permit. But something of the diversity of the period can be sketched by looking at the lives of those prominent at the time. By reducing the past to a human scale, recognition may be easier. However distant, the people themselves encourage the effort to understand.

England: The Shires c. 1085

North
Sea

Newcastle

Durham

ST CUTHBERTS LAND

UNSHIRED LANDS
ANNEXED TO
YORKSHIRE

YORK

Lancaster

York

BETWEEN RIBBLE
& MERSEY

LINCOLN

CHESHIRE
Chester

DERBY

Lincoln

STAFFORD
Stafford

Derby

Nottingham

NORFOLK

Shrewsbury

Tamworth

LEICESTER

Norwich

SHROPSHIRE

Leicester

Thetford

WORCESTER

WARWICK

NORTHAMPTON

HUNTS

CAMBRIDGE

SUFFOLK

HEREFORD

Worcester

Warwick

Huntingdon

Northampton

Cambridge

Bury St Edmunds

Hereford

Gloucester

Bedford
BEDS

Ipswich

Buckingham

OXFORD

Hertford

Colchester

GLOUCESTER

BUCKS

HERTFORD

ESSEX

BERKS

Oxford

MIDDLESEX

London

Bristol

WILTS

Reading

Rochester

Canterbury

Sandwich

SOMERSET

HANTS

Guildford

KENT

Taunton

Salisbury

Winchester

SUSSEX

Dover

DEVON

DORSET

Southampton

Lewes

Exeter

Dorchester

English Channel

Launceston

CORNWALL

0 10 20 30 40 50 miles

England and Northern France

Newcastle
Durham
Richmond
York
Chester
Lincoln
Nottingham
Shrewsbury
Lichfield
Stamford
Peterborough
Norfolk
Coventry
Worcester
Warwick
Cambridge
Bury
Hereford
Ely
Gloucester
Colchester
Oxford
Bristol
London
Bath
Rochester
Canterbury
Salisbury
Winchester
Dover
Hastings
Pevensey
Exeter
Dorchester

North
Sea

English Channel

FLANDERS
PONTHIEU
Amiens

CHANNEL
ISLANDS
Bayeux
Rouen
Jumièges
Caen
Lisieux
Évreux
Coutances
NORMANDY
Paris
Mt. St. Michel
Avranches
Dol
Martain
ISLE DE FRANCE
Pontorson
Fougères
Rennes
MAINE
Le Mans
BLOIS
Orleans
BRITTANY
Angers
ANJOU
Tours
TOURAINE
POITOU

0   20   40   60   80   100 miles

THE ROYAL DYNASTY OF ENGLAND
1066-1272

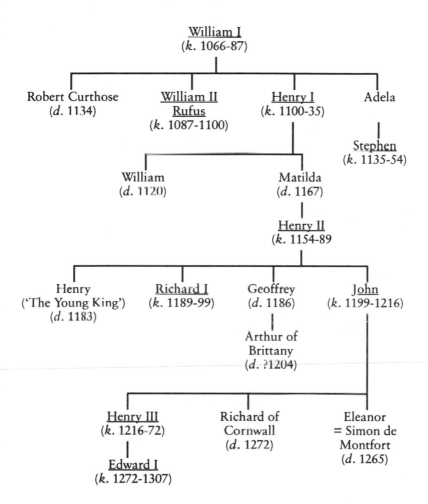

Monarchs are underlined

LIST OF ILLUSTRATIONS
& ACKNOWLEDGEMENTS

The author and publisher wish to thank the following for permission to reproduce materials in their care and possession. Where requested, shelf marks are shown after the name below.

L'Abbaye Royale de Fontevraud for illustration nos. 9, 10, 12, 15
La Ville de Bayeux for illustration no. 3
The British library for illustration nos. 1, 6, 7, 11, 21, 22
The British Museum for illustration nos. 8, 16
The Bodleian Library, Oxford for illustration no. 2
Chetham's Library, Manchester for illustration no. 13
The Master and Fellows of Corpus Christi College, Cambridge for illustration nos. 17, 18, 20
The President and Fellows of Corpus Christi College, Oxford for illustration no. 5
The Provost and Fellows of Eton College for illustration no. 4
The Dean and Chapter of Westminster Abbey for illustration no. 19
The Dean and Chapter of Worcester Cathedral for illustration no. 14

1. William I (MS Cotton, Domitian A II fol. 22)
2. Lanfranc (MS Bodl. 569, fol. 1r)
3. Odo of Bayeux
4. William II
5. Henry I
6. Stephen (Seal no xxxix. 10 obverse)
7. Robert of Leicester (Seal HARLEY Charter 84.H.19)
8. Henry of Blois
9. Henry II
10. Eleanor of Aquitaine
11. Thomas Becket (MS Cotton, Claudius B II, fol. 341)
12. Richard I
13. Hubert Walter
14. John

15. Isabella of Angoulême
16. Robert Fitzwalter
17. Stephen Langton
18. Peter des Roches
19. Henry III
20. Richard of Cornwall
21. Simon de Montfort (MS Cotton Nero D II fol. 177)
22. Matthew Paris (MS14 C.vii fol. 218 b)

WHO'S WHO IN
EARLY MEDIEVAL ENGLAND

WILLIAM I, known as the Bastard or the Conqueror (*c.*1028-1087; duke of Normandy 1035-1087; king of England 1066-87) exemplified with unsurpassed clarity a favoured theme of medieval writers, the unexpected turns of Fortune's wheel. He overcame adversities of birth, circumstances and opposition to seize the most glittering prize of the century and to die the most feared and respected ruler of his age. His deeds resounded through Europe and remain to this day a source of controversy and debate, of admiration and horror. If in no other respect, the accession of a duke of Normandy and his heirs to the English throne fundamentally altered the perspective of English politics by opening an inescapably intimate continental dimension which formed a major theme of English history for the next few centuries and provided the chief distinctive feature of post-Conquest English history.

Born the illegitimate son of Robert the Devil, duke of Normandy and Herleve, daughter of Fulbert of Falaise, allegedly a tanner, William was recognised in 1034 by the Norman magnates as heir to the duchy on the insistence of his father, who was about to embark on a pilgrimage to Jerusalem. Robert's death in Asia Minor on his return from the Holy Sepulchre in 1035 provoked a long and bitter struggle for power within and beyond the ducal dynasty during which ducal authority crumbled and from which William himself barely escaped with his life. It is said that his guardians were less fortunate: two were murdered; another poisoned and a fourth, the seneschal Osbern, killed in the very room in which the young duke was sleeping. William's survival largely depended on the assistance of Henry I, king of France, whose intervention culminated in the defeat of the anti-ducal rebels from Lower Normandy at Val-ès-Dunes in 1047. However, in the face of continued internal dissent, the rise of a hostile Anjou to the south and a change in French policy, William's

1

William I with the symbols of authority, the crown and sceptre
(From the Chronicle of Battle Abbey)

position was precarious until a French invasion was repulsed at Mortemer in 1054.

William's subsequent consolidation of control over both church and magnates depended crucially upon military success and his consequent ability to reward loyalty, attract support and punish opposition. Northern France, a patchwork of competing lordships and conflicting claims of allegiance, offered considerable scope for a vigorous and well-organised power. Between 1054 and 1064 William extended his influence and authority to

Ponthieu, the Norman Vexin, Brittany and Maine. A Flemish alliance was achieved by his marriage (c.1051) to Matilda (d.1083) the diminutive but forceful daughter of Baldwin V, count of Flanders. William also allied with the counts of Boulogne. This network of alliances proved vital when William planned his invasion of England. Norman expansionism was considerably assisted by the chance of the deaths of Henry of France and Count Geoffrey Martel of Anjou in 1060. Both had been hostile to William's advances but were replaced respectively by a sympathetic minority government in France and a succession dispute in Anjou.

William, as all medieval rulers, relied for his success on co-operation with leading landholders and the church. The Norman military aristocracy was of recent creation and heavily dependent on ducal patronage. The church was dominated by prelates appointed either from the ducal and other noble families (such as William's uncle Mauger at Rouen or his half-brother Odo at Bayeux) or by ducal appointment (such as Lanfranc of Pavia at Bec and Caen). William's skill lay in identifying mutual self-interest: lands and military activity for the lay aristocracy; ducal patronage for ecclesiastical reform, endowments, buildings and the fashionable Truce of God movement for churchmen. The Truce of God movement, supported by William's government as early as 1042, required knights to swear to keep the peace for specified periods and to police that agreement, if necessary by taking arms against transgressors. For William this was a highly convenient combination of political control, social cohesion and ecclesiastical authority all under ducal protection.

The eleventh century saw acquisitive lords and knights from Normandy seek their fortunes far beyond the confines of the duchy, in the eastern Mediterranean, southern Italy, and England. William's great-aunt, Emma, a daughter of Duke Richard I, married, in turn, Ethelred the Unready (king of England 978-1016) and Cnut (king of England 1016-35). Her son by Ethelred, Edward, spent his exile after 1016 at the Norman court and after becoming king himself in 1042 he introduced a number of Normans into England, notably his nephew Ralph the Timid as earl of Hereford and Richard Champart of Jumièges successively as bishop of London and, briefly, archbishop of Canterbury. Whether the childless Edward offered William the inheritance of the throne in 1051-2, as Norman propagandists insisted after the Conquest, must remain speculation. Despite some evident falsehoods in the Norman version, it is possible that Edward took the opportunity of the disgrace of the powerful Godwins to cement an Anglo-Norman alliance and solve the chronic uncertainty over the succession. However, other sources, no less partisan and unreliable than the Norman chroniclers, tell different stories. Perhaps it is worth noting that in 1051-2 Edward had a number of male relatives closer in blood than William; that William was far from secure in Normandy; that it would have been gross political folly for Edward to close options so soon and so completely; and that, despite later Godwin special pleading and Westminster Abbey hagiography, Edward himself could have expected to have heirs, especially as he had just put aside his first wife presumably in the hope of a second, fruitful marriage. If an attempt is made to reconcile the various accounts, Norman, Scandinavian, Godwin and non-Godwin English, then Edward must appear the most eccentric, foolish and politically profligate and devious ruler in English history, promising his throne to anybody, indeed everybody, as whim and circumstance dictated. The fact is that there are no trustworthy sources for the period leading up to 1066. All are to some extent wise after the event and concerned to justify or explain or refute. Above all, the Norman writers, William of Poitiers and William of Jumièges are apologists determined to establish William's claim. But as they wrote after 1066, their interpretation cannot, as many modern historians have done, be taken at face or perhaps any value.

What can be suggested is that by 1064 William was interested in the succession to England as a natural further extension of his power, especially as he could — and did — assert a dynastic claim. Edward may actually have been trying to secure William's support for a non-Norman inheritance by sending to him Godwin hostages and then, in 1064, Harold Godwinson himself, the leading magnate in England. It is clear from Norman and English written sources, and the Bayeux Tapestry (perhaps devised under the patronage of Odo of Bayeux at Canterbury, a suggestion lent some support by its similarities to the account of

1066 by the Canterbury monk Eadmer) that the 1064 embassy of Harold was a diplomatic triumph for William. Eadmer even records Edward's sharp displeasure at the turn of events, an image perhaps preserved in the Bayeux Tapestry's cringeing figure of Harold reporting back to an admonishing Edward. According to the Norman sources, Harold had sworn to be William's man and to help him secure the English succession. Whatever the truth, just as he confidently insisted on the legitimacy of his rights to overlordship in Brittany, the Vexin or Maine, William portrayed himself as believing in his absolute right to the English throne, a posture lent subsequent validity by friendly propagandists, supported by the verdict of events.

On hearing that Harold had been crowned king of England after Edward's death (January 1066), William began elaborate preparations. In a series of councils he attracted the support of his nobles. He publicised his claim at the Papal Curia, emphasizing the oath-breaking of Harold and the irregularities of the English church, which would be grist to the slow, sure-grinding mills of the holier-than-thou, purist elite then in control of the papacy. He received the blessing and a banner from Pope Alexander II, a signal, as he saw it, of the justice of his cause. Throughout, William laid claim to what modern historians call the moral high ground: at Hastings he wore a necklace of holy relics. His patronage of militant clerics and the Truce of God movement bore spectacular fruit.

William's wealth, reputation and carefully laid diplomacy attracted lords, knights and mercenaries from all over France and, it was said, beyond. Throughout the summer of 1066, ships were built and fitted in the Channel ports; equipment and horses were gathered. Modern assessments of the scale of William's enterprise tend to be conditioned by the weight of evidence. Yet, as we do not have much information about earlier amphibious operations, which, in English history, go back at least to Edwin of Northumbria's attack on the Isle of Man in the 620s, we should be wary of investing William's preparations with a uniqueness which may only be apparent because of the surviving evidence. Angles, Saxons, Jutes, Franks, Danes, Swedes and Norwegians, all had invasion fleets. Was William's so different?

William had not only isolated Harold diplomatically, but had also probably been in contact with Harold's brother Tostig and Harald Hadrada who were themselves planning an attack on England. A bloody crisis was inevitable, the tension being heightened by the appearance of Halley's Comet in the spring of 1066. In August William assembled his fleet in the River Dives, but contrary winds, and, perhaps, knowledge of English defences, delayed his sailing. The fleet was transferred to St Valéry on the Somme whence, at dusk on 27 September, it embarked for England, arriving, unopposed and intact, at Pevensey the next morning. The English defensive forces in the south had been disbanded on 8 September, as William probably knew, and Harold was in the north, having just defeated and killed Tostig and Hadrada at Stamford Bridge (25 September). The ensuing campaign showed William's skill and his luck in equal proportions. Establishing a fortified base at Hastings, William proceeded with the normal medieval tactic of concerted pillaging with the intention of drawing Harold to precipitate action. It worked. Arriving with a hastily levied army, Harold offered battle immediately. The battle of Hastings, fought on Saturday, 14 October 1066, left Harold and his brothers dead, his army destroyed and the road to London and the crown open. William had barely survived the battle himself, but he acquitted himself well as a field commander in what was his first pitched battle in sole charge (Henry I took the lead at Val-ès-Dunes and William was not at Mortemer). The rarity of set-piece battles is a feature of warfare in this period, some great warlords, for example Henry II of England (1154-1189), never fighting any battles at all. Hastings reminds us why.

After a cleverly conceived and ruthlessly executed campaign of devastation, William forced the submission of the surviving English magnates, led by Aldred, archbishop of York, the legitimist claimant, Edgar Atheling and the earls Edwin and Morkere. The military *fait accompli* was sanctified on Christmas Day, 1066 when William was hallowed king of the English in Westminster Abbey, a scene of reconciliation and acceptance, William being attended not only by his French companions but also his English nobles and bishops. By adding an arc to the crown of Edward the Confessor, a sign of almost imperial pretentions, William indicated the grandeur of his designs in the British Isles.

The manner in which William held his kingdom was as impressive as the way in which it had been won. Between 1067 and 1075 a succession of rebellions were dealt with firmly. In one nine month period in 1068 the new king subdued Exeter, parts of the West Country and Midlands and York. The northern rising in 1069, when native earls allied with Scandinavian invaders, led to a winter campaign of deliberate cruelty. The so-called Harrying of the North lasted three months (January- March 1070), embraced parts of Wales, Lincolnshire, Yorkshire, Teesdale, Chester and Stafford, and left areas of Yorkshire wasted for a generation. Calculated violence was a noted and consistent instrument of William's policy. Twenty years earlier he had ordered that thirty-two citizens of Alençon have their hands and feet cut off, ostensibly because they had jeered at his illegitimacy, but more probably to encourage loyalty from this vital frontier town in southern Normandy. By the end of 1071, the Danish fleet had been paid off and Hereward the Wake flushed out of his base at Ely. William's regime fell heavily on French as well as English, but its effectiveness was not in doubt, as witnessed by the suppression of the 1075 revolt of the French earls of Norfolk and Hereford in the king's absence.

Although there was little threat from Wales, the king of Scotland, Malcolm III Canmore, eagerly fished in the troubled waters of English politics. In response, in 1072 in an effort to secure his northern frontier as he had his northern subjects, William launched one of his most remarkable campaigns. In a classic demonstration of the use of concentrated military aggression in pursuit of political advantage, William marched his army, shadowed by a fleet, up the east coast as far as the Tay where, at Abernethy, a cowed Malcolm was forced to come to terms. This, as all William's military success, was based on the employment of disciplined troops, mainly household knights and mercenaries, mobility and castles, such as those at Hastings, Exeter, Dover, London, Newcastle, Warwick and York built variously as part of aggressive military strategy, as focal points for controlling an occupied country and as centres of administration.

From 1072 William could concentrate on France, in particular his ambitions in Brittany, Maine and the Vexin. Defeats at Dol (1076) and Gerberoi (1079) at the hands of Norman rebels, the disloyalty of his brother Odo and his eldest son Robert Curthose, placed William on the defensive in his later years, which makes his achievements in England the more remarkable.

With interests so far flung, William had to rely on a small group of faithful magnates, men such as his half-brother Robert of Mortain, William FitzOsbern, Roger of Beaumont, Bishop Geoffrey of Coutances and Archbishop Lanfranc. Their consistent support says much for William's ability to inspire loyalty. After the risings of the late 1060s and the execution of Earl Waltheof in 1076 for complicity in the 1075 rebellion, attempts to reconcile the surviving English lords were abandoned. By the end of his reign power and property had shifted wholesale from Englishmen to Frenchmen or Normans. The Domesday Survey of 1086 recorded only 5% of the land held by members of the families of pre-Conquest owners, not all of them English, and only two Englishmen, Coleswein of Lincoln and Thorkell of Arden, held land directly from the king. The church presents the same picture. After 1070 many English bishops were dismissed and no new Englishmen were appointed. William and his archbishop, Lanfranc, introduced reforms in ecclesiastical law and diocesan organisation based on continental models.

The tenurial, aristocratic and ecclesiastical revolution was sweeping and profound, but it was consequent on the replacement of English with French landlords and the new interests of the rulers rather than on any deliberate or accidental alterations of the structure of society, landholding or law. William did not introduce a new system of 'feudalism'. English thegns had held land in return for military service for centuries, their obligations becoming more regulated as the demands of central government became more effective. If William and his successors introduced a more precise method of assessing obligation, *servitium debitum,* and the so-called knights' fee, that was because of their need for defined resources to support their wars. The technology of war in pre-1066 England was not so very different from that in pre-1066 Normandy, as shown, for example, in the Bayeux Tapestry and descriptions of thegns' military equipment contained in Old English law codes. The new rulers were careful to assert that their land was held in all respects in the same way and with the same rights as those enjoyed by their English predecessors. Even the great Oath of Salisbury (1086), seen by some historians as demonstrating the feudalisation of England, can be compared with the general oaths imposed by English kings over the previous century. What undoubtedly changed, not immediately but inexorably, was the idiom describing and defining tenurial relationships among the landed elite and, in a similar process, the language and articulation of the law. An early example of French management of an English system of rule is found in the record of the Penenden Heath inquiry (c.1072) into the rights in Kent of Archbishop Lanfranc and Odo of Bayeux. Although the case involved two leading tenants of the king, it was heard in the traditional English shire court. Although the presiding justice was the Norman Geoffrey of Coutances, he called upon the legal knowledge of the deposed English bishop of Selsey, Aethelric: English law in a French context. What affected the French rulers was suitably rearticulated. What did not, namely the activities of the mass of the population, for example the manorial system, continued to develop as if Hastings had not been fought.

In 1066 England possessed a mature structure of government, administration and law, in most respects the superior to those of France and Normandy. William always insisted that he was a legitimate English king who respected English customs as surely as any of his predecessors. He wanted England to exploit not to change. Many historians have claimed that the Normans 'modernised' England. Recently, however, it has been observed how incompetently the new rulers managed traditional mechanisms of royal control, for instance the shire system and the coinage. Certainly, William's chief concern was less to understand the intricacies of English administrative habits than to obtain money in order to enhance and protect his position, especially in France. This desire attracted contemporary accusations of avarice and extortion. But, as the last crisis of his reign illustrates, William was no simple-minded thug.

At Christmas 1085, faced by the prospect of a huge Danish invasion and a fresh continental campaign, William and his advisors ordered the compilation of the Domesday Survey, which appears to have had the dual purpose of identifying the bases for innumerable disputes over possession of land and of reassessing income from property preliminary to a new, increased land tax. The resulting Domesday Book, although overtaken as an immediate administrative weapon by William's death, stands as a unique monument to English governmental tradition and Norman political initiative, and provides information unparalleled for any eleventh century kingdom. At Salisbury, on 1 August 1086, William, about to depart for Normandy, extracted oaths of loyalty from his tenants-in-chief and their followers (one source says their knights; others their tenants).

Such harnessing of clear perceptions of political and fiscal needs with vigorous military and administrative action is typical of William's role. If not all his ambitions were achieved, if Maine and the French Vexin remained outside his grasp, if luck had played a vital role throughout his career, William's achievements remain stupendous. Determined, energetic, ruthless, William possessed a personality and practical intelligence which, more often than many rulers in history, allowed him to dominate his contemporaries and to control his destiny, from the precarious life of a hunted bastard to the most powerful position in western Europe. William's success transformed the political map of Europe and the course of English history. The Norman Conquest gave English politics a fresh context, English government and law a different language, English society a new ruling class, and English culture an additional perspective.

William himself was impressive in manner and, on the evidence of a surviving bone recovered after the desecration of his tomb during the French Revolution, tall (c.5ft 10ins). Contemporary physical descriptions are almost entirely formal, although he may have had a noticeably harsh voice, and, like so many medieval aristocrats, have run to fat. A man of at least conventional piety, he was an active and generous patron of the church. He died at St Gervais near Rouen on 9 September 1087, his final illness possibly resulting from a riding accident suffered during a characteristically vicious attack on Mantes. Active to the end in pursuit of his interests, William was a man who seized his opportunities with unrivalled vigour, and, as many contemporaries said, with unrivalled cruelty as well. Whatever judgment is made on the nature and extent of his influence on his time and his new kingdom, whether he is regarded as cypher or architect, William the Conqueror was and is one of the most notable figures in English history.

D. C. Douglas, *William the Conqueror*, 1964.
D. Bates, *William the Conqueror*, 1989.

EDGAR ATHELING (*c*.1057-*c*.1125) was the son of Edward the Exile (*d*.1057) and so the grandson of Edmund Ironside and great-grandson of Ethelred the Unready. There is some evidence that Edward the Confessor, his great-uncle, intended Edgar to succeed him as king of England in 1066. After the death of Harold II at Hastings he was chosen as king by the remaining English magnates in London, but was soon forced to submit to the victorious William of Normandy. For the rest of his career, Edgar fulfilled the frustrating and ultimately barren existence suggested by his cogomen: an atheling was a member of a noble or royal family with a claim to the throne. By virtue of his position as the male heir of the House of Wessex, Edgar enjoyed patronage and hostility beyond his deserts, by turns an exile and a boon companion to the great. A rootless, restless, charming and feckless man, he had the personal qualities to attract supporters and lead troops, but neither the experience nor aptitude for political success. His career was a wheel of fortune which never reached the top. Initially accepted at William I's court, Edgar, with the rest of his family, fled to Scotland in 1068, where his sister Margaret married King Malcolm III. After the Treaty of Abernethy (1072) between Malcolm and William I Edgar was again on his travels, to Flanders and France, where Philip I hoped to use him to foment trouble against William. Soon reconciled with William, Edgar received some small estates in England, a place at court, a pension of £1 a day (which he casually exchanged for a horse) as the price of political emasculation. During this period, Edgar may have formed his attachment to Robert Curthose, whose character and career matched his so well. In 1086, Edgar was allowed to raise a force of two hundred knights to fight in southern Italy. On his return he was established with lands in Normandy where Curthose was now duke

(1087), only to be expelled from them in 1091 as part of a treaty between Curthose and his brother William II, who evidently found Edgar's independence as unsettling as had his father. However, Edgar's Scottish connections proved useful to William Rufus in his attempts to destroy the hostile regime of King Donalbane (1094-7), and in 1097 Edgar was put at the head of an English-sponsored invasion of Scotland which placed Edgar's nephew, also called Edgar, on the Scottish throne. Despite his family's hold on Scotland and Henry I of England's marriage to his niece, Matilda (1100), Edgar remained excluded from political power. In 1101-2, he, and one of his English supporters who had been with him in Scotland, Robert FitzGodwine, went to the newly captured Holy Land. Back in Europe, Edgar once more found himself on the losing side when he supported Curthose at the battle of Tinchebrai (1106). Thereafter, Edgar lingered on in obscurity, a relic of an increasingly irrelevant past, a curiosity, perhaps, to a generation in which Edgar's freelance adventurism had little or no place.

D. C. Douglas, *William the Conqueror,* 1964.
F. Barlow, *William Rufus,* 1983.

LANFRANC OF PAVIA (*c.*1010-1089; archbishop of Canterbury 1070-89) by circumstance and skill was one of the most influential archbishops of Canterbury. After the Norman Conquest, his political alliance and personal friendship with William I reset the pattern of Church/State relations which, despite a few well-publicised exceptions, were characterised by cooperation. Lanfranc maintained the intimacy between king and archbishop which had been established by Dunstan and Edgar a century earlier. Jealous of his authority within the church, where his concentration on rights and canon law bred episcopal arrogance and rancour, when the ecclesiastical and secular worlds met Lanfranc saw his role as the king's adviser, not challenger or competitor. He expressed this policy succinctly, the Latin giving a flavour of the clarity and vigour of his mind: 'contra preceptum regis nil rogare et nil iubere praesumo' ('I cannot take the responsibility for giving any directive or order that is contrary to the king's instructions').

Lanfranc
(A Norman depiction c.1100)

In 1070, William I engineered the deposition of Archbishop Stigand, ostensibly on the canonical grounds of irregular appointment and pluralism, but in reality because of Stigand's suspect loyalty. The king's choice of successor was risky yet understandable. Lanfranc was an ageing monk and scholar whose administrative and political experience had been confined to the world of Norman monasteries. Yet, as abbot of the ducal foundation of St Etienne at Caen, he was an intimate of William's household and family. From William's perspective, Lanfranc offered the moral integrity of a monk; the personal devotion of a friend; and the clarity of intellect and purpose of a lawyer. Although Lanfranc was never really at home in England, he effectively managed to mould the English church as he and his master desired.

Lanfranc's early career was not one which suggested his later hierarchical eminence. In the early eleventh century important

Western European bishops were usually from the ranks of the high nobility and, except in tenth century England, tended to be secular clerks, not monks. Even in England, the habit of appointing monks as bishops was waning in the decades before the Conquest. Lanfranc, from an urban professional background, had begun his career as a student of law in northern Italy. About 1030, he crossed the Alps into Burgundy and France where he seems to have studied and perhaps taught the traditional trivium — grammar, rhetoric and logic — before settling to teach at Avranches c.1039. Around 1042, Lanfranc underwent a conversion and joined the religious community at Bec where, despite his complaints about its lack of eremitic rigour, he stayed for twenty years, from c.1045 as prior. During the 1050s he resumed teaching, his interests still centred on law, grammar and rhetoric, traditional subjects to which he contributed little that was not soon superceded. Although he engaged in controversy, attacking Berengar of Tours' views on the Eucharist in the 1060s, Lanfranc as an academic, as later as a churchman, was a conservative. Unlike his successor as prior of Bec and archbishop, Anselm of Aosta, Lanfranc did not engage in the higher flights of speculative philosophy or theology. However, as an expert in canon law, Lanfranc was concerned with ecclesiastical discipline and the moral standard of the clergy. In this he was in tune with contemporary church reformers who enjoyed the support of Duke William and made him a suitable candidate in 1063 for the abbacy of the duke's Abbey of St Etienne, the so-called Abbaye-aux-Hommes, at Caen.

As in Normandy, Lanfranc's policies in England were those of an old-fashioned reformer, looking to a partnership with the secular ruler to achieve an improvement in the organisation, manners, morals and buildings of the clergy. In his insistence on legal precedent and rights, Lanfranc had much in common with the reformers who, in the late 1040s had captured the papacy, their vociferous campaign against the abuses of simony, lay investiture and clerical marriage reaching a crescendo during the pontificate of Gregory VII (1073-85), after whom the movement is commonly known. But on the issue of authority and the subjugation of temporal to spiritual power, Lanfranc parted company with the Gregorians who wished to enforce fealty from secular rulers and subservience from the ecclesiastical hierarchy. Thus in 1080, Lanfranc was not prepared to agree that the king of England was, by virtue of the payment of Peter's Pence, an annual gift to the pope, a papal vassal. Equally, within the church Lanfranc respected the pope's position, but not without qualification. As he wrote to Pope Gregory: 'I am ready to yield obedience to your commands in everything *according to the canons*' (my italics). Throughout his reign, Lanfranc maintained mutual support with the king and the independent rights of Canterbury.

Lanfranc's rule of the English church mirrored and sustained the secular conquest of the country. Like the king, he pursued his rights through law and, failing that, violence. In 1088, when meeting resistance from the monks of St Augustine's, Canterbury to his nominee as abbot, he dispersed some of them, imprisoned others and had one publicly flogged: 'thus did Lanfranc enforce obedience, and so long as he lived he broke down the opposition of the rest by dread of his name'. He presided over an almost wholesale exclusion of Englishmen from the highest posts in the church: not one native was appointed to a see during his nineteen years at Canterbury. He sponsored the introduction of continental monastic practices, and even some foreign monks. Where William built castles, Lanfranc encouraged the construction of new cathedrals which in their size and austere regularity of design were visible symbols of the new order in church as in state. Using the model of his abbey at Caen (and importing stone from there too), Lanfranc rebuilt his own cathedral in the 1070s on a grand scale, dedicated to Christ Himself. At Canterbury, he disparaged English saints, removing their relics from the cathedral and their names from the calendar of feast days. Even St Dunstan was demoted in this fashion and he thought so little of local sentiment that Archbishop Elphege, murdered by the Danes in 1012, only narrowly avoided a similar fate. Some of his early predecessors and other saints from the heroic age of the Conversion Lanfranc moved to his new foundation of St Gregory's which thereby was lent an instant, potentially lucrative, if spurious aura of venerable sanctity. At the very least there was an intrusively abrasive quality about Lanfranc's behaviour. As the Canterbury monk Eadmer (who revered Elphege as a 'holy martyr') commented, Lanfranc was 'a somewhat unfinished Englishman' (*quasi rudis Anglus*). In this he was just like most of the others who ruled the kingdom after 1066.

Yet if he had little time for English customs, he was unflagging in establishing what he saw as the traditional rights of his office. Claiming primacy over all Britain, in addition to English prelates he consecrated, either personally or by delegation, Irish and Orcadian bishops. In 1072, he secured a papal judgement acknowledging the supremacy of Canterbury over York, although this failed to resolve what became one of the longest running ecclesiastical feuds in Europe. The method of establishing Canterbury's primacy shows Lanfranc at his most characteristic. The case was heard at a council presided over by the king, held at Winchester, at which Lanfranc, the lawyer to his core, produced an impressive array of evidence, including chronicles, Bede's *Ecclesiastical History,* and papal privileges (possibly forged for the purpose).

Canterbury's temporal rights were not neglected either. At the famous trial at Penenden Heath (1072 or, possibly, 1075/6), Lanfranc not only made good his claim to certain estates in Kent against Odo of Bayeux and others, but also, in the words of one account, 'vindicated afresh the liberties of his church and the customary jurisdiction which he was entitled to exercise' over his lands. The judgement effectively recognised the immunity of Lanfranc's lands from the scrutiny of royal officials.

In ruling the church, Lanfranc was equally keen to establish a legal basis, often agreed at church councils, of which he held seven. At Winchester in 1072, apart from the dispute with York, issues of the church calendar, simony, wandering clergy and monks, treason and an instruction to secular priests to say masses for the king (an extension of tenth century English practice) were discussed. The Council of London in 1075 was the largest of the reign chaired, in the absence of the king, by Lanfranc himself. The main business was the transfer of sees, usually to towns, a sign of both political necessity and the growing urbanisation of England: Sherborne to Old Sarum; Selsey to Chichester; Lichfield to Chester; Dorchester-on-Thames to Lincoln and North Elmham to Norwich. Characteristically, justification for these removals was found in precedent and canon law. The latter also provided the basis for decisions on pastoral care; discipline of the clergy; good order within monasteries; lay marriage customs, and, even, prohibitions on white magic : 'the bones of dead animals must not be hung up anywhere as a charm against cattle-disease'.

However, despite such admirably reformist procedures, it is salutary — and very far from the Gregorian ideal — to note that the removal of spiritual pleas from secular to episcopal courts 'according to the precepts of the holy canons' was ordered by royal writ. All that Lanfranc achieved was in the context of royal power. Whatever independence he had in church matters was delegated from the king, a situation typical of both England and the continent over the previous century and more. What was different was Lanfranc's insistence upon legal, canonical precedent and his grip of the church structure expressed through patronage, regular meetings with his fellow bishops and occasional church councils.

Much of this successful exercise of archiepisopal *auctoritas* depended on Lanfranc's own personality and his willingness to identify his interests with those of the king. At least twice, in facing down the serious rebellion of 1075 in the king's absence and in the securing of the succession of William II in England in 1087-88, his active political support for the monarch was crucial. His loyalty, on a public level, is understandable. One great advantage Lanfranc had as archbishop was that he had no independent network of influence, patronage or power. He had no family or landed connections in the Anglo Norman nobility. He was unaffected by faction as all he had came from the king's favour. Thus isolated, Lanfranc, as has recently been written, 'could only be the king's man'.

That he embraced this position with enthusiasm cannot be doubted. He was one of the few men that William I trusted and cherished: on one occasion Lanfranc was forced to rest and submit to a medical regime 'on the king's orders'. No less important was his concept of obedience and hierarchy. At the trial of the rebel bishop of Durham in 1088 against William II, Lanfranc adopted a position entirely at odds with Gregorianism: 'We judge the bishop not as a bishop but as a vassal, as we judged Odo of Bayeux [in 1082] . . . by his original breach of faith and by accusing the king's magnates of deceit the bishop has lost the safe-conduct which he has invoked'. This outburst provoked spontaneous applause from the king's barons who shouted 'Seize the bishop! The old bloodhound's right!' For Lanfranc, the right order of the world was one which recognised the importance of the secular ruler in maintaining peace: that was not a function of a monk. Early in the 1070s he summed up his view: 'While the king lives we have peace of a kind, but after his death we expect to have neither peace nor any other benefit'. Lanfranc saw temporal things as ephemeral, papal pretentions to dominate the world no less transitory than those of princes.

From the sources, Lanfranc does not emerge as a particularly warm or attractive personality. He was apparently uninterested in the spiritual life of the laity, more concerned with legally proper forms of administration and organisation. His contempt for local English cults is revealing. Even his apparently generous gesture in allowing women who had fled to nunneries 'for fear of the Normans' to re-enter the world and marry was dictated by pragmatism and an acknowledgement of the legal as well as emotional fragility of vows made under exceptional compulsion. To Lanfranc's obsession with legality and rights and his creation of an ambitious, able but self-conscious episcopal elite has been attributed one of the least creditable yet most tenacious aspects of the post-Conquest church; the endless round of infra-ecclesiastical litigation and bickering over shares in the church's chest of temporal wealth, jurisdiction, status and power. Lanfranc could be cruel and, if not necessarily vindictive, then sternly unyielding. Small wonder he and William I got on so well. Yet although he contributed much to royal government, for all his forensic intellectual skills and his legal clarity of language, he kept his independence. Unlike Geoffrey of Coutances or Odo of Bayeux, he was never a glorified member of the king's administration. He rarely even witnessed royal charters.

The apparent contradictions of medieval monks who adopted public roles are probably impenetrable to modern observers. Yet for all his worldly prestige, wealth and power, Lanfranc's monastic vocation was central to his personality and, hence, his effectiveness. Unlike some famous medieval holy men, he did not flaunt his spirituality. Neither did contemporaries accuse him of hypocrisy. He belonged to a generation of monks less self-consciously obsessed with their own virtue than their successors. He reconciled his public labours and private faith through a sense of rectitude which could be unforgiving but was untainted by self-righteousness. In England he was able to avoid the posturing of the continental Investiture Contest partly because he achieved what the militants of Gregorianism missed entirely. He was able to see that necessary political action for the benefit, as he saw it, of God's church was not dependent on the constant scrutiny of first principles which owed nothing to accepted precedence, custom or efficiency. If anything, his legacy to the church in England consists of a pragmatic and independent appreciation and application of universal canon law which encompassed both royal control and ecclesiastical autonomy.

M. Gibson, *Lanfranc of Bec*, 1978.
H. Clover and M. Gibson, *The Letters of Lanfranc*, 1979.

REGENBALD (*fl.*1050-67; *d.* after 1086) was the head of Edward the Confessor's writing office, in effect, and possibly in name, his chancellor. He seems to have continued in this office under William I until replaced in 1067, in which year the new king confirmed all his previous holdings and added some estates formerly held by Harold II. Regenbald still held extensive benefices and property in 1086 when he was described in Domesday Book as *canceler*. A clerk, who under Edward the Confessor enjoyed the status although not the office of a bishop, his retention of land suggests he may have done the new regime some service as an agent of administrative continuity. His wealth and power in 1066 reflects the growth of a central royal writing office whose professionalism was reflected in the well-fashioned writs of the last Anglo-Saxon kings, an administrative tradition exploited and extended by the Norman rulers. His estates in 1086 indicate that the Norman tenurial revolution had limits. Regenbald, perhaps originally German, had another qualification to be an adhesive tenant. He was vicar of Bray. His acceptance of the changing governments of the 1060s merely foreshadowed his two more notorious successors, Simon Aleyn, who survived the religious upheavals of the 1530s to 1560s, and

Francis Carswell, who trod delicately through the ecclesiastical minefields of late Stuart and early Georgian England. Aleyn was supposed to have denied being a turncoat: 'I alwaies kept my Principle, which is this, to live and die the Vicar of Bray', the exact sentiments attributed to Carswell in the famous eighteenth century song. Regenbald would have recognised their achievement.

S. Keynes, 'Regenbald The Chancellor (sic)' *Anglo-Norman Studies*, x, 1988.

WALTHEOF (*d*.1076) was the last of the Old English earls to survive under William I, his execution for treason in 1076 marking a significant stage in the aristocratic and tenurial revolution which followed 1066. Younger son of Earl Siward of Northumbria, Waltheof became earl of Huntingdon probably in 1065. As one of the few English magnates not from the Godwin faction, he accepted and was accepted by William I, witnessing royal charters and remaining loyal to the new regime until in 1069 he joined with the Danes in their invasion of Northumbria. He was prominent in their capture of York, hoping, no doubt, to be restored to his father's position. This opportunism is perhaps more characteristic of English magnate reactions to the political turmoil of 1065-70 than any supposed national feeling. However, the revolt and invasion were defeated by William I's winter campaign of 1069-70. It is a measure of William's insecurity that when Waltheof submitted in 1070 he was restored to royal favour and, in 1072, added the earldom of Northumbria to his holdings. To bind him more tightly to the Norman dispensation, William gave him his niece Judith in marriage. But in 1075, Waltheof was implicated in the largely French revolt led by Ralph, earl of Norfolk and Roger, earl of Hereford. Despite his lack of military action, his confession, apparent contrition and the support of Archbishop Lanfranc, Waltheof was executed on 31 May 1076.

The king's motives are obscure. Waltheof was the only prominent Englishman to be executed in the reign. Perhaps his removal was part of William's justifiably nervous response to the problem of controlling Northumbria. It may have made sense to take the chance to remove a potential — and proven —focus of northern discontent. Yet Waltheof's heirs were not harried, one daughter marrying David I of Scotland (1142-53), another Ralph IV of Tosny, a leading Norman baron.

Waltheof is a significant reminder that the period around 1066 was transitional, with no necessarily definite beginnings or endings. Waltheof adapted to the new order, falling foul, it seems, of the ambitions and schemes of others, not least of par-venus Frenchmen. He married into the new elite, yet embodied the old. Heir to both English and Anglo-Danish traditions, it was he who completed one of the most celebrated of Anglo-Saxon blood-feuds. In 1016, Uhtred, earl of Northumbria was murdered by a northern nobleman called Thurbrand. He was, in turn, killed by Uhtred's son and successor, Ealdred who was himself slain by Thurbrand's son, Carl. Waltheof's mother was Ealdred's daughter and he avenged his great-grandfather and grandfather by massacring a number of Carl's sons.

Waltheof himself was buried at Crowland Abbey where, as did many martyrs to royal policy in the middle ages, he found posthumous fame in a cult which, by the mid-twelfth century, was venerating him as a saint. Yet his career in the north shows that not far beneath the measured tones of Norman propagandists or the efficient gloss of English bureaucratic procedures simmered the violence of Dark Age epic.

F. Stenton, *Anglo-Saxon England*, 1943.

WULFSTAN OF WORCESTER (*c*.1010-1095; bishop of Worcester 1062 95), was the last surviving pre-Conquest bishop who, while revering the traditions of Anglo-Saxon episcopal monasticism, actively supported the Norman regime. Unlike some contemporaries and modern historians, Wulfstan saw no contradition in this. A patron and preserver of English learning, he sent a favoured pupil, Nicholas, to study under the rigorous Lanfranc at Canterbury. Wulfstan was son of one of the bishop of Worcester's servants. After education at Evesham and Peterborough Abbeys, he returned to Worcester where he spent most of the rest of his career. Ordained when a member of the household of Bishop Brihtheah (1033-38), he soon abandoned his secular living at Hawkesbury and returned to Worcester to become a monk. In the cathedral priory he rose to become prior. When the pluralist Aldred of York was induced to give up the diocese of Worcester in 1062, Wulfstan was the unexpected choice as his successor. Perhaps his appointment was not so surprising: steeped in Worcester tradition, Wulfstan continued to fight for its privileges long after 1066. As a diocesan bishop, he was conscientious and efficient, seeing his role as extending beyond the focal points of monasteries. Capitalising on the recent extension of the parochial system, Wulfstan perambulated his diocese, preaching and personally supervising baptisms and confessions. In this, he was in step with continental practices and his episcopate suggests that the well publicised discrepancy between England and the rest of the western church was somewhat exaggerated. With his colleague Aethelwig, abbot of Evesham, he not only accepted the new dispensation after 1066, but convinced William I of his loyalty. Probably it was this as much as any apparent holiness or efficiency which enabled him to survive the purge of Anglo-Saxon bishops in 1070-72. A trusted associate of Lanfranc, he repaid the Anglo-Norman state with energetic service. In 1075 and 1088 he supported the king against rebels and rivals. His posthumous reputation depended heavily on his legacy at Worcester, which produced at least two considerable historians in the following century, Florence and John, and his biography written in English by Coleman, Wulfstan's chaplain. Coleman's Life was given wider circulation on being translated into Latin by William of Malmesbury for whom Wulfstan was an emblematic figure: a holy Englishman, noted for piety and simplicity, who recognised and embraced the virtues of the French conquerors without disclaiming his inheritance. Of Wulfstan's local status there was no doubt. A cult sprang up at Worcester soon after his death and he was canonised in 1203. In 1216, King John, in extremis, chose to be buried at Wulfstan's shrine in Worcester cathedral. John may have wished to be identified with a national, English interest against the rebels who had sought assistance from Prince Louis of France. After Edward the Confessor, whose shrine at Westminster was inaccessible to royalists in 1216, Wulfstan represented the best known and most respected example of English sanctity. But Wulfstan was more. He was no solitary monk yearning for escape from his episcopal duties. While remaining true to his self-denying vocation, he cared not just for the laity but as keenly as any twelfth century legist Wulfstan was determined to secure the rights and privileges of Worcester. In pursuit of this policy he commissioned a Cartulary from Hemming, a Worcester monk, of documents crucial to the defence of Worcester property and estates. In this Wulfstan was a link between the fierce corporate ecclesiastical identities of the tenth and twelve centuries.

E. Mason, *St. Wulfstan of Worcester*, 1990.

ODO OF BAYEUX (early or late 1030s-1097; bishop of Bayeux 1049/50-97) was one of the most powerful men in England in the twenty years after the Norman Conquest. Although famously ambitious, ruthless and energetic, Odo's position depended on his half-brother, William the Conqueror. To him Odo owed the immensely lucrative see of Bayeux when he was still a teenager. After playing an active part in the Conquest, Odo was granted the strategically important earldom of Kent as well as vast estates throughout England which, by the 1080s, were worth over £3,000 per annum, making him the richest tenant-in-chief in the kingdom. In the king's absence, Odo regularly acted as one of his deputies in England. Unlike other magnates, Odo travelled the kingdom settling, ostensibly in the king's name, small land disputes, of which there was no shortage in the messy aftermath of conquest. His motives were hardly altruistic, his intervention in land tenure becoming notorious. As a man and a politician Odo acquired a bad reputation for luxury, vice and cruelty. Viewed objectively, he was both wealthy and efficient: he reorganised the diocese and extended the chapter at Bayeux; he proved a vigorous military commander in the north of 1080; and he increased the yield from his own demesne in England by 40% in twenty years. However, his power relied entirely on royal favour. Unlike the prince-bishops of the Rhineland, he had no real independence. In 1072, he lost claims to lands in Kent against Lanfranc by the judgement of a royal agent. In 1082, for reasons still obscure, but possibly connected

Odo of Bayeux (left) conferring with
William the Conqueror and Robert of Mortain
(From the Bayeux Tapestry *c*.1080)

with Odo's continental ambitions or his support for William's impatient eldest son, Robert, the king decided to destroy his brother. He was arrested and spent the rest of William's reign a prisoner at Rouen. Although restored by Rufus, Odo rebelled in 1088 with other members of the 'old guard'. His defeat led to the final confiscation of his English lands. His last years were spent on the continent, presiding over a thriving cathedral community at Bayeux. In 1095, he cut an incongruous figure at the Council of Clermont, at which Urban II proclaimed the First Crusade. Odo embodies much of what the reforming popes detested: lay appointment; secular office; a love of material wealth and power; a layman in all but dress and, perhaps, education. Nonetheless, Odo, seeing his favoured nephew lose his grasp on Normandy to Rufus, joined Robert on crusade. Odo got no further than Palermo, where he died early in 1097 while visiting a Norman soul-mate, the tough, successful adventurer Roger, the Great Count of Sicily. Odo's career touched greatness but ended in failure. His lasting achievements came from his local power: his endowment and building at Bayeux; his probable sponsorship of the Bayeux Tapestry, almost certainly embroidered in Kent; and, above all, his patronage of gifted secular clerks from Bayeux who went on to scale the heights of church and state, including three archbishops of York (Thomas I, 1070-1100; Thomas II, 1109-1114; Thurstan 1114-1140); William of St Calais, bishop of Durham (1080-97), the compiler of the Domesday Book; and Ranulf Flambard, Rufus's feared chief minister. They formed a fitting epitaph for a man described a generation later as 'more given to wordly affairs than spiritual contemplation'.

D. Bates, 'Odo of Bayeux', *Speculum*, 1975.

ROBERT OF MORTAIN (*c*.1031-90), half-brother of William the Conqueror, became the wealthiest subject of the English crown in the generation after the Conquest. The second son of the Conqueror's mother, Herleve and Herluin, vicomte of Conteville, Robert was appointed by William count of Mortain in south-west Normandy around 1055. Robert's elevation was part of William's policy of creating a close network of loyal nobles, often related to the ducal house, with and through whom William controlled his duchy and, later, was to conquer his kingdom (Robert's full brother, Odo, was bishop of Bayeux). Robert's prominent part in the invasion of England was remembered in his depiction in the Bayeux Tapestry advising William with his brother Odo after the landing at Pevensey. Both at Hastings and during the often difficult pacification of England 1066-69, Robert proved an effective military subordinate to William. His reward was massive. By 1086, with almost eight hundred manors from Sussex to Yorkshire to Cornwall, as well as valuable castles, such as Pevensey, Robert was the greatest secular landholder after the king and the church. Together, his and Odo's estates were worth £5,000: the next richest lay holdings were valued at c.£750. However powerful his grip on his vassals, William preferred to keep power in the family. This presented problems; both his brother Odo of Bayeux and son Robert Curthose openly rebelled. Unlike the restless Odo, Robert of Mortain made little individual mark on events. He spent much time with his half-brother in a career, until 1087, conspicuous by its loyalty. In 1087, Robert persuaded the dying king to release Odo from prison and was probably one of those who insisted that Robert Curthose succeed to Normandy. Although initially accepting William Rufus as king, in 1088 Robert threw in his lot with Odo and Curthose. He held Pevensey for the rebels, withstanding a six-week siege by Rufus in person. After his submission, he was pardoned but withdrew to Normandy to die. Robert emerges dimly from the records, the least colourful or defined of a family of striking personalities. He seems to have been on close terms with both his brothers and to have harboured a soft spot for Robert Curthose. Alternatively, he wished to preside over his lands free from superior exactions, an independence fostered perhaps by his paternal inheritance (it was in his father's monastery of Grestain that he was buried), and later offered by the policies of Odo and the character of Curthose. Only the accident of his mother's liaison with Duke Robert I elevated this child of provincial aristocracy to the greatest heights of the Anglo-Norman baronage. In the eleventh century at least, nobility could be acquired by favour and fortune, not just by blood.

GEOFFREY OF COUTANCES. Geoffrey de Mowbray, bishop of Coutances (*d.*1093; bishop 1048/9) was one of William the Conqueror's closest advisers. From a prominent Norman family, before 1066 Geoffrey played a leading part in the ecclesiastical reforms patronised by Duke William. In the early 1050s he visited Rome and, in an early display of his talent for secular business, raised money for a new cathedral from the Hauteville rulers of southern Italy, who had originally come from the Cotentin. By 1066 an intimate of Duke William, he accompanied the invasion of England, was present at Hastings and at William's coronation at Westminster on Christmas Day 1066 when the acclamation Geoffrey led caused a near-riot. Although retaining his Norman see, Geoffrey spent much of William's reign governing England. He was especially prominent in settling major land disputes, for example at Penenden Heath in 1072 (re. lands claimed by Lanfranc) or Kentford in 1082/3 (re. lands claimed by the abbey of Ely). These involved important political interests and the need to establish formal continuity of possession between current claimants and their English predecessors before 1066. Such shows of legal propriety legitimised individual tenures specifically and Norman rule in general. Geoffrey also attended all major lay and ecclesiastical councils in England and Normandy during William's reign. In 1069 and 1075 he helped crush rebellions, brutally on both occa- sions: in 1069, prisoners were mutilated; in 1075, each had his right foot cut off. Geoffrey's dedication to William was rewarded with massive estates. In Somerset alone, Geoffrey received almost eighty manors and, by 1086, he was one of the top ten wealthiest magnates in England, with as many as two hundred and eighty manors. After William's death, he joined Odo of Bayeux's revolt against William II in 1088. When this failed, he unsuccessfully tried to ingratiate himself with the new king at the council which condemned his fellow rebel the bishop of Durham. Faced down by Lanfranc's hostility, he withdrew to Normandy for the rest of his life. Geoffrey was one of a close- knit group of friends and advisers who made the Norman Conquest possible in 1066 and thereafter. Great though his rewards were, his power depended upon the king's favour. The unity, coherence and survival of the Norman achievement in England were forged by such bonds of loyalty responding to authority.

D. C. Douglas, *William the Conqueror*, 1964.

WILLIAM FITZOSBERN (*d*.1071) was a military adventurer on a grand scale. The son of Osbern the Seneschal, one of William the Conqueror's murdered guardians, he became a close friend and steward of the duke. At the Council of Lillebonne in 1066 he urged the Norman barons to invade England and later played a leading role in the campaign, according to the twelfth century writer Wace commanding the right wing at Hastings. His importance was signalled by the vast English estates with which he was rewarded, notably in the Welsh Marches. Within six months of Hastings FitzOsbern was earl of Hereford and, with Odo of Bayeux, viceroy of England during William's absence in Normandy (March-December 1067). Heavily engaged in defence and assault against the Welsh, he assumed a task vital to rulers of the English since the seventh century. FitzOsbern set about his responsibilities with particular vigour and acumen. He became notorious for his generosity to his knights, lavishing special legal immunities and large wages on those who served him, this dispersal of treasure incurring, so William of Malmesbury two generations later claimed, the disapproval of the king. To reward his knights further, he settled many of them on lands previously belonging to the church. Uninhibited in exploiting his power over laity as well as clergy, he built a number of castles, for example at Clifford, Wigmore and Chepstow, with local forced labour. Such a policy was merely a continuation of earlier public obligations to contribute to the construction of ramparts which had been fully employed by rulers at least as far back as Ethelbald and Offa of Mercia in the eighth century. Now it provoked a revolt by an English dissident, Edric the Wild, in Herefordshire who allied with Welsh princes. Two years later, in 1069, FitzOsbern helped King William suppress the Northern insurrection and dealt with more trouble from Edric. He attracted further hostile comment from ecclesiastical writers by apparently advising a financially hard-pressed king in 1070 to seize treasure from the English monasteries. The main source for FitzOsbern's life, Orderic Vitalis, is torn between admiration at his material success and disapproval of his methods. Of the former there was no doubt. At Christmas 1070 he was in Normandy helping administer the duchy. Early in 1071 he was sent to Flanders to protect the regent, Richildis, and her son, Arnulf, the young count (and William I's nephew), against a rival claimant, Robert 'le Frison', Arnulf's uncle. To secure FitzOsbern's aid, Richildis offered him her hand in marriage. The air of chivalric romance was caught by the contemporary observation that FitzOsbern travelled to Flanders 'as if to a game'. If so, it proved fatal. He was killed in the decisive battle with Robert 'le Frison' at Cassel in February 1071.

FitzOsbern's dramatic career showed that the immemorial skills of warrior and warlord remained as central to the success of William the Conqueror as to that of any of the great fighting kings and heroes of the early Middle Ages. Whatever their political or administrative talents, which now seem rather less compelling than once they did, the French invaders of 1066 secured their conquests by violence, often crude and extreme. But it should be noticed that FitzOsbern secured his military support by rewards of cash and privileges as much as by grants of land: he relied on a paid host , not a 'feudal' levy in the classic sense. His life also suggests that in the eleventh as in other centuries, there was only a fine line separating art and nature: a murdered father; personal bravery; cruel conquest; great wealth and friendship with the great won by the sword; international fame for arms; a dowager in distress; the offer of marriage as well as power; and a death in the defence of a widow and orphan. Compared to the images manufactured by Norman apologists for King William himself, FitzOsbern may appear a throwback to a nastier, more vicious age. Yet in achieving great power and transforming his destiny through the exercise of military strength and the expenditure of large sums of money, FitzOsbern and his master, ruthless opportunists both, had much in common.

D. C. Douglas, *William the Conqueror*, 1964.

HEREWARD THE WAKE (*fl.*1060-70) was a Lincolnshire noble and outlaw who became a popular figure of legend in the twelfth century. At some date before 1066, Hereward fled his lands in south Lincolnshire, banished, according to local tradition, on his father's petition by Edward the Confessor as a troublemaker. After the Conquest, his lands were distributed to newcomers, for example Oger the Breton. This may have supplied the motive for Hereward's brief career of Fenland banditry. Leading his own gang, he joined the invading Danes under King Sweyn when they seized Ely in 1070. Although Ely became the focus of what the one version Anglo-Saxon Chronicle (later kept locally at Peterborough) described in terms of a general uprising, Hereward had his own interests to pursue. A former tenant of Peterborough Abbey, he led a raid which looted the abbey, perhaps in revenge for the new French abbot's refusal to restore Hereward's estates. After Sweyn had come to terms with King William and withdrawn, Ely continued to hold out into 1071, its resistance attracting some distinguished Anglo-Danish opponents of the Norman regime, including Morkere, formerly earl of Northumbria, and bishop Aethelwine of Durham. Starvation and self-preservation finally led to the rebels surrendering to the king, but not before Hereward had broken out to escape with some followers. Although apparently reconciled with William, it seems that he was subsequently killed by other Frenchmen, possibly nervous lest he made good any claims to their newly acquired property. What is more remarkable than this career of violence and failure is the rapid elevation of Hereward as a local, later national hero. By 1140, at Ely, Peterborough and in Gaimar's *Histoire des Engleis*, Hereward's deeds were recorded in detail and romanticised. That the reality was more prosaic is suggested not only by the raid on Peterborough but by the evidence of Domesday Book concerning conflicting claims to lands supposedly held by Hereward before 1066. Personal vendetta; the opportunities offered by the Conquest for outlawry and self-advancement; the coincidence of individual ambition with foreign invasion and national rebellion are all involved in Hereward's story showing that, in its earliest years, the Norman Conquest was neither as neat nor as secure as it later appeared. 1066 added to rather than initiated violent tenurial disputes and local rivalries. Hereward, described in the admittedly hostile Peterborough *Gesta Herewardi Saxonis* as 'cruel in act and severe in play', was an outlaw to Edward the Confessor as well as William the Conqueror. He became, however, a figurehead in the sentimental tradition of English resistance: by 1200, local Fenlanders were naming their sons after him. Unlike his surplanter as the symbol of anti-French English solidarity, Robin Hood, Hereward not only existed but actually did do some of the things claimed for him. (His nickname, 'the Wake', means watchful.)

J. Hayward, 'Hereward the Outlaw', *Journal of Medieval History*, xiv, 1988.

HERFAST, (*d*.1084; bishop of the East Angles 1070-1084) was possibly the first royal servant to be called chancellor, in 1069. A Norman clerk, he was witnessing ducal charters from 1060. Sometime after the Conquest, perhaps in 1068, Herfast was appointed to head the royal writing office, in succession to Regenbald, who had served Edward the Confessor as well as William I. As chancellor, Herfast made no obvious innovations: for example, the English vernacular in royal writs was retained. In 1070, he received the East Anglian bishopric which was then sited at Elmham but which he moved to the more prosperous centre of Thetford. His episcopate was notable for a strenuous contest with the abbey of Bury St Edmund's over the monks' immunity from the bishop's jurisdiction. The dispute, which concerned the vital interests of both wealthy abbey and impoverished diocese, drew a testy rebuke for Herfast from Archbishop Lanfranc: 'Were you to devote less time to gambling and games of chance, to read the Bible for a change and to learn some canon law . . . you would cease to argue with your mother church'. This attack reveals less about Herfast's relaxed morality (he may have been married and was reputed to have fathered a son) than of the widening gulf between old style curial clerks and the new intellectual puritans, a divide which transcended any supposed contrast between 'backward' English and 'progressive' Normans. Herfast was as much a creature of court life and the traditional habits of aristocratic clergy as the disgraced Stigand and, as such, hardly less offensive to the stern reformist Lanfranc.

MAURICE OF LONDON (*d*.1107; bishop of London 1086-1107) was one of those public servants whose private life, although notorious and scandalous, scarcely interrupted his successful career. A Norman by birth, he was appointed archdeacon of Maine as part of William the Conqueror's annexation of the county after 1063. He became William I's chancellor c.1078, an office he held until his appointment to the see of London in 1086. Evidently an efficient organiser, he reconstructed his cathedral of St. Paul's on a lavishly grand scale. His legal experience failed to prevail, however, in 1094 when he unsuccessfully contested Anselm's right to consecrate the parish church of St. Mary's in the archbishop's manor of Harrow. In 1100, he played a central role in the succession of Henry I to the throne after the sudden death of William Rufus, crowning the new king only three days after his brother died. His influence in royal administration is reflected here and in the earlier rise to dominance of his protégé, Ranulf Flambard. Like Flambard, Maurice, even though not in full priestly orders until shortly before his consecration as bishop, was a libertine, his pursuit of women attracting considerable monkish condemnation. Apparently, Maurice justified his sexual exploits by claiming that, on medical grounds, they were essential to his health.

GUNDULF, (?1024-1108; bishop of Rochester 1077-1108) was typical of the ecclesiastical administrators introduced after the Conquest, earning himself an equal reputation for saintliness as a champion of monasticism and for efficiency as Archbishop Lanfranc's business manager and supervisor of the construction of the Tower of London. Born in the Vexin and becoming a clerk in Rouen cathedral, he vowed to become a monk after a difficult pilgrimage to Jerusalem, entering Bec c.1060, at about the same time as Anselm. There he soon became the protégé of the prior, Lanfranc, whom he followed to St. Etienne, Caen in 1063 and to Canterbury in 1070. In England, Gundulf acted as Lanfranc's proctor and helped run the new archbishop's estates. Rewarded by William I and Lanfranc with the see of Rochester in 1077, Gundulf continued to be closely associated with the fortunes of Canterbury, providing the ecclesiastical administration during the archiepiscopal vacancy 1089-93. In 1095, he refused to disown his fellow Bec alumnus, Anselm, at the Council of Rockingham, but in general he remained loyal to the king. He undertook building work at Rochester Castle for William II, in whose cause he defended it during the civil war of 1088. In 1100 he witnessed Henry I's Coronation Charter and, in Archbishop Anselm's absence, baptised the king's son, William, in 1103. Like his mentor and patron Lanfranc, Gundulf saw no contradiction in the power of Church and State. He used his evidently considerable skills as an organiser to the benefit of his diocese. In tune with earlier eleventh century thinking, the secular canons at Rochester were replaced by sixty monks with an independent endowment and new conventual buildings. Rochester Cathedral was rebuilt as was the shrine of St Paulinus, Gundulf's most famous predecessor and, like him, a foreigner who got on well with kings. At the episcopal residence at West Malling, Gundulf erected a tower, an indication, perhaps, of the constant anxiety for security which characterised the first generation of French conquerors.

It is, however, for his involvement in the construction of the White Tower in London that Gundulf is most remembered. At about the time he was promoted to Rochester, Gundulf was appointed by William I to supervise work on 'the great tower of London'. His precise role is unclear. Although being described a decade later as being 'very competent and skilful in building in stone', and having commissioned a number of construction projects, civil, military and ecclesiastical, it is unlikely that Gundulf was himself an architect. For instance, there is no evidence to link him with Colchester Castle (completed by 1087) which appears to have been designed by the same architect as the White Tower, although on an even grander scale, Gundulf probably acted in a financial and administrative capacity, although he supervised building at close hand, lodging in the London house of one Eadmer the Lefthanded. Perhaps Gundulf had gained experience of construction work during his time at Caen which saw the building of both St. Etienne and its sister house Holy Trinity. Yet, although castles were a commonplace of the Conquest, there was nothing quite like the White Tower or Colchester in England or on the continent. Four-square to the ground, they are unlike the donjons of northern France, such as that at Falaise. It has been suggested that the apsidal chapels built out from the walls indicate a function beyond the purely military. The White Tower was built for what it remained, a royal palace as well as a stronghold, an idea confirmed, perhaps, by William II's need to provide a wall around it in 1097. For centuries, the White Tower acted as a centre of government, a respository of archives and, as no doubt it had been intended by the Conqueror, a symbol of power.

Gundulf emerges vividly as the archetypal administrator-bishop from two separate sources, an early twelfth century *Vita* and the contemporary collection of Rochester records, the *Textus Roffensis*. Combining lacrymose piety with a knack for business, Gundulf was a monk of the world. This duality, so common and so essential in effective medieval bishops, finds expression in Gundulf's dying words, reported in his *Vita*: 'Thanks be to God for giving me such wealth that I can help the poor and still leave my successor enough to cover his expenses even if he has to support thirty followers.'

H. M. Colvin *et al.*, *History of the King's Works*, i, 1963. M. Rudd, 'Gundulf of Rochester', *Anglo-Norman Studies*, xi, 1988.

THOMAS OF BAYEUX (archbishop of York 1070-1100) was a member of a remarkable ecclesiastical dynasty: his brother Samson became bishop of Worcester (1096-1112); one nephew, Thomas, was archbishop of York (1109-1114); another, Richard, was bishop of Bayeux 1108-1133). The family owed much to the patronage of Odo of Bayeux, whose influence almost certainly lay behind Thomas' appointment to York. The son of Osbert, a priest, and Muriel, he and his brother Samson were sent by Bishop Odo to Liège, presumably to complete their studies. Before his elevation to York he had been a canon and treasurer of Bayeux. By 1070 he seems to have become one of William I's chaplains. His had been the well trodden high road to ecclesiastical preferment. However, Thomas's tenure of the archdiocese was no sinecure. In particular, he had to cope with two intractable problems: externally the assertion of York's independence from the primacy of Canterbury; and internally the restoration of the church's finances and administration.

Although the status of York as a subservient archbishopric was anomalous in Western Christendom, neither Lanfranc of

Canterbury nor, even less, William I were prepared to concede the point. Politically, subjugation of York was one part of William's policy of subduing the north and reducing the prospects of local particularist support for any invader or rival claimant. For the same reason in the tenth century the kings of England had attached York to the see of Worcester and entrusted both to loyal West Saxons. William's and Lanfranc's way was ostensibly more legalistic. Thomas waged a stern but unavailing campaign to establish the equality of York as a metropolitan see. After expressing reservations before his consecration by Lanfranc in 1070, he urged his claims to autonomy at Rome when he and Lanfranc went to collect their *pallia* in 1071. In 1072, a council at Winchester found in Canterbury's favour and Lanfranc had his primacy and right to York's profession of obedience upheld. The archbishop of York was left with only Durham as a suffragan (Carlisle was not founded until 1133). Royal pressure not canon law or precedent determined the judgement; the papacy significantly failed to ratify the position. Indeed, the dispute rumbled on, occasionally flaring into spectacular, if often petty, rows, until the Reformation. The archbishop of York still cannot wear his pontifical robes in the southern province, a lasting legacy of the Norman political and ecclesiastical settlement.

Within his province, Thomas met with more success. At York he organised a chapter of secular canons and introduced a system of prebends (ie. lands and revenues owned by the cathedral but specifically attached to support individual canonries), no mean feat given the poverty and disruption of cathedral finances and personnel. The arrangement, although in tune with continental practice, contrasted with the monastic chapters of many southern cathedrals which Lanfranc, a monk, continued to support, not least at Canterbury itself. Indeed, the monk's customary disdain and suspicion of the secular priest may account for an edge in Lanfranc's relations with Thomas. It is possible, for instance, that Thomas, in common with many contemporary clerics, was married. The professional celibate would not approve. Yet as well as being a skilled administrator, Thomas was no philistine: a noted musician and patron of scholars, he was remembered by Hugh the Chantor a generation after his death as having rebuilt York Minster and restored the fortunes of a shattered diocese.

G. Aylmer and R. Cant, *A History of York Minster*, 1977.
F. Barlow, *The English Church 1066-1154*, 1979.

WILLIAM WARENNE (*d*.1088) was one of those followers of William of Normandy who made their fortunes by the conquest of England. The younger son of Rudulf of Varenne in Normandy (*d*.1074), he distinguished himself in ducal service as a very young man in the early 1050s. After the ducal victory at Mortemer (1054) he received estates in upper Normandy, but it was only after the English invasion that he attained the front rank. He fought at Hastings and was rewarded with lands which by 1086 extended into thirteen counties, most notably strategically important estates in Sussex centred round Lewes. By the end of William I's reign he was one of the dozen largest individual landowners in England. He repaid his debt with vigorous loyalty in both England and France. In 1075 he played a leading role in supressing the revolt of the earls of Hereford and Norfolk. After the Conqueror's death, Warenne supported William Rufus in 1087-88 against Robert Curthose and Odo of Bayeux. Rufus encouraged his service by creating him earl of Surrey in 1088. The same year Warenne was seriously wounded by an arrow in his leg at the siege of Pevensey and died at his foundation of Lewes Priory on 24 June 1088. Warenne's career was more than meteoric. A younger son of an obscure minor Norman nobleman, he had risen through conspicuous loyalty to his lord to become not only one of the richest men in one of the richest kingdoms of Europe but also the founder of a dynasty which, powerful, wealthy and influential, survived as earls of Surrey until 1347. Warenne's foundation at Lewes (1078/80) was the first Cluniac house in England, another sign of the Conquest's effect on establishing institutional as well as personal links across the Channel. Warenne's success depended on the traditional chivalric virtues of loyalty, bravery and prowess in arms. His life illustrates the stupendous prizes and the personal dangers on offer to those who joined the conquest of England. It was appropriate that Warenne's direct descendent, John de

Warenne, earl of Surrey (1231-1304), when challenged in 1278 by royal commissioners to produce title to his lands, produced an old rusty sword declaring 'Here, my Lord, is my warrant (*warrantus*: a pun which no doubt appealed to the somewhat intractable sense of honour of the time). My ancestors came with William the Bastard and won their lands with the sword, and by the sword I will hold them against all comers'. Earl John won his case. William of Warenne would have approved.

ROGER OF MONTGOMERY (*d*.1094), first earl of Shrewsbury, created one of the most powerful and strategically important lordships in post-Conquest England. The son of a Norman *vicomte*, he first appears in the army of Duke William in 1051-2. Probably only a few years younger than the duke, thereafter he enjoyed William's special confidence. In the early 1050s he greatly increased his estates by marrying the forceful Mabel, heiress to the extensive lordship of Bellême. Although closely involved in planning the invasion of 1066, Roger remained in the duchy to help the administration of the Duchess Matilda. It was only the later romances of Wace that put him at Hastings, a tribute to his subsequent fame and reputation. In 1067, however, he accompanied William to England where he received huge estates in Sussex and Shropshire. By the end of 1074, he was titled earl of Shrewsbury. His administration of his Marcher lands provide an insight in how the Conquest was secured. Roger had a more or less free hand. Before 1066, there had been no crown lands or royal thegns in Shropshire: by 1086, apart from Roger, there were only five other lay tenants-in-chief in the whole county. To support him, Roger gave out land to men already his vassals in Normandy with whom he set about building castles (as at Shrewsbury and Montgomery) and extending his power into Wales. Orderic Vitalis, whose father, Odelerius, was Roger's chaplain, described the earl as wise and prudent 'a lover of justice, who always enjoyed the company of learned and sober men'. His English subjects were as unimpressed as they were unfavoured. The citizens of Shrewsbury complained that they still had to pay the same level of geld after the castle had been built as before, perhaps because of the loss of houses incurred in its construction, let alone the forced labour. Roger's rule was effective and ruthless; his authority based on ties of personal allegiance; a network of castles; successful protection from the Welsh; and brute force. In many ways he remained a conqueror and exploiter rather than a settler. But he left his mark on the Marches, in his castle mounds and the perpetuation of his name in the Welsh town and county of Montgomery. As J. Le Patourel wrote, Roger's career 'shows what was possible in Norman society during the eleventh century'.

WALKELIN OF WINCHESTER (*d.*1098; bishop of Winchester 1070-98) was William Rufus's chief minister in the 1090s. Although not on the intimate terms of advisers such as Robert of Meulan, Walkelin was prominent in the king's council, often heading witness lists to charters and writs, and seems to have had charge of the king's financial affairs, in which he worked closely with Ranulf Flambard. It was said that Rufus's incessant demands for cash finally killed him. A Norman, royal clerk of William I and canon of Rouen, whose brother became abbot of Ely and nephew bishop of Hereford and archbishop of York, at Winchester Walkelin was typical of the new continental episcopate appointed by the Conqueror. Initially hostile to the local tradition of monastic chapters, his attempts to secularize Winchester were thwarted by Lanfranc and, despite the anomalous position of a secular clerk presiding over monks, came to be regarded with affection by them. In 1079, he began to rebuild his cathedral on a grand scale in monumental romanesque: austere, regular, massive, a statement as much about the new secular order as religion. Much of Walkelin's work survives, in the nave and transepts. As bishop of Winchester, Walkelin was in a position to oversee the main royal treasury houses in the city's castle. Additionally, he acted as a royal commissioner in both secular and ecclesiastical matters: in 1089 he dealt with the restive monks of St Augustine's, Canterbury; in 1095 he investigated the rights of Herbert Losinga, bishop of Thetford/Norwich; in 1096, he led a judicial circuit of the South-West to hear royal pleas. At court his authority grew in the early 1090s. After the death of Bishop William of Durham in January 1096, Walkelin was the dominant figure in the administration of England, organising the geld of that year and acting as regent in Rufus's absence in France in 1097. Although he did not work alone, some historians have seen in Walkelin's activities the origins of the office of Chief Justiciar. This seems to be an exaggeration. Walkelin was the king's main administrative deputy, not his Prime Minister.

F. Barlow, *William Rufus*, 1983.

ROBERT LOSINGA, *i.e.* the Lorrainer (*d*.1095; bishop of Hereford 1079-95) was a distinguished mathematician, computist, chronologist and astronomer (*i.e.* astrologer). An unusual choice as a post-Conquest bishop, he was neither a royal clerk nor a Norman monk, his experience being of scholarship not administration. To England and his diocese, Robert brought a range of influences. Notably, he rebuilt Hereford cathedral on the model of Aachen and attempted to popularize the eccentric chronological system of the Irish recluse Marianus Scotus (*d*. 1082). (This added twenty-two years to the AD calculation.) Robert sent a copy of Marianus's *Universal Chronicle* to his friend Wulfstan of Worcester in 1082, where it was incorporated into the cathedral chronicle, and himself wrote a commentary on it, wrongly described as *Excerpts* from Marianus, in 1086. This included a uniquely contemporary description of the Domesday Survey then in the process of being conducted. Perhaps Robert's greatest fame came from his study of the stars, by which he claimed to have successfully predicted the future, famously when he declined to set out for the consecration of Lincoln Cathedral in 1095 because he rightly foresaw it would not take place. It is possible that Robert also introduced the western, two-dimensional abacus into England, thus facilitating the computing revolution which transformed royal and baronial auditing in the following century, the abacus being a chequered cloth which gave its name to the Exchequer. It is likely that Robert's brand of cosmopolitan learning would have reached England regardless of the Conquest, but the employment of Robert reveals how closely England was drawn into movements of European culture. Rather than his acknowledged skill at computing time and numbers, where his high reputation despite gross error made him a model of academic achievement, perhaps

Robert's main attraction to William was his expertise as an astrologer. If so, Robert was not alone. The Conqueror's doctor, Gilbert Maminot, bishop of Lisieux (1077-1101), a scholarly sybarite who spent much of his time gambling and hunting, was also a *sagax horoscopus*, a learned astrologer. Medieval monarchs were nothing if not superstitious; they greatly favoured those who convinced them that divination was a science.

OSMUND OF SALISBURY (*d*.1099; bishop of Salisbury 1078-99) was probably a distant relative of William the Conqueror whom he accompanied to England as a chaplain. From c.1070-78 he was the king's chancellor, head of the small writing office which drew up royal documents, mainly charters and writs. Described in the Northamptonshire Geld Roll (*c*.1070/78) as the king's *writere*, it is even possible that during his chancellorship he was effectively the sole court scribe, the rest of the writing for the government being farmed out to cathedral and monastic *scriptoria*. Certainly, William of Malmesbury later described Osmund as bookish who, even as bishop, 'did not disdain writing or binding books'. In his time as Chancellor, Latin fully replaced English as the sole official language of government. Following almost invariable custom, Osmund's reward for his services came in the form of a bishopric. At Salisbury (what is now Old Sarum), he built a new cathedral and reformed the cathedral chapter, installing a hierarchy of officials and thirty-two secular canons. Osmund does not appear to have played a very prominent part in national or ecclesiastical politics. However, he was closely involved in planning Domesday Book, probably being a commissioner for the survey of South-Western counties, now contained in the so-called Exon Domesday which may have been written at the Salisbury *scriptorium*. Of even more lasting significance was his institution of new orders for liturgical services, the so-called 'Use of Sarum', a compilation designed to establish uniformity of worship. Whether or not it was introduced in response to the reluctance of English clergy to adopt Norman styles of chanting, the Sarum Use, with emendations especially in the thirteenth century, came to dominate the liturgy of the English church for the rest of the middle ages.

When Osmund was finally canonised in 1457, the work he had started almost four centuries before had left an indelible mark on the religious life of his adopted country.

WILLIAM OF ST CALAIS (*d.*1096; bishop of Durham 1080-96) was trained under Bishop Odo at Bayeux, the Anglo-Norman administrative Sandhurst. Unlike many of his colleagues, William became a monk, his first offices being prior of St Calais in Maine and abbot of St. Vincent-des-Près at Le Mans. He caught the eye of William I as a diplomat, but his experience of a frontier province may have influenced the king's decision to appoint him to the see of Durham in 1080 after the murder of Bishop Walcher. A conscientous and efficient diocesan, in 1083 he introduced monks to Durham cathedral, thus founding a priory which remained a centre of scholarship and learning until the Reformation. If pious, William was also intelligent and ambitious. By the end of William I's reign he was a leading royal servant. Largely on manuscript evidence which associates the scribes of Domesday Book with the Durham *scriptorium*, it has been suggested that William was in overall adminsitrative charge of the Domesday Survey. There are other references to William of St Calais's concern with the details of which baron owned what, and it may be significant that every writ of William II referring to Domesday Book is witnessed by Bishop William. He was thus probably responsible for one of the most remarkable governmental achievements of the age. The absence of returns from north of the Tees, William's diocese, might also suggest his involvement as a relatively neutral organiser.

The Domesday Survey was conducted between Christmas 1085 and 1 August 1086. The kingdom was divided into seven circuits, each with its own commissioners, who were deliberately not drawn from local landowners. To reduce fraud, a second batch of commissioners was despatched shortly after the first to check the declarations. The material collected concerned the extent of holdings, ownership and revenues, calculated in terms of tangible assets such as mills, ploughs, ploughteams and labourers. The commissioners asked three further questions: what was the estate worth and whose was it a) '*tempore regis Edwardi*' (*i.e.* in the time of Edward the

Confessor, 1066); b) when the present owner took possession; c) in 1086. The information was collated under counties, arranged by tenants-in-chief, *i.e.* those who held their lands directly from the king. Thus each county entry would begin by listing the holdings of the king, then the archbishop/bishop, then the leading barons and so on.

In fact Domesday Book is three separate texts:

1. The Exon Domesday, which covers the south-western counties, seems to be an early draft of material collected by one group of commissioners and is organised by tenants-in-chief and then by counties and not, as the others, vice versa;

2. Little Domesday, which contains a fair copy of returns from East Anglia;

3. Great Domesday, apparently a final, condensed text, covers all England south of the Tees except East Anglia and the City of London. The scale of the enterprise is only matched by its monumental result. Domesday was an apt nickname as the survey established, or sought to establish, title to land to which government officials referred for over a century after. Medieval rulers frequently surveyed their holdings, usually for fiscal reasons. In spirit, therefore, Domesday is not unique. But in size, detail and deliberation it stands alone as a towering monument to Anglo-Norman administrative skill. For it was a non-racial product. The main scribe of Great Domesday was, given his penchant for anglicising place names, most likely English. But the guiding force, William I, and the executor, William of St Calais, were French.

One mystery surrounding Domesday is its purpose. It has variously been interpreted as a tax book preparatory to a new assessment of the land tax or a more efficient collection of the old; a schedule on which new feudal and military obligations could be calculated; a statement of ownership of land which confirmed title or provided the basis for the settlement of tenurial disputes; or an immediate reaction to a political crisis (the threatened Danish invasion) in which landowners cooperated in the assessment in order to curtail royal misuse of the right to billet troops. What can be said is that potentially Domesday Book had fiscal and tenurial application and must have had considerable magnate approval for the survey to be completed so quickly. It is intriguing, however, that for all its bureaucratic grandeur, Domesday was still-born. It existed, and exists, and was, and is, used as a mine of information. But it led to no obvious political or fiscal initiative. In part this may have been because its originator, William I, died in 1087. It may also have been because the minister most closely responsible, within fifteen months of the Conqueror's death, was on trial for treason.

On his accession, William II, says the *Anglo-Saxon Chronicle*, treated Bishop William 'so well that all England went by his counsel and did exactly as he wished'. This was hardly surprising if the bishop had the evidence of Domesday at his disposal: knowledge is power. However, during the civil war of 1087-88 between William II and his brother Robert Curthose and their uncle Odo of Bayeux, Bishop William deserted the king and refused to fight against the rebels. His reasons are obscure as he seemed to have got on well with Rufus, supplying smooth talk for a tongue-tied monarch. The king's reaction at what he saw as treachery was commensurately vigorous. The bishop was arraigned for treason at a royal court at Salisbury on 2 November 1088. The king, vocally supported by Archbishop Lanfranc, insisted that William was being tried as a secular lord: his ecclesiastical position and office were not in dispute. William, ever nimble in debate, adopted the mantle of Gregory VII, claiming canonical immunity from secular prosecution or trial, arguing that he could only be judged by fellow bishops or the pope. Lanfranc dismissed such posturing as irrelevant. William forfeited his temporalities and went into exile, possibly to the court of Robert Curthose. Lanfranc's rejection of William's arguments may have been prompted by disbelief at this royal clerk's sudden conversion to clerical immunity, which, ironically, William may have derived from Lanfranc's own collection of canon law. But this early example of the clash between royal and ecclesiastical jurisdiction reveals that the English clergy were traditionalists: unlike advanced Gregorians they continued to recognise the practical distinction between the spiritual and temporal spheres.

It is perhaps a sign of William's ability or Rufus's magnanimity that the bishop was restored to favour in 1091 and resumed his position as one of the king's closest advisers. In 1095, at the Council of Rockingham, he led the bishops in their repudiation of Archbishop Anselm, accusing the primate, unblushingly despite the events of 1088, of polluting his fealty to the king. William evidently chose arguments that would serve his immediate turn, and would, no doubt, have agreed with Winston Churchill that consistency is a mark of mediocrity. But the violence of his attack on Anselm lost William the support of the barons: he was, perhaps, too clever by half. He died on 2 January 1096, appropriately enough at the king's court at Windsor, for his career was crucially bound up with the government of the first two Norman kings. Yet he never neglected his diocese. Under his auspices, a new cathedral was begin in 1093. He thus lays claim to have been the begetter of two of the most impressive surviving monuments of his age: Domesday Book and Durham Cathedral.

J. C. Holt, *Domesday Studies,* 1987.

HUGH, COUNT OF AVRANCHES, and EARL OF CHESTER (*c.*1047-1101) presents the world of the eleventh century nobleman in its full diversity. A violent military adventurer, a student of vice and self-indulgence, he was a friend of Anselm. Profligate with his income, he was a patron of monasteries. His household contained a bunch of rowdy thugs; it was also cultivated, even pious. Nicknamed 'the fat' or 'the wolf', Hugh died in the habit of a Benedictine monk. If contemporaries saw a contradiction, they have left no sign. Hugh, the son of the count of the Avranchin in western Normandy and nephew of William the Conqueror, probably fought at Hastings. Early in the 1070s he was granted palatine powers over a wide area of the northern Welsh Marches centred on Chester within which, except for church lands and pleas, he, not the king, was sovereign. This grant allowed Hugh complete freedom to establish, by force, French control over the northern frontier with Wales and to penetrate along the coast of North Wales towards Anglesey. Hugh was outside royal supervision, a law unto himself, a tactic copied with the Montgomerys in Shropshire. Taking full advantage of his opportunity, he campaigned relentlessly against the Welsh, extending his power to Bangor, where he established a bishopric in 1092, and Anglesey. Beyond the English frontier, however, his authority could only be sustained by castles, garrisons and repeated raids which, in turn, provoked continual resistance and rebellion. On its fringes, the Norman Conquest remained a messy affair. Elsewhere, Hugh was one of the leading magnates in the Anglo Norman realms, inheriting Avranches from his father in the 1080s and, by 1086, holding land in twenty counties outside Chester. In the succession disputes after the Conqueror's death, he supported William II and Henry I. Hugh acquired a foul reputation: vicious; violent; addicted to gambling and sex; and so greedy 'that, weighed down by a mountain of fat, he could hardly move'. He was also generous, which explains why his household was always crowded with many as debauched and sybaritic as he. But there was another side. Hugh was, according to Eadmer, an old and close friend of Anselm whom he persuaded to come to England in 1092 to supervise the installation of a community of monks at St Werburgh's Chester. Open-handed to 'good men, clerks as well as knights' as well as bad, he employed a Norman clerk, Gerold, who took upon himself the moral instruction of his fellow courtiers, using admonitory stories from the Bible and, no doubt more popular, stirring tales of Christian warriors and 'holy knights'. In such a raucous atmosphere of passion, carnality, militarism and piety, was nurtured the mentality which, in Hugh's lifetime, generated the Crusades. The knights who, in 1099, stormed Jerusalem and massacred its inhabitants, some of them Hugh's relatives and friends, shared this heady brew of self-righteous, self-pitying extremes of hedonism, brutality, guilt, obligation, spirituality and remorse.

ROGER BIGOD (*d*.1107) was one of the tight-knit group of second-rank Norman nobles who did well out of the conquest of England. Prominent in the Calvados region before 1064 as an under-tenant of Odo of Bayeux, he rose in ducal and royal service to become, by 1086, one of the leading barons in East Anglia, holding wide estates to which he added Belvoir by marriage and Framlingham by grant of Henry I. His territorial fortune was based on his service in the royal household, where he was a close adviser and agent for the first three Norman kings, and the propitious circumstances of post-Conquest politics. Much of his honour in East Anglia was carved out of lands previously belonging to the dispossessed Archbishop Stigand, his brother Bishop Aethelmar of Elmham and the disgraced Earl Ralph of Norfolk. A royal justice 1076-9 and regularly sheriff of Norfolk and Suffolk, under Rufus — if not before — Roger was one of the king's stewards. Usually in attendance on the king, he regularly witnessed writs but was also sent out to the provinces as a justice or commissioner. Apart from a flirtation with the cause of Robert Curthose in 1088, he remained conspicuously loyal to Rufus and Henry I, for whom he continued to act as steward and to witness charters. The adherence of such men was vital to the Norman kings. Through them central business could be conducted and localities controlled. Small wonder they were well rewarded. Roger established a dynasty which dominated East Anglia, from the 1140s as earls of Norfolk, until 1306. Roger's byname and the subsequent family name was derived from a word (*bigot*) meaning double-headed instrument such as a pickaxe: a tribute, perhaps, to Roger's effectiveness as a royal servant; certainly an apt image of one who worked hard both for his masters and himself.

F. Barlow, *William Rufus*, 1983.

SAMSON OF WORCESTER (*d*.1112: bishop of Worcester 1096-1112), a chaplain to William I and William II, was claimed by V. H. Galbraith in 1967 as the compiler and scribe of the so-called Great Domesday Book, the surviving fair copy of the survey of 1086. A Norman of noble origins, son of Osbert, a priest, like so many administrators of the first and second generations after 1066, Samson was a protégé of Odo of Bayeux, becoming a canon and treasurer of Bayeux Cathedral. In royal service by 1074, he apparently declined the see of Le Mans in 1081 saying that he was a man of this world not the next. Although having been married and still only in minor orders, Samson was appointed by William II to the bishopric of

Worcester in 1096: a striking, and possibly deliberate, contrast to his saintly predecessor Wulfstan. Samson was at the centre of a remarkable ecclesiastical dynasty: his brother Thomas of Bayeux was archbishop of York (1070-1100), as was one of his sons, Thomas, (archbishop of York 1109-1114); another son, Richard, was bishop of Bayeux (1108-1133). This scale of preferment for one clerical-administative family is impressive but not unique; it was matched if not surpassed by the rise of Roger of Salisbury and the Le Poers under Henry I. Samson was one of those secular minded ecclesiastics so mistrusted and vilified by the reformers clustered around the late eleventh century papacy. According to William of Malmesbury, Samson was an '*antiquorum homo morum*' a man of the old school. Although personally given to the pleasures of the flesh, particularly food ('a veritable sink of eatables' in William of Malmesbury's phrase) Samson does not seem to have been a bad bishop. However, recent scholarly opinion denies his authorship of Domesday, not least because there are inconsistencies and errors in the valuation attached to one of Samson's own estates, Templecomb (Somerset), by the scribe Galbraith sought to identify as Samson himself. Whatever their other shortcomings, Norman curial officials and landowners were unlikely to make mistakes of that sort.

J. C. Holt, *Domesday Studies*, 1987.
F. Barlow, *The English Church 1066-1154*, 1979.

WILLIAM II (*c*.1060-1100; king of England 1087-1100) has attracted more personal opprobrium than most English kings. His relatively brief reign has tended to be recalled for his morals, bad language, viciousness and dramatic death, not for his achievement in mastering the Anglo-Norman lands and, from inauspicious beginnings, becoming one of the most feared and respected rulers of his time.

William was the third, but second surviving, son of William the Conqueror. His red face as much as his hair earned him the nickname Rufus. Unlike his eldest brother Robert Curthose, the younger William remained conspicuously loyal to his father during the family conflicts of the 1070s and 1080s: he was wounded at Gerberoi (1079) fighting against a rebellious coalition led by

Curthose. His reward was designation as heir to England by the Conqueror on his deathbed in 1087, even though William had previously received no lands or titles. Seizing his opportunity with speed, William was crowned by Archbishop Lanfranc at Westminster on 26 September 1087, only seventeen days after his father's death at Rouen. Curthose, supported by his uncle Odo of Bayeux, refused to accept the division of the Anglo-Norman lands and disputed the succession in England. But after a short, vigorous campaign in 1088, Rufus suppressed opposition in England, in the process establishing his reputation as an effective warrior.

Between 1090 and 1096, Rufus bent his energy to consolidate his kingdom and reunite the Anglo-Norman dominions. He regularly invaded Normandy and, by vigorous military action and a skilful use of money, he managed to occupy or gain the allegiance of large parts of the duchy. In 1091, in alliance with Curthose, he ousted his younger brother Henry from the Cotentin in western Normandy, but from 1094 he and Henry cooperated against Robert. William's task was made easier by Curthose's failings as a ruler. An ineffectual politician, Curthose was unable to control his self-interested nobility. Instead, he fell back on a rootless charm and a name for bravery: he was no match for William. In 1096, the First Crusade provided unexpected relief for Robert and opportunity for William. In return for a mortgage of 10,000 marks to pay his brother's crusade expenses (raised in England by a heavy and unpopular tax of four shillings to the hide), William received the whole duchy for three years in pledge. From 1096 *de facto* duke of Normandy, Rufus had reunited his father's possessions with much of the Conqueror's skill, determination and opportunism.

In England, apart from the civil war in 1088 and a revolt by the Mowbrays in 1095, Rufus's main concern was the protection of his frontiers. He campaigned against the Welsh (1095 and 1097) and Scots (1091) and in 1092 Cumbria was annexed. In 1097 Rufus was behind the establishment of Edgar as king of Scots who then acknowledged him as overlord. However, France continued to be Rufus's main concern as he attempted to make good his father's claims to the Vexin (1097-8) and Maine (1098 and 1099). Rufus's ambition ranged widely.

William II
(From the reverse of his seal 1091/2: the king as warrior)

With his bullish and seemingly limitless self-confidence, some even thought he aspired to the French crown itself. He certainly cut a rather more impressive figure than the obese and lethargic King Philip. A characteristically bold plan to annexe Aquitaine in the same manner as he had acquired Normandy, through a mortgage for the count of Poitiers departing on crusade, was thwarted only by Rufus's death on 2 August 1100 when he was killed by a stray arrow while hunting deer in the New Forest.

The king's sudden death was a political sensation and a

moralist's dream. No respector of ecclesiastical privileges, William in death attracted the censure and hostile comment that few dared address to him in life. To die without time to confess or repent sins was seen as particularly awful in the Middle Ages, a judgement of God. Lurid stories filled with blood-curdling omens were soon embroidered around the fatal hunt. The reality was probably more chaotic than dramatic. Hunting accidents were commonplace: William's own brother, Richard, had been killed in the New Forest *c.*1070 and a nephew, a bastard of Curthose, had suffered an almost identical fate to William's only three months earlier. Some historians have smelt conspiracy rather than divine retribution in the king's death. Its timing was opportune for Henry, Rufus's younger brother, to seize the throne before Curthose had reached Normandy on return from his crusade. The man who most probably fired the deadly arrow, Walter Tirel of Poix, was a connection of the Clares who were close adherents of Henry. What we know of Henry suggests that he stopped at little that stood between him and his ambition. Cruel, violent, unsqueamish and unscrupulous, in fact just like Rufus, Henry, who happened to be one of the king's fellow hunters, certainly took full advantage of the situation. But beyond the circumstantial there is no evidence of premiditation: Henry's chance was fortuitous, not planned. Of that, contemporaries were more or less unanimous.

One cause of the suspicious, hostile, sanctimonious and scurrilous accounts in ecclesiastical chronicles of Rufus's life and death was his relationship with the Church. Not only was his quarrel with Archbishop Ånselm of Canterbury notorious, but his concerted exploitation of church land, especially during deliberately prolonged episcopal vacancies (during which time the king enjoyed the bishopric's revenues), earned him the posthumous dislike of clerical writers, ever fearful for their collective and corporate rights, privileges and, always, income. The confrontation with Anselm has received so much attention largely because of the work of Anselm's biographer and companion, Eadmer. It is worth noting, however, that despite the later clerical disapproval and condescension, Rufus never lost his grip on what he regarded as his Church. Some writers, such as Orderic Vitalis, evidently preferred a vigorous if brusque ruler to the inept drift of a Curthose, even if strict canonical immunities suffered. The conflict with Anselm was unusual, if predictable. In 1088, Archbishop Lanfranc had sided with the king in deciding that the bishop of Durham, William of St Calais, a rebel sympathiser, should be answerable in the royal court as a tenant-in-chief and not be able to claim clerical immunity or appeal to the pope. This was Norman convention. Anselm himself was only too willing to cooperate with royal power: in 1096, for example, he and Rufus combined to prevent some monks of Cerne Abbas from illegally setting out on crus-ade. In principle, Anselm had little objection to working with the monarch. However, his over-precise academic intellect made him a tactless, over-fastidious and undiplomatic coadjutor of a king who suffered fools marginally better than those he deemed muddle-headed or obstructive. From William's point of view, Anselm was both. Their relations were fraught from the beginning, when, in 1093, a dangerously ill William had, in fear for his soul, forced a reluctant Anselm to become archbishop. Much of the antagonism was based on personal and local issues: the archbishop's military contribution; whether the archbishop or king had the right to decide which of two competing popes to recognise; and the right of the archbishop unilaterally to appeal to Rome. Although failing to oust Anselm at the Council of Rockingham (1095), Rufus managed to force the archbishop into exile in 1097 to the king's considerable financial and political benefit. It may be significant that none of Anselm's episcopal colleagues saw fit to share his exile: the dispute was between the king and archbishop, not State against Church. Up to his death, Rufus was the clear winner.

The ineffective eccentricity of Anselm was the familiar consequence of the don in politics. Rufus relied, as had his father, on more practical sons of the Church to effect his policies, men like Bishop Walkelin of Winchester and Ranulf Flambard, whom he elevated to the see of Durham in 1099 as reward for outstanding (some would say infamous) service in filling the king's coffers. But he was unafraid to destroy the unfaithful, as he showed when he broke his father's minister William of St Calais, bishop of Durham, in 1088.

Rufus's reign was marked by heavy financial exactions

commensurate with the scope of his political and military designs. National taxes, such as those of 1094 and 1096, were required to pay for constant war and the Normandy mortgage. It is possible that, in 1096 at lease, the information gathered in Domesday Book (1086) was employed to increase revenue. Local justiciars extracted as much as they could from royal rights and dues in the counties. More notoriously, the profits of vacant bishoprics were ruthlessly exploited, although only two vacancies, Canterbury (1089-93) and Durham (1096-99) were in royal custody for more than a couple of years. His dealings with abbacies were equally a matter of profit and patronage. Yet, despite the injured hostility of ecclesiastical chroniclers, Rufus was no tyrant. He surrounded himself with a loyal group of administrators, nobles and household companions. He consulted, as well as employed, his magnates, as over the 1096 tax, for it was on them that the king relied to fight his wars, to govern his country, secure his justice and collect his taxes. Testimony to his political as well as financial success is found in his achievements and his contemporary reputation. Abbot Suger of St Denis, writing a generation later, acutely described William as 'magnanimous', 'prodigal with the treasures of England, a brilliant recruiter and paymaster of soldiers'.

However, English chroniclers, from Eadmer to William of Malmesbury, Orderic Vitalis and Henry of Huntingdon, developed an increasingly unflattering portrait of a foul-mouthed, loutish homosexual; an almost demonic character for whom few good words could be found; an oppressor of the Church whose death was a blessing and whose burial without ceremony or prayers just deserts. Of his bad language there are so many references as to be credible (his favourite oath being, somewhat obscurely, 'By the Face of Lucca' — a reference to a popular Italian icon of the time). All chroniclers note his blunt manner of talking, which matches a career driven by a practical intelligence as much as fierce energy. The earliest observer, Eadmer, noted that William's court in 1094 was crowded with effeminate young men, parading girlishly long hair, mincing walks and flirtatious glances. Predictably, Anselm, although interested, was unamused. William of Malmesbury added a quarter of a century later details of elaborate and garish shoes and tight-fitting clothes. Such stories were coupled with dark mutterings about the king's own sexual habits. When Anselm, in 1094, proposed holding a Church Council to condemn sodomy, William refused. But it was only many years after his death that explicit accusations of homosexuality were levelled against William himself. Much of the surrounding disapproval can be explained by an odd cultural barrier between France and England which amounted to little more than different fashions. As early as 1077, William of Poitiers had recorded the Norman astonishment at the English habit of men wearing their hair long, something only women did in macho Normandy. The association of long hair with degeneracy and moral turpitude was pursued by a Council at Rouen in 1096 which publically condemned long hair. This obsession has had a remarkably tenacious hold on the English aristocracy and their imitators by no means extinguished even today.

It is probable, therefore, that the chroniclers, uniformly monastic, were voicing prim, prudish, perhaps prurient dislike of a fashion they regarded as alien or out of date but which William and his courtiers had adopted rather ostentatiously: an English Conquest, perhaps. That Rufus was content if not eager to go his own way cannot surprise. After all, he is one of the very few whose first title was that of king: he had no previous claim to a lordship, earldom, county or principality. What is more remarkable was his failure to marry. Although his brothers left marriage until relatively late (Curthose at forty-seven; Henry I at thirty-two), for a monarch not to make provision for legitimate offspring is exceptional. The only clear parallel to Rufus's behaviour is remote: Aethelbald, king of Mercia and overlord of southern England (716-757). Otherwise the only adult monarch bachelors or spinsters since 1066 are Elizabeth I and Edward VIII, and he married as soon as he could after abdicating. It is possible that William was homosexual. Unusually for his family, no bastards are attributed to him. Given the manner of his death, the rumours of his life and the interests of his successor, it is understandable that writers coloured their accounts. William of Malmesbury depicts Rufus as a short, pot-bellied, red-faced braggart with long, combed fair hair who, despite these obvious physical disadvantages, nonetheless insisted on wearing the gaudiest of the latest male fashions.

Whatever the truth, William Rufus left few observers indifferent. Although it is impossible to be certain how, he made a powerful impression on those he encountered. His actions reveal him as a man of extraordinary, if occasionally undisciplined, energy, singular determination and exalted ambition. His career exudes self-confidence of a high order. But there was more to him than blustering activity. One July afternoon in 1099, while dining at Brockenhurst in the New Forest (another source has him hunting), he learnt that his garrison at Le Mans was under siege. He immediately set off towards the coast and, despite stormy weather and reluctant ferrymen, landed unscathed in Normandy at dawn the next day ready to raise an army. Such speed of reaction was, to say the least, unsettling to his opponents and cheering to his supporters.

Rufus effectively harnessed the resources of England to pursue deliberate policies of consolidation and aggression in France and the English marches. If he was impatient and tolerated no opposition, he was also remarkably successful in achieving his designated ends. Much of the responsibility for the permanence of his father's conquests and the scope of his brother's dominance can be credited to Rufus. The anecdotes about him make him more vivid than either. Begun in 1097, Westminster Hall, which in spite of evidently hasty construction stands to this day, was, at 240 feet by 67 feet 6 inches, by far the largest secular building in western Europe. It is typical of its builder that when he first saw it, William Rufus complained that it was too small.

F. Barlow, *William Rufus*, 1983.

ANSELM (1033-1109; archbishop of Canterbury 1093-1109) was one of the most original thinkers of the western middle ages. By using reason and logic, his proofs of the existence of God and the importance of the Incarnation for the first time went beyond the traditional Scriptural and Patristic foundations of Christian theology. He wrote not just to confirm but to convince. Anselm's talents were not restricted to academic speculation: forty-six of his forty-nine years as a monk were spent in administrative or political positions, as prior, then abbot of Bec, and archbishop of Canterbury. His life is unusually well-documented in a biography written, much of it during his lifetime, by a close companion, Eadmer of Canterbury.

Born of noble parents in Aosta in northern Italy, his youthful desire to become a monk clashed with his status as an only son who was expected by his father to inherit the family estates. In the late 1050s he left Italy in search of education and vocation. In particular he was attracted by the reputation of another expatriate Italian, Lanfranc of Pavia, who had settled in Normandy. In 1060, Anselm became a monk at Bec, where Lanfranc was prior. He had earlier rejected the idea of entering the great Burgundian monastery of Cluny because its emphasis on reciting the liturgy — a sort of eternal choir-practice — left little time for academic study. In 1063, Anselm succeeded Lanfranc as prior of Bec; in 1078 he was made abbot. Although concentrating on study and teaching, Anselm presided conscientiously over his institutional responsibilities. At Bec, scholarship and administration walked hand in hand: it is no coincidence that so many of Anselm's pupils went on to positions of high responsibility in church and state, Bec becoming the Sandhurst of the Anglo-Norman church militant. On Lanfranc's death in 1089, Anselm appeared as his obvious successor to many, not least the monks at Canterbury who had already made him an honorary member of their community. William II was, however, in no hurry to fill the vacancy until, in March 1093, he fell seriously ill. It happened that Anselm was at court. In what appears to have been a coordinated ploy by some of William's lay advisers and the bishops, William was persuaded to appoint Anselm archbishop if he wished to recover. The advantages to both church and state of having a new primate, preferably in the Lanfranc mould, were obvious: leadership for the church; control for the state. Anselm regarded the prospect with horror: he protested his age; his loyalty to his vocation and monks at Bec; and, rather disingenuously, his lack of aptitude for secular affairs. He may also have been wary of the irascible and volatile temperament of the king. The courtiers, barons and bishops would have none of it. He was manhandled into the royal presence and the crozier forced into his clenched fist. As he put it, after his hurried consecration, 'you have yoked together in the plough the untamed bull and the old and feeble sheep'.

As archbishop, Anselm was by no means as inept as he pretended. By denying the validity of his initial appointment, he managed to negotiate terms with William for six months before finally doing homage and fealty to the king in September 1093. The central issue was property: Anselm accepted the archbishopric only after William had agreed that all lands held by Lanfranc in 1089 should be restored. Legalistic and plain-speaking, Anselm did not behave in a sheep-like manner. Relations with the king deteriorated as the two men found themselves incompatible and unable to reach agreement on anything without argument. Although the disputes concerned perceptions of royal and archiepiscopal rights, the essential conflict appears to have been personal and temperamental: a foul-mouthed, aggressive, self-confident king and a silver-tongued, prim and obstinate prelate. Events early in 1094 were typical. Anselm offered a gift of £500 to support William's projected campaign against his brother, Robert, in Normandy. When the king demanded more, Anselm withdrew the offer completely. Anselm continued to send out contradictory signals. He was willing to put the question of recognition of Pope Urban II, one of the conditions of his acceptance of the archbishopric the previous year, on one side, yet publicly condemned the vices at William's court; proposed a church council to discuss sexual morality; and challenged William's policy of holding abbeys vacant. The king was by turns angry and dismissive. The pattern continued the next year. Anselm was eager to receive his pallium from the pope in Rome, but this required recognition of Pope Urban II, rather than the anti-pope, Clement III, or, as William I and William II had preferred since 1085, neither. Anselm did not deny his fealty to William but placed more weight on his allegiance to Urban, given when abbot of Bec. The matter was discussed at a council at Rockingham in February 1095. The bishops, led by William of St Calais, bishop of Durham, tried to bully Anselm into accepting William's authority over papal recognition. There were threats of deposition. The barons, ironically, took Anselm's part. The deadlock was resolved by a royally initiated compromise with the help of a papal legate, Walter of Albano. William recognised Urban II; confirmed Anselm in office and favour (*i.e.* the king would refrain from harassment: anything more positive was out of the question). Anselm, faced with papal support for the king, had to accept traditional royal rights over the church. In return, he received the pallium the legate had brought.

Anselm's agreement to the compromise of 1095 suggests a more pragmatic strain than Eadmer would allow. Once the issue of principle was settled, Anselm fell in with royal policy, even to the extent of accepting the military command of Canterbury and eastern Kent in the face of a projected invasion by Robert Curthose. It is understandable that this episode was ignored by Eadmer. Conflict broke out, however, again initially on a secular matter. William was furious at what he considered to be unsuitable and poorly trained knights provided by Canterbury for his campaigns in Wales in 1097. For his part, Anselm was increasingly angered by William's refusal to countenance a church council to reform morals. In the fact of royal hostility, Anselm insisted on being allowed to appeal to Rome. William took this as braking the 1095 agreement and presented Anselm with a choice: either swear to abide by English customs and never again appeal to the pope or go into exile. Anselm, almost happily, chose the latter, hoping perhaps that, once at Rome, he could resign his office.

What was at stake between Anselm and William II was neither the prerogatives of the newly reformed papacy, nor the freedom of the English church from secular tyranny. At issue were the rights of the see of Canterbury regarding lands, political influence, moral authority and secular obligations. Above all, perhaps, at the heart of the problem was Anselm, a tender conscience backed by an adamantine will. Unlike Becket, however, Anselm never identified his own cause with that of the church as a whole. His exile was solitary — no bishop shared it — and personal. In many areas, he had no quarrel with traditional practices and fully acknowledged the rights of the king, except where they conflicted with his principles or his see's interests. Long taken as a champion of the papal side in the Investiture Contest between lay control and ecclesiastical independence, Anselm was nothing of the sort. His acts were political, but his vision was not. He did not see himself as belonging to any terrestrial party.

If Anselm hoped to be relieved of his duties by the pope he was disappointed. His presence added lustre to the increasingly self-confident papal curia. In 1098, at the council of Bari, he debated the nature of the Procession of the Holy Ghost with Greek theologians and was present at the Council of Rome in April 1099 when the most extreme decrees prohibiting lay investitute were promulgated. This was a ticklish issue for Anselm, as he himself had been invested with the staff of office, if not the ring, and had sworn homage and fealty to the king, both of which were condemned at Rome.

Anselm returned to England after the death of William II in 1100. Soon he was in difficulties again. Acting in accordance with the Rome decrees of 1099, he refused to pay homage to the new king, Henry I, for his Canterbury lands, even though, as the king insisted, it was customary. This time, the problem was not Anselm's personal fastidiousness, but his loyalty to the pope. On one level, Anselm worked well with King Henry I. He officiated at the king's marriage in 1100; he was allowed to hold his reforming council at London in 1102; and, while the pope was considering his case, permitted Henry to invest bishops. There was not the personal bitterness with Henry as there had been with his brother. Unfortunately, circumstances and Anselm's logic made a compromise difficult to broker. It was his obedience to Rome, not any hostility to lay investiture, which conditioned his actions. As a Benedictine monk, obedience was central to his understanding of the religious life. For Pope Paschal II (1099-1118), any retreat from the 1099 decrees would weaken his position in the struggle against the German king, yet he was reluctant to alienate Henry I. For Henry, abandoning control of episcopal appointments could, quite literally, put his power over England at risk, so great were ecclesiastical land holdings. For Paschal and Henry, the issue was political; for Anselm it was of principle. The final compromise agreed at Bec (1106) and confirmed in London (1107) outlawed lay investite while allowing episcopal homage. Additionally, and for the king, crucially, royal approval of elections was permitted. Anselm was perfectly content with this. Free elections had never held much appeal to him: he had been chosen by the king and confirmed by personal agreement between them. He had, more or less, chosen his successor at Bec. For Anselm, good men not good procedures were what mattered. Thus fealty and homage were permissible, as neither contradicted the priestly office, whereas lay investiture did: how could a layman grant a cure of souls? Anselm's final years were marked by close co-operation with the king, for example over the creation of the diocese of Ely (1109). His identification with his see, a dominant *leitmotif* of his episcopate, he retained to the end. One of his last public acts was to insist that the archbishop-elect of York acknowledge the supremacy of Canterbury. Discipline and obedience were the hallmarks of Anselm as thinker and monk. What made him a controversial archbishop was that he had his own often highly individual scale of allegiances. Above all was his conception of what he owed to God. This high idealism proved inconvenient to friends and foes alike.

As archbishop, Anselm cannot be judged a great success. His obstinacy had engineered a change in procedure, without altering the substance of the political relationship between church and state. His absences had done little to protect and nurture the interests of the monks at Canterbury, as some of them noted. His influence on affairs was personal. According to Eadmer, a man of lively wit and robust conversation, his clarity of mind impressed, exasperated or annoyed all who encountered him. He possessed to a fault the donnish habit of discovering intractable problems of principle behind apparently innocent situations. Yet — another donnish fad — he found public affairs irresistible. He may not have been a willing politician; he certainly was not an effective one. But Eadmer fails to persuade when he has his hero declare 'I have shunned all wordly business': God's purpose for the military commander of Canterbury in 1095 was more complicated than that.

What is unquestionable is his stature as a theologian, the more remarkable as some of his greatest works were composed amidst the distractions of abbatial and archiepiscopal affairs. His thought revolved around the ontological proof of God and His nature *i.e.* because it is impossible to conceive of that which does not exist, the idea of a perfect God must, of necessity, imply the existence of such a God, as is argued in the *Monologion* (1077). This is inductive, taking the conclusion, 'I believe in God', and working back to the proof of the reality of the statement. In the *Proslogion* (1078), he demonstrates the same point from a different, deductive direction, beginning with the statement 'there is no God' which, Anselm argued, is self-contradictory as it implies the idea of a God as a being 'than whom no greater can be conceived'. Thus, Anselm did more than re-affirm God's existence according to Christian texts: he relied on reason and logic. In *Cur Deus Homo* (*c*.1095-98), he went further. To show that the claims of Christianity were specifically valid, consistent and without flaw, he demonstrated the necessity of the Incarnation as the only means whereby Man's debt to God could be discharged and Man redeemed. Throughout his theological works there runs a clear line of concise reason and precise argument, supported by a lucid Latin style. Anselm was no free-thinking rationalist. He wrote that men might obey the teachings of the Church. Reason depended on faith, not *vice versa*: 'I do not seek to understand that I may believe, but I believe that I may understand, for this also I believe, that unless I believe I shall not understand'.

But there was another side to Anselm. As a monk at Bec, he showed an intense devotion to Christ, the Virgin Mary, saints and other monks. His *Prayers and Meditations* and his friendships with pupils reveal a passionate, occasionally tortured nature, the human emotion which drove him to explain the mystery of God to his fellow men. His personality comes down the centuries, that of a lively, charming, considerate, but intellectually tough, uncompromising and rather intimidating tutor of the best sort, a friend to his pupils rather than their inquisitor. His intellectual reputation has never dimmed. He was in Dante's *Paradiso* among 'the spirits of light and power in the sphere of the sun'. His contemporaries, particularly at Canterbury and at court, were perhaps somewhat more equivocal in their reactions. Eadmer, to still criticism, had to append lists of his miracles to his biography in the 1120s. Anselm was not the stuff of martyrs; to many he must have seemed a nuisance. It is intriguing that his canonisation had to wait until 1494 and the rather unlikely auspices of the Borgia pope, Alexander VI.

R. W. Southern, *St Anselm*, 1963.

Eadmer, *Life of St Anselm,* ed. & trans. R. W. Southern, 1962.

RANULF FLAMBARD (*c*.1060-1128; bishop of Durham 1099-1128) was one of the most powerful and controversial figures of the reign of William II. His actions and personality excited resentment, admiration and anecdote. His character and reputation are suggested by his nickname, 'Flambard': flamboyant, fiery, glittering, scorching, prompting William of Malmesbury's pun, 'a torch of iniquity'; definitely dangerous to know if he were against you, but a generous benefactor to family and friends. His work for William Rufus earned him the obloquy of ecclesiastical commentators but his monks at Durham remembered him with affection. The remarkable attention lavished on him by contemporary writers suggests that Ranulf was not easy to ignore. Ranulf is one of the few people of his generation (barring saints) for whose personality there is plentiful and plausible evidence. From the excavation of his tomb, it is possible to know what he chose for his episcopal staff and ring and even what he looked like. Five foot nine tall, he had a short, broad head, a strong jaw and sloping forehead: witnesses thought him good-looking.

The son of Thurstin, an obscure parish priest in the diocese of Bayeux, Ranulf was probably introduced to the royal court by Odo of Bayeux. By 1086, as well as a royal chaplain, he had become keeper of the king's seal, working under Maurice the Chancellor. Already Ranulf had amassed lands, houses and churches across southern England worth about £30. For Ranulf, royal employment was always a means to profit. It is characteristic that when Maurice, now bishop of London, reputedly denied him a deanery, Ranulf looked elsewhere for patronage. Precisely what tasks he performed for William I is unclear, but it is likely he was involved in producing and executing royal writs, and hence in legal business and finance. By 1087 he may have had experience in what became one of his specialities, the administration of vacant churches on behalf of the crown.

After 1087 Ranulf rose rapidly in the household of the new king. The two men were of a similar age; neither, in the words of R. W. Southern, 'can be called respectable'; they shared a certain exuberant enjoyment of life. Although Ranulf was always a servant, and their relationship never reached the intimacy of that between Henry II and Becket, they got on well. In his unceasing search for money and the exploitation of royal rights, Rufus had, in Ranulf, an agent as predatory as himself.

Within the royal household, although never holding any office other than royal chaplain, Ranulf soon emerged as a key administrator. Regularly witnessing royal writs, in 1093 his name appeared immediately after the bishops and chancellor; in 1096, his name headed the witnesses to a writ ordering tenants of Worcester to pay a relief to the king. It may be no coincidence that these years saw an increased use of the writ for communicating royal orders to the localities, there being a substantial fine of £10 imposed for non-compliance. Throughout William II's reign, Ranulf witnessed more writs than anybody else (35), but he acted as part of a team of officials, including the grand curial bishops William of St. Calais of Durham and Walkelin of Winchester, and the household servants: the chancellors William Giffard and Robert Bloet; the stewards Eudo and Haimo; and Urse d'Abitot. Ranulf's dominance was, perhaps, exaggerated by later chroniclers searching for a scapegoat for Rufus's harsh ecclesiastical exactions, but Ranulf did emerge in the 1090s as the king's leading man of business. In part, this was because he was unafraid to appear in public on his master's behalf, as in 1093 when he appeared at Canterbury to serve a writ on Anselm on the very day of the archbishop's enthronement. Ranulf was also able to roam across a wide area of royal administration, unhampered by any formal designated duties, when, in 1097-99, he acted as one of the regents left in England during the king's absences.

Contemporaries were in no doubt about his power, calling him 'justiciar' and *totius regni procurator*, titles later applied to Henry I's chief minister, Roger of Salisbury. The two areas beyond the royal household in which Ranulf was most active were finance and the law, both liable to provoke hostility and publicity in equal measure. Although Orderic Vitalis portrayed Ranulf as measuring England with a rope in his eagerness to reassess royal dues, most evidence comes from the exploitation of existing feudal incidents, such as reliefs, and the exploitation of the church. As bishops and abbots technically were tenants-in-chief of the king, during vacancies the crown had the right to administer the church's lands. That this was profitable, and that William to some extent manipulated his rights by delaying appointments, was widely recognised, even if exaggerated, especially when compared to the similarly lucrative secular custodies which, affecting lay lordships, failed to incite the chroniclers' corporate wrath. Ranulf was appointed administrator of Ely Abbey possibly by William I. During Rufus's reign he was involved in the custody of Ramsey; New Minster, Winchester; Christ Church, Canterbury; and the bishopric of Worcester in 1095. Between 1096 and 1099, Ranulf made £300pa as custodian of the see of Durham. Other abbeys which fell under Ranulf's frankly commercial control included Thorney, where he ordered a re-assessment of services (presumably upwards), and Hyde Abbey which he sold to a close associate, Herbert Losinga, in 1090. It is small wonder that Ranulf was seen by monkish chroniclers as a rapacious asset-stripper.

Called by some the king's *placitator* or advocate, Ranulf was equally heavily engaged in the endless litigation involving land rights and jurisdiction. Whatever else, the Norman Conquest and subsequent land settlement had left uncertainty and, as Domesday revealed, a host of disputes, many involving the crown. Part of Ranulf's job was to travel the realm in pursuit of royal claims. This line of business took Ranulf to Canterbury in 1093 and Bury St Edmunds in 1095; in 1096, he toured Devon and Cornwall asserting royal rights to lands in a manner which looked back to the circuits of Odo of Bayeux under the Conqueror and forward to the itinerant justices of Henry I and Henry II. Ranulf's handling of suits demonstrated that medieval royal justice usually meant deciding cases in favour of the crown, its friends and its allies. Justice was neither neutral nor blind. As with ecclesiastical and secular custodies, the currency of civil law was property; so were the profits, to king, to Ranulf and to his associates. Ranulf, as the king's representative, could intimidate or favour litigants.

It is hardly surprising that such a vigorous royal servant should be feared. However, he was resented because he was a *parvenu* who lined his own pockets. Whether or not in 1094 he took a cut of the money he received from the fyrd of Hastings in lieu of military service, he certainly exploited his custodies and amassed a fortune in lands, revenues and ecclesiastical preferment. Archbishop Anselm called Ranulf a prince of publicans, implying that he exploited royal taxes for his own advantage. By the late 1090s, Ranulf enjoyed a string of lucrative benefices across southern England, as well as canonries at Salisbury, London and Lincoln. These last perhaps indicate a network of old government hands with whom Ranulf had worked, including the three former royal chancellors, Bishops Osmund of Salisbury, Maurice of London and Bloet of Lincoln. Ranulf also took care of his family, including his own sons, his brothers and nephews for whom he worked hard, and with some success, to place throughout the Anglo-Norman church. However, the gravy train of government service had a precise destination. Hitherto wholly dependent on royal favour, in 1099 Ranulf bought himself independent power and position with £1,000 for the bishopric of Durham. The *arriviste* had arrived.

Just as suddenly, Ranulf's career as royal minister was ended with the death of his master on 2 August 1100. Within a fortnight, Ranulf was arrested, deprived of his bishopric and sent to the Tower of London, earning himself the distinction of being the first political prisoner to be incarcerated there. His fall was primarily symbolic. In tune with his coronation Charter of Liberties, Henry I was trying to distinguish his regime from that of his predecessor in order to garner the widest support for his coup. Ranulf, more than any of Henry's subsequent favourites, a man 'raised from the dust', was expendable, whereas, for example, his former boss, Maurice of London, or Rufus's last chancellor, William Giffard, were not, and were received into Henry's favour. Ranulf's reaction to adversity showed his mettle. In February 1101 he escaped from the Tower (later romancers said by rope) and placed his services at the disposal of Robert Curthose in Normandy in attempting to unseat Henry from the English throne. Ranulf may have acted as one of Curthose's leading advisers for the invasion of England in 1101 which led to the inconclusive Treaty of Alton, but was probably unimpressed by the quality of his new master. Once peace had been agreed, there was a reconciliation with Henry which restored Ranulf's bishopric and his English lands. An unspoken condition seems to have been that Ranulf stayed in Normandy as a double-agent for Henry in the methodical campaign to annexe the duchy. He visited his see only occasionally, as in 1104 for the translation of relics of SS Cuthbert and Bede, despite his apparent doubts as to their authenticity. Meanwhile, he exercised his energies in administering the diocese of Lisieux, which he attempted to convert into a family sinecure, first for his brother, then his son.

After 1106, and the successful conquest of Normandy by Henry I, Ranulf returned to Durham for good. No longer the king's protégé, materially in reduced circumstances, Ranulf set about organising the monastic priory at Durham which his predecessor, William of St Calais, had founded. Inevitably, as in most medieval cathedrals, there were disputes between bishop and chapter over money, in this instance over the income from priory lands to be used to pay for the building of the great new cathedral church. The row emphasised the straitened circumstances of the northern diocese. The idea of the wordly former civil servant cloistered with his monks inevitably gave rise to ribald stories. On one occasion it was alleged the bishop provided a lavish meal of food normally forbidden the monks served by waitresses in tight fitting clothes; Ranulf sat back watching the brothers' surreptitious glances at the women and chiding them for their hypocrisy. In fact Ranulf was generous to his monks and relations were normally good. Ranulf's business acumen brought stability to Durham's finances; he attracted scholars to his household, including the future archbishop of Canterbury, William of Corbeil. He was a friend and benefactor of the influential and respected local hermit, Godric of Finchale. In Durham and the surrounding area, Ranulf was remembered with affection. There is a flattering portrait of him in a later twelfth century *Life* of St Godric by one Durham monk; another recalled: 'that was our golden age, under Ranulf our bishop'.

That Ranulf was heartily disliked by many cannot be denied. Yet hatred and condemnation were often tinged with respect, as in the story of his escape from kidnap and attempted murder by Thames pirates when keeper of the king's seal or in the account of his daring escape from the Tower. He lived life to the full. Handsome, intelligent, witty, he was an attractive figure, fond of clothes, food, drink and sex. His attempted seduction and failed rape of his wife's niece Theodora in 1114 has become notorious because his intended victim later became the well-known hermit, Christina of Markyate. Yet after he had become a bishop he provided for his wife Aelfgifu by respectably marrying her off to a prosperous man in Huntingdon. He neglected neither her nor his children. In the eleventh century, for able children of humble parents like Ranulf, the only hope of advancement lay either in the church or in especial skill at martial butchery. Inevitably religious vocations could be affected or strained. Yet in all the calumny heaped on Ranulf, nobody accused him of hypocrisy, for which he was perhaps too honest, too aware of human weaknesses, both excellent credentials for his role as royal extortioner. Ranulf's sins were venal and venial. To compensate for social insecurity he sought to establish a dynasty. He understood that to be great a man had to be generous, as his household and monks as well as his family discovered. He fascinated even those whom he terrorized. The monk Simeon of Durham, who knew him, summed up his quality: 'impatient of leisure, he went on from labour to labour, thinking nothing done unless new enterprises pressed on the heels of those already accomplished'. To this restless energy was allied acute intelligence and organising genius. His career had a wider significance than that of Rufus's henchman. Again in the words of Southern, 'the great line of administrators who fashioned and finally destroyed the medieval system of government in England begins with Flambard'.

R. W. Southern, *Medieval Humanism*, 1970.
F. Barlow, *William Rufus*, 1983.

ROBERT, nicknamed **CURTHOSE** (*c.*1053-1134; duke of Normandy 1087-1106) twice failed to make good his claim to the English throne. The eldest son of William the Conqueror, he had been designated count of Maine in 1063 and duke of Normandy in 1077-8. Impatient for power and easily led by dissident Norman barons, from 1078 he persistently rebelled against his father. Nevertheless, on his deathbed, William confirmed Robert's succession in Normandy, leaving England to his more capable son William Rufus. Between 1087 and 1088, Robert and his allies made a concerted but unsuccessful bid to wrest

England from his brother. Thereafter, his rule in Normandy was constantly undermined by William and his youngest brother Henry. In 1096, having mortgaged his duchy to William for 10,000 marks, he departed on the First Crusade, during which he won for himself glittering fame. On his return he found William dead and Henry installed in England. Once again, his invasion of England failed, terms being agreed at Alton in 1101. In 1106, Henry exploited his growing political advantage in Normandy, defeating and capturing Robert at the battle of Tinchebrai. Thereafter, Henry held his brother in comfortable but close confinement. It was said that Henry mitigated the harsh treatment usually meted out to his political prisoners in deference to Robert's status as a former crusader. Most of Robert's captivity was spent in Cardiff Castle where, according to tradition, he learnt Welsh and composed at least one poem, on a tree he could see from the window of his cell. His threat to Henry I was maintained by his son, William Clito (d.1128). Robert was a poor ruler, vain and malleable. He was, however, a fine warrior, who once wounded his own father in battle at Gerberoi (1079) and earned such fame on crusade that even in his lifetime chroniclers invented improbable deeds of valour and spread the false story that he had been offered the crown of Jerusalem in 1099. His legendary deeds were enshrined in stained glass by Abbot Suger at St Denis. As an effective, disciplined ruler, Robert was a failure, but as a military leader and companion, he won renown, a paradox central to many political tensions of the period.

C. W. David, *Robert Curthose,* 1920.

ADELA OF BLOIS (?1062-1137) was a daughter of William I and his wife,, Matilda of Flanders, and the mother of King Stephen (king of England 1135-1153). In 1080 she married Stephen, count of Blois and Chartres. She appears to have played an active role in the administration of her husband's lands, regularly witnessing his charters. A noted bluestocking, among her friends were two of the leading intellectuals of her day, the canonist Ivo of Chartres and Anselm. Having inherited her father's appetite and ability to rule, Adela persuaded her popular but weak-willed husband to join the First Crusade in 1096, assuming the regency of his counties herself. Her role was not nominal, Hildebert, bishop of Le Mans commenting that 'in you . . . is all that is needed to steer the ship of state'. Her husband was less fortunate. Although in charge of the central funds of the Crusade, Stephen deserted at Antioch in 1098, understandably enough in the face of overwhelming odds. Unfortunately for his reputation, the crusaders survived and succeeded in capturing Jerusalem in 1099. According to Orderic Vitalis, Adela was unamused by a disgraced husband, 'mocked by almost everyone'. She waged a sustained campaign of bullying and moral blackmail that extended into their bedroom where, between intercourse, she would urge Stephen to think of his reputation and return to the Holy Land. In the end, her nagging worked and Stephen departed East once more in 1101, to meet a satisfactorily noble death at Ramlah the following year. No longer a coward's wife but more congenially a hero's widow, Adela continued to rule Blois-Chartres until 1107 when she formally transferred authority to her son Theobald. Nevertheless, she maintained her network of active political contacts, not least with her brother, Henry I, who lavished patronage on another son, Stephen, and appointed a third, Henry, bishop of Winchester, the richest see in England. Adela retired in 1120 to the abbey of Marcigny-sur-Loire, where she died in 1137. By all accounts a forceful personality, Adela's qualities were not uncommon among women aristocrats, although more often they found an outlet in the running of nunneries. Adela's secular career, as *de facto* ruler of one of the most powerful principalities of northern France for more than a decade, is exceptional, testimony to the power of breeding as well as to her own determination. Although married to a French count and living to see a son crowned king of England, she significantly chose to be buried beside her mother at Caen under an inscription 'Adela, filia regis'. She was always the Conqueror's daughter.

WALTER TIREL III (*fl.*1100), lord of Poix, was notorious in the early twelfth century as the man who shot dead William II king of England during a deer hunt in the New Forest on 2 August 1100. His repeated and strenuous denials of responsibility made under oath to Abbot Suger of St Denis, chief minister of Louis VI of France, suggest that public infamy was as intrusive and tenacious as it is today. Castellan of Pontoise in the strategically important Vexin between Normandy and the lands of the king of France and related by marriage to the powerful Anglo-Norman Clare dynasty, Walter Tirel received lands from William I and was a close friend of William II. All contemporary accounts attribute William's death to a stray arrow, a hunting accident. Most, including William of Malmesbury, the Worcester chronicler and Orderic Vitalis, name Walter Tirel as the unwitting culprit. It seems likely that he shot the arrow that missed a deer and killed the king. He certainly fled the scene immediately afterwards. Some modern conspiracy theorists have used this to support their reconstruction of a plot hatched by the Clares and William's brother, Henry. It is true that Henry was present on the fatal hunt and grasped the opportunity to sieze the throne. For him, the circumstances and timing of his brother's death were convenient, but probably fortuitous. William Rufus was not the first to die by accident in the New Forest. His brother Richard had been killed hunting there c.1070 and a nephew, also called Richard, had met a fate eerily similar to the king's in May 1100. Walter Tirel was not a scapegoat or a fall-guy. Subsequently, he neither suffered retribution nor enjoyed preferment. But to kill a king, even by accident, was an uncomfortable burden for a boon-companion to bear. As his confessions demonstrated, Walter Tirel was less concerned with the schemes of men than with the opinion of his peers and the designs of God.

HENRY I (1068-1135; king of England 1100-1135) was one of the most effective and successful of all English monarchs. It is no coincidence that he was also one of the most ruthless, violent and vicious. According to Henry of Huntingdon, writing after his death, his public virtues of wisdom, military success and wealth were complemented by private vices of greed, cruelty and lust. A demanding patron and a frightening enemy, Henry constructed a royal dominance over England that was more than personal; one that was recalled with awe, respect and, in the civil war under his successor, even nostalgia; one that provided the basis in propaganda and in fact for the rule of his grandson,

Henry II. The cost of Henry's achievement was great: to the noble houses he ruined; to the dynastic rivals he destroyed; to the subjects, lay and clerical, he taxed with unsurpassed ferocity; and to himself. He was as stern and cruel as his father, the Conqueror; as energetic as his brother Rufus; but he was more suspicious of those around him than either. More than one contemporary chronicler recorded Henry's fearfulness and acute anxiety: fear of those whom he had made suffer for his ambition; anxiety lest his success turn to ashes. However harsh his actions and self-confidently lordly his official pronouncements, Henry appears to have understood the cost of success and the fragility of his achievement. He suffered from nightmares and at times feared being murdered in his own bed.

Henry's career cannot be viewed solely in an English perspective. The unifying factor of his life was his ambition to secure for himself as much of his father's Anglo-Norman inheritance as possible. Between 1087 and 1100, this meant balancing his interests between his competitive elder brothers Duke Robert of Normandy and King William of England. On Rufus's death, it required a determined and unending struggle to establish control and authority in England, then Normandy against rival claims and baronial hostility. The pursuit of security in France led to long absences from his kingdom; just over 50% of his entire reign: from the Summer of 1111 to his death at the end of 1135, the proportion rose to 67%. The effect on England, however, was direct through the king's demand for men and especially money to finance his diplomacy and wars. These requirements were the engines which drove the notable developments in English government organisation, financial management and legal administration which marked Henry's reign.

The fourth surviving son of Wiliam the Conqueror, although the only one born after 1066 (thus *porphyrogenitus*, a point emphasised in his later propaganda), Henry may have been intended for the church. There is some evidence that he understood Latin. It is unlikely, however, that he could write, the nickname 'Beauclerc' being a thirteenth century invention. The eulogising William of Malmesbury claimed Henry had been introduced to the liberal arts when young and had obtained learning 'by snatches', although the chronicler admits that the king 'never read much in public and displayed his skills sparingly'. The death of his second son, Richard, in 1075 may have persuaded the Conqueror to keep his youngest son available for secular lordship. Even so, the old king declined to grant him land (Rufus was similarly denied). On his deathbed, when he disposed of Normandy to Robert and England to William Rufus, the Conqueror bequeathed Henry the substantial sum of £5,000, but no property. (This memory may have prompted Henry, on his own deathbed forty-eight years later, to leave his son, Robert of Gloucester, an even greater sum of money.) Henry had to make his own way. In the 1090s the opportunities lay in Normandy where Henry built up a significant lordship in the west of the duchy. Henry's prospects were determined by his relations with his brothers. In 1091, when they combined against him, he was temporarily deprived of the Cotentin, Avranches and Mont-St-Michel. From 1092, however, Henry, now established at Domfront, threw in his lot with Rufus in his attempts to increase his power in the duchy between 1093 and 1096. After Robert mortgaged the duchy to Rufus to pay for his crusade in 1096, Henry was rewarded with Coutances and Bayeux. Thereafter Henry appears loyal to Rufus, an intimate at his court. His choice was dramatically vindicated. He was in the New Forest with the royal hunting party on 2 August 1100 when Rufus was fatally wounded. Because he was present, Henry was able to seize the opportunity and the crown.

Although not the most glorious passage of Henry's life, the 1090s were formative. Forced to live off his wits as much as his birth, Henry gained experience of war, diplomacy and the subtler political arts of managing men, winning people to his cause, exploiting the weaknesses of rivals and calculating his own long-term advantage. He learned patience and, in the performance of his brother Robert, saw how not to rule. He could have plotted against Rufus after 1096; he could have sought his fortune elsewhere. He chose loyalty and gained a kingdom. The combination of patience and decisive action, demonstrated in his *coup* of 1100, were characteristic of Henry's later rule. The 1090s also provided Henry with practical lessons in lordship. It is no chance that many of Henry's advisers when king originated in his western Norman lands and neighbouring Brittany including Brian

Henry I dreaming of threats from peasants,
knights, clerics and a storm at sea
(From the Chronicle of John of Worcester *c.*1140)

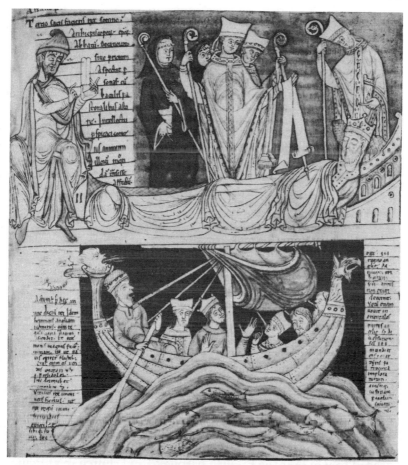

FitzCount; Richard de Redvers; Geoffrey de Clinton and Roger of Salisbury. Such men established and maintained Henry's power in England. Their support for him and his patronage of them probably stemmed from the contacts established during his apprenticeship in Normandy in the 1090s. However, familiarity and sentiment never swayed Henry's choice of servants: even the closest and most highly favoured, such as Geoffrey de Clinton, could be dismissed. Of all his qualities as ruler, one of the most important was his skill in picking men of ability to serve him. Young knights flocked to his court to bask in his hospitality, reputation and employment. For all his many disagreeable traits, Henry had a capacity for affection. Richard de Redvers (d.1107) was a close friend; Henry seems to have been genuinely fond of his nephew Stephen of Blois; and he was an extremely indulgent guardian of the Beaumont twins Waleran and Robert, sons of his chief minister Robert of Meulan (d.1118). Friendship and generosity, the creation of a loyal, privileged *familia* were not simply aspects of a gregarious personality; they were essential tools of government.

The speed with which Henry grabbed the English throne in August 1100 has prompted some historians to suggest there was a conspiracy to kill Rufus. There is no real evidence for this beyond the circumstantial. It was, however, a piece of massive good fortune for Henry, coming as it did just before Robert Curthose had returned to Normandy after the First Crusade. In his exploitation of Rufus's death, Henry displayed the energy, decisiveness, and a precise understanding of where power lay and how to obtain it which subsequently marked his reign. Within hours of the arrow striking Rufus, Henry had secured control of the royal treasury in nearby Winchester; within three days he had been crowned king of the English at Westminster (Sunday, 5 August). Speed was of the essence. Henry acted before a Robertine faction could form. He did not wait until Archbishop Thomas of York could officiate at his coronation, still less for the exiled Archbishop Anselm. Instead he was anointed by his father's former chancellor, Maurice, bishop of London. Control of the royal treasure and hallowing by Holy Oil provided only the basis for Henry's assumption of power. He needed to win over the English baronage and church in anticipation of a challenge from Curthose. He immediately issued a manifesto, later known as his Coronation Charter, in which he promised not to tax vacant churches; to avoid arbitrary alterations to rules governing baronial inheritance and marriages; to exempt lesser royal tenants from the geld and other non-military levies. Such concessions may have depressed royal income by as much as a third; a high but necessary price for political support. However, Henry did not abandon royal rights over the Forests and, in a number of clauses, he significantly instructed his barons to treat their tenants as he treated them and warned that anyone guilty of disseisin during the interregnum (2-5 August) was liable to pay a penalty to the king regardless of whether the land taken was royal or not. Designed to curry favour with those who had suffered from Rufus's rapacity, while at the same time reassuring the royal administration, in its implicit guarantees of the liberties of all royal tenants and sub-tenants it was recalled as a model by the framers of Magna Carta in 1215. In 1100, it was one part of Henry's consolidation of power. Another sop to political opinion was the arrest and detention in the Tower of Rufus's notorious leading adviser, Ranulf Flambard. Others in Rufus's administration were retained, such as the chancellor, William Giffard. Henry was adept at political symbolism.

His marriage, in November 1100, to Edith (also known as Matilda c.1080-1118), daughter of Malcolm III of Scotland, was symbolic and practical. When he became king Henry was unmarried with no legitimate children: he and his adherents needed the security of a clear succession as soon as possible. The choice of Edith was, in English terms, imaginative. Something of a bluestocking, through her mother, Queen Margaret, she was the great-granddaughter of King Edmund Ironsides (d.1016), great-great niece of King Edward the Confessor (d.1066), and niece of Edgar Atheling, who had claimed the throne after Hastings. The marriage served a triple function for Henry. It promised heirs; it united the new dynasty with the old; and it secured the Scottish frontier and thus helped solve the perennial problem of controlling the north, which Henry visited only once, in 1122. It created, therefore, a potential dynastic balance, Anglo-Norman-Scottish, to measure against candidates to the English throne from among William I's other son and grandsons. The association with the Old English kings was celebrated by English writers, including William of Malmesbury whom Queen Edith/Matilda encouraged to write his *Gesta Regum Anglorum*. Some of the grander Anglo-Norman barons were less impressed, contemptuously referring to the royal couple as 'Godric and Godgifu', no better than English yokels. Whatever else, the marriage was a dynastic success; two surviving children were born, Matilda (1102) and, crucially for Henry's hopes, William (1103). However, marriage did little to make Henry monogamous. In his efforts to excuse Henry's sexual appetite, William of Malmesbury claimed that the king's fornication was driven not by lust but by desire for children. If for nothing else, Henry was notorious for the number of his bastards, at least twenty, nine sons and eleven daughters. Unlike his great-grandson King John, Henry prudently did not prey on the wives and daughters of his barons. Most of his known mistresses came from the lesser nobility, with the exception of the colourful Nest, 'the Helen of Wales', daughter of Rhys ap Tewdwr, prince of South Wales.

The political problems confronting Henry were focussed on establishing his power in England; the annexation and subsequent defence of Normandy; and securing the succession for his son, William, then, after the White Ship disaster in 1120, his daughter, Matilda. At no stage in his reign could Henry rest; although England after 1102 was quiescent, his hold on Normandy was never wholly unchallenged. Henry's achievements came from a shrewd combination of diplomacy and war. Robert Curthose's invasion of England was bought off at the treaty of Alton in 1101. Henry's counter-attack on Normandy was gradually prepared by winning Norman allies (1104-6), before the decisive military victory at Tinchebrai in 1106. His control of the duchy was threatened by Curthose's son, William Clito and his followers (to 1128); by the hostility of Louis VI of France and, until 1128, Fulk, count of Anjou; and by unreconciled Norman barons, notably Robert of Belleme (to 1111) and Amaury de Montfort. There were serious revolts on behalf of Clito 1116-1120 and 1123-4. The Angevin threat only receded through the treaties and marriage alliances of 1120 and 1128, although at the very end of his reign Henry had to resist attacks on the duchy by his impatient son-in-law, Geoffrey of Anjou. The king of France never ceased to fish in the troubled Anglo-Norman waters, even though Henry routed Louis at the pitched battle of Brémule in 1119. Throughout, Henry was forced to react rather than control.

Where Henry could influence events in his favour was with the church. As promised in his Coronation Charter, his fiscal demands fell less heavily on the church than had his brother's. Although he exploited episcopal vacancies without much scruple, he was eager to be cooperative. The church was the greatest single landowner after the king; it provided great scope for aristocratic patronage and for rewarding royal clerks. Henry sought reconciliation with Archbishop Anselm. The issue between them which led to Anselm's renewed exile (1102-7) was lay investiture not as a principle but as a sign of obedience to papal authority. Once agreement had been reached in 1106-7, which preserved royal influence on episcopal elections while honouring clerical scruples about lay interference, Henry worked closely with ecclesiastical leaders, for example over the creation of the see of Ely in 1108. Personally, Henry was a generous benefactor, especially to the Cluniacs and the Austin Canons. His own major foundation was Reading Abbey (1121), a Cluniac house lavishly endowed and richly built, where he was buried. His interest in the Austin Canons was confirmed in the founding of the see of Carlisle (1133). Henry's handling of the church was a model of firm but uncontroversial control, using techniques more pacific than required by his dealings with his secular magnates.

One of Henry's weapons was fear. One story had Henry, in 1090, personally hurling a Norman rebel called Conan to his death from the top of a tower in Rouen. His political violence was little less extreme: in 1106, he had his first cousin William of Mortain blinded; after the 1123-4 rebellion, he ordered three leading rebels to have their eyes put out, including the literary Luke de la Barre, whose main offence had been to mock Henry's appearance and habits in public: apparently Luke preferred to take his own life. Henry's treatment of his daughter Juliana and her children in 1118/9 was reputedly sadistic and barbaric, noted because beyond the normal currency of acceptable political retribution. In 1125, as punishment for debasing the coinage (not entirely their fault) Henry ordered all English moneyers to have their right hands cut off and to be castrated, one of the more extreme examples of a government finding a scapegoat for failed financial policy. Even if physical mutilation were avoided, Henry's opponents risked long imprisonment: Robert Curthose (1106-34) and Robert of Bellême (1111 to after 1130) died as prisoners; the blinded William of Mortain was held incarcerated even longer, from 1106 until after Henry's death, when, in 1140, he was allowed to enter the Cluniac monastery at Bermondsey instead. Even Waleran of Meulan, once Henry's spoilt and pre-cocious ward, was loaded with chains when imprisoned 1124-9 for his part in the 1123-4 rebellion.

In England, Henry made conspicuous loyalty the test of royal favour. Those suspected of sympathy for Curthose or other dis-loyalty were dealt with severely: the great Norman house of Grandmesnil was ruined in 1101; more spectacularly, Robert of Bellême and the Montgomeries were destroyed in a crucial trial of strength in 1102; in 1104, William of Mortain lost his English fiefs and was banished. The technique employed by Henry became almost standard: a charge to be answered in the royal court; a demand for the surrender of castles or other property; then, if these orders were resisted, the threat or reality of armed force leading to confiscation, banishment or worse. Henry was unafraid to use such methods to discipline former allies, such as Geoffrey de Clinton who was accused of treason in 1130. Such draconian techniques of political discipline proved highly effec-tive, but they were hardly new. As far back as the laws of Alfred in the late ninth century, disloyal English magnates had been liable to confiscation, exile or death.

As the effectiveness of such methods depended upon the king having sufficient baronial support, Henry had to reward those who remained faithful, such as the Beaumont brothers Robert of Meulan and Henry of Warwick. To replace those he ruined and to balance those who retained favour, Henry promoted newcom-ers to the higher ranks of the landed nobility, disparagingly and somewhat misleadingly described by Orderic Vitalis as 'men raised from the dust'. The result was a baronage, part derived from older families with provincial power, such as the Bigods in East Anglia, and part from a newer class of curial magnates who had risen through service to Henry, all secure only through royal authority. The currency of this royal power was patronage; its coin land. In his Coronation Charter Henry promised to abide by traditional rules of inheritance and marriage, but often neither were simple: families died out in the male line; there were more than one potential heir, minorities and wardships; and the increasing subdivision of fiefs and commercialisation of the land market gave wide scope for royal intervention in land suits and the disposal of estates even without political confiscation and property transfers. Possession of land was complemented by the enjoyment of rights, exemptions and liberties, some of which the king could influence directly. For example, the term of sheriffs' tenure was reduced over Henry's reign, which allowed for greater financial efficiency as well as political control. The almost frenetic insistence on discipline and royal authority signified both Henry's dominance and insecurity.

If his skills in managing the political nation were in most respects traditional Henry's contribution to royal administration and justice were more innovatory. Although good at delegation, Henry presided directly over his government. He heard the most important royal pleas; he confirmed existing charters and issued new ones; he gave orders to his officials in the localities. A flavour of Henry's style is found in a famous writ to his agents in Worcestershire c.1110: 'I order my county and hundred courts to sit where and when they sat in King Edward's time (*i.e.* pre-1066). I forbid my sheriff to make them sit anywhere else to suit some need of his. But I myself, whenever I wish, may have these courts summoned for my lordly needs at my will'. Even more than his administrative direction, Henry's policies determined how England was governed, especially the need for money. His return from France in 1109 seems to have sparked a period of administrative activity. In 1110, to meet the requirements of collecting the massive aid to renew a £500 money fief paid to the count of Flanders and the 10,000 marks dowry on his daughter Matilda's marriage to the German emperor Henry V, the royal accounting office was reorganised as the Exchequer. The king's absences gave unique prominence to his chief minister, Roger of Salisbury, *procurator regni* or justiciar. Roger's task as head of Henry's administration was to run the government on the king's behalf in Henry's frequent absences, represent royal justice and secure income. Whatever administrative reforms occurred in Henry's reign — or, indeed, any other — came about not through any spontaneous combustion of bureaucratic inventiveness but as pragmatic responses to the demands of the ruler. The government of England was the king's in the sense that it served his personal needs, domestic and public: *L'etat c'est lui*. However, in the process of providing for the king's needs there developed institutions of government — the

Exchequer or the Chancery — that operated independent of daily or direct royal scrutiny. In the development of distinct government departments, the reign of Henry I was of considerable significance.

The spur to change came in response to royal needs. However, the government's reaction to the crisis of 1123-4 also shows a continuing intelligent self-appraisal by the king and his advisers. During his regency (1123-6) Roger of Salisbury reduced the sheriffs' terms; established or extended the system of itinerant judges (justices-in-eyre); and punished the moneyers for debasing the coinage. Between 1128 and 1131, a thorough overhaul of the administration was effected. This last exercise may explain the unique survival of the 1130 Pipe Roll. A Pipe Roll recorded the money owed the Exchequer, the amounts paid in, the sums pardoned and any expenses incurred by the sheriffs in their duties. Omitted were money paid directly to the king and royal loans. Given the sophistication and detail of the 1130 Pipe Roll, it must be presumed not to have been the first since the Exchequer was created in c.1110. It may have been preserved because, as part of the administrative reforms, it recorded fully all outstanding arrears as well as current payments. This may explain the huge sums mentioned, larger than on any subsequent Pipe Roll until 1177. The 1130 Pipe Roll confirms the chroniclers' opinion that Henry was massively wealthy: £23,000 had been received; £5,000 were pardoned; expenditure was recorded as £1,500; and £39,000 remained owing. Small wonder that Orderic Vitalis fancifully thought Henry could leave 60,000 marks to Robert of Gloucester.

With his wealth, Henry was particularly remembered for his maintenance of law and order. He was easily identified with the 'Lion of Justice' in Geoffrey of Monmouth's prophecies of Merlin, written at the end of Henry's reign. Significantly, Geoffrey's Lion of Justice fought the French and taxed his subjects heavily. Justice itself was a source of income, through fines for example, as well as a sign and instrument of authority. As his Coronation Charter emphasised, justice was central both to Henry's self-image and his rule. In his reign, there was some attempt to codify and unify both criminal and civil law which, a generation after the Conquest, still divided into the law of the conquerors and the conquered, an untenable position as the two increasingly impinged on each other. By 1135 royal power of confiscation and fines had largely surplanted the older Anglo-Saxon system of compensatory payments. The Crown heard pleas on serious offences; on infringement of royal rights; on the king's role as feudal overlord; and, increasingly, on appeals from tenants and subtenants unable to obtain justice in private, seigneurial courts, usually on matters concerning title to or occupation of land. This last function was to provide the basis for the sweeping reforms of the administration of justice under Henry II. Although it is difficult to talk of the establishment of a recognised Common Law in England much before the end of the thirteenth century, some of the expedients under Henry I certainly presaged it.

The need to define what constituted the law was evident. The 1100 Coronation Charter referred to the laws of Henry's predecessors. To clarify what these may have been, accounts of the laws of Edward the Confessor and William the Conqueror were produced during Henry's reign as well as, c.1110, two collections of the Laws of Cnut. A synthesis of past and current theory and practice was attempted, probably by a royal justice, in the *Leges Henrici Primi* (1114/18) and the *Quadripartitus,* which included Anglo-Saxon laws. Such works show an awareness of the practical, judicial importance of determining agreed laws and an attempt, if only at a rarified literary level, to emphasize the image of kingship, what the *Leges Henrici* described as the *tremendum regie majestatis imperium,* the tremendous power of the royal majesty. Away from the heights of legal theory, however, when king or chronicler thought of law and order they were just as likely to think of the sort of justice meted out by the royal judge Ralph Basset at 'Hundehoge' in 1124 when he sentenced forty-four thieves to be hanged and six more to be blinded and castrated.

If the administrative and judicial institutions survived at least as models for future governments, Henry was only too aware that his own authority would die with him. With the passion of a usurper, Henry spent much of his reign trying to guarantee the succession to his territories for his children. In 1115, the Norman barons did homage to his son William; in 1116 the English tenants-in-chief recognised the prince as heir. In 1120, the marriage between William and the daughter of the count of Anjou was designed to provide diplomatic cover in case the king of France intervened on behalf of William Clito. All Henry's schemes, however, drowned with his son off Barfleur on the evening of 25 November 1120 when the White Ship foundered. Well might Henry now have had nightmares. The only remaining grandson of the Conqueror in the male line was William Clito, the implacably hostile son of Henry's elder brother Robert Curthose who was himself still languishing in prison in Cardiff castle. Other candidates included Henry's other nephews, the sons of his sister Adela of Blois, Stephen and Theobald (whose young son had been chosen to tell Henry the terrible news of the White Ship disaster, a task older and stronger men quailed at). Stephen had, before 1120, received substantial grants of English lands and had married the heiress to the county of Boulogne. But this did not signal that Henry wished to make him his heir. Instead, Henry tried to solve the problem by marrying again within two months Adela of Louvain. When it became evident that there would be no children from this marriage, Henry took the gamble of imposing his daughter Matilda, a widow since 1125, as his successor and marrying her to Geoffrey, son of Count Fulk of Anjou. There never had been a Queen Regnant in England, indeed the prevailing literary topos was distinctly hostile to women wielding political power (*e.g.* Asser's comments on Queen Eadburh of Wessex which were reproduced by William of Malmesbury). Moreover, the Angevin alliance proved widely unpopular in Normandy and, thus, with the greater Anglo-Norman magnates with estates on both sides of the Channel. Henry's predicament was not unique at the time. Both Alfonso VI of Castile and Baldwin II of Jerusalem designated daughters as their heirs, Urraca (1109) and Melisende (1131) respectively. In 1127, and again in 1131 and 1133, the English barons swore allegiance to Matilda who married Geoffrey in 1128. After the death of Clito in 1128, Henry sought to balance rivalry among potential claimants, Stephen and his eldest illegitimate son Robert of Gloucester, by rehabilitating the Beaumont twins. The pivot of Henry's plan was the birth in 1133 and 1134 of Matilda's sons, Henry (the future Henry II) and Geoffrey. Now Henry, apparently a doting grandfather, could see his dynasty's future: more importantly so could the Anglo-Norman barons on whom the succession in reality depended. In the event, Henry's fears were justified. Masterful in life, in death he was powerless.

The failure of Henry's succession plan which led to a civil war which almost destroyed his achievements may prompt questions about his judgement. Certainly, he was perhaps obstinately determined to retain for his heirs all that he had fought for so long to attain. It is difficult, however, to see that any alternative plan would have been any more assured of success. The succession of every monarch between 1066 and 1272, except Richard I's in 1189, was decided by force of arms. Against that political law of nature, Henry I could do little.

Henry was by no means uniformly successful. His two visits to Wales (in 1114 and 1121), for instance, achieved little. Although he reunited the Anglo-Norman realm of his father, he failed to resolve the tensions within Normandy. But if greatness is measured by the size of difficulties overcome, the complexity of problems solved and the constructive methods employed, then Henry has more than a slight claim to greatness. For contemporary ecclesiastical observers, Henry presented a dilemma. Henry of Huntingdon could not decide whether he was 'a tyrant or a true king'. It is inevitably difficult to know much, if any, of the inner personality of medieval kings. They can only be described through their actions. Like many powerful men, Henry attracted stories. From many of these, he emerges as cruel and selfish, distinctly unpleasant. Apart from his nightmares and fear of assassination, he was known to have worried about his health and retained a large number of doctors, including the Spaniard Pedro Alfonso. He was also an enthusiastic patron of hospitals. Of middle-height, broad-chested, stout, with dark hair, Henry could be cheerful: some nervous subjects feared his jocularity more than his sterner moods. Conventionally pious, his spirituality has been described by J. A. Green as being marked by 'almost morbid awareness of sin and repentence'. His intellect was distinguished by curiosity, in the law, in investigating his rights, even in the natural world; at Woodstock, Henry housed a menagerie of exotic animals. Determined, greedy for treasure, food and women, Henry leaves an abiding impression of energy, even in old age. It was entirely in character that his final illness came on him after a hard day's hunting and that his death was hastened by rejecting his doctor's advice by eating lampreys; according to Henry of Huntingdon, a surfeit.

J. A. Green, *The Government of England under Henry I*, 1986.

ROBERT OF MEULAN, LORD OF MEULAN and BEAUMONT, EARL OF LEICESTER (1046-1118), was the leading lay adviser to both William II and Henry I. Although in the course of a long public life he amassed extensive estates in England, Normandy and France, Robert was the nearest thing to a king's minister that contemporary circumstances allowed, the more remarkable as his successors as royal lay advisers — with the exception of his own son Robert of Leicester, justiciar to Henry II — tended to come from less exalted ranks of the nobility, men such as the justiciars Ranulf Glanvill, Geoffrey FitzPeter and Hubert de Burgh. Robert's career made a distinctive impression on contemporaries and affords a rare glimpse into how eleventh century politics worked.

The son of a prominent Norman magnate, Roger of Beaumont, Robert made his name by his deeds at his first battle, Hastings. Thereafter, during his father's lifetime, Robert sought his fortune in England. By 1087, he had become one of William I's active *curiales* and held land in England worth a significant but not spectacular £254. In the early 1080s he had inherited the county of Meulan from his maternal uncle but, despite succeeding to his father's Norman lordships a decade later, his interests and loyalties remained Anglo-Norman. Unusually, he faithfully supported all of the first three post-Conquest kings. After spending much of 1087-93 in France securing his inheritance, from 1093 he emerged as William Rufus's closest counsellor, playing a prominent role in the dispute with Anselm and the king's French campaigns.

On the sudden death of Rufus in August 1100, Robert smoothly transferred his allegiance to Henry I. For the last eighteen years of his life, Robert appears as the most frequent witness to the new king's charters, a reflection of his influence.

By 1107 when, perhaps in reward for his part in Henry's acquisition of Normandy, Robert was given the earldom of Leicester, he had become a major landowner in England as well as northern France, with estates especially extensive in the Midlands. While Roger of Salisbury ran the royal administration, centred upon the Treasury and Exchequer, Robert's influence was in politics, diplomacy and the law. Robert played a crucial role in furthering Henry's cause in Normandy 1103-6 and undermining that of the duke, Robert Curthose, with whom Robert of Meulan had long had strained relations. He continued to be closely involved in the dispute with Archbishop Anselm, his prominence recognised by Pope Paschal II who identified Robert by name for excommunication in 1105. However, Robert was instrumental in securing a compromise with Anselm, finally concluded at Bec in 1106, and in persuading Henry I to stick to the agreement, to moderate church taxes and restore church lands. In 1109, Robert 'with flattery, coaxing and apology' tried to persuade Archbishop Thomas of York to profess obedience to the see of Canterbury, an attempt repeated with Thomas's successor, Thurstan, in 1116.

As a significant Norman lord, wealthy French count and English earl, with experience of public affairs stretching back to the 1060s, Robert was well placed to further his own interests. He established an elaborate, almost quasi-regal administration for his English and continental lands: in England he had his own exchequer, in imitation of the new royal accounting office. At Leicester, he restored the Anglo-Saxon court of Portmanmote, a tribunal of twenty-four, to replace trial by combat. He insisted that his twin sons, Waleran and Robert, both of whom were to play leading political roles in the next generation, received good educations. He was tenacious of his own rights and lands. In 1111, in revenge for an attack on Meulan, he ravaged the French king's capital at Paris causing so much damage that the Ile de la Cité required extensive rebuilding. Ruthless in manipulating his position and the law to acquire new estates, on his deathbed he characteristically refused to restore any lands he had illegally seized. Robert's private life may not have been untroubled. He had married late (c.1096) Isabel of Vermandois who was alleged to have eloped with William of Warenne, whom she subsequently married, before Robert's death. As in contemporary Romances, so in life, infidelity and chivalry could be close companions.

Robert's interest in public affairs and desire to influence royal business, although personally enriching, was not solely self-seeking. To Robert was attributed Henry I's less aggressive, less ostentatious and more conciliatory tone of government, notably towards the church and in the delicate handling of the prickly Norman baronage. William of Malmesbury wrote of Robert as 'the persuader of peace, the dissuader of strife . . . urging his lord the king rigorously to enforce the law; and himself not only abiding by existing laws but proposing new ones'. Not the least of Robert's achievements may have been to temper Henry's notorious personal brutality. Orderic Vitalis, who may well have met Robert, attributed to him a remarkable political testament delivered to Henry I in 1101. This may stand as a blueprint for effective medieval political management which, even if the chronicler's invention, suggests what policies contemporaries associated with Robert.

'We . . . to whom the common utility is committed by Divine Providence, ought to seek after the safety of the kingdom and of the Church of God. Let our chief care be to triumph peacefully without the shedding of Christian blood, and so that our faithful people may live in the serenity of peace . . . Speak gently to all your knights; caress them all as a father does his children; soothe them with promises; grant whatever they might request and in this manner cleverly draw all to your favour . . . do not hesitate to make magnificent promises, as is fitting to royal munificence. It is better to give away a small portion of the kingdom than to lose both victory and life to a host of enemies. And when . . . we have come to the end of this business (withstanding the threat of Robert Curthose), we will suggest useful measures for recovering the demesnes usurped by rash deserters in time of war'.

It is worth noting that the 'useful measures' mentioned included accusations of treason, deprivation of patrimonies and forced exile. As with all successful medieval politicians, Robert of Meulan knew that violence and the threat of violence was the strongest supporter of conciliation.

S. N. Vaughn, *Anselm of Bec and Robert of Meulan*, 1985.

ROBERT OF BELLEME, EARL OF SHREWSBURY (1052/6-
c.1130) was one of the most powerful Anglo-Norman magnates
of the second generation after the Conquest. Son of Roger of
Montgomery, first earl of Shrewsbury, he had already acquired
large estates in Normandy and Maine before his father's death in
1094 when he received, as the elder surviving son, the patrimonial lands in the duchy. In 1098, on the death of his younger
brother Hugh, he received the extensive Marcher earldom of
Shrewsbury and the family property in Sussex, to which Robert
added the Midland fief of Tickhill by purchase and the county
of Ponthieu by marriage. He thus controlled lands stretching
from the Somme estuary and northern Maine, through Normandy, southern England to the Midlands and into Wales. He
personified a Norman 'Empire' linked rather than divided by the
Channel. In Rufus's reign he was notorious for two things: his
cruelty and interest in military architecture, both useful attributes for a man in his position. If his power was spectacular, so
was his fall. Robert had supported Robert Curthose for the English throne in 1088 and, although he had formally accepted
Henry I in 1100, retained this loyalty, possibly calculating that
his own power would be the greater under the ineffectual
Curthose. In 1102, all his English lands were confiscated after an
abortive attempt to resist Henry, who, unable to trust Robert,
had determined to destroy him. The rest of Robert's political
career was spent in Normandy, his opposition to Henry persisting even after Curthose's defeat in 1106. In 1112 Henry lost
patience. Robert was arrested and incarcerated, first in Normandy then, from 1113, at Wareham in Dorset. There he spent
the rest of his life, hidden from view except for a reference in the
Pipe Roll of 1130 to payments for his maintenance and clothing.
The wheel of Fortune had come round. His grandfather had
been a minor ducal official in Normandy. Through good marriages, the patronage of William the Conqueror and their own
predatory instincts, the family had reached the highest rung of
the nobility. Their rise had been spotted with blood, of their
opponents and subjects; sometimes their own: Robert's mother,
Mabel, had been brutally murdered; his brother Hugh killed by

a Viking on a raid to Anglesey. The ascent and destruction of Robert's family provides an object lesson in how Anglo-Norman politics worked away from the sanitized niceties of government book-keeping.

ROGER OF SALISBURY (*c*.1065/70-1139; bishop of Salisbury 1102-39) was the dominant figure in English royal administration for a generation. As chief financial and judicial minister of Henry I and Stephen for thirty years, he created lasting institutions of central government, notably the Exchequer, and provided a model for the later Chief Justiciars of the Angevin kings. The shadow of 'Roger the Great', as some called him, lies heavy across all descriptions and discussions of the origins of effective departments of state and national bureaucracy. To his admiring great nephew, Richard FitzNeal, in his *Dialogue of the Exchequer* (1179), Roger was 'the chief mover in great matters'; to his modern biographer, he is 'one of England's greatest statesmen'.

Yet the character, mind and motives of this most powerful of ministers of the crown remain elusive. No minutes of meetings or personal correspondence survive, only a small proportion of the official documents issued or received by him. What exists suggests a man of energy, talent and ruthlessness, but also seriousness and resilience. Like a surprising number of English leaders, he was self-made. In his delight in ostentation and power, he was perhaps more of a Wolsey or a Thatcher than a Thomas Cromwell; in venality more a Lloyd George. As with all these, at his plenitude Roger was both innovative and feared; with them, too, his fall was sudden and complete; but, uniquely in this company, Roger's legacy was incontestably durable.

Roger first came to the notice of the future Henry I as a priest from the Avranchin region in south-west Normandy, probably in 1091. According to legend, Roger recommended himself by the speed with which he said Mass. If this story — written a century later — was designed to cast doubt on Roger's vocation, it may have been wide of the mark. It was unusual for ambitious secular clerks of the time to proceed to full Holy Orders so young. There are signs that Roger's spiritual life, while overlaid with secular employment, was neither assumed nor dormant. The chronicler William of Malmesbury, who knew Roger, mentioned his reluctance to stay in royal service after he became a bishop. Although he amassed an awesome fortune, he was not obviously corrupt and claimed he received no formal salary after becoming a bishop. In 1114, he successfully opposed what he regarded as the king's poor choice of candidate for the archbishopric of Canterbury. A cultured man, with interests in education and the arts, throughout his public career Roger was an active patron of Augustinian canons, a new order with a particular mission to the laity and one popular with some of Roger's contemporaries with unimpeachable spiritual credentials. His most notable benefaction was to St. Frideswide's priory in Oxford. At the end of his life, his contrition for harming the interests of certain religious houses appears focused and genuine. No saint, indeed a notorious sinner with an openly acknowledged mistress, Roger was probably a traditionally committed priest, who saw the separation from secular matters and the imperatives of canon law in a rather more relaxed light than the Gregorian reformers around him. Except to the noisy puritans of his day, this did not make him a hypocrite.

However he caught Henry's eye, by 1100 Roger was a chaplain, possibly steward, in his household in Normandy. After Henry's accession in 1100, as the king's chaplain, he began witnessing charters in England. Early in 1101, Roger became Henry's chancellor, in which capacity he used to dictate charters on the king's behalf. His prominence in the chancery was recognised by his appointment as bishop of Salisbury in 1102 (although consecration by Archbishop Anselm had to await the resolution of the dispute over investiture in 1107). His status within the regime as a whole was clearly signalled by a succession of lucrative grants of castles, estates and benefices beyond those attached to his see. Soon his interests stretched across southern England, from London to Wiltshire. Roger's political prominence was notably confirmed in 1106 by the commital to him of the captive Richard Curthose, the king's elder brother, who remained imprisoned in Roger's castle of Devizes for the next twenty years. The bishop's menage at Devizes was bizarre, the eldest son of the Conqueror rubbing shoulders with the bishop's articulate mistress, Matilda of Ramsbury, and their children. Whether they conversed and, if so, what they had to say to each other, is matter for speculation.

By 1109, Roger had advanced to the forefront of royal administration acting in concert with the regent, Queen Matilda, during the king's absences in France. His activities had become primarily judicial (he had acted as a local justiciar at least since 1106) and financial. Here, at the centre of government, Roger established his authority and wielded power, in the phrase of more than one observer, 'second only to the king'. Here, too, he laid the foundations of a system of central fiscal scrutiny and control that survived for centuries.

The pre-Conquest English kings had apparently kept track of what was owed and paid them by means of tallies, sticks notched according to the amounts received and split into two, so that each party held a record. It seems that this system, operated by 1066 at the main royal treasury at Winchester, was *ad hoc*, there being no regular, central audit to scrutinize revenue. After the Conquest, a larger royal demesne; higher demands on expenditure; the introduction of sheriffs' farms; the perceived necessity for accurate accounts of revenue paid and owing; and even, perhaps, the Domesday Survey, prompted the establishment in the 1090s of regular meetings of royal officials to audit receipts, identify debts and settle disputes. It was this central audit that Bishop Roger reorganised and transformed, almost certainly in response to raising the marriage aid for Princess Matilda in 1110. From that year, at the latest, the office of the household which collected levies, assayed receipts, adjudicated complaints and recorded payments, debts and pleas, was known as the Exchequer.

The Exchequer derived its name from the 5' by 10' cloth marked with white columns of an abacus against a black background (so not actually chequered) which covered the table at which the audit was conducted. The use of this visual computer was, with the various methods of checking the number, weight and content of the coins received, designed to establish the Exchequer calculations beyond doubt. It also speeded up the process of demonstrating to the sheriffs whose accounts were being audited the sums, especially deficits, involved. The unimpeachable accuracy of the Exchequer's accounting was essential as much of its business, and most of its importance, depended on its role as a court, where judgements were delivered on the whole range of the king's fiscal affairs, including fines and profits of justice. In a similar move to secure acceptance of decisions, records of the annual audit held at Winchester each Michaelmas were committed to rolls of parchment and stored. The first mention of these so-called Pipe Rolls was in 1114, although only one survives from Roger's career, that of 1130. As in earlier centuries and across Europe, officials were almost automatically suspect, the distinguished contemporary Arabist and astrologer Adelard of Bath accusing England's chief men of violence, 'the magistrates wine lovers and the judges mercenary'. Given this ritualised suspicion, openness and accuracy were at a political as well as financial premium.

The adoption of the abacus as a tool of bureaucracy was no accident. In and around the English court c.1100 there was considerable interest in mathematics and computing. Adelard of Bath himself translated Euclid, studied the abacus and computed horoscopes. The Lorrainer, Robert Losinga, bishop of Hereford (1079-95) may have introduced the abacus into England. One of Henry I's prominent sheriffs, Hugh of Buckland (d.c.1115), provided administrative information to the author of a treatise on the abacus, Turchil: either of them may have helped devise the Exchequer itself. Another influence was the school where Adelard had taught at Laon in northern France, with its leading *magister*, Anselm, and his brother, the mathematician Ralph, who also wrote on the abacus. To Laon, Roger sent his nephews, Alexander and Nigel, and employed a Laon graduate, Guy of Etampes as master of the school at Salisbury. Whatever else, the Exchequer was introduced by a circle of clerical administrators well abreast of the most recent developments in scholarship. It needed the practical skills of Roger to translate theory of such as Turchil's into a durable instrument of government.

By the early 1120s, Roger's ascendancy was complete. As early as 1113, his authority was described by a suppliant bishop as 'procuration' (*vestra procuratio*) implying control and management. This Roger particularly displayed in matters fiscal and judicial, but his wider political role steadily grew. The deaths of Queen Matilda (1118) and Prince William (1120) left him the sole viceroy in name as he had been before in action. During Henry's absence 1123-26 Roger ruled England, described by one witness as 'guardian' (*provisor*), by himself as *procurator* of the realm. As viceroy, Roger oversaw all aspects of government and issued writs in his own name authorising expenditure or fiscal pardons. In 1124/5 he organised a major reform of the coinage after Henry's troops had complained of the debased content of the money with which they were being paid. Roger's tactics give an insight into the rougher side of twelfth century administration. Ninety-two minters were summoned to Winchester where most were blinded and castrated. By 1124, Roger had also instituted a system of *ad hoc* itinerant justices to hear royal pleas and supervise the activities of sheriffs. In this period Roger demonstrated the efficacy of a more impersonal rule, a model exploited fully after 1154 when the king of England held more extensive lands and interests overseas. Under the Angevins the Exchequer consolidated its position as the pivotal fiscal and judicial institution of royal control over his subjects and provinces; the tactic of itinerant justices was formalised, after 1168, into regular circuits by justices-in-eyre; and the post of viceroy and king's *alter ego* was vested in the office of Chief Justiciar.

In fact Roger's years of power did not win him total security of royal favour. In 1126, on the king's return, Robert Curthose was transferred into the keeping of Robert, earl of Gloucester, Henry's illegitimate son. In 1128-9, a special audit was held by Robert of Gloucester and Brian FitzCount, which uncovered extensive indebtedness among the sheriffs, many of whom had been appointed by Roger a few years earlier. This audit produced a thorough reorganisation of administration, revealed by the unusually full Pipe Roll of 1130. Not only were some of Roger's associates, such as Geoffrey de Clinton, attacked, but the use of Earl Robert and Brian FitzCount to scrutinize administration as well as their findings implied criticism of Roger's management. Roger never again acted as regent.

One explanation for this apparent decline in royal confidence may have lain in Henry's plan to secure the succession for his daughter Matilda and his son-in-law Geoffrey of Anjou. Although Roger swore to uphold this succession in 1127 and 1131, he may have had misgivings: in 1135 he quickly embraced the claim of Henry's nephew Stephen of Blois. Henry's schemes for the succession had been worked out among intimates outside Roger's circle, two of whom, Earl Robert and Brian FitzCount, both strong Matildine partisans, conducted the 1128-9 investigation. Alternatively, this apparent reining in of his authority may have reflected royal unease at Roger's pre-eminence: in 1129 one royal clerk put Roger's name on a charter instead of the king's.

If Roger's power was restricted, he remained administratively indispensible. Throughout his long tenure of high office, he attracted no whiff of scandal or charges of corruption in his conduct of business. Yet, unafraid to enjoy the fruits of office and the patronage of a grateful monarch, Roger built up a powerful temporal position and, with two nephews installed as councillors and bishops (Alexander at Lincoln 1123 and Nigel at Ely 1133), established a unique dynastic influence. He also found time to be an energetic and effective diocesan. His capacity for work was evidently considerable.

If anything, the death of Henry I in 1135 temporarily restored Roger's position. As guardian of the treasury at Winchester and head of the Exchequer, he played a crucial role in supporting Stephen's successful *coup*. His son, Roger, became chancellor and Adelelm, probably another son, acted as the king's treasurer. Yet the appearance of government as a family firm was deceptive. Roger retained his grip on administration, his style as peremptory as ever, as in a writ of 1138: 'On behalf of the king and myself, I order . . .'. But politically, his star was waning. Roger, now ageing, was unable to control the new king's expenditure, the treasure amassed by Henry I being rapidly and disastrously dissipated. This financial failure, over which Roger presided perhaps helplessly, revealed that the main political decisions were being taken by the king and his own close advisers, notably Waleran of Meulan.

It may have been fears of Roger's entrenched power combined with his possible disapproval of the management of affairs that led to Stephen succumbing to Waleran's determination to destroy Roger and his family. It was rumoured that the bishop harboured sympathy for Matilda, although this is circumstantially unlikely. The fall of Roger was encompassed at Oxford in June 1139, when his men were embroiled in a contrived affray, the bishop then being charged with a breach of the king's peace. Roger was personally treated very badly, at one point being committed to a cowshed. His castle of Devizes, defended by his mistress and nephew, Nigel of Ely, surrendered to the king after Stephen had threatened to execute one of Roger's sons. Although Roger and his episcopal nephews were allowed to retain their sees, their goods and property were confiscated. Such was the gigantic size of Roger's treasure, that this may have been one motive for the bankrupt king's actions. To signal the change of ministry, a new royal seal was made.

The charges against Roger were heard in a church council at Winchester, when the king's breach of clerical privilege was also challenged. In the event Roger was neither convicted nor exonerated; he kept his see but the bulk of his possessions and wealth were lost. Out of office, the ailing bishop spent his last months organising restitution for those he had harmed or neglected, especially in the church. It is said that all political careers end in failure; there are few for whom that failure was seemingly so complete. When Roger died in December 1139, his and his family's fortunes were in ruins; the treasury over which he had presided was empty, except for his own wealth which had been pillaged; his country was embarked on civil war; the administration which he had created was disrupted to the point of extinction. Yet for all that, his method of rule and his institutions of government survived to ensure that Roger's legacy was the most constructive of any single royal official in the early middle ages.

E. J. Kealey, *Roger of Salisbury*, 1972.

GILBERT CRISPIN (*c*.1045-1117; abbot of Westminster 1085-1117) was one of the distinguished intellectual Norman clerics who came to dominate the English church in the generation after the Conquest. A fellow graduate of Bec and close colleague, pupil and contemporary of Anselm, he combined administrative skills with academic power. A member of the Norman nobility, he owed his preferment in England to Lanfranc, whom he joined at Canterbury in 1079 before being promoted, on the archbishop's advice, to the politically prominent abbacy of Westminster in 1085. In 1092-3, Anselm took refuge with Gilbert to avoid pressure to accept the archbishopric of Canterbury. Throughout Anselm's episcopate (1093-1109), the abbot was a loyal ally.

At Westminster, showing an awareness of history and the need for indigenous legitimacy, Gilbert nurtured the cult of Edward the Confessor, the ceremonial translation of whose relics he supervised in 1102, to the material advantage of the abbey and monks, whose numbers and buildings he extended. His literary work combined historical interests with a command of the latest developments in Anselmian theology of the proof of the existence and nature of God. His *Vita Herluini* (1109-17) was less of a biography of the founder than a history of the foundation of Bec and Lanfranc's career there. In his theological works, in contrast to the abstract thought of his *magister*, Gilbert applied his arguments to specific problems of dogma, such as the number of places available in Heaven or the identity of Mary Magdalen; the religious life (monasticism as the perfection of Christian life or simony); or the superiority of the claims of Christianity over other religions. Gilbert's *Disputatio Judei et Christiani (Debate between a Jew and a Christian c.*1093) was possibly based upon an actual conversation, although the Jew's remarks were clearly adapted to include the latest Anselmian tags, such as the definition of God as 'that than which nothing greater or more sufficient can be thought' from Anselm's *Proslogion.* The *Disputatio* is, however, a sign of a greater realisation of the existence of the non-Christian world only a few years before the First Crusade. In the 1090s there cannot have been many Jews resident in England, although the community in Normandy was well established. Royal patronage and even Gilbert's building programme itself may have attracted Jewish financiers to Westminster. Gilbert later claimed that a Jew had been converted to Christianity by the debate he recorded and had become a monk at Westminster. The *Disputatio* was immensely popular, twenty manuscripts surviving from the twelfth century alone. For Christians it provided a neat, one-sided confirmation of the truth of their religion, at the expense of another. However, parts were translated for the reverse purpose of refutating Christianity by the Jewish Biblical exegete Jacob ben Reuven in *Sefer Milchamot Ha-Shem (Wars of the Lord)* (1170). Gilbert's attempt to prove the existence of God without recourse to Scripture, his *Disputatio Christiani cum Gentili* (c.1093), was not successful.

Works of Gilbert Crispin, abbot of Westminster ed. A. S. Abulafia and G. R. Evans, 1986.

EADMER (*d.c.*1125), a monk of Canterbury and historian, was Boswell to Archbishop Anselm's Dr Johnson. His reputation rests on two works, the *Life of Anselm* and the *Historia Novorum (History of Recent Events)*. The twin objects of Eadmer's devotion were Christ Church Canterbury and Anselm. From 1093, he was Anselm's constant companion. As a member of the archbishop's household, Eadmer accompanied him in exile (1097-1100 and 1103-6), organised his chapel and looked after his collection of relics. From 1093 to 1100, Eadmer kept extensive notes, which Anselm himself corrected before, in 1100, asking Eadmer to destroy his draft history. Eadmer complied to the extent of destroying one copy and not pursuing his account until after Anselm's death in 1109. However, both the *Life* and *Historia* up to 1100 are based on Eadmer's contemporary observations. After 1109, Eadmer revised and completed the *Life*, but, in response to growing criticism of Anselm particularly at Canterbury, he first added two chapters (before 1114), then a whole book (*c.*1122) on Anselm's miracles. His fellow monks had to be convinced of Anselm's sanctity to deflect their unhappiness at his neglect of their communal interests when he was alive. The *Historia* also suffered a change in emphasis after Anselm's death. Although earlier Eadmer may have exaggerated Anselm's importance, he now added two books justifying the claims of Canterbury to primacy over the English church and, in particular, over York. To support his case, he was unafraid to copy into his work forged papal bulls, concocted between 1121 and 1123 by Eadmer's fellow monks. Eadmer went along with the deception even to the extent of inventing a story of how these documents were 'discovered' in an old Gospel book. The special pleading and polemicism of his later years should not obscure Eadmer's achievement as an historian. In the *Life*, his picture of Anselm is vivid, intimate and convincing. To demonstrate

Anselm's character, Eadmer relies on recounting his conversations and table-talk which at least sound authentic. Eadmer resisted the temptation to reduce his hero to a stereotype, although the insistence that Anselm disliked business, when obviously being very good at it over more than half a lifetime, may be taken as, in some part, a formal disclaimer. The *Historia* was probably intended for a wider circulation than the Canterbury community and it still offers unique insight into how the events of the late eleventh century appeared to one well-informed, self-interested audience. Eadmer's other works included lives of three Anglo-Saxon archbishops and, at the request of the monks there, two bishops of Worcester. In 1120, Eadmer had the chance to put his principles into action when he lost the chance of the see of St. Andrew's by insisting on the primacy of Canterbury over Scottish dioceses. As a historian, Eadmer combined Anglo-Saxon biographical traditions (e.g. Asser's *Life of Alfred* or the eleventh century *Lives* of Queen Emma and Edward the Confessor), with the Bec habit of intimate and immediate biographies of community heroes (e g. Gilbert Crispin's *Life of Herluin*), bound together by his passionate love of his archbishop and his monastery.

R. W. Southern, *St. Anselm and his Biographer*, 1963.
Eadmer, *The Life of St. Anselm*, ed. & trans. R. W. Southern, 1962.

STEPHEN HARDING (*d*.1134, abbot of Cîteaux 1108-1133) was one of the founders of the Cistercian Order of monks which led a spiritual and institutional reform of western monasticism in the twelfth century. Originally simply called Harding, he was born at Sherborne (Dorset) where his parents, who were of middling social rank, presented him as an oblate to the cathedral priory. As a monk, Harding soon found the intellectual and spiritual life at Sherborne stifling and he left to find learning and deeper religious experience. He travelled to Scotland and France, where he received a grounding in the Liberal Arts, and, with a fellow Englishman called Peter, he made a pilgrimage to Rome, during which he adopted the name Stephen. On their return from Rome, the two pilgrims entered the recently founded abbey of Molesme in Burgundy. Stephen's search for a purer, stricter form of religious life, although conducted largely on the continent, may have been inspired by reading the works of Bede of Jarrow preserved in the priory library at Sherborne. On their trip to Rome, Stephen and Peter recited the whole of the Psalms every day, as, according to Bede's *Ecclesiastical History*, had the exiled priest Egbert during his *peregrina vita*, a spiritual and physical journey to God. Some of Stephen's later ideas on monastic organisation perhaps show the influence of Bede's *Lives of the Abbots of Monkwearmouth and Jarrow*.

Molesme had been founded c.1075 as a place of seclusion and monastic simplicity, its monks dedicated to following the literal observance of the Rule of St Benedict which in most Benedictine houses had been severely modified and, in the eyes of some, diluted. Stephen rose to be sub-prior. But in 1098, finding that the original ideals were increasingly compromised at Molesme, he joined the abbot Robert and the prior Alberic and eighteen others in seceding from the abbey and establishing a new haven of ascetic perfection in the nearby forest of Cîteaux. Here Stephen was prior under Alberic's abbacy from 1099 to 1108, when he was elected abbot himself. It was Stephen, through his work as abbot and his writings, who established Cîteaux as a model for a fresh sort of Benedictine monasticism and as the centre of a growing family of monasteries, daughter houses linked together by observance and constitution. Although the survival and expansion of the Cistercian Order was secured primarily by St. Bernard who entered Cîteaux in 1112, it was Stephen who established and preserved the early ideals, traditions and rules of the order in his account of the foundation of Cîteaux, the *Exordium Cisterciensis Coenobii* (c.1115) and the *Carta Caritatis* (1114-1119) which laid down details of how the order was to be governed and decreed uniformity of practice and observance.

Many of the innovations of the White Monks, as the Cistercians became known, were institutional. Each Cistercian abbey had to submit to annual visitations by the abbot of their founding house. Every year a general assembly of Cistercian abbots was held at Cîteaux. Any formal control by laymen was prohibited, all lands being held independent of secular obligations.

Within the monasteries, there were to be no servants, the monks being assisted in their work by lay brothers, *conversi*. To facilitate running the often huge monastic estates, monks were allowed to spend nights away from the monastery in farm houses set at a distance from the abbey known as granges. The literal interpretation of the Rule of Benedict, complete with the injunctions to manual labour, was central. Cistercians, to preserve their ideals, sought remote places to build their monasteries, as far as possible outside existing social, political and economic structures. For an order wedded to strict poverty it was ironic that their organisation proved economically efficient and profitable. Much exploitation of marginal and new lands for cultivation, livestock and settlement was generated across Europe by Cistercians. For all the hopes of Stephen Harding and the other founding fathers, many Cistercian abbeys became large propertied corporations scarcely distinguishable from other Benedictine houses, a sobering fate for an order ostensibly dedicated to living lives of poverty and simplicity, 'the world forgetting, by the world forgot'. Within a dozen years of Stephen's death, a White Monk, Bernardo Pignatelli, sat on the throne of St. Peter as Eugenius III. Nevertheless, in their brief prime, to the mid-twelfth century, the Cistercians set a rigorous tone and example for other monks, such as the Cluniacs, to follow.

To Stephen Harding himself may be credited certain essential features of the new order: the strictness of observance; the emphasis on unity and uniformity; monastic independence from outside influence; the emphasis on trying to establish the best texts of the Scriptures; and the tradition that abbots continue to be part of the monastic community and not, as in other Benedictine houses, set apart. Intriguingly, all have Bedan parallels. However, many are the customary baggage of fundmentalists and, whatever their intellectual origins, owed their adoption in no small measure to the personalities of their proponents. What sustained the early Cistercians was their self-belief. Their discipline they interpreted as *caritas,* a form of love for the souls of others. They were unafraid of self-publicity. An account of the coming of the order to England preserved at Fountains Abbey, the English Cistercian house founded in Skeldale in 1133, describes the Cistercian missionaries as 'men of outstanding holiness and perfect religion' who 'had converse with angels', 'by their virtues glorified the monastic name' and 'whose hearts had been touched by God'. Cistercian pride was the pride of self-abnegation and spiritual rectitude: exciting, strenuous, uneasy, impressive and vulnerable. It is a measure of Stephen Harding's achievement that he lived to see his challenging views accepted across western Christendom. By the time infirmity forced him to resign as abbot of Cîteaux in 1133, the year before his death, he was the titular head of an international order, a far cry from the pilgrim who presented himself at Molesme eager to escape to a purer life. Without Stephen's grasp of management and organisation it is hard to imagine the flight to Cîteaux of 1098 as having led to anything more than an actual wilderness.

H. E. J. Cowdrey, 'The English background of Stephen Harding', *Révue Bénédictine*, ci, 1991.

GEOFFREY DE CLINTON (*d*.1130/35) was the first named and most prominent of those advisers of Henry I memorably described by Orderic Vitalis as 'men raised from the dust'. Rather than a sociological fact, Orderic was reflecting the resentment of traditional Anglo-Norman oligarchs at Henry's agents who were challenging their provincial hegemony. Clinton provided a prime example of this. In the 1120s he was raised to the position of a major landowner and sheriff in Warwickshire in order to balance the power of Roger, earl of Warwick, who was suspected of sympathies for William Clito. A prominent curial official, who had been witnessing the king's charters since 1108/9, Clinton was a royal chamberlain and treasurer by the mid-1120s and by 1130 had been appointed to hear royal pleas in eighteen counties. What angered those to whose gossip Orderic Vitalis listened was not his place in the king's household, but the estates and consequent social status with which his services were rewarded, including the marriage of his son to one of the earl of Warwick's daughters and the elevation of his brother, Roger, to the see of Coventry in 1129 (reputedly at a cost to Geoffrey of 3,000 marks). The sudden creation of new provincial dynasts was very unsettling for the old. In fact the charge of obscure origins is inaccurate. Clinton came from small landowning stock in the Cotentin. That his elevation was wholly dependent on royal favour was emphasised in 1128 when, the threat from Clito removed by death, Clinton found himself cut down to size by royal charges of treason. Although he cleared himself and retained very extensive property throughout the Midlands, he was never again quite the local force he had been. Nonetheless the establishment of his dynasty and tenants, many coming from the Cotentin, in Warwickshire demonstrated that a forceful monarch could exert more than passing influence on the localities of his realm. The method, however, was not through novel administrative or legal procedures, but through essentially traditional manipulation of tenurial patronage.

J. A. Green, *The Government of England under Henry I*, 1986.

RALPH d'ESCURES (*d*.1122; archbishop of Canterbury 1114-22) is one of the more shadowy occupants of the chair of Augustine. The son of a Norman baron, Siegfried d'Escures, Ralph spent all his early career at the abbey of Séez, a monastery patronised by the Montgomery family. Ralph rose from child oblate to abbot (*c*.1089). There he became friendly with fellow abbot, Anselm of Bec. Having fallen out with the violent and irascible Robert of Bellême, Ralph fled to England where he became a familiar figure at court. In 1104, he played a prominent part in the lavish ceremonies surrounding the translation of the relics of St. Cuthbert at Durham. In 1108, Anselm consecrated him bishop of Rochester, in succession to Gundulf, another of Ralph's friends. Ralph was well-educated and eloquent: a number of his homilies survive. He acquired a reputation for wit which — to some eyes — bordered on the frivolous. He may not have taken his monastic vows as solemnly as others, as he spent eight years outside the cloister before becoming a bishop. He was probably good company. This may have been important when, in 1114, he was the magnates' candidate for Canterbury, instead of the king's doctor, the Italian Fabrizio. A member of the Norman baronage himself, Ralph was seen as congenial: he was one of them. As archbishop, much of Ralph's energies were occupied with an increasingly bitter and tortuous contest with the archbishop-elect of York, Thurstan. In 1120, he suffered a stroke, which left him seriously incapacitated and, apparently, very bad-tempered.

WILLIAM (1103-1120), the only legitimate son of Henry I, was more famous in death than in life. Through his mother, Matilda, descended from Ethelred the Unready, on him rested his father's dynastic ambition. To secure acceptance of his son's authority and succession, in 1115 and 1116 Henry made the barons of Normandy and England swear homage and fealty to William. Although designation was not unknown in England, such a formal ceremony was unprecedented, a sign of Henry's own sense of vulnerability. In 1118-19, William acted as regent for his absent father before joining him in Normandy where, the following year, he married Matilda, daughter of the count of Anjou and did homage to Louis VI for Normandy. But Henry's schemes came to nothing when, on the evening of 25 November, the White Ship, carrying William back to England, foundered off Barfleur. The prince had embarked late and so missed high tide; both passengers and crew were reported to have been drunk. As a result, the ship was driven hard into a rock in Barfleur harbour revealed by the ebb tide. In the ensuing panic, William was put into a lifeboat, but, seeing his half-sister still on board the stricken vessel, he ordered the boat to return to her rescue, only for it to be capsized by others desperate for rescue. Few if any on board that or any other Norman ship could swim. William, his sister, another illegitimate brother and many prominent courtiers and barons were drowned. Only Berold, a butcher from Rouen, survived to tell the tale — which he did, frequently. The disaster was so horrific in its political, let alone personal, implications, that none dared tell the king: they left it to a boy. By depriving Henry of a legitimate son, or the prospect of a grandson in the male line, the White Ship disaster changed the course of English history. The last fifteen years of Henry I's reign was spent trying, in the event unsuccessfully, to restore an ordered succession to his dominions. More immediately, the drama of the catastrophe was heightened by its unexpectedness. Between 1066 and 1144 there are no reports of any loss of life or even injuries as a result of a shipping accident in the English Channel, and only one reference to a vessel dragging its anchor in port.

Small wonder contemporary monastic chroniclers had a field day in pointing the moral: man proposes; God disposes.

ROBERT, EARL OF GLOUCESTER (*c*.1090-1147) had all the kingly attributes except one: legitimacy. The eldest of Henry I's twenty or so bastards, literate, intelligent, brave, adept at the factional politics of court and a patron of both the church and the arts, Robert had to stand back to watch others compete for the throne, literally so in 1127 when he lost his claim to precedence over his cousin Stephen of Blois when doing homage to his half-sister the Empress Matilda. It was some measure of an increase in orderliness and legal propriety that William the Bastard could inherit a duchy and win a crown, while his grandson, Robert, whose personal credentials were second to none, had to be content with a supporting role.

Under Henry I, Robert was prominent in a party consistently loyal to the king. In 1119, Robert fought at Brémule against the king of France and in 1123 against the Norman rebels; in 1126, he was given custody of his uncle Robert Curthose. Despite acquiescing in Matilda's succession, he still fought against the Angevins on Henry's behalf in the 1130s. Robert's reward was in lands in South Wales and the West Country and the earldom of Gloucester (1122). After Henry's death in 1135, it was not his loyalty to the Empress which swayed him so much as his own self-interest: arguably, his hesitation in deciding where that lay allowed Stephen to grab the throne.

Admired by William of Malmesbury, Robert has traditionally been seen as a noble, chivalrous defender of the hereditary rights of his half-sister. His actions between 1135 and 1139 suggest more selfish motives. His unusual conditional homage to Stephen in 1136 signalled his importance to the new king but it may also have been forced on him by his isolation among the English baronage and the threat to his lands in South-East Wales posed by a Welsh revolt, the crushing of which, it has recently been suggested, may have prompted Robert's literary protégé, Geoffrey of Monmouth, to write his *History of the Kings of Britain*. Although Robert cooperated with Stephen at the siege of Exeter in 1136, he soon became alienated from the new regime, not least because of the favours granted to the Beaumont twins, Waleran of Meulan and Robert of Leicester, old rivals from the court of Henry I. Opposition to the Beaumonts provide a *leitmotif* in the rest of Robert of Gloucester's career, not least in the fighting at Wareham (1138), Worcester (1139) and Tewkesbury (1140).

It was probably the growing influence of Waleran of Meulan in particular that led to Robert distancing himself from the king in Normandy in 1137 and his fears of assassination by the royalist mercenary, William of Ypres. In 1138, the formal break with Stephen occurred, but after the failure of the Angevins to capture Normandy in 1138-9, Robert, perhaps in desperation lest his English estates would be lost, landed at Arundel with Matilda to dispute the English throne. In England, Robert provided the judicious advice, material support and personal charm that Matilda so conspicuously lacked. That she retained followers at all may in part have been the achievement of her gregarious and generous half-brother with his knack for friendship. Although playing the leading military role on the Empress's side, Robert also managed to use the civil war to build an almost impregnable power-base for himself in South-West England, centred on Bristol, a control that the vicissitudes of the wider dynastic struggle did little to challenge. 1141 saw his greatest triumph in the crushing defeat of the king at Lincoln in February, but his victory exposed the vulnerability of his position. Unless he looked after his own interests, he would have no more guarantee of security at an Angevin than at a Blois court. The former suddenly looked a forlorn prospect after the Rout of Winchester in September, where only Robert's personal courage and chivalry secured Matilda's escape at the price of his own capture.

The subsequent exchange of Robert for Stephen inaugurated stalemate, during which Robert consolidated his hold over the South-West (just as his rival Robert of Leicester extended his grip on the Midlands). To the end, Robert was inflexible, not only over the Angevin claim but, more damaging to prospects of civil peace, in harbouring the factional rivalries and grudges of the 1130s. Robert's death in 1147 allowed English magnates to make private accommodations with each other: Robert's own son, William, even married Robert of Leicester's daughter c.1150. It may be no coincidence that only a few months after her faithful defender died, Matilda left England.

If Robert of Gloucester was a vigorous politician, he was also one of the leading literary patrons of his generation. Apparently something of an intellectual himself, eager at quoting Biblical analogies, Robert was the focus of a group of writers which included the historian William of Malmesbury and the historical romancer Geoffrey of Monmouth, writers of secular narrative histories whose interest in the epic past of Britain was presumably shared by their patron. William of Malmesbury's revised *Gesta Regum* was dedicated to him, as was his *Historia Novella* which extensively eulogises the earl. Not only was Robert one of the dedicatees of Geoffrey of Monmouth's *History*, but he circulated copies of it to his monastic foundations and to his friends, including Walter Espec. Inside the nobility's metal helmets and chain mail were men of cultivation and intellectual curiosity. Robert employed mercenaries such as the bestial psychopath Robert FitzHubert; at the same time he fostered a literary genre that captured the imagination of the civilised world.

D. Crouch, 'Robert, earl of Gloucester and the daughter of Zelopheliad', *Journal of Medieval History*, xi, 1975.

WILLIAM OF CORBEIL (*d.*1136; archbishop of Canterbury 1123-1136) was the first post-Conquest archbishop of Canterbury not to have been a monk. A scholar, who had studied under the influential Anselm of Laon; a close friend of Anselm of Canterbury; a clerk of Ranulf Flambard (apparently acting as tutor to Flambard's bastards); and canon of Dover, in mid-career William sought a more rigorous religious life as an Augustinian canon, becoming prior of the new foundation of St. Osyth's in Essex. After the death of Archbishop Ralf d'Escures in 1122, William's past as a well-connected secular clerk and his present as a canon regular (*i.e.* living under a rule) commended him as a candidate for Canterbury to Roger of Salisbury who, with royal backing, was eager to appoint someone who was not a monk. As archbishop William proved himself a vigorous reformer. At three councils at Westminster in 1125, 1127 and 1129, decrees were promulgated extending the definition of simony; limiting the number of fees permitted to be collected by clergy; outlawing clerical marriage and fornication; and prohibiting the inheritance of benefices. As most of these measures challenged traditions and appetites, they were widely ignored. William was more effective in resolving the long running dispute with York in Canterbury's favour, helped by some convenient forged documentary evidence. However, William was most notorious in the twelfth century for crowning King Stephen in 1135, in direct contravention of the oath he and the other bishops had sworn to Matilda in 1128. It was this act of perjury — or policy — which probably lay behind Henry of Huntingdon's damning verdict that William could not be praised 'because there is nothing to praise'. This was harsh, as William, although possibly avaricious, led an austere and blameless life, the priority he gave his spiritual and religious commitment being evinced in his Augustinian vocation. He must also have possessed some distinctive qualities of personality to be friends with both the saintly Anselm and worldly Flambard.

SIMEON OF DURHAM (*fl.* 1100-1150), precentor and monk of Durham Cathedral in the early twelfth century, has had ascribed to him some important historical works. The *Historia Regum*, a compilation of annals, legends and extracts from other historians covering the period from the seventh century to 1129, contains original material for the years 1119-29. It also preserves much of value from earlier sources, including, it has been argued, material collected in the tenth century of especial interest for the history of Northumbria and the claims of the church of York to ecclesiastical independence from Canterbury. The *Historia* is, therefore, potentially a text of great interest and originality for Anglo-Saxon history. Simeon's attribution as author depends on a reference in a later twelfth century manuscript of the *Historia* by which time, in any case, several modifications had been made. To Simeon has also been ascribed, with no more certainty, the *Historia Dunelmensis Ecclesiae (History of the Church of Durham)*, a history of his diocese down to 1096. Even if the authorship of either book cannot be definitively ascertained, they both point to the growing interest in the past in twelfth century monastic communities. Both try to demonstrate the continuity of the traditions and privileges of the community of St. Cuthbert at Durham, despite the reality that monks were only reintroduced there in the late eleventh century after a gap of three centuries or more. In such works the past was pressed into service of the present. Simeon has also been linked, appropriately perhaps, with an account of the Translation of St. Cuthbert in 1104.

A. Gransden, *Historical Writing in England c.550-c.1307*, 1974.

THURSTAN (OR THURSTIN) OF YORK (*c.*1070-1140; archbishop of York 1114-40), royal clerk, combative and independent prelate, patron of new religious orders, protector of hermits, and founder of a new diocese, embodied many of the distinctive features of the twelfth century church, not least the capacity for controversy. His early career was conventional. Like so many Anglo-Norman bishops, he came from Bayeux, the son of a priest, Auger, who later became a canon of St. Paul's. Either at Bayeux or at St. Paul's Thurstan became the protégé of Ranulf Flambard, chief minister of William II and bishop of Durham (1099-1128), joining a tight-knit group which dominated government of church and state. From the 1090s, Thurstan rose through the royal chapel, becoming a clerk of William II, chaplain and almoner of Henry I, and, like his father, a canon of St. Paul's. In 1114, he followed many loyal servants of the crown onto the episcopal bench as archbishop of York. (His brother was made bishop of Evreux at much the same time.) Presumably Henry I thought he had placed a dependable ally in the potentially troublesome northern province. If so, he was wrong. To all appearances one of the old school, Thurstan immediately displayed an obstinate legalism in refusing consecration or ordination from the archbishop of Canterbury. From 1114 to 1121, with the support of Popes Paschal II (1099-1118) and Gelasius II (1118-19) and of Flambard (in exile at Bayeux, but technically his leading suffragan), he defied the king's attempts to force his submission to the primacy of Canterbury, spending much of that period in exile. After formally resigning his see in 1116, he was reconsecrated by Calixtus II (1119-24) in 1119. Weakened by the rebellion of 1118-19 and the death of his son in the White Ship disaster, in 1120 Henry I agreed to Thurstan's return. The arch-bishop was enthroned at York in 1121 and was soon back in favour, conducting royal business. Compromise with Canterbury was reached in 1125, when Pope Honorius II (1124-30) gave the archbishop of Canterbury legatine authority over the whole English church but did not insist on any formal submission by Thurstan.

Thurstan was notable for his personal piety. He protected and lent support to the hermits Godric of Finchale and Christina of Markyate against institutional jealousy and suspicion from the ecclesiastical hierarchy. A patron of the Augustinian canons who established their mission in the north western counties of Eng-land, he was instrumental in the consequent establishment of the see of Carlisle whose first bishop he consecrated in 1133. A year before, Thurstan had sanctioned the exodus of monks from St. Mary's, York to found the Cistercian monastery of Fountains on 200 acres the archbishop gave them in Skeldale, near Ripon. Thurstan, as few others, combined religious enthusiasm, politi-cal contacts and administrative efficiency. This ensured him an excellent press from contemporaries, particularly Cistercians. His extended contacts with what could be called the eremitic tendency within the church suggests a religious network of some complexity beyond the formal structures of dioceses, monaster-ies and parishes. A poweful patron, he seems to have possessed a share of the holiness of Anselm and the dogmatism of Becket, but with an eirenic quality all his own. His reputation was further enhanced by his organisation of northern resistance to the Scottish invasion of 1138 which culminated in the English victory at the battle of the Standard. The chaotic divisions which afflicted the see of York after his death are perhaps the true measure of his skill in reconciling northern interests.

D. Nichols, *Thurstan of York*, 1964.

ORDERIC VITALIS (1075-1142/3), author of the *Ecclesiasti-cal History of England and Normandy*, was one of the most important chroniclers of the Anglo-Norman empire, a union he embodied in his own life. He was born at Atcham, near Shrews-bury, but spent the whole of his career as a monk at the Norman abbey of St. Evroul. Orderic's father, Odelerius, was a Frenchman who had come to England to increase his fortune with Roger de Montgomery between 1066 and 1068. His mother was English and, as must have been common for children of such mixed marriages, until he was ten Orderic probably knew no French. His separation from his family in 1085 left its emotional scars. Over fifty years later Orderic recalled the moment when his father 'weeping . . . gave me, a weeping child, into the care of the monk Reginald, and sent me away into exile for love of God, and never saw me again. And so, a boy of ten, I crossed the English channel and came into Normandy as an exile, unknown to all, knowing no one.' The habit of sending children away, tenacious in the English upper classes, had, for Odelerius, a positive justification: 'he promised me that if I became a monk I should taste of the joys of Heaven with the Innocents after my death.' St. Evroul provided Orderic with the surroundings, the books, the time and the incentive to write history, often in his own hand. The description of him as 'one of the finest calligraphers of his day', is borne out by his own holograph manuscript of the *Ecclesiastical History* which survives in the Bibliothèque Nationale in Paris. Orderic began writing history before 1109. The *Ecclesiastical History*, commissioned by the abbot of St. Evroul, was begun in 1114/15 and completed in 1141. The original scheme was to include a history of Normandy and the Normans in England to the reign of Henry I. In 1136, he added two books of universal history and, at about the same time, inserted a digest of earlier Anglo-French history. He also included, at the request of the monks of Crowland whom he visited in 1115, Lives of their patron, St. Guthlac (*d.c.*714), and their benefactor, Waltheof (*d.*1076). Certain passages were revised in 1141. Initially conceived for the community of St. Evroul, as it grew the *Ecclesiastical History* became a history of the Normans for the Normans. Orderic's main inspiration was Bede's *Ecclesiastical History*, of which he made his own copy. His researches were extensive: documents; over fifty literary sources; and oral evidence. St. Evroul attracted important visitors and Orderic himself travelled in Normandy, England and France gathering material. Safe in his cloister, Orderic attacked the lax morals of courtiers and nobles, writing with some objectivity about the Anglo-Norman kings. Like Bede, he was careful to establish the provenance of his oral information: for example his information on the White Ship disaster (1120) came from the sole survivor, Berold, a butcher from Rouen, who apparently did the rounds of the duchy relating his ordeal to packed houses. Orderic's attitude to the English was understandably equivocal: he attacked the violence and greed of the Norman conquerors; but condemned the English as degenerate and justified the Conquest as providing necessary church reform. Orderic's vision of the secular world is in the mainstream of Christian historigraphy: the wages of sin are death; there is no help in this world even for the most powerful. Thus, in a typically vivid passage, William the Conqueror's naked, abandoned and rotting corpse testifies to the transience of earthly glory. History was didactic, a series of examples to inspire men to reform their lives. Anglo-Norman society gave Orderic plenty of scope.

The Ecclesiastical History of Orderic Vitalis, ed. & trans. M. Chibnall, 1969-80.

WILLIAM OF MALMESBURY (*c*.1095-*c*.1143) was one of the most distinguished English historians. The twelfth century witnessed a recrudescence of historical writing, stimulated by a general western European revival of learning and by events. On the continent, polemicists on both sides of the Investiture Contest between Pope and Emperor looked to the past to justify present policies. The First Crusade (1096-99) provoked an avalanche of contemporary narratives seeking to place this remarkable episode in a suitably providential frame as new, incontrovertible evidence of God's immanence. In England, although the unique vernacular tradition of historical narrative of the Anglo-Saxon Chronicle had become attenuated after 1066, the Norman Conquest provided a fresh spur to historical investigation. Monks had to justify their privileges; clerics were forced to reassess the insular Christian tradition in the new circumstances of largely foreign leadership; and scholars felt compelled to explain and judge the cataclysm which had overtaken Anglo-Saxon England. William of Malmesbury did all three.

Born of Anglo-Norman parents, William rose from a child

oblate at Malmesbury to be the abbey's librarian and perhaps, in 1140, an unsuccessful candidate for the abbacy. As a historian he regarded himself as successor to Bede of Jarrow (672-735) whose *Ecclesiastical History of the English People* was the greatest and most influential historical work of early medieval England. Like Bede, William was a polymath whose scholarship found its basis in his monastic library. Through his reading, William mastered scripture, the classics, theology, hagiography, civil and canon law. But he did more. A prominent feature of his writing is his use of topography and buildings as evidence. He appears to have travelled widely in England and his *Gesta Pontificum Anglorum* (1125) (*Deeds of the Bishops of the English*) has been described as an ecclesiastical gazetteer. Elsewhere, he points a wider political and moral argument by contrasting the meanness of Anglo-Saxon dwellings with the magnificence of new building by the Normans.

Such an eclectic approach to source material is parallelled by his extensive use of both past and contemporary literary narratives from Suetonius's *Lives of the Caesars*, Bede, and local historical traditions to eleventh and twelfth century authors such as William of Poitiers, William of Jumièges (for the Norman Conquest) and Fulcher of Chartres (on the First Crusade). Unafraid to flaunt his classical learning, his anthology of texts on Roman history, compiled in 1129, survives in a manuscript now in the Bodleian Library, Oxford. William's range embraced on the one hand archival documents (some, it must be said, forgeries, perhaps in the case of evidence on Malmesbury's antiquity concocted by William himself) and on the other a string of Rabelaisian anecdotes of debauchery and self-indulgence.

Part of William's posthumous reputation has depended on his leaving a substantial corpus of different literary works, the first English historian to do so since Bede. In 1125 he completed the first versions of his *Gesta Regum Anglorum*, a history of England from the arrival of the Saxons in the fifth century down to 1120, and the *Gesta Pontificum Anglorum*, a history of the English church to 1125. Between 1135 and 1143 he revised the *Gesta Regum* twice and the *Gesta Pontificum* once; he wrote a hagiographical Life of St. Dunstan, in which he tried to demonstrate the ancient origins of Glastonbury, with the help of some dubious documentary material from Canterbury; and he completed his *De Antiquitate Glastoniensis Ecclesiae* on the origins of Glastonbury Abbey. In the last three years of his life William, by now an embittered and isolated figure at Malmesbury, compiled a *Historia Novella*, an account of recent events 1128-1142, which was probably cut short by his own death

Apart from local corporate pride, William's historical work was centrally concerned to reconcile the histories of pre- and post-conquest England. His position is unusually ambivalent, which makes it more interesting. He wished to preserve the reputations of Anglo-Saxon saints; he called 14 October 1066 'a fatal day'; he stressed the continuity of English history. Yet he also sought to justify the Norman Conquest by condemning the English for sins of the flesh and casual religious observance. Harold II may have been personally brave, but his people were sinful and effeminate: William was always hot in disapproval of long hair and fancy clothes.

Of particular technical interest was William's development of a critical method in handling his sources. For example, he had little time for stories of Arthur, although this may have had as much to do with his dislike of the Welsh as his distrust of Geoffrey of Monmouth's fables. William laid claim to objectivity, although much of his account of 1066 is derived from Norman propaganda and his treatment of the early years of the civil war under Stephen is clearly that of a Matilda partisan. What is notable is that he admitted as much. Although happier in relating past events, his description of his own times in the *Historia Novella* is possibly the more intellectually remarkable, as he had no sources to guide him. Here his central interest in human affairs comes to the fore. More strongly than many medieval historians, William is prepared to speculate on human motive not just Divine judgement. For example, he attributes Urban II's launching of the First Crusade to the pope's 'little known' desire to exploit any political disruption caused by the crusade to win back papal lands in central Italy. Among western writers, this secular analysis of the supreme sacred political event of the age is unique.

But there was another side to William of Malmesbury. Like many another apparently humane Benedictine scholar, he was snobbish; anti-Semitic; a toady to patrons such as Robert of Gloucester, Matilda's chief supporter; a political time-server, as in his mealy-mouthed description of the distinctly unlikeable Henry I; and, for instance in his account of William Rufus, priggish to the point of prurience. But his achievement in restoring an English past to the Anglo-French elite of his day and subsequent generations remains one of the most impressive academic and intellectual feats in twelfth century England.

R. Thomson, *William of Malmesbury*, 1987.
A. Gransden, *Historical Writing in England c.550-c.1307*, 1974.

WALTER ESPEC (*d*.1153/58) was a second generation Anglo-Norman landowner who did well out of the reign of Henry I. Probably the son of William Spech (*fl*.1086) from western Normandy, Walter first witnessed royal charters in 1122. Inheriting lands in Bedfordshire, he acquired, possibly from the king, substantial property in Yorkshire, centred upon the castles of Wark and Helmsley. These grants made Walter a leading figure in the north as one of the king's most loyal agents in a potentially troublesome region. By 1130 he was a royal justice in Yorkshire, Northumberland, Carlisle and Westmorland and was responsible for receiving royal income from Yorkshire and the vacant see of Durham. He played a central role during the Scottish invasion of 1138 when his castle at Wark had to withstand a vigorous siege. Although already an old man, he organised and led the northern barons in the victory over the Scots at the Battle of the Standard. His friend Ailred of Rievaulx described Walter as the *dux et pater* of northern barons. Walter was supposed to have delivered a rousing speech before the battle summoning up the fame and traditions of the Normans as a spur to valour. Yet, for all his pride in his Norman ancestry, he was also regarded as a protector by influential English northerners such as Ailred. But Walter was more than soldier and administrator. His most lasting contribution to the north was as a patron of new religious orders. Without surviving children of his own, he used his wealth to found an Augustinian priory at Kirkham (1121), the Savignac monastery at Byland (1138) and the Cistercian house at Rievaulx (1132), as well as another

Cistercian house at Wardon in Bedfordshire (1136). He is most identified with Rievaulx, close to his castle at Helmsley. Rievaulx was the most successful of his foundations, one in which he kept a firm interest, and to which he directed its most famous abbot, Ailred in 1134. Ailred, in return, praised his patron in his account of the battle of the Standard. In the *Relatio*, Walter is described as being tall, with black hair, a full beard, broad features and a loud voice. Whether literate or not (and his official duties make it a possibility), Walter had a genuine enthusiasm for history and its imaginative counterpart the *chansons de geste*. From Robert of Gloucester, he borrowed an early copy of Geoffrey of Monmouth's *History of the Kings of Britain*, perhaps the greatest work of fiction masquerading as history of the middle ages. This Walter almost certainly showed to his neighbour, Ailred of Rievaulx, sometime before 1143. Walter's career touches many important themes of the early twelfth century: the skilful use of patronage to impose royal control across the kingdom; the development of a system of itinerant justices with local ties and central loyalties; and the establishment of the new continental orders of monks in English society. Walter may appear typical, but no cypher. He was, it seems, rather more than a pious thug.

For his role as literary patron,
A. Gransden, *Historical Writing in England c.550-c.1307*, 1974.

GILBERT OF SEMPRINGHAM (1083/89-1189), apart from being one of the few probably authentic centenarians of the Middle Ages, was the founder of one of the more unusual new orders of the twelfth century. Of Anglo-Norman parentage, after education in France, Gilbert was presented by his father with the living of Sempringham in Lincolnshire, although he spent most of his time, perhaps as a teacher, in the households of successive bishops of Lincoln, Robert Bloet(1094-1123) and Alexander (1123-48). The latter ordained him. In 1131, he withdrew to Sempringham and built an enclosure next to the parish church to house a group of seven devout women. On the advice of Abbot William of Rievaulx (1132-45), Gilbert added lay sisters to his embryonic order of nuns. To support this community with agricultural labour and the collection of rents and dues, Gilbert provided for lay brethren on the Cistercian model. In 1147, after being refused incorporation by the Cistercians, Gilbert was authorised by Pope Eugenius III to rule the order himself and he established a fourth branch of his order, that of Canons, to act as chaplains. Thus the final constitution of the order, which Gilbert himself only joined in the 1170s, comprised nuns, under a Cistercian rule; lay sisters; canons, under the Augustinian rule, and lay brothers. For lay members, there were initially very strict rules regarding food and clothing, which Gilbert had to modify c.1186. The community lived in double monasteries, divided architecturally. The Gilbertine joint houses were the first such since the great early Anglo-Saxon monasteries of the seventh century, such as Whitby or Hartlepool. Gilbert's highly eclectic, not to say eccentric system proved locally popular. By 1150, three other houses had joined the order, and it has been estimated that by 1200 there were over nine hundred nuns and lay sisters and more than five hundred canons and lay brothers in the order as a whole. Some of the problems the order encountered were predictable. The different branches complained of the behaviour of others, the lay brothers being particularly resentful of the canons. With the proximity of the sexes, scandal and rumour were never far away, although nothing compared to the real life horror of the nun of Watton (see NUN OF WATTON). Other problems were self-inflicted, such as the admission of girls to be nuns from the age of four. Despite the difficulties, the order survived and prospered, playing its part in the economic expansion of England through the drainage and cultivation of the fens, and in the religious life of the country by the acceptance of the vocation of pious women. Gilbert's own reputation was unsullied. Despite his support for Becket, Gilbert was protected by Henry II. Blind and infirm, he gave up administration of the order in 1178, although he retained ultimate authority until his death in 1189. Never an international order, the Gilbertines nonetheless were evidence of the variety of entrepreneurial opportunities in the religious as well as secular life provided by an expanding society and economy.

The Book of St. Gilbert, ed. R. Foreville & G. Keir, 1987.

RICHARD OF FOUNTAINS (*d.*1139), the first abbot of the great Cistercian Abbey of Fountains in Yorkshire, presents a revealing example of how the new wave of spirituality associated with the Order of Cîteaux became established; how it differed from existing practices; and how, equally, it grew from traditional monasticism. Richard was prior of St. Mary's, York, a wealthy Benedictine house, under an aged, easy-going abbot, Geoffrey. In 1132, with the help of his friend the ascetic Archbishop Thurstan, patron of hermits and sponsor of the first Cistercian house in the north at Rievaulx, Richard led a schism, not unlike that from Molesme to Cîteaux in 1098. With the example of the white monks recently settled at Rievaulx, and the encouragement of Bernard of Clairvaux, Richard and a few of his fellow monks established a new monastery in Skeldale on land given them by Thurstan. Soon known as Fountains Abbey, this became the leading Cistercian house in Yorkshire and exerted a profound influence throughout the northern province. Richard's departure from St. Mary's was caused by his impatience at the failure there to follow the pristine Rule of St. Benedict, in particular over time for prayer, study and work; silence; and diet. He sought a more eremitic existence. Initially he had hoped to find it in reforming St. Mary's. Only when this was rejected did the archbishop effectively allow him to break his vow of obedience in order to follow a new vocation. Yet in spite of the inter-order polemic that characterised much of the monastic debate in the twelfth century, relations and exchange between Benedictines and Cistercians continued close and frequent, in both directions. It was the logic of institutional inertia; the ties of custom; the responsibilities of possessions; and the wishes of the majority that prevented reform within established houses as much as any burning radical desire by reformers to secede. Richard and his abbey quickly found that they too became part of a not entirely other-worldly organisation. Richard himself died not in Skeldale, but in Rome in 1139 on Archbishop Thurstan's business. His career suggests that the Cistercian démarche was far less a rejection of traditional forms of regular religious life than either the hermit movement of the twelfth century or the friars in the thirteenth.

ADELARD OF BATH (*b.c.*1080-after 1151) was one of the most versatile intellectuals of his generation whose interests stretched from falconry to astronomy, from Euclid to magic, from Arabic science to playing the harp. His father was a tenant of the bishop of Bath and Wells and Adelard himself witnessed charters of Bath priory in the early twelfth century. Educated at Tours and familiar with the schools of northern France, by the 1130s he had established contacts at court, perhaps as an astrologer. In the 1140s he wrote a book explaining the use of the astrolabe in predicting the movements of stars and hence the future for the young Henry FitzEmpress. About 1110, Adelard visited southern Italy and Salerno in Sicily and it was probably there that he came into contact with Arabic and Greek learning. Although there is no direct evidence that he could read either language, he is credited with supervising the translation, perhaps by commissioning local scribes, of numerous Arabic works on astronomy and astrology, in particular the astronomical tables of al-Khwarizami (1126). Adelard was also responsible for a Latin version of Euclid's Elements of geometry, a textbook on the abacus, glosses on Boethius's *De Musica* and a book on magic. His book on falconry marks Adelard's social status, a scholar with the background of a country gentleman. His fascination with astronomy, which formed part of the formal academic curriculum of the period, was shared by many of his contemporaries, for example Walcher, prior of Malvern who produced an astronomical treatise *c.*1120 with the help of one of Henry I's many doctors, the converted Spanish Jew Pedro Alfonsi. The abacus was also of wide interest. Introduced into England probably by another learned cleric, Robert Losinga, bishop of Hereford, the abacus was not only of use to mathematicians, but also provided the essential method of computing royal accounts in the newly organised Exchequer at Westminster. In his travels and his translations, Adelard exemplifies the opening up of Europe and the increasingly cosmopolitan nature of academic life in the twelfth century, the precursor to the age of the great international universities. In presenting Arabic and

Greek knowledge to a western audience, Adelard, and others of his and the next generation, enriched and extended traditional classical and christian philosophical and scientific learning. Adelard himself, however, presents a series of contrasts which warn against any facile perception of a new rationality or modernity in his or his contemporaries' thought. On the one hand he had a genuine interest in the natural sciences for their own sake, producing at least two substantial works on the subject, *De eodem et diverso* and *Questiones naturales* based on his acquaintance with Arabic texts. He could write in the spirit of empirical observation: 'Of course God rules the universe, but we may and should enquire into the natural world. The Arabs teach us that'. On the other hand he cast horoscopes, wearing for the purpose a special green cloak and ring. The horoscope he cast for Henry FitzEmpress in 1151 at Bristol still survives in Adelard's own hand in the British Library. This apparent paradox of the scientist magician, the philosopher and mathematician who predicted the future by reading the stars exposes the very distinctive, inclusive approach to knowledge typical of a period before specialis–ation, when knowledge scholars sought to embrace was universal. Reason and divination were thus two aspects of the systematic and comprehensive attempt to understand God's creation and Man's place in it.

C. Burnett (ed.), *Adelard of Bath*, 1987.

HENRY OF HUNTINGDON, (?1080s-*c*.1155), archdeacon of Huntingdon wrote the most extensive work of history composed in the reign of King Stephen, the *Historia Anglorum*. Born in Huntingdonshire or Cambridgeshire, Henry spent his career attached to the households of successive bishops of Lincoln, Robert Bloet (1093-1123), who appointed him archdeacon of Huntingdon in 1109, and Alexander (1123-48), nephew of Roger of Salisbury, whose lifestyle was notoriously lavish, and whose contacts with court may have proved valuable to Henry who wrote his history at Alexander's commission. Henry also wrote a number of formal letters, designed for publication, and a collection of miracle stories, both of which he incorporated into the *Historia*. Henry wrote the *Historia* between 1129 and 1154 in a number of volumes and editions which he constantly expanded and revised. From 1130 onwards he was describing contemporary events, different instalments being issued throughout the 1130s and 1140s. His models, however, were Bede and the *Anglo-Saxon Chronicle*. By 1150, a number of copies of the *Historia* were in circulation, at least one in northern England, others at Bec and Mont-Saint-Michel in Normandy. Henry had good contacts. On his visit to Rome with Archbishop Theobald in 1139, he may have taken the opportunity to publicise his own work, for example when he met the Norman historian Robert of Torigni at Bec. The *Historia* was popular and widely used by later historians of the twelfth and thirteenth centuries. This must partly have been due to Henry's good stories and dramatic accounts of fighting, which appealed alike to writers of vernacular historical romance and fiction, such as Geoffrey of Monmouth and Geoffrey Gaimar, and conventional historians, such as William of Newburgh or Roger of Wendover. But Henry was scrupulous in his work, ranging widely for his sources, and copying documents into his text. It is for his stories that he is best remembered: Cnut and the waves and Henry I dying of a surfeit of lampreys first appeared in Henry's *Historia*.

A. Gransden, *Historical Writing in England c.550-c.1307*, 1974.

ROBERT PULLEN (*d*.1146) was one of the very few English cardinals in the twelfth century, but his domestic fame rests more with the assertion that he was one of the earliest Masters at the embryonic University of Oxford. The truth is more prosaic. Born in Dorset, he studied theology in northern France before returning to England as an itinerant scholar. By 1133, he was teaching in Exeter, presumably at the cathedral school at which Baldwin of Ford (archbishop of Canterbury 1184-90) was educated, almost certainly after Pullen's time. Between 1133 and 1138/9, Pullen taught Scriptural theology at Oxford and acquired the archdeaconry of Rochester before moving to Paris, where he taught 1139-44. Among his pupils there was John of Salisbury. In 1144, he was summoned to Rome to become papal chancellor. In this position he probably attracted a number of Englishmen to the Papal Curia, including, perhaps, the future pope, Nicholas Brakespeare. Although highly spoken of by Bernard of Clairvaux, Pullen remains a shadowy figure. He is said to have refused a bishopric offered by Henry I: but such claimed refusals, in all ages, tend to indicate ambition or reputation rather than actual fact. As a scholar, his theological works follow the critical methods of Abelard, although his own *Sentences of Theology* were soon overtaken by those of Peter Lombard. He evidently gained renown as a teacher, as the Parisian schools of the early 1140s were not for the second-rate, although they were, in the aftermath of the recent condemnation of Abelard, a place for the orthodox. Pullen must have had a reputation for administrative as well as intellectual skills to become papal chancellor: we know from Bernard of Clairvaux's correspondence that he had influential friends. The significance of his time in Oxford is clearer. The only previous known Master to teach in Oxford had been Theobald of Etampes, who seems to have lectured on the liberal arts from before 1100 to the early 1120s. There was no continuous school at Oxford. Pullen had no successor until late in the century, the university being a creation of the early thirteenth not early twelfth century. Many English towns boasted academic Masters: Northampton, for example, gaining an earlier reputation for its schools than Oxford. But Pullen's presence in Oxford coincided with the residence there of men such as Geoffrey of Monmouth and suggests that the town, with its many religious foundations, castle and royal palace, was beginning to be attractive to scholars and their clients.

J. Catto (ed.), *History of the University of Oxford*, vol i, 1984.

STEPHEN OF BLOIS (*c.*1096-1154; king of England 1135-54) is chiefly remembered as an unsuccessful king whose reign formed a chaotic interlude between the masterful rule of Henry I and Henry II. The damning verdict of the Peterborough version of the *Anglo-Saxon Chronicle* has stuck: 'People said openly that Christ and his saints slept'. English historians and their audience prefer strong kings, whatever their cost in terms of misery. For eight and a half centuries Stephen, who eminently failed to control events, has received short shrift. Yet it is not entirely obvious that conditions in England, when viewed from a

Stephen
(From the obverse of his seal: the king in majesty)

perspective other than that of royal government or hostile and judgemental monastic chroniclers, were markedly worse than under more effective monarchs. Devastation was local, confined to areas most affected by civil war, such as parts of the West Country, or temporary, as in East Anglia during Geoffrey de Mandeville's ravaging of 1144 or the areas affected by Henry FitzEmpress's destructive campaign of 1153. When compared to other parts of Europe, for example Stephen's native northern France where baronial banditry and terrorism were endemic in the early twelfth century, the contrast is less apparent. Stephen was faced with identical problems to those which confronted all new kings in this period: how to secure his position and to manage his kingdom and magnates. His lack of success speaks loudly of the scale of his difficulties and his personal and political incapacity to deal with them. It is less clear that his reign witnessed particular social or political disintegration. What his accession did reinforce was the tradition that the kingdom of the English was reigned over by foreigners: Danes and Norman French in the eleventh century; French in the twelfth and thirteenth; Welsh (of a sort) in the late fifteenth and early sixteenth; Scots in the seventeenth; and varying sorts of Germans ever since. England's place in Europe was never more underlined than in its rule by King Stephen whose previous interest in the realm had been purely tenurial. That he became king at all demonstrates that modern concepts of nationalism, so intrinsic to the medievalists of three and four generations ago, cannot be applied to English politics of the twelfth century.

Stephen was the third son of Stephen, count of Blois and Adela, daughter of William the Conqueror. His forceful mother, widowed in 1102, sent him to be educated at the court of her brother, Henry I of England. Stephen soon became the recipient of regular and lavish grants of titles and lands from his uncle in Normandy and England. By 1113, he was count of Mortain and received the extensive honour of Eye in Suffolk. The following decade saw his holdings extend into at least twenty-one counties. In 1125, he was given the valuable and strategically important county of Boulogne on marrying its heiress. By 1130, his demesne property in England alone amounted to at least 1,339 hides making him one of the richest magnates in the realm.

Although, with the other barons, Stephen had sworn to uphold the rights to Normandy and England of Henry I's sole surviving legitimate child, the Empress Matilda, as the king's nephew and favourite, and supported by an influential faction of barons, he retained a keen interest in the succession. Henry I died on 1 December 1135 at Lyon-la-Forêt in Normandy. Immediately on hearing the news, Stephen crossed from Boulogne to England and, within three weeks, had secured the support of London, Henry's government officials and the church. Recognition by the royal administration based at Winchester under Roger, bishop of Salisbury was crucial as it gave Stephen access to the royal treasure. Stephen was crowned by the archbishop of Canterbury, William of Corbeil, on 22 December 1135.

The speed of Stephen's *coup* took his rivals — Matilda and her husband, Geoffrey of Anjou; Stephen's elder brother, Theobald; and Henry's illegitmate son Robert of Gloucester — off-guard. News of Stephen's coronation ended plans of the Norman barons to offer the duchy to Theobald. Stephen's quick action was reminiscent of Henry I's seizure of the throne in 1100: once the king was crowned the only alternative to acceptance was rebellion and civil war. By May 1136, all the English barons, including Robert of Gloucester, had recognised the *fait accompli*; the Church had been granted a Charter of Liberties as the price for its support; and the hostile King David of Scotland, who himself could have constructed a claim from his direct descent from Ethelred the Unready, had been bought off. But Stephen's success had not been achieved without cost. Whatever he and his ally Hugh Bigod implausibly claimed, he had not been designated king by his uncle, and he did not have the best hereditary right. Internally, his position depended on the forbearance and cooperation of those who had acquiesced in his 'election', even though, as the contemporary chronicler Henry of Huntingdon gloatingly pointed out, such approval meant breaking their oaths to Matilda. Externally, he could hardly expect his cousin and the Angevins to surrender their expectations without a fight. To combat possible disaffection, Stephen was precariously dependent on the support of a few powerful individuals, such as Robert of Gloucester or Stephen's brother, Henry, bishop of Winchester, who had been energetic on his behalf in December 1135.

The new king's vulnerability was emphasised by his inability to prosecute the siege of Exeter (1136) against Baldwin de Redvers because of his troops' lukewarm support and the fiasco of his campaign against Geoffrey of Anjou in Normandy (1137), when his army disintegrated into rival fighting groups of Normans and Flemish mercenaries. The massive treasure left by Henry I was dissipated for little tangible gain. Stephen tried to build a faction of his own to control government centred on the glamorous but feckless Waleran, count of Meulan. Experienced sheriffs were replaced and, in 1139, Roger of Salisbury and his nephews, who had run the royal financial administration for a generation, were crudely ousted from power, and their castles seized. Henry of Winchester, who, as papal legate (1139-43), was effectively head of the English church, was alienated by the appointment of Theobald of Bec as archbishop of Canterbury in 1138. Disenchantment and self-interest in the face of a king who seemed alternately aggressive and inept, led to defections, notably Robert of Gloucester's in 1138. In an attempt to exploit this dissatisfaction, in 1139 Matilda landed at Arundel opening the way to civil war.

Matilda's support came less from those wedded to her hereditary claim than from those who had felt cheated of lands by Henry I or preferment under Stephen, and those whose allegiances were determined by local rivalries or the need to protect their lands. Although enjoying military superiority, Stephen appeared to lack adequate resources or resolve to crush his opponents, whose strength was based around Robert of Gloucester's estates in the West Country. Increasingly the conflict turned on the control of strategic towns and castles, such as Wallingford, Cricklade and Oxford in the Thames valley. The only prospect of a decisive end to the struggle came in 1141. On 2 February, Stephen himself was captured at the battle of Lincoln and imprisoned at Bristol. For a brief moment, the accession of Matilda looked possible, especially when both Henry of Winchester and Waleran of Meulan came over to her side, although the latter only did so to protect his continental possessions from Angevin attack and the former was soon alienated. Matilda's victory was clouded by her boorishness, especially her off-hand treatment of the Londoners which prevented her consecration. Her support remained tentative, and crumbled in the face of a vigorous offensive by Stephen's wife (also called Matilda) and his mercenary commander William of Ypres. In September 1141, Robert of Gloucester was captured at the so-called Rout of Winchester, from which the Empress only narrowly escaped, and was promptly exchanged for Stephen. To signal his rehabilitation (and emphasize a crucial distinction with Matilda), the king attended a legatine council at Westminster in December 1141 at which the legate, Henry of Winchester, and the clergy reaffirmed support for Stephen as the anointed king. Thereafter, neither side established a clear military advantage in England. Matilda's partisans held important castles in the South West and East Anglia, but Stephen secured London, Winchester and the Midlands, improving his position in 1142 by capturing Oxford whence Matilda had to flee by night through the enemy lines across the snow and frozen Thames camouflaged in a white cloak. On the continent, however, Stephen lost ground decisively between 1141 and 1145 as Geoffrey of Anjou completed the conquest of Normandy. This further strained loyalty to Stephen as some, like Waleran of Meulan, were forced to submit to the Angevins to protect their Norman patrimonies.

Relations with the Church, since the arrest of the bishops in 1139, were soured. Personally conventional in his patronage of religious orders such as those of Savigny and Cluny, Stephen was the first English king for centuries to lose control over some major ecclesiastical appointments, such as the election to the archbishopric of York after 1140. He was further undermined by the consistent opposition of Bernard of Clairvaux, the self-appointed and widely acknowledged keeper of the public conscience of Christendom, and his pupil, Pope Eugenius III (1145-1153), both members of the increasingly influential Cistercian order which in 1147 swallowed up the Savigny order. Archbishop Theobald's flight to the council of Rheims (1148), in defiance of a royal prohibition, and his later sympathy for the Angevins confirmed Stephen's weakness. After failing to retain his legateship, Henry of Winchester's authority and ability to deliver ecclesiastical support faded. One damaging political result of the coolness between king and Church was the latter's refusal to crown Stephen's eldest son, Eustace, in his father's lifetime. Stephen and James II are the only post-Conquest monarchs of England to fail to secure the succession of living legitimate sons. Perhaps that is the true measure of Stephen's failure. Even King John did better.

In England, Stephen pursued an erratic course. Anxiously eager to win quick advantage, he cast an essential prerequisite of good lordship, trustworthiness, into doubt. He spectacularly broke his own safe-conducts when he arrested at court the powerful and potentially dangerous magnates Geoffrey de

Mandeville (1143) and Ranulf of Chester (1146) at times when they were professing loyalty to him. Hardly surprisingly they both rebelled as soon as they were released. If Stephen could not be trusted, neither could he be feared as his uncle had been. Although a vigorous campaigner, Stephen lacked ruthlessness; withdrawing from Bristol in 1138; allowing Matilda safe-passage from Arundel to Bristol in 1139; releasing Geoffrey and Ranulf; paying for Matilda's son, Henry's withdrawal from England in 1149. A typical incident occurred in 1152 when Stephen was besieging John Marshal's castle at Newbury. To allow time for a parley, John sent his son William to Stephen's camp as a hostage promising that, during the lull in hostilities, the garrison would not be reinforced. John broke the conditions, but Stephen failed to execute the five-year old William, who thought the whole thing a game, especially as he and the king had played 'knights' (a tournament game played with straw figures) in the royal pavilion. The future regent of England was unlikely to have learnt much statecraft from this encounter, but he later recalled the old king with some affection. Yet in the twelfth as in other centuries, nice people rarely make effective rulers.

By the late 1140s, the civil war had reached stalemate. Despite the death of Robert of Gloucester (1147), the final withdrawal to Normandy of Matilda (1148) and the failure of Henry FitzEmpress's invasion of 1149, final military victory eluded Stephen. However, his grip on most of England seemed secure. Central government continued to work. The chancery seems to have been little affected by the troubles although, with a number of counties outside royal authority, the exchequer operated on a reduced scale. To combat local insecurity and to try to prevent a collapse of law and order, Stephen appointed earls in many counties whose office supplemented existing royal agents, such as the sheriff. However, the weakness of royal power was obvious. Between 1149 and 1153 a series of private treaties were agreed between magnates on opposing sides designed to limit mutual hostility in case of a renewal of the civil war, the most famous being the 'final peace and concord' arranged by Robert of Leicester and Ranulf of Chester. Although these treaties were not, in fact, very effective in keeping the peace, they signal the king's inability to provide justice and a common desire among the barons to protect themselves from unnecessary or excessive damage in the protracted struggle for the throne.

Increasingly this struggle was one Stephen could not win. After 1150, the rival candidate was Matilda's son, Henry, who held unchallenged control of Normandy and, after his father's death in 1151, Anjou and enjoyed the tacit approval of the papacy. In 1153, Henry invaded again and after a deliberately violent campaign in the south and Midlands, the magnates, fearful of the destruction promised by the Angevin's scorched earth tactics, forced each side to negotiate for peace at Wallingford. During the subsequent negotiations, Stephen's son Eustace conveniently died. The final treaty of 1153, accepted in principle at Winchester (in November) and promulgated at Westminster (in December) provided for Stephen to remain king for his lifetime then for Henry to succeed as the hereditary heir of Henry I. Stephen remained active, but king only on sufferance of his successor. He died on 25 October 1154.

The events of Stephen's reign have proved fertile for historical debate and have been interpreted variously as 'feudal' anarchy; a war of succession; and a struggle by the baronage to establish recognised hereditary succession to their fiefs. The causes of the collapse of royal control have been attributed to Stephen's lack of financial resources by 1138; to a baronial desire to maintain or recreate Anglo-Norman unity; to a noble reaction against weak kingship; and to accident. The circumstances of 1135 made civil war almost inevitable and Stephen, his *coup* achieved, failed to master the problems of faction and local baronial disputes. So soft-spoken that, it was alleged, he had a spokesman to address his troops before battle; chivalrous; energetic; by turns foolhardy and indecisive, Stephen, for all his lineage, opportunities and position, appears as rather colourless, unimpressive in an age when personal impressions counted for much. He was no match for the forces which, in order to succeed, he needed to dominate.

R. H. C. Davis, *King Stephen*, 1967.

MATILDA (1102-1167), for a few months in 1141, seemed about to become the first queen regnant in English history. Her failure to do so rested as much on her own mistakes as on the deep-seated mysogyny of twelfth century public life. Two of her contemporaries, Urraca of Castile (in 1109) and Melisende of Jerusalem (in 1131) inherited their fathers' crowns, although not without controversy. Matilda's inability to make good her claim may have been predictable, but not inevitable. Her career falls into three periods: marriage to the Holy Roman Emperor (1109-25); heiress and claimant to the Anglo-Norman realm (1127-42); patroness of the inheritance of her son, Henry, in England (1142-48) and Normandy (1148-53). Like all noble heiresses outside the cloister, Matilda's life and actions were defined by men: her father, husbands, rivals, allies and son. Unlike many, however, Matilda played an active role in her own destiny, provoking one contemporary to call her 'a woman of the stock of tyrants'.

The eldest child of Henry I, Matilda received a blue-stocking education, first in England at the cultivated court of her mother, Queen Matilda, then, after 1110 and her betrothal, in Germany by Archbishop Bruno of Trier. This training for a politically influential life was hard, Matilda later recalling being beaten regularly by a terrifying aunt. The marriage alliance with Germany, concluded in 1109, was of considerable diplomatic importance for Henry I, witnessed by the dowry of 10,000 silver marks he offered. Henry stood to gain an ally against the king of France and, equally important to a monarch whose authority rested on *coup d'etat* and military conquest, enhanced status as the emperor's father-in-law. For Matilda, her marriage to Henry V, solemnised in 1114, was a defining moment. Although she survived Henry by over forty years, took another husband, and identified herself with Normandy and England, she retained the title of Empress: her son by her second marriage was known as Henry FitzEmpress. Matilda was no passive consort; she witnessed royal *acta*; channelled petitions to the king; performed as titular regent in Italy (1118-9); corresponded with her father; and, on her husband's death from cancer in 1125, was entrusted with the imperial insignia. On the election of Lothar of Supplinberg as the new king of Germany, Matilda returned to her father, laden with jewels and relics, ready to be groomed for a new, no less exalted position than the one she left behind.

In 1120, Matilda's brother, William, drowned in the White

Ship, leaving her Henry I's sole surviving legitimate child. Although he remarried in 1121 (Matilda's mother having died in 1118), Henry had no more legitimate children, nor, by 1126, as he neared sixty, was he likely to after five years of childless marriage. Henry's choices were limited. His elder brother, Robert, was still in one of his prisons and, unsurprisingly, the king rejected Robert's son, William Clito. Of his own bastards, the eldest, Robert of Gloucester, was suitable in all things except his unacceptability to the church and, increasingly, to a lay baronage whose titles to land rested on legitimacy. Henry had showered lands and honours on his nephew, Stephen of Blois, son of his sister Adela, but more as a means of building up a loyal family block of support for his designated heir rather than as a signal of preference for the inheritance itself. His choice was eased by what he may have seen as his daughter's aptitude for public business. Her training had ensured she had a mind of her own and sufficient, perhaps excessive, self-confidence to act independently. Whatever his emotional attachment (hardly strong in practice as he had scarcely seen her between her ninth and twenty-fourth year), Henry decided that his dynasty was to hold the throne, not those of his siblings.

His decision is explicable in the context of his rise, against expectations, to power through his own initiative and skill. It was also not unique. At precisely the same time, another self-made monarch, Baldwin II of Jerusalem, was facing death with no sons. Like Henry, he settled the succession on a daughter, Melisende. The parallel was hardly coincidental, as the Jerusalem and the Anglo-Norman arrangements were closely linked. To secure Matilda's succession, two things were necessary: her formal acceptance by the magnates and a husband, to provide heirs and military leadership. Henry extracted oaths of allegiance to Matilda in 1127, 1131 and 1133 (and possibly 1128); and in 1128, she was married to Geoffrey of Anjou whose father, Count Fulk, departed immediately after the ceremony to become the consort of Melisende of Jerusalem, leaving Geoffrey as count of Anjou and, thus, a suitable match for Henry I's heir. There was, however, a difference in Baldwin's and Henry's succession settlements: under the former, Fulk became king of Jerusalem on Baldwin's death alongside his wife; Geoffrey was designated no such status, the allegiance sworn to Matilda in 1131 being to her alone. She was to be more than the vessel of the dynasty's continuity.

In fact that continuity was by no means easily secured. Matilda had been reluctant to marry Geoffrey, a decade her junior. The match made good diplomatic sense, protecting Normandy's southern flank and balancing the perennial hostility of Capetian France and the prospective antagonism of Blois. But the Angevins were traditionally suspect to the Norman baronage, with whom, especially with loyalists such as her half-brother Robert and Brian FitzCount, Matilda had forged close political links. Matilda possibly contrasted the status and surroundings of her two husbands. Equally, she had a notoriously sour nature and he a famously shallow one. Despite the urgency to provide Henry I with a grandson, they lived apart between 1129 and 1131 and perhaps only the prospect of the succession to Anjou going to his Jerusalem half-brothers in Palestine (the first of whom was born in 1131) persuaded Geoffrey to a reconciliation. More certain was Henry I's hostility towards Geoffrey which could only be assuaged (and then only partially) by producing the desired heir. Thus a combination of duty and greed led to the births of Henry (1133); Geoffrey (1134) and William (1136).

While Henry I denied his son-in-law any influence in Normandy, still less England, Matilda spent much time at Rouen where her father and his ministers could introduce her to government administration. But Henry's preparations came to nothing after his death in December 1135, his failure to admit Geoffrey into favour being perhaps crucial, as it left the field free for Stephen of Blois's *coup d'etat*. By Easter 1136, only one English tenant-in-chief had not acknowledged Stephen as king, including those most closely associated with Matilda. Her attempts to reverse the decision of 1135-6 were hampered by the fact of Stephen's coronation and anointing; the near-unanimity of secular and ecclesiastical acceptance of his title once he had been crowned; and Geoffrey's lack of interest in England: throughout his marriage his main concern was to further Angevin interests by annexing Normandy.

If Stephen had proved a successful ruler, Matilda's claim

would have languished and lapsed. But a series of mistakes, blunders and defeats, most notably the failure to gain firm control of Normandy in 1137, opened a path for Matilda to contest the throne. Although the Welsh and Scots, whose king, David, was Matilda's maternal uncle, failed to dent Stephen's regime in 1138, dissaffection grew in 1139, encouraging Matilda to assert her rights. Landing in Bristol in September 1139, she attracted the support of former allies, officials and favourites of Henry I, including her half-brothers, Robert of Gloucester and Reginald of Cornwall; Baldwin de Redvers; Miles of Gloucester; Bishop Nigel of Ely and Brian FitzCount. Her followers shared no obvious guiding principle (although political disappointment and the desire for recognised tenurial legitimacy have been suggested) other than loyalty to Henry I's wishes — and self-interest. Matilda's power was confined largely to the west country and her supporters' estates. For most of the next decade, victory or defeat were impractical, as neither Matilda nor Stephen attracted overwhelming baronial backing. The king usually enjoyed majority allegiance, but Matilda's adherents were a powerful, loyal and tight-knit group that could not be destroyed by the royalists. In addition, after 1137 Stephen could not rely on Normandy, which was finally lost to Geoffrey in 1144. Military equilibrium was matched by political *impasse*. There were no grounds for compromise. Either Stephen was king or not: only death or decision of war could alter that.

The stalemate was briefly broken in 1141 after the defeat and capture of Stephen at the battle of Lincoln (February). From his prison at Bristol Stephen released his vassals from their allegiance; his brother, the papal legate Bishop Henry of Winchester, accepted Matilda as 'Lady of the English' in March; Stephen's party began to collapse; Normandy rapidly gave way to Count Geoffrey, who overran the duchy except for some pockets of resistance only finally overcome in 1144. But Matilda's support was fragile. There was a disappointing attendance at an assembly at Winchester intended to confirm her authority (April) which was disrupted by royal partisans who were being rallied by Stephen's wife. More serious was Matilda's failure to secure the surrender of significant garrisons between her and London, notably Wallingford and Windsor. With Kent and

London itself in the hands of royalist sympathisers, Matilda's hopes of coronation at Westminster depended on further appeasement. In June, she bought the adherence of Geoffrey de Mandeville, castellan of the Tower. This allowed her in June to establish herself temporarily at Westminster. Here her high-handedness, arrogance and lack of tact alienated baronial support and infuriated the Londoners. She even managed to fall out with Henry of Blois, on whose continued support she depended for her chance of success. When she haughtily threatened the Londoners with a heavy tax, they attacked Westminster, forcing her to flee unceremoniously to Oxford. A few weeks later, the Rout of Winchester (August), from which Matilda herself barely escaped, reversed the verdict of Lincoln with the capture of Robert of Gloucester. By the end of 1141, after the exchange of prisoners, Stephen was restored and, if anything, Matilda's position was worse than it had been twelve months earlier. Her behaviour, domineering towards allies and vindictive towards opponents, exacerbated doubts as to the suitability of a woman as monarch.

Although remaining the focal point of resistance to Stephen until 1148, Matilda's chance of the throne had gone. A new pattern emerged. After her dramatic escape through enemy lines from Oxford on a snowy winter night in December 1142, Matilda maintained her base at Devizes. The beneficiary of Stephen's political mistakes, such as his ill-judged mistreatment of Ranulf of Chester (1146), she was unable to make headway against secure royalist domination to the east and north. Her pleas for assistance to her husband, who completed the conquest of Normandy in 1144, were ignored. From the moment of his perilous landing in England in November 1142, Matilda's hopes were concentrated on her son, Henry. Increasingly irrelevant to the future of English politics, in 1148, a year after the death of Robert of Gloucester, Matilda settled in Normandy leaving her son to make good his own claim in England. It might have been more prudent for Henry I to have designated his grandson heir in the first place: perhaps his daughter refused to countenance being by-passed; it would have been in character.

The rest of Matilda's life was spent nurturing her son's interests, as viceregent in Normandy and in diplomatic dealings with

Germany and France. To the end of her life, when she attempted
to mediate between Henry II and Louis VII of France, she
refused to embrace dignified inaction. Perhaps that was one of
her problems: against the logic of the times she had insisted on
an effective political role as the head of her own party. By doing
so, in some eyes she compromised her cause. Her qualities of
energy, arrogance, bravery, commendable in a man, were condemned in a woman. In all senses she could not win. Described
by contemporary writers as a striking, forceful and unbending
woman, her attempts to rule were seen as unfeminine. On the
other hand, she successfully retained the loyalty of important
English magnates and displayed considerable tenacity in adversity. It was her failure to match this with charm and magnanimity that sealed her fate. Constitutionally, it is hard to see that
Matilda represented anything except herself and her family
interest. Her eagerness to disinherit Stephen and his heirs of the
Honour of Boulogne in 1141 demonstrated she stood for no
principle of inheritance or legitimacy. Her career emphasised
that, in spite of largely clerically-inspired theories of election
and consecration, and the secular lip-service paid to inheritance
and designation, royal power depended chiefly on occupancy.
This Stephen achieved in 1135-6 and Matilda failed to grasp in
1141. Yet her career was not entirely unsuccessful: all subsequent
monarchs of England have been her descendants, not Stephen's.

M. Chibnall, *The Empress Matilda*, 1991.

DAVID I, KING OF SCOTS (*c*.1085-1153; king 1124-53) was
the sixth son of Malcolm III and his second wife, Margaret,
great-grand-daughter of Ethelred the Unready (king of England
978-1016), and sister of Edgar Aetheling who the English legit-
imists had briefly tried to make king of England in 1066. David's
English connections were reinforced by education at Ramsey
Abbey and at the court of his brother-in-law, Henry I who had
married David's sister Matilda (also known as Edith). In 1113,
he further tied himself to English affairs by marrying Matilda,
daughter and heiress of Earl Waltheof, in whose right David,
already since 1107 earl of Cumbria, became earl of Huntingdon.
After his accession in 1124, his English connections had two

main repercussions, one on English politics, the other on Scottish. In Scotland, his reign saw an influx of Anglo-Norman lords being granted fiefs, especially in the Lowlands. Royal relations with the nobility were increasingly articulated in vassalic terms familiar to the southerners. At court and in local administration, David's government was penetrated by Anglo-Norman procedures, offices and methods. David's impact on England was twofold, as a prominent baron and as the representative of one branch of English royalty. In 1127 David had sworn to uphold the rights of his niece, Matilda, on whose ostensible behalf he invaded England in 1136, although his more likely object was to secure the earldom of Huntingdon for his eldest son, Henry. His second invasion in 1138 ended in a military catastrophe at the battle of the Standard to rank beside the famous Scottish defeats at Alnwick (1093), Neville's Cross (1346) and Flodden (1513). Despite military failure and the barbarity of his Galloway troops, David managed to extract favourable terms from the weak King Stephen at the Treaty of Carlisle which confirmed David's son Henry as earl of Northumberland. In 1141, David hurried to join Matilda's triumph after the battle of Lincoln, withdrawing hurriedly after her rout at Winchester. During this period, it cannot have been beyond imagination that if the new Anglo-Norman dynasty failed (and between 1128 and 1133 its survival after Henry I hung on his daughter alone), David's claim could have been asserted. It was surely of some significance that Henry FitzEmpress, the future Henry II, chose to be knighted by his Scottish uncle in 1149 as being, in one sense, the senior male of the royal family. It also signalled the end of any lingering dynastic ambitions for David. Away from politics, David was apparently a keen gardener, in particular a fruit-grower who took an interest in improving fruit cultivation by grafting cuttings from one plant onto the stems of others.

MATILDA OF BOULOGNE (?1103-1152; queen of England 1135-52; wife of King Stephen) was the daughter of Eustace III, count of Boulogne. Matilda proved herself a vigorous and effective politician in her own right, one of a number of such tough twelfth century bluestockings such as her namesake and rival the Empress Matilda; Eleanor of Aquitaine; or the two Languedoc

Ermengards, of Narbonne and Béziers. As well as being heiress to one of the more strategic counties of north west Europe and a large fief centred on Essex, Matilda was closely related to the kings of Jerusalem, the counts of Flanders, and the kings of Scotland (Malcolm III was her maternal grandfather). Through her mother she was a direct descendent of Ethelred the Unready: through her father, of Charlemagne. Married to Stephen of Blois in 1125, Matilda brought to her husband spectacular lineage, significant wealth and a determination and energy which he often lacked. It was from her county that Stephen launched his successful coup in 1135. In 1138, Matilda supervised the capture of Dover castle from the Empress's partisans. The following year, she negotiated a treaty with her uncle, David I of Scotland. In 1140, she arranged a marriage alliance with France and discussed the prospects of peace with Robert of Gloucester at a conference at Bath. In 1141 Matilda's role was crucial for the survival of Stephen's cause. She rallied his supporters after the king's defeat and capture at Lincoln; harried diplomatically the turncoat bishop of Winchester, finally winning him back to Stephen's side; manipulated the favours of the Londoners against the Empress; and played an important role in the rout of the king's enemies at Winchester. The royalist *Gesta Stephani* admiringly described Matilda as 'a woman of subtlety and a man's resolution' who 'bore herself with the valour of a man'. In later years she seems to have concentrated on the prospects of her children, in particular her son and heir, Eustace. In her vigorous pursuit of her family's interests and her ability to replace her husband when required, Matilda conformed to a type of medieval heiress far removed from the blushing, playful, politically neutered objects of contemporary romancers' imagined devotions.

R. H. C. Davis, *King Stephen*, 1967.

WALERAN, LORD OF MEULAN, EARL OF WORCESTER (1104-1166), for a few years at the beginning of Stephen's reign was possibly the most important man in England after the king. A descendant of Charlemagne, vain, rash, ambitious and proud, Waleran's career was one of brilliant failure. The elder of the twin sons of Robert of Meulan (*d*.1118), Henry I's chief adviser, Waleran and his brother Robert, later earl of Leicester, were well educated, precocious and spoilt, not least by Henry I. After achieving majority in 1120, Waleran, having received the family lands in Normandy and France, experienced sharp changes of fortune. Eager for martial glory, Waleran rebelled against Henry I in 1123-4 on behalf of William Clito only to be crushingly defeated at the battle of Bourgtheroulde (March 1124). Imprisoned for five years, some of the time in chains, he was suddenly released and restored to high favour in 1129. One reason for this royal *volte face* may have been Henry's desire to balance the court factions as part of his plans for the succession of his daughter Matilda. Another may have been the king's seduction of Waleran's sister, Elizabeth, who subsequently bore one of Henry's twenty or so illegitimate children. Whatever the cause, Waleran's restoration was complete. For the rest of Henry's reign, he and his brother was regularly at court and enjoyed extensive royal patronage. On Henry I's death in 1135, the twins, in return for large grants of land, supported Stephen. With his wide estates and political contacts in northern France, between 1136 and 1139 Waleran played a central role in trying to secure Norman allegiance to Stephen and repelling invasions by the rival Angevin claimants. Created earl of Worcester late in 1138, between 1139 and 1141 Waleran was the leading adherent of the king's party in England, especially after he had engineered the fall of the Justiciar, Roger of Salisbury (in the words of one royal sympathizer, because of 'a furious blaze of envy') and Robert of Gloucester had defected to Matilda. It was probably Waleran who obtained the unexpected appointment of Theobald of Bec as archbishop of Canterbury. In the early years of the civil war, Waleran was vigorous in the king's cause, especially in Worcestershire and Gloucestershire where the fighting was fiercest. 1141 brought disaster. Although fleeing in panic from the royalist defeat at Lincoln in February, Waleran remained loyal to Stephen and stood by Queen Matilda. However, the Angevin advances in Normandy put his French lands in jeopardy. In order to save them, in September 1141, under a truce negotiated by his brother, Waleran changed sides, accepted the claims of the Empress Matilda and left England, never to return. By virtue of his wealth and lineage, Waleran was welcomed by the Angevins, but as Henry FitzEmpress grew to maturity, his influence waned. Absent from France on pilgrimage (1144/5) and crusade (1146-9), after 1150 Waleran was gradually excluded from power in Normandy. His Worcester lands were confiscated in 1153 and, unlike his brother, there was no place for him at Henry II's court after 1154. Thereafter, his sympathies lay increasingly with French rather than Angevin interests. Waleran, an impulsive politician and notable intriguer, was unwilling to compromise self-interest to achieve power. He proved a destructive friend to Stephen by alienating other royal support and, ultimately, ruined himself, brought down by the circumstances of a divided Anglo-Norman state and his own pride. It is revealing that on at least three occasions he described himself as 'by Grace of God count of Meulan', a typical insistence on his own importance and independence that proved fatal to his ambitions. There was another side. Waleran inspired personal devotion; he was loyal and generous; a patron of learning who himself dabbled in Latin verse. On the contemporary scale of values, such attributes commended respect and gained applause.

D. Crouch, *The Beaumont Twins*, 1985.

ROBERT, EARL OF LEICESTER (1104-1168) was the younger of the twin sons of Robert of Meulan (*d*.1118), Henry I's chief adviser. While his brother, Waleran, was mercurial, even flashy, Robert was renowned for patience and circumspection. Until the 1140s very much under Waleran's shadow, Robert slowly built up one of the largest baronies in England and a major political position through alliances with other magnates and a growing network of vassals whose loyalty was secured by firm discipline. By 1154, Robert was perhaps the most powerful baron in England as well as being a political veteran whose experience embraced over thirty years. He had also gained a reputation as an administrator, negotiator and lawyer, (in the words of Richard FitzNeal who knew him 'a man of sound judgement, well educated and practised in legal affairs'). Something of an intellectual, his views on royal authority and treason were quoted by John of Salisbury in his *Policraticus* and he himself wrote on philosophy and astronomy. In 1155, Henry II harnassed both Robert's territorial power and his personal talents to the new regime by appointing him Justiciar, an office which he held, as the senior partner to Richard de Lucy, until his death.

Under his father's will, Robert received the family lands in England, including the earldom of Leicester, but in 1121 his marriage to Amice, heiress of Breteuil brought him a strategically important fief in Normandy. Brought up at Henry I's court, by the early 1130s, Robert shared in the high favour bestowed on his family and their connections; he also witnessed fifteen royal charters between 1130 and 1135, a sign of things to come. With the death of Henry I and the accession of Stephen, Robert shared in the heyday of Beaumont power, taking the opportunity to settle old scores with territorial rivals, such as the Tosnis in Normandy. In 1139 he helped his brother destroy Roger of Salisbury, receiving from Stephen the city and earldom of Hereford the following year. Robert's diplomatic skills were exercised in 1141 when he negotiated the division of the family lands so that he could retain his English estates as a supporter of Stephen and his brother Waleran his French lands as an adherent of the Angevins. Although remaining a close associate of King Stephen, Robert spent much of the rest of the reign securing his own position. Independent of the king, he formed treaties with Angevin magnates, such as Ranulf of Chester, in order to reduce the prospects of damage to his landed interests, especially in the Midlands. He was notorious for controlling his tenants over whom he lay the constant threat of disseisin. In 1153, he changed sides, soon becoming one of Henry FitzEmpress's chief counsellors and having his Norman estates restored.

As Justiciar, he acted as Henry's main adviser at court and his representative when the king was abroad. Although prominent in the Becket controversy, he avoided the excommunications of 1166, perhaps because the archbishop saw him as of independent mind, a possible mediator. His duties as Justiciar included presiding at the Exchequer; carrying out royal writs; overseeing local royal officials; acting as a judge in hearing major pleas of the crown; provisioning royal castles and palaces; paying troops and transporting treasure. Robert was a dominant figure in government and aristocracy, with unrivalled royal confidence and

Robert of Leicester
(From his seal)

estates to match, stretching from Wales to East Anglia. Much of
the later prestige attached to the Justiciarship derived from
Robert's own reputation as a politician of unequalled experience; a royal servant of expertise and a baron of the highest lineage and unsurpassed wealth. Yet sometimes his dual role found
him out. In *c.*1167, he had obtained a special writ of exemption
from demands on his lands under the Forest Laws. This caused
outrage among the old Exchequer hands led by Nigel of Ely who
insisted that anyone who sat at the Exchequer possessed *ex-
officio* exemption which did not require specific royal approval.

It is one case of many where Earl Robert's first thought was to promote and protect his own property and interests while at the same time serving the king. FitzNeal described Robert as strong-minded and diligent. Henry II recognised his quality and, again in FitzNeal's words, made him 'head not only of the Exchequer, but of the whole kingdom'.

Born to greatness, Robert acquired further greatness by doing well out of the civil war of Stephen's reign and was thus in an unrivalled position to exploit his opportunities when high office was thrust upon him. Robert has been called 'the model of the curial magnate' and his career, taken with those of his father and brother, expose how unrealistic is the historical cliché which pits kings against barons. Medieval realms only operated through intimate cooperation between ruler and the most powerful of the ruled. Such relationships were inevitably at times tense and could degenerate into acrimony and violent confrontation especially if, as under Stephen, the king was a poor manager of men. But such dislocation was the product of mutual dependency not separation of interests. Robert did well out of kings and did well for kings: in him and those like him, we can see how effective medieval government operated to the desired benefit of all involved. Sectional interests as often as not united monarch and magnate as divided them. Twelfth century kings had no option or desire to base their rule on others than the natural leaders of society of whom few were more effective than Robert of Leicester who combined self-interest and loyalty to the material advantage of master and minister alike.

D. Crouch, *The Beaumont Twins*, 1985.
F. J. West, *The Justiciarship in England*, 1966.

HENRY OF BLOIS (*c*.1100-1171; abbot of Glastonbury 1126-71; bishop of Winchester 1129-71) was a prince-bishop of a kind familiar in continental Europe, but uncommon in England. Henry was a grandson of William the Conqueror, fourth son of Adela and Count Stephen of Blois. He became a monk at the grand and influential Burgundian monastery of Cluny. In 1126, his uncle, Henry I, secured for him the abbacy of Glastonbury, to which he added the wealthy see of Winchester in 1129, the younger Henry holding the two in plurality for the rest of his life, to the disgust of monastic purists such as the Cistercians. Whatever spiritual lead he gave, Henry was an energetic administrator, his abbey's and see's profits being channelled into lavish building programmes as well as his own capacious pocket. Henry possessed a taste for the finer things of life, but he was also a serious churchman in the Cluniac mould. His political ideal was of an independent church, run by monk-bishops, basking in the protection and cooperation of pious kings and noble patrons who deferred to their spiritual advisers. Heavily criticised by many for his political involvement and worldly machinations, it was nonetheless in keeping with his principles that he was one of the most sympathetic English bishops towards the hounded Becket in the 1160s, earning for himself the saint's praise as 'a wall of Israel'.

Henry was ambitious, for himself, his family and, after his own fashion, the church. In 1135, he was instrumental in securing the English throne for his brother, Stephen, from whom he extracted formal guarantees of the freedoms of the Church (in the so-called Oxford Charter of Liberties 1136). Hopes of a dominant political role were undermined by Stephen's reliance on others, notably the Beaumonts, whose influence ensured the elevation of Abbot Theobald of Bec to the archbishopric of Canterbury in 1138, instead of Henry, who had expected the job. But Henry's good contacts at the papal curia led to his appointment as papal legate in England (1139-43) with jurisdiction even over the archbishop. Henry used his power to effect. After Stephen's brusque arrest of Bishop Roger of Salisbury and his clan, the king was summoned to appear before Henry's legatine court to answer for his actions. Although Henry failed to make any charges stick, the king's recognition of the court's jurisdiction was a significant concession to church authority. The legateship allowed Henry to pursue an independent policy in the civil war, but only to 1143. In his attempt to retain effective control over the English church, he failed; in his political trimming, he attracted opprobrium from the papacy and diehards on both sides of the succession dispute. Throughout the 1140s, his position was precarious, between pope, king and claimant, to each of whom he had been alternately lieutenant and enemy.

Henry of Blois
(From an enamel plaque commissioned by the bishop during his lifetime)

In 1140, his attempts at mediation between Stephen and
Matilda failed; in 1141, Stephen's defeat at Lincoln forced him to
come to terms with Matilda, but her refusal to compromise soon
led him back into Stephen's camp, a translation sealed by the
royalist victory at the Rout of Winchester. Subsequent loyalty to
Stephen was offset by the loss of his legatine commission in 1143
on the death of Innocent II; his ultimate defeat at the hands of
the new pope, the Cistercian Eugenius III over his attempt to
maintain his protégé and relative William FitzHerbert as archbishop of York; and by the collapse of his plan to elevate

Winchester into an archdiocese to compete with Canterbury. In 1148, he was suspended for failing to attend the papal council at Rheims; yet in 1150, he was attacked at a council in London by Archbishop Theobald for his ultramontane behaviour as legate. As a consequence, Henry had to plead his case personally at the papal curia. However, Henry was nothing if not resilient. In 1153, he played a significant role in arranging acceptable peace terms, finally agreed at Winchester and Westminster.

Despite his part in the Angevin succession, after Henry II confiscated his castles in 1155, Henry withdrew to Cluny for a few years. In Stephen's reign, he had been a considerable secular political force: apart from the castles he built (*e.g.* at Winchester, Farnham and Taunton), he was *de facto* earl of Hampshire. The new reign was characterised by the king's refusal to tolerate any autonomous focus of power. Furthermore, Henry was too compromised by his relationship with Stephen and his prominent place in royal councils in the years Henry FitzEmpress was trying to make good his claim (1142-53). On his return to England (*c.*1158), Henry adopted the role of senior statesman. He continued to attend court. In 1162, he presided over the election of Becket as archbishop; in 1166, he acted as a papal judge delegate in a case of mutinous Gilbertine lay brothers. But his days of power were gone.

His behaviour during the Becket controversy showed that he retained an independent spirit. His contact with Becket may have been of long standing: one source suggests he was party to Becket becoming chancellor in 1155. Henry ordained the new archbishop at his consecration in 1162 and earned Henry II's displeasure by his support for the beleaguered primate at Northampton in 1164. Although he probably disapproved of Becket's extremism, and went along with royal attempts at papal arbitration in 1166-7, he kept in touch with the exile, keeping him informed and financially solvent. On his deathbed in 1171, he rebuked Henry II for his handling of the Becket affair. It is hard to conceive a greater contrast between the suave, urbane and worldly Henry and the intense, dogmatic and tactless martyr. Yet the proud prelate was also a monk. Throughout his career, he had taken sabbaticals at Cluny: his appears to have been more than a vocation of convenience.

But as a Cluniac, he saw it as his duty to influence secular events.

Henry's abilities were only little less than his ambitions. It is hard not to think that his mother had chosen the wrong younger son to go into the church: Henry could have made a more formidable monarch than Stephen. As it was, there have been few English bishops to match the elevation and extent of his contacts, the boldness of his political and ecclesiastical aspirations, or the opulent magnificence with which he surrounded himself. His interests were as expansive as his style of living. He collected birds and animals; he may have commissioned some of the finest manuscripts of the so-called Winchester school; he brought international motifs as well as money to the elaborate rebuilding schemes at Glastonbury as well as to his palace at Wolvesey, near Winchester. If he ordered the commemorative enamels which bear his portrait, his taste was as good as it was expensive. He liked large jewels and rings. Contemporaries found it hard to make him out. John of Salisbury preserves a vivid picture of him on a visit to Rome: a quiet, solemn figure, with an unfashionably large beard who, between exchanges of barbed wit with the pope and pleading his case against his ecclesiastical enemies, took the opportunity to purchase a large collection of classical statues.

R. H. C. Davis, *King Stephen,* 1967.
John of Salisbury, *Historia Pontificalis,* ed. M. Chibnall, 1956.

HERVEY DE GLANVILL (*fl.*1140-50) was a member of an Anglo-Norman family which had, by 1086, already established itself among the significant landholders in East Anglia, especially Suffolk. Except for two moments in his career, almost nothing is known of Hervey's life. His son, Ranulf, rose to become Henry II's justiciar 1180-89, and a number of other family members achieved royal office. In 1147, he appears as leader of a group of East Anglian crusaders who combined with others from England, Normandy, Flanders and the Rhineland to travel by sea to the Holy Land. At Dartmouth, where the fleet mustered, the leaders of the separate contingents formed a sworn commune, under which they agreed to be ruled in matters of discipline, justice and policy. During their passage along the

Atlantic seaboard, the crusaders were asked to help the king of Portugal capture Lisbon from the Moslems. In the debate over the proposal Hervey's strong appeal to martial honour and the unity of the commune apparently secured agreement. There survives a vivid, eye-witness account of this and the Lisbon campaign, the *De Expugnatione Lyxbonensi,* probably written by a member of Hervey's own entourage. Whether or not Hervey subsequently proceeded to Palestine is unclear, although many of his colleagues did. In 1150, Hervey appears again, at a joint meeting of the shire moots of Norfolk and Suffolk, held at Norwich in the bishop's garden, attended by the king's steward, the bishop of Ely and other East Anglian barons. The case hinged on the rights and immunities of the abbey of Bury St Edmund's which the royal advocates were attempting to set aside in order to prosecute one Hubert and his accomplices. Once again, Hervey's eloquence swayed the meeting, this time, as far as can be ascertained, according to a neutral witness. Hervey pleaded for the traditional jurisdictional independence of the abbey to be upheld against royal encroachment, citing in support of his testimony fifty years' experience of shire court business. As in Portugal a few years before, Hervey stood his ground on precedent and established legal agreements. It has been assumed that the two Herveys, crusader and shire court veteran, are the same man. The eloquence and conservatism of both support this. Furthermore, Hervey's legal interests and skills were inherited by his son Ranulf. However, Hervey's age presents a problem, especially if, as is possible, he was still alive in 1166. Could the crusader have been, as the 1150 evidence requires, about seventy at the youngest? Was he in his fifties when his son Ranulf was born? Hervey, as is the way of public speakers, may have exaggerated his seniority for effect at the shire moot. Alternatively, there were two Hervey de Glanvills, although there is no proof of that either. The sharp focus of the two incidents and the obscurity surrounding them demonstrate the pitfalls awaiting medieval historians. Whether one or two, Hervey de Glanvill nevertheless indicates the complexity of experience in the ranks of the second-rate provincial nobility: military adventure; idealism; horizons at once local and limitless; practical expertise in law as in the management of men or estates.

C. W. David (ed), *De Expugnatione Lyxbonensi*, 1975.

H. M. Cam, 'An East Anglian Shire Moot of Stephen's Reign', *English Historical Review*, xxxix (1924).

RANULF II EARL OF CHESTER (before 1100-1153), nicknamed *aux Gernons* (*i.e.* moustaches), played a prominent and vacillating part in the civil war of Stephen's reign, his actions, in common with most of his peers, springing from personal grievance rather than dynastic loyalty or principle. Ranulf's father, Ranulf I, had been granted the earldom of Chester in 1121 after his maternal uncle had drowned in the White Ship disaster (1120) but, in return, had been compelled to surrender Cumberland and his patrimony of Carlisle. The restoration of these lost estates was the mainspring of much of Ranulf II's political life. Inheriting the Chester earldom in 1129, he initially supported Stephen as king after 1135. However, successive treaties between Stephen and King David of Scotland in 1136 and 1139 gave the Scots large tracts of lands in Cumberland coveted by Ranulf who reacted by seizing the town and royal castle at Lincoln in 1140. Stephen retaliated early the following year by driving Ranulf from the town and beseiging the castle. Ranulf now allied with the Empress Matilda in defeating the king at Lincoln in February 1141. Ranulf's association with the Angevin party was cemented by his marriage in 1141 to the daughter of Robert of Gloucester. However, his territorial ambitions were no closer realisation as the king of Scots was also a close ally of Matilda. In 1145, Ranulf was reconciled to Stephen. However, there was no love lost between Ranulf and the king's entourage, many of whom had suffered at his hands. In August 1146, at Northampton, Ranulf was suddenly arrested and put in chains when he refused the king's demand to restore all lands he had taken. He was only released when he surrendered all former royal property, including Lincoln. Stephen's arrest of Ranulf was a public relations disaster. He had broken his oath of reconciliation of 1145 and his own promise of protection, thus detering any more defections from the Angevin faction. Stephen had breached a central tenet of effective medieval rule, that of being a good — *i.e.* fair — lord. In 1149, Ranulf joined Henry FitzEmpress and was reconciled with David of Scotland who, in return for the lavish

grant to Ranulf of most of Lancashire, retained Carlisle. But
Ranulf was never a party man. His priorities remained centred
on his own territorial and dynastic advantage, as shown by his
conventio with a leading royalist baron Robert of Leicester
(1149/53). Under this treaty, the two magnates, independently of
their rival liege-lords Stephen and Henry FitzEmpress, agreed to
limit any hostilities forced between them by their masters and to
protect their respective tenurial positions. Ranulf's career, notorious for his arrest in 1146, is more significant as evidence that
the drama of high politics was played against a dense background of baronial competition for rights, lands and inheri-
tances which took precedence over any claims of royalty.

R. H. C. Davis, *King Stephen*, 1967.

BRIAN FITZCOUNT (*d.*1147/49) was the son, possibly illegitimate, of Alan Fergant, count of Brittany. Brian, with a number of other Bretons, found favour at the court of Henry I, who
knighted him. By 1114, Brian appears as a witness to royal charters and rose to become one of the king's constables. By 1119,
marriage had brought him the rich and strategically vital honour
of Wallingford and royal grant the no less important Marcher
lordship of Abergavenny. One of Henry's intimate circle, in 1127
he played a leading role in securing Matilda's marriage to
Geoffry of Anjou. At about the same time, he and the king's
bastard son, Robert of Gloucester, conducted a special audit of
the exchequer. Although he recognised Stephen in 1136, he
declared for Matilda as soon as she had landed to stake her claim
to the throne in 1139. Thereafter, his loyalty never wavered, even
though, as castellan of a stronghold surrounded by enemies, his
estates were ravaged and he lost the fortune he had amassed as a
protégé of Henry I. He was an unusually articulate supporter of
Matilda's cause. Around 1143, he wrote or dictated a stinging
rebuke to the vascillating bishop of Winchester on the virtues of
consistency. From this letter something of the authentic voice of
a twelfth century nobleman may be caught, in his concern for
the destruction of his crops; in his respect of the First Crusaders
as models not of piety but of honour; and in his robust impatience with clerical casuistry. In response to the bishop's

injunction to remember the fate of Lot's wife and not look back to the past and the oath to Matilda, Brian's letter spat: 'as for Lot and his wife, I never saw them not knew them or their city, nor were they alive at the same time (as me)'. Whatever this may reveal of laymen's grasp of Scripture, it certainly suggests irritation with donnish pretentiousness. Brian was also the author, probably by dictation, of a book or pamphlet in which he set out the validity of Matilda's claim. Brian's career, royal poodle to principled rebel, suggests the image of the barons of Stephen's reign as self-seeking boors is flawed. In common with contemporaries such as Robert of Gloucester and Walter Espec, Brian was intelligent and thoughtful, as capable of expressing ideas as of leading a charge or counting profits.

H. W. C. Davis, 'Henry of Blois and Brian FitzCount', *English Historical Review*, xxv, 1910.

MILES OF GLOUCESTER (*c*.1100-1143) was a leading protagonist in Matilda's attempt to win the English throne. Sometimes regarded as one of Henry I's 'new men', Miles was the hereditary sheriff of Gloucestershire and castellan of Gloucester, position first acquired by his grandfather, Roger of Pitres, in the reign of William the Conqueror. Miles succeeded his father, Walter, sometime before 1126. By marriage, he secured the Welsh lordship of Brecknock and from Matilda in 1141-2 the sub-tenancy of Abergavenny. His power in the west was consolidated by his acting as local justiciar. Loyal to Henry I, he nevertheless soon recognised Stephen and by Easter 1136 was acting as his constable. Miles remained close to Stephen in the early years of the reign, playing an important role in the supression of the Welsh rising of 1136.

In 1139, however, he joined Matilda almost as soon as she landed. Given the adherence to Matilda of Miles's more powerful neighbour, Robert of Gloucester, this change of allegiance may have been prompted by self-preservation as much as legitimist devotion. Whatever his motives, Miles proved one of Matilda's most effective commanders: in 1139 alone he secured Gloucester and Hereford; relieved Wallingford and sacked Worcester. In 1141, however, he only managed to flee the Rout of

Winchester by abandoning his weapons and stripping off all his armour so that he arrived at Gloucester 'weary, half-naked and alone'. Earlier that year, at the height of her power, Matilda had created Miles earl of Hereford, confirming his position as a sort of military viceroy in the southern Marches. One of his duties was to raise finance for Matilda's campaigns, but he encountered stern opposition when he attempted to tax the church. Even though supported by Gilbert Foliot, then abbot of Gloucester and his protégé, Miles was placed under an interdict by Robert of Béthune, bishop of Hereford. Such fiscal expedients, common to both sides in a civil war, no doubt played a part in colouring the gloomy and hostile tone of ecclesiastical commentators on the conflict. Few issues aroused the moral indignation of medieval established clergy more certainly than heavy financial exactions levied on their institutions. Miles himself came to an unfortunate end, accidentally shot dead by one of his companions when out hunting in the Forest of Dean, an accident eerily reminiscent of the death of William II.

Despite his apparent fickelness, Miles was far from being a representative of any so-called 'feudal anarchy'. His local authority depended on his maintenance of a combination of public justice, royal favour and private acquisition of land; thus did he calculate his political advantage. Once decided, he seems to have acted with conspicuous loyalty. Nearly the last thing he, or his fellow magnates, wanted was a baronial free-for-all with its promise of the last thing they wanted: loss of estates and titles.

D. Walker, 'Miles of Gloucester', *Bristol and Gloucester Archeo-logical Society,* 1958-9.

GEOFFREY DE MANDEVILLE (*d.*1141) has been regarded as the archtype of the violent, factious, self-interested and venal magnate, the overmighty subject who took advantage of a weak monarchy to indulge his private ambitions, sell his loyalty to the highest bidder and provoke 'feudal' anarchy. To generations of historians wedded to the idea that firm central authority was 'good' and baronial autonomy was 'bad', Geoffrey represented all that was reactionary and regressive in medieval England, a

warning of the disintegration of the realm which might have
occurred but for the stern yet beneficent rule of Henry I, Henry
II and Edward I. More recently the disapproval of J. H. Round
has given way to a more sympathetic and realistic view, champi-
oned by R. H. C. Davis, of a baron whose family tradition of
royal favour and service was compromised by the strains and
contradictory pressures of civil war; whose especial difficulties
were the result less of inherent anarchic tendencies than of the
uniquely important strategic position of his lands and castles.

Before Stephen created him earl of Essex in 1140, Geoffrey,
like his father before him, had been sheriff of Essex and castellan of the Tower of London. He also possessed castles at Saffron
Walden and Pleshey (both in Essex) as well as extensive lands
strung across the Home Counties north of London. Inevitably, in
the crisis of 1141 and the struggle for London, Geoffrey was pivotal. Far from the cynical, ruthless turncoat of tradition, Geoffrey, while exploiting the situation for advantage, leant towards
loyalty to Stephen, only reluctantly and briefly entering into
Matilda's allegiance after the king's capture at Lincoln. Despite
his public support, and Matilda's confirmation of his possessions, the Empress failed to secure control of London. By September 1141, before the Rout of Winchester restored the royalist
cause, Geoffrey was back on the king's side. With Stephen in
prison, accommodation with Matilda had been prudent and
inevitable, but, in common with others, Geoffrey found Matilda
less than congenial and reverted to his original loyalty: hardly
the actions of a mercenary thug with eyes only for his main
chance.

Geoffrey was able to extract a very high price, Stephen confirming him as keeper of the Tower of London and justicar and
sheriff of London, Middlesex, Essex and Hertfordshire in hereditary right ('and his heirs after him' the charter reads). In effect,
Stephen was contemplating granting away from the crown,
apparently permanently, the most important castle in the kingdom and authority over four shires closest to the seat of government. Such a hereditary grant was a measure of the precarious
or naive nature of Stephen's regime as it implied, in the words of
M. T. Clanchy, that 'the English monarchy . . . would have ceased
to exist as an effective government'. Perhaps Stephen, under-

standably, had no great faith in the durability of political alliances or the agreements made to secure them. In 1143 Geoffrey was suddenly arrested by the king and forced to hand over all his castles. A pro-Stephen chronicle, the *Gesta Stephani*, hints that he was contemplating going over to the Empress, but this is unlikely. A more probable explanation is Stephen's lingering outrage at Geoffrey's detention in the Tower in 1141 of his daughter-in-law, Constance of France and his unease at Geoffrey's power.

In response, Geoffrey rebelled, launching a vicious campaign of ravaging in the Fens and East Anglia, attracting excommunication for his seizure of Ramsey Abbey, which he used as a base. Geoffrey now fought for himself, with ferocity born of betrayal and isolation. Noted for his shrewdness, courage, firmness of purpose, skill in war, as well as savagery, Geoffrey was as much a victim of the collapse of political order as its instigator. He was mortally wounded in the siege of Burwell, dying on 16 September 1144. His final mistake, apart from taking off his helmet and being wounded in the head by an arrow, was to be perceived as a persecutor of the church. His reputation paid dear for his attack on Ramsey. More widely, the last phase of his career helped establish the conventional view of the misery and chaos of Stephen's reign. It was at Peterborough Abbey, near to Ramsey and the scenes of Geoffrey's final mayhem, that the most famous and lurid account of these years was written, words which condemned a whole reign as a time when 'men said openly that Christ and his saints slept'. If true, Geoffrey, for all his grasping nature, suffered in their neglect as much as any.

R. H. C. Davis, 'What Happened in Stephen's Reign', *English Historical Review*, lxxix, 1964.

GEOFFREY OF MONMOUTH (*d*.1154/5) was the author of the *Historia Regum Britanniae (History of the Kings of Britain)*, one of the most popular and influential secular works of the Middle Ages. Purporting to recount the history of the British from pre-Roman to Saxon times, the *Historia* invented a Celtic past which exerted a tenacious hold on subsequent generations with stories of Cymbeline, Gorboduc, Old King Cole, Lear,

Merlin and, most famously, King Arthur. Geoffrey's *Historia* inspired a new genre of vernacular romantic fiction, in verse and prose, the so-called 'Matter of Britain', adding a new dimension to the collective imagination of western Europe.

Geoffrey came from the Monmouth area, possibly of Breton origin. By 1129, he was in Oxford where, until 1149, he was a secular canon of St George-in-the-Castle, which was then absorbed by Osney Abbey. He may have done some teaching, as he is occasionally referred to at this time as *magister*. In 1151 he was elected bishop of St Asaph's, being consecrated the following year, although he never visited his diocese. He witnessed the peace treaty of Winchester between Stephen and Henry FitzEmpress in 1153, the only Welsh bishop to do so, recognition, perhaps, of his contacts with leaders of the Angevin party. He died soon after.

Geoffrey's literary works date from his time in Oxford. The *Prophetie Merlini* (before 1135), dedicated to Bishop Alexander of Lincoln (in whose diocese Oxford lay), was a collection of prophecies, allusive to the point of obscurity, of a sort popular throughout the Middle Ages. Geoffrey claimed the *Prophetie* were copied from a British verse version of prophecies delivered by Merlin to King Vortigern in the fifth century. Spurious authenticity and provenance was a hallmark of Geoffrey's work and not only followed medieval convention (often fully justified) to disclaim originality, but also supported the fiction. Merlin was again pressed into service after 1148 in a verse *Vita Merlini*, a collation of legend, false history, philosophy and astrology, probably aimed at an educated audience.

The *Historia Regum Britanniae* was begun before 1135 and finished in 1138. Geoffrey insisted it was based on an ancient Breton book shown him by an Oxford colleague, Archdeacon Walter of Coutances. There is no evidence this was true. There are two Latin Breton texts with narratives similar to parts of the *Historia* which may pre-date it, but probably do not. In fact, Geoffrey used Gildas, Bede, Nennius's *Historia Brittonum*, classical Latin literature, genealogies, possibly Welsh and Breton legends, and folklore on the origins of places. Above all, Geoffrey used his own imagination. The achievement was remarkable, from the sustained narrative of events in a legendary history of many centuries, through the weaving of the fiction into existing knowledge, to the ingenious use of phoney etymology to support his inventions (thus King Lud, founder of London; king Cole, founder of Colchester). Geoffrey's fame is that of a creative artist not a historian. As history, the *Historia* is worthless. From Russia to Italy, the twelfth century saw histories written or invented to legitimise present political circumstances or aspirations. None had the literary and cultural impact of the *Historia,* nor were as creative or original.

Circulation was rapid; its impact immediate. Geoffrey wrote three separate dedications: to Robert, earl of Gloucester; Robert and Waleran, count of Meulan; and Robert and King Stephen, *i.e.* the three most powerful men in the kingdom. This cultivation of the great helped circulation. One copy was borrowed from Robert of Gloucester by Walter Espec. He showed it to Ailred of Rievaulx, and then passed it on to Ralph FitzGilbert, the patron of the vernacular poet Geoffrey Gaimar who, by 1140, had incorporated Geoffrey's work into his popular *L'Estoire des Engleis.* Another copy found its way to the Norman abbey of Bec by the beginning of 1139, where it was seen by the English historian Henry of Huntingdon, who was asked why his *Historia Anglorum* ignored the British past revealed by Geoffrey. Few books have changed received perceptions of the past so quickly and radically.

Why did Geoffrey write such an elaborate pseudo-history? There is an element of parody of established contemporary historians of England's past, William of Malmesbury and Henry of Huntingdon. There was, too, a positive purpose, to provide Britain with a heroic and distinguished past. It is unclear, however, whether this was a backhanded compliment to the Normans as conquerors of most of Britain, including parts of Wales or, as some have argued, a reaction to the French habit of denigrating the Welsh in general and to the unsuccessful Welsh revolt of 1136/7 in particular. Was Geoffrey, the well-connected Oxford *littérateur,* indulging in covert sedition at the expense of his patrons? Were his creations, Merlin and Arthur, the first heroes of Welsh nationalism? If so, they were soon transmuted into central figures in the chivalric traditions of north-west Europe: Celtic warriors into French knights.

Whatever his intentions, Geoffrey of Monmouth invented, in Arthur, a figure to match the greatest epic heroes. His alternative fantasy history gained almost universal acceptance. It troubled Henry of Huntingdon, aroused the disapproval of Ailred of Rievaulx. Some, like William of Newburgh dismissed it as impudent lies. Significantly, Geoffrey's fellow countryman, Gerald of Wales, was also sceptical. They were isolated voices. Within a generation, Arthurian romances by poets such as Chrétien de Troyes had become all the rage. It is even possible that a passage from the *Historia* indirectly influenced one of the most renowned clauses in *Magna Carta,* no 12 on the levying of scutages or aids, by providing the inspiration for the phrase 'unless by the common counsel of our kingdom'. In 1301, Edward I even cited Geoffrey in refutation of papal claims to jurisdiction over Scotland. Geoffrey's protean creation pervaded the mentality of the west. He remains particularly what he called himself: 'Galfridus Arturus'; Geoffrey the Arthur man.

Historia Regum Britanniae, vol i, ed. N. Wright, 1985.

WILLIAM OF NORWICH (1132/3-1144) was an apprentice leather worker in Norwich whose unexplained murder provoked the first accusations of ritual killing of Christians by Jews and was the excuse for the creation of a cult which lasted until the Reformation. The charges against the Jews were not immediate on the discovery of William's body in a wood on the outskirts of Norwich, but his family, especially his uncle, a priest called Godwin, soon concocted a case for the Cathedral authorities. Unnamed Jews were accused of kidnapping William and torturing him before crucifying the boy on Good Friday. The elements of blasphemy and ritual slaying, long part of medieval Christendom's myths about Judaism, were a potent mixture. There is not a shred of evidence to support the family's claims. The Jewish community in Norwich, there under the protection of the French authorities, was of very recent import. The growing prosperity of the third wealthiest town in England may have increased their business in providing financial services. Resentment, and the initial popularity of the cult, seems to have come from those with modest means, urban artisans who, perhaps for the first time, were sufficiently well-off to get into debt. Whatever social or economic tensions the slanders concealed, the cult itself was manufactured by three people: Godwin; William Turbe, prior of Norwich, then bishop 1146-74; and Thomas of Monmouth, who took over from Godwin as the cult's manager in 1150. Thomas supervised numerous translations of the pathetic corpse which, on one occasion, he relieved of some teeth for his private relic collection. In 1173, he composed the *Life and Miracles of St William.* The desire of the Norwich monks for an attractive cult of their own was as powerful as their anti semitism. In the early years the pilgrims who received the saint's cures were very local, although by the time Thomas wrote the *Life,* the novelty had worn off in the immediate neighbourhood. The cult survived until the 1530s. The story of young William's killing was copied repeatedly, most famously in the events leading to the grisly pogrom surrounding the supposed martyrdom of nine-year-old Hugh of Lincoln in 1255. Chaucer's Prioress's Tale is very similar. The corruption of innocence made it an attractive literary device. More sinisterly, the cynical exploitation of an obscure tragedy set a pattern for self-righteous prejudice which increased as Jewish communities spread across Angevin England. The intolerance towards the Jews may have been fed by ignorance and a fear born of the endless repetition in words and images of the Passion and Crucifixion. But the outbreaks of anti-semitic violence, notably the massacres of Lent 1190 in Stamford, King's Lynn and York, were rarely spontaneous. Like the cult of St William, they were concerted expressions less of religious zeal than of secular antagonism for which horror stories such as the one invented by Godwin and his relations in Norwich in 1144 provided convenient fuel.

R. Finucane, *Miracles and Pilgrims,* 1977.

WULFRIC OF HASELBURY (*c.*1090-1155), a parish priest in Wiltshire turned anchorite, lived in a small cell attached to the parish church of Haselbury Plucknett (Wiltshire) for thirty years from 1125 until his death. In the 1180s Prior John of the Cistercian house at Ford wrote an admiring biography which allows sharp insights into the function of a holy man in twelfth century society. The central feature was the most obvious. By virtue of being restricted to his cell or the adjacent parish church and his extreme religious exercises, such as praying all night in the church or even in a tub of cold water, Wulfric was dissociated from the world. He was thought of as neutral in the social tensions of an economically prosperous and expanding locality, but powerful through his personal relationship with God. In fact, Wulfric had an unrivalled network of local information and gossip and a keen self-interest which showed itself in his lethal habit of cursing his enemies — from mice to men — who tended to drop dead on demand. A combination of a one-man Citizen's Advice Bureau, consultant psychologist and local ombudsman, Wulfric established his credentials as social arbitrator, prophet and healer by results, for which he was financially rewarded by grateful clients. He amassed wealth, which he used to distribute alms and endow monasteries. Although his food came from the Cluniac house of Montacute, Wulfric was particularly close to the Cistercians for whom he conducted recruitment interviews. It was this connection which probably explains John of Ford's enthusiasm. Wulfric's education and knowledge of French allowed him to upstage the parish priest in dealings with the aristocracy, and thus provided an important and seemingly dispassionate link between social groups. Having apparently opted out of the secular and ecclesiastical rat race, Wulfric acquired considerable power, certainly more than if he had remained a parish priest. With his wide contacts, energetic servant, full-time scribe and full treasure chest, Wulfric was running a profitable business under the guise — genuine or not — of simplicity and self-abnegation. His wealth included livestock, gold, silver and expensive textiles. His advice, especially medical, was often common sense, but it was authoritative and acceptable from a man uniquely placed to resolve local disputes and negotiate with external forces such as landlords, other villages and God. Wulfric's curses and manipulation of gossip reveal a nastily vindictive, neurotic personality for whom less restricted or contrived contact with the outside world might have proved disastrous. His proclaimed purpose was moral improvement of his fellow men. To this end he acted as a relief agency. An unusual entrepreneur in an age of opportunism, his career demonstrates that holiness can be materially significant but that holy men are not necessarily nice people.

H. Mayr-Harting, 'The Functions of a Twelfth-Century Recluse', *History* lx, 1975.

HADRIAN IV (*c*.1100-1159; pope 1154-59) to date is the only Englishman to become pope. His career was almost entirely outside England, evidence of the opening of twelfth century Europe to an international clerisy of ambitious, mobile and educated ecclesiastics whose careers could be as cosmopolitan and opportunist as any freebooting Viking of earlier centuries. Born Nicholas Breakspear(e) at Abbot's Langley, near St Alban's, his father was a minor royal official who entered St Alban's as a monk. This suggests that there was money in the family. Sometime after 1120, Nicholas left England, studied in France, and entered the community of canons regular at St Rufus, near Avignon. He rose through the ranks to become abbot *c*.1137/40. He was not popular, the canons complaining to Rome of his strictness. This quality of determination (or alternatively tactlessness) was to make him a brilliant papal legate and a maladroit pope. Sometime in the late 1140s he visited Rome, perhaps making contact with Englishmen at the Curia, such as Robert Pullen. What prompted Eugenius III to create him Cardinal Bishop of Albano in 1149 is obscure. Nicholas made his name as papal legate to Scandinavia (1150-53) when he brought the Norwegian and Swedish churches decisively into the orbit of the Roman church. He established Trondheim as the metropolitan see for Norway; laid the foundation for the archbishopric of Uppsala; and gained local agreement to the payment of Peter's Pence. The Danish historian Saxo Grammaticus thought him a skilled administrator and diplomat. His unanimous election as pope in December 1154 after his return to Rome is, nevertheless, hard to understand. He had no obvious patrons or curial pedigree. His time as cardinal had been spent mainly abroad. Perhaps, as in other leadership elections, he had an indefinable aura of success which attracted the jaded power brokers in Rome. Since the reign of Paschal II (1099-1118), popes had become victims rather than directors of events. Perhaps his colleagues hoped Nicholas, the

Apostle of the North, would break the mould of compromise, stagnation and failure which had so recently been confirmed in the fiasco of Eugenius III and the Second Crusade. If so, they were to be disappointed. Nicholas took the unusual papal name of Hadrian, the first for two hundred and seventy years, perhaps in honour of Hadrian I (772-95) who, it was claimed, had given the first papal privileges to the abbey of St Albans's. Certainly, the new pope extended papal protection to St Alban's (1156). Hadrian's main challenge was his political weakness in Italy, especially in Rome. Initially he relied on an alliance with the German experor, Frederick Barbarossa, but when it became apparnt that papal and imperial interests in Italy were incompatible, Hadrian performed a diplomatic somersault at the Treaty of Benevento (1156) by allying with the papacy's adversary, the king of Sicily. This *démarche* in fact did little to secure Hadrian's permanent hold on Rome. Relations with the emperor deteriorated further in 1157 when Hadrian's envoys at Besançon implied that Frederick was the pope's vassal. Despite attempts to mollify the emperor, Frederick pressed ahead with his territorial claims in Italy. By the time of his death, Hadrian had confirmed the papacy's political vulnerability. At the Curia, Hadrian gathered around him Englishmen such as John of Salisbury and his nephew Boso, whom he placed in charge of papal finances. Through John of Salisbury and his own letters, Hadrian tried to encourage Archbishop Theobald to adopt a more robust stance over papal jurisdiction in England, to little immediate effect. As in Scandinavia, Hadrian wished to reassert, under papal control, episcopal authority over the church after a generation when the lead in reform and church government had been increasingly in the hands of monks and abbots, especially Cistercians: during his reign the papal title of Vicar of Christ became current. It was in this context that Hadrian, probably at the request of John of Salisbury and Archbishop Theobald, issued the bull *Laudabiliter* (c.1155/6) which ostensibly encouraged Henry II to incorporate Ireland in his empire. One consequence of any such conquest, the clerics hoped, would be the extension over the Irish church of the jurisdiction of Canterbury and, ultimately, Rome, an arrangement which Hadrian had perfected in Scandinavia. Personally, Hadrian, like so many successful clerics, was said to have had a good singing voice. According to Boso and John of Salisbury, he was a generous host and a good companion. Such was local pride in Hadrian's pontificate that Walkelin, archdeacon of Suffolk, named one of his bastards Adrian and proposed to call the next, if a girl, Adriana.

R. W. Southern. 'Adrian IV', in *Medieval Humanism*, 1970.

WILLIAM OF YPRES (*d.*?1165), one of the leading mercenary captains of the mid-twelfth century, played a prominent role in support of King Stephen in the late 1130s and early 1140s. The illegitimate son of Philip of Loo and a wool-carder of Ypres, and a grandson of Count Robert I of Flanders (1071-93), he may have been involved in the plot to assassinate Count Charles the Good in 1127 and certainly was one of the competitors for the county in 1127-8. Expelled from Flanders in 1133, William found refuge in England. For a decade after 1135 he led Stephen's Flemish mercenaries, proving himself the king's most loyal and effective commander. In the process he acquired an evil reputation for ruthlessness and violence, beginning in Normandy on Stephen's ill-fated visit in 1137, when he and his troops antagonised and frightened the Norman aristocracy in equal measure. In 1141, he apparently abandoned Stephen to capture at the battle of Lincoln (February). But at least he and his soldiers lived to fight another day and in the following months when Stephen's cause hung in the balance he showed unswerving loyalty. It was William's tactical skill which led to the capture of Robert of Gloucester and the Rout of Winchester (September 1141) which restored the king's fortunes.

Later in the 1140s, as the general fighting died down, William appears to have mellowed, perhaps because he went blind. He turned his energies to ecclesiastical patronage, founding Boxley Abbey (1144-6), and political mediation, as in 1148 between Stephen and Archbishop Theobald. Stephen rewarded William with large estates and revenues in Kent which Henry II allowed him to keep, at least until 1156/7. As did many violent men of the time, William ended his days in the cloister, at St Peter's, Loo, in his native Flanders

Although the civil war highlighted his importance, it should be remembered that he was engaged by Stephen at the height of the king's power early in the reign. Mercenaries, *i.e.* paid soldiers, were not emergency expedients in the armies of the central middle ages, but a permanent and necessary presence. For instance, William II's reputation as a powerful warlord depended, according to Abbot Suger, on his being a 'brilliant recruiter and paymaster of knights'. William of Ypres's career presents a striking contradiction to the supposed norms of chivalric society. Against the topos of devoted martial valour of men serving their lords out of 'feudal' loyalty so carefully nurtured by predominantly clerical writers at least since the eighth century, William, who openly served for material profit, proved both more skilful and more loyal than his baronial colleagues. He, William Marshal and Richard I's mercenary commander Mercadier give the lie to the politically and socially comfortable conceit that trust could not be bought. Indeed, their activities suggest that it was not profit but the traditional bonds of aristocratic society that bred untrustworthiness. The barons who forced King John to sign *Magna Carta* in 1215 tacitly accepted this in their condemnation, by name, of the king's mercenary leaders in Clause 50. Gerard d'Athée, Engelard de Cigogné and the rest were dangerous precisely for the firmness of their devotion to the king: a marked contrast to their noble critics.

R. H. C. Davis, *King Stephen*, 1967.

WILLIAM FITZHERBERT (*d.*1154; archbishop of York 1141-7 and 1153-4; canonised 1226) was one of the more unlikely saints of medieval England. The son of the half-sister of King Stephen and his brother, Henry of Blois, bishop of Winchester, by 1138 he had risen to be Treasurer of York. In January 1141, on the orders of the king, he was elected archbishop of York. Although no enemy to the monastic reformers in the North, William had defeated a Cistercian candidate. That alone was enough to excite the fury and vindictiveness of Bernard of Clairvaux. Worse still was the obvious interference by the king and his brother Henry, then papal-legate in England. Both parties appealed to Rome. Initially, Henry of Blois held the advantage and, with the approval of Innocent II (1130-43), consecrated

William archbishop in 1143. Henry drew the full force of St Bernard's invective ('here I say is the enemy, . . . the man who walks before Satan, the son of perdition, the man who disrupts all rights and laws'). The deaths of Innocent (1143), Celestine II (1143-44) and Lucius II (1144-45) delayed the granting of the *pallium* to William. The accession in 1145 of St Bernard's pupil Eugenius III (1145-53) put it out of reach. At Rome, Eugenius upheld his Order's interests by deposing William in 1147, rejecting another royal candidate and instead consecrating the Cistercian Henry Murdac, abbot of Fountains. The struggle symbolised the political weakness of King Stephen, who could not even get his candidates into the second see of the realm, and the new power in the North of the Cistercians. Self-righteousness allied to landed wealth made them confident and aggressive, and provoked conflict. After 1147, William retired to the protection of Bishop Henry at Winchester. That his fate had been largely a matter of politics not principle, despite St Bernard's fulminations, was tacitly recognised after the deaths of Murdac, Eugenius and Bernard when Anastasius IV (1153-54) restored William to his diocese in 1153. William died in 1154, it was rumoured from a chalice poisoned by the archdeacon. To the end, William aroused controversy. According to his enemies, a lazy man of lax morals, William was caught between the traditional structures of ecclesiastical patronage and the demands for recognition by the newly endowed purists of the Cistercians who, far from being content to 'forget the world, and be forgotten by it' as their founders claimed, wished to capture the strategic heights of ecclesiastical power in a region they had come to dominate. William's canonisation owed nothing to either position, but to the desire of the clergy of York Minster for a saint of their own to compete with the local cults at Ripon and Beverley. Honorius III obliged in 1226.

HENRY MURDAC (*d.*1153; abbot of Fountains 1144; archbishop of York 1147-53) took full advantage of the brief period when the Cistercian order combined political power and moral authority to achieve high ecclesiastical office in the face of royal hostility and local opposition. A Yorkshireman who held lucrative preferments under Archbishop Thurstan, he abandoned teaching as a secular clerk to enter Clairvaux under its charismatic and forceful abbot, St Bernard. Murdac, a man of intellect, asceticism and conviction, became one of Bernard's favoured disciples, being appointed successively abbot of Vauclair and then Fountains, in his native Yorkshire. At Fountains, Murdac proved himself combative, rigid in imposition of strict Clairvaux rules and entrepreneurial. Daughter houses were sponsored, even as far away as Norway. Locally, he began to assert Cistercian influence beyond the cloister in opposing the election as archbishop of York of William FitzHerbert, a secular clerk and close relative of King Stephen. In his campaign Murdac was able to recruit his patron Bernard, seen by many — himself included — as the conscience of Christendom, and, crucially, Bernard's pupil, Pope Eugenius III (1145-53). At one point in the conflict, William's men sacked Fountains itself: they knew who their enemy was. Murdac's motives may or may not have been selfless. What is certain is that after William's desposition by Eugenius in 1147, Murdac attracted enough support in a divided election for the same pope and fellow Cistercian to appoint him archbishop in William's stead.

As archbishop, as when abbot, Murdac scarcely conformed to the often proclaimed Cistercian model of the retiring eremite, shunning the world, finding spiritual fulfilment only in the cloister. Despite the refusal of the king and the York clergy to accept him, Murdac pursued a vigorous policy of asserting archiepiscopal rights often in the direct interests of the Cistercian order. He also maintained close control over the affairs of Fountains, using his archiepiscopal authority as a cover for hiring and firing a series of abbatial stooges. Recognised by the King in 1151 in return for his help in persuading Pope Eugenius to consecrate Stephen's son king, Murdac remained energetic in imposing what he saw as the highest ecclesiastical standards throughout the church, but his effectiveness was limited and transitory. After his death, a non-Cistercian pope, Anastasius IV, restored Archbishop William. Murdac, for all his personal qualities, exposed flaws in Cistercian policy eagerly siezed upon by opponents. His rectitude appeared self-righteous; his probity smug; his conviction arrogance; his actions no better than those of any other self-interested ecclesiastical faction. Such were the contradictions of success. To them Murdac added his own abundant taste for acrid controversy. York never again had a Cistercian archbishop.

F. Barlow, *The English Church 1066-1154,* 1979.
D. Knowles, *The Monastic Order in England,* 1949.

AILRED OF RIEVAULX (1110-1167) was one of the most influential twelfth century leaders of the Cistercians in England whose widely acknowledged spiritual standing was reinforced by an unsurpassed network of contacts with the secular great as well as the religiously good. His family history embodied much of the reality of church and monastic reform. Ailred came from a long line of prosperous married clergy. His great-grandfather, Alured, sacrist of St Cuthbert (*c.*1020), spent his time stealing relics of Northumbrian saints to add to his community's collection. Thus did Bede's bones find their way to the shrine of Cuthbert. Ailred's father, Eilaf, was a priest at Hexham. In 1113, Archbishop Thurstan of York imposed Augustinian canons at Hexham, although Eilaf retained a life-interest in his benefice, a compromise perhaps more common than purist zealots would have liked and one which allowed institutional change without the friction of dispossession. In 1138, Eilaf joined the monastic community at Durham.

Ailred's roots were, therefore, in the English clerical aristocracy of north-east England, a background which influenced his preferment but also instilled an affection for the English past, its saints, such as Cuthbert and Edward the Confessor, and language, which he spoke even on his deathbed. Probably educated initially at Hexham, Ailred was subsequently attached to the court of King David of Scotland, where he made friends with the king's son, Henry, and stepson, Waldef. The easy contacts between the Scottish court and the nobility of northern England were those to be expected in what was still a disputed frontier area. Perhaps, additionally, David, a direct descendent of Ethelred the Unready, attracted ambitious Englishmen when most power in England remained firmly in the hands of the Anglo-French. Ailred rose to be *dispensator* (steward) of the king's household, as well as following his family tradition in becoming a canon of Kirkham. Although in his later incarnation as a monk, Ailred tended to depict his time at court as one of spiritual anguish, the education, personal contacts, and experience of court politics and administration served him well in his future life; they could, despite his own testimony, be said to have been the making of him.

In 1134, Ailred abandoned life in the secular world by joining the newly founded (1132) Cistercian abbey of Rievaulx, near Helmsley in north Yorkshire. Although described as a profound spiritual conversion, his entry into the Order of White Monks proclaimed Ailred as no ordinary recruit. He had been on an embassy from King David to Archbishop Thurstan of York, both of whom were early supporters of the new order. He had heard of Rievaulx from a friend, probably Waldef (who had entered Rievaulx a couple of years before) and was introduced to the abbey itself by its founder, patron and protector, Walter Espec, lord of Helmsley, with whom Ailred was staying. Far from diminishing his vocation, such elevated social contacts were not untypical of those who joined the Cistercians, an order which insisted on the ascetic dimension of a purer, pristine exercise of the Rule of St Benedict. Ascetism flourished in the midst of affluence, particularly amongst the affluent. Institutionally, too, the Cistercians, as befitted a self-conscious elite corps of spiritual warriors, tended to be lead by men of noble or well-to-do origins. The poor layman wishing access to the order were usually confined to the role of lay brother (*conversus*). Cistercian monks were no more socially egalitarian than any other established twelfth century community.

At Rievaulx, Ailred thrived, as a writer, teacher and administrator. According to his biographer, and from his own works, he emerges as handsome, charming, undomineering, well-educated with an almost nineteenth century public school passion for close friendship. Ailred soon rose in the hierarchy. In 1142, while on a visit to Rome to protest against the election of a non-Cistercian archbishop of York, William FitzHerbert, he visited Bernard of Clairvaux, the dominant figure in the order. Apparently, Bernard was impressed, urging Ailred to write his first book, *Speculum Caritatis (The Mirror of Charity)*. Returning to Rievaulx, Ailred became novice-master (1142-3) and abbot of Rievaulx's daughter house of St Laurance at Revesby in

Lincolnshire (1143-7) before being elected abbot of Rievaulx in 1147.

As abbot (1147-67), Ailred's impact was threefold, through his administration of the abbey; his contacts with the secular world; and his writing. In fact the three were inextricably entwined. As with all successful twelfth century abbots, Ailred's main achievement at Rievaulx was to increase its numbers and wealth. He was notorious for encouraging all comers, a *laissez-faire*, open house attitude which swelled the community at Rievaulx from three hundred in 1142 to six hundred and fifty in 1165. By ignoring the suitability of recruits, Ailred was storing up trouble for his successors and was placing a strain on the operation of the strict Cistercian Rule. It was only Ailred's forceful personality that saved the monastery from division and laxity. Popularity brought its own rewards in the form of attention and donations. Just as, in Ailred's words, 'the strong and the weak alike' found the gates of Rievaulx open, so did their lay relatives and acquaintances. During the civil war of Stephen's reign, Ailred encouraged gifts of land 'because he realised that in this unsettled time such gifts profited knights and monks alike . . . the possessors of goods were helped to salvation'. The benefit to the monks was more material. The close embrace between monastery and nobility was crucial to the very nature and achievement of twelfth century monasticism.

Ailred had a more individual role in secular affairs. His friends included the English justiciar Robert, earl of Leicester and Gilbert Foliot, bishop of London. Even before 1154, he had ingratiated himself with Henry of Anjou by dedicating to him a *Geneaology of the Kings of England* (1152-3), which emphasised to the future king the union of English and Norman lines: Henry II was the first post-Conquest king to be descended from both Alfred the Great and Rollo of Normandy. Ailred's political and personal loyalties could be divided, as when, c.1155-7, he wrote his account, *Relatio de Standardo (Story of the Battle of the Standard)*, of David of Scotland's invasion of 1138 which was defeated by Walter Espec. Characteristically, perhaps, Ailred solved the problems by praising both his patrons. His audience was probably confined to his monastery.

Away from Rievaulx, Ailred frequently acted as an arbitor or judge in ecclesiastical disputes, including anything from the precedence of the prior of Durham to a lurid sex scandal at the nunnery at Watton. He was a patron of the hermit, Godric of Finchale, whose biography he commissioned from Reginald of Coldingham. He was a sought-after preacher. Alone, however, such activity would not explain his reputation. To a large extent, this depends on the affectionate biography of him by one of his own monks, Walter Daniel, and on his own writings.

Modern historians have been convinced that they know something of Ailred's personality because his surviving works not only reflect his interests and career but are often composed in a manner which invited sympathy and in a tone which suggests intimate revelation. This is especially true of Ailred's most famous work, *De Spirituali Amicitia (Spiritual Friendship)*, written between 1150 and 1165. Based on Cicero's *De Amicitia,* Ailred's book purports to use his own emotional experience to assert the spiritual importance of friendship: 'it is easy to pass from man's friendship to God's by reason of their similarity'; 'suddenly and unawares love changes its object and being so near touches the sweetness of Christ . . . thus rising from that holy love which reaches the friend to that which reaches Christ, he will joyfully pluck the rich fruit of friendship'. It is, in fact, difficult to know whether to take apparent confessions of emotion at face value, especially as the object of the work was to confirm and enhance the faith of monks living in a community within which a cult of spiritual friendship was of evident value. Walter Daniel's account of Ailred was designed to serve a similar purpose.

Firmer evidence of Ailred's interests are found in his other works. His sermons and theological works, for example on the Soul or the Book of Isaiah, show him as a teacher. Rievaulx possessed a tradition of scholarship before Ailred's abbacy, in particular local hagiography. Ailred's contribution was typical. His *De Sanctis Ecclesiae Haugustaldensis* (1154/55) is a tract on the relics preserved at Hexham. Hexham was Ailred's family church and he took the opportunity to emphasise, and probably exaggerate the role that successive generations of his ancestors had played in the history of Hexham and its relics. Perhaps Ailred was the more conscious of family pride as he had chosen celibacy (as had his sister). His admiration of Northumbrian saints was matched by his affection for Edward the Confessor, canonised in 1161, at whose translation at Westminster in 1163 Ailred preached. He followed this with a *Life of Edward the Confessor* (later translated into French by Matthew Paris for Henry III's queen). Whatever national or local political or ecclesiastical points he wished to make, such diverse literary output places him in the forefront of the intellectual monastic world in England. More learned than many efficient abbots, he was also less credulous: he dismissed Geoffrey of Monmouth's Arthurian stories as fiction as early as 1142-3.

However much his vocation was particularly novel or Cistercian, the chief impression Ailred has left is that of a traditionally scholarly ecclesiastical administrator, whose provincial connections and pride in local saints place him firmly within the expectations of his own ancestors as much as those of his new, more abrasive colleagues in the Order of Cîteaux.

Walter Daniel, *Vita Ailredi*, ed & trans F. M. Powicke, 1950.

THE NUN OF WATTON (*fl.* late 1150s or 1160) was one of the victims of a monastic system which is more often remembered for its heroes. Although her name is unknown her story was recounted by Ailred of Rievaulx who was consulted over the case. Watton was a Gilbertine house in which nuns, canons, lay sisters and lay brothers lived, although rigidly segregated. The story reveals a darker side of the religious life, a world of tense closed communities in which a breakdown in discipline caused dislocation when spiritual harmony could be replaced by vengeance, cruelty, and barbarous violence; in which a social crisis released pent up forces of sexual jealousy or anxiety which, in turn, demanded harsh repression before an ordered norm could be recovered. There are elements of social ritual as well as religious extenuation in Ailred's account. The nun was caught in an affair with a lay brother. After she confessed, her fellow nuns beat her up; the younger nuns even wanted her burnt, flayed and branded. Although she avoided that, the nun was incarcerated in solitary confinement, her legs in chains, and fed on bread and water. When she was found to be pregnant, she was prevailed upon to disclose where her lover, who had fled the monastery, was living. By this time, the business had reached the ears of the founder of the order, Gilbert of Sempringham. On his orders, some other lay brothers caught and mugged the miscreant who was then handed over to the nuns. What happened next almost defies belief. The nuns 'wished to avenge the injury to their virginity'. While the man was held down by the other nuns, his mistress was forced to cut off his testicles, which were then thrust into her mouth 'just as they were, befouled with blood'. The man was returned to the lay brothers, and the nun to her prison. There, although this is concealed by a story of heavenly visitations, her baby was either aborted, still-born or disposed of, killed most likely, at birth. At this, the nun appeared 'virginal' again, and was released. God, as Ailred commented, had protected the nuns whose prayers throughout had been that He should be 'mindful of their virginal shame' and 'counteract the infamy and ward off danger'. As to the scenes of sadistic violence and sexual humiliation, Ailred expressed himself unhappy at the shedding of blood, although he commended the nuns' zeal in exacting revenge for what he, as they, saw as an insult to Christ. For Gilbert and Ailred, the matter was of discipline and upholding the sacred vows of the nuns, particularly in a new order which was bound to run risks of such liaisons. What they ignored were the dangers of admitting oblate nuns as young as four years old. The honour of the community is throughout seen as paramount over the individual: that, after all, was a central theme of rigorous monasticism. However, the problems of communal celibacy were heightened by an official imagery shot through with sublimated sexuality: Christ the bridegroom; the Church his Bride; the nun 'marrying' Christ etc. Even Ailred talks of nuns' 'ineffable raptures' at Mass. Above all, whatever the emotions and feelings of the actors in the drama, the events were seen, perhaps even by the participants, through a prism of absolute belief in a determining Divine Providence which stripped actions of temporal meaning by endowing them with spiritual significance. Ailred, making an edifying story out of the sordid scandal, was eager to avoid criticism of the community and, by implication, the monastic vocation. What is intriguing is that most educated contemporaries may have agreed with him.

G. Constable, 'Ailred of Rievaulx and the Nun of Watton', *Mediaeval Women*, ed D. Baker, 1978.

GODRIC OF FINCHALE (*d*.1170) was a merchant-turned-holy man who settled at Finchale, on the River Wear near Durham, who received wide attention during his life and around whom there developed a strong local cult which lasted to the end of the Middle Ages. As with other twelfth century ascetics, Godric's reputation depended not on his poverty or isolation (he had neither) but on his simplicity, his contact with nature, and his openness to rich and poor alike. His cult was unusual in the very high proportion of women it attracted.

Much of the information of Godric's life comes from a biography written by Reginald of Coldingham, one of three Durham monks who wrote contemporary *Lives* of the hermit, evidently in the hope of annexing his fame to their priory. Reginald's *Life*, commissoned by the prior of Durham and Ailred of Rievaulx, was reluctantly authorised by Godric himself who supplied details of his early career and lived to receive a finished copy. Whether the subject's cooperation makes the *Life* more or less accurate is a moot point. Certainly, Reginald frequently introduces Godric's apparent devotion to Durham's own patron saint Cuthbert. However, the *Life* reveals much about the nature of the eremitic vocation and its uses in twelfth century England.

A Norfolk man of English parentage, Godric began his career as a merchant. From modest beginnings as a local pedlar, as his business grew he took to the sea, trading throughout the North Sea and beyond. His travels took him to the major pilgrimage centres of Compostella in Spain, Rome, and St Gilles in Southern France, as well as British shrines at St Andrew's and the Farne Islands. Godric twice visited Jerusalem, although whether in the course of his international trading or, as the *Life* implies, as part of his renunciation of Mammon, is unclear. Godric's business interests also included acting as steward to rich landowners in Norfolk. Godric evidently took full advantage of the varied entrepreneurial opportunities offered by the growing economy of the early twelfth century.

Retiring from commerce, Godric wandered around northern

England until, under the patronage of Ranulf Flambard, bishop of Durham, he settled (c.1112) at Finchale where he built a chapel and was joined by a substantial entourage, including his own priest. His holiness had practical application. A French speaker, he could mediate between the English locals and their masters, lay or clerical. Credited with the useful powers of prophecy and healing, he also acted as a banker, amassing a large treasure: 'the wealth of many had been . . . entrusted to him'. The hoard was a target for thieves and, in 1137/8, Scottish invaders who, frustrated in their search for it, slaughtered his livestock. Adjacent to the major centre of ecclesiastical and secular authority in the north-east, Godric was ideally placed to give spiritual, medical or financial advice unencumbered by the constraints of the established social or clerical hierarchies. In a sense, he remained an entrepreneur, a trader in conspicuous holiness with which he eased or solved his clients' problems. His services encouraged donations. Apart from guardianship of the riches of others, he kept livestock; had the materials to paint and sculpt; and could afford to rebuild his original wooden chapel in stone.

Of course his effectiveness, as financial consultant or thaumaturge, was attributed to his being a 'man of God'. As such, he came to the notice of Becket, Ailred of Rievaulx, King Malcolm of Scotland, even Pope Alexander III. But his appeal was essentially to a smaller, humbler audience. After he died, apparently in extreme old age, in 1170, the monks of Durham began to nurture a cult. From 1172, Godric's relics performed miracles of healing which drew a regular stream of pilgrims over the next few centuries. The cult was strictly local: almost all known pilgrims came from a forty-mile radius of the shrine which, in the thirteenth century, was extended as part of a new priory built on the site of Godric's hermitage. Godric's cures appealed especially to women (comprising ⅔ of the 244 recorded miracles) and those without social pretentions. This may say something about the expense and misogyny of the more famous, elite shrines run by monks, not least that of neighbouring St Cuthbert.

Libellus de Vita et Miraculis S. Godrici Heremitae de Finchale, ed. J. Stevenson (Surtees Society), 1847.

CHRISTINA OF MARKYATE (*c.*1096/98-*c.*1155/66) was a recluse under the patronage of the monastery of St. Alban's. Her contemporary importance is witnessed by her possession of an elabrate luxury Psalter (now at Hildesheim) and the elevation of her hermit's cell into a nunnery in 1145. Her posthumous reputation rests on a surviving *Life*, written at St. Alban's in the twelfth century, probably by a close acquaintance.

Christina came from a family of wealthy English landowners in Huntingdon. Her reaction to puberty was to take a vow of virginity on a visit to St. Alban's. The crisis of her life came around the year 1114 when her aunt's former lover, Ranulf Flambard, bishop of Durham, tried to seduce her. Although fearful of rape, Christina successfully resisted. In revenge, Flambard helped arrange a forced marriage for Christina to a local man, Burhred. Even then, Christina defended her chastity. In the end, released from her marriage and cut off by her parents, Christina fled from home and was placed under the care of a group of hermits near Dunstable, first Alfwen of Flamstead and then Roger of Markyate, a former monk of St. Alban's. On Roger's death, *c.*1122, she attracted the protection of Archbishop Thurstan of York before finally establishing herself at Markyate *c.*1123. From then on, with the patronage and friendship of Abbot Geoffrey of St. Alban's, Christina became an established and respected figure in influential religious circles. She resisted offers of preferment to nunneries in York, Marcigny-les-Nonnains and Fontevrault. In 1155/6, Henry II himself made her a grant of fifty shillings. Although her influence was largely personal, on her important friends, such as Abbot Geoffrey or by the example of her eremtic privations, a nunnery was established at Markyate by 1145. It is clear from the richness of the Psalter prepared for her use and the *Life* that her vocation had a practical dimension. One charge of her detractors was that she was 'just a worldly-wise business woman'. The were right although her admirers attributed her material as well as spiritual success not to 'earthly prudence' but to 'a gift of God': a distinction without a difference, perhaps.

Many of Christina's contemporaries affected to flee the world and, like Wulfric of Haselbury or Godric of Finchdale, set themselves up profitably as mediators between God and man, man and nature and, most importantly, man and man, across class or race. There was, in a changing and increasingly affluent society, a clear place for the professional outsider whose escape from the world was more apparent than real. In England, the complexity of social and economic relations was compounded by the barriers of French and English. It is no coincidence that most of the twelfth century recluses were *bien pensant* English (Wulfric; Godric; Christina herself and her companions, such as Alfwen of Flamstead) who could converse in French. They were of a social or economic status to compete with the French-speaking elite, symbols not so much of any Ivanhoe-like Anglo-Saxon nationalism as of social contact, protection, even power; aloof and therefore useful; social as well as spiritual interpreters.

Christina, in her cell almost on Watling Street (the present A5), one of the main highways of medieval England, close to, and protected by the neighbouring abbey of St. Alban's, one of the leading Benedictine houses, fitted this pattern. Well connected, patronised by the great of the church, her seclusion was relative, and operated within semi-formal constraints which became official when, after sixteen years as a freelance, she took the veil at St. Alban's in 1131. Hermits were organised, as witnessed by the group under Roger of Markyate, and, in a sense, licensed by more orthodox or regular clergy, very different from the eccentric liminal figures of contemporary Arthurian romances. Two features, according to the *Life*, distinguished Christina from other hermits. Her miracles seem to be confined to prophecy (a useful commodity in any age), and restricted to her own circle with only a few externally useful acts; indeed only one cure is mentioned. This may suggest that the *Life* had a limited purpose of praise of an example for the inspiration of Markyate priory, which lasted until the Reformation. The other eccentricity was her recorded obsession with sex, or rather, the lack of it.

Christina's sexual status, as a virgin, is the *leitmotif* of her biography. It is littered with thwarted seducers, frustrated husbands, lecherous hosts and guilt-ridden clerical associates. Temptation is everywhere, and recognised by Christina herself who worries about her feelings towards her friend, the abbot of St. Alban's. It could be that the reader is supposed to take these stories allegorically; Christina's embattled virginity representing the difficulties of spiritual purity, a metaphor of the religious life, or even the Church itself. The vivid circumstantial details, however, suggest actuality. The dramatic scene in Bishop Flambard's bedroom is a classic:

> Satan put it into his heart to desire her. Busily, therefore, seeking some trick of getting her into his power, he had the unsuspecting girl brought into his chamber where he himself slept, which was hung with beautiful tapestries, the only others present with the innocent child being members of his retinue. Her father and mother and the others with whom she had come were in the hall apart giving themselves up to drunkenness. When it was getting dark the bishop gave a secret sign to his servants and they left the room, leaving their master and Christina, that is to say, the wolf and the lamb, together in the same room. For shame! The shameless bishop took hold of Christina by one of the sleeves of her tunic and with that mouth which he used to consecrate the sacred species, he solicited her to commit a wicked deed. What was the poor girl to do in such straits? Should she call her parents? They had already gone to bed. To consent was out of the question: but openly resist she dared not because if she openly resisted him, she would certainly be overcome by force.
>
> Hear, then, how prudently she acted. She glanced towards the door and saw that, though it was closed, it was not bolted. And she said to him: 'Allow me to bolt the door: for even if we have no fear of God, at least we should take precautions that no man should catch us in this act.' He demanded an oath from her that she would not deceive him, but that she would, as she said, bolt the door. And she swore to him. And so, being released, she darted out of the room and bolting the door firmly from the outside, hurried quickly home. This was the beginning of all the frightful troubles that followed afterwards. Then that wretch, seeing that he had been made a fool of by a young girl, was eaten up with resentment and counted all his power as nothing until he could avenge the insult he had suffered. But the only way in which he could conceivably gain his revenge was by depriving Christina of her virginity, either by himself or by someone else, for the preservation of which she did not hesitate to repulse even a bishop.

The Life of Christina of Markyate, ed. C. H. Talbot, 1959.

C. Holdsworth, 'Christina of Markyate' in *Mediaeval Women*, ed. D. Baker, 1978.

THEOBALD (*d.*1161; archbishop of Canterbury 1138-61) was one of the most effective medieval archbishops of Canterbury, although by no means one of the most colourful. He came to Canterbury with the classic credentials of an abbot of Bec, but, unlike his illustrious predecessors Lanfranc and Anselm, his elevation was unexpected and controversial. In 1138, Theobald, a native of Lower Normandy, was unknown in England, a political nonentity who had only become an abbot two years previously. Perhaps his inexperience and lack of involvement in the factional manoeuvring of the early years of Stephen's reign actually commended Theobald in preference to the obvious candidate, Stephen's brother, Henry, bishop of Winchester. In the event, his abbacy proved of less importance than the influence of Bec's lay patron, and Stephen's closest lay advisor, Waleran, count of Meulan. However, as with so many of Stephen's political calculations, the appointment of Theobald, rushed through on 24 December 1138, failed to bring the expected benefits. The king had alienated his powerful brother, while, initially, the *ingénu* archbishop was unable to provide any balancing weighty support. Once Theobald did establish his political bearings, although whenever possible observing public loyalty to Stephen, he proved a closet Angevin, resistant to royal control and the king's increasingly urgent demands for the coronation of his son.

Overshadowed between 1139 and 1143 by Henry of Winchester's appointment as Papal Legate in England, Theobald was content to follow events. In December 1141 he recrowned Stephen and his queen in Canterbury, but after the Angevin conquest of Normandy (1141-44) Theobald pursued an increasingly independent role. In this he was aided by the Angevin sympathies of Popes Celestine II (1143-44) and Eugenius III (1145-53) and Stephen's enfeebled control over the English Church. Henry of Winchester's legateship expired with Innocent II in 1143 and Stephen's failure to impose his candidate as archbishop of York led to a schism in the northern province which left Theobald unchallenged in leadership of the Church, a dominance confirmed in 1149/50 by his own appointment as papal legate.

In 1147 he visited Paris at the same time as Geoffrey of Anjou. The following year he defied a royal ban and travelled, at some personal risk, to the papal Council of Rheims. Once there, he characteristically interceded to prevent Pope Eugenius from excommunicating King Stephen. During this exile, he and the young Henry FitzEmpress persuaded the pope to create Gilbert Foliot bishop of Hereford: securing jobs for people was one of Theobald's chief attainments. Theobald wished to establish the firm authority of both church and state. A weak king meant a threatened church. For the remainder of Stephen's reign, Theobald sought political compromise with his ultimate objective being an Angevin succession. Thus he attempted mediation in 1148 and played a central role in the final agreement of 1153 between Stephen and Henry FitzEmpress, but he refused point blank to crown Stephen's son Eustace in 1152, preferring another brief exile. Seeing royal and ecclesiastical authority as complementary, Theobald was nevertheless concerned to assert his rights as archbishop of Canterbury, not least against unnecessary papal interference. He regarded Henry of Blois's legateship as doubly threatening in its reliance on papal power and usurpation of Canterbury's primacy. Even the crisis of 1148 can be seen not so much as an assertion of papal authority, more a vindication of Canterbury's right to represent the English church at the Council. This view may have rubbed off on one of Theobald's companions in the open boat which took the archbishop across the perilous Channel on the way to Rheims: Thomas Becket.

Under Henry II, Theobald continued to promote ecclesiastical authority, particularly his own in harmony with the king. It must be uncertain how Theobald would have reacted if Henry had insisted on defining the jurisdictional parameters of Church and State as he was to do at Clarendon in 1164. He certainly desired a demarcation of the spiritual and temporal spheres in justice as elsewhere. But his response to the Papal Schism of 1159 is perhaps typical. Two popes had been elected, Alexander III and Victor IV. Theobald adhered to the former, but he wrote to Henry: 'while the matter is in suspense we think that it is unlawful in your realm to accept either of them without your approval', although he urged the king to take the advice of the clergy, which the king did.

As archbishop, Theobald maintained the traditional hostility towards the monks of Canterbury, particularly over their administration of estates and revenues. Although a Benedictine monk himself, Theobald preferred the company of secular clerks, men of intellect rather than conspicuous piety. There can have been few more distinguished clerical households in the Middle Ages to compare with the men assembled by Theobald, and fewer still on whom the golden rewards of patronage and preferment were showered more lavishly. Roger of Pont l'Eveque became archbishop of York (1154-81); John of Pagham, bishop of Worcester (1151-7); John of Canterbury, bishop of Poitiers (1162), archbishop of Narbonne and finally archbishop of Lyons (1182-93); Bartholomew, bishop of Exeter (1161-84); Theobald's brother Walter, bishop of Rochester (1148-82). Also attracted to Theobald's househod were John of Salisbury, one of the leading European intellectuals of his generation, who wrote many of Theobald's official letters; Master Vacarius, a canon lawyer of international repute from Bologna; Jordan Fantosme, later master of the cathedral school at Winchester and author of a French verse account of the great rebellion of 1173-4; and Thomas Becket, the drama of whose career has tended to cast his old mentor in the shade. Yet it was Theobald who chose these men and, in many cases, provided their opportunity for public prominence.

Personally, Theobald presented an apparent contradiction. In private he was sharp tongued, garrulous and short tempered, but, according to Robert of Cricklade, trimmed his conversation when talking to powerful men. Patient, occasionally obsequious to superiors, Theobald could be aggressive, overbearing even violent towards inferiors. But, unlike his archdeacon and successor, Becket, he did not over-react to people or events. Publicly cautious and patient, he calculated his advantage with care, as when he arranged for Becket to become Henry II's chancellor in 1155 as the young, untried, foreign king's minder. Unglamorous; by no means a saint, even posthumously; a nepotist and a far from passionate monk, Theobald achieved much. He saw off the challenge of Henry of Blois to ecclesiastical dominance; he checked the business incompetence of the Canterbury monks; he firmly established the de facto primacy of Canterbury over York; he secured a reasonably smooth Angevin succession after a generation of civil war; he successfully promoted his protégés; he defined a semi-detached working relationship between the English church and the increasingly intrusive legalism of the papacy; he maintained the independence of the church without challenging its interdependence with the state. The measure of his achievement is perhaps to be found in the explosive chaos which followed his death: even that can be attributed in part to his success as a patron.

A. Saltman, *Theobald, Archbishop of Canterbury*, 1956.

NIGEL OF ELY (*d*.1169; bishop of Ely 1133-69) was a member of the remarkable family of royal administrators established by his uncle, Roger, bishop of Salisbury, Henry I's justiciar. This included his brother, Alexander, bishop of Lincoln; his cousins, Roger and Adelelm, respectively chancellor and treasurer in the early years of Stephen's reign; and his own illegitimate son, Richard FitzNeal, treasurer to Henry II and Richard I. Educated at Laon under the renowned *magister* Anselm and his brother, the mathematician Ralph, Nigel became treasurer to Henry I in the mid-1120s, the post probably being created for him by his uncle Roger when (1123-6) viceroy of England. As treasurer, Nigel, who may have picked up the latest computing techniques at Laon, coordinated the financial operations of the king's chamber and the treasury. He remained at the heart of government after his appointment as bishop of Ely in 1133 until he shared in his uncle's ruin in 1139. Nigel's response to Bishop Roger's arrest was characteristic. Used to a substantial military entourage, Nigel withdrew to Devizes castle prepared to fight, only surrendering when the king threatened to hang his cousin Roger. Excluded from court and stripped of office, Nigel retained his see and from there continued to resist Stephen, hiring troops and fortifying the Isle of Ely. Driven out by royalist forces, Nigel joined Matilda in the west country, being at her side throughout the triumphant months of 1141. When the pendulum swung against the Empress, Nigel became an especial target of the king, fearful lest the bishop combine with other East Anglian rebels. In 1143, Nigel was forced to appeal to Rome against charges brought by the papal legate, Stephen's brother, Henry of Winchester. On his return in 1145, he made peace with the king, giving his teenage son Richard as hostage.

In 1154, at the repeated and urgent requests of the new king Henry II, he came out of retirement to help reconstruct administration at the exchequer which had been severely run down during the civil war. Nigel's reluctance was understandable. Most of his new colleagues, including the two justiciars, had served Stephen, one of them, Robert of Leicester, being implicated in the coup of 1139. The urgent problems at the exchequer were re-establishing control over sheriffs; restoring procedures of effective audit; and the revival of clear, comprehensive and coherent records on the Pipe Rolls. All these, by the time Nigel retired through ill-health in 1164-5, had, to a great extent, been achieved.

For Henry II, Nigel represented expertise and experience. In the flattering account by his son in the *Dialogue of the Exchequer*, he appears as a master of procedure and exchequer business. Although his position was informal, Nigel was influential enough to be able to give the justiciar, his old enemy Robert of Leicester, a severe dressing down when he breached precedent over exchequer privileges: the exchange must have given the aged bishop some pleasure. The impression given in the *Dialogue* that Nigel recreated the exchequer is probably untrue, but he did restore it on the same lines as it had operated under his uncle, providing Henry II with effective means to implement his wishes. To his son, Nigel was a heroic bureaucrat. He certainly was industrious. At Ely, he instituted inquests into the see's lands; established a diocesan exchequer; and vigorously pursued resumption of estates lost in the severe depredations of the civil war. Combined with his actions under Stephen and his charters, the evidence shows Nigel to have been, as his enemies portrayed him, a man more adept at secular lordship than spiritual leadership.

JOHN OF SALISBURY (*c.*1115/20-1180) had an international career typical of the well-connected and highly-educated twelfth century ecclesiastic. Although in the second rank of academics, lawyers and administrators, John was a prominent member of the closely interlaced clerisy of clever secular clerks who glided seemingly effortlessly between the courts of kings, popes and prelates. John's contacts are a roll-call of the intellectual and spiritual leaders of western Christendom in the mid-twelfth century: Abelard, Pullen, Becket, St. Bernard, Eugenius III, Hadrian IV, Alexander III, Archbishop Theobald. John's contribution to this circle was literary and secretarial. Education at Exeter and Paris was followed by travel and employment across Europe. Although no lawyer, he spent much of his career advising on legal matters, for example on appeals from the English church to Rome. An ability to get on with people secured him an ill-defined administrative post at the papal curia in the late 1140s, followed in the 1150s by employment as secretary to Theobald of Canterbury. In England he became a friend of Thomas Becket, whom he preceded into exile in 1164, only returning in 1170. Apart from the letters he composed for his masters, John's main literary works were the *Metalogion*, a defence of the study of the liberal arts; the *Historia Pontificalis* a gossipy account of the papal curia between 1148 and 1152, written in exile during the 1160s; lives of Anselm and Becket; and the *Policraticus*, written in the 1150s, which combines a critique of contemporary rulers with a treatise on political thought. The *Policraticus* presents a moral view of rule. There is a single principle of government derived from the teaching of the Church. However, although God's law is sovereign, in the secular sphere the monarch possesses unassailable authority. John describes a republic (*i.e.* secular state) as a living organism whose head governs the other members. Only where the monarch is illegitimate, and, in John's terms, therefore tyrannical, was there a right to depose or kill him to restore the moral order. The very unoriginal practicality of the *Policraticus* commended it to later humanist lawyers of the fourteenth century and after who were attempting to construct a theory of authority not dependent upon the self-validating minutiae of lawyers and theologians. John's writing was characterised by a lack of dogmatism and a sense of irony, even objectivity in assessing men and events. John's eye for detail, imagery and allusion made up for his lack of intellectual depth, a fact of which he may have been conscious, as a number of his classical references and quotations are entirely bogus. But they look impressive. There is a refreshing humanity in John. An observer more than an actor, when caught up in the century's most famous act of violence, the murder of Becket, he made his position clear to the archbishop: 'We are sinners and not yet prepared to die: I see no-one here except you who is anxious to die for dying's sake'. At the entry of the knights into the cathedral, John quickly hid. Yet his association with the martyr did him no harm, perhaps even identifying him as a candidate for the high office he attained at the very end of his career as bishop of Chartres. John confessed to another human weakness: drink. He regarded himself as something of a connoisseur of wine, being particularly harsh on Sicilian, Greek and Cypriot wines which he thought lethal. But he was no wine snob. In 1157, he wrote to a friend: 'I am fond of both wine and beer, and do not abhor any liquor that can make me drunk'. As has recently been written, 'John's fame is as a mirror of his age'.

M. Wilks, ed., *The World of John of Salisbury*, 1984.

HENRY II (1133-1189; king of England 1154-89) has been seen as one of the most important English monarchs. To nineteenth century constitutional historians, he was the 'gravedigger of feudalism', the 'father of the common law', a king whose sagacity and insight put England and Englishmen on a path to equality under the law. In the twentieth century, what has impressed is the scale of Henry's activities and his energy, the man who pacified England; held together a French empire that stretched from the Channel to the Pyrenees; had designs on hegemony in the British Isles; whose itinerary embraced Dublin and Toulouse; and whose policies set the political agenda for half a continent. Where his regime has been criticised for harshness it has been praised for efficiency and effectiveness. Although there are many other candidates, Henry II is possibly the most overpraised monarch in English history.

In fact, Henry II had no grand design of rule, no lucid strategy for law or government, and no especial interest in England. His accession to the throne honoured a dynastic obligation but returned England to the status of a province of a continental ruler. Henry, born at Le Mans, dying at Chinon, buried at Fontevrault, saw the world from the patrimony of his ancestors, counts of Anjou and dukes of Normandy. Henry spent two thirds of his long reign out of England; his main concern with his kingdom was the exploitation of his rights and collection of revenue. Many previous views of Henry have been distorted by an anachronistic or insular perception of what constituted government in the twelfth century and, specifically, what role in government was played by the monarch. The king may have been the soul of the polity, but the workings of administration and society possessed free will. Henry's achievement was not as a builder of political structures, legal systems or administrative coherence, rather that he survived, almost to the end, as undisputed ruler of his dominions, whose lordship validated the power of his magnates and who maintained the inheritance of his predecessors, counts of Anjou, dukes of Normandy and kings of England. With only a consort's interest in Aquitaine, there he was content to allow his son, Richard of Poitou, autonomous control provided it did not clash with his own concerns. Although owing more to hostile imagination than truth, Henry's deathbed words

Henry II
(From his effigy at Fontevrault Abbey in Anjou)

invented by the splenetic Gerald of Wales have a ring if not of authenticity then of empathy: 'Shame! Shame! on a vanquished king'; less a lament on traduced regality, more an apostrophe of self-pitying failure.

From the moment of his birth, Henry had great expectations. As eldest son of Matilda, heiress of England and Geoffrey, count of Anjou, one of his grandfathers was Henry I, duke of Normandy, also king of England; the other Fulk, formerly count of Anjou, then king of Jerusalem. Henry's potential inheritance included England, Normandy, Maine, Touraine and Anjou. The aura of destiny which clung to the young prince was explicit in the name by which contemporaries knew him: Henry Fitz-Empress (his mother's first husband had been Holy Roman Emperor). Throughout his adult life, Henry displayed the insouciant disregard and dislike for the trappings of power and lineage in which only those totally secure in both can afford to indulge.

However magnificent, every piece of Henry's inheritance had to be won: England and Normandy from King Stephen and the house of Blois; and the Angevin patrimony against the claims of Henry's younger brother, Geoffrey, to whom they had been promised by family agreement in 1151. Duke of Normandy in 1150; count of Anjou on his father's death in 1151; duke of Aquitaine and count of Poitou by virtue of his marriage with Eleanor of Aquitaine in 1152, Henry's accession to the throne of England in 1154 marked a personal fulfilment rather than an inevitable progress or political epoch. His accumulation was literally unique, fortuitous and apparently transient. That it came to be seen as something rather more than that owes much to Henry himself.

Henry received an excellent education, academically from some of the best scholars in England and northern France; politically and militarily from his own experiences in the struggle for his English inheritance. Henry posed as something of an intellectual and scholar; he was a good linguist, fluent in French and Latin; he was reputed to have helped compile his own legislation. He was renowned for his political deviousness (or skill depending on the point of view) and has also been credited with contributing to a military revolution in his concentration on castles

as the key elements in warfare. Whatever Master Matthew at
Bristol or Adelard of Bath taught him, Henry, figurehead of his
dynasty's cause since his first visit to England in 1142, learnt
most about ruling and statecraft from his English campaigns of
1147, 1149 and 1153. He was knighted in 1149 by David I of
Scotland, who, as a great-grandson of King Edmund Ironsides
(d.1016), had a claim to the English throne which he effectively
renounced. In 1153, Henry determined the issue of the succession by force. Agreements at Winchester and Westminster were
brokered by a baronage whose security had been undermined by
constant shifts in political prospects and alliances. With a
scorched-earth campaign reminding them of the possibility of a
continued struggle and his refusal to abandon his hereditary
rights, Henry secured approval for his succession, his path eased
by the death of Stephen's eldest son, Eustace.

The key to the 1153 compromise, hereditary right, was a
theme to which Henry repeatedly returned in official pro-
nouncement for the rest of his reign. But it also posed a problem.
If his succession guaranteed the rules of legitimate inheritance,
where did those rules end? Were all holdings, titles, lands,
offices, castellanies etc., to be included, as in France? One of the
features of Henry's rule was the distinction drawn between what
was considered a royal office — a sheriff or local justiciar — and
what was allowed as a heritable title — earldoms, baronies etc.
There was little logic to this: an earl was originally just as much
a royal officer as a sheriff. Equally, both Stephen and Matilda
had created hereditary sheriffs. Yet Henry tenaciously sought to
restrict, limit and supervise the rights of all freemen, culminating in the so-called Inquest of Sheriffs of 1170 which investigated, as the commission had it, 'archbishops, bishops, abbots,
earls, barons, sub-tenants, knights, citizens and burgesses, and
their stewards and officers'. However, Henry was not trying to
establish a coherent framework of property law or a new system
of public jurisdiction taking precedence over private franchises,
although this ultimately was the effect. His motives were primarily political not legal. To secure his new dynasty in England
— his policies in his continental lands were subject to other constraints — Henry wished to eradicate autonomous franchises
prejudicial to royal authority. Hence his consistent vigilance over

the custody of castles, which had played such a crucial role in the civil war of Stephen's reign and were to prove pivotal in the Great Rebellion of 1173-4. In terms of law, England was similar to northern and western France. Differences lay in the political ramifications. Whereas in France the count or seigneur held his castles free from royal interference, this was not the case in England under Henry II.

But even here, Henry was supported by tradition not invention. Unlike in France, from the tenth century English kings retained formal control of public jurisdiction. All freemen were liable to swear a general oath of obedience to the king; there was no tradition or right of private war; earls were regularly disciplined, their lands confiscated or restored according to political circumstance and royal will; there existed a working central administration. After the Conquest royal powers were confirmed or reinforced. William I and Henry I were among the most powerful and assertive monarchs of their time. It was to this legacy that Henry II appealed, explicitly. Again and again he insisted that he was intent on restoring the rights held by his grandfather alienated by Stephen. However, Henry's main concern was the pursuit of his rights, unfettered by tradition. It was this constant manipulation and extension of his prerogatives that earned Henry the reputation simultaneously as a creator of new laws and a ruler who governed by selfish caprice, in the phrases of the time *ira et malevolentia* and *vis et voluntas*: anger, malice, force and wilfulness.

Henry's power was personal. His conception of rule, for all his and his courtiers' scholarly idealising, was practical, the advice and support of his magnates counting for more than any philosophical statement of monarchical authority. The lack of coherent ideology is most obvious in the contrast between his treatment of his subjects in England and his king in France. His theory of good government comprised what was good for him. Henry, like any other contemporary ruler, wished to secure his rights for his own advantage and his possessions for his dynasty. Thus his rule tended to the piecemeal and *ad hoc* rather than the ordered or systematic. To take a famous example, Henry's dispute with Becket (1163-70) was conducted by the king both as a pesonal vendetta and an intellectually incoherent attempt to safeguard royal rights to justice and ecclesiastical patronage. Against Becket's protestations of universal laws and definitions of authority, Henry proposed an empirical appeal to tradition and expediency. Ironically, although Henry lost the academic debate and the propaganda war so disastrously, his pragmatism was vindicated in church/state relations in the years after Becket's murder. What was true for the church was also true for the state. Henry wanted what he thought was owed him from England, chiefly wealth. To secure this he was unafraid to regulate and codify legal procedures and practice or to discipline his subjects, where necessary and possible. He was no philosopher king; no legal genius in huntsman's disguise.

The impression of farsighted creativity in part derives from the sources for Henry's reign, particularly the increasing use of writing in law and administration. Legal procedures long determined orally in courts that kept records in the memories of the wise appeared more orderly when committed to writing and, indeed, became more standardised — or fossilized as Michael Clanchy has it — as a result. The chroniclers of Henry's reign were either Angevin apologists who lauded the advent of 'the peacemaker' after 1154; or were courtiers and officials, often directed by hindsight to compare Henry's reign with the uncertainties of Richard's and the disasters of John's. Thus, a king almost universally disliked and mistrusted in life, in retrospect became a by-word for good government.

The essence of twelfth century government was the king, his personality and desires. Despite the Exchequer's role in administering his will, royal influence was controlled from the king's chamber. Despite itinerant justices after 1168 and the beginnings of a central bench of judges at Westminster (1178), justice followed the household of the king. Henry was literally mobbed and jostled by petitioners wherever he went. The king personally presided over important cases involving lay or clerical tenants-in-chief. In such circumstances, Henry's character and habits determined the nature of his rule far more certainly than developments in fiscal or judicial bureaucracy. Belying his posthumous reputation as a lion of justice, Henry was a dilatory judge and his officials notoriously venal and corrupt. Some suitors died before their cases came to judgement. He left the Bigod inheritance unresolved for the last twelve years of his reign. Richard of Anstey was luckier, but he had to chase Henry across England and France for over five years, at great personal cost, before he finally secured a decision in 1163. Royal caprice, inattention, absence and indifference may all have contributed; but there was also method. According to one of his courtiers, Henry's forceful mother — not known as a paragon of patience herself, it must be said — had advised him to 'spin out all the affairs of everyone'. She was thinking primarily of patronage, the allocation of offices, but legal judgements were a comparable aspect of royal largesse. Complaints about access, delay and corruption in the judicial process feature prominently in Magna Carta (cc.17-19 and 40).

During Henry's reign there were numerous codifications and clarifications of customary law: the Constitutions of Clarendon (1164); the Assizes of Clarendon (1166), Northampton (1176), of Arms (1181) and Woodstock (1184). The feudal obligations of tenants-in-chief was investigated in the *Cartae Baronum* of 1166 and the administrative duties of his subjects and officials in the great Inquest of 1170. From official documents and the memoirs of courtiers there emerges a picture of an intellectual court, intent on using the fashionable techniques, or at least vocabulary, of inquiry to reveal the truth and of employing the technology of writing to facilitate the running of government. From 1168, justices-in-eyre, itinerant judges, were sent out on regular circuits of counties, to hear royal pleas, including the imposition of fiscal rights as well as criminal and civil cases. Legal historians see the justices as harbingers of effective, rational government: contemporaries saw them as extortioners.

Central to Henry's image as a legal innovator are the so-called possessary assizes. Between 1166 and 1176, Henry and his advisers perfected new procedures in minor pleas over the occupation or inheritance of property (respectively novel disseisin and mort d'ancestor) and, for major pleas of right, replaced trial by battle. The new system depended on plaintiffs initiating a writ from the king to his sheriff to investigate and settle cases. Juries, of knights for 'grand' assizes and freemen for 'petty' assizes, were sworn in to testify to the evidence. Increasingly, itinerant justices delivered the final judgements. These procedures give the impression of a legal revolution mainly because of the survival of writs and records of the judicial eyres. The reality was less novel. The suits were the same; the law was the same as before; the traditional weight of local opinion continued to be felt through the jurors. Justice was not blind, even if now its operation was more transparent. No new law was made, although the increasing bulk of recorded cases exerted a profound influence in establishing a coherent or, at least, standard common law in the thirteenth century. There was no greater guarantee of equity under the new system than previously. There was considerably greater potential for royal exploitation of both plaintiffs and defendants. Above all, there was no strategy of reform on Henry's part beyond attempting more efficiently to pursue his rights and exercise his responsibilities.

It is away from those areas traditionally associated with Henry's supposed genius that his character and intentions must be sought. The events of his reign reveal no especial control over events. Throughout, Henry's course seems to have been determined by a vigorous pursuit of his rights and a tenacious insistence on the establishment of his dynasty through the preferment of his four adult sons. It was not entirely fortuitous that Henry bequeated his lands essentially intact in 1189. Although he had settled his wife's lands of Poitou and Aquitaine on Richard, Brittany on Geoffrey and Ireland on John, there was the presumption that the eldest son, Henry, to whom was allocated the patrimony of England, Normandy and Anjou, was to be the head of the family firm, to whom the others were to pay homage and whose precedence was recognised by his designation and coronation as king of England in 1170. Although there was no strategic aim or intellectual concept of an Angevin 'empire', the association in the Young Henry's inheritance of Anjou with England and Normandy was novel. With the death of the Young King in 1183 and the succession of Richard of Poitou in 1189, to this patrimony was added that of Aquitaine, all of which consisted of John's inheritance in 1199. By 1216, Henry III could lay claim to all Henry II's lands except Brittany as his patrimony, even though he was incapable of making good that claim.

Henry's reign falls into distinct periods. In the 1150s came the re-establishment of royal authority: the seizure of castles; the reconstitution of the Exchequer; the reconciling of factions by the appointment of two former Stephen partisans as justiciars, Richard de Lucy and Robert of Leicester; and the elevation of a protégé of Archbishop Theobald to chancellor and confidential adviser, Thomas Becket. Henry felt sufficiently secure that, from 1158 to 1163, he could leave the administration of England to proxies. The 1160s became dominated by the Becket dispute and Henry's plans for his dynastic settlement. Whereas the latter required defining his relations with magnates and his French overlord, the former imposed a definition of his rights over his subjects, clerical (Constitutions of Clarendon 1164) and lay (Assize of Clarendon; *Cartae Baronum*; justices-in-eyre; Inquest of Sheriffs). The two strands came together in 1170 with the coronation of the Young Henry, the Inquest into ecclesiastical as well as lay officials, Becket's excommunication of those who crowned the Young King and Becket's murder. That Henry had risked the fragile accommodation with Becket for the coronation was a sign of his eagerness to avoid the fate of his predecessor who had consistently failed to engineer the coronation of his son during his lifetime. This sense of insecurity was genuine, almost usual. Every English monarch from 978 to 1189 either possessed a disputed title or was establishing a recent claim.

However, Becket's murder threw Henry's rule into the hazard, not least because of the personal venom which had infected the dispute and the king's alleged encouragement of the murderers. The early 1170s witnessed a crisis in Henry's affairs. In 1171, he attempted to portray himself as a loyal sword-arm of the church by invading Ireland, ostensibly to effect the wishes of the papacy expressed in the bull *Laudabiliter* (1155). The expedition also had the advantage of asserting Henry's power over potentially unruly Marcher vassals who had already begun to dabble in Irish politics and expanding the scope for Angevin dynastic aggrandizement: in 1177, John, Henry's youngest son, was designated lord of Ireland. However, the brief foray into Ireland was hardly an attempt to create a sovereignty over the British Isles. With Scotland, Henry was content to restore English control of Northumberland (1157) and impose English garrisons in some strategic Scottish castles (at the Treaty of Falaise 1174). In

Wales, Henry shared the fate of his predecessors. The failure of a large-scale invasion in 1165 led to accommodation with the Welsh princes in 1170.

The breach with the church and his dynastic plans continued to undermine Henry. Only at the Compromise of Avranches of 1172 did Henry obtain absolution for his part in Becket's murder. Only in 1174 did he perform personal penance at Canterbury, driven, it must be suspected, as much by his parlous political situation as by acute remorse. In 1173, a dangerous coalition of Henry's elder sons, Henry, Richard and Geoffrey, egged on by his wife, Eleanor, allied with the king of France, Louis VII, William, king of Scots and Philip, count of Flanders, and supported by a jumbled assortment of ambitious and disaffected magnates in England and Normandy, launched a series of invasions and revolts. The loyalty of key barons and officials, led by the justiciar Richard de Lucy; lack of coordination among his opponents; and his own unflappability enabled Henry to survive and to trounce his enemies. The aftermath of the Great Rebellion showed Henry in characteristic light. Although lenient towards his chief opponents, he set about reinforcing the exercise and exploitation of royal rights. The writ of mort d'ancestor was devised to ease access to royal courts of plaintiffs who had lost out in the quickening land market: what went to royal courts avoided or superseded baronial ones. Castles, such as those of the rebel Hugh Bigod in East Anglia, were destroyed. The itinerant justices system was overhauled with new orders for criminal justice decreed giving them greater authority (Assize of Northampton 1176). Forest Laws were resumed in their full severity. To emphasise how much Henry depended upon his standing administration in England, Richard de Lucy was allowed, as Roger of Salisbury had been under Henry I, to issue writs in his own name, a royal *alter ego* indeed. Although all these measures have come to be seen as typical of Henry's robust and intelligent governmental style, none of them was inevitable, all were the children of expediency rather than ideology.

What made Henry's rule work was not administrative genius but physical energy. Henry was almost pathologically restless; his household and court were always on the road, sometimes at very short notice. If his courtiers were exhausted, their master never was. The speed with which Henry travelled from Ireland to Normandy via Wales and England in the Spring of 1172 — Wexford to Savigny in a calendar month — prompted the rather sour comment of Louis VII: 'the king of England seems rather to fly than to travel by horse or ship'. One courtier, Walter Map, declared that Henry 'covered distances like a courier', adding bitterly 'showing no mercy to his household'. Constantly on the move, Henry was able more easily to impose his personality on his subjects and his will on events. Where he was absent, his interests were pursued by agents acting in his name and, crucially, answerable to him for their conduct. This habit of scrutinizing his officials provided the incentive to efficiency. Another acute observer, Peter of Blois, described Henry as 'hunting through the provinces inquiring into everyone's doing, and especially judges those whom he has made judge of others'. Henry did not govern his people; he governed his interests.

The effectiveness of Henry's authority depended on local acquiescence obtained by identifying mutual self-interest or coercion. It was as a politican that Henry earned respect, because he rarely chose outright military action if it could be avoided. Indeed, as king he led only three major military expeditions — to Toulouse in 1159; Wales in 1165 and Ireland in 1171 — none of which were unqualified triumphs. Henry's tactic was the siege, the threat of ravaging, the pressure of gaining local loyalties, the agreed settlement. Although from youth he campaigned almost every summer of his life Henry never fought a pitched battle. It was as a negotiator, a man who understood the political as much as military weaknesses and anxieties of his enemies, that Henry got his way. Where he resorted to brute force — at Toulouse or with Thomas Becket — he failed. There was something of the showman in Henry. One of his favourite roles was that of humble penitent. The very public penance at Canterbury was only one of a number of convenient displays. In 1187, in trying to reach a truce with the French, he appeared before their negotiators in floods of tears, confessing his sins and protesting that he would reform his ways as signal of which he intended to go on crusade. The performance had some effect, although the king of France, Philip II, justly twitted his negotiators: 'You believed all that?'.

W. L. Warren argued that when Henry made a will in February 1182, he was at the peak of his career. He had imposed his will on his dominions; England in particular was peaceful, which is not the same as being content. Henry's victory in 1174 led to an extended period of internal peace: no royal army had to tackle a concerted rebellion in England until 1215. In that, if in nothing else, Henry II had emulated his grandfather. The church was now an ally, under his protection and subject to his patronage. His revenues were substantial and growing, from England running in the last decade of his life at over £20,000 per annum. But there remained intractable problems. His sons champed at the bit of his continuing authority. A new king of France, Philip II (1180-1223), would prove a more skilled adversary than his father Louis VII in the unending fencing match between Capetain king and Angevin vassal. In 1183, a major rebellion by the Young Henry was only averted by his death. In 1185, John's attempt to enforce his lordship in Ireland ended in fiasco. To many observers there appeared a weakening of Henry's grip. Gerald of Wales, who was close to Henry at this time, recognised this, fancifully attributing it to Henry's refusal to go to aid the Holy Land or accept the crown of Jerusalem (itself arguably a family possession; its kings were the direct descendants of Henry's grandfather Fulk of Anjou). In 1188, Henry did take the cross and was rewarded by the chance to levy a highly efficient tax, the Saladin Tithe, on all those of his free subjects who had not followed suit. The money helped pay for the wars of his last months.

The fundamental cause of Henry's troubles in his later years were his children. Even the deaths of Henry (1183) and Geoffrey (1186) did not remove the problem of the succession. After some years of increasing strain, in 1188-9 Richard of Poitou openly rebelled to assert his claim to the full Angevin inheritance, fearful, perhaps, lest Henry disinherit him for his younger brother John. With the support of Philip of France, Richard brought Henry to bay. Illness, age and political odds forced Henry to surrender the initiative. At the end, he simply gave up the struggle, dismissing his army, withdrawing to die at Chinon. The last act of the drama was played out, appropriately, in Anjou. Henry, however conscious of being the legitimate king of England was not, in any meaningful sense, English. His kingdom was just one of many possessions which he claimed as of right and to the control and exploitation of which he expended his immense vitality.

Inevitably, Henry's person and character attracted immense interest. If not quite the cynosure of all eyes, he was reputed to have introduced the short cloak of Anjou into England, prompting his nickname of Curtmantle. Contemporaries described him as dressing simply and rejecting the trappings of pomp. He rarely appeared at formal crown-wearings, unlike his Norman predecessors. Of medium height, powerfully if stockily built, with grey-blue eyes, bow-legs, rough hands and a ruddy and freckled complexion, he tended to look rather unkempt and grubby. Obsessed by hunting, his physical restlessness some attributed to this fear of getting fat, a fate he combatted by vigorous exercise. Whatever the cause, his impatience of repose, apart from presenting appalling logistical problems for his household staff who trailed along in his wake, 'disturbed almost half Christendom'. Most vividly, to Becket's disciple Herbert of Bosham, Henry was a human chariot, drawing all after him.

Admired, Henry was not well liked. Politically, he earned a reputation as an oath-breaker. Personally, he got on notoriously badly with his immediate family. Although he was affectionate towards his cousins, he kept his two brothers Geoffrey and William out of any significant possessions. His wife, the formidable Eleanor of Aquitaine, he kept under house arrest for the last fifteen years of their marriage. His indulgence of his sons was returned by treachery and hatred. Perhaps Henry was too much his own man to admit intimacy; perhaps as a father he expected too much character and too little independence. According to Gerald of Wales, Henry had had painted in Winchester castle a picture of an eagle being attacked by four young ones who, he explained to his friends, represented his four sons 'persecuting me even unto death'. Henry had a number of mistresses throughout his life, notably Rosamund Clifford (*d*.1176) whom he openly acknowledged after 1174. It is ironic that, in the final crisis of his reign, such an obsessive dynast should find loyalty only in an illegitimate son, his chancellor Geoffrey.

Yet where he chose to bestow it, his friendship was strong. Those he liked and admired most were often his opposites, men of inflexibility and calm: Hugh of Avalon; Baldwin of Ford; William Marshal; and Thomas Becket. All showed independence of mind and courage in the face of Henry's will. The difference between them was that the first three were embraced for their integrity, however awkward. But Becket, the friend of his youth, mentor, companion, guide, attractive, worldly but not corrupt, intelligent and seemingly loyal, had, in Henry's eyes, betrayed affection and friendship. For that there was no forgiveness.

Of all his personal traits, the image of Henry's anger is most indelible. His rages were Homeric. When opponents talked of the *ira* of the king, perhaps they had in mind more than a term for political or legal impropriety. Henry's tantrums were awesome, transcending mere petulance. When roused, he tore his clothes and literally chewed the carpet (easier to do then as they were made of straw). Such was the mood that condemned Becket: 'Will nobody rid me of this turbulent priest?'. Yet at other times he could be judicious, witty, generous, eager to understand the problems or people he encountered. He suffered from always being the centre of others' attention, which may explain why in his household he often withdrew in private, in marked contrast to his public accessibility. He held unexpected, even awkward views. He disdained the fashion of chivalry and tournaments. Brave in battle and a campaigner of renowned and proven stamina, he disliked battles and was distressed by casualties. A thoughtful monarch, his recorded conversation suggests a man of some humanity. When the patriarch of Jerusalem tried to persuade Henry to lead an army to the Holy Land in 1185, Henry remarked in private 'These clerks can incite us boldly to arms and danger since they themselves will receive no blows in the struggle, nor will they undertake any burdens which they can avoid'.

A war-hating warrior, Henry's piety presents a similar paradox. An unenthusiastic attender at services, he spent over twenty years toying with going on crusade before taking the Cross in 1188. Yet he quietly sent treasure for use in the defence of Jerusalem. A critic of secular clerks, he was a patron of the strict orders of Grandmont and Chartreuse and promoted the Cistercian Baldwin of Ford and the Carthusian Hugh of Avalon. Impatient with hypocrisy, Henry admired faithfulness and clarity; yet he himself was a notorious perjuror and dissembler. His interest in legal procedures, which gave rise to the thirteenth century story of him spending sleepless nights with his advisers perfecting the wording of the writ of novel desseisin, may have sprung from his intellectual self-confidence. As Peter of Blois optimistically put it 'with the king of England it is school every day'. This sits ill with the impression derived from others of a court seething with low life as well as the great and of a lord who delighted in inconveniencing his servants and courtiers. It is impossible to know what Henry was like, how much of his undoubted charisma was derived from his personality or his position. That is why historians have been able to cast him in their own image.

Henry's rule marked no great epoch. He presided over social and cultural developments on which he could, in the nature of things, exert little control. His achievements were pragmatic, in response to events and circumstance, the greatest of them being survival. There were no great triumphs to match those of the first William, Richard or Edward. What made Henry remarkable was the hold he kept over remarkably diverse lands for a remarkably long time. Above all, for contemporaries, he knew how to act regally. As Walter Map put it, he 'brought honour on good men'. When Henry compensated sailors of his fleet who had lost their ships during a Channel crossing, Map added 'perchance another king would not have paid this just debt'.

W. L. Warren, *Henry II*, 1973.
J. Gillingham, *The Angevin Empire*, 1984.

ELEANOR OF AQUITAINE (*c.*1122-1204) epitomised the constrained role allotted to medieval heiresses. Although by inheritance from her father, William X of Aquitaine, she was in her own right duchess of the largest duchy in France, stretching from Poitou to the Pyrenees, for sixty-seven years (1137-1204) her authority was exercised first by her two husbands, then by two of her sons. She merely conveyed and validated power. Her importance lay in her dynastic value which, in turn, depended on her ability to produce sons and heirs. In 1137, she married Louis VII of France (king 1137-80), but after fifteen years they had

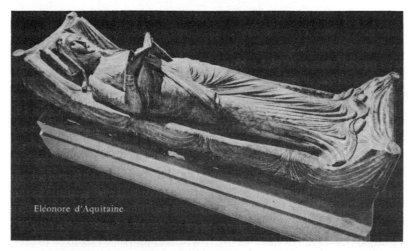

Eleanor of Aquitaine
(From her effigy at Fontevrault Abbey in Anjou)

only had two daughters. Louis, despite the risk of losing such a large province, divorced Eleanor. There had been rumours of her sexual indiscretions with Geoffrey of Anjou (Henry II's father) and, most notoriously, with her uncle, Raymond of Poitiers, prince of Antioch, during the Second Crusade, on which Eleanor accompanied her husband (1147-9). This last piece of gossip may well have been embroidered as a *post facto* justification for the divorce in 1152. However, Eleanor's position and marital career(s) encouraged such talk, the more so when, a few weeks after her divorce from Louis, she married, around Whitsun 1152, his most powerful vassal, Henry of Anjou, who was only nineteen.

Not only did she bring her vast inheritance to extend the Angevin dominions from the Channel to the Spanish marches (to which England was added in 1154), but she bore Henry five sons, as well as three daughters (William, 1153-56; Henry 1155-83; Matilda 1156-89; Richard 1157-99; Geoffrey 1158-86; Eleanor 1163-1215; Joan 1165-99; and John 1167-1216). Yet during Henry II's life, her political role was formal, except for one disastrous intervention in 1173 when she joined her elder sons in their plot to depose their father. Eleanor was arrested as she tried to escape Henry's court at Chinon disguised as a man. For the rest of Henry's reign, she was virtually under house-arrest. But even before 1173, she was only a cypher, acting as titular head of the royal administration in England during some of Henry's absences, and agreeing to the investiture of her son Richard as count of Poitou and Aquitaine in 1170.

This impotence had, it seems, little to do with personality. As the young queen of France, she had been notably vivacious and, after Henry II's death, she assumed, for the first time, a prominent political role. As in 1173, she acted in her sons' interests, securing Richard I's succession in England in 1189 and John's in Anjou in 1199. In 1191, she escorted Berengaria of Navarre to Sicily to be married to Richard before returning to France: one crusade was, perhaps, enough to last a lifetime. In 1192-4 she tried to preserve Richard's rule in France, against Philip II (1180-1223), and in England against John. She saw herself, or was cleverly manipulated by the justiciar, Hubert Walter, to be seen as the guarantor of Angevin legitimacy. As such Eleanor was instrumental in raising the huge ransom for Richard in 1193-4 and in receiving the king from his captor, Henry VI of Germany, in February 1194. As she grew older, she may have begun to operate a dynastic policy of her own, with the aim of securing Aquitaine for her descendants — Angevin; Castilian; Toulousain; or French. She helped John secure his throne, not least by laying waste parts of rebellious Anjou in 1199 with Richard I's mercenary captain Mercadier, and, in 1202, held Mirebeau against her grandson Arthur of Brittany for long enough to allow John to relieve the castle. But Eleanor also arranged, in 1200, for another grandchild, Blanche of Castille, to marry the heir to the king of France, the future Louis VIII (1223-26). Until the birth of John's first son in 1207, any marriage of Eleanor's grandchildren was of potential significance for the succession to Angevin lands. In extreme old age, Eleanor retired to the abbey of Fontevrault where she died and was buried, appropriately enough, beside Henry II and Richard I. In death, as in life, Eleanor was defined by her relationship with husband and son.

Yet her life was sufficiently long and occasionally dramatic to have spawned a myth which placed her, with her daughter by

Louis VII, Marie of Champagne, at the centre of a cult of courtly love which was supposed to have grown up at her court in Poitiers between 1167 and 1173. Fostered by these independent feminine spirits and nurtured by troubadours under the leadership of the great Champagnois poet Chrétien de Troyes, the essence of this cult was the glorification of adulterous love of a man, usually unmarried, for a married woman, attainable (as with Guinivere in Chrétien de Troyes' Lancelot) or not. In a treatise De Amore or The Art of Courtly Love, written c.1186 by Andrew, a Champagne court chaplain, Eleanor and Marie are shown at Poitiers adjudicating lovers' quarrels. The whole paraphernalia has been seen as essentially seditious, undermining male dominance and authority as well as the teachings of the church. Unfortunately for romantics and feminists alike, it is all fiction. Eleanor was not at Poitiers consistently from 1167-73. There is no evidence that Marie or Chrétien visited her there or anywhere else. Andrew's treatise was written after he had left Marie's service and was composed in the spirit of irony, especially when depicting the aged Eleanor condemning consanguineous marriages (of which she made two) and marriage to worthless younger husbands (Henry was eleven years her junior). Marie of Champagne's notorious denial that love in marriage is impossible was dated by Andrew to May 1174 — when Eleanor was a prisoner of her husband at Chinon. If Eleanor was a patron of artists, her husband was more so. If she had a liking for formalised smut, we do not know of it. That she attracted such stories was perhaps explicable in terms of her marital adventures and her position as the last representative of the old, independent line of Aquitainian/Poitevin counts. Many of the Arthurian stories were hostile to the authority not only of husbands but of kings: Eleanor, countess of Poitou and duchess of Aquitaine would have been a suitable, if fictitious patroness. The reality was that she lived and died an appendage to her father, husbands, sons (and lovers, if she had any). Her resting place lay not in the pages of romance but beside her second husband and her favourite son in the abbey of Fontevrault. Eleanor's personal legacy were her descendants: her grandchildren included an emperor of Germany, Otto IV, as well as a king of England, Henry III. From her, all subsequent English monarchs were descended as were all French kings from Louis IX (1226-70) to Louis Philippe (1830-48). Impersonally, her legacy was even greater. Through her, Gascony was attached to the English crown until 1453, a source of constant tension and lengthy wars with the kings of France. With Gascony came Bordeaux, its wine trade, prosperity for Bristol and Southampton and the uniquely English, or rather Anglo-French word for red Bordeaux wine. In claret, Eleanor of Aquitaine's inheritance still lives.

W. W. Kibler, ed. *Eleanor of Aquitaine: Patron and Politician*, 1976.
J. F. Benton, 'The Court of Champagne as a Literary Center' in *Speculum* xxxvi, 1961.

GILBERT FOLIOT (1105/10-1188; abbot of Gloucester 1139-48; bishop of Hereford 1148-63; bishop of London 1163-88) has emerged from the polemics of the Becket dispute as a cold, devious, envious pharasaical church politician. The murder of his rival turned an ecclesiastical dispute into a cosmic judgement against Foliot and what he represented. Yet he had all the qualities of a remarkable bishop, more, in fact, than Becket: intelligence; education; good connections; literary skill; legal expertise; political sensitivity; personal piety; and monastic austerity.

Foliot's family were tenants of the earls of Huntingdon who were, for much of the twelfth century, also kings of Scotland, which might explain Gilbert's association with Ailred of Rievaulx, to whom he may have dedicated his *Homilies* (1163/67). Other relatives included Miles of Gloucester, earl of Hereford and Richard of Ilchester, a leading royal clerk under Henry II. In the 1130s, after a thorough education in the liberal arts, scriptural exegesis and canon law, which possibly took him to Paris and Bologna, Gilbert entered the great Burgundian monastery of Cluny, rising to be its prior and then abbot of its daughter house at Abbeville. Appointed by Miles of Gloucester to the abbacy at Gloucester (1139), he followed his patron in support of the Angevin claim although, when promoted to the see of Hereford by the pope in 1148, he proved a successful navigator of the political shoals of support for the future Henry II and public allegiance to King Stephen. As abbot and bishop Foliot was noted for combining personal austerity with administrative skill, which extended to condoning some important forgeries in support of his abbey's claims (a not uncommon twelfth century monastic pastime). Characteristically, he wanted to retain his abbacy when bishop: pluralist greed, or a yearning for the company of monks? Perhaps a bit of both.

In 1162, Thomas Becket, the king's chancellor, was chosen by Henry as archbishop of Canterbury. The only evidence that Foliot was a disappointed candidate comes from his enemies, and is unlikely. Translation between sees was uncommon, Foliot's own to London in 1163 requiring a special papal licence. Henry may, however, have regarded Foliot's promotion as balancing the preferment of a royal clerk with a distinctly secular reputation. Foliot was supposed to have complained at Becket's appointment that Henry had performed a miracle by transforming a soldier into an archbishop. The witness is hostile, but the sentiments may be genuine enough. Foliot, with his impeccable religious credentials, never fully believed in the sincerity of Becket's transformation from royal stooge to champion of the church. Events did little to alter his assessment.

The bitterness between Foliot and Becket was personal and political. From the start there was conflict, with Becket trying to insist that Foliot renew his oath of allegiance to Canterbury as bishop of London, while Foliot, with precedent and law on his side, argued that he was still bound by his profession of obedience as bishop of Hereford. Foliot thought Becket tactless and foolish in his handling of the king over clerical immunities in 1163-4. For Foliot, the issues at stake were not doctrinal or moral but administrative. Accommodation was possible without compromising principles or confrontation with the king. Becket managed to do both at the council of Clarendon (1164). For three days, the bishops had remained united in the face of verbal abuse and physical threats when, unilaterally, Becket capitulated to the king's demands that the bishops swear an oath to abide by the customs of the realm regarding church and state relations. As Foliot later put it: 'it was the general of our army who deserted, the captain who fled'. He did not trust Becket again. At Northampton, he tried to force Becket to accept the secular authority of the king's council and to allow the bishops to mediate. In the face of the archbishop's intransigence, Foliot shouted 'you always have been a fool, and always will be'.

With Becket in exile, Foliot became the king's leading ecclesiastical adviser on how to handle the controversy. He was skilled at gaining clerical support, including that of Becket's former tutor and theological expert Robert of Melun, bishop of Hereford (1163-7), and marshelling arguments to present to the pope. The invective and mutual recriminations intensified, not least because Foliot had been assigned the administration of the Canterbury see. Becket may not have been an effective archbishop, but he was an excellent propagandist, supported as he was by most fashionable donnish opinion.

Foliot's response to the calumnies against him came in his letter *Multiplicem* written in 1166. On the principle that attack is the best method of defence, this was a stinging and savage indictment of Becket as a simoniac (which was untrue), a coward and a traitor to his fellow bishops. Foliot argued that Henry was best handled by quiet remonstrance not violent insults. Crucially, but, except for Becket, uncontroversially, Foliot admitted the royal right to judge bishops in secular cases (an argument accepted by Lanfranc in 1088), as well as the king's quasi-sacerdotal position by virtue of being annointed with chrism at coronation. Accusations aside, *Multiplicem* sums up Foliot's basic belief that the two swords of church and state must and could cooperate. Whatever Becket's allies said, Foliot was personally and professionally committed to church reform and freedom from secular domination. The Cluniac ideal was of separation from but influence over the laity. Shouting across an unbridgeable divide of prejudice would achieve nothing. Throughout the controversy, Foliot sought to detach the Becket case from the wider issue of *libertas ecclesiae*, which he felt the archbishop had hijacked. More specifically, with slick legalism he pressed, as at Argentan in 1167, for the pope to depose the archbishop, at the same time protecting his own back from possible excommunication. To achieve his ends, Foliot was as ready as his opponent to stoop into the gutter, as his self-seeking, disingenuous charges against Becket in *Multiplicem* showed.

Becket's language also became more personal and intemperate. In 1167, he wrote to Foliot: 'Your aim has all along been to effect the downfall of the Church and myself' (the association is typical). In 1169, he excommunicated Foliot. On the pope absolving him in 1170, Becket exclaimed: 'Satan is unloosed for the destruction of the Church'. On hearing that Foliot had assisted at the coronation of the Young Henry, Becket again excommunicated him. This time, because of Becket's murder (December 1170), Foliot was not released until 1172. In 1174, at Henry's public penance at Canterbury, it was appropriately Foliot who preached the sermon; not surprisingly he protested the king's innocence of blame for the murder. Unfortunately for the bishop, the Becket cult and the attendant cottage industry of histories of the controversy were already in full swing, with Foliot cast as a leading villain, a new Achitophel, corrupter of princes. After all, some of the pro-Becket writers still hoped for preferment from the king.

Carrying such uncomfortable baggage, Foliot could not resume a prominent political role. Although not a great scholar, he was fluent in Latin, French and English, an apparently notable accomplishment. In his later years he wrote commentaries on the *Pater noster* and the *Canticles*. He lingered on into extreme old age, but not as a representative of a past age. The English church of the 1180s bore more similarities with that of the 1150s than Becket's apologists would have welcomed. Foliot, a clerical grandee who, in his thirty-nine years as a bishop, appointed five archdeacons and every one a relative, was not out of place on an episcopal bench sporting names such as de Lucy, Ridel, Bohun, FitzJocelin, another Foliot, let alone the king's cousin, Roger, and son, Geoffrey. In one sense, Gilbert Foliot had lost the battle but won the war or, rather, hostilities had been suspended. On all sides, moderation and accommodation had prevailed after the histrionics of the 1160s. The ambitious prelate would have felt his defeat keenly; the austere monk may have been satisfied with Walter Map's description of him, when old and blind, as 'a treasure-house of goodness and wisdom'.

A. Morey and C. N. L. Brooke, *Gilbert Foliot and his Letters*, 1965.

THOMAS BECKET (c.1120-1170; archbishop of Canterbury 1162-70; canonised 1173) was the most famous Englishman of the Middle Ages. He remains perhaps the most controversial. Chaucer's 'holy, blissful martyr' redeemed a life of fame, conflict, vanity, pride and failure by being hacked to bits by four probably rather drunk knights one dark December evening in Canterbury Cathedral. His most famous death transformed his life into something beyond biography; for believers beyond history. His life and death became Providential, his sacrifice a lesson in the mysterious workings of God. The reality, however, if not the stuff of legend, is almost that of fiction.

Becket was born around 1120 in London the son of a merchant, perhaps a mercer, Gilbert Becket, and his wife, Matilda. Both parents were Norman, Gilbert originating from the Eure region of Lower Normandy. The surname Becket was Gilbert's and was never used by Thomas himself, who preferred to style himself 'Thomas of London'. (Nobody until the Reformation concocted 'à Becket'.) The acquisitive entrepreneurial spirit of a self-made London merchant may have influenced Thomas. Certainly, his background — urban, non-noble, commercial — forced him to live on his wits and personality as something of an outsider, not part of the established social hierarchy, nor in the traditional channel of social betterment, a monastic order. Although educated at the Augustinian Priory at Merton, at a London grammar-school and briefly at the Schools in Paris, Thomas was never part of the ambitious, self-congratulatory clerisy of schoolmen who so dominated later twelfth century church and state. Intelligent, but no scholar, a late entrant into clerical orders, Thomas never lost a secular air, to the suspicion of his critics and the unease of his supporters.

Becket's adult life falls into distinct periods, a fact which itself aroused contemporary comment on the fickelness of his personal and professional allegiances. Handsome, tall, thin, with pale skin, dark hair, a big nose and bright eyes, his personality invited friendship: he attracted people. But there were also signs of an inner nervousness. He was susceptible to stress-related illnesses and he had a slight stammer. A young man on the make, from a prosperous London mercantile family, it was perhaps

The murder of Thomas Becket
(From a Canterbury manuscript of John of Salisbury's account
of the martyrdom)

natural that his first attempt at a career (*c*.1143-45) was as
accountant to a leading London banker Osbert Huitdeniers (*i.e.*
Eightpence — perhaps his rate of interest in the pound?) In
1145/6 Becket found a greater patron when he joined the household of Archbishop Theobald of Canterbury, where he stayed
until 1155, rising to become archdeacon of Canterbury in 1154.
With Theobald, Becket gained his entrée to the world of politics.
He made contacts with future leaders of the church, such Roger

of Pont l'Evêque. Accompanying Theobald to the Council of Rheims (1148) he would have had the chance to meet the likes of Bernard of Clairvaux, Suger of St Denis and Peter Lombard, each of them pivotal figures in their respective fields of government, spirituality and theology. In the early 1150s Theobald sent Thomas for a year's study of civil and canon law at Bologna and Auxerre. He was introduced to diplomacy on visits to the papal Curia. His capacity to charm and talent for inspiring devotion in others was thoroughly exercised on Theobald and his colleagues in the archbishop's household.

Another Knight's Move, to become, on Theobald's recommendation, chancellor to the new, foreign and untried Henry II, opened up a fresh heady career which lasted from 1155 until his elevation to the see of Canterbury in 1162. He became the young king's intimate councillor and close friend. Although he performed official duties, witnessing royal letters and charters, sitting occasionally at the Exchequer and infrequently acting as a royal judge, it was his informal influence that counted. He and the king were inseparable: which of them learnt or benefited more is impossible to gauge.

Still in minor orders, Becket steadily amassed ecclesiastical benefices and was rewarded for his professional services by the king with a number of estates. As a sign of especial favour, the king excused his chancellor from rendering account at the Exchequer on lands he held in custody, i.e. on behalf of the king. This was potentially dangerous as Becket revealed a taste for outward magnificence which was fuelled by these royal grants of custodies which included vacant bishoprics and secular baronies such as the extensive Honor of Eye. Henry's assessment in 1164 that Becket had made £30,000 out of these lands was probably an exaggeration, but of the chancellor's wealth there can be no doubt. One of his biographers states that most of his fifty-two clerks were assigned to administer his estates. He had a military household of 700 knights. On an embassy to Paris in 1158, he took with him two hundred and fifty servants; eight large waggons laden with furnishings, plate and provisions; and twenty-four changes of clothes. Small wonder locals were astonished: 'What a wonderful king he must be to have such a great chancellor'. The effect was no doubt deliberate, but the extravagance went beyond diplomatic point-scoring: in Paris a single dish of eels eaten by Becket cost 100 shillings.

As well as a taste for the good life, Becket absorbed secular manners even to the extent of actively campaigning with his troops. In 1159, on Henry II's ill-fated expedition to subdue Toulouse, Becket, in full armour, led successful attacks on three towns. On the Vexin campaign of 1161, commanding a retinue of, according to one biographer, nearly six thousand cavalry and infantry, Becket led the royal vanguard. On one occasion he defeated a French knight, Engelram of Tric, at a joust, claiming his charger for his prize. Few Archbishops of Canterbury until Dr Robert Runcie (MC) could claim as much. Becket could play the great magnate, but his wealth and position was entirely dependent on the king. That had been his opportunity and still offered hope of advancement. But it spelt his doom.

When Archbishop Theobald died in 1161, Henry appointed Becket in his place, a characteristically bold yet pragmatic act. The tradition of monks being appointed to Canterbury had been strong since the tenth century, the sole royal clerk being the infamous Stigand. Becket's reputation and lifestyle were bizarre, if not offensive qualifications. Yet Theobald had favoured him, not least because of his knowledge of Canterbury and his close relationship with the king. In making the appointment, Henry did not intend to dominate the church, merely continue to cooperate with it. If he also wished to reclaim royal rights lost under Stephen, Becket was an even more ideal choice. There were continental precedents and parallels, most obviously in Germany where Frederick Barbarossa had appointed Rainald von Dassel his chancellor in 1156 and archbishop of Cologne in 1159: Rainald, an almost exact contemporary of Becket's who shared his delight in military exploits, continued to serve his temporal and spiritual masters without conflict or strain. Henry expected Thomas to do the same.

The final priod of Becket's life, as archbishop 1162-70, forms an apparent contrast to what had gone before. Yet, psychologically, his reaction to his changed circumstances is perhaps not so inconsistent. Once he had identified the nature of his responsibilities, he tried to suit them. Historians, then and now, have insisted on a transformation between the worldly chancellor and the ascetic champion of the church. In fact, Becket's perspective depended, not unnaturally, on his position: thus his advocacy in the king's interest of the harsh scutage of 1159 matches his later insistence on ecclesiastical immunities. Theobald had taught him that the church and the state were dependent but separate; Theobald's career had been conditioned by his attempt to retain independence in order best to protect the interests of his church, English or Canterbury (not always synonymous). Whatever and whenever internal conversion occurred, Becket was keen to act as fully the archbishop as he had the chancellor. If the externals required were different, so be it. Equally, if they were the same, Becket was not unwilling to comply. His hospitality as prelate was little changed in lavishness to that as royal favourite, his table no less luxurious.

What had definitely altered was Becket's status. As archbishop he was, for the first time, his own master. The sense of authority and liberation proved too much for what discretion he may have possessed. On receiving the *pallium* from the pope, he surrendered the chancellorship and almost immediately began to adopt extreme and provocative stands on ecclesiastical immunities and jurisdiction, to the annoyance of the king. Becket's initial posturing may have been designed to win acceptance and respect from the Canterbury monks and his fellow bishops suspicious of this royal nominee. Just as, when chancellor, he had aggressively pursued royal rights, so, as archbishop, he argued for the protection and recovery of all traditional rights belonging to Canterbury. One difficulty was Becket's style. He was tactless and aggressive, over-eager to assert himself, too sensitive to the possibility of being ignored.

Wider issues soon precipitated open conflict with the king, but personal hostility coloured all their dealings. By the autumn of 1163, relations with the king had disintegrated. In October, Becket was stripped of all secular honours acquired as chancellor: it is perhaps significant that he had not resigned them previously. At Westminster in October 1163, Henry raised the issue of the immunity of convicted criminous clerks from secular punishment. He argued tht secular crimes should be punished in secular not ecclesiastical courts. With the support of the other bishops, Becket insisted on clerical immunity and condemned the concept of double jeopardy, trial and punishment by two courts of the same offence. They only agreed to existing royal customs 'saving their order'. Attempts to find a compromise were unsuccessful. Relations with the king were further damaged at Clarendon in January 1164 when Henry tried to force the bishops to accept existing customs unconditionally. After three days'intransigence, Becket unexpectedly capitulated, to the shocked surprise of his episcopal colleagues. But Henry pressed his advantage by enshrining what he saw as the existing conventions in writing in the Constitutions of Clarendon. Further conflict was inevitable.

By now Becket's arrogance and inconsistency had alienated many of his colleagues, notably Archbishop Roger of York and Bishop Gilbert Foliot of London, and had aroused vindictive fury in the king who now plotted Becket's ruin. The archbishop was summoned to Northampton in October 1164 ostensibly to answer a charge brought against him by John the Marshal of unlawfully withholding property. Once there, Becket faced additional charges of peculation, dating back to his chancellorship, and treason. He was threatened with deprivation. Ignoring the legal and physical threats and the angry pleadings of the bishops, Becket defied his critics. On the day of his trial, with a characteristic sense of drama carrying his own cross, he denied the jurisdiction of the royal court, declared that the issue was one of ecclesiastical independence and appealed to Rome. He then fled in disguise into exile.

The six years Becket spent in exile turned what had been a local dispute into an international *cause célèbre*. This was no accident. To garner international support, Becket played on French political hostility to Henry and the weak position of Pope Alexander III, to whom he loudly protested his allegiance, somewhat to that cautious man's disquiet. He waged a relentless and increasingly heated and extravagant propaganda campaign. To further his cause he immersed himself in canon law and recruited sympathetic academics in the Schools. As is their wont, these intellectuals were happy to discuss the cosmic principles behind what others, such as Bishop Foliot and King Henry, regarded as matters of practical policy and administration. For all his protestations, Becket could not rely on the English church for support. Most bishops opposed his methods which, as Foliot pointed out in an acerbic attack in 1166, achieved nothing except to weaken the church. However, the king could not entirely ignore the controversy. Like his predecessor, Henry was keen to see his son crowned king in his lifetime to secure the new dynasty and was reluctant to close the door completely on compromise, whatever his personal feelings towards his former friend. The dispute had all the makings of drama: observers were not to be disappointed.

As if to emphasise his rightness as well as righteousness, in his private life Becket began to assume more recognisable features of rigorous piety. From 1165, he seems to have worn some form of monastic habit, perhaps adopted at the Cistercian house of Pontigny where he stayed 1164-66. About this time he also began to wear a hair shirt next to his skin and to indulge in violent flagellation. Once more, chameleon-like, he assumed the appearance most fitting his station: not the flamboyant royal *familiaris*, nor yet the primate of England, but now a symbol of persecution.

Frequent attempts at reconciliation organised by the pope or Louis VII of France foundered on the obstinacy of both parties. In 1169, with the dispute in stalemate, personal interviews between Henry and Becket at Montmirail and Montmartre failed to achieve anything: king and archbishop were alike in their obstinacy and their hatred of losing face. However, in June 1170 Henry II had his eldest son, Henry, crowned king by the archbishop of York, in blatant contravention of one of the most cherished rights of Canterbury. Ironically, this blow to Becket's position led to a reconciliation with Henry at Fréteval in July 1170 which restored Becket's lands, allowed his return to England but left the substantive issues of dispute untouched. The agreement had little chance of success.

Returning to England to a mixed reception in December 1170, Becket proceeded with a typical lack of tact, travelling ostentatiously across southern England and refusing to lift the excommunication of the bishops involved in the coronation of the young Henry. Angered by news of this, and possibly alarmed at reports of Becket's popularity, King Henry, in Normandy for Christmas, lost his temper. In one of his notorious passions, possibly exacerbated by seasonable junketings, Henry was reputed to have declared 'What miserable drones and traitors have I nourished and promoted in my household who let their lord be treated with such shameful contempt by a low-born clerk' or, more popularly and more succinctly, but less reliably, 'will nobody rid me of this turbulent priest?' This was the cue for four knights, Hugh de Moreville, William de Tracey, Reginald FitzUrse and Richard le Breton to embark for England. Their motive may have been simply to arrest the archbishop, but, once they reached Canterbury on 29 December, events slid out of control. Argument turned to anger and anger into violence. Becket's last moments were the noblest of his life, heroic, even if we discount the embellishments of the many hagiographers who retold the tale. He was unafraid of death and remained calm amid the confusion and horror. Uncompromising to the end, his pride and rashness were transmuted into a steely resolve to meet his fate. Refusing to go with the knights, he was cut down and butchered in the north transept of his cathedral, the second of five archbishops of Canterbury to meet a violent end.

The manner of his murder ensured for Becket a possibly desired martyr's crown. His was the single most chronicled death in English history, its impact and legacy matched only, perhaps, by that of Charles I. There are five accounts of the martyrdom written by those actually in the cathedral at the time of Becket's death, including John of Salisbury (who hid behind the altars); Benedict of Peterborough (who collected the first stories of miracles); and Edward Grim who, in trying to protect his master, had his arm sliced through to the bone by a blow from Reginald FitzUrse's sword. What confirmed the unique significance of the assassination were the miracles which began within days. Within a decade, 703 miracles were recorded. In 1173, Becket was canonised, by which time his tomb had already become a focus of pilgrimage and healing. Becket's cult and shrine rapidly gained international popularity which survived to the Reformation. Apart from its carefully documented efficacy, the cult was sustained by the production of Canterbury Water, allegedly an inexhaustible supply of the martyr's diluted blood, but probably a sort of medieval Ribena, which pilgrims would carry away with them in specially crafted ampullae which the monks sold to the faithful. Whatever the transcendent benefits of Becket's cult, materially it secured the prosperity of Canterbury and its tourist trade for more than three and a half centuries.

His death transformed Becket's career and achievement. In life he had proved one of the least successful archbishops in English history. Effectively he performed his duties for under two and a half years. He alienated former friends, such as Roger of York and Arnold of Lisieux; exasperated allies, including Pope Alexander III; and convinced enemies such as Foliot of his unsuitability. Proud, inflexible, sincere but unimaginative, Becket had a love of the grand gesture but a weakness for exaggeration. His assessment of issues was unsubtle, if vigorously and skilfully defended. The mess he made of his great opportunity in 1162 suggests that he was promoted beyond his abilities: an excellent lieutenant, a poor leader. Unable to compromise, as archbishop his frenetic behaviour and nervous outbursts mark him as being overwhelmed. Intelligent, he lacked schooling; efficient in the ways of the world, he never mastered patience. Perhaps he would have been a better soldier than statesman.

The great issues for which he claimed he fought were resolved after his death by negotiation, not confrontation. A chastened Henry II, who did penance at Becket's tomb in 1174, agreed to the principles of free elections to bishoprics, the right of appeal to Rome, independent ecclesiastical jurisdiction and clerical immunity. However, over the subsequent twenty years, less exclusive perameters of cooperation were settled: for instance civil secular suits involving clergy were heard in royal courts and, crucially, the king retained a decisive voice in episcopal appointments. Henry II saw the problem of criminous clerks as one of law and order, legal equity, perhaps royal sovereignty; Becket defined it as a central to *libertas ecclesiae*, freedom of the church, the old battle cry of church reformers for the past century and more. Others interpreted that freedom as more complex than Becket would allow. Developments in canon and civil law made tension inevitable but accommodation imperative for the well-being of both church and state. This Becket failed to understand. No less damaging was his habit of regarding his defence of the particular rights of his church of Canterbury as synonymous with the universal contest: both his arraignment at

Northampton and his fury over the coronation of the Young Henry actually concerned the privileges of his diocese, not the whole clerical order, as he pretended. The violence of his language, the obstinacy of his opinions and the narrowness of his vision gained his cause little but publicity. Even his death was a triumph for the Faith rather than a vindication of his policies. By the end, he had come to identify his cause with himself: in his dying agony he murmured: 'For the name of Jesus and the protection of the church I am ready to embrace death'.

F. Barlow, *Thomas Becket*, 1985.
B. Smalley, *The Becket Controversy in the Schools*, 1973.

RICHARD DE LUCY (*d.*1179) was the most prominent royal administrator of mid-twelfth century England. He came from a knightly family with land in Kent and East Anglia which originated from Lucé on the Normandy/Maine border, an area in which Henry I had interests before he became king. Although modern observers emphasise his lack of baronial background, Richard's family had significant connections, one of his relatives being the successful Abbot Geoffrey of St Albans (1119-46). By the early years of Stephen's reign, Richard was castellan of Falaise, while his brother Walter, with some help from Queen Matilda, had been appointed abbot of Battle (1139-71).

Richard remained in Stephen's service throughout his reign, by the end of which he had acted as local justiciar in Essex and was castellan of the Tower and Windsor, two of the three most important castles in south-east England (Dover being the third), Richard's position being recognised in the Treaty of Winchester which secured the end of the civil war in 1153. After 1154, despite his continued association with Stephen's surviving son, William, Richard, with Robert, earl of Leicester, was made jointly responsible for the supervision of the royal administration. Henry II was careful neither to alienate those who had run the country under Stephen nor to create another viceroy like Roger of Salisbury. Both justiciars had been supporters of Stephen, and while Robert of Leicester was one of the most powerful barons in his own right, Richard owed his growing landed fortune to loyal service to the king, continuing the tradition of secular advisers drawn from the lesser nobility which had been a notorious feature of the rule of Henry I.

In the early years of Henry II's reign, Richard concentrated on the administration, rather than politics, where Earl Robert took precedence, possibly because he remained in England while Richard followed the court. During this period the justiciars acted as intermediaries rather than viceroys, particularly during the king's visits to England. Nonetheless, Richard was involved in a wide variety of business, financial, judicial and diplomatic. In 1162, he managed the appointment of his friend and colleague, the chancellor, Thomas Becket, as archbishop of Canterbury which, in the careful handling of the Canterbury monks and the other bishops, required tact and authority. Richard's concern with ecclesiastical issues was recurrent. No doubt well briefed by his brother, in 1157 he advised the king to uphold the franchises of Battle Abbey in a dispute over the jurisdiction of the bishop of Chichester. In 1164, at least so Becket believed, Richard helped draft the Constitutions of Clarendon, being excommunicated for his pains in 1166.

With the defection of Becket as chancellor (1162) and the retirement of the veteran treasurer, Nigel of Ely (1164/5), the justiciars' influence grew. Increasingly, Richard took the lead in implementing policy, at the exchequer and in supervising royal justice. In 1164, he unsuccessfully tried to persuade the exiled Becket to come to terms with the king. In 1166, in order to enforce the Assize of Clarendon, Richard and Geoffrey de Mandeville visited seventeen counties before Geoffrey's death that October. The Clarendon assize had instructed sheriffs to apprehend and try felons through juries of presentment and trial by water, sheriffs being allowed to hunt down criminals regardless of local franchises. Convicted felons forfeited their lands to their lords and their chattels to the king. The presence of Richard and Geoffrey was highly effective, the Pipe Roll showing that sheriffs were markedly more vigilant in those counties the royal justices visited than the rest. The 1166 visitation set the pattern for regular judicial circuits — or eyres — conducted by teams of justices which began in 1168. It also demonstrated the failure of many sheriffs to carry out royal instructions without supervision: this was one motive for the general Inquest of the

Sheriffs of 1170, which led to twenty out of twenty-six being replaced. Thus both administratively and judicially, Richard's 1166 visitation marked a significant step towards greater central scrutiny of provincial royal agents and barons. Richard was probably also closely concerned with the establishment of procedures by which non-baronial freemen could resolve litigation over possession and ownership of property, the so-called possessory assizes *novel disseisin* and *mort d'ancestor*. Thus, though no legal expert himself, Richard presided over the inception and administration of a judicial system that profoundly enhanced the role of the crown in the affairs of its subjects. This proved a double-edged weapon. The reforms were popular: by 1176-8, the general eyres were overloaded with work. But they were equally seen by some — not unjustly — as vehicles for royal extortion and rapacity.

In royal service, Richard had become a baron of some consequence, his estates being assessed in 1166 at thirty knights' fees, centred upon Ongar in Essex. His political authority, which had been increasing steadily, was confirmed after the death of Robert of Leicester in 1168, when he was left the sole justiciar. However, his power, and, in consequence, that of his office, was transformed by the rebellion of 1173-4 when for some months he held England for the king, vigorously combating the military manoeuvres of the new earl of Leicester and the king of Scots. Earlier in the reign, in the king's absences abroad, the regency had been filled by members of the royal family: Henry's mother, wife or son Henry. In 1173, Matilda was dead and Eleanor and the Young Henry ranged against the king. Richard was left in sole charge and his energy and loyalty in large measure saved England for Henry. Richard's rewards were territorial and political.

After 1174, he acted as the king's *alter ego* in the manner of Roger of Salisbury. On his own authority he could issue writs and command expenditure. He dominated the exchequer; acted as a justice in the north; assessed tallages in the Midlands and the south; implemented the new possessory assizes; fortified castles; organised defence against the Welsh; and acted generally as the king's paymaster and chief executive. Even then, he remained the king's servant. It was the king's presence that prompted the Assize of Northampton, which dealt with enforcing criminal and civil law, in 1176. In the same year, Richard argued unavailingly against Henry's retrospective cancellation of the suspension of the Forest Laws granted during the rebellion of 1173 and, in common with other barons, had to surrender his main castle at Ongar. Furthermore, he had powerful and influential colleagues such as Richard of Ilchester, bishop of Winchester, and Geoffrey Ridel, bishop of Ely. Even so, between 1173 and 1178, Richard set the pattern for the justiciarship elaborated and perfected by his successors Ranulf Glanvill, Hubert Walter, Geoffrey FitzPeter, Peter des Roches and Hubert de Burgh. Significantly, all of them depended on the king. As ambitious clerics and knights with backgrounds in the lesser nobility of the Angevin dominions, they were royal creatures.

Richard de Lucy had shown his frequently absent king the usefulness of a chief official in England, dependent on royal favour and command but with status as great as any baron, whose prime qualification was that, as proxy, he used the king's power in relentless pursuit of royal rights and interests. Henry regretted Richard's resignation in the winter of 1178-9 for he had lost a minister who, however personally ambitious, deserved the nickname the king gave him: Richard the Loyal.

At his retirement, Richard was probably an old man. He had been active in government for forty years. He withdrew to the house of Augustinian canons he had founded at Lesnes, in Kent, where, before his death in 1179, he adopted the habit of the order. Such gestures were not uncommon, but Richard appears to have possessed a high degree of conventional piety. In 1164, he apparently went on pilgrimage to Compostella and, in reaction to the Becket dispute, he may have taken the cross, and even gone to the Holy Land. More certainly, whatever the state of his soul, Richard died leaving both a barony — inherited by his grandson — and a political dynasty: one son, Godfrey, became bishop of Winchester (1189-1204); his grandson was prominent under John and Henry III. However, like the other lay justiciars (Glanvill, FitzPeter, de Burgh), he failed to found a dynasty that could sustain itself at the top of the English baronage for more than a couple of generations.

Richard's career was, in one way, replicated across twelfth century Europe. With the growth of written records, the study of law and developments in accounting, monarchs increasingly trusted their affairs to curial knights rather than risk conflicts of interests and time inevitable with ministers drawn from the upper nobility. However, the scope of administrative activity over which Richard presided and to some extent initiated was peculiar to England: the regular central audit; the control of localities through itinerant justices, confiscations of castles and supervising sheriffs; the inauguration of legal mechanisms to resolve the social dislocation of persistent litigation over land; the imposition of rules to govern the apprehension and trial of felons; and the institution of national inquiries as a means of government. Royal authority — as Richard himself showed in 1173-4 — was based on the skilful or fortunate manipulation of force and patronage, on politics and people not bureaucracy and parchment. But Richard de Lucy and his colleagues gave Henry II weapons with which he could take unusual advantage of whatever political success he achieved.

W. L. Warren, *Henry II*, 1973.
F. J. West, *The Justiciarship in England*, 1966.

ROGER OF PONT L'EVEQUE (*d*.1181; archbishop of York 1154-81) has suffered from being judged by his role in the Becket controversy. Although this perspective aptly reflects the corrosive embrace of the affair, it does not give Roger his due. A well educated Norman, a good Latinist and able church lawyer, Roger was one of the talented group of erudite secular clerks Archbishop Theobald gathered around him in the 1140s. Later hostile gossip suggested that Roger was condescending and antagonistic to the less academically groomed Thomas Becket. Yet until the parting of the ways in 1162-4, there was no especial antagonism between Roger and Thomas, beyond perhaps inevitable rivalry for preferment and attention in the competitive, self-consciously superior hot-house of Theobald's household, the twelfth century's equivalent of Jowett's Balliol, just as Bayeux was the eleventh's. Roger, indeed, had little to be jealous about. One of Theobald's favourites, in 1148 Roger became archdeacon of Canterbury and in 1154, largely through Theobald's influence, archbishop of York.

Theobald may have hoped that in Roger he would have a pliant archbishop of York who, with his Canterbury background, would forego the usual disputes with the southern metropolitan. In fact Roger turned native, becoming an aggressive and skilful advocate of York's claims to equality with Canterbury and authority over the Scottish episcopacy. In York itself he extended the Minster with the construction of a new choir, east end and lavishly endowed chapel of St Sepulchre, as well as building himself a substantial palace. To his scholarly interests may be attributed surviving twelfth century manuscripts still in the Minster Library. Perhaps it was because of his benefactions, made possible by the considerable fortune he amassed, or his absences on national business that he retained good relations with his chapter. His household included the renowned Italian canon lawyer Master Vacarius, another old boy of Theobald's entourage. He accompanied Roger north in 1154 and never went back, his presence testimony to Roger's stature and the attractions, under his rule, of the northern province. Roger brought to the province of York a stability not seen for more than a decade before his election and not witnessed again for another thirty-five years after his death.

As archbishop of York, Roger's finest hour should have been when he crowned Henry II's son king in June 1170. Instead, this formed a prime charge in the indictment levelled at him by the supporters of Becket for whom Roger had been an invader of the rights of his superior metropolitan, a malicious inciter of royal anger and, even, a conspirator and paymaster of the saint's murderers. By 1162, when Becket was appointed archbishop of Canterbury, Roger was already an experienced prelate. Outside his diocese he served as a papal judge-delegate; he undertook diplomatic missions for the king; he regularly attended the king's court; and, in the Canterbury vacancy after the death of Theobald in 1161, he had acted, with papal approval, as head of the English church. Historically and perhaps personally, tension with the new archbishop of Canterbury was likely, if not inevitable. After 1163, Roger sided with the king — as in the end did all his brother bishops. Appointed a papal legate in 1164, Roger's connivance at the Young Henry's coronation was unsurprising, but it attracted Becket's especial wrath and his disciples' particular venom. It was Becket's excommunication, on the eve of his return to England in November 1170, of Roger and two colleagues for their part in the coronation that prompted Roger's visit to Henry at Bar-le-Roi over Christmas; the king's outburst of rage at his former chancellor; and the retaliation of the four knights. Some later said that Roger helped plan the knights' attack. This probably owes more to the hysteria of Becket's bereaved followers than truth. Although he was suspended by the pope, by the end of 1171 he had been rehabilitated: the charges of the Becket faction had not stuck.

Throughout the Becket controversy, Roger had played his own game. While Foliot took the polemical lead, Roger exploited the situation to consolidate, where possible, the rights of York. He disagreed with Becket's position; deplored his methods; and had little regard for his powers of argument, but he was motivated not by personal spite or ideological disagreement but institutional advantage. In the aftermath of the martyrdom, such expedient opportunism was damned by hindsight but was more representative of how the church operated than Becket's histrionics. Roger persisted with his attempts to establish York's independence from Canterbury under Becket's successor, Richard of Dover, and continued to assert his claims over Scotland. He played a significant role on the king's side in the rebellion of 1173-4. Looked at from his new palace, his career was neither blighted nor peripheral.

Dangerously for the historian, Roger's opposition to Becket ensured that his personality received close and unflattering scrutiny from the martyr's apologists. Even the high-minded John of Salisbury in 1172 dragged up a twenty-year-old scandal about Roger's sex life. In the early 1150s Roger apparently had a homosexual affair with a beautiful boy, possibly an oblate, called Walter. When Walter later told others about the liaison, Roger, perhaps fearing blackmail and the ruin of a career so promisingly launched, used his authority as archdeacon to have the unfortunate Walter's eyes put out. Then, to silence him for good, Roger persuaded some secular judges to convict Walter as a felon and have him hanged. There followed a cover-up, smoothly orchestrated by Archbishop Theobald, ending with absolution from the pope. As a story, it had much to titillate:

illicit sex; the abuse of power; the murky private lives of the great; the establishment closing ranks. How much, if any of it, is true is impossible to estimate. It is hard to credit that Roger, so soon after these events, would have been selected by Theobald as archbishop of York, nor that he could, as he did, have kept on such civil terms with the rest of Theobald's high-minded, priggish protégés. John of Salisbury's salacious story probably tells us more about him and the sort of scabrous tale popular in twelfth century educated circles than it does about Roger. Nevertheless, Roger would not have been the last archbishop of York whose sexuality was a grey area.

F. Barlow, *Thomas Becket*, 1986.
A. Aylmer and R. Cant, *A History of York Minster*, 1977.

ROSAMUND CLIFFORD (*d.c.*1176) was the most favoured of Henry II's mistresses. Daughter of Walter de Clifford, a marcher lord, Rosamund appears to have been openly acknowledged by Henry after the Great Rebellion of 1173-4 and the consequent disgrace of his wife, Eleanor of Aquitaine. Legends soon began to cluster around Rosamund, including romantic tales of her seclusion at Woodstock and her poisoning by a jealous queen. What is certain is that she did not long enjoy her status as Henry's *maîtresse en titre*, dying perhaps as early as 1176. She was buried at Godstow nunnery near Oxford, with which her family had connections and on which a devastated Henry lavished donations for her shrine. In 1191, a convenient four years after her lover's death, Rosamund's tomb was removed from before the altar at Godstow by an outraged Hugh, bishop of Lincoln. Immune from the censure of Henry II, the moralising bishop had Rosamund's body reburied in the cemetery because 'she was a harlot'. Described on the inscription on her grave as 'Rose of the world', Rosamund appears to have been, in the words of Henry's most recent biographer, 'the great love of his life', prominent enough to excite rumour and gossip among contemporaries and to feature in salacious stories a century after her death. Discernable political influence she had none, as Henry recognised in not divorcing Eleanor in 1175, which he was rumoured to be contemplating. The inadequate evidence concerning 'Fair Rosamund' is a reminder of how little can be reconstructed of the private lives even of the most famous medieval people. Henry II had a number of mistresses, and at least two bastards, Geoffrey FitzRoy, archbishop of York and William Longsword, earl of Salisbury, their mother possibly being an Englishwoman, called Ykenai, with whom Henry had a liaison in the early 1150s. We know nothing of Henry's, or his mistresses', emotions, although the king was probably a generous lover. The Pipe Roll of 1184 records payment of £55 17s for 'clothes and hoods and cloaks and for the trimming for two capes of samite and for the clothes of the queen and of Belle-belle, for the king's use'.

W. L. Warren, *Henry II*, 1973.

HUGH BIGOD (*c*.1094-1177), second son of Roger Bigod, on the death of his elder brother William in the White Ship disaster (1120) inherited vast estates especially in East Anglia, a region he bent most of his energies over an exceptionally long and active political career to dominate. Where his father had been a loyal servant of successive kings, Hugh, although a hereditary steward in the royal household, exploited the civil war under Stephen to try to establish quasi-autonomous power in East Anglia, a policy which, when pursued in more settled times under Henry II, led to conflict with the king and near ruin. Hugh's priorities were the reverse of his father's. Roger Bigod had served his king well and had in consequence been created a great provincial magnate; Hugh had inherited a great provincial position and, therefore, expected to play a part in national politics. His loyalty was conditional on what suited his local interests. Thus Hugh regarded Stephen, who possessed extensive personal lands in eastern England, as a local competitor as much as king. Hugh's defection to Matilda in 1141 was to serve his own ambitions, not hers: he received the title of earl of Norfolk as a reward. Under Henry II, rivalry with Stephen's son, William, continued until 1157 when the king confiscated the castles of both men. Hugh bought only partial restitution on payment of a large fine in 1165. This grievance made Hugh well-disposed towards the rebellion against Henry in 1173-4 but, despite capturing Norwich, he was forced to submit, with his stronghold of Framlingham being dismantled. Hugh's failure to escape royal control was, in one way, ironic, as in 1135 he had played kingmaker when he swore — almost certainly falsely — that the dying Henry I had designated Stephen his successor. That one moment of influence typified Hugh's career of earnest, not always prescient and often frustrated seeking after personal and dynastic advantage.

W. L. Warren, *Henry II,* 1973.

THOMAS BROWN (*d.c.*1180), an Englishman by birth, had a remarkable career as a leading counsellor and administrator to two of the dominant rulers of twelfth century Europe, Roger II of Sicily (1105-54) and Henry II of England. He appears in Sicilian charters as a royal chaplain possibly as early as 1137. A cleric, customarily called 'Master' (*Magister*), he is also mentioned as 'familiaris regis' and, in a Greek charter (Roger's scriptorium being trilingual: Latin; Greek and Arabic), 'Thomas the Brown' (θωμα τοῦ Βρουνου). Later described as being 'almost at the head of King Roger's confidential business', apparently his fame was such that there were 'many kingdoms in which he would have been received with honour'. It was said that Henry II repeatedly offered Thomas a post in his native England. But it was only the death of Roger II and the subsequent persecution of the late king's servants by his son, William I, that forced Thomas to flee in search of new employment. His international reputation may be testimony to the cosmopolitan world of the Norman connection and of court gossip throughout western Europe. Alternatively, Thomas's fame may have been embroidered by his colleague, Richard FitzNeal, from whose book, *The Dialogue of the Exchequer* (1178), most of the information comes. Whatever the means of his preferment at the Angevin court, Thomas, who was in England by 1159, rapidly moved to the centre of the royal administration. He appears as Henry II's almoner (officially the royal officer who distributed alms on behalf of the king) in 1166, having been appointed perhaps some years earlier. His actual importance was far greater. According to FitzNeal, Thomas had a special privileged seat at the Exchequer audit, with his own clerk who noted down all Treasury receipts and expenses. Thomas's competence seems to have ranged across all royal business. He kept a third roll to complement those of the Treasurer (the so-called Pipe roll) and the Chancellor, an innovation in customary Exchequer practice devised uniquely for Thomas. With his 'lynx-eyed' clerk scrutinising all Treasury transactions, his own association with all important Exchequer decisions and his private roll containing, says FitzNeal, 'the laws of the realm and the secrets of the king', Thomas appears to have acted as Henry's personal representative, presumably briefed to check on how the audit was conducted. As the later troubles of Angevin government illustrate, how equitably or efficiently the Exchequer operated was of prime political as well as financial significance for the king. Thomas's position was entirely personal and unofficial. The king may have been eager to have his own ears and eyes in an institution which, as FitzNeal's description of it hints, had already developed a sense of corporate tradition, even self-importance. FitzNeal's rather prim comment that Thomas's private roll was contrary to the Exchequer's 'ancient custom' may show a recognition of this intrusion, which itself reveals that royal government was still not rigidly bureaucratised. Furthermore, the ease with which Thomas, and others in the twelfth century, moved between courts, argues either for similarity or simplicity of governmental procedure. Thomas's administrative career provides a mirror to those of aristocratic opportunists such as William Marshal: mobile; cosmopolitan; precarious; dependent on personal ability, luck and the friendship and trust of princes; crowned by great rewards in profit, influence and power. Thomas was a knight-errant and an aristocrat of civil servants.

HERBERT OF BOSHAM (*d*.1194) was a notable scholar, a pupil of Peter Lombard in Paris and a Hebraist whose career was devoured by his loyalty and devotion to Thomas Becket. He first worked for Becket before 1157 as a royal clerk when the future archbishop was Henry II's chancellor. There developed a close bond between them, Herbert remaining with Becket after 1162. In the archbishop's household, Herbert was Becket's teacher, counsellor and, on a number of occasions, his confidential agent. At Becket's side at Clarendon and Northampton in 1164, he shared the archbishop's exile. Others in Becket's entourage found him rather trying. He was difficult, obstinate, intemperate and extreme in the advice he offered. Devastated at not being present at Becket's murder, he found it almost impossible to reconcile himself to the compromises necessary afterwards. In 1172, he complained hysterically to the pope of shabby treatment, but his inflexible hostility to all who were not as fanatical in honouring Becket's memory as he made it difficult for him to be treated any differently. In 1184-6, he wrote his *Life of St. Thomas of Canterbury*, dedicated to Archbishop Baldwin, which, although containing the best account of Becket's exile, relies heavily on turgid sermonising. In 1189 he briefly entered the household of William Longchamp, regent for Richard I, but he clearly was past holding down any responsible post. He spent his last years in a Cistercian abbey in Artois writing a commentary on Jerome's *Hebrew Psalter* to make ends meet. Herbert, who thought of himself as privileged to have served Becket, was a victim of the conflict. It had been the most exciting period of his life; he could not cope with the drabber days that followed. He felt betrayed. To the trimmers who inherited Becket's legacy, he was an awkward reminder of the saint's own extremism and passion.

E. Barlow, *Thomas Becket*, 1986.
A. Gransden, *Historical Writing in England c.550-c.1307*, 1974.

AILNOTH INGENIATOR, or the Engineer (*fl.*1157-90), was one of, if not the most expert of Henry II's overseers of royal buildings. For over thirty years, from 1157/8 until 1189, he drew a salary of 7d a day (£10 12s 11d a year). His main position was that of Keeper of the Palace of Westminster, but this minimises the variety of tasks entrusted to him as well as his own versatility. At Westminster, his responsibilities included repairs of the fabric of the complex of houses which comprised the royal palace, cleaning them, providing fresh rushes, replacing broken windows (in 1179, early evidence for royal houses of domestic glazing), erecting a cloister linking the king's chambers, and the planning and construction of a new wharf and landing stair. At

Westminster Abbey he repaired the refectory in 1175, built a stone arch in 1187 and possibly designed the Chapel of St. Catherine in 1160. Elsewhere, Ailnoth supervised the building of the Fleet gaol in London during the 1170s and 1180s and was regularly engaged on work at the Tower where he provided lead for the Chapel roof (1176) and hired carpenters to find timber for building work there in 1175. He was also active at various times at Windsor Castle, Woodstock and Rayleigh. It is probable that Ailnoth was involved with, perhaps even designed Orford Castle, with its novel polygonal keep, built between 1165 and 1173. Certainly his duties were not confined to civil works alone. In 1175 and 1176 he led a team of royal carpenters and masons who pulled down the motte and bailey castle at Framlingham, stronghold of Hugh Bigod, earl of Norfolk and one of the defeated leaders of the Great Rebellion against Henry II in 1173-4. As with many contemporary engineers, although he dealt with lead, glass and stone, he had probably begun his career as a carpenter and had most likely worked on war- and siege-machines, useful talents in a country recovering from civil war, as England was in the 1150s. It is only in the twelfth century, with the financial record of payments made at the Exchequer recorded on the Pipe Rolls, that we are able to trace careers of men like Ailnoth. But whether he acted as a superviser, designer, architect, builder or manager of the king's works is impossible to say. Ailnoth seems to have retired in 1189/90, as his wages in 1190 were recorded as being only £2 10s. He was certainly dead by 1197, when his wife Maud is described as a widow. He seems to have acquired or was given property in Westminster and was probably the father of Roger Enganet, who was active in West-minster c.1177-1216. It was on men like Ailnoth that the grander facade of Angevin government depended if only for the reason that kings needed experts to maintain their palaces, build their castles and tear down those of their enemies.

J. Harvey, *English Mediaeval Architects*, 1987.

GEOFFREY FITZROY (1151/3-1212), illegitimate son of the future Henry II and an Englishwoman, Ykenai, possessed much of the ability of the Angevins, not least their capacity to make enemies. Destined for the church, he was elected bishop of Lincoln in 1173, although not yet a priest. For nine years, Geoffrey enjoyed the revenues as bishop-elect but made no moves to be consecrated, which says much for the ineffectiveness of the ideals of the martyred Thomas Becket. In all, Lincoln remained vacant for over sixteen years (1166-1183), although Geoffrey was a benefactor, as when he redeemed cathedral ornaments for £300 from the banker Aaron of Lincoln. Politically, Geoffrey proved more loyal to his father than his legitimate half-brothers, especially during the Great Rebellion of 1173-4 and the civil war in France with Richard (1187-9). In 1182, he became his father's chancellor. Alone of Henry's sons he was at his father's deathbed at Chinon in 1189. Richard I put an end to Geoffrey's lingering political ambitions by sacking him as chancellor and having him forcibly made a priest in 1189 shortly after nominating him as archbishop of York. After a challenge from the York chapter, Geoffrey was consecrated in 1191. Although reconciled with Richard, Geoffrey was regarded by most, including his half-brother John and the justiciar Hubert Walter, as a troublemaker. The rest of his career was spent fending off ecclesiastical challenges to his position and dabbling ineffectually in national politics. An educated man, possibly with a speech impediment, his career as absentee and pluralist sits oddly beside the respectability and, in a few cases, vocation of his contemporary bishops. Geoffrey did not take Holy Orders very seriously but they were all that were left. Any political ambitions were stifled by his illegitimacy, a comment less on his talents than on the effectiveness of the church over the previous century in changing secular attitudes to marriage. Thus Geoffrey was condemned to obscurity or notorious frustration. He chose the latter, with, it seems, his father's approval. After the Great Rebellion by his other sons the king reputedly declared of Geoffrey: 'Baseborn indeed have my other children shown themselves; this alone is my true son'. Unsurprisingly, the 'other children' disagreed.

Gerald of Wales, *Vita Galfridi* in *Opera*, ed. J. S. Brewer, J. F. Dimock & G. F. Warner, 1861-91, vol iv.

HENRY (1155-83; crowned king of England 1170) was the eldest son of Henry II and Eleanor of Aquitaine. To secure his dynasty, the elder Henry followed French practice by having the Young Henry crowned in his lifetime. Although the ceremony itself, performed by the archbishop of York at the height of the conflict with Becket, proved controversial, its validity was unchallenged, thus creating a situation unique since the Conquest of there being simultaneously two crowned kings of England. In 1169, Henry II had assigned the succession to his dominions to his three eldest sons: Henry was to inherit the patrimonial lands of England, Normandy and Anjou; Richard his mother's duchy of Aquitaine; and Geoffrey the county of Brittany. In the event the Old King was compromised by the very thoroughness of the arrangement. His sons, as legally constituted rulers, wished for actual power which their father denied them. This was especially true of the Young King. Richard was given an increasingly free hand in Aquitaine and Geoffrey in Brittany, but Henry, despite his title of king, was left with no political authority and no lands to rule as his own. This anomaly was largely his father's fault, but was also a consequence of the Young Henry's personality. Like other heirs to forceful royal parents, Robert Curthose, the Prince Regent, Edward VII or Edward VIII, Henry's charm was vitiated by restless shallowness, a bored pursuit of pleasure rather than duty. Refusing to play a constructive role in government as his father's subordinate or representative, Henry sought vicarious excitement in an obsession with tournaments and the burgeoning fashion of chivalry. At no stage did he suggest anything but political fecklessness and incompetence; his influence was almost wholly destructive. Impatient for power, if not responsibility, Henry fomented the Great Rebellion against his father of 1173-4 in alliance with his two elder brothers, the king of France and the count of Flanders. Despite reconciliation with his father in 1174, Henry remained dilatory in performing even the modest political tasks entrusted to him while maintaining a taste for disruptive intrigue. In the months before his death, with Geoffrey of Brittany and Philip II of France, he once more unavailingly confronted his father, dying unreconciled and unsuccessful. His political failure was balanced by his contemporary popularity. Open-handed

chivalric poseurs won more plaudits than tight-fisted administrators. Yet it is significant that even his tutor-in-arms, William
Marshal, lost patience and favour. Whether Henry's fickleness
came from stupidity or petulence, his career as a gilded playboy
touched pathos. Energetically, even desperately convivial, flat-
tered, cosseted and irresponsible, Henry was heir to a destiny
too great for him to grasp. For all his heart-winning generosity,
capacity for friendship, ambition and pretensions, in the end
Henry ruled nothing, not even his own appetites.

W. Warren, *Henry II*, 1973.

   GEOFFREY OF BRITTANY (1158-86) was the fourth son of
Henry II and Eleanor of Aquitaine. As part of his father's plans
to secure and extend his family lands in France, as a child he was
betrothed (1166/7) to Constance, the heiress to the count of Brittany (Conan the Little, *d*.1171). At the family settlement at
Montmirail on 1169, Geoffrey did homage for Brittany to his
eldest brother, the Young Henry, who, in turn, did homage to
Louis VII of France. With his elder brothers, he allied with the
French king against his father in 1173-4. In 1175, he began his
rule in Brittany, doing homage for the county to the new French
king, Philip II, in 1179. He finally married Constance in 1181. In
1183, he goaded the Young Henry into revolt against the old
king and Richard of Poitou, the future Richard I; a year later, he
allied with his younger brother John against Richard, disappointed, perhaps, at not being given Anjou on the Young
Henry's death (1183): it had gone to Richard. In Brittany he promulgated the so-called 'Assize of Geoffrey' (1185) which was
aimed at protecting lords' rights. Knighted by his father in 1178,
Geoffrey developed a passion for tournament and intrigue which
finally killed him. It was at a tournament in Paris, whither he
had gone to plot with Philip II in 1186, that he was mortally
wounded. His son, Arthur, who was to contest as unsuccessfully
as his father for the Anjevin inheritance (1199-1203), was born
posthumously. The contemporary royal clerk and historian,
Roger of Howden, called Geoffrey 'that son of perdition'.
Gerald of Wales, with his acute dislike of all the Angevins,
described Geoffrey as 'of tireless endeavour, a hypocrite in

everything, a deceiver and a dissembler' 'able to corrupt two kingdoms with his tongue'. Geoffrey's career testifies to the ambition and the weakness of Henry II's schemes.

WILLIAM CADE (*d.*1166) was a financier of Flemish origins whose business activities reveal the existence and something of the extent of the credit market of twelfth century England. A moneylender on a massive scale, in the 1150s and 1160s he numbered among his clients some of the greatest in the land, including the king. At his death, he was owed around £5,000. Although his surviving accounts are not explicit about the interest he charged, it is probable that, as with contemporary banking transactions by monasteries, the sums outstanding include hidden usury. His Flemish background could point to a mercantile base for his operations, as England traded extensively with the Low Countries. The size of his loans, and those of other twelfth century Christian moneylenders, such as the merchant Gervase of Southampton, combined with the banking activities of religious houses and the growing Jewish community indicate one central difficulty confronting contemporary social elites. How could extensive landed wealth and rights over markets, trade, and tenants be converted into ready cash to meet the rising costs of aristocratic life, in particular the expenses of military retinues in peace as well as war, and the price of land. Few historical orthodoxies are as bogus as that which suggests that in a so-called 'feudal' society all land, in a sort of tenurial pyramid, was held ultimately of the king in return for personal military service and that all armies were raised by a feudal levy of knights provided by tenants according to a fixed quota, the knight's fee. Such appearances were, at best, legal fictions. Thus the *Cartae Baronum* of 1166, which purported to be a survey of the knights' fees possessed by all tenants-in-chief was designed to reveal not how many troops Henry II could call upon but the basis for a fiscal re-assessment of the scutage tax. Just as soldiers had been paid, even where they owed homage and fealty, so too had land changed hands after financial transactions, at least since the eighth century. Wages and purchase prices rose while fixed rents lost value in the twelfth century, on top of which many families had to suffer the often crippling costs of crusading, high taxation, and heavy feudal incidents (*e.g.* reliefs and wardships). The cycle of debt, encouraged in some instances by Angevin government, or so believed the instigators of *Magna Carta*, offered scope and, no doubt, rich pickings for those with access to bullion and cash. Despite ecclesiastical prohibitions, lending money for profit was flourishing among the Christian as well as Jewish community, with monks as well as merchants leading the way. Men like Cade provided an essential service to a society and economy which refused to be pinned down by church dogma or modest and laboriously realised annual rates of return on land.

H. Jenkinson, 'William Cade' in *English Historical Review*, xxviii (1913) and in *Essays in History Presented to R. L. Poole.*

RALPH OF BETHLEHEM (*d.*1174; bishop of Bethlehem 1156-74), an Englishman, was chancellor of the Latin Kingdom of Jerusalem for the last thirty years of his life. The Queen Regnant Melisende, his patroness, had tried unsuccessfully to appoint him archbishop of Tyre, the second see in the kingdom, in 1146. It was said by his successor as chancellor that Ralph owed his promotion to Bethlehem in 1156 to being a fellow countryman to the then pope, Hadrian IV. A learned but worldly man, Ralph played a significant role in the affairs of the kingdom as administrator, diplomat, even military commander: he was wounded on campaign in Egypt in 1165. Under Bishop Ralph the remarkable Byzantine mosaics were installed in the Church of the Nativity in Bethlehem, which survive to this day: Greek designs, commissioned by an English bishop for a Latin church in Palestine, symbols of the cosmopolitan world which allowed Ralph to find employment two thousand miles from his homeland. Ralph was a Levantine counterpart to Thomas Brown, the English minister of Roger II of Sicily. It is likely that Ralph came from a noble family who, frustrated by career prospects in Europe, sought his fortune in the less congested ecclesiastical world of Outremer where western also-rans could come in winners. Ralph was not the only successful Englishman in the east. Another was William, prior of the chapter of the Holy Sepulchre who became the first Latin archbishop of Tyre in 1128. The horizons of twelfth century Europe were widening,

offering, as Ralph's career showed, new and attractive opportunities for the educated, well-connected and pushy.

B. Hamilton, *The Latin Church in the Crusader States: The Secular Church*, 1980.

RICHARD OF CLARE (*d*.1176), nicknamed by some contemporaries 'Strongbow' (a play on one of his titles, lord of
Striguil), was the most prominent of the Anglo-Norman lords
who began to colonize Ireland in the reign of Henry II. The son
of Gilbert, earl of Pembroke, he inherited his father's estates in
south Wales in 1148. His loyalty to King Stephen cost him his
earldom on Henry II's accession. In consequence, as Gerald of
Wales commented, 'his pedigree was longer than his purse'. In
common with many disinherited noblemen, Richard was open
to any proposal likely to restore his fortune. Ireland offered just
such an opportunity.

As with England in the 1060s and Scotland in the 1090s, internal Irish political tensions attracted foreign intervention. There
had been ecclesiastical pressure on Henry II to consider extending his overlordship to Ireland since the 1150s, but it was only on
the invitation of Dermot, king of Leinster, that intervention
began. In 1167, Henry II gave Dermot permission to recruit supporters to help him win back control of Dublin from the king of
Connaught. A few Marcher lords, led by Robert FitzStephen and
Maurice FitzGerald landed at Wexford in 1169. Richard of Clare
joined them in August 1170 having reached a very favourable
deal with Dermot: Richard was to marry Dermot's daughter and
in due course inherit his kindom.

The Anglo-Normans were immediately effective, using military techniques new to Ireland, such as the motte-and-bailey castle, and mounted knights operating in conjunction with archers
and infantry. In September 1170, Dublin was taken and by the
time Dermot died in 1171, his power over Leinster had been
restored. Richard of Clare now asserted his claim to Leinster.
This not only ran counter to Irish law but also aroused the suspicion of Henry II, anxious lest any vassal of his dare establish
himself as a ruler independent of his authority. In the autumn of
1171, therefore, Richard was faced by a siege of Dublin by Rory

O'Connor, king of Connaught; withdrawal of royal aid from England; and the imminent arrival of Henry himself armed to conquer all, including Richard, who stood against him. Richard defeated King Rory, but had to obey Henry. Paying homage for his Irish lands, Richard was confirmed in control of Leinster, but only received the key towns of Waterford, Wexford, and Dublin in 1174. From 1173 to 1176, he seemed to have acted as Henry's viceroy in Ireland, a position he adopted from Henry's initial agent, Hugh de Lacy who was established as lord of Meath. However, if Henry had hoped that by formally imposing his lordship on Irish and Anglo-Normans alike (Rory O'Connor submitted in 1175) he had solved the problem of his authority in Ireland, he was wrong. But the violence and instability in Ireland, which had attracted Richard of Clare in the first place, cannot be seen in nationalist terms. The Irish kings fought each other; they fought the Anglo-Normans; they allied with the Anglo-Normans against Irish rivals. It is true that beneath this carapace of feuding and flouted legality, Anglo-Norman settlement began, especially in the east, adding yet another fault-line along which Irish society could tear and break. But it must be remembered, when any facile condemnations about English involvement in Ireland are trotted out, that opportunists like Richard of Clare had been given their chance and their stake in Ireland by indigenous Irish leaders. Henry II reluctantly became involved only when Richard of Clare's success seemed to threaten his interests elsewhere.

WILLIAM OF SENS (*d*.1180) has often been credited with introducing French Gothic style into English ecclesiastical architecture when he was placed in charge of the extensive remodelling of Canterbury Cathedral between 1174 and 1177. A fire had conveniently gutted the cathedral choir, giving the monks the opportunity to redesign it as a monument to Thomas Becket. To find the right mason, the monks held a medieval equivalent of an architects' competition. A number of master masons were interviewed before William of Sens was chosen. Our main source for the rebuilding, the eye-witness Gervase of Canterbury, described William as 'the most cunning craftsman in wood and stone'. One of his techniques was to make moulds which were then sent to the individual masons for cutting the stones. William oversaw the rebuilding for about three years before badly injuring his back in a fall of fifty feet from the wooden scaffolding. Crippled and bed-ridden, William struggled on for a short time giving instructions to a young monk (possibly Gervase himself) who supervised the work. This arrangement proved unsatisfactory. William soon relinquished his post to his namesake, William the Englishman, returning to France where he died on 11 August 1180.

While there are evident similarities between the new design of Canterbury in the 1170s and the cathedral of Sens, begun in the 1140s and one of the earliest to be built in the new Gothic style, the most stylistically innovative parts of the rebuilding, for example the Trinity Chapel and Corona, date from after William of Sens had departed and must be credited to William the Englishman who completed the work in 1184. The latter was, according to Gervase, 'small in body, but in workmanship of many kinds acute and honest' and may have pursued a career as architect, engineer or carpenter at Canterbury and for the king until 1214. As for William of Sens, he was evidently widely travelled and experienced before 1174. It is possible he was attracted to Canterbury by the link between Sens and Becket, who had stayed there during his exile. It is as likely that he was on the look out for lucrative employment. William of Sens's appearance at Canterbury indicates a lively international traffic in masons and thus in artistic and architectural influences. However, the contribution of William the Englishman is a reminder of the equally significant role of local inspiration.

J. Harvey, *English Mediaeval Architects*, 1987.

RICHARD OF DOVER (*d*.1184: archbishop of Canterbury 1173-84) was the unlikely choice as Becket's successor. A previously obscure mediocrity, he nevertheless demonstrated, to the anger of the Becketeers, that effective cooperation with the king was possible. Although not glamorous, Richard's credentials were appropriate. He had been a monk at Canterbury and, unusual in a household dominated by secular clerks, one of Archbishop Theobald's chaplains before being promoted as prior of St Martin's, Dover in 1157. His suitability for the primacy seems to have become apparent on a visit he made to Henry II in 1173 as part of a delegation to discuss the election of a new archbishop. While the form of a free election was preserved, as, in the circumstances of the king's submission to the pope earlier in the year at Avranches was essential, it represented a deal struck between Henry, his Justiciar, Richard de Lucy, and the prior of the Canterbury monks, Odo. Such outward compliance with canonical precept and practical compromise with secular authority set the tone for Richard's tenure of Canterbury. The contrast in style and concerns between Richard and his predecessor could hardly have been greater. Richard was interested in the reform of the clergy. A canonist of some enthusiasm, he collected papal decretals for circulation in England and acted as a papal judge-delegate. But he was also a royalist. In 1173-4, he went along with the appeal against his election by the Young King Henry because he knew that he had the Old King and the bishops on his side: this appeal to Rome looked good but was wholly ineffectual. He consistently defended the king's role in episcopal elections (to the irritation of Pope Alexander III); he allowed the king to sit in on his judgements as papal delegate; he approved of the use of bishops as royal justices; he argued for the trials of murderers of clerics to be held in secular courts; and he specifically repudiated Becket's hostility to what he had called double punishment in cases where clerks were tried by secular as well as ecclesiastical courts. In a letter of 1176, Richard put forward the view that if one court 'supplements the other's insufficiency, that is not a double punishment but a combined punishment'. Such opinions provoked accusations that he lost for the church every point for which Becket had fought. But it was Richard's policies, not Becket's, which charted the relationship between the English church and state for the rest of the Middle Ages.

H. Mayr-Harting, 'Henry II and the Papacy', *Journal of Ecclesiastical History,* 1965.

MAURICE (*fl.*1174-87) was probably responsible for building two of the most impressive English stone keeps of the twelfth century, at Newcastle-upon-Tyne and Dover. Described in 1174-5 as a *cementarius* (mason) at Newcastle, he may have been involved throughout its building 1171-77. Between 1181 and 1187 he was in charge of construction at Dover as an *ingeniator* (engineer), being paid at the unusually high rate of one shilling a day. In 1181, he received over £3 as a gift from the king. This value placed on his work and the similarities of design between Newcastle and Dover points to Maurice as their architect. In style, both are dominated by traditional donjons: regular, rectangular stone towers, like the Tower of London of the previous century. These were being superseded by polygonal keeps (such as at Orford 1165-73) which gave defenders greater coverage of besiegers. Nevertheless, Maurice's keeps were impressive defences. They were also very expensive: Newcastle cost up to £1,000, while the price for Dover was nearly £4,000, perhaps a quater of the English king's annual income. Maurice has been described as 'the greatest, as he was the last, of the exponents of the square donjon'.

That financially hard-pressed monarchs were prepared to spend such vast sums on castles demonstrates their importance as centres of administration, political control, military garrisons and defence. From William the Conqueror's makeshift pallisades at Pevensey and Hastings in 1066, to the motte and baileys which helped secure the French conquest of England, to the great stone fortifications at London, Colchester, Rochester, Windsor, Winchester, Nottingham or Norwich, castles played a crucial role in English political life. Henry II spent over £20,000 on some ninety castles over thirty-three years. Much more than success in set-piece battles, control of castles formed the pivotal objectives of kings and their opponents in every major crisis of the period, for example the establishment of William I's power 1066-1069 and Henry II's in the 1150s or the civil wars of 1088, 1139-53, 1173-4, 1215-17 and 1263-65. The royal garrison at Orford effectively hampered Hugh Bigod's manoeuvres in East Anglia in 1173-4, while, on the other hand, Brian FitzCount's castle at Wallingford in Stephen's reign, Falkes de Bréauté's fortress at Bedford in 1224 and the Montfort stronghold at Kenilworth in 1265-66 proved intractible obstacles to royal supremacy. Thus the work of servants such as Maurice was central to royal government, a role brought to its apogee by the building of the Edwardian castles in North Wales, symbols of almost imperial might, by the Savoyard James of St George in the 1270s and 1280s.

J. Harvey, *English Mediaeval Architects*, 1987.

AARON OF LINCOLN (*d.*1185/6) was a leading banker in twelfth century England, a prominent member of the modest but significant Jewish community which had established itself in the second half of the twelfth century. Given the formal restrictions on Jewish commercial and civil rights, the scale and scope of Aaron's business was remarkable. On his death, his property, including outstanding debts owed him, escheated to the Crown. The amounts owing were so great that a special government office was established to chase them up, the *scaccarium Aaronis* — 'Aaron's exchequer': it took more than twenty years to finish its work. Aaron's deals were spread across the kingdom and throughout the secular and lay establishment. He had clients in twenty-five counties; they included the king of Scotland, the archbishop of Canterbury as well as nine Cistercian abbeys, who owed Aaron 6,400 marks. He arranged funding for the new cathedral at Lincoln and the abbeys at Peterborough and St Alban's. He also took on debts owed to other Jews, presumably because of his larger and more effective operation for administering and collecting debts. It is sometimes said that Jews made so much money out of lending because of their high interest rates, 43½%, even 60% in some instances. The inflexibility in the land market and the chronic problem of liquidity in an economy based on the exploitation of land, made such rates acceptable, attractive even, especially when compared to what was offered by others. Although sometimes in need of liquid capital themselves, monasteries were another source of cash. Some of them actually had agents scouring the land touting for trade at propitious moments, such as an impending crusade. However, unlike transactions with the Jews, monastic loans were hedged around with legal fictions or pious facts about grants for the good of the monastery and the debtor's soul. Monkish interest rates, however disguised, were definitely competitive: for example in the

1140s St Benet's Holme (Norfolk) made at least a profit of 133% over seven years on a deal with a departing crusader. The problem of debt was endemic amongst the ruling classes, despite, or perhaps because of an expanding economy. The costs of capital projects, such as constructing castles or churches, and war required immediate payments out of reach of even the most grasping landlord or government. The Jewish success in this market depended ultimately on their usefulness to the Crown whose special protection they alternately enjoyed and suffered. The king regularly received offerings from Jews *pro recto debiti sui*, *i.e.* to help them recover their debts. Jews could be tallaged at will by monarchs (as with the massive levy of £60,000 imposed at Guildford in 1186); but in consequence the Jews had to be allowed to prosper for the king to profit. When, in the thirteenth century, the wealth of the Jewish communities declined, they became more vulnerable. It was their poverty not their riches which led to their expulsion by Edward I in 1290. Aaron of Lincoln, however, prospered relatively unhindered, free at least from the worst excesses of visceral prejudice which emerged with destructive force in 1190. Whether feared or respected, he performed a vital service in Angevin England.

C. Roth, *A History of the Jews in England*, 1978.
R. B. Dobson, *The Jews of Medieval York and the Massacre of 1190* (Borthwick Papers No 45), 1974.

RANULF GLANVILL (1120/30-1190), one of Henry II's chief ministers, came from a family of Suffolk landowners. His father, Hervey, had been one of the leaders of the English fleet which had helped capture Lisbon in 1147 during the Second Crusade. His uncle, Roger, also had a successful career in royal service, and his wife's nephew, Hubert Walter, having begun his career in Ranulf's household, rose to become justiciar 1193-98 and chancellor 1199-1205. Ranulf seems early to have been destined for an official career, his first appearance in the records (1144/54) being as a witness to a charter of Nigel, bishop of Ely, Henry I's treasurer and restorer of the Exchequer after 1154. He also witnessed charters in the 1150s of King Stephen's second son,

William (*d*.1159). His early official career was centred on the north, as sheriff of Yorkshire (1163-70; 1175-89), and, at various times, custodian of Richmond, Westmorland and Lancaster. Although he lost his shrievalty in the Inquest of Sheriffs in 1170, he retained royal favour, which he cemented with his victory at Alnwick over William the Lion, king of Scots, in 1174 during the Great Rebellion against Henry II. Thereafter, Ranulf moved to the centre of affairs as a justice-in-eyre, diplomat and, from 1180 at the latest, justiciar in succession to Richard de Lucy, a man of similar background and dependence on royal patronage with whom Ranulf may have been associated since the 1150s. Ranulf, by all accounts, became one of Henry's closest personal advisers, as well as his leading official in England. Apart from financial, administrative and military responsibilities, Ranulf was especially active as a judge, both centrally and, unusually, in the provinces. His tenure of the justiciarship coincided with the definition of the judicial organisation required by Henry II's legal reforms, particularly the possessory assizes. Ranulf gained a reputation as an effective judge, eager to settle cases rapidly, although a number of observers close to the court noted that he was not above twisting the law and his position to his own advantage. It was under his auspices, although not by his own pen, that the law-book associated with his name, *Tractatus de legibus et consuetudinibus regni Angliae* (1187/89), was composed. The *Tractatus* is both a statement of principles and a guide to what was evidently still tentative practices. The main thrust of Henry's legal innovations had been to guarantee royal justice to all freemen in matters of land tenure and property rights. To make this anything more than pious hope or arbitrary interference, a system of coherent procedures and consistent judgements was essential. Ranulf, as justiciar, was central to this process to which the *Tractatus* bears authoritative witness. But Ranulf's authority depended on his ability and usefulness as a politician more than as a jurist. His loyalty to Henry II never wavered, as commander of campaigns against the Welsh; negotiator with Philip II of France; executor of the king's will; or supporter of Henry against his sons in 1188-9. Ranulf did not make policy; he executed it with the full freedom of royal favour. His rewards were tangible, from royal grants to the profits of office: in 1176/77, he was allowed to keep over £1,500 in cash, valuable horses and silver plate acquired in the course of his duties as sheriff of Yorkshire. Although he founded no dynasty, he was an important patron of the church in his native Suffolk where he founded an Augustinian priory at Butley (1171) and a Premonstratensian abbey at Leiston (1182). Given his support for Henry II, it was inevitable that, when the king died in 1189, Ranulf would be sacked, a fall accompanied by the usual charges of peculation which hounded finance ministers of dead monarchs throughout medieval Europe. In addition, it was said that the new king, Richard I, fined Ranulf the huge sums of £15,000; if true a tribute to the avarice of both parties. Although ruined politically, Ranulf retained enough power to follow his father's crusading example and lead a contingent on the Third Crusade. With him was his nephew Hubert Walter, newly promoted to the see of Salisbury, a fact which may suggest Ranulf's fall was not as complete as some contemporaries would have us believe. With Archbishop Baldwin of Canterbury, Ranulf left the king's army at Marseilles and hurried to Palestine in the autumn of 1190 as an advance-guard to the main English force which wintered in Sicily. There, in the appalling conditions of the besiegers' camp outside Acre, Ranulf died in October 1190. His life can be treated as typical of the Angevin lay civil servant, raised not from the dust but from the lesser nobility; supported by a network of patrons, family and protégés; lining his own and his master's pockets; loyal, energetic, and flexible as judge, financier, administrator and general. Ranulf's personality is irrecoverable, but his use to Henry appears to have been not simply that of the efficient bureaucrat but as a trusted adviser. Something of the atmosphere he created and the personal and political talent the king valued may be caught in the description of Ranulf by a close observer of Angevin government in the 1180s, Richard of Devizes. According to him, Ranulf was 'the king's eye'.

R. Mortimer, 'The Family of Ranulf de Glanville' *Bulletin of the Institute of Historical Research liv, 1981*
Glanvill, *Tractatus de legibus et consuetudines regni Angliae* ed G. D. G. Hall, 1965.

BALDWIN OF FORD (*d*.1190; bishop of Worcester 1180-84; archbishop of Canterbury 1184-90) combined a secular clerk's knowledge of worldly affairs with a Cistercian' s exclusive moral rectitude. Depending on occasion or point of view he was fearless or tactless in the pursuit of his aims. Although one of the less famous or notorious twelfth century archbishops, neither a saint nor a great scholar, his career throws light more evenly than those of more glamorous figures on a number of salient features of the church infra-diocesan feuding; the practical problems of implementing canon law; the relations of church and state, kings and churchmen; and the crusade, its preaching, organisation and conduct. For these alone, Baldwin's life repays attention.

Born at Exeter, he received a good education, probably at the cathedral school in his native town, earning by 1150 an international reputation as a teacher. He became an expert in canon law under the patronage of Bishop Bartholomew of Exeter (1162-84) who appointed him archdeacon of Totnes. A satisfying career in the service of church and state seemed to beckon. However, Baldwin, as a number of mildly surprised contemporaries noted, took his religion very seriously and, in about 1170, abandoned his prospects as a secular clerk and entered the Cistercian monastery at Ford on the Devon/Dorset border. It was while a monk at Ford that Baldwin produced most of his surviving works, including a *Penitential*, various sermons and treatises on the Sacraments and the Scriptures. His literary output was orthodox, conventional, even mundane. His particular interest in the anchorite Wulfric of Haselbury, also his later commitment to the Third Crusade, may suggest an inner spiritual life of some force. Whatever the power of his vocation, he soon resumed a successful public career. By 1175, he had become abbot of Ford and, in 1180, he was raised to the see of Worcester. In 1184, he intervened to prevent the execution at Worcester of Gilbert of Plumpton, a convicted robber, kidnapper, seducer of a royal ward and a victim of Justiciar Glanvill's particular hatred. Instead of anger at having his justice deflected, Henry II, displaying a penchant for stiff-necked prelates he repeated two years later by his preferment to the see of Lincoln of Hugh of Avalon, insisted on Baldwin's election as archbishop of Canterbury.

Independence of spirit may have counted with the king for less than Baldwin's unique perspective on ecclesiastical politics. As a Cistercian whose reputation was laid as a secular clerk specialising in canon law, Baldwin could be expected to keep his distance from the vested interests of the Benedictine monks of Christ Church, Canterbury, who acted as the cathedral chapter, as well as holding credentials for piety and administrative acumen. Given the internecine feuds and jealousies between the competing religious orders of the later twelfth century, the appointment of a Cistercian to Benedictine Canterbury, especially one intellectually suspicious of monastic as opposed to secular cathedral chapters, was provocative, not least as the Canterbury monks' preferred choices had been three Benedictines. Henry may have calculated that Baldwin would not, as had so many of his predecessors, 'turn native' and, thus dependent on royal patronage, would be willing to make Canterbury resources available for royal causes, as indeed happened in 1187/8 for the crusade. In fact, Baldwin's pontificate was marked by spectacular rows with the monks that threw into relief the long-standing eccentricity of the English tradition of monastic cathedral chapters whose relationships with their bishops were nowhere defined by increasingly rigid continental (*i.e.* universal) canon law. Baldwin's policies, not surprisingly, attracted the institutional hostility of contemporary monastic writers, especially exciting the venom of Gervase of Canterbury whose relentless bias against Baldwin stands in striking contrast to Eadmer's eulogies on Anselm. Our views of twelfth century archbishops are conditioned more than is sometimes acknowledged by the acceptability of the prelates to their clerical constituencies rather than to their effectiveness or holiness.

Baldwin began by wresting some estates from the control of the Canterbury monks who, he claimed, had degenerated into luxurious living in the first flush of the massive exploitation of the cult of Becket since 1170. There are echoes here of the long running twelfth century debate between Cistercians and Benedictines over the degree of asceticism required by the Rule of St. Benedict. Such controversies were marked by justice and hypocrisy on both sides. However, the question of estates and revenues paled into insignificance in the face of Baldwin's

scheme to found a college of secular canons at Hackington, on
the outskirts of Canterbury, dedicated to St. Stephen and St.
Thomas. The monks of Christ Church regarded this not only as
a threat to their prestige but also as providing a model and an
excuse for replacing them with secular canons in the cathedral
chapter, as both the king and most of his bishops apparently
desired. Baldwin reacted vigorously to the sustained monastic
opposition to his plans, at one period imprisoning the monks in
their own buildings for over eighteen months (January 1188-
August 1189) and later imposing on them a prior of his choice.
The new king, Richard I, eager to resolve such conflicts before
embarking on crusade, imposed a settlement on the disputants
in November 1189 which largely favoured Christ Church, Baldwin transferring his plans for a college to land he acquired at
Lambeth. The dispute had drawn much attention to it throughout western Christendom and was to rumble on in some form or
another for years after Baldwin's death. His conduct is difficult
to judge given that the most detailed account of it, by Gervase of
Canterbury, is eloquently hostile, but his actions show Baldwin
as provocative, reluctant to compromise, aggressive and dicta-
torial. The end of the dispute in 1189 also suggests that royal
approval and support was crucial and its withdrawal fatal.
One thing that Becket's death had failed to achieve was
archiepiscopal independence from the crown: the position was
too important for that.

Not all Baldwin's energies were expended on his dispute with
the monks of Christ Church. He played an active role as adviser
and diplomat for the king, one which he combined with his
ecclesiastical position most famously during Lent 1188 when he
lead a tour of Wales to preach the Third Crusade. One of Baldwin's companions was Gerald of Wales who wrote a detailed
account of the trip, *The Journey through Wales*. Part preaching,
part recruiting, part diplomatic mission to secure Angevin overlordship over the Welsh church and princelings, Baldwin's tour
was ostensibly a success, even though, on Gerald's self-serving
evidence, Baldwin was an indifferent and uninspiring preacher.
As an organiser, though, Baldwin was careful and thorough. In
1188 he insisted that his unfit entourage dismount, lead their
mounts and walk the steep valleys of mid-Wales in preparation

for the arduous journey to Jerusalem. On his new estate at Lambeth in 1189 he erected the tents he intended to take east with him, presumably to test their suitability or to practise putting them up. One of only two English bishops to fulfil their crusade vows(the other was Hubert Walter, bishop of Salisbury who later succeeded Baldwin at Canterbury), Baldwin played a brief but significant role in the campaign. Leaving Richard I at Marseilles in August 1190, he, Ranulf Glanvill and Hubert Walter led an advance party of the Angevin army to the Holy Land arriving at the siege of Acre in October. With the Patriarch of Jerusalem ill, Baldwin found himself the most important cleric among the besiegers. As such he made strenuous efforts to prevent the erosion of the power of King Guy of Jerusalem who, as a Lusignan, had been a vassal of King Richard. However, conditions in the crusader camp were atrocious and Baldwin died on 19 November 1190. In his will he left some money to provide wages for twenty knights and fifty sergeants to act as sentries, the remainder going to the central fund established to look after the increasing number of impoverished and destitute crusaders.

Whatever his faults and limitations as a pastor, Baldwin's noble death probably tempered more adverse judgements by contemporary chroniclers. Gerald of Wales, who had observed him at close range, thought him gloomy and highly-strung but patient, without malice and scholarly; a somewhat grey figure. All commentators outside Christ Church, Canterbury agreed on his religious sincerity, but there hung about him a whiff of failure. For one in his position, piety was not enough. Pope Urban III (1185-87) was said to have described Baldwin as 'a most fervent monk, a zealous abbot, a lukewarm bishop and a careless archbishop'. This rather jaundiced opinion, coming from an ageing pontiff who allegedly died of shock on the news of Saladin's victories in the Holy Land, may seem too glib, a reflection of a widely shared irritation at Baldwin's bellicose handling of his monkish chapter. Of Baldwin's capacity to inflame Benedictines there can be no doubt, a trace of such resentment even colouring Dom David Knowles's account of his career written in the 1940s. Baldwin lacked the heroic stature (or folly) or the clearly defined principle (or good press) that made memorable the careers of Anselm, Becket or Langton. He was no quietly efficient administrator in the Lanfranc or Hubert Walter mould. With these shortcomings he was fairly representative of the English episcopacy, clergy and church: a man of some firm beliefs who enjoyed good academic training and munificent secular patronage, but who still found the complexities of lay and ecclesiastical politics open to no simple solutions.

W. L. Warren, *Henry II*, 1973.
D. Knowles, *The Monastic Order in England*, 1949.

HUGH DU PUISET (*c.*1120/5-1195; bishop of Durham 1153-95; justiciar 1189-90), reputedly one of the most avaricious public figures in twelfth century England, owed his glittering career in church and state largely to his birth. A great-grandson of William the Conqueror, his mother was Agnes of Blois, sister of King Stephen; his father, Hugh III of Le Puiset, was a notorious gangster who terrorized wide areas of northern France before retiring to Jerusalem in 1128/9. Blois patronage brought the younger Hugh to England *c.*1130 and preferment in the church. Bishop Henry of Winchester, an uncle, made Hugh his archdeacon in 1139; in 1143 he became Treasurer of York and archdeacon of the East Riding under Archbishop William, another relation, whose cause he strenuously maintained against his surplanter, the Cistercian Archbishop Murdac. A taste of Hugh's arrogance is preserved in how he described himself at this time: 'By the Grace of God, treasurer and archdeacon'. He felt quite free to excommunicate his own archbishop: the feeling was mutual. Tactically withdrawing to assist his uncle at Winchester in 1149/50, he returned north as bishop of Durham, apparently a popular as well as royal choice, commending himself to locals and to the pope alike as an opponent of the increasingly abrasive Cistercian mafia which at the time looked set to dominate the northern church. Consecrated by Pope Anastasius IV himself at Rome in December 1153, he proved a moderately active diocesan, especially in periods when excluded from court in the 1150s and 1190s, although his most permanent legacy was in buildings rather than administration. Both his office and his background gave Hugh a certain independence, precariously so after the end of the power of the house of Blois in England in

1154. By the 1160s, he had ingratiated himself with Henry II, remaining in conditional favour for the rest of his reign. In some ways Hugh was an unlikely bishop. For royal service, although well-connected and adequately secular in outlook, he lacked learning or bureaucratic experience; for spiritual leadership, he possessed neither theological grasp nor monastic training. It is perhaps unsurprising that he held aloof during the Becket controversy. His diocese uneasily placed on the frontier, Hugh's loyalty was tested during the Scottish invasion of 1173-4, his policy of self-interest leading to the confiscation of his castles, the return of which remained a source of tension with Henry II for many years. However, he was increasingly regular in attending the king's court and in royal service. In 1188, he went to Scotland to try to extract the Saladin tithe. All the time he was assiduously expanding his wealth by purchase or exchange. When he took the cross (in 1185 or 1188), although temporarily adopting a hair shirt, he made rich preparations for his crusade. These came to nothing in 1189 when the death of Henry and the accession of Richard I opened new opportunities. Richard was desperate for money. Hugh, probably using the treasure he had raised for the crusade, obliged with a total of 3,600 marks for property, release from his crusade vow, a half share in the justiciarship and the earldom of Northumberland, prompting Richard to the sardonic quip that he had made a young earl out of an old bishop. Perhaps Hugh's promotion was made with a view to keeping Scotland quiet in the king's absence on crusade. However, Hugh's foray into national politics was brief and disastrous. The actual work was done by a committee of which Hugh was not a member. Appointed in September 1189, in March 1190 he was stripped of formal power in the south, and in June sacked altogether. He was no match for the ambitious chancellor William Longchamp, who effectively replaced him.

Although restored to uneasy favour after Longchamp's fall in 1191, his sphere of influence was largely confined to the north, where he remained loyal to Richard I's interests in the face of John's attempted *coup* of 1193-4. He died, after apparently overindulging at a Shrove Tuesday feast, in 1195, a not inappropriate end for a man who lived lavishly, surrounded by material luxury. He died immensely wealthy: after his debts had been paid, there was a surplus of at least £3,000. His domestic life was equally extravagant. His affair with Alice de Percy gave him four sons, one becoming chancellor of France, another a Yorkshire landowner, the others archdeacons. As William of Newburgh commented, his public career had seemingly been framed by his insatiable thirst for money. He found, however, that even if he could afford to buy favour, he could not purchase success. A prince of the church, he lacked the skills to rule.

G. V. Scammell, *Hugh du Puiset*, 1956.

RICHARD FITZNEAL (or FITZNIGEL) (*c*.1130-1198) was an illegitimate son of Nigel, bishop of Ely, treasurer of Henry I. A leading civil servant under Henry II, Richard's fame rests on his *Dialogue of the Exchequer*(1178), an account of the history and practices of the central royal accounting office. His whole life was bound up with the small administrative elite employed to run the king's household government. During the civil wars of the 1140s, Richard had been taken hostage by King Stephen to secure the good conduct of Bishop Nigel, who had been disgraced in 1139. In 1154, Nigel was restored to office by Henry II in order to revive the financial system of Henry I. Richard may then have become the Chief Writing Clerk. In 1156/8, Nigel bought his son the Treasurership from the king for £400, a post Richard held for most of the rest of his life (until 1195/6), In common with other royal officials, Richard's activities were not confined to one part of royal administration. He acted as a justice-in-eyre and a judge of Common Pleas at Westminster. In 1176, with his colleague Richard of Ilchester, Richard went to Normandy to reorganise the Rouen exchequer. Parallel to his bureaucratic career, Richard attracted the ecclesiastical preferment to be expected by a royal official in a period before substantial civil service salaries, pensions or systematic bribery. Archdeacon in his father's diocese of Ely in 1160, he added a canonry at St. Paul's and the archdeaconry of Colchester before becoming dean of Lincoln in 1184. Rejected as bishop of Lincoln in 1186 in favour of the dynamic Hugh of Avalon, Richard secured the bishopric of London during Richard I's initial orgy of patronage in 1189. Although adequately versed in the law,

a)

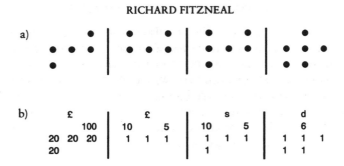

b)

£			£			s			d		
		100	10		5	10		5			6
20	20	20	1	1	1	1	1	1	1	1	1
20						1			1	1	

How the Exchequer Board worked:

a) is how £198 19s 11d was shown on the board;
b) is the key.

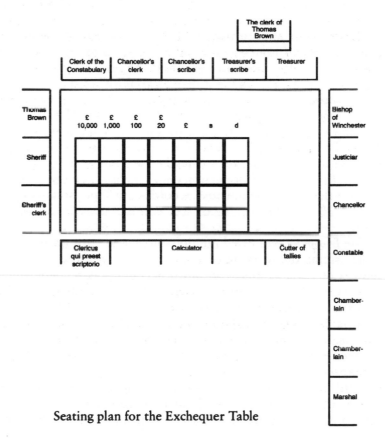

Seating plan for the Exchequer Table

Richard was no scholar, and his ecclesiastical role did not extend beyond the administrative. As the *Dialogue* showed, his career and heart lay in the Exchequer and royal business.

Apart from his duties at the Exchequer in examining the accounts rendered each Michaelmas by the sheriffs and organising the annual audit, the Treasurer also controlled the royal treasuries, in which were stored the king's money, mainly in the form of barrels or sacks of £100 worth of silver pennies. Treasuries were located in convenient royal castles, such as Gloucester, Salisbury or Oxford, with larger depositories at Winchester (convenient for journeys across the Channel to Normandy) and London, near the Exchequer at Westminster, The Treasurer was a slightly detached figure in the king's household. Concerned with securing the king's treasure and valuables, collecting revenue and debts, and, through the audit, scrutinising the behaviour, loyalty and honesty of local officers, his job ensured long absences from the itinerant court and the presence of the king, where power lay. Yet his function was vital for royal government for he supervised the transfer of funds to the king's Chamber, the financial department of the royal household. The Chamber was the key financial office, through which huge sums were directed to warfare, the costs of the royal court and the king's entertainment. Yet, because Chamber accounts do not survive from before the thirteenth century, its role has been obscured by that of the Exchequer, whose records, the Pipe Rolls, survive from 1130 and, in a more or less continuous sequence, from 1155.

The *Dialogue* pioneered administrative and corporate history. In describing the working of the Exchequer, Richard details all sources of royal revenue for which account was rendered there and, in many instances (e.g. Danegeld and Domesday Book) provides historical accounts, often of doubtful accuracy, of the origins of payments and procedures. The *Dialogue* casts the bureaucrat as hero. In part this is because the history of the Exchequer was, for Richard, family history. The importance, perhaps even the existence of the Exchequer was due to Richard's great-uncle, Roger 'le Poer', bishop of Salisbury; its re-establishment under Henry II, to Richard's father. Writing of Bishop Roger, Richard remarked 'it is from the overflow of his learning that I have received, in my blood, the little I know'. As with most family histories , Richard's may not be as objective as it at first appears. For example, it is evident that the Exchequer was a place where important people met rather than, as Richard would have it, of great political importance *per se*. The *Dialogue* conveys a sense of corporate identity associated with the physical surroundings of the office, its halls, seating plans, tables etc. The Prologue begins 'In the twenty-third year of the reign of King Henry II (i.e. 1176-77), as I was sitting at a turret window overlooking the Thames . . .' Some things have changed little for the English mandarin.

The most famous item of office furniture in English history was the Exchequer board, a table covered with a chequered cloth which was used to show the figures being audited (see diagram). The board acted as a two-dimensional abacus, a device which probably was introduced to England *c*.1100. Of great interest to mathematicians, to whom it opened up calculation of high numbers, its adoption by royal financial officials is an early example of the application of information technology to government: the twelfth century Exchequer was the first English computerised department of state. Its efficiency was not lost on those who sat around the Exchequer board. One of them, Robert of Meulan (*d*.1118), Henry I's chief minister, had his own exchequer for revenues from his English estates. The Exchequer board provided the intimidating focal point of the annual Michaelmas audit of sheriff's accounts, which was conducted in front of an impressive array of officials and specially appointed experts, including *ex officio* the Justiciar, who presided, the Treasurer who led the scrutiny and supervised the compilation of the official record of the audit on the Pipe Rolls; and the Chancellor, who kept his own copy of the audit, the Chancellor's Roll, for use by the royal household and, presumably, the Chamber. (In the thirteenth century, when pressure of judicial work kept the Chancellor away, a deputy attended on his behalf, known as the Chancellor of the Exchequer.) Underlying this system, however, was an older method of keeping accounts and records, the tally stick. Notches representing the amounts rendered were cut in sticks which were then split, one being given to the renderer of the account, the other kept at the Exchequer. None of the latter survive, as in 1834, during a fit of bureaucratic efficiency, the Exchequer tallies were burnt. The resulting conflagration of timber, some of it dried over eight centuries, not only carried off an irreplacable historical archive, but destroyed the old Palace of Westminster too. As one who revered tradition (even where spurious), Richard might have thought it served his successors right.

C. Johnson, ed., *The Dialogue of the Exchequer*, 1950.

RICHARD I (1157-99; king of England 1189-99) was one of the most glamorous of medieval monarchs and, judged by what mattered at the time, one of the greatest. Yet, admired and feared by contemporaries, he has been reviled by modern historians. No English king has had more legends woven about him, by scholars no less than romancers. Until the seventeenth century, he was a hero. Since then, while retaining a popular image as a knight, he has been condemned as an absentee warlord who capriciously milked England of its wealth to fund campaigns in France and the Mediterranean, by implication far away places of which good Englishmen know nothing. Yet for more than a century after his death, his aura lent lustre to his successors. Henry III was proud to dine beneath his uncle's shield and decorated his palaces with murals and titles depicting Richard's heroic exploits on crusade. Edward I's crusading provoked the comparison: 'Behold he shines like a new Richard'. Another observer contrasted the uneasy first six years of Edward II's reign with the drama and success of Richard's first three. Far from being a shameful example of royal neglect and princely self-indulgence, Richard I was the yardstick for admirable English monarchy.

Born in Oxford, the third son of Henry II and Eleanor of Aquitaine, Richard spent most of his early years in England. Whether acquired then or later, in adult life Richard displayed particular affection for the insular saints Alban and Edmund of East Anglia. He had some fond memories of childhood: when king in 1189, he gave estates in Wiltshire to his former wet-nurse, Hodierna, whose reward is recalled in the parish of Knoyle Hodierne. Apart from military training, Richard received an excellent education. Belying his popular image as being little

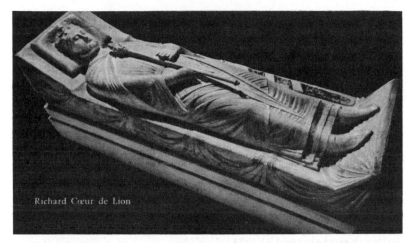

Richard Cœur de Lion

Richard I
(From his effigy at Fontevrault Abbey in Anjou)

more than an effective killing machine, Richard was a talented
linguist. He could tell jokes in Latin and recite poetry in French
and Provençal. He exhibited interest and skill in choral music.
For all his passion for tournaments, the trappings of chivalry
and the reality of fighting, Richard was no mindless thug. He
brought his intellect and insight to the conduct of war, initially
in consolidating his rule in Aquitaine then, as king, in launching
a massive amphibious force on the Third Crusade and subsequently in regaining territory in France. There was more to successful warfare than mastery of riding, holding the lance and
sword-play. Raising money, men, ships and supplies for the
crusade; building castles; and, above all, leading men and con
vincing them to fight, demanded skills of a high order. Richard's
own family history was littered with those unequal to such tasks:
Robert Curthose; Stephen; John.

In 1167, it was decided that Richard should inherit the lands
of his mother, the county of Poitou and the duchy of Aquitaine,
for which he did homage to the king of France in 1169. From
1172, when he was formally installed as duke, Richard's career
was chiefly spent in asserting ducal power over a recalcitrant
nobility in a large and diverse province: excellent training for

kingship. Politically, Richard faced tensions within his family: he joined his mother and brothers in the Great Rebellion against Henry II in 1173-4 during which he held his first independent command; in 1182-3 his authority was challlenged by his elder brother Henry; finally, in 1187-9, he was heavily engaged in securing inheritance to all the Angevin lands. Throughout, Richard showed himself energetic, single-minded and resourceful. A sign of his self-confidence is shown by his willingness to ally with Philip II of France in order to secure his inheritance. Philip's price was Richard's public acceptance of Capetian overlordship. As king, whatever the political favours, personal obligation or legal status, Richard felt no constraints in dealing with Philip. As ever, the effectiveness of Capetian attempts to exploit their overlordship depended on the behaviour of their vassals rather than their own efforts.

Richard's accession as king of England, for all the uncertainties of 1187-9, was the most harmonious and least challenged of any English king between 1042 and 1272. His coronation at Westminster, the first for which we have a detailed account, was lavish, the feast afterwards even more so. Behind such ceremonies lay atavistic traditions of sacral kingship — the centrepiece of the coronation being the anointing of the king on his head, hands and bare chest — and the assertion of power. Richard had especial need to signal his authority as he had determined to lead an army to the Holy Land to recapture Jerusalem. Richard needed to establish an effective regency and raise vast sums of money. It is no small tribute to Richard as a political leader that Angevin authority survived his absence and his people contributed to his crusade in almost unprecedented amounts.

Few things reveal the absolute gulf between the Middle Ages and our own time more than the crusades. Modern experience of war has stripped away the last vestiges of noble, chivalric veneer. The squalid ends of empires have cast suspicion over stereotypes based upon cultural or racial superiority and antagonism. Religious wars have too often contradicted the Faith ostensibly in dispute. Yet, for many of Richard I's contemporaries, few ideals were nobler, for the layman none more meritorious than taking the sign of the cross to defend or recapture the scene of Man's Redemption, the Holy Sepulchre and the Holy City of

Jerusalem. To achieve either required personal commitment of a very high order: many failed to reach their destination; more did not return. Crusading demanded material resources and organisation usually beyond an individual. The First Crusade (1096-99), which captured Jerusalem, had attracted only sparse support from Englishmen, although many from the Anglo-Norman aristocracy took part. The second large-scale expedition (1146-9) elicited a more widespread response. Nobles used it as a respectable excuse to escape political dilemmas at home. Contingents from London, East Anglia and the Channel ports made a significant contribution to the crusading fleets which succesfully besieged Lisbon in 1147. By 1187, a tradition of interest in and visits to the Holy Land had become well-stablished in England. News that the armies of the Christian king of Jerusalem had been annihilated by the Egyptian sultan Saladin at the battle of Hattin (July 1187) and that Jerusalem itself had fallen (October) galvanized the West. The Angevin lands, including England, were swept up in the huge military effort now known as the Third Crusade. In November 1187, Richard was the first prince north of the Alps to take the cross.

The Third Crusade became a central pre-occupation of Angevin government and a major dimension of English politics. Where Henry II had temporized for decades, Richard acted decisively: nine months after his coronation and just under a year after his father's death, Richard set out on crusade from Vézelay in northern Burgundy. On the evidence of his organisation and conduct of the crusade alone, Richard is revealed as a most formidable politician and administrator, as well as a commander of stature. An experienced general, Richard realised that there was no limit to the treasure needed for the crusade: its first year cost at least as much as the king's annual income. Roger of Howden, a royal clerk and former justice who himself went on Richard's crusade, recalled that the new king 'put up for sale all he had, offices, lordships, earldoms, sheriffdoms, castles, towns, lands, everything.' Officials of his father, including the justiciar Ranulf Glanvill, were sacked and heavily fined, their offices auctioned to the highest bidder. Episcopal sees, such as London and Ely; forest rights; town charters; even his own demesne lands were all sold off. Richard told his friends that he would have sold London itself if he could have found a buyer.

Richard's preparations were precise, effective and breath-takingly large. He raised and pre-paid a fleet of over a hundred ships, carrying perhaps 8,000 men. His own land army which met the fleet at the pre-arranged rendezvous ports of Marseilles and Messina, may have totalled as much as 9,000. Having wintered in Sicily, but for a storm which blew his huge fleet off-course (allowing him, with typical aggression, to capture Cyprus) Richard would have arrived in Palestine as he had planned, a year after embarkation. To exert such control over logistics and strategy by land and sea over the length of a conti-nent is a feat unparallelled in previous English history. Although from 1189 significant private contingents departed for the Holy Land, notably from London, the core of the English response to the crusade was very much that of central government, from the hiring of ships from Cinque Port merchants to the ordering of horse-shoes from the Forest of Dean, cheeses from Hampshire and bacon from Warwickshire. The dynamism behind such operations was that of the king himself. Where other crusader princes — the king of France or the emperor of Germany — relied on leading a coalition of self-financing vassals, Richard made sure that his leadership was supported by a massive force in his direct control and pay. The Third Crusade was a triumph of Angevin organisation, in scope, imagination and execution, one of the most remarkable governmental achievements of the Middle Ages.

To medieval observers, Richard's crusading exploits con-firmed him as the ideal prince. Modern criticism, by contrast, condemns Richard for leaving his lands dangerously exposed to internal wrangling and external threat. Dynastically, Richard was taking a risk. Like Louis VII of France before him (in 1146), he set out for the East without a male heir. He compounded pos-sible confusion by recognising, for immediate diplomatic advan-tage, his infant nephew Arthur of Brittany as his successor at Messina in October 1190, whilst having only recently built up the landed position of his brother John to almost viceregal sta-tus in parts of England. However, the regency arrangments worked, with the little local difficulty of the fall of his chosen viceroy Longchamp being smoothly resolved by his replacement with Walter of Coutances, archbishop of Rouen (1191) and, finally, by the appointment of Hubert Walter as archbishop of Canterbury and justiciar in 1193. If Richard had returned, as planned, in the spring of 1193, all would have been well, Furthermore, Richard did not cut himself off from problems at home. On rumours of political tensions in England, Walter of Coutances was despached as royal troubleshooter from Sicily early in 1191. Richard was kept in close touch by a stream of messengers: in return he sent regular newsletters announcing his triumphs, such as the capture of Acre (July 1191) and the defeat of Saladin at Arsuf (September 1191). News from England could have reached the Holy Land in little more than two months: the king knew of Longchamp's deposition in October 1191 by the following January. For England, Richard on crusade was only different from Richard in Aquitaine by degree.

The problem was Richard's failure to return in 1193. He had begun his journey East in July 1190. Having sent an advance guard to the siege of Acre in the autumn of 1190, Richard and the bulk of his army wintered at Messina in Sicily before embarking for Palestine. Having almost casually overrun Cyprus, Richard arrived at Acre in July 1191: the city fell a month later, after a siege of two years. Philip II of France left for the West three weeks later, leaving Richard as the dominant commander. After repulsing Saladin and occupying Jaffa, Richard twice tried an assault on Jerusalem, each time withdrawing a few miles from the Holy City because of the vulnerability of his supply lines and the realisation that, even if he could take Jerusalem, he would not be able to hold it. Such careful campaigning and agonising, but militarily enlightened decisions mark Richard as an outstanding general. Persuading his followers to obey him, to have the prize of their efforts dashed from them at the last moment, reveals a remarkable leader of men. As 1192 progressed, military stalemate forced a three-year truce to be agreed between Richard and Saladin in August 1192 (they never actually met, *pace* thirteenth century myth-makers and twentieth century Ladybird books). Although the Holy City remained in Muslim hands, the littoral of Palestine was restored to an attenuated Christian kingdom of Jerusalem. Part of the deal was that crusaders were allowed to fulfil their vows and pray at the church of Holy Sepulchre under Saladin's safe-conduct, no doubt the source of his laudatory reputation in the West thereafter. Richard declined the offer, prefering to leave his own vow unfulfilled for future redemption. Richard sailed from Acre in October 1192. So far, so good.

What transformed Richard's crusade from orderly and digni-fied, if limited success into potentially fatal personal and politi-cal disaster was his capture on his way home in December 1192 by Leopold of Austria, whom Richard had insulted during the siege of Acre. Within a few weeks, Leopold had sold Richard to Henry VI of Germany. Richard stayed in captivity for a year while Henry conducted an auction for the king's release. One side of the bidding was Richard, backed by the resources of the Angevin empire. On the other were Philip of France and Prince John, in 1193-4 allies in a partially successful attempt to dis-member Richard's continental possessions. Richard won, offer-ing a ransom of 100,000 marks, the bulk of which was paid before the king's release in February 1194. Such was the impor-tance of Richard's freedom that, on hearing of the deal with Henry VI, Philip II wrote to John: 'Look to yourself: the devil is loose'.

But the damage had already been done. Although the regency in England held firm under Eleanor of Aquitaine, Walter of Coutances and Hubert Walter, strategically important parts of Normandy were lost to the French king in the year of Richard's captivity, the recovery of which dominated the last five years of the reign. Imprisonment of medieval rulers was not unknown, but, as in the cases of Stephen, Henry III, Edward II, Richard II, Henry VI *etc.* was usually the result of internal discord. Not all precedents were reassuring. Richard's great-great-uncle, Robert Curthose, duke of Normandy, spent twenty-eight years in prison. Like him, Richard took to poetry to while away the time, although there is no truth in the legends of his being sought out and discovered by a faithful minstrel Blondel. Observers were impressed at Richard's demeanour. One usually hostile French writer enthused that Richard bore himself in adversity as if 'seated on the throne of his ancestors at Lincoln or Caen'. Even at the nadir of his fortunes, Richard knew how to cut an impressive figure. But part of the blame for his predicament must be his. Alone of the great leaders of the major crusades, he had failed to arrange safe passage home. If the consequences for his power and dominions were limited partly by his own effort, the severity of the threat was no less his responsiblity. The obverse of his self-confidence was a streak of recklessness.

During his brief, and as it transpired final visit to the land of his birth (March-May 1194), he ostentatiously rededicated his rule to two national saints closely identified with English crusaders, Thomas Becket and Edmund. Like Stephen on his release in 1141, at Winchester in April 1194 he revived the custom of ceremonially wearing his crown. But Richard never fully escaped the repercussions of his captivity. One of the terms of his release was that he had to perform homage to Henry VI for England, technically thus reduced to a fief of the empire. Richard was able to ignore any practical implications of this, helped by the early death of Henry (1197) and subsequent German civil war. His homage had only personal advantage, easing the speed of his freedom. By contrast, when John, in a move much criticised by later commentators, submitted England to the overlordship of the papacy in 1213, he gained practical support from successive popes which proved vital in keeping the Angevin dynasty on the English throne. More seriously, the loss of lands in France, particularly in the Seine valley, significantly weakened the external defences of his lands, as well as showing how continental loyal ties, at least, could be swayed away from the Angevins, a lesson repeated more devastatingly a decade later.

Richard's ransom and consequent wars with Philip of France cost his subjects a fortune. The ransom of 1193 necessitated the levy throughout the Angevin lands of a tax on moveables and 25% on incomes. A year's wool crop was requisitioned from the great Cistercian sheep ranches of upland England, as well as ecclesiastical gold and silver plate. The speed of collection — at least 70,000 marks were paid in six months before Richard's release — is testimony to the efficiency of royal administration and, more strikingly, the loyalty of taxpayers. Richard's officials could not have coerced such sums from an unwilling populace: the support, particularly, of the baronage was vital, fiscally as it was politically, in resisting the schemes of John. Richard was alert to the political dimension. Even in his German prison, he wanted to know how much each baron had contributed to the ransom 'so that we may judge how far we must return the compliment'. Angevin kings forgot nothing but learnt much.

No less remarkable were the sums raised 1194-99 for Richard's French wars realising tens of thousands of pounds and necessitating a new land tax — the carucage — in 1194. Typically, Richard's officials, in a manner powerfully reminiscent of his father's reign, took the opportunity of the king's return to launch an extensive general investigation into what they called 'royal pleas' , meaning all the king's potentially lucrative rights. Whatever else, Richard's reign saw no slackening of the grip of Angevin government. Apart from the characteristic ploy of extracting protection money from wealthy individuals, towns and the vulnerable Jewish community, those who had bought offices in 1189 were now informed that they had in fact only purchased a short lease and had to pay a further sum to retain possesion. Richard understood that success in war which revolved around sieges and scorched-earth campaigns, went to the general with the most money. Wages, food, siege engines: all were expensive. Castle-building was astronomically so: Château Gaillard, built on the Seine as an offensive bastion against the French, in two years (1196-98) cost £11,500. (The total royal expenditure on English castles for the whole reign was only £7,000.)

The question often posed is whether Richard's military enterprises bled his dominions white, leaving them vulnerable to French attack after his death. Evidence from England and Normandy for the early years of John's reign suggest that these milch cows were by no means exhausted. What differed was the willingness to shoulder the burden which was related directly to the popularity of the ruler and his success or, in John's case, lack of it. Richard's exploitation of his resources depended as much on perceptions of him as a ruler as on the bureaucratic skills of his officials. Thanks to both, Richard's rule went unchallenged despite his extravagant demands on his subjects. By 1199, almost all the lands lost to Philip II had been recaptured, with some others added. Richard's supreme ability to harnass men and materials to specific political objectives continued to pay rich dividends.

Richard died on 6 April 1199 from a crossbow wound suffered during a siege of the castle of Chalus-Chabrol, near Limoges in Aquitaine. He is one of eight post-conquest kings so far who have died violent deaths, This alone makes the event notable. But the manner of it has encapsulated much of the criticism of Richard: foolhardy in pursuit of ephemeral, capricious greed. It was later claimed that Richard believed that Chalus-Chabrol housed hidden treasure. Such claims miss the mark. His death was in keeping with his adult life but not in the way his insular critics imagine. Apart from the years of the crusade, Richard's career was largely spent in maintaining, protecting and extending his inherited lands and jurisdiction, chiefly on the continent where they were most vulnerable. For Richard, England demanded no especial attention. At Chalus he was policing a troublesome rebellion in a strategically vital part of his dominions.

However, Richard received his fatal wound because he exposed himself to enemy fire without the protection of armour. Richard's personal bravery and recklessness in battle was no small part of his reputation. It is also remarkable how many medieval commanders died because they could not bear to wear full armour in the front line (testimony to quite how uncomfortable it all was). Richard's lack of caution may have been part of his political personality. Literary convention urged enjoyment of war, well expressed by Richard's own protégé Bertrand of Born: 'once he has entered the fray let each man of high birth think of nothing but the breaking of heads and arms; for it is better to die than to be vanquished and live'. The reality may have been less gung ho. Henry II, for one, was circumspect about fighting and revolted by casualties in which Bertrand seemed to delight: 'I find no such pleasure in food, wine or sleep as . . . in seeing men great and small go down on the grass by the ditches; and in seeing the dead, with the pennoned stumps of lances in their sides'. Richard appears a creature inhabiting Bertrand's world. Yet he consistently refused to impose his own foolhardy heroism on his troops. Richard fought in the front line, as when he famously waded ashore at the head of a relief force to save

Jaffa falling to Saladin in 1192, beacuse that is where leaders who expected to be obeyed fought. Such behaviour was deliberate. The example was not one to follow but to inspire.

Richard's personality, as opposed to his legend, has left scant trace. Indifferent to personal safety, he was capable of calculated cruelty, as when he had executed 3,000 Muslim captives after the fall of Acre. His crusade testifies to militant piety. A man of few but decisive words, he could be eloquent when occasion demanded, as in his defence of himself at Speyer in 1193. He lacked pettiness and vindictiveness. Many of his father's loyal servants found in him a generous master. He forgave the crossbowman who fired the fatal shot at Chalus. Richard can be considered negligent in failing to produce an heir after eight years of marriage to Berengaria of Navarre, but there is little evidence to support accusations of homosexuality. These reflect misunderstandings of medieval habits, where sharing a bed, which Richard is said to have done with Philip II, was a symbol of brotherhood, of a contractual rather than erotic relationship. In any case, almost nobody suggested Richard was a homosexual until the mid-twentieth century. A maverick hermit in 1195 accused him of 'illicit acts' and reminded him of the fate of Sodom, but other observers criticised his voracious appetite for girls, even on his deathbed. Richard's one acknowledged bastard was sufficiently well-known for Shakespeare to give him the leading role in his *King John*, where Richard — complete with the thirteenth century story of ripping out and eating the heart of a lion — is held up in heroic contrast to his shifty brother.

Richard ruled England in his own interests, as did all medieval kings. The difference was that, unlike so many of them, he did it rather well. His captivity was partly his fault, The uncertainty about his preference for Arthur or John allowed Philip II to cause trouble after his death. But while he lived he held most of his vast territories together, bequeathing his successor the most extensive inheritance in western Europe. It was hardly Richard's fault that John squandered it. His early death can be counted a blessing, as in the case of Henry V. But Richard achieved a huge amount in a brief decade. Supremely, he won the acquiescence of his subjects and the respect of his enemies. A French chronicler called his performance in captivity 'lionhearted'; a thirteenth century Muslim observer called him the most remarkable ruler of his times.

J. Gillingham, *Richard the Lionheart*, 1978.

WILLIAM LONGCHAMP (*d*.1197; bishop of Ely 1189-97), who briefly ruled England during Richard I's absence on crusade 1190-1, was one of the most vilified public figures of the Middle Ages. Not content to demolish his policies and motives, his enemies portrayed him as a physically grotesque, ugly, misshapen, dwarfish, leering, pot-bellied pederast. Whether or not Longchamp resembled a gargoyle or could not, as some alleged, be trusted with the sons of the nobility, his chief failings were political tactlessness and personal arrogance which, in the eyes of his employer King Richard, were, initially at least, outweighed by his effectiveness in conducting royal business. A Norman clerk and expert in civil law, he graduated from Henry II's chancery to the service of the future Richard I, rising to be his chancellor before 1189. After Richard's accession, Longchamp, now the royal chancellor in England, was selected as the king's chief representative in England, being appointed joint justiciar and bishop of Ely, the traditional civil servant's see. The following year Longchamp ousted his colleague, Hugh of Le Puiset, bishop of Durham, leaving himself supreme. Richard clearly calculated that he needed a viceroy of complete personal loyalty, without existing potentially conflicting ties of interest. To provide the necessary institutional status, Richard not only agreed to the demotion of Le Puiset but secured (for a cool 1500 marks) Longchamp's appointment as papal legate. This concentration of authority was no irresponsible whim: Longchamp's power over church and state was replicated after 1194 in Richard's appointment of Hubert Walter as archbishop of Canterbury and justiciar.

In his eighteen months in power (March 1190-October 1191), Longchamp proved himself vigorous and effective. The central administration continued to function smoothly, Longchamp's management even provoking what passed for humour from one of his bureaucrats compiling the Pipe Roll:

The bishop of Ely owes £20 of that (*i.e.* Welsh) scutage on account of his knights. But he had them and a great many more in that same army in the king's service. And therefore with angels and archangels he is quit.

Longchamp pursued royal rights energetically, especially in controlling strategic castles. In 1190, he toured the north, disciplining royal officials who had allowed the massacre of the Jews in York and dissidents at Lincoln. He twice campaigned in the Welsh Marches. He held a church council at Westminster in 1190. As measure of his success, the majority of the bishops supported his petition to the new pope Celestine III in 1191 for his legation to be renewed and he retained the support of senior barons, such as the earls of Warenne and Aumale.

Longchamp's tactics were no more draconian than those of Henry II's servants, but in the absence of the king he was vulnerable. Office had not yet been divorced from person, and baronial resentment at government action could express itself more easily against a parvenu minister rather than the king. Longchamp fell foul of the xenophobic snobbery of the English elite, which, rather than nascent constitutionalism, was an increasingly marked feature of this period. Longchamp also had to contend with the restless ambition of Richard's surviving brother and adult heir presumptive, John, to whom the king had alloted considerable estates in England. Together, John and discontented barons set out to destroy the chancellor, whose high-handed methods proved poor politics. In the summer of 1191, civil war was only averted by a treaty between Longchamp and John mediated at Winchester by the king's special envoy, Walter of Coutances. The compromise included criticism of arbitrary disseisin by royal officers, an anxiety which reached mature expression in Clause 39 of *Magna Carta*. Certainly, Longchamp had, with Hugh of Le Puiset, Gerard de Camville or Roger Mortimer, acted ruthlessly on his own authority, but it could be argued that was what he had been appointed to do. His opponents talked of his disregard of what they described as the legitimate customs of the realm, but their motives were hardly altruistic. John wanted to run England by and for himself. His chief propagandist, Hugh of Nonant, bishop of Coventry, was a self-important, opportunist turn-coat whose main talent, it seems, lay in the invention of colourfully venomous anecdotes about the chancellor.

Longchamp's fall was dramatic. In trying to prevent the king's half-brother, Geoffrey, archbishop of York, from entering the country, some of Longchamp's men had violently dragged him from sanctuary into custody. Geoffrey and his allies ensured that no-one would miss the parallels with Becket's murder. Although politically trivial in itself, the incident provided an excuse for all Longchamp's enemies to combine to force him from office. This they achieved by mid-October 1191, when Longchamp surrendered the seal. According to Hugh of Nonant, Longchamp's initial attempt to flee the country disguised as a woman — 'a sex which he always hated' — ended in humiliating farce: waiting on Dover beach, he was picked up by a fisherman whose attempted rape was only thwarted after he lifted Longchamp's skirts.

Although excluded from England, Longchamp retained Richard's favour and continued to show his worth. In 1193, he arranged terms for the king's release from captivity in Germany and visited England to arrange payment of the ransom of 100,000 marks. He was in England again during the king's visit in 1194. As a servant of the king, Longchamp showed skill and tenacity, two traits which especially irritated the factious barons and prelates he so conspicuously failed to control during his period of office in England.

W. Appleby, *England without Richard*, 1965
J. Gillingham, *Richard the Lionheart*, 1978.

HUBERT WALTER (?*c*.1140/5-1205; bishop of Salisbury 1189-1193; archbishop of Canterbury 1193-1205; justiciar 1193-1198; chancellor 1199-1205) has been described as 'one of the greatest royal ministers of all time'. In organising royal justice, finance, warfare or administration, he was supreme, his authority matched by his competence. For more than a decade, as chief minister, primate of England and papal legate, he dominated church and state with a thoroughness unmatched until Thomas Wolsey three centuries later. While his reputation among modern historians has been enhanced by his instituting efficient government record-keeping of lawsuits and official correspondence, of his achievement there is no doubt. Fifty years afterwards, the inventive Matthew Paris had King John exclaim on hearing of Hubert's death 'Now, for the first time am I truly king of England'. Although apocryphal, the sentiment was not inappropriate: if a litigant went over Justiciar Hubert's head directly to King Richard, he was liable to be punished; and in 1205, Chancellor Hubert effectively scuppered King John's projected invasion of France. Wherever he was active, Hubert, combining efficiency with ruthlessness, was a force to be reckoned with.

Born, probably at West Dereham, Norfolk, into the ranks of the lesser baronage, Hubert was educated in the household of his uncle, the powerful royal official Ranulf Glanvill (justiciar 1180-89), whose right-hand-man Hubert became in the 1180s. First appearing as a witness to royal charters in 1181/2, Hubert's rise was swift. A justice from 1184 and dean of York in 1185, Hubert worked in the Exchequer and chancery. In 1189, Richard I elevated him to the bishopric of Salisbury, a move perhaps not uninfluenced by the presence at Salisbury of the depository of the Saladin Tithe. The Third Crusade was the making of Hubert. Accompanying his uncle Ranulf with the English advance-guard to Acre in 1190, the deaths of the other leaders left him in effective control of the beleaguered English force in the winter and spring of 1190-1. He rose to the challenge: he conducted the tortuous diplomacy with other contingents; administered a central fund to pay soldiers and provide for the provisioning of the destitute; and even led forays against the Muslims. On Richard's arrival in 1191, he became his close adviser, acting as his chief negotiator with Saladin and leading the first group of crusaders allowed to visit the Holy Sepulchre in Jerusalem under the terms of the treaty of 1192. Hearing of Richard's captivity on his way home, Hubert visited the king in Germany in 1193 and was sent to England to supervise the collection of the massive ransom. His reward was the archbishopric of Canterbury and the justiciarship, becoming, in effect, Richard's viceroy.

The justiciarship had elastic powers but two specific functions: the control of royal finances and the administration of justice. As a finance minister, Hubert was notoriously

Hubert Walter (left) anointing King John at his coronation
(From mid-thirteenth century drawing)

successful. The Ransom of 1193 raised 100,000 marks; scutages were extracted in 1195 and 1196; tallages on royal demesnes, including towns, in successive years from 1194; levies on wool were imposed on the sheep-ranches of the Gilbertines and

Cistercians; and in 1194 a new land tax, the carucage, was instituted. According to the former royal justice Roger of Howden, Hubert raised 1,100,000 marks in two years 1194-96. Allowing for taxpayers' exaggeration, Hubert was collecting huge sums to pay for wars in Wales and France. Additional revenue came from feudal dues; miscellaneous, often large, debts to the Exchequer; and the profits of justice. These latter included fines (often levied as security for good behaviour), payments for writs and hearings, as well as innumerable *douceurs* from anxious litigants eager to ensure prompt and/or favourable judgements. Thus, Hubert's judicial role was linked to the financial. The general judicial eyres he organised in 1194 and 1198 were occasions to call in money owing as well as to dispense royal justice. Hubert also gained a reputation for his knowledge of legal custom. The permanent *curia regis* which sat at Westminster was attracting more business and the justices, inevitably, grew more professional than their predecessors whose activities had ranged more widely across royal business. Increasingly, *curiales* specialised in finance or law. A symptom of the increase in legal work may have been the introduction under Hubert of formal records of *curia regis* cases on rolls of parchment. With more business, the need to establish precedent and case law became more pressing. These rolls formed the basis of the first legal text-books in the following century. It is also true that Hubert had a tidy mind. The appearance of newly detailed evidence should not automatically persuade historians of significant developments in practice: Hubert's changes may have been motivated by considerations of bureaucratic efficiency, not more work. The same can be said of the enrollment of royal letters and patents during Hubert's period as chancellor under King John.

Away from Westminster, Hubert was involved in general royal policy. His major political achievement as justiciar was the pacification of the realm after the turmoil of Richard's absence, the opposition to Longchamp and the rebellion of Prince John. Involved in Richard's continental diplomacy, as well as providing for the king's wars, he also fought some of them. As at Acre in 1190-1, Hubert directed military operations at the sieges of Marlborough (1194); the Welsh campaigns of 1196 and 1197; and he helped raise the relief force for the siege of Painscastle shortly-before he retired from the justiciarship in 1198. Hubert was not a desk-bound bureaucrat: he was the king's chief agent, executive and minister.

Hubert was also archbishop and, from 1195 to 1198, papal legate. Most contemporaries were fairly sure where his priorities lay, especially those clergy whom he taxed. When secular circumstances demanded, Hubert ignored clerical privileges. But he worked with characteristic energy as an ecclesiastical judge; he conducted diocesan visitations; he chased up recalcitrant crusaders from Cornwall to Lincolnshire; he held a legatine council for the Northern province in 1195, and a council for the south in 1200. In John's reign he protected monastic immunities and helped in the canonisation of Wulfstan of Worcester and Gilbert of Sempringham (1203 and 1202 respectively). Unlike many, including perhaps Pope Innocent III (1198-1216), Hubert saw no contradiction in wielding the two swords of *regnum* and *sacerdotium*. He embodied the normal practice of twelfth century Europe. In a sense, Hubert was what Henry II had hoped Becket would be. It was frankly hypocritical for Roger of Howden, a royal clerk who had spent years in government service instead of tending his flock in the East Riding, to condemn Hubert for prefering worldly office to spiritual ministry. Hubert was not a great religious leader and was no theologian, but he was efficient and thorough in church business, which is more than can be said of some other primates, more inspired, intelligent or passionate than he. At least in his ferocious conflict with the monks of Canterbury over his scheme to establish a college of secular canons at Lambeth, Hubert maintained the highest traditions of his office.

This is not to deny to Hubert a spiritual life. He embraced a variety of religious insurance policies. In 1193, he adopted the habit of an Augustinian canon at Merton priory, a gesture which may or may not have been prompted by the new archbishop's desire to associate himself with his famous predecessor Thomas Becket who had gone to school there. In 1195, he became a *confrater* (*i.e.* an associate member) of the Cistercians, a connection which paid dividends when he persuaded the Cistercian abbots in England to write him a glowing testimonial to the pope. More intriguing was his reaction to a visit to the Carthusian house at Witham where he was so impressed by the sanctity of the monk

Adam of Dryburgh that he insisted on receiving from him 'discipline with the rod'. What either party made of this scene where an obscure holy man beat the naked body of the most powerful man in England is not recorded.

Hubert's resignation as justiciar in 1198 scarcely interrupted his influence, if it lessened his load. His protégé Geoffrey FitzPeter succeeded him and he remained an intimate adviser of the king. In 1199, although initially reluctant, he decisively supported the accession of John, receiving the chancellorship as immediate reward. To consolidate his hold on England John, whose main interests were then continental, may have wished to recruit Hubert as an ally as much as a servant. Either way, it signalled that there would be little change in the tenor of English government which, in the long term, John may have regretted. Only after Hubert's death did John promote his own clients into posts of great influence. Immediately, Hubert displayed his talents in the chancery. Within a month, a fixed schedule of fees for documents issued under the Great Seal was produced and chancery writs and charters began to be enrolled. His experience and relationship with other leading officials gave the new chancellor a brief far beyond his formal duties. He was active in diplomacy; in May 1202 he was sent to England to convey the king's commands to officials and to lead their counsels; in 1203, he was in charge of levying a seventh from the clergy; he continued to sit as a judge; he advised the king on all matters fiscal, political and administrative; he kept the church quiescent. The defeat in France in 1204 may have led to a cooling of relations with the king, but Hubert retained enough clout to dissuade John from his 1205 campaign. It may be that, at the end, within weeks of his own death, Hubert felt doubts or even remorse at the rapacity which was the inevitable accompaniment to war. Perhaps he saw that the administrative and political costs were proving too high. Perhaps he knew that John was no Richard, and that another French defeat could fatally compromise his position in England, especially as there was at the time no direct heir. Whatever the motive, the old minister prevailed; a familar circumstance.

If a definition of a great minister is that he fulfils his master's wishes, Hubert Walter was one of the greatest. Seemingly unencumbered by sophisticated education or lofty ideals, he was a practical genius who could organise anything, anywhere, anytime. Contemporaries noted his lack of learning: his Latin was apparently poor and he was an indifferent public speaker. But he had a clear mind and a huge capacity for work. His brilliance as an administrator, first prominently displayed in the unlikely surroundings of a disease-ridden army camp in Palestine, underpinned his success as a finance minister and judge. He knew how things — and presumably people — worked; he knew what he and his masters wanted. In relations with his monarchs he showed conspicuous skill, unassuming and indispensible. He carefully built up a network of contacts in government service and, with equal care, and unlike his potential rival William Longchamp, did not dabble in politics on his own account. He made sure that his enemies were the king's. Despite his high ecclesiastical office, he espoused no political independence; not for him the mistakes of Henry of Blois or Stephen Langton. Loyalty, as he knew better than any, had its own reward.

His *modus operandi* was quietly and effectively self-interested. From the number of disseisins he had perpetrated which needed special investigation after his death, it is clear he used his judicial position for personal gain. In office, he had the use of large sums which passed through his hands for which rendering account could be delayed for years. He received money direct which normally went to the Exchequer. Although one modern apologist talks of Hubert's 'speculative investment' in royal wardships, corruption is a better word. In 1203, he paid 1,000 marks down, with a promise of a 3,000 more over three years for a rich royal wardship which netted 2,000 marks a year. In a sense, as justiciar and chancellor, he was dealing with himself, and so could make profits for all concerned, except the ward's family. Hubert used his public position to strike private deals as well. Thanks to his official intervention, the abbot of Bury St. Edmund's secured control of the wardship of Adam de Cokefield's grand-daughter, which he then sold (freely?) to Hubert for 150 marks, although the going rate was 300. Hubert then sold the wardship on for 500 marks. Such manipulation of rank allowed Hubert to live lavishly and ostentatiously. He died a very wealthy man.

At its height, Hubert's power was awesome, but not invulnerable. When threatened, he showed his steel. In 1196, complaints that Hubert's regime was corrupt and rife with official peculation were directed at the king from two sources: William Fitz-Osbert, a prominent London citizen and rabblerouser, and Robert, abbot of St. Stephen's, Caen. The latter was sent by Richard to London to head an investigation into the conduct of the Exchequer and the honesty of the sheriffs rendering account there. The day before Abbot Robert arrived in London, Fitz-Osbert was hanged on the justiciar's orders for resisting arrest (by Hubert's men), causing an affray and manslaughter. At dinner with Hubert the following day, the newly arrived abbot was taken ill: he died five days later. William of Newburgh commented 'those who feared his coming, did not mourn his going'. The inquiry was cancelled.

Tall, handsome, diffident on the public stage, relentless behind it, Hubert Walter may appear the archetypal English mandarin. Yet he was a ruthless and effective politician too, not in the sense of competing with the baronial magnates in loud gestures of support or opposition to royal acts or in open, bitterly fought land disputes, but rather in council, on the bench and in administration. He provided the king with money and solutions to problems. Familiar with Exchequer, chancery, the court, the church, the siege and the battlefield, his versatility and command over the whole range of government business made him much more than a serviceable bureaucrat. It was Hubert's voice which was crucial in the acceptance of John as king in 1199. Hubert was formidable, unscrupulous but, it was said, sensitive to criticism. Many suffered at his regime's bullying, often vindictive pursuit of royal rights, fiscal exploitation and personal greed. Yet he set a standard of efficiency that his successors could but try to emulate. In his capacity for official business; administrative expertise and imagination; determined financial management; skill at handling kings, politicians and opponents; personal venality; political ruthlessness; and success, Hubert Walter bears comparison with another Norfolk man — Robert Walpole.

C. R. Cheney, *Hubert Walter*, 1967.

HUGH OF AVALON (*c.*1135-1200; bishop of Lincoln 1186-1200) combined noble birth, spiritual integrity and unusually outspoken self-confidence to become one of the most distinguished prelates of his age. His life was commemorated in two contemproary biographies, a character sketch by Gerald of Wales and a more hagiographic account by his own chaplain, Adam of Eynsham. A nobleman from the Burgundy/Savoy region of France, Hugh had tried various religious vocations before joining the Carthusian order *c.*1160, attracted by its eremitic strictness and refusal to compromise its original principles. Unlike the Cistercians, the Carthusians remained few in number, an elite group the rigour of whose life, based on solitary devotions rather than communal ceremony, was never weakened to accommodate popularity. Although protesting his dislike of official business, Hugh was good at it, becoming successively *procurator* (*i.e.* bursar) of the Grande Chartreuse, the mother house of the Order; prior of Witham (Somerset); and bishop of Lincoln. Hugh was an ascetic, but not a contemplative. He fulfilled his stern vocation in ruling and guiding others. Hugh owed his career in England, however, to being well-connected. Henry II was looking for a prior to rescue his under-endowed foundation of Witham; Hugh was recommended by a neighbour of the Grande Chartreuse, the count of Maurienne. Immediately, Hugh improved conditions and appealed — impressively but not very successfully — for more royal funds. Hugh's plain speaking avoided the common pitfall of clerical admonition by never being hysterically vituperative. There was always some specific point to his famed obstinacy, a practical purpose behind his inflexible determination. He was no Thomas Becket. To the surprise of many, Henry II lapped this up. He took Hugh's rebukes so well that rumours circulated that Hugh was Henry's bastard son. In fact, in 1186, Henry replaced his actual bastard, Geoffrey, bishop-elect of Lincoln, with Hugh, who thus became the only Carthusian directly to become an English bishop. As bishop, Hugh successfully juggled his vocation as monk, diocesan and self-appointed moral censor of secular, especially court politics. Whilst retreating at least twice a year to Witham, he issued reform decrees; instituted regular alms to lepers and the poor; took a keen interest in the rebuilding of the cathedral after the earthquake of 1185; insisted on a high standard in the clergy he licensed; resisted attempts to instal unworthy courtiers into lucrative prebends; attacked, even excommunicated, royal officials he regarded as guilty of excessive exploitation, people not hard to find in Angevin England. Nationally he sat as a papal judge-delegate, sometimes with that very different monastic leader, Abbot Samson of Bury St. Edmund's; he opposed the rule of Longchamp and the attempted *coup d'etat* of Prince John in 1194; in 1197 he refused Hubert Walter's demand for a clerical aid; in 1199 he assisted at Richard I's burial at Fontevrault. There were many anecdotes of his idiosyncratic treatment of his monarchs: turning Henry II's anger to laughter with a jibe at the king's illegitimate ancestry; manhandling Richard I into giving him the kiss of peace; forcing John to delay his dinner by a lengthy sermon. He delighted in exposing the vanity and hypocrisy of power. His principles were adamantine. He returned Henry II's gift to Witham of the Winchester Bible, one of the finest twelfth century manuscripts, because the king had purloined it from St. Swithun's, Winchester. When Hubert Walter sought the dying Hugh's repentence for his harsh words about the archbishop, all he received was regret that they had not been stronger. Although like an Old Testament prophet, a scourge of backsliding kings, Hugh's reputation depended as much on his wide human sympathy. Unlike many monks, he was no misogynist, allowing a place in Heaven for married women; he liked babies; he was sceptical of miracles and uninterested in apparent natural prodigies. Hugh's consistent impatience with human foibles made him an irritable chairman of Chapter meetings at Lincoln as well as a prickly courtier. It may also explain why his most famous companion was the swan he adopted at his estate at Stow, near Lincoln. One of the more distinctive and unusual bishops of his time, he was canonised in 1220.

H. Mayr-Harting, ed., *St. Hugh of Lincoln*, 1986.

WILLIAM FITZOSBERT (*d*.1196), nicknamed 'Longbeard', came from a prominent London family, members of which, according to a thirteenth century legend, affected beards 'as a mark of their hatred of the Normans'. In 1190 he and a fellow

Londoner, Geoffrey the Goldsmith, fitted out and commanded a ship for the Third Crusade. On his return, FitzOsbert placed himself at the head of a popular party, critical and suspicious of the ruling oligarchy which ran London's affairs after the establishment of a Commune in London in 1191. FitzOsbert repeatedly complained that the Commune was hand in glove with the government, to the detriment of the ordinary Londoners. Litigous and demogogic, in 1194 he accused his own brother of treason when he was refused a loan and campaigned vigorously against what he saw as the underpayment of the King's ransom by the City fathers who, reluctantly, were forced to accept him on the City council. Extravagant in behaviour and language, FitzOsbert used his prominent position to oppose the harsh financial regime of the justiciar Hubert Walter, complaining against government corruption, especially in the form of unequal tax assessments in which he suspected the connivance of the City elite. His tactic was to use the regular folkmoots at St. Paul's Cross to condemn the justiciar while claiming that he was protecting the interests of the king. That Hubert Walter almost certainly had things to hide made FitzOsbert's attacks more dangerous. In 1196, FitzOsbert took his grievances to the king in Normandy and Richard, possibly coincidentally, appointed the abbot of Caen to investigate charges of peculation at the Exchequer. Threatened with FitzOsbert's popular agitation and an official enquiry, the justiciar's position was precarious. His reaction was characteristically thorough. His agents provoked an affray when trying to arrest FitzOsbert. After futile resistance, FitzOsbert fled to the sanctuary of Bow church whence he was dragged to a summary trial and execution at Smithfield. As for the abbot of Caen, he died suddenly soon after arriving in London to investigate the justiciar, and before he had had time to start inquiries, let alone report to the king. The inquiry was dropped. Events had fallen out remarkably conveniently for Hubert Walter, whether by accident or not.

FitzOsbert's posthumous repuation was mixed. To some, he was a martyr, to others a rabble-rouser. His career provides a revealing footnote to the methods and impact of Angevin government and to the history of the development of self-government in London. Successive post-Conquest kings had tried to retain control of London while granting certain fiscal privileges and administrative autonomy. Whenever royal power was weak, Londoners took advantage. In 1141, they declared themselves to be a Commune, a sworn body sovereign unto itself. Although this was crushed under Henry II, the need for good relations with the rich merchants and bankers of the city tempered government hostility. In 1191, with the king on crusade and the regency government of William Longchamp in tatters, another Commune was established, with a leading merchant Henry FitzAilwin as mayor. This marked the beginning of London's continuous tradition of self-government. The London Commune was in no sense egalitarian, whatever the suspicions of the more traditional powers of king, church and nobility. Fitz-Osbert's actions exposed the reality of a tight-knit, wealthy oligarchy who maintained their independence for their own narrow self-interest, not that of the citizenry or inhabitants as a whole. Then, as now, there was little democratic about the City of London.

G. Williams, *Medieval London*, 1963.

ODO (*d*.1200; abbot of Battle 1175-1200) provides an example of the two faces medieval abbots can show posterity. For the writer of the *Chronicle of Battle Abbey*, Odo was a figure of spiritual power, simplicity, eloquence, humility and learning, the leader who worked and ate with his community and only refrained from sleeping in the common dormitory because of an unpleasant bowel condition. It is of this man that Dom David Knowles waxed lyrical: 'one of the most attractive of all those that appear in the literature of the time . . . had others cultivated the simplicity and sobriety of Odo the subsequent history of the monastic order in England would have been happier and more peaceful'. Yet Odo, as sub-prior and prior of the monks of Christ Church, Canterbury, played an active and distinctly equivocal, if minor role in the Becket affair. It was his business acumen as much as his sanctity that appealed to the monks of Battle when they elected him abbot in 1175. No man who twice was considered for the archbishopric of Canterbury or who provoked papal accusations of conspiracy to murder was entirely unworldly.

Already prominent in Canterbury circles by 1159, Odo became the leading figure in the Canterbury priory at a time when all the attention was sought and taken by the secular clerks of the households of Archbishops Theobald and Becket. Yet Odo was not overawed in such company. John of Salisbury respected his quality and, in 1163, as sub-prior, Odo acted as Becket's proctor in Rome in the dispute with York. Becket's absence (1164-70) presented the monks with a severe conflict of loyalty, to their archbishop or convent. Odo seems to have been faithful to his institution. In 1166-7, he cooperated with the king's agent Richard of Ilchester and in 1167 was chosen as prior without Becket's approval. Although Odo temporarily withdrew from Christ Church in 1169, this did not spare him from coming under suspicion of collusion with the archbishop's enemies in 1170. Yet Becket's disciples were predominantly members of his household without permanent status or affiliation at Canterbury, so during the vacancy 1170-73, the convent, led by Odo, once again assumed prominence. Although passed over for Richard of Dover in 1173, Odo continued to act as Christ Church's business manager and legal spokesman. As such he attracted the notice of the monks of Battle. The abbey of Battle acted as both a war memorial and, as the justiciar Richard de Lucy observed, a symbol of Norman victory and legitimacy. As abbot, Odo continued his predecessors' defence against the bishop of Chichester's claims to jurisdiction. Although again losing out at Canterbury to Baldwin of Ford in 1184, Odo established a reputation for holiness partly through his public sermons, in which he expounded the scriptures with clarity and style. To his monks he spoke in Latin or French; to the people he spoke in English. That we think of Odo as a saint rather than a man of affairs reflects not a dichotomy in twelfth century monasticism so much as the slant of our records. Odo may have been an admirable man — although not all contemporaries thought so — but he was also an effective manager of a monastic community and its secular interests.

D. Knowles, *The Monastic Orders in England*, 1949.

DANIEL OF MORLEY (*fl*.1180-1200) was one of a growing number of western European scholars who devoted themselves to transmitting Arabic learning to Christendom. Having studied in Paris, perhaps after Oxford, Daniel spent twenty years or so in Toledo, where he studied under an Italian scholar and translator, Gerard of Cremona. Daniel was primarily interested in mathematics and science, subjects which naturally drew him to the work of Islamic writers. In Toledo he attended Gerard's lectures on astronomy (*i.e.* what would now be called astrology) and engaged in translation of Arabic works perhaps, like Gerard, on medicine, astronomy, alchemy, mathematics, philosophy and logic. He probably did not have a reading knowledge of Arabic, relying instead on locals, probably Mozarabs (*i.e.* Arabic speaking Christians), to translate the texts into Spanish which he could then turn into Latin. Daniel wrote at least two books himself, one on Philosophy and one on Natural Science. To the latter, the *Liber de Naturis inferiorum et superiorum*, he appended an autobiographical preface. Apparently he returned to England with a collection of translated texts, but found the intellectual life of his native country sterile. He was especially disappointed at the quality of science, which is ironic as it was to science that one of the most original English medieval thinkers, Robert Grosseteste, made some of his more significant contributions in the next generation. Daniel was, however, persuaded to stay by John of Oxford, bishop of Norwich. It was on the almost professional teams of translators like Daniel, working in Spain, Southern Italy and Sicily, that the great triumphs of Scholastic synthesis of Albert the Great and Aquinas were based.

J. Catto, ed, *History of Oxford University*, volume i, 1984.

ROGER OF HOWDEN (*d*.1201/2) a Yorkshireman from the East Riding, was vicar of Howden from 1173/6. A royal clerk by 1174, he was involved in diplomatic missions, led an inquiry into vacant abbeys (1175) and was an itinerant justice 1185-90. In 1190, he accompanied Richard I on crusade. At the siege of Acre he was in close touch with a group of crusaders from his part of Yorkshire. In 1191, Richard sent Roger back to Europe to keep an eye on Philip II of France. One of Roger's patrons was Hugh du Puiset, bishop of Durham whose fall from power as justiciar in 1190 may have led to Roger's exclusion from office in the 1190s as he retained close links with the bishop, who died in Howden in 1195. Roger wrote two major chronicles, the *Gesta Henrici II et Ricardi (Deeds of Henry II and Richard)*, which covered events to 1192 and a *Chronica*, which revised and edited the *Gesta*, extending it to cover a wider span, 732-1201. The *Gesta* has been attributed to another chronicler, the so-called 'Benedict of Peterborough', but it is now clear that Roger wrote both. For the reigns of Henry II and Richard I, Roger is an indispensible source. Drawing heavily on official records, Roger provides a detailed account of central government, diplomacy, international affairs and high politics, while keeping an eye on local events in south Yorkshire. He preserves a detailed itinerary of Richard I's journey to Sicily and Palestine in 1190-1, and an eye-witness account of the siege of Acre. Reflecting his own career and interests, Roger copied into his text Henry II's assises, the law book attributed to Ranulf Glanvill, names of Henry's justices, papal letters and diplomatic treaties. Roger set a standard for dispassionate narrative and official history not often met by other chroniclers of the political scene. His private life may have been more turbulent. A story did the rounds in the late 1180s of the parson of Howden's mistress (his *belle amie*) whose immorality was exposed by a miracle at a local shrine which led to her being publicly beaten up. Perhaps Roger's crusade was of penitence or escape.

D. Corner, 'The *Gesta Regis Henrici Sewind*' and *Chronica* of Roger parson of Howden, *Bulletin of the Institute of Historical Research*, LVI, 1983.

J. Gillingham, 'Roger of Howden on Crusade', *Medieval Historical Writing*, ed. D. O. Morgan (1983).

RALPH DICETO (1120/30-1201) spent most of his career at St Paul's Cathedral, London, as canon in the 1140s, archdeacon of Middlesex (1152/3) and dean (1180/1). He was active in reorganising the cathedral archives and, as dean, conducted a survey of churches owned by St Paul's. A secular clerk, his energies were not confined to the cathedral chapter. He spent time in

Paris and knew other parts of France well, particularly Anjou. He may have been born there, although, alternatively, 'Diceto' could have derived from Diss in Norfolk. As a prominent member of the St Paul's chapter, Ralph was inevitably involved in politics. In the 1160s he was closely associated with Gilbert Foliot's opposition to Becket and, through Foliot, gained an entré to Henry II's court. He came to know most of the church leaders of his time, men who also ran the state: Hubert Walter, William Longchamp, Walter of Coutances, Richard FitzNeal as well as Foliot. Towards the end of the 1180s, Ralph began writing history. His main works are the *Abbreviationes Chronicorum,* a potted history of the world from the Creation to 1148, and the *Ymagines Historiarum (Images of History)*, which dealt with the years 1148 to 1202, from 1188 written contemporaneously. Ralph also composed short digests of historical information, *opuscula,* as he was concerned to communicate his material in acceptable form: hence the *Abbreviationes;* the summary of events which prefaced the *Ymagines*; and his system of marginal signs to indicate certain subjects. Well-informed, not least by his extensive political contacts, Ralph's perspective is broad. He is equally at home describing French affairs, Sicilian politics, the plight of crusaders in the dire winter at Acre in 1190-1 or the machinations at the English court. His portrait of Henry II is flattering, emphasising the king's generosity, love of justice and his legal reforms. Ralph applauds the appointment of leading churchmen to secular positions of judicial or political power. In this, Ralph was no more than acknowledging an established fact. For all the rhetoric, usually monkish, of separation of functions, the church provided the state with its rulers and, Ralph thought, a good thing too.

A. Gransden, *Historical Writing in England c.550-c.1307,* 1974.

PETER OF BLOIS (*c.*1130-1212) was one of the most popular western writers of the Middle Ages: over five hundred manuscripts of his works survive. After a conventional upper class education in law, at Bologna, and theology, at Paris, Peter became a freelance tutor, lawyer, and attendant cleric to any household willing to employ him. His story was that he spent his time warding off would-be patrons. He held an influential post at the Sicilian court (1166-8), acting as keeper of the royal seal and tutor to the young William II. In the 1170s he was attached to the households of the archbishop of Rouen; Reginald Fitz-Jocelin, archdeacon of Salisbury; and, from 1174, the archbishop of Canterbury, Richard of Dover, whose chancellor Peter became. He also made contact with the royal court. In 1182, FitzJocelin, now bishop of Bath, appointed Peter his archdeacon. Between 1184 and 1190, Peter worked for the new archbishop of Canterbury, Baldwin of Ford. He was closely involved in presenting Baldwin's legal case against the monks of Canterbury, in which cause he was prepared to lie in court and tamper with evidence. He accompanied Baldwin on crusade in 1190. Thereafter, he drifted between service to Eleanor of Aquitaine, Hubert Walter and Archbishop Geoffrey of York. Further preferment came with the deanery of Wolverhampton and the archdeaconry of London, but despite these and other benefices, Peter complained of poverty and neglect. What he really wanted was a bishopric. His inability to speak English — and his refusal to learn — may have played a part in this.

Peter was in the second or third rank of secular clerks, competing for but never achieving high office. Perhaps because of this, he became a more or less professional writer of letters, pamphlets and short treatises. Some, such as the panegyric on Henry II c.1174, were designed to impress potential patrons. Others, such as his three tracts on the Third Crusade, had a wider purpose, to influence opinion. In 1184 he compiled a collection of his letters to which he added over the next decade. They formed the basis of his posthumous reputation, and were read into the fifteenth century as models of style as much as anything more profound. Peter was not an original thinker: for his treatise on friendship he plagiarised Ailred of Rievaulx. His strength was rhetoric. In many of his letters he advocated moral reform, a return to individual apostolic poverty as a protection against the evils consequent on material extravagance. Whether this implied indigence or humility is not entirely clear, nor is it plain to what extent Peter's arguments were personally felt or literary exercises. Well-travelled, vain, self-righteous, a regular in the ante-chambers of the great, Peter was a twelfth century pundit, a sort of proto-journalist. Like a modern leader-writer, he took an event, for instance the rebellion of 1173-4 or the death of Raynald of Châtillon at the hands of Saladin (*Passio Reginaldi* 1187/90), and proceeded to tell his audience what its significance was and what they should think and do about it. He articulated ideas for others to use.

R. W. Southern in *Medieval Humanism*, 1970.

GERALD OF WALES (1146-1223), royal clerk, chronicler, ethnographer, polemicist, observer of nature and frustrated careerist, was one of the most prolific writers of his generation. The central theme of his life was his uneasy position as a member of a mixed, frontier Franco-Welsh aristocracy. Too French for the Welsh; too Welsh for the Angevin rulers of England; too cosmopolitan to have anything but contempt for the English, his intellectual inquisitiveness was matched by a political restlessness which ultimately secured for him a position of marginal impotence from which he railed at his erstwhile patrons. With justice he has been compared with Jonathan Swift: 'another disappointed man with literary and invective talent who suffered from the ambiguities of his national position'.

Gerald was the grandson of Nesta, daughter of Rhys ap Tewdwr, prince of South Wales. A remarkable woman, a mistress of Henry I and twice married thereafter, her descendants littered the higher reaches of the Welsh marcher nobility and the Anglo-Norman colonists in Ireland. Gerald, the son of Nesta's daughter Angharad and William of Barry, was, in fact, only a quarter Welsh by blood. This inheritance bred in Gerald an almost schizophrenic attitude towards the kings of England. On the one hand, they offered the path to preferment; on the other they threatened the independence of Welsh marcher lords and their cousins in Ireland. Between these two stools of loyalty and resentment, Gerald leapt and fell.

Educated at Brecon, Gloucester and Paris he was appointed, *c.*1175, archdeacon of Brecon. He cannot then have dreamt that this was the highest post his talent and his family's influence would obtain for him. As a churchman, Gerald displayed the intellectual's inflexible adherence to principle and blindness to hypocrisy. A provocative reformist, he nonetheless condoned nepotism when he was exercising it. The central goal of his clerical life was, however, to secure the diocese of St David's, which had been held by an uncle. Three times, in 1176, 1198-1203 and 1214, the prize eluded him. His background and conduct were against him. In 1199, his one serious chance, although gaining election from the chapter, his insistence on the independence of St David's from Canterbury ensured the opposition of Hubert Walter and, through his influence, the pope. Gerald's pursuit of his claim in Wales merely served to enrage King John, who outlawed him, while failing to secure the see. With only the support of Welsh princes, he was regarded as a proponent of dangerous autonomy. Yet this was the man who had spent a decade or more ingratiating himself with the great of the English church and state; the man who, in 1188, had accompanied the then archbishop of Canterbury on a tour of Wales which included a very public assertion of the supremacy of Canterbury over St David's. What counted against him were his contacts with the Marcher families who repeatedly in the twelfth and early thirteenth century threatened the power of the Angevin kings.

Gerald was attached to the royal court from 1184 to 1194, where his contacts were fully exploited. In 1185, he accompanied Prince John on his ill-fated journey to Ireland and in 1188 he helped Archbishop Baldwin preach the Third Crusade throughout Wales. In the early years of Richard I, he was sent more than once to protect royal interests in Wales. His withdrawal from court in 1194 may have been connected with the failure of John's coup and the appointment of Hubert Walter as justiciar, a man who showed himself no friend to Marcher lords. Gerald's alienation from the Angevins was complete after his defeat at St David's, but it had begun in the mid-1190s when, in his disappointment at the lack of patronage, he called the court 'that image of death and model of Hell'. There is no evidence that Gerald possessed any administrative ability. He does not seem to have had any particular legal skills, still less political aptitude. Cleverness and literary ability alone were not enough to gain preferment from the Angevin kings who perhaps looked askance at this provincial *manqué*, this middle-aged *enfant terrible*. In time, as so often, disappointment turned to hate. After his retirement to Lincoln in 1207, Gerald's pen poured forth vitriol against the Angevins culminating in 1216 with a declaration of loyalty to Louis of France.

If his later work is saturated by self-pity and hate, Gerald's writings nevertheless reveal a talent for observation and description, whether in chronicle narratives, political polemics, or accounts of peoples and places. His output was prodigious and his curiosity protean: substantial chronicles dealing with high politics; descriptions of Wales and Ireland; works of semi-auto-biography; biography; saints' lives; pamphlets in support of the rights of St David's; poems; a map of Wales; and a book on tides. Many of these works were revised and rewritten over decades. He worked on his most popular book, the *Topographia Hibernica* for over thirty years. His polemical history of the rise and fall of Henry II, misleadingly hiding under the title *De Principis Instructione (Concerning the Education of Princes)* was begun *c.*1190 and completed *c.*1217. His chronicles, although widely quoted, are more expressions of spite than balanced history. What sets him apart from his contemporaries are his works on the topography and ethnography of Ireland and Wales, the *Topographia Hibernica* (1188); the *Expugnatione Hibernica* (1189), the *Descriptio Kambriae* (*c.*1194) and, to a lesser extent, the account of his preaching tour of 1188, the *Itinerarium Kambriae* (*c.*1191). In these Gerald not only describes the natural world as he saw it, with, for the time, rare, as well as vivid, empirical, almost scientific detachment. He also analyses the societies he found. A man of many nations and, ultimately, none, Gerald was sensitive to differences in culture and social behaviour. His work reminds us that twelfth century Europe was a place of frontiers, of strangers, of ethnic and cultural clashes beside which the Norman Conquest of England appears a squabble amongst siblings.

Gerald's own position was, typically, equivocal and occasionally disingenuous. Strident about his Welshness, he spoke no Welsh, only French and Latin. A champion of Welsh national aspirations, at least ecclesiastical, he despised the Welsh. His contempt for the native Irish was even greater. The indigenous Irish Christian tradition was second to none in western Europe. Only by portraying them as barbarians could Gerald hope to justify, in the name of civilisation and the church, the invasion of Ireland and its attempted subjugation by, amongst others, his own relatives. Gerald of Wales was rarely neutral. He wrote for a purpose as much controlled by vanity and prejudice as intellect. He dropped names with professional intensity, to vilify them later. He glorified his own deeds (we only have his word for his exceptional preaching talent). In 1187 or 1188, he took the unusual step for a twelfth century author of promoting his own book. On three consecutive days, he gave public readings from his *Topographia Hibernica* in Oxford. Yet for all his pride and venom, Gerald was one of the most distinguished and original writers of his day, widely quoted in subsequent generations. His vision of the new frontiers of Ireland and Wales, as much as of the old drama of princes and power, was highly individual because, to his deep hurt, he never ceased to be an outsider when being 'one of us' was never more important.

R. Bartlett, *Gerald of Wales,* 1982.

SAMSON OF BURY (1135-1211; abbot of Bury St. Edmund's 1182-1211) was perhaps a more typical abbot than the saints and scholars who are so often taken to represent twelfth and thirteenth century religious and monastic life. Unusual for his time in having an intimate biography written of him which is far from unthinkingly or consistently laudatory, Samson's spirituality, whatever it was, is hidden behind practical affairs. Yet such mundane matters as balancing accounts and managing estates were fundamental to contemporary monasticism. Without the sometimes predatory acquisitive instinct none of the great monastic revivals would have been possible, nor would the exercise of learning or holiness. The successful man of God had to be adept in dealing with Mammon, Few were more energetic or notorious in their pursuit of the essential material basis for the spiritual life than Samson of Bury.

The chronicle written by another monk at Bury, Jocelin of Brakelond, presents a uniquely rounded portrait of Samson; its richness of texture prompted Thomas Carlyle to celebrate Samson's life in his popular *Past and Present* (1843). Jocelin's biography reflects the author's own changing relationship with his subject. From Samson's election as abbot in 1182 until 1187 Jocelin was his chaplain and acted as his secretary; thereafter he became more closely involved in other areas of the abbey's life, becaming guestmaster in 1200. As Samson spent much of his time trying to restrict the monks' administrative freedom, control of property and independence of action, Jocelin's tone became increasingly critical, at times even hostile towards his former hero. Although his *Chronicle* ends in 1202, Jocelin's picture of Bury and its abbot is one of the most vivid medieval accounts of monastic life.

Samson, like a number of twelfth century abbots (*e.g.* Baldwin of Ford), began his career as a secular clerk. A Norfolk man, he followed the fashion of studying in Paris. He first served the great local Benedictine house of Bury St. Edmunds in 1160, ironically as spokesman for the monks in an appeal to Rome against the abbot: this earned him a spell in the abbatial prison at Castle Acre. Seeing, perhaps, the opportunity for advancement within a protected corporate structure, Samson took monastic vows at Bury in 1166. He soon proved himself an effective administrator, holding a series of offices, including, in the 1170s, that of novice master. Jocelin of Brakelond was one of his charges. This wide experience of how the abbey was organised not only helped build for Samson support among the monks, in whose interests he had once more been confined briefly to Castle Acre, but also was ideal preparation for his period as abbot. He knew, none better, where lay the monks' interests, weaknesses and inefficiencies.

On his election as a compromise candidate in 1182, Samson's objectives were clear: the restoration of the abbey's finances through a recovery of temporal rights and vigorous management of property. A thorough investigation of abbey estates was conducted. Within two years, all debts had been paid off and by 1186 a book, known as *Abbot Samson's Kalendar*, had been completed listing all the rights and revenues owed to the monastery from each of its holdings. The increased revenues that ensued were used by Samson to pursue contested rights, for instance in the 1190s over the number of knights' fees attached to the monastery, and to rebuilding the abbey church and other monastic quarters (he had been master of the workmen 1180-82 when the choir of the church was rebuilt). Although vigilant in protecting the abbey's privileges and immunities, Samson also encouraged the liberties of the town of Bury, not least as a counterweight to the pretensions of his monks. Similarly, as had his predecesors, he allied with the king to control the aspirations of the Bury monks. It was little wonder that their resentment at his autocratic manner and behaviour, as well as to the detail of his policy, grew. At one stage, in 1199, Samson feared for his life. The sustained opposition was based on legitimate anxieties as well as corporate self-interest. Samson saw his responsibility in running Bury as that of a royal tenant-in-chief accountable to the king for his barony: hence his determination to control as much of the community's property as possible. The monks, on the other hand, feared that, during any protracted abbatial vacancy (as occurred in 1180-2 and 1211-15) the lands that the abbot had taken from the community would be dealt with by the king as part of the abbot's barony and controlled by the crown. However, it is also clear from Jocelin's politically alert account that the monastic body itself was a network of disputing factions, based on age and personal loyalties. Where other writers give only the merest hint of such institutional discord, Jocelin exposes in detail what must, nevertheless, have been a commonplace of life in such wealthy, cloistered communities of men or women, where pettiness could be interpreted as principle and prejudice as piety.

Inevitably, by taste and position, Samson was heavily engaged in national secular as well as local ecclesiastical politics. Perhaps his most memorable intervention was in the 1190s when he defended Richard I's administration from John's attempted *coup*. In 1193 he excommunicated John and the other rebels and, with his military retinue, besieged John at Windsor. Later he visited Richard in Germany. As with his policies towards his abbey, Samson's characteristically firm stand suggests not only a strong personality but a substratum of principle and conviction beneath his actions. However, Samson realised the importance of royal favour and was reconciled to John after he became king in 1199.

Samson was no saint. An effective administrator, he was more at home with the intricacies of politics and estate management than with ascetic rigour or spiritual endeavour. Jocelin describes him as disliking introverted scholarly monks, preferring good organisers. Apparently he harboured the unfulfilled wish to have been the abbey's accountant. Although adequately versed in-Latin, he preached in French and English, the latter with a Norfolk dialect, a habit he shared with another expert administrator, Robert Walpole. Something approaching local pride may be deduced from his devotion to St. Edmund, on whose miracles he compiled a largely derivative treatise between 1166 and 1182 and whose body he examined in 1198 while constructing a new shrine for the saint. Although, on hearing of the loss of Jerusalem and the True Cross in 1187, he took to wearing hair shirts and drawers and abandoned eating meat, he was not noted for personal privation. and, in any case, he preferred 'fresh milk and honey and such like to any other food'. Energetic, at times almost frenetic, he could be impulsive or showy, as when he appeared in front of his guest Henry II in 1188 carrying a needle, thread and a cloth cross and demanding to be allowed to go on crusade. The king refused.

Jocelin's detailed physical description of Samson is a mirror of his personality:

> Abbot Samson was of middle height, and almost entirely bald; his face was neither round nor long, his nose prominent, his lips thick, his eyes clear as crystal and of penetrating glance; his hearing of the sharpest; his eyebrows grew long and were often clipped; a slight cold made him soon hoarse. He had a few white hairs in a red beard and a very few in the hair on his head, which was black and rather curly; but within fourteen years of his election he was white as snow. He was a man of extreme sobriety, never given to sloth, extremely strong and ever ready to go either on horseback or on foot, until old age prevailed and tempered his eagerness.

Jocelin of Brakelond, *Chronicle*, ed. and trans. H. E. Butler, 1949.

JOCELIN OF BRAKELOND (*fl.*1180s-after1200) became a monk at Bury St Edmund's in Suffolk in 1173. Shortly after 1202 he completed a *Chronicle* of events in the abbey from 1180 to

1202, effectively a biography of Abbot Samson (abbot 1182-1211), who had been Jocelin's novice master in the 1170s. Jocelin was ideally placed for his work, as he had been Samson's chaplain and secretary (1182-7). At the time of writing, Jocelin was the abbey's guestmaster. Adequately trained in the Latin classics (Virgil, Horace, Ovid *etc.*), Jocelin kept abreast of contemporary historical writing, quoting Ralph Diceto's *Ymagines Historiarum* (finished by 1200), and included considerable information about the customs, administration and tenants of the abbey. His account of Samson is tinged with hagiography, although, when considering the events after he had ceased to be the abbot's secretary, Jocelin allows a more objective, occasionally critical tone to intrude. Most striking, however, is the vivid description of Samson's physique and personality which, unlike most monastic chroniclers, is convincingly drawn from life, not from an honoured exemplar. The accounts of the internal factions; the struggles over Samson's administrative and financial reforms; and the tensions between young and old in the monastery are sharply observed, conveying a sense of reality. Jocelin's purpose may have been to praise Samson and, ultimately, the patronal saint, Edmund, but in the process he left the clearest and most lively description of the life and aspirations within a community of monks written in the medieval England. Jocelin also wrote a now lost *Life of St Robert,* a boy supposedly killed by Jews in Bury in 1181. Jocelin and his *Chronicle* were popularised by Thomas Carlyle's *Past and Present* (1843) as evidence of the virtues of a pre-industrial society run by heroic individuals, a sentimental view wholly of the nineteenth not the thirteenth century.

The Chronicle of Jocelin de Brakelond ed & trans H. E. Butler, 1949.

WILLIAM MARSHAL (1147-1219) had a most remarkable career. Born the son of a prosperous minor baron, he made his name first as a roistering but shrewd manager of a team of tournament fighters. With good looks and a loyal disposition, he established an enviable reputation for the newly fashionable qualities of courtliness and chivalry. The protégé successively of

Eleanor of Aquitaine, her son the Young King Henry and Henry II, the originally landless William netted one of the greatest heiresses in the Angevin Empire. Prominent in the service of Richard I and John, despite the latter's ingratitude, William stood firm in support of the king in the years of disaster for the Angevins 1213-16, so much so that when John died, leaving as heir a child of nine, the septugenarian William became the young Henry III's protector and regent of England for the last three years of his life.

William's distinctive life was nonetheless a palimpsest upon which were successively written the obsessions of his age and class: war; tournaments; courtly intrigue; the caprice and generosity of the great; pilgrimage to the Holy Land; the hunt for heiresses; the hard choices of men with more than one lord; loyalty; dynastic greed; and the balance of rule between monarchs and their nobles. That William, despite nasty setbacks, emerged triumphant in most of these itself deserved notice: he was clearly more than a pretty face, a silver tongue and a strong right arm. There is a tenacity of ambition and ruthless determination which framed and lent purpose to the outward glitter of his life.

No less remarkable is that William was the subject of the first medieval biography of a layman who was not a king. The *Histoire de Guillaume le Maréchal,* a vernacular poem of over 19,000 lines finished between 1226 and 1229, was written by a member of the Marshal's circle, called John. The author is hardly objective; but he is informative. Behind the glamorous veneer, a man considerably less of a bland archetype can be detected, one whose deeds nevertheless inspired enough interest and devotion to warrant such a unique surviving tribute.

Although not from one of the great landed dynasties of Anglo-Norman England, William spent his whole life in or near royal courts. In 1152, still a very young boy, his pro-Angevin father, John Marshal, gave him as a hostage to King Stephen to buy more time at the siege of Newbury. William later recalled that in his tent Stephen played him at 'knights', a tournament game with straw men, a scene which says much about the amiability of king and the charm of the child.

In the decade before his death in 1165, John Marshal's fortunes declined so much so that William was left nothing.

Entering the household of William de Tancarville, in 1167 he was knighted, and for the first time saw action (at the battle of Neufchâtel-en-Bray) and fought in a tournament. Despite earning praise for his courtliness, William lacked cultural refinement. Nicknamed 'gaste-viande' (*i.e.* 'guzzle-guts'), he was unusual for one of his background in never learning to read or write. His education was more or less exclusively fitted for a career as a professional soldier. Yet he was quick-witted enough to spend his life extracting profit from tournaments and royal service.

After spending a couple of years attached to the court of Eleanor of Aquitaine, in 1170 William joined the extravagant and glamorous entourage of the Young King Henry, where, while keeping up his semi-professional tournament business, he fulfilled the role as the prince's tutor-in-arms. Henry was a tournament fanatic, so William's place in his favour was sure. In 1173, William's prestige was singularly recognised when he knighted the Young King, a ceremony which he repeated in vastly different circumstances for young Henry's nephew and namesake forty-three years later. Except for a brief period in the early 1180s, William remained close to the Young King, but Henry's death in 1183 transformed prospects. Entrusted with carrying the dead prince's cloak bearing his crusader's cross to the Holy Land, William received a promise of employment on his return from Henry II. William brought back with him in 1186 the rich cloth which was to serve as his own pall thirty-three years later.

Having lost the reversionary interest of the Young Henry, William rapidly compensated by service to the Old Henry. The secure foundations of his later grandeur were laid in 1186-89. He made close contacts with influential members of the king's household, such as the future Justiciar Geoffrey FitzPeter and began to receive patronage, in the form of lands, lucrative wardships and the promise of the hand of Isabel, heiress to the extensive lands in the Marches, Wales and Ireland of Earl Richard of Striguil. On Henry II's death in 1189, despite having been unhorsed by William in a recent encounter at Le Mans, the new king, Richard I, confirmed and extended his father's grants on both sides of the Channel. On his marriage to Isabel of Striguil, William at last entered the baronage and independence.

However, he owed his fortune to his loyalty. Richard I had elevated him for a purpose, to help guard his dominions during his absence on the Third Crusade. This proved a test of William's political skill and prescience, as the conflict between the Chancellor Longchamp and Prince John careered towards civil war. William backed John and led the movement which ousted Longchamp in October 1191. Although faithful to King Richard, remaining at his side through his French campaigns of 1194-99, William kept in with John. In 1194, he refused homage to Richard for his Irish lands, instead reserving it for John, as Lord of Ireland. Such ambivalence had a precise purpose. As his enemy Longchamp acutely remarked 'Planting vines, Marshal?'

After Richard's unexpected death in 1199, William harvested the fruits of his husbandry. Instrumental in securing John's succession, he was rewarded with the earldom of Pembroke and a significant extension of his estates, especially in Wales and Ireland. Enjoying the favour of a new and grateful king and the friendship of both justiciar (Geoffrey FitzPeter) and chancellor (Hubert Walter), William appeared at the summit of his career. But his self-interest could not long remain compatible with that of a monarch whose power was crumbling and whose suspicion was pervasive and venomous. William played a vigorous if unavailing part in the defence of Normandy. But when Philip II gained control of the duchy in 1204, William looked to his own, managing to negotiate a deal with Philip in 1205 whereby he did the king liege homage for his French lands. This implied that William would be unable, on risk of forfeiture, to fight Philip in France. As the recapture of his French lands was King John's central policy, William's homage to Philip at one stroke questioned his loyalty and negated his usefulness. Between 1205 and 1212, William suffered the humiliations and political insecurity of loss of royal favour. Initially, he was not even allowed to retire peacefully to his possessions in Ireland, as John was fearful for his own lordship there. When summoned to court in 1207-8, it was to be publicly humiliated, personally teased, politically undermined and legally threatened. From 1208, William lived in retirement in Kilkenny, for the first time acting as a settled ruler of his estates, as well as indulging in a favoured pastime of beating up the native Irish: as the imaginative Matthew Paris put it a generation later, he was 'a Saturn to Ireland'.

The extraordinary transformation of William's fortunes between 1212 and 1216 from distrusted exile to regent of England reveals the extent of the collapse of John's authority as well as the Marshal's almost robotic loyalty. Yet even in his late sixties, William never altered his conviction that the greatest rewards were to be found at the hands of the richest provider, the king. He, as very few then did, remembered the failure of the 1173-4 rebellion and the ultimate futility of hoping for preferment in opposition to the monarch. If he had been tempted to forget, his experiences of 1205-12 served as a raw reminder. When, in 1212, magnate discontent with John's methods of rule expressed themselves through an ill-concealed assassination plot, William ensured that Ireland stayed loyal. In a sense he had no option: a successful *coup* would not have advantaged him much more than a vengeful king. As for John, the plot of 1212 and the opposition to the French campaign of 1213-14 demonstrated that there were fewer and fewer men of substance and experience on whom he could rely. Patronage in the Middle Ages was never entirely efficient in binding the loyalty of subjects, but it was with William Marshal, perhaps because he had started with nothing.

Returning to England in 1213, William immediately began to reap the landed rewards of service. He also emerged, with the earl of Chester, as the leading loyalists among the magnates as the English baronage slid from the defeat in France in 1214, to the failed compromise of *Magna Carta* and open civil war in 1215. Nevertheless, whether by accident or design, family interests were protected by William's eldest son's support for the baronial side. As the crisis deepened for the Angevins, William's importance grew. He organised the royalists in the southern Marches and Wales. In 1216 he unsuccessfully tried to dissuade Philip II from sending his son Louis to England: such an invasion obviously placed William in a uniquely difficult position. But he did not flinch in his adherence to John. After the king's death in October, when to many it must have seemed that a Capetian triumph was inevitable, William assumed guardianship of the young Henry III and, with the approval of the earl of Chester, the regency: 'rector noster et regni nostri' as he was styled in royal documents. The sight of the venerable warrior, who had buried three kings (four if you include the Young Henry), whose memories stretched back to King Stephen, with the boy-king were the stuff of romance — and maybe of actual emotion. There is a Churchillian sentimentality in William's recorded remarks to three friends the evening of his acceptance of the regency: 'If everyone abandons the boy but me, do you know what I shall do? I will carry him on my back, and if I can hold him up, I will hop from island to island, from country to country, even if I have to beg for my bread'.

The first task facing the new regent was survival. This William achieved in 1217 primarily through military victories over the French and the rebels at Lincoln and in the Channel. At Lincoln, William himself fought energetically, forgetting his helmet in his eagerness for the fray in which he killed Robert of Roppesley. The naval battle off Sandwich he merely observed with the king from the cliff-tops. But the royalist success was consolidated by a lack of vindictiveness. Already in November 1216 he had *Magna Carta* reissued, a symbol of a fresh start and a more consensual method of governing. Now, after the French defeat, William negotiated the withdrawl of Prince Louis for the sum of 10,000 marks. As Louis was the son of William's French overlord, perhaps this generosity was not wholly altruistic.

In the last two years of his life, William laid the foundations for the rebuilding of royal authority. Given the poverty of the crown and the divisions of the civil war, it was inevitable that he had to conciliate rather than coerce. *Magna Carta* was again reissued in 1217; the Exchequer was restored; the judicial bench returned to Westminster in 1217, with salaried justices to minimise corruption; a general eyre was instituted in 1218-19; and regular councils gave the magnates the impression that they were involved in rule through common consent. Helping the regent were the papal legates, Guala and Pandulph; the Justiciar Hubert de Burgh; and the bishop of Winchester, Peter des Roches. But none of them could (or were to) inspire wide enough confidence, especially vital as there was no prospect of effective independent royal government dealing with intransigent rebels or grasping partisans of the late king, not least because of the failure to restore royal finances. Of course, William never ignored the interests of his family: in 1217 he recovered Marlborough which his father had lost almost sixty years before. But whatever the limitations of his rule, William had kept the centre intact. By the time he died in 1219, there was a system of royal government for others to expand and develop.

The verse biography of William Marshal makes it both easier and more difficult to approach the man as an individual. Opinions and remarks attributed to him have to be treated with care. But something of the private man can be detected. He seems to have been a faithful and certainly uxorious husband: he and Isabel had ten children. Although over forty when he married, he left no recorded bastards. He was a brave, vigorous and deadly fighter into his seventies. He turned his prodigious skill at tournaments (he claimed to have taken prisoner over 500 knights) into a thriving business in the 1170s, with his Flemish partner Richard de Gaugy: they had a disciplined team with a deliberate strategy calculated to maximise captives and minimise risk of injury, all conducted on a professionally commercial footing. Of his dynastic ambition there can be no doubt: it provided the most prominent *leitmotif* of his life. His success can be judged that when he died, possibly of cancer, on his own manor, surrounded by his own extended household, he had made his family one of the greatest in the British Isles. His loyalty was not disinterested. Neither, presumably, were his extensive religious donations. He died, in the habit of a Templar, the model of a good Christian lord and knight, firm in his Faith and his social position. Rather typically, the biographer's account ignored the inconvenient detail that William died still under excommunication by the Irish bishop of Ferns, a penalty dating back to some Irish-bashing of 1212.

William's political apotheosis was the result of longevity — he knew personally all the kings who ruled England from 1135 to 1272 — and clear political vision. It may also have been because he was liked. William had the qualities contemporaries admired and a personality to match. He was no routine toady: on his deathbed, holding Henry III by the hand, he prayed that the king's life might be short if he followed the example of 'alcun felon ancestre' ('a certain criminal ancestor'). Famously impassive in public, here the dying courtier perhaps let slip his true feelings for at least one of his Angevin masters. William's life shows that there was more to being a courtier than literature might imply. In warfare, chivalry, politics, faction, intrigue and self-advancement, William Marshal fought his way to the top and managed to stay there. As Richard I once said of him, he was indeed 'molt corteis', most courtly.

D. Crouch, *William Marshal*, 1990.

WALTER MAP (*c*.1130/5-1209/10) was a successful royal clerk and church administrator who gained a great reputation as a *reconteur*. Many of his stories are preserved in his *De Nugis Curialium (Courtiers' Trifles)* compiled between 1181 and the early 1190s. Born in the Welsh Marches (Map = ap = son of in Welsh), his family had served Henry II before 1154. Educated at Gloucester and in Paris, he became a canon of Hereford under the patronage of Gilbert Foliot. In the king's service by 1173, when he was an itinerant justice in Gloucestershire, he remained a prominent royal clerk for the rest of Henry II's reign. Walter attended the Third Lateran Council in 1179 as one of Henry's representatives and was attached to the household of the Young Henry until the prince's death in 1183. As his official career developed, he amassed a comfortable living as a pluralist. Already a canon, in 1186 he became chancellor of Lincoln and precentor in 1189. In 1196 he was appointed archdeacon of Oxford. By this time, he had finished *De Nugis*, a rambling compendium of court gossip and satirical anecdotes, with as much organisation, Walter himself admitted, as a timber yard. At its serious moments it compares with a parody of the *Mirror of Princes* genre supported by edifying moral or cautionary tales. Walter attempted some historical portraits, all worthless except his vivid, surprisingly unbiased and convincing description of his patron Henry II — an objectivity which may account for Walter not publishing it. *De Nugis* sheds light on the rather chaotic mind of a leading member of the chattering classes of the late twelfth century. His interests are human; his eduction classical; his style urbane, witty, informed and spacious, devoid of the portentous anxiety or academic pretentiousness displayed by so many of his contemporaries. One curiosity is that *De Nugis* is the earliest known work to nickname Ethelred II 'the Unready' or, more properly 'un-raed', bad counsel, a pun which would have been right up Walter's street.

Walter Map, *De Nugis Curialium* ed M. R. James, C. N. L. Brooke and R. A. Mynors, 1983.

GEOFFREY FITZPETER (*d*.1213) was the epitome of the successful and versatile royal servant. His rise from holding one knight's fee to the earldom of Essex demonstrated how great were the rewards of office in Angevin England. Soldier, administrator, politician, landowner and judge, he played an increasingly important role in Henry II's and Richard I's administrations until succeeding his close associate Hubert Walter as justicar in 1198, a post he held until his death. Although not of 'grant linage', his promotion to the highest ranks of the nobility did not arouse such hostility as did that of another modestly born justiciar, Hubert de Burgh. It may be that, from his activities as judge and tax collector, the enemies he made were the king's enemies, the friends his own. He was fortunate not to have lived to witness the near-collapse of Angevin control of England, his posthumous reputation being enhanced by the chaos after 1213. Matthew Paris lamented: 'after his death England was like a ship in a storm without a navigator'.

Originally from Wiltshire, where in 1166 he held a knight's fee at Cherhill, Geoffrey entered royal service in the late 1160s, perhaps as a household knight. How he caught the king's attention is unknown, although in the household he may have attracted the interest and patronage of Ranulf Glanvill, himself a future justicar (1180-89), whose nephew, Hubert Walter, became one of Geoffrey's closest colleagues. Geoffrey's progress was swift. He witnessed royal charters from 1181; in 1184 he was appointed sheriff of Northamptonshire and Chief Forester (which meant that he led the regular Forest eyres to uphold royal rights, collect dues and hear grievances); by 1189, he had been a justice-in-eyre and sat on the bench of justices at Westminster. Geoffrey's importance was recognised when the pope allowed him to postpone his crusade vow in 1189 on the grounds of his being indispensible to the government of England in Richard's absence.

Office brought riches. Before 1185, Geoffrey had married Beatrice de Say (*d*.1197), one of the heiresses to the wealthy earldom of Essex; various royal wards were assigned to him; and his own estates were, by 1189, worth at least twelve knights' fees. Throughout the 1190s, Geoffrey continued to hold sheriffdoms, act as an itinerant justice and sit on the central bench of justices at Westminster. Opposed to the wilful rule of Longchamp, he was a member of the regency council which replaced him in 1191. On Hubert Walter's appointment as justiciar in 1193, Geoffrey's influence grew further. So regularly did he witness Hubert Walter's writs that court clerks tended simply to abbreviate his name to 'G. fil. P.'. When Walter resigned in 1198, Geoffrey was a natural successor, ensuring continuity.

Retained in 1199 by John, whose claim he had supported, Geoffrey continued to supervise the exchequer; the collection of taxes; the justices at Westminster; and the general eyres. In 1204, he organised an overhaul of the system of raising money from the shires, replacing sheriff farms (agreed annual fixed sums payable to the Exchequer by the sheriffs in lieu of royal dues, any surplus being kept by the sheriff) by custodian sheriffs (the actual, varying amounts owing to the crown being payable). This involved replacing twenty-two out of thirty-one sheriffs, a major political undertaking. Geoffrey was the king's regent in his absences and chief executive when John was in England, which he was increasingly after 1204. The king's presence reduced Geoffrey's independent political role and, unsurprisingly, led to tension. After granting Geoffrey the title of earl of Essex and showering him with gifts (including fifteen tuns of wine) in 1199 in gratitude for his support, and lavishing property on him in the awkward aftermath of the loss of Normandy in 1204, John seems to have cooled towards his minister. In 1209, cases for the justices at Westminster were diverted to the *coram rege* for the king to adjudicate. After 1210, John introduced more of his own officials into government, such as Peter des Roches. In 1212, Geoffrey was implicated, by association, in the plot to kill the king: two of his daughters had married sons of the archtraitor Robert FitzWalter. As an inducement to loyalty, John allowed the dispute over the succession to the lands of William de Mandeville, earl of Essex (*d*.1189) to be reopened. The case was a politico-legal *cause célèbre*. In 1189, Geoffrey de Say had won the Mandeville inheritance against Geoffrey PitzPeter's claim on payment of a relief of 7,000 marks. When, however, Geoffrey de Say defaulted, Geoffrey FitzPeter secured the inheritance with 3,000 marks. Even to withstand a new legal assault on his claim opened the prospect of massive new payments to the king: the loss of the lands themselves was hardly to be contemplated by one so avaricious and successful in pursuit of property. John seemed to be harassing his justiciar. There were policy disagreements, as in 1209 when Geoffrey tried to engineer a reconciliation with Innocent III. By the time of Geoffrey's death, John had reportedly lost confidence in him. Hearing the news, the king remarked: 'when he enters Hell let him salute Hubert, archbishop of Canterbury, whom no doubt he will find there'. A good story, but laced with the possibly accurate sense of royal dissillusion with the men who had ruled England in the king's name for a generation.

Geoffrey was a man of many parts. A *miles literatus*, he knew Latin and was interested in mathematics. He kept his own file of copies of his charters and, with Hubert Walter, presided over the increasingly efficient system of government record-keeping. He was a conscientious and meticulous judge, one of those who established a system of law which provided a relatively stable and unified framework within which the expanding political nation could operate. Immensely industrious, Geoffrey used the Tower of London as a permanent office. But he was not just a desk-bound official. His career had begun in military service for Henry II and, even at the height of his administrative and judicial responsibilities, he led campaigns in Wales in 1192, 1198 and 1210. On one level, his career appears successful, effective, even beneficent. This was far from true. Geoffrey was one of the architects of the system which broke down in 1215. At the centre of public business for thirty years, he tenaciously pursued royal rights; closely supervised payments to the Exchequer: ruthlessly imposed and collected scutages and carucages, all of which, allied to political failure, precipitated the near-collapse of Angevin government after his death. There is little evidence that he could have prevented it. Geoffrey conducted a regime increasingly perceived as rapacious; and in the process lined his own pockets. Not as glamorous or lurid as other leading figures in the dramatic events of the reigns of Richard I and John, he was no less responsible for what happened.

R. V. Turner, *Men Raised from the Dust*, 1988.
F. J. West, *The Justiciarship in England*, 1966.

JOHN (1167-1216; king of England 1199-1216) is the most notorious English king, one of the most unfairly maligned but also one of the least successful. The legend of his awfulness as a person as well as a ruler dates from his own lifetime. Even now, when his positive qualities as a conscientious judge, a careful adminstrator, a man of culture and a ruler of energy are widely recognised, his personality and style leave a nasty taste in the mouth. 'Foul as it is . . . Hell itself is defiled by the fouler presence of King John'. This verdict of Matthew Paris of St. Albans in the thirteenth and J. R. Green in the nineteenth century sums up the 'Bad King John' theory, investigated with more pathos and psychological sympathy by A. A. Milne in his wistful poem 'King John's Christmas' where the monster is reduced to loneliness, self-knowledge and child-like yearning. Other opinion portrays John as able but flawed, 'the ablest and most ruthless of the Angevins' (J. R. Green again) with, in the words of a post-war biographer, W. L. Warren, 'the mental abilities of a great king, but the inclinations of a petty tyrant'. This interpretation too has a long pedigree. In the 1220s, the annalist of Barnwell priory near Cambridge, commented 'he was a great prince certainly but hardly a happy one'. For Shakespeare in the 1590s, John was the unprincely prince, the schemer whose schemes all came unstuck, whose outward show of regality and power concealed a character unstable and deceitful but not monstrous.

More recently, the arguments have moved away from John's character — more or less irrecoverable — to his rule. Thus John's arbitrary government has been studied by J. A. Jolliffe without going down the *cul-de-sac* of moral judgment. Rehabilitation has come with scrutiny of offical records, from which John appears hard-working and competent. J. C. Holt has even

John
(From his effigy at Worcester Cathedral *c*.1225-30)

compared John's administrative achievement with that of Henry II or Edward I. This has drawn the retort from J. Gillingham that 'John is the most overrated king in English history', only the accident of record-keeping making him seem busier and more industrious than his predecessors. After all, the contemporary Ralph, abbot of Coggeshall, awarded only faint praise: John governed 'satis laboriose', with enough effort. The problem with assessing King John is that he presents an image of contradictions: energetic and slothful; judicious and corrupt; sensitive and myopic; intelligent and brutish; cultured and violent. Such, to the confusion of contemporaries and historians, was the sum of John's humanity.

Critics and apologists are faced with one supreme fact. Tactically successful — in gaining the throne, defeating his rival Arthur of Brittany, exploiting the fiscal potential of England, gathering a coalition against France, supervising English administration, recruiting vital political and material aid from the pope when he needed it most — as a whole John's reign was a disaster. Having lost much of his continental inheritance by 1204, by his death he had forfetied the loyalty of most of the English baronage and was facing civil war and a foreign invasion. He left his dynasty's future in the hazard, its survival dependent on the repudiation of John and his style of rule. Even King Stephen had retained more support than John. His responsibility for this is related to why his personality inspired such a loathesome reputation. The vilification of John is comparable in English history only to the Protestant slander of Mary I. Other kings had angered the church by their policies, yet clerical and monastic chroniclers reacted much more violently to John and the Interdict than to Henry II and Becket's murder. Why did the normally sober William of Newburgh call John 'nature's enemy'?

John was born in 1167, like his brother Richard at Oxford, the last child of Henry II and Eleanor of Aquitaine, who was forty-seven at the time of John's birth. Significantly younger than his brothers, John was excluded from the dynastic settlement of 1169, but in the 1170s various schemes for John's endowment were proposed. Interestingly, with four healthy sons, Henry II ignored the option of directing any of them to the church. A plan for John to marry the heiress to the county of Maurienne, which controlled the western Alpine passes vital for access to Rome and the Mediterranean, came to nothing. (Both John's sons, Henry III and Richard of Cornwall, actually did marry into the family which controlled this strategically important region.) In 1177, John was created lord of Ireland, an empty title carrying opportunity and risk rather than authority or profit. This was especially true after John's unsuccessful visit in 1185 designed to establish his position. With hindsight, chroniclers saw a pattern in John's political adventures. In Ireland, he frittered away the money his father had provided and indulged with his young friends in luxurious living and mockery of the locals: ridicule of the hairy Irish; disdain for the Anglo-Norman settlers. John was not the last insensitive and futile English proconsul in Ireland. But a reputation for failure clings.

The Irish fisaco of 1185 did not prompt Henry to moderate his devotion to his youngest child, There were rumours — which the future Richard I believed — that Henry was contemplating making John his heir. None of this prevented John from deserting his father at the last, a betrayal that caught the disgust of contemporaries. Small wonder the well-informed Richard of Devizes thought him flighty, an habitual traitor. On his accession in 1189, Richard I provided John with an heiress to marry — Isabella of Gloucester — and vast estates in England, the honour of Lancaster and the counties of Nottingham, Derby, Dorset, Somerset, Devon and Cornwall; in Normandy the county of Mortain which the young Henry I had held. There was no doubt that John was then regarded as Richard's heir. In the king's absence on crusade, he set about reinforcing his position. Almost in defiance of the regency government under Longchamp, John established his own court complete with justiciar, chancellor, *etc.* Nobles earlier in the century had had their own exchequers, but John's establishment had the air of a rival government. Perhaps resentful at not being given the regency himself, John led opposition which forced Longchamp's removal in 1191. Continued exclusion from power thereafter, combined with his brother's designation at the treaty of Messina (1191) of their nephew Arthur of Brittany as his heir, drove John to take advantage of the king's captivity in Germany (1193-4) to ally with

Philip II in dismembering Richard's continental lands. This second betrayal, especially of a crusader, did little to enhance John's reputation: nor did his subsequent *volte face*. In 1194, John had been given Evreux by Philip; after submitting to a remarkably forgiving Richard, he returned to Evreux and massacred his French garrison. Henry II had been a notorious liar and cheat, and yet earned grudging respect. The same traits in John just made him appear shifty.

Richard I's sudden death in April 1199 propelled John to his inheritance. In a possibly apocryphal story circulating twenty years later, William Marshal and Hubert Walter, archbishop of Canterbury, debated whether to support Arthur of Brittany or John as king of England. William persuaded Hubert that legally and politically John should be prefered, but the archbishop warned: 'So be it . . . but mark my words, Marshal, you will never regret anything in your life as much as this'. Yet the early signs must have encouraged both. After a vigorous diplomatic and military campaign, by September John had been accepted by all the Angevin provinces in France and had been crowned king of England; Arthur of Brittany and his mother Constance had submitted; and Philip of France had agreed to parley. At the treaty of Le Goulet (May 1200) Philip recognised John as rightful heir to all Richard's lands in return for a relief (payment to a lord by a vassal entering into possession of an inherited fief) of 20,000 marks. The fact of acknowledging Capetian overlordship was neither novel nor degrading. Henry II and Richard I had openly acknowledged it, as had, tacitly, Henry I. What the Capetians made of their recognised suzerainty depended less on them than their vassals, Angevin, Burgundian, Flemish or Champagnois. Here lay the difference between John and his predecessors: they coped with Capetian overlordship; John did not. The relief, however, was new, and an added drain on John's finances. There is little evidence that John's, or Richard's, demands exhausted Angevin territories. However, whereas Richard's demands led to results that were popular — the crusade; the king's release; the counterattack in France — John's exactions, heavy from the start of his reign, produced no such positive results. Furthermore, where Richard could persuade English nobles to support his continental wars, John had much greater difficulty. The elusive element of personality was central. The task of a medieval monarch was to convince a few hundred men, and a few women, to follow his lead. Richard could do it; John could not.

John's reign had three distinct phases. During the policing and ultimate loss of Normandy and Anjou to 1204, John was as absent from England as much any of his predecessors. Between 1204 and 1214 most of his energies went in amassing the funds to recapture his continental lands, his presence in England presenting novel circumstances for a political nation used to an absentee overlord, The failure of the reconquest led directly to the final challenge to his authority, the civil war and French invasion 1215-16. It is largely a consequence of the clerical monopoly on chronicles and later attempts to place John's resistance to the papacy in a suitably Anglican light that have exaggerated the importance of the papal Interdict (1208-13), making John a monster of godless depravity or, as in *The troublesome reign of King John* (1591), a flawed Protestant champion. In fact, as far as John's control over the church and his nobility, the Interdict made little difference; its resolution if anything strengthening John's position by gaining a useful ally against enemies both foreign and domestic.

Throughout his reign, John showed vigour and intelligence comparable to his father and brother. His hurried divorce and subsequent marriage to the twelve-year-old Isabella of Angoulême in 1200 secured a strategically important alliance in Aquitaine. In 1202, decisive military action and a forced march of eighty miles in less than two days out-manoeuvred his enemies at Mirebeau, where Arthur of Brittany was captured. Angevin control of Poitou was consolidated by the limited expedition of 1206. Careful naval preparations were rewarded by the first major English victory at sea at the battle of Damme in 1213. During the dark days of civil war in the winter of 1215-16, John wrong-footed the rebels with a lightening three-month campaign through their territory, his march from Winchester to Berwick taking less than five weeks. This was coercive warfare in the best style of Henry II. Elsewhere in the British Isles, with only the threat of force, John imposed a harsh treaty on the inveterate troublemaker, William the Lion, king of Scots, in

1209. In 1210, a brief expedition to Ireland established royal authority over the Anglo-Irish barons in the east. In 1211, Llywelyn, prince of north Wales was subdued so that, in the words of the Barnwell chronicler, 'now no one in Ireland, Scotland or Wales . . . did not bow to his nod'. From such successes, John derived not only political clout but substantial booty.

John was no slouch as an administrator. He personally supervised the work of the Exchequer. He was an assiduous judge: in 1209-12, the central judicial bench which customarily sat at Westminster was suspended, the justices following the king around the country. During the reign there were significant developments in bureaucracy: household offices became increasingly specialised; systematic collection of administrative and judicial records was instituted; a royal privy seal was employed to expedite business; the distinction was established between the civil (Common Pleas) and criminal (King's Bench) jurisdiction of the Westminster judges. John presided over the creation of a national customs system based upon standardized weights and measures and the organisation of a royally funded and built navy. The tone of John's government is captured in his instructions to agents in Southampton in 1206 to carry out his orders with 'immediate haste', whether 'night or day' 'as you love us, our honour, the peace of our kingdom, and regard your own safety and welfare'. All the ingredients of Angevin success and failure are present: urgency; attention to detail; authority; menace.

Yet John was no bureaucrat. His close involvement in the government of England was largely enforced by the loss of Normandy and Anjou. Thereafter, John, whose restlessness was notorious (only once in his reign staying more than a month in any one place), travelled incessantly in his kingdom, as some saw it meddling in his subjects' affairs. In areas such as the north, rarely visited by kings since the tenth century (indeed even Henry III only went north three times in fifty-six years), the presence of an inquisitive and acquisitive monarch on the doorstep came as a rude shock. It was no accident that the rebellion of 1215 was initiated by a group known as 'the Northerners'. The impression of John's conscientiousness, no less than that of a more specialised household, may simply reflect the creation of new ways of recording business which coincided with John's reign. Consequently, by accident, John can be studied in far greater detail than any of his predecessors. The administrative initiatives probably owe more to John's civil servants than to the king. Under John England was run by veterans of Angevin service who had been ruling the kingdom for years before 1199, such as the justicar, Geoffrey FitzPeter, and the chancellor, Hubert Walter. It was for political rather than bureaucratic reasons that John introduced his own men into English government, such as the Tourainers Peter des Roches (bishop of Winchester from 1205; justicar 1213-15), Peter de Mauley, Engelard de Cigogné and Gerard d'Athée and the Norman Falkes de Bréauté.

Whatever his achievements, John consistently undermined them. The nickname 'Softsword' stuck because of a willingness to give up a cause before decisive action. John left Normandy in December 1203, six months before the fall of Rouen, and three before the fall of Château Gaillard. The month before Rouen capitulated in June 1204, the archives of Norman government were shipped to England and taken to London in carts provided by the king, hardly an encouraging sign to those still at their posts in the duchy. In 1214, on the news of the defeat of his allies at Bouvines, John withdrew. Eighteen months later, instead of combating the invasion of Prince Louis of France, John allowed him to land without resistance. With the exception of the Welsh campaign of 1211, John, in marked contrast to his father and brother, lacked tenacity in adversity. On each occasion, however, he feared treachery and would not expose himself to the risk of battle or campaigns against the odds.

Suspicion ate at the heart of John's personality and rule, vitiating his triumphs. In 1200, instead of compensating Hugh of Lusignan for the loss of his intended bride, Isabella of Angoulême, John siezed his duchy of La Marche. This prompted Hugh to appeal to his and John's overlord, Philip of France, thus setting in train the formal confiscation of John's continental lands and the loss of Normandy and Anjou between 1202 and 1204. After the spectacular *coup* at Mirebeau in 1202, John willfully alienated William des Roches, seneschal of Anjou. Thereafter, John could no longer rely on the loyalty of the barons of Anjou. Most damaging was the disappearance and presumed murder inside one of John's prisons of Arthur of Brittany in 1202-3. Rumours swirled around Arthur's death. Hubert de Burgh, custodian of Falaise where Arthur may have been held, denied responsibility for his death. Some accused John's henchman Peter de Mauley of the murder. One account, possibly derived from an eye-witness, accused John in person, saying that he murdered Arthur in a post-prandial alcoholic rage at Rouen at Easter 1203, disposing of the body in the Seine. Whatever the truth, Arthur's fate and John's inability to produce him, lent Philip II a telling propaganda weapon and ensured the hostility of the Bretons.

In dealings with English nobles, John was no less malevolent. Even the loyalist earls of Chester and Pembroke were harried and threatened for no better reason than that they were powerful. More notoriously, John's former favourite, William de Briouze, was ruined and exiled, his wife and son starved to death in prison. Such violence fostered an atmosphere of fear. It was one thing to execute thirty Welsh hostages in 1212 or allow captives from Mirebeau to starve to death in Corfe Castle after a failed attempt at a mass break-out. But the persecution, without trial, of English barons was different.

Yet this is precisely what John's policy seemed often to be. At every turn he exploited wardship, relief, and his sovereignty as king to discipline his nobles. A favoured technique was to force barons to become royal debtors. Again, the Briouze family provides a most dramatic example, Matilda de Briouze being compelled to offer the huge sum of 50,000 marks (equivalent to the Exchequer revenue for one year) for the king's grace (*i.e.* protection money) when her assets amounted to 24 marks and some gold pieces. Geoffrey de Mandeville forced to offer 20,000 marks for John's ex-wife and the earldom of Gloucester. Reliefs varied according to loyalty. 10,000 marks were imposed on William FitzAlan and Nicholas Stuteville, but William de Forz, the son of John's mistress the dowager countess of Aumale, inherited for free. The purpose was political control not financial profit. Stuteville had, by 1230, almost £10,000 still outstanding on debts contracted under John. Given the average annual baronial income of £200, very few being worth even as much as £400, the threat of foreclosure was potentially ruinous. If the debtor had recourse to Jewish bankers for a loan, he again confronted the king who regularly taxed the Jews and received all their property — including notes of credit — on their deaths. Other avenues of extortion were explored. The venality of Angevin justice and adminstration, exactly matching its pretentions, could be turned to the king's advantage. William Mowbray was encouraged to offer a bribe of 2,000 marks to the king to obtain a favourable outcome in a land suit. John accepted the bribe — and allowed Mowbray to lose the case, insisting he pay up nonetheless. It is unsurprising that the sale of justice, judgement without trial and the cost of reliefs and wardships appeared prominently in *Magna Carta*

John's unpopularity went further. His style of rule and his personality repelled affection and loyalty. Even his gambling and drinking crony, his half-brother William of Salisbury, briefly deserted him in 1216. John's suspicious nature was matched by gracelessness and the insensitivity of a cunning, introverted cleverness. Many of his hobbies were innocuous enough. John was an avid collector of jewels, which he liked to wear round his neck. He drank and gambled and, like his father, was an obsessive huntsman. Well-read and cultivated, he read both French and Latin, possessing his own portable library, including a copy of Pliny. John was also a predatory lecher, with a repuation for seducing his nobles' sisters, daughters and wives. He had numerous mistresses and at least five bastards. Outrage at John's sexual licentiousness may have added an edge of bitternees to political resentment. One of John's alleged intended victims was the wife of the northern baron Eustace de Vesci who for no obvious political reason played a central role in stirring rebellion in 1215. John also had a penchant for blackmailing others for their sexual adventures, accepting bribes as 'hush-money'. He may have had a dirty sense of humour, which may explain the famous, if enigmatic entry on the Oblate Roll of 1204: 'The wife of Hugh Neville promises the lord king two hundred chickens that she might lie one night with her husband'. Whether or not John was a smutty-minded groper, it does seem that many thought him personally unsavoury. In a world where private relationships were the stuff of high politics, that was a distinct problem.

John had a gift for making enemies, but policies as much as personal quirks caused friction. John was determined to recapture his inheritance. Money was raised by any means possible. There were national property taxes in 1203 and 1207. As the latter raised £60,000 it is difficult to argue that the fiscal exactions of the 1190s had bled England dry. However, the political price was high, there being considerable resistance to the 1207 levy. Thereafter, John was forced to more piece-meal expedients. As feudal overlord, John levied reliefs, wardships and scutages at unprecedentedly high rates. On top of the scutage, a tax in lieu of military service, calculated on the number of knights owed, each baron had to pay a fine for personal exemption. This was hardly popular. Sheriffs were required to account for every penny owed the crown instead of, as previously, paying an agreed lump sum (or 'farm'). Inevitably, this encouraged sheriffs to greater rapacity (or efficiency as Exchequer clerks no doubt saw it). Towns were encouraged to purchase mercantile privileges. Infringements of the onerous Forest Laws were assiduously pursued, as were more general profits of justice and the ubiquitous imposition of amercements, fines for petty misdemeanours, often merely protection money. To such sources of income were added the profitable campaigns of 1209-11, Jewish legacies and tallages, and the proceeds of the deserted benefices during the Interdict. Small wonder John was accused of being 'a pillager of his subjects'. More dangerous than the pious clichés of monastic chroniclers, such high and persistent demands for money excited concerted resistance and, in 1213-14, refusal to pay the scutage. In the insistence that aids and scutages be levied with the consent of the barons (Clause 12), *Magna Carta* was passing political judgement on John's preparations for the great reconquest in France. But by then John's hopes had been dashed. The road from Bouvines to Runnymede was direct.

The last years of John's reign were some of the most extraordinary in English history. Confident in his treasure and his own leadership, two obstacles to a return to Normandy remained. To forestall a projected French invasion blessed by the church, in 1213 John submitted his kingdom to the pope to remove both his personal excommunication and the country's Interdict. When Richard I had done homage for England to the Emperor Henry VI in 1194, he gained merely his own freedom. John, by becoming a papal vassal for his kingdom, acquired a staunchly loyal ally which played a crucial role in sustaining the Angevin dynasty. The root of the dispute had been the king's traditional right to appoint the archbishop of Canterbury, which the pope had contradicted by appointing Stephen Langton archbishop in 1206. Although not overtly a pious man (again like his father), John's response had little to do with religion. At stake was royal control over church appointments which, given the irrevocable increase in the church's estates, was essential for royal authority to be maintained. An independent church or one wholly controlled by an ultramontane papacy would present immense difficulties in ruling England. As it was, the settlement of 1213 acknowledged the pope's legal authority, but with Innocent III (and his successors) committed to support of their newly repentent vassal, there ceased to be any challenge to royal wishes. For most practical purposes, provided the king and pope cooperated, royal manipulation of the church could continue.

Less tractable was the mounting irritation of sections of the baronage. In 1212, there was a plot to assassinate the king. It is significant of what John had to face that one of the ring leaders, Robert FitzWalter, had surrendered the vital town of Vaudreuil to the French in 1204. John's enemies were champions of no liberty except their own. In 1215, FitzWalter trumpeted himself as 'Marshal of the Army of God', yet personal vendetta and grievance not constitutional, still less religious principle lay at the heart of opposition to John. Neither side could claim the moral advantage. Robert's fellow traitor of Vaudreuil, Saer de Quincy, was another to rebel in 1215. John was confronted by men exasperated but no less duplicitous and self-seeking than he. John's failure was to woo enough interests and individuals to his side. One problem was that his interests and those of his leading barons increasingly diverged. In 1205 and 1213 he was prevented by magnate indifference and hostilty from attacking Normandy. In 1213, his attempt to circumvent the higher nobility and widen the scope of political action by summoning knights from the shires to a national assembly backfired: they were as

unenthusiastic as the barons about the French wars. All might
have been transformed by victory in 1214. Failure, however, is
contagious.

The civil war of 1215-16 showed John at his best and worst. A
master of tactics, he wrong-footed his enemies, led by a hard
core of northern malcontents, by assuming the protection of the
crusader when he took the Cross at Easter. At Runnymede in
June, *Magna Carta*, into which all the baronial fear and distaste
for the operation of Angevin government was untidily poured,
provided some basis for compromise, except that its final clause
(61) provided for a committee of twenty-five barons to supervise
government. If implemented (which inevitably it was not), this
would have placed the English crown into commission. Yet at the
very time he was ordering his sheriffs to execute the terms of the
charter, John was seeking its annulment by the pope. Militarily,
John had the beating of the rebels until the invasion on their
behalf by Louis of France, son of Philip II, in the summer of
1216. John's characteristic refusal to challenge Louis on the field
led to a haemorrage in his support. Misfortune, such as the loss
of some of his treasure near the Wash, and illness took its toll.
John himself recognised the desperation of his plight. In his
will, dictated on his deathbed, he urged his executors to 'render
assistance to my sons for the recovery and defence of their
inheritance'.

By October 1216, the central issue in the civil war was no
longer Angevin government but John himself. Immediately after
his death, the regency, on behalf of the nine-year-old Henry III,
issued a modified *Magna Carta* signalling a new, more consensual style of rule. Already, the image of Bad King John was
abroad. Ironically, John is most remembered for *Magna Carta*,
in the drafting of which he was little involved and whose content
he quickly repudiated. The true measure of John's reign is not in
the temporary truce between two mercenary and self-interested
factions, which the charter represented. It lies in the contrast
between the magnificent inheritance of 1199 and the legacy of
1216, with the enemy already within the gates and almost ready
to take possession. John may not have been the worst English
monarch, nor yet the most tyrannical; but it hard not to
judge him, on any terms other than his own, as one of the most

unsuccessful. However, John's family did not entirely reject his memory. Fifty years after his death on a windy October night at Newark, John's grandson, the future Edward I, named his first-born son John.

W. L. Warren, *King John*, 1961.
J. C. Holt, *King John* (Historical Association Pamphlet), 1963.
R. V. Turner, *King John*, 1994.

ARTHUR OF BRITTANY (1187-?1203) was one of the many kings England almost but never had. His father was Henry II's fourth son, Geoffrey, who died after a tournament accident some months before Arthur's birth; his mother was Constance, heiress to the county of Brittany. In 1190, at Messina, on his way to the Holy Land, Richard I designated his young nephew heir to all the Angevin lands, a move that helped provoke Arthur's other surviving uncle, John, into rebellion. Richard's gesture was probably merely symbolic, as he was about to marry and could have expected heirs of his own. In April 1199, however, on Richard's sudden death, Anjou, Maine and Touraine declared for Arthur and he had the support, so it is said, of Archbishop Hubert Walter for the succession to England and Normandy. Whether John or Arthur was the rightful heir was unclear in contemporary English law, and different areas of the Angevin Empire had their own inheritance customs. The matter was resolved by force and diplomacy. By September Arthur had been deserted by his Angevin followers and compelled, with his mother, to make peace and accept John as overlord. In 1202, Arthur seized the opportunity of Philip II's formal confiscation of John's French dominions by doing homage to the French king for all Angevin fiefs except Normandy, which Philip was determined to keep for himself. Philip also knighted Arthur. However, in the ensuing campaign Arthur was captured in Mirebeau where he was beseiging his grandmother, Eleanor of Aquitaine, and incarcerated at Falaise. He then vanishes from view. How, when and where he died was at the time and has remained ever since a source of speculation and debate. The Annals of Margam Abbey in Glamorgan have John killing Arthur in a drunken fury one evening at Rouen in April 1203, a story which may have come from the abbey's patron, William of Briouze, Arthur's captor at Mirebeau. John is known to have been at Rouen at the time. However, John's later barbaric treatment of the Briouze family may have coloured the tale. Other sources adopt a very different line, insisting that Arthur was a traitor and oathbreaker who deserved his obscure and shameful death. Both the reliable Barnwell Chronicle and the *Life* of William Marshal mention Arthur's pride, leaving an image far removed from the innocent, beguiling and rather nauseating child depicted by Shakespeare in his play *King John*. Most of Arthur's life was spent as a pawn in others' political and dynastic contests. On the threshold of manhood, he was no match for his generous-seeming patron, Philip of France, nor his determined rival, King John. Arthur's significance, in fact, may lie elsewhere, as a symbol of the creation of national identify myths. A common twelfth century phenomenon, these fantasies were fuelled by distorted or invented histories which constructed fabulous and honourable pasts to confirm present aspirations. The greatest pseudo-history of the twelfth, perhaps any post-Classical century, was Geoffrey of Monmouth's *History of the Kings of Britain*, after whose central hero Constance of Brittany deliberately named her son.

W. L. Warren, *King John*.

ISABELLA OF ANGOULÊME (*c*.1188-1246) was the daughter and heiress of Aymer (*d*.1213), count of Angoulême, a strategically important county in south-west France. Although betrothed to Hugh IX, count of Lusignan, Isabella was married to King John in 1200. Whether diplomacy or an allegedly uncontrollable passion for the twelve-year-old were uppermost in John's motives, it proved an expensive move. His subsequent hostility to Hugh led to the count's appeal to the king of France which was the pretext for the formal confiscation of John's French lands in 1202. From 1213, when she inherited Angoulême, Isabella attracted rumours about her infidelity. John may have believed them, as there is a story he placed her under house arrest at Gloucester in December 1214. After John's death, and the establishment of a stable regency for her son Henry III in 1217, she returned to her county. In 1220 she married Hugh X of

Isabella of Angoulême
(From her effigy at Fontevrault Abbey in Anjou)

Lusignan, the son of her suitor of 1200. For the rest of her life she was perched precariously between the interests of her two families. Her Poitevin sons may have sought their fortunes at Henry III's court, to that king's ultimate detriment, but Hugh betrayed him at Taillebourg in 1240. She died and was buried at Fontevrault in 1246, beside Henry II, Eleanor of Aquitaine and Richard I. From her perspective, the collapse of the Angevin empire was not a defining moment of national history, but one episode in French comital relations in which her role was that of territorial pawn. At least until the 1250s, it was a perspective shared by her sons in England.

WILLIAM OF BRIOUZE or Braose (*d.*1211) was at the centre of one of the most damaging *cause célèbres* of John's reign. After succeeding to his father's lands in Sussex, Devon and Wales in 1180, he proved himself a tough and ruthless fighter in the Angevin cause in the Welsh Marches and France. He was with Richard I at Chalus in 1199 and with John in Normandy 1202-3, when he captured Arthur of Brittany at Mirebeau in 1202. An arrogant and unpopular man, with a shrewish wife,

William was showered with favour by John, receiving the extensive Irish lordship of Limerick in 1200-1, more castles in 1205 and lucrative marriages for his many children. For reasons not entirely clear, from 1205 John began to harry his former favourite, perhaps out of fear of his independent spirit or a desire to show that even those powerful by royal creation were subject to the king's will. It is certain that John determined to make an example of William and that William reacted with obstinacy, rashness and incompetence. The weapon William had placed in John's hands were his pledges of huge sums in return for royal grants (5,000 marks for Limerick in 1201; 800 marks for the castles in 1205) on which he subsequently defaulted. Not only did John undermine William's position in Ireland and deprive him of offices in England, he also had a legal case against him at the Exchequer. When the king demanded hostages in 1208, William initially blustered and his wife, Matilda, fatally for her, apparently excused her refusal to deliver her sons as hostages by accusing John of murdering his nephew Arthur. This was particularly provocative as William was probably one of the few who actually knew what had happened to Arthur and who could lend credence to the rumours that John himself had murdered his nephew in a drunken rage at Rouen in April 1203. Whatever the personal edge, John proceeded vigorously. In 1209, William's chattels were distrained, castles surrendered, hostages promised and his English and Welsh lands pledged as security for repayment of his loan. To add pressure, John sent troops to attack William's Marcher lands. William and his family fled to Ireland, but returned in 1210 to avoid John's armies there. This was unavailing. Matilda and her eldest son were captured, taken to Windsor Castle where, despite offers of ransom, they were starved to death. William fled to France, where he died a broken man in 1211, his funeral being conducted by another exile from John's anger, Stephen Langton.

It was not William's harassment which shocked. As the king, supported by many leading barons, insisted in 1210, William was a contumacious debtor and rebel. It was the inexorable quality of the pursuit and the obscene cruelty of the treatment of Matilda and her son, attested by contemporaries, which made the case notorious. William could be said to have brought about his own ruin by failing to submit. There is little objective evidence that John was especially vindictive in the early stages of his attack. In the campaign to increase the effectiveness of the Exchequer's collection of revenue owing to the crown, William's fate was to show other barons that none were immune from royal authority. Whether John's subsequent cruelty was informed by personal spite or misjudged sternness is impossible to say. However, the case of William and Matilda de Briouze showed an increasingly resentful baronage the lengths to which the king could go and, in time, would stand as a major indictment of John's policy, judgement and personality, a significant part of the myth of 'Bad King John'.

W. L. Warren, *King John*, 1961.
J. C. Holt, *The Northerners*, 1961.

ROBERT FITZWALTER (*c.*?1170-1235) was an irascible baronial troublemaker who attempted to elevate treason and personal spite into a crusade for liberty. A bully who threatened violence when faced with the workings of the law and surrendered a vital fortress when confronted with a fight, his career makes the rapacity, paranoia and brutality of King John's government explicable. With impeccable credentials (one grandfather was Henry II's justiciar, Richard de Lucy, another, Robert, had been Henry I's steward; one uncle was bishop of Winchester), he held important lands in the south, including the lordship of Dunmow (Essex) and Baynard's Castle in London, as well as extensive estates in northern England through his wife. Perhaps because of his London base, he was involved in the wine trade, owning a number of wine ships. In John's reign he was soon notorious. In 1203, he surrendered the castle of Vaudreuil in Normandy to Philip II of France without a fight. In the circumstances, John's refusal to pay Robert's ransom was understandable, although it made him an enemy for life as Robert had to sell land to raise the money himself. There is a story of Robert arriving at the trial of his son-in-law for murder with five hundred armed men, a reflection if not of the truth then of his reputation for violence and wealth. In 1212, he had to flee the country when a plot he instigated to assassinate the king was

Robert Fitzwalter
(From his seal)

discovered. In exile in France, he made contacts with the French court which proved useful during the English civil war 1215-17. Robert managed to convince enough influential people on the continent that he was a martyr to the harsh regime of an excommunicate monarch with such success that he was named as one with whom the king must be reconciled in the treaty of 1213 between John and the pope which ended the Interdict. From 1214, Robert was a militant leader of the rebels. Even after the compromise at Runnymede, Robert, now calling himself Marshal of the Army of God (perhaps as a counter to John's status as a crusader), kept a baronial force in being under the guise of holding tournaments. In the subsequent civil war, his influence in London was important, as were his links with the French which he used in 1215-16 to secure the intervention of Prince Louis, to whom he and the other baronial leaders swore allegiance. Taken prisoner at Lincoln in 1217, he was soon released. Rehabilitated in a general political amnesty in 1218, his departure in 1219 on crusade suggests that he was content in the protection of his lands during his absence. It is ironic that in 1223-4, when the justiciar, Hubert de Burgh, was destroying Robert's old adversary, Falkes de Bréauté, Robert appeared at court at Hubert's side. The link may have been Archbishop Langton, a fellow opponent of King John, but if Hubert was going to assert his authority over veterans of John's administration, such as Peter des Roches, all aid was welcome. For Robert, the justiciar's favour helped the security of his lands. He may have appreciated the further irony in 1225 when he, one of the committee of twenty five set up by *Magna Carta* to control royal actions, witnessed the royal re-issue of the Charter in 1225. Perhaps he had mellowed with age. Only, however, one blinded by hysterical hatred of John and fanatical devotion to an anachronistic view of *Magna Carta* as the foundation of English liberty, law and parliamentary democracy could share T. F. Tout's view that Robert had been 'the first champion of English liberty'.

Robert's *D.N.B.* entry was by Tout.
J. C. Holt, *The Northerners*, 1961.

EUSTACE DE VESCI (1169-1216) was one of the leaders of the so-called 'Northerners', who provided the nucleus of the rebellion against King John in 1215. The son of a substantial northern landowner who had served Henry II as a sheriff, Eustace held estates in Northumberland, Durham and Yorkshire, with his principal castles at Alnwick and Malton. In 1193, by marrying Margaret, the illegitimate daughter of William the Lion, king of Scots, he added lands in the Scottish Borders. Under Richard I and John he appears as a loyal and frugal baron, employed in diplomacy with Scotland and paying military service and scutage as demanded. Unlike other barons, he avoided running up large debts at the Exchequer; perhaps having to pay off his relief of 1,300 marks in 1190 taught him a useful lesson. Nonetheless, he stood as pledge for the debts of others, and so was involved in what became under John a major source of grievance against the crown as the Exchequer increasingly insisted on strict terms of repayment. Whereas his father had benefited from the beginnings of systematic royal intervention into northern affairs, Eustace never served as a sheriff or profited from the king's closer exploitation of revenue and justice after 1204. Yet even in the face of the increase in the weight of government in the north 1204-14, there is no obvious explanation for Eustace's career of treachery and rebellion between 1212 and 1216. The records suggest a cautious character who spent modestly in litigation or purchases of land and franchises. In one recorded action, Eustace secured the manor of Rotherham at a cost of only 100 marks — and a successful duel. Independent, unafraid to match his claims with physical violence, careful with money, resentful of southern interference, Eustace emerges as something close to the stereotype of the touchy, blunt northerner.

For whatever reason, in 1212 Eustace joined a widespread baronial conspiracy to assassinate King John. The motive behind the plot may have been connected with a proposed Inquest on baronial tenures and obligations. Eustace was not the most prominent of the conspirators, but he, like Robert Fitz-Walter, was the most important to be found out. Eustace fled to Scotland (actually only a few miles from his Northumberland estates); he was outlawed and his English lands confiscated. Rather skilfully, he managed to persuade the circle around archbishop Langton that his exile was because of his opposition to the Interdict, so as part of the settlement between pope and king in 1213 he regained his estates. However, John was not so easily taken in: Eustace's compensation was paltry and the castles of Alnwick and Malton were razed to the ground. Restoration left Eustace unreconciled. In 1214, with a group of fellow northern barons, he refused military service or scutage for the Poitou expedition. After the failure of John's continental campaign, these 'Northerners' became the focus of armed opposition to John which led to *Magna Carta*. Eustace's role was recognised by his being named as one of the baronial committee of Twenty-Five set up by the charter to supervise royal policy. More practically, he managed to have restored his right to hunt his dogs in the forest of Northumberland. With the collapse of the *Magna Carta* compromise and the outbreak of full-scale civil war, Eustace took an active part in operations in the north, helping negotiate the entry on the baronial side of Alexander II king of Scots, his brother-in-law, with whom he campaigned in the summer of 1216, meeting his death at the siege of Barnard's Castle on the Tees.

Eustace appears the model of an irreconcilable, self-interested provincial baron. His treason is evident; his unforgiving rebellious nature attested by the pope himself in 1214. But his career should not be seen solely through the prism of royal interests. There is no denying Eustace's violent and aggressive nature. It was rumoured, not entirely convincingly, that his hatred of John sprang from the king's lecherous advances to his wife. Such stories may be more credible as metaphors. Eustace may have thought rebellion the only price to pay for what he regarded as direct, insidious attacks less on his wife's virtue but on his own traditional way of political life in the north. Almost alone of those opposed to John, there was no evident financial grudge, although he may have regretted exclusion from the royal gravy-train. Eustace's actions reveal that the disturber of the king's peace may also be the defender of regional independence. But medieval history has tended to be written by admirers of the state, for whom local thuggery is condemned with far greater acerbity than the violence of central government.

J. C. Holt, *The Northerners*, 1961.

FALKES (or FAWKES) DE BRÉAUTÉ (*d*.1226) has suffered from nationalist prejudice from his own time to this. An entrepreneurial soldier and self-made politician, loyal to John but ultimately unable to find a settled role in the apparently more respectable regime of Henry III's minority, Falkes, as much as any, was responsible for there being a King Henry at all. Much of the hostility directed at Falkes was due to endemic snobbery: he was foreign and he lacked pedigree. Equally damaging to his reputation, he offended the abbey of St Alban's, home to two of the most influential historians of the thirteenth century, Roger of Wendover and Matthew Paris, who embellished his account of Falkes's death from food poisoning by drawing a picture of the devil shoving the offending bad fish into his mouth.

Falkes was the illegitimate son of a Norman knight. According to a contemporary story his first name alluded to a falx, or scythe, with which he had killed a knight on his father's land. He entered the service of King John as a serjeant, but rose to become one of his most trusted associates, whose loyalty was as unquestioned as his fortune was dependent upon royal favour. He acquired a reputation for brutality as sheriff of Glamorgan and, by 1217, had amassed a number of other shrievalties as well as the custody of six important castles: Bedford, Buckingham, Cambridge, Hertford, Northampton and Oxford. In the civil was of 1215-16, he was one of the leading royalist commanders. In 1216 he captured and plundered Worcester and attacked Ely; in 1217 it was the turn of St Alban's. He played a conspicuous part in the royalist victory at Lincoln (1217). His rewards were great, being assigned the heiress of the earldom of Devon, the lands (although not the title) of which he received as his wife's dower in 1218. During the regency, he cut a substantial figure, often in alliance with Peter des Roches, the bishop of Winchester, with whom he abortively planned to go on crusade in 1221. However useful his considerable military skills, Falkes was politically vulnerable. He was resented as a parvenu who openly disdained royal letters and accused 'all native-born Englishmen' of being traitors. Most of all, he had no patrimony of his own in England, his lands and offices depending on his wife, who had a son by a previous marriage; royal grants, which could be revoked; and his own acquisitions, each achieved at a political cost. His vulnerability was demonstrated by a series of suits of disseisin against him, many successful. More used to the independence of the war years, Falkes was impatient at the attempts of the justiciar Hubert de Burgh to regulate his activities in the shires under his control. Although he cooperated with the justiciar in quelling riots in London in 1222, Falkes was increasingly alienated by the government policy of resumption of the royal demesne (1222), royal castles and sheriffdoms (1223-4). His anxiety was in proportion to what he stood to lose. It was, however, his other land deals which precipitated his fall, when in 1224 he lost sixteen suits of disseisin. The kidnap of one of the justices by Falkes's brother, William led to the siege and capture of Falkes's castle at Bedford; the execution of William; and the ruin of Falkes himself. After pleading his case before the pope and composing an ingenious complaint at his treatment (known as his *querimonia*), he died in exile in Rome in 1226. Falkes had been a mainstay of Angevin government who sunk in the shifting political sands of the Minority. No more ambitious than his rivals, he lacked their established positions in the church or the English baronage. Self-made, he self-destructed. An arrogant man, in his pomp called by one chronicler 'more than a king in England', his turbulent career was a product of his dependence on royal patronage: it created him and ruined him. So far from being an over-mighty subject, Falkes demonstrated the difficulties facing the political adventurer: it is hard to buck the established order. Falkes seemed to have had an idea of this. His son was given the English name of Thomas and became an Oxfordshire county knight, a respectability his father, for all his fame and wealth, never quite achieved.

W. L. Warren, *King John*, 1961.
D. Carpenter, *The Minority of Henry III*, 1990.

STEPHEN LANGTON (*c*.1165-1228; archbishop of Canterbury 1207-28), one of the foremost Biblical scholars of his time, found himself, through little fault of his own, one of the most controversial archbishops of Canterbury at the centre of the most serious and acrimonious dispute between the king of England and the pope in the Middle Ages. Born in Lincolnshire, Langton studied in Paris in the 1180s, remaining there to teach and write. The schools of Paris then attracted the intellectual and ambitious elite of western Europe. One of Langton's fellow students was a well-connected Italian nobleman, Lothar dei Conti of Segni who, as Pope Innocent III (1198-1216), was to determine the course of his later career. Together, the two of them may well have visited the Canterbury shrine of Thomas Becket, a saint for whom Langton held a persistent, patriotic admiration.

Langton's academic studies were mainly scriptural. Although his *Quaestiones,* which revealed a practical mind when applied to textual or theological problems, were popular, his fame rested upon his preaching and his work as a Biblical commentator, his re-organisation of the chapters of the Bible in the late 1190s gradually winning general acceptance across the whole of western Christendom. His other works included religious verses such as the hymn *Veni, Sancta Spiritus.* A later English chronicler ascribed to Langton, somewhat improbably, a life of Richard I. Orthodox and unoriginal, it is unlikely that it was his pedagogic influence that led to his only pupil known by name, one Master Guerin of Corbeil, to be condemned for heresy in 1210. Langton, whose academic reputation was recognised by preferment to canonries at Paris and York, was typical of a group of his Paris contemporaries, including fellow Englishman Robert of Courçon (*i.e.* Curzon). Not satisfied with purely speculative theology, Langton and his colleagues were concerned with the systematizing of doctrine and its application to the actual world: one of his own famous sermons was on usury. Of particular relevance to the future was Langton's teaching at Paris that it was lawful to resist a tyrannical king who acted by his own will, not the law, a precept he had to defend in practice as King John's archbishop.

This pragmatic quality, allied to occasionally inflexible intellectual rigour, was characteristic of a generation of ecclesiastics which came to the fore under Innocent III. Among these Langton was prominent. In 1206, he was appointed Cardinal Priest of St Chrysogonus (an obscure, possibly fictional martyr of the early fourth century), testimony to his Parisian eminence. The timing was fortuitous. By the end of the year. Langton had been elected archbishop of Canterbury after an almost unprecedented display of papal authority. After the death of the previous archbishop, Hubert Walter, in 1205, one faction among the monks of Christ Church, Canterbury had elected their fellow monk Reginald, another the king's candidate John de Gray. The parties appealed to Rome, where Innocent set aside both candidates and presided over the election, by the Canterbury monks present at the Papal

Stephen Langton re-crowning Henry III in 1220
(From Matthew Paris's Chronica Majora)

Curia, of Cardinal Langton who was in Rome at the time. The new archbishop was consecrated by the pope at Viterbo in June 1207. According to the agreements reached between English kings and the papacy over the previous century, although the election by the monks was canonical, the consecration, without royal assent, broke accepted precedent. King John felt his rights of patronage and hence control over the English church, were threatened; he refused to recognise Langton as archbishop.

This led to a bitter six-year conflict, with Langton, except for a brief foray to Dover in 1209, exiled from England. Significantly and deliberately, he spent much of this period at the Cistercian monastery at Pontigny where Becket had stayed in the 1160s. King John was excommunicated and England placed under a papal Interdict. Deadlock was only ended in 1213 by the pope's threat to depose John at the very time the king's plans to recover his lost patrimony in France were nearing fruition. Faced by a possible papally sponsored French invasion, King John yielded in May 1213, receiving absolution from Langton himself in July.

Having been a symbol of a papal vision of ecclesiastical authority, Langton in office proved to be his own man. From 1213-15, he clashed with successive papal legates, a result of the novel and anomalous circumstance of the king having submitted his kingdom to papal overlordship as a price of reconciliation in 1213. From being the traditional head of the church, the archbishop now had to contend with a papal representative whose main brief was to support a now-faithful papal vassal, the king. In 1213/14, Langton clashed with Legate Nicholas over the extent of royal patronage. During the early months of 1215, Langton attempted to mediate between John and the rebellious magnates. According to the unreliable St Alban's chronicler, Roger of Wendover, Langton suggested the Coronation Charter of Henry I as a legitimate basis for the baronial demands against the king. This is credible, if only because two years earlier Langton had presided over the council of St Alban's where John had sworn to abide by the laws of Henry I, by which may have meant the Coronation Charter. Whatever his role in drafting *Magna Carta*, Langton's failure to support the king wholeheartedly excited the anger of the pope and led to the archbishop's suspension by Legate Pandulf and summons to Rome. After attending the Fourth Lateran Council, Langton remained abroad from 1215 until 1218. He had demonstrated that, like other occupants of the chair of St Augustine, he possessed inconvenient singlemindedness.

The political landscape to which he returned was very different from that which he had left. The Minority government of William Marshal operated on the basis of consent rather than coercion. After the Marshal's death in 1219, Langton continued as an ally of the justiciar, Hubert de Burgh, in protecting the authority of the crown, in particular against former partisans of King John such as Falkes de Bréauté. He remained wedded to finding just agreement between magnates and king: between 1221 and 1223, he played a leading role in mediating between the young Henry III's counsellors; in 1223, he called for the reissuing of *Magna Carta*, as he did again in 1225 in return for support for a fifteenth for a campaign in Poitou. In 1223, in order to bolster the independent effectiveness of the king's government, he helped secure the papal bull which granted Henry III control of his own seal.

As archbishop, Langton proved loyal to the traditions of his office and the national church. He recrowned Henry in 1220 (the Legate Guala and the bishop of Winchester had performed an unavoidably perfunctory ceremony in the dark days of 1216). In 1221, he persuaded Pope Honorius III (1216-27) to remove the resident papal legate; to limit papal provisions in England, a system whereby the pope imposed candidates to benefices, often absentees or papal cronies; and to restate the superiority of Canterbury over York. In 1226, Langton further emphasised his independence by resisting an attempt to reserve a prebend in each collegiate church for papal funds. In tune with the reforms encouraged by Innocent III at the Fourth Lateran Council, probably at an assembly held at Osney Abbey near Oxford in 1222, Langton issues a set of Constitutions concerning ecclesiastical discipline and organisation which were widely imitated across the English dioceses over the next generation.

By the time of his death in 1228, Langton had shown himself as a constructive church leader and a politician of pragmatism. He was no Becket. Unlike the martyr, whose relics he moved to a new shrine amidst great ceremony in 1220, he sought to translate general principles into effective practice. If he lacked the silken skills of the adept political infighter, he also lacked the brittle prigishness of many intellectuals in public life. It is rare for such a distinguished academic to cope even as well as Langton with the pressures of political leadership, but in this, as in much else, Langton conformed to the reforming approach and programme of his circle of Parisian scholars and of Innocent III in particular. It is often said that Innocent's pontificate marked the apogee of papal monarchy in the Middle Ages. If so, his success and lasting influence depended on men of the calibre of Stephen Langton.

But Langton was not simply a general in the papal army, however much he came to symbolise the pope's claims to authority in Christendom during the dispute with King John. As a figurehead for Innocent III's vision of the world order, he could encounter trouble, as on the occasion one of his sermons was heckled shortly after his return to England in 1213. But in contrast to any identification with the ultramontane implications of Innocent's policies, Langton was proud of his Englishness. Like many exiles through choice or compulsion (and Langton was both), he lauded his love of his country. In 1207 he declared that 'from our tender years we have loved our kingdom with a natural love'. This may have been no more than politic for the newly appointed ex-patriot archbishop establishing his local credentials. But it was a theme to which he returned. At the translation of Becket's relics in 1220 he talked of 'the triumph of an Englishman' and in a sermon of 1224 he refered to men like Falkes de Bréauté as 'the affliction of the natives to whom the people of England were so often given over as booty . . . take heed so that aliens are no longer permitted to act against you'. The thirteenth century saw a growing awareness amongst the political elite of national identity. It is entirely in keeping with this development that Langton, one of the most cosmopolitan of archbishops, should have issued, in January 1215, a charter in Anglo-Norman French, one of the first such documents not written in Latin, the universal language of government, law and religion, since the reign of William I.

Stephen Langton was neither a hero nor a saint. He was at times as much a victim as a champion of the cause he was chosen to represent. From his politics, sermons and writings, he emerges as a highly practical man, of sharp but flexible intellect, who prefered to achieve than to strike propagandist poses or escape into intellectual obscurantism. To have helped compose *Magna Carta* or to have re-organised the Vulgate text of the Bible would each have been notable: to have done both was remarkable.

F. M. Powicke, *Stephen Langton*, 1928.

PETER DES ROCHES (*d.*1238; bishop of Winchester 1205-1238; Justiciar 1213-15) was a central figure in English politics for over thirty years. He acquired an awesome reputation as a hard-faced and ruthless exponent of unrestricted royal authority. Many observers, from the thirteenth to the twentieth century,

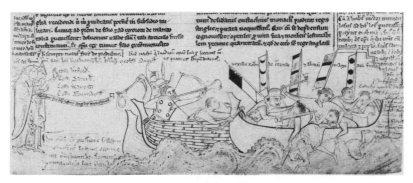

*Peter des Roches blessing the royalist fleet
at the battle of Sandwich 1217*
(From Matthew Paris's Chronica Majora)

have seen him as head of a sinister invasion of 'aliens', derisively
described by contemporaries as 'Poitevins' (*i.e.* notoriously
untrustworthy) who were held to have conspired, over half a century, against the interests of native-born Englishmen. In fact,
Peter, who was actually from Touraine, was an extremely effective administrator on behalf of John and Henry III whose chief
political fault was that he did not suffer gladly or silently the
self-interested posturing of the English baronage or their greedy
attempts to feed on the carcass of royal rights. The idea that the
magnates could provide good government he brusquely dismissed on intellectual and pragmatic grounds. As a foreigner, his
views were less obscured by local sentiment, family networks
and group solidarity. Peter's career was international, embracing
Italy and the Holy Land as well as France and England. Like any
other great lord, he surrounded himself with and promoted
those he found congenial and useful, often men who literally
spoke his own language, a group which included his three royal
masters, Richard I, John and Henry III. To them, Peter was certainly not an alien; rather he was very much 'one of us'. Therein
lay the secret of his tenacious influence.

Although the hostile Roger of Wendover described him as
having been in youth a 'knight, expert in warfare', this may be
wishful thinking: Peter was not the only cleric who showed
military aptitude. His early career was as a clerk in the house-

hold of Richard I, firmly rooted in the ecclesiastical aristocracy of his native region and Poitou where he held a number of significant benefices. As treasurer of Poitiers, he may have impressed Richard with his financial abilities, because it was in household finance that he first made his mark. Retained by John as one of his clerks after 1199, he worked closely with the king, authorizing payments to and from the Chamber, the royal household's financial office. Until 1205, the chamberlain was Hubert de Burgh, but Peter's role became increasingly important. It may be that Peter des Roches was one of King John's few genuine friends (*pace* A. A. Milne). By 1204, he was working alongside great barons and leading ministers. After Hubert's removal to France from 1202, Peter progressively took over the running of the household finances, being rewarded with custody of the English lands of the court of La Perche and the vacant bishoprics of Chichester and Winchester.

In 1205, John appointed Peter to the see of Winchester, perhaps the richest in England. Although hardly the model of the concerned reforming diocesan so energetically promoted by the pope at the time, Peter found in Winchester a power-base that was to give him invaluable political security. Ironically, in view of the exactly contemporary disputed election at Canterbury, in order to render his appointment incontestable, John sent Peter to Rome to receive consecration by Pope Innocent III. The importance John attached to Peter's elevation is indicated by his gift to the new bishop on the day of his enthronement at Winchester in 1206 of gorgeous vestments and chapel ornaments belonging to the recently deceased Hubert Walter.

Peter returned John's favour with interest. Despite the papal Interdict and the king's excommunication, Peter remained at his post, by the end of 1209 the only bishop left resident in England. Both in the king's household and at the Exchequer he extended his activities. A satire from this period sums up one view of his activities:

> 'The warrior of Winchester, presiding at the exchequer, keen at accounting, slack at Scripture, unrolling the king's roll, ignoring Luke for lucre, valuing marks more than Mark and putting money above books.'

Peter acted both as one of the king's finance ministers and his personal financial agent. His enthusiasm for this sort of work is reflected in the pipe roll for the Winchester estates he had compiled.

As one of the small group of advisers who ran the central institutions of government, Peter's power was considerable, especially as John's main policy in these years was to acquire sufficient treasure for the reconquest of his French lands. Peter displayed political as well as financial skills during the negotiations to end the Interdict. Despite his lack of any legal experience or expertise, on Geoffrey FitzPeter's death in 1213 Peter was a logical choice as justiciar. The appointment was, however, double-edged. In his handling of the regency in John's absence in France, in overseeing the 1214 scutage, the more sensitive law suits at Westminster and the disposal of castles and patronage, Peter proved himself capable but aggressive. It was not simply that he presided over some of the most notorious incidents of the king's manipulation of his rights, such as the infamous Mandeville inheritance case where it appeared superficially that Geoffrey de Say (15,000 marks) and Geoffrey de Mandeville (20,000 marks) had both paid the king huge sums for the same property. It was Peter's peremptory viceregal manner which added insult to injury, at least in the eyes of barons sensitive about the deference due to their eminence. A flavour of Peter's style is to be found in this summons to David, earl of Huntingdon to appear at a council in 1214 (David, it should be noted, was the brother of the king of Scots):

'Know that we have many things to say to you concerning the business of the lord king and of his kingdom, wherefore we order you, as you love his honour and yourself and your hostages and whatsoever you hold of him, that, without delay or excuse, you shall be in the neighbourhood of London, wherever you hear we are, about the octave of the Assumption of the Blessed Mary (*i.e.* 22 August) to treat concerning his aforesaid business.'

It is no surprise that Peter was a casualty of the compromise reached between the king and the rebellious barons at Runnymede in 1215, being replaced as justiciar by the less abrasive

Hubert de Burgh. Peter regarded the proceedings and *Magna Carta* itself with some contempt. However, his loss was not, in practice, so very great. The civil war of 1215-17 effectively suspended the justiciar's traditional duties. Peter retained his wealthy bishopric and his position at court. But he was never again to hold formal office, a measure of the lack of trust his behaviour as justiciar 1213-15 generated among the English magnates in whose favour the balance of power shifted during Henry III's minority. Writing perhaps in 1219, the Waverley Annalist remembered Peter's policy as justiciar was that 'little by little he might subject the most powerful men of the land to the will of the king', adding that anger against him 'is sedated not even now'.

This made little or no difference to Peter's attitudes or conduct. Ironically, it was he who imposed the papal suspension of Langton from office in 1215. In 1216, under the direction of the Legate Guala, he crowned Henry III. The following year he played an active and crucial role in the victory at Lincoln. In pursuing royal rights, he had not changed his spots: in 1218 he imposed extortionate terms on some Lincolnshire debtors. From 1216 Peter had the guardianship of the king, a sign of the trust placed in him at least by the king's mother, the Poitevin Isabella of Angoulême. Although after 1219 he retained considerable influence as well as the tutorship of King Henry, his position was gradually undermined by Hubert de Burgh. In 1221, Peter's ally, Peter de Mauley, was exiled and he himself accused of treason and deprived of the royal tutorship, although some may argue that his views on kingship had already left their mark on the teenage monarch. His political eclipse became almost total in 1223-4 when, with other former servants of King John, he lost castles and the shrievalties and was again accused of treason by Hubert de Burgh who apparently blamed the bishop for all the evils of John's reign and the Minority. Peter vowed vengeance: 'if it cost him all he had, he would cause the justiciar to be removed from power'.

Despite this exclusion from power, Peter lost none of his ambition or resourcefulness. His horizons were international. It was reported even that he had been elected, *in absentia*, bishop of the Egyptian port of Damietta after its capture by crusaders in 1219. He had taken the Cross in 1221: after 1224 he prepared to fulfil his vow. His crusade of 1227-29 greatly enhanced his reputation. Even the xenophobic Matthew Paris had a good word to say, praising the bishop's expedition as being 'to the salvation and honour of many, especially of all Englishmen'. Paris may have been influenced by Peter's gift, on his return, of a book on the marvels of the East. On crusade, Peter struck up a close relationship with the German Emperor Frederick II, witnessing his treaty with the Sultan of Cairo (18 February 1229) which restored Jerusalem to Christian rule. Equipped with considerable funds, Peter supervised the rebuilding of Jaffa and militarized the English Order of St Thomas of Acre by giving it a new rule, based upon that of the Teutonic Knights. A lasting monument to Peter's crusade may be the chapel of the Holy Sepulchre in Winchester cathedral which has been associated with the bishop. Peter stayed at Frederick II's side on his return to the West, helping negotiate the peace of Ceperano between the emperor and Pope Gregory IX in 1230. On his way back to England, he assisted in arranging a truce between Louis IX and Henry III. There was far more to Peter des Roches than his English critics allowed.

After a triumphant return to England, Peter capitalized on the increasing problems of Hubert de Burgh and the king's growing impatience with his justiciar. Supported by a coalition of disparate magnates, including the earls of Cornwall, Chester and Pembroke, Peter managed to secure the appointment of his son, Peter des Rivaux, as head of royal finances in March 1232 and the overthrow of Hubert a few months later. Between 1232 and 1234, Peter was dominant. Peter des Rivaux held the shrievalties of twenty-one counties; old companions such as Peter de Mauley and Engelard de Cigogné, returned from exile; strategic castles were manned by dependable Flemish and Breton mercenaries. A series of disseisins were effected 'per voluntatem regis', in contradiction of Clause 39 of *Magna Carta* which had guaranteed judgement by peers not royal whim. Peter justified such acts by referring to the king's 'plenitude of power' over his subjects, an idea fashionable in many royal courts at the time, including the pope's and Frederick II's whose most grandiloquent statement of a ruler's authority, the *Liber Augustalis,* appeared shortly after Bishop Peter had left him in 1231.

As two decades before, Peter's methods aroused hostility, fear and revolt, led by Richard Marshal, earl of Pembroke, son of Peter's former colleague, the regent. In response to Richard's complaint that he had suffered judgement without trial by peers, Peter sneeringly repudiated the idea that there were peers in England, as there were in France (where Richard had spent most of his time). Peter insisted that the king could sentence anyone on the judgement of whomsoever he wished to appoint as judge. While the barons saw Clause 39 of *Magna Carta* as a defence of liberties, Peter saw it as protection of sectional privilege. The lesson he drew from recent legal history was that all free Englishmen were equal before the law, the king's law, obedient to the monarch. He was not tolerant of special interests. However, politics prevailed over ideological niceties. After baronial threats of deposition and royal demands for special oaths of fealty, open war flared up on the Welsh Marches in 1233, as Richard allied with Llewelyn of Wales. Attempted ecclesiastical mediation in 1234 was overtaken by the death, in Ireland, of the Marshal. Suspicion clung to Peter des Roches, leaving the king little option but to repudiate the bishop and his allies in June 1234. For the last time, Peter had fallen foul of the factional politics of the English nobility he professed to despise. Peter had himself become the obstacle to the implementation of his own policies. These were not solely concerned with the forceful assertion of royal rights. More quietly, but effectively, his associates began reforming the procedures of the Exchequer and other financial institutions to bring them more firmly under royal control. If the politics of Hubert de Burgh allowed Henry III to survive the Minority, the reforms of Peter des Roches enabled him to rule as king. It is significant that three central figures in the bishop's administration of 1232-34, Peter des Rivaux, Robert Passelew and Stephen Segrave, all returned to office in 1236.

Once more rejected by his adopted homeland, Peter found an outlet for his restless energy abroad. In 1235-6 he was again in Italy, placing his military skills at Gregory IX's disposal. In 1236, with the count of Toulouse, he defeated the pope's Roman enemies at Viterbo. Back in England later that year, he died at his castle of Farnham in 1238.

Peter's career was, by any standard, remarkable in its length and scope. Yet precisely the qualities that made it distinctive rendered it unintelligible to English observers who inhabited a more constricted universe. Viewed from his own perspective, the association of Peter with an 'alien' conspiracy in England was no less incomprehensible. His masters were French, if his estates were English. His ecclesiastical offices stradled the Channel. His career exemplified the practical unity of Christendom, from the British Isles to Syria, where a man of talent, contacts and ambition could play many parts. Diplomat, bishop, statesman, civil servant, minister, general, crusader and courtier, Peter des Roches, far from the malign intriguer of English legend, proved himself a loyal servant and a valuable colleague. His taste for magnificence, his generosity to relatives and clients, fidelity to his *familia* and companions mark him as possessing the attractive qualities of an admirable lord. Like all effective medieval rulers, he was feared, yet his consistency stands in marked contrast to the shifting allegiances of his fiercest critics. Those who criticised Peter and the other 'aliens' were the very same who queued up to swear allegiance to Louis of France. Peter's loyalty was based not on spurious nationalism but faithful service to a succession of demanding masters — Richard I, John, Henry III, Frederick II — in whose service he was not found wanting. But there was more. With many clerics of his generation he identified principles of authority behind political action. Furthermore, there was an observed strand of lordly faith; he was an active crusader and his last public words were of the extirpation of all infidels and the triumph of the one catholic church. Whatever the truth of Peter's personality, it is hard to disagree with the punning monks of St Swithin's, Winchester, who described him as 'hard as rocks'.

D. Carpenter, *The Minority of Henry III*, 1990.
F. J. West, *The Justiciarship in England*, 1966.
N. Vincent's magisterial study on Peter des Roches is forthcoming.

RALPH OF COGGESHALL (*d.* after 1224) was abbot of the Cistercian abbey of Coggeshall in Essex from 1207 until ill-health forced him to resign in 1218. He gave his name to a *Chronicon Anglicanum*, covering the years 1066-1223, the last section of which, 1187-1223, he wrote himself. Although head of an obscure provincial house, through extensive personal contacts with the nobility and the international Cistercian network, Ralph was well-informed. His information about the Third and Fourth Crusades, for instance, came from returning crusaders and monks. Much of his chronicle is based on oral evidence, which lends it a diffuse character. Not a witness of political standing or academic distinction, Ralph displays the orthodox prejudices of a conventional monk content to follow the harsh judgemental view of a sinful world familiar to his predecessors. The great, Richard I or Hubert Walter, are punished for their vanities or sins; the Jews deserved death in the massacres of 1190. His portraits of Richard I and John may represent a barometer of contemporary opinion, moulded by the hindsight of events. Richard is a flawed hero, his chivalric reputation sullied by greed and anger. Ralph's dislike of John grew as his reign progressed, until by 1216, he is shown as a bad-tempered liar, cheat, glutton and coward. Henry III's minority, however, is regarded more positively, perhaps because of the reconciliation between royalists and most of the baronial opposition between 1217 and 1219. Ralph's description of the ravages of the civil war of 1215-17 explains his enthusiasm at the return of peace. He, like many others, transferred their loyalties from the baronial faction to the royalists, a conversion tinged with overt nationalism. Just as Ralph was suspicious of John's foreign officials, such as Peter des Roches, so he scorns the French Prince Louis as one 'who had come to destroy the English people'. Such xenophobia, initially useful in rallying support behind Henry III, was to grow to deafening, irrational proportions in the hands of later writers, such as Matthew Paris, and some discontented politicians in the late 1250s. Ralph's nationalism suggests that the future of an Anglo-French Angevin empire would have been precarious regardless of the outcome of John's battles with Philip II of France, a fact largely lost on the cosmopolitan courtiers of Henry III.

A. Gransden, *Historical Writing in England c.550-c.1307*, 1974.

RANULF III, earl of Chester (c.1170-1232) was one of the old school of Anglo-Norman barons whose loyalty to the Angevin dynasty was consistent but contingent on the receipt of lucrative favours. Bishop Stubbs described him as 'almost the last relic of the great feudal aristocracy of the Conquest' and, however his career is viewed, he was — and thought himself — very grand. Small in physical stature, he was a giant in terms of family relationships and estates, the twin pillars of his ambition and political career. Succeeding to the earldom as a minor in 1181 and attaining majority and control of his estates in England and Normandy in 1187, in 1189 he married Constance of Brittany, widow of Henry II's son Geoffrey (d.1186) and mother of Arthur of Brittany, with whom King John contested the Angevin succession 1199-1202. Although bringing Ranulf control of the honour of Richmond in England as well as the duchy of Brittany, the marriage was not a success, being finally dissolved in 1199. The following year Ranulf cemented his power in Normandy by marrying Clemencia of Fougères. Relations with John were initially tentative. Ranulf had opposed John's attempted *coup* of 1193-4; he retained many contacts with partisans of his former stepson, Arthur; and his second wife's family joined Philip II. Spending most of 1199-1204 in France, Ranulf's continued loyalty was bought by John with further patronage. But the king was suspicious of Ranulf (as, indeed, he was of most people), perhaps with reason. In the winter of 1204-5, Ranulf, suspected of dealings with the rebellious Welsh and of contemplating revolt himself, had extensive estates temporarily confiscated by the king. The episode demonstrated the limits of independent action even by the most powerful English magnate, which may have persuaded Ranulf that loyalty was good business. Thereafter, Ranulf basked in an uninterrupted flow of royal favours. In return, he fought John's Welsh wars 1209-12; helped secure the peace with the pope in 1213-14; and was with the king in Poitou in 1214. Loyal to John in 1215-16, one of the few barons to witness *Magna Carta* of 1215 *ex parte regis*, Ranulf played a leading military role in the civil war by virtue of his extensive estates and numerous castles. On John's death, Ranulf's influence increased further. Although he stood aside to allow William Marshal to assume the regency for the young

Henry III, he put his political weight behind the reissuing of
Magna Carta (1216 and 1217); his military experience in defeating the rebels at Lincoln (1217); and his diplomatic skill in negotiating the treaty with Louis of France (1217) and peace with the
Welsh (1217/8). His rewards from the government he partly ran
were immense, including the earldom of Lincoln, a clutch of
sheriffdoms and estates in the north, East Midlands and East
Anglia. In 1218, his decision to honour the crusade vow he had
taken in 1215 may point to a genuine piety beyond that of the
customary ecclesiastical patronage expected of the great. It may
also reflect a degree of thwarted ambition: relations with the
regent were not always easy. In the East, Ranulf played a leading
role in the Fifth Crusade's siege and occupation of Damietta
(1218-19). On the Crusade's failure, he returned to England in
1220, to find William Marshal dead and the government in the
hands of Hubert de Burgh. Ranulf was not alone in finding the
shoals of faction difficult to navigate in 1220-1224 as tensions
grew between government officials and old John loyalists. These
flared into open conflict in the winter of 1223-4 when Ranulf,
among others, briefly tried to resist de Burgh's policy of resumption of sheriffdoms and royal castles. Ranulf's final years saw
him acting as an elder statesman, witnessing the 1225 re-issue of
Magna Carta; playing a prominent role in the dispute in 1227
over Forest Laws; and, as a veteran, leading Henry III's army on
the ill-fated Poitou expedition of 1230-1. He never lost sight of
his private advantage. In 1220, some of his estates avoided the
carucage; the 1225 Aid was not levied in Cheshire; and in 1229,
he successfully resisted the ecclesiastical tax collector. It may
have been a sign of age and declining influence that he failed to
stop the levy of the 1232 Fortieth on his lands. The whole of
Ranulf's career had been determined by the maintenance and
acquisition of rights and property. It must therefore have been
galling that he had no heir, on his death his estates being divided
between his four sisters. Ranulf's political career reinforces the
folly of historical periodisation. Knighted by Henry II, with
estates on both sides of the Channel, Ranulf cut a European figure after 1204, on crusade 1218-20 and on two campaigns in
Poitou, 1214 and 1230-1. A witness to all first four issues of
Magna Carta, he had little thought of running his estates

according to new constraints of political or legal behaviour. Historians seek the origins of change: in Ranulf III of Chester they have a good example of the tenacity of tradition.

J. W. Alexander, *Ranulf of Chester*, 1983.

HENRY III (1207-72; king of England 1216-72) reigned for longer than any other English monarch until the eighteenth century. Yet his personality has often been obscured by the rush of events, his achievements clouded by the incessant problems of sustaining royal power. To nationalist and constitutional historians of the last century or more, Henry has appeared as a tyrannical hindrance to the progress of parliamentary government or as a cosmopolitan traitor to the growth of English independence. Henry has tended to be overshadowed by the stronger personalities of his own courtiers and contemporaries: Hubert de Burgh, Peter des Roches, Robert Grosseteste, Louis IX, Simon de Montfort and the Lord Edward. He has suffered at the hands of chroniclers opposed to foreigners or sympathetic to the reform movement of 1258-65. Even royalist writers seem lukewarm, his son attracting the credit for the successes of his final years.

Henry III is the first English king whose daily life can be followed through the sources. He is also the first of whom we have a clue of what he looked like. Henry had a drooping eyelid which shadowed one eye; it was genetic: his son Edward had one too. Henry was a ruler of stature who defied the maxim that all political careers end in failure: his end was physically pathetic, but politically triumphant. He suffered humiliations at the hands of his own subjects beyond those of any king since the Conquest, but his policy ultimately prevailed. In 1216, he ascended the throne as the child figurehead of a beleaguered faction of baronial oligarchs. When he died, royal authority was such that his son succeeded without a murmur, even though he was hundreds of miles away.

Henry was the first monarch since Harthacnut (1040-42) born to be king; he was the only king until the late fourteenth century to be educated as king. Publicly and privately his Minority (1216-27) shaped his future. The restoration of the monarchy through resumption of estates and administrative and judicial functions was achieved by consensual government where magnates and royal officials joined together to decide policy and household appointments. The principles were those of the re-issued *Magna Carta* of 1216, 1217 and 1225. The crown was expected to operate through consultation and within agreed limits of custom and law. However, it was not resolved how this system could work when there was an adult, sane monarch. The clause placing the king under the scrutiny of twenty-five barons (Clause 61 of the 1215 charter) had been dropped in 1216. There was no agreed mechanism to interpret law and custom. Even the stipulation of trial by peers (Clause 39)could be challenged, as by the pugnacious Peter des Roches in 1233 when he questioned what was meant by peers: all freemen or a privileged elite of barons? The charter contained no rules for appointing royal officials, still seen for what they still were, personal agents of the king not officers of an impersonal state. The behaviour of sheriffs and justices were conditioned in certain circumstances, but not their recuitment or terms of service. The insistence that the king do justice to his people and respect their liberties was as flexible as each lawsuit was individual. On royal patronage, the very stuff of politics, the charter was silent.

Yet the repeated re-drafting, re-issuing and confirmation of the Charter (or Charters, as clauses dealing with Forest law were published separately from 1217) created expectations of baronial consultation and control, particularly over policy. During the Minority, successive regents had carefully balanced the factions and consulted widely in order to make policy acceptable. In any case, men such as William Marshal (regent 1216-19) and Hubert de Burgh (justiciar 1215-32) were themselves barons. Problems arose when, of age, Henry wished, perfectly legitimately, to restore the royal prerogative in areas traditionally governed by it: patronage; foreign policy; justice; appointment of household officials. There was nothing except the experience of the Minority to suggest that the king, like any other lord, had not full freedom in these areas. After 1216, the king may have been seen as being under the law. But resurrecting the prerogative was a political not a legal matter and, inevitably, caused friction with baronial interests. Henry III was happy to confirm the

Henry III
(From his effigy at Westminster Abbey finished in 1291)

Charters in 1237 and 1253; he had no wish to rule as a tyrant, nor in general did he. The problem was that there remained the desire of many barons to influence the exercise of the royal prerogative to their collective or individual advantage. The Minority left the Charters fundamental to political debate, positively, in the parameters of behaviour they set and negatively, in what they left unsaid.

Henry provoked anger because he behaved as king not as chairman of a baronial Round Table. Thus much criticism was directed at his appointments, his distribution of patronage and, as in 1238, 1242 and 1255-8, his failure to consult over controversial, expensive or disastrous decisions, respectively the marriage of his sister Eleanor to Simon de Montfort, his botched attempt to recapture Poitou and the Sicilian business. There were two possible solutions to this inherent tension. Formal baronial control of the royal prerogative; or the strengthening of royal authority as the undisputed head of the community of the realm supported by consent and obedience. The verdict of Henry's reign, uneasily and bloodily reached, was clear. The conundrums bequeathed by the Minority were resolved by 1272 in the monarchy's favour.

Privately, Henry's experiences and education during his minority were also formative. Whatever he learnt from the grammarian Hugh of Avranches, whose enthusiasm to show off his skills led him to produce a primer 2,200 lines long, Henry grew up on politics and administration. His mentor was Peter des Roches, the most dynamic royal official of his generation. Throughout his reign Henry understood how government worked and often manipulated it skilfully. Gradually brought into political prominence, crowned for the second time in 1220, given the use of his own seal in 1223 and formally declaring himself of age in 1227, Henry had his own household and was consulted on matters of state from an early age, as in 1220 over Welsh affairs. There were even suggestions that his majority would be declared on his fourteenth birthday. Unlike the young Henry VI, Henry III clearly showed some aptitude. From whatever source, Henry imbibed a heightened ideology of kingship, fashionable among the rulers of the time. The king was God's minister who had responsibilites to all his people; whose liberties transcended sectional interests but whose prerogative was untrammelled by other terrestrial jurisdictions, lay or ecclesiastical; to whom obdience must be unconditonal and absolute. Henry was fond of insisting on the majesty of his office; and keen to accuse those he disliked of treason. He increased the occasions on which the *laudes regiae* (chants praising the king) were sung. But, unlike his father, King John, his rhetoric was not matched by deeds. His concept of his office was grand but his use of the prerogative bounded by practical limits. He may have learnt from Peter des Roches,who he made his first minister of his personal rule (1232-4) and whose son, Peter des Rievaux, remained an influential advisor and servant for two decades.

How far the circumstances of his youth affected Henry's personality is impossible to say. Matthew Paris recorded him saying once 'You English want to hurl me from my throne as you did my father'. He harboured a lifelong and not unjustified suspicion of the selfishness of the English baronage, just as he retained a devotion, sometimes more sincere than sensible, to the papacy which had sustained his monarchy in his youth. Henry grew up to be a petulant, injudicious man, quick-witted with a waspish, unguarded tongue. Possibly as a consequence of youthful isolation, Henry was lavish with affection, but over-sensitive to betrayal. Impetuous, lacking wisdom, Henry was, however, neither especially vindictive nor did he share the taste for violence showed by his father and son. In government, he was industrious and alert. He understood how to articulate his policies if less able to implement them. He was not a good general. In public he cut a figure lacking *gravitas* or self-possession. The chronicles are full of his rude, aggressive and provocative outbursts. But as he got as good as he gave, he evidently did not inspire fear or even respect from those who knew him. He seems to have been a nervy chairman of meetings of his council or assemblies, often with good reason. But he was not unpersuasive, on more than one occasion, for example, using private blandishment to encourage abbots to part with their money.

Henry was famously pious, in a rather showy way, a hostile witness commenting: 'the less he was clever in his actions on earth the more he indulged in a display of humility before God'. An addicted pilgrim, he regularly toured English shrines such as

Bromholm, Walsingham, Bury St Edmund's and St Alban's He adored ceremonies, such as the reception in Westminster Abbey of a relic of the Holy Blood in 1247 which the overexcited Henry insisted Matthew Paris, who was in the audience, record for posterity. Extravagant in lifestyle, Henry, like his brother-in-law Louis IX, was obsessed by the poor. Like many devout rich people in the Middle Ages, Henry confronted the criticism inherent in the Gospel stories of the wealthy man's path to Heaven, or Lazarus and Dives, by using charity to the poor as a passport to redemption. Riches used in this way could circumvent the apparent clarity of Christ's teaching. In religion as in politics, Henry's motto was that he had inscribed over the gable in the Painted Chamber of Westminster Palace: 'He who does not give what he holds does not receive what he desires'.

In fact, Henry had a childlike passion for presents. A generous giver, he loved receiving them. At his eldest son's baptism, his relish in the christening gifts prompted a courtier to remark: 'God has given us this child, but the lord King is selling it'. Unusually for his family, Henry was chaste, a loyal and faithful husband. He directed much energy into a love of artefacts. Like his father, he delighted in jewels. He took an interest in all aspects of public display: vestments, sacred vessels, pictures, interior decoration, sculpture and architecture, as witnessed by his rebuilding of Westminster Abbey (completed 1269) and his work on his residences, for example Westminster Palace or Clarendon. His love of books does not seem to have extended far beyond their bindings or illuminations. A moody, affectionate, excitable, energetic, thoughtful and devout man, Henry was unfortunate that his virtues were unheroic and his weaknesses damaging. Yet, while there may have been better monarchs to rule England, there have been few better men.

In one aspect of his rule, Henry's youth was probably decisive. His father had enjoined his executors in 1216 to assist Henry and his brother Richard regain their inheritance. Henry's titles were king of England, lord of Ireland, duke of Normandy and Aquitaine and count of Anjou. Even as late as the 1230s, he styled himself in official documents, such as the statute of Merton (1236), 'king Henry son of King John'. Under the guidance of Peter des Roches and his father's former Poitevin cronies such as Peter de Mauley, Henry grew up with a firm sense of his inheritance and the inescapable obligation to reconquer those lordships lost under John (Normandy and Anjou) and during the Minority (Poitou in 1224). Henry saw himself as a European figure. If anything, he extended his continental interests by marrying, in 1236, Eleanor of Provence, giving him a link to the western Alpine passes, and, in the 1250s, bidding to establish his own family in place of the Hohenstaufen. In 1255, he accepted, on behalf of his second son, Edmund, the crown of southern Italy and Sicily. In 1257, his brother, Richard of Cornwall, bought himself the crown of Germany. For thirty years, first through military means, the invasion of Brittany in 1230 and Poitou in 1242, then by diplomacy, Henry tried to regain the Angevin provinces in France. These claims were only abandoned at the treaty of Paris (1259) when Henry needed a French alliance to extricate himself from the Sicilian mire and against pressing foes at home. The surviving possession of Gascony was defended at huge and often fruitless expense, a major priority as well as financial drain, and the scene of Henry's one successful military expedition in 1253-4.

However, Henry's cosmopolitan interests were not shared by his English magnates to whom he had to turn for assistance to achieve his ambitions. Almost none of the barons had any concern with lands in France and those who did, such as Richard Marshal (d.1233) and Simon de Montfort, were just as likely to be leading the opposition. This lack of sympathy with Henry's dearest schemes underpinned much of the mutual suspicion between king and noble. There was an even wider gulf separating royal concerns and those of the increasingly influential lesser baronage, knights and shire gentry, whose anxieties probably lie behind the repeated refusal of assemblies in the 1240s and 1250s to taxation. While Henry surrounded himself with foreigners speaking southern French (*langue d'oc*) and dreamt of an Angevin empire stretching across France to Germany, Italy and the Mediterrean, his subjects saw no further than the Channel. In 1258 the Provisions of Oxford were circulated to the shires in Latin, French — and English.

Such tensions were exacerbated by Henry's penchant for advisers and favourites from southern France who were seen as either imposing alien rule or syphoning off decreasingly available royal patronage. Between 1232 and 1234, the government was run by Peter des Roches. In the years after his marriage in 1236, Henry welcomed his wife's uncles from Savoy: in 1236-7, William, bishop-elect of Valence was prominent at court; Peter of Savoy became lord of Richmond in 1240 and remained a major figure at court for two decades; in 1241, Boniface of Savoy was appointed archbishop of Canterbury. With them came other Savoyards: Peter d'Aigueblanche, given the see of Hereford in 1239; or Henry de Susa, the celebrated canon lawyer, better known as Hostiensis, who was the king's proctor in ecclesiastical cases until 1243. Such men were not only useful in Henry's continental diplomacy, but provided loyal service in England as magnate and official factions on whose loyalty the king could rely. They also had the advantage, perhaps, of being more congenial to the king, who seems to have a liking, again possibly dating from childhood, for Occitans (people from southern France). In 1247, Henry welcomed his Lusignan half-brothers, sons of his mother Isabelle, who had married, as her second husband in 1220, Hugh de Lusignan. They were showered with lucrative favour: William of Valence was given the heiress to the earldom of Pembroke; Aymer received the see of Winchester, one of the richest in the kingdom; Guy and Geoffrey were richly provided for.

This policy of promoting foreigners aroused widespread dismay. Many, lay and clerical, saw it as proof that the king, by depriving natives and prefering aliens, was intent on imposing absolutist tyranny. Henry was accused of having a distorted — *i.e.* selfish — view of national priorities. This feeling was most keenly voiced by clergy who associated it with Henry's willingness to allow the pope to interfere in church appointments and, most worrying to the comfortably beneficed or cosily cloistered, to levy church taxes. If anything, Henry was being rather conservative. He saw government in terms of pursuing his and his family's rights. His lands were possesssions to be ruled fairly to serve his ends. Kingship was personal, even if elevated by doctrines at once theocratic and Roman. Ruling was nobody else's business. Ideas of power being derived from the community, that there was a test of justice beyond his own or that his lands

constituted a unitary state would have had little meaning for
Henry, not least because they had little practical reality. Ironically, this dislocation between Henry's cosmopolitan, conservative, pesonal kingship and the concerns of a widening political
nation did more than anything to implant such ideas into English politics. Henry's internationlism was a powerful force in
developing English national identity. Henry had no intention of
subverting his own realm, although his failure to communicate
and gain the approval of his magnates and their vassals almost
destroyed his regime. Henry's failings were less tyrannical than
imaginative.

Unlike other child-kings, Richard II or Henry VI, Henry III
was an effective monarch for a quarter of a century. Although
the Poitevin *coup* of 1232, which released Henry from the tute-
lage of Hubert de Burgh and marked his political emancipation,
was unsustainable in the face of united baronial and episcopal
opposition, there was no return to limited monarchy. From 1234,
Henry was master of the government. Away from high politics,
he restored royal administration. Despite his public pronouncements, he wisely left baronial adminstration of their affairs
alone, concentrating on enforcing royal rights, through the
reform of the Exchequer, scrutiny of sheriffs, increased regularity of judicial eyres, and use of the central courts at Westminster.
A sign of Henry's refusal to challenge the maladminstration of
the magnates in the localities is found in the wave of complaints
against baronial officials which emerged in 1258-9. By 1250,
Henry was solvent and at peace, he (or rather his cleverer and
more dynamic brother Richard) had reformed the coinage and
he was even salting away a considerable fortune in gold preparatory to going on crusade.

There had been difficulties with the barons over policy, the
appointment of officials, and taxation. Despite regular meetings
of what came to be called parliaments, in 1242, 1244, 1248, 1252,
1255 and 1257 lay subsidies were refused. Anger over their exclusion from administration and policy-making led to baronial
schemes for controlling the crown such as the 'Paper' Constitution of 1244. However, the recovery of royal government since
1232 was real, significant and unchallenged. But Henry's
manipulation of his magnates was less effective than his

exploitation of his rights. Henry was not a particularly good soldier. His campaigns in France in 1230 and 1242 had been fiascos; his expeditions to Wales hardly decisive. That he could maintain his authority being so militarily limp says much for the efficiency of his bureaucracy. However, relations with many of the nobles were poor or equivocal and his handling of the church vitiated by his alliance with the papacy with whose fiscal demands he generally concurred.

Three things led to the temporary collapse of Henry's power in 1258: foreign policy; finance; and the Lusignans. Maintaining Gascony was massively expensive, as were the campaigns there in 1253-4 and in Wales in 1257. The need to pay for these expeditons in the absence of lay subsisdies forced royal officials to exert greater pressure on the localities, already burdened by poor harvests. The Sicilian business seemed to encapsulate Henry's faults as a ruler: lack of consultation; subservience to the pope; wild fantasies of international power; and financial idiocy. The agreement called for Henry to provide, as a sort of entry fee, over £90,000. Although Henry hoped this would come from the church, there was the cost of the actual campaign to conquer Sicily. The idea may not have been absurd: indeed one of Henry's brothers-in-law, Charles of Anjou, achieved in the 1260s precisely what Henry had hoped for in the 1250s. But the commitment had been made without any consultation of those on whom the burden of sustaining the enterprise would fall. In addition, Henry was in the undignified position of promising to go on three crusades at once: to Palestine (according to his vow of 1250); North Africa (with the king of Castile); and Sicily (elevated by the pope to crusade status to ease funding and recruitment). Perhaps typically, he went on none.

The Sicilian obligation came at precisely the moment Henry was increasingly strapped for cash. This had a direct political effect. Some of his magnates were his creditors. If the king wanted subsidies he had to agree to greater baronial involvement in government. Traditionally, kings bought support by patronage, but Henry's policy was here myopic and provocative. In the 1250s, the land available to the king to give out to his nobles was severely limited, yet he continued to shower the Lusignans with whatever was available, to the fury of those, like Simon de

Montfort, who regarded their own claims to a place at the trough as superior. Equally, if not more damaging, was the riotous and rapacious behaviour of the Lusignans themselves and Henry's willingness to protect them even to the point of denying justice to those who entered pleas against them. Such actions held strong echoes of John's reign. As a sign of Henry's failure to manage his barons and the essential factionalism, rather than nationalism, that lay behind the baronial coup of 1258, among the seven who banded together against the king in April 1258 were Peter of Savoy and Simon de Montfort, both aliens who had done well out of the king — but not as well as the threatening Lusignans.

The reform programme known as the Provisions of Oxford, devised between 1258 and 1259 at parliaments at Oxford and Westminster, effectively placed the crown into commission. Policy and offical appointments were to be conducted by a standing council, regularly answerable to parliaments. Grievances of knights and gentry were to be met in a new general eyre which ostensibly was to investigate baronial as well as royal administration. Affecting to solve the problems left outstanding in *Magna Carta*, the Provisions solved little. Control of the king lay at the heart of the scheme, a matter of authority not law. By skilful use of a loyal bureaucracy and playing off baronial factions, Henry easily outmanoeuvred the reformers, a success which should not be overlooked in assessing his political ability. By 1261 he was back in power. In the unrest of 1263-4, especially after the Mise of Amiens vindicated his position, the king could even appear as the best guarantor of justice against the hotheaded self-interested rebels. But whatever the failings of Montfort and his allies, without Henry's duplicity, misjudgements and mismanagement of the 1250s, there would have been no need for such a conflict.

The outcome was settled by force of arms. In May 1264, Henry was unexpectedly defeated at Lewes and captured. In some senses this marked the end of his rule. Montfort's prisoner, he played no part in the royalist victory in 1265, narrowly avoiding being killed by friendly troops at Evesham. Thereafter his son, Edward, and his friends increasingly controlled events. But the final settlement, enshrined in the Dictum of Kenilworth

(1266) and the Statute of Marlborough (1267) owed not a little to Henry's careful handling of his opponents in 1260-3. Whilst rejecting any control of the prerogative, Henry nonetheless had not closed the door on judicial changes directed especially at answering the grievances of the wider political nation. Henry was always suspicious of baronial hegemony: now he was quite happy to assert royal justice as the defence of the commuity against the rapacity of men like Simon de Montfort.

Henry's achievement was mixed. To allow the restoration of the royal prerogative in the 1230s and 1240s, he was prepared to loosen the hold on baronial power in the localities in return for an extension of royal authority elsewhere. Yet, from Henry III's reign, the Common Law administered and protected by royal judges and royal courts became the medium through which Englishmen perceived — often wrongly — their rights and liberties. Despite the fine words of 1258-9, it was the crown not the barons which summoned the new political classes to redress the self-interested factionalism of the old. Henry's personal rule had ended in bloody civil war and near-deposition. To survive, Henry had abandoned, in 1259, all his cherished hopes of recovering his birthright in France. The victory of 1265-7 established the undisputed authority of the crown, if not the person of the king, for the next three and a half centuries, in some part the result of Henry's fixed dermination not to compromise the royal prerogative, even when it seemed possible, an attitude in marked contrast to the vacillating caprice of his son, Edward. Both Matthew Paris and Dante, who had little else in common, characterised Henry III as 'simple'. The legend underestimates the fact.

More widely, Henry III instituted a new image of monarchy, one deliberately theatrical, associated with gorgeous public ceremonies, surrounded not by the trappings of the hunt or battlefield but the paraphenalia of quasi-ecclesiatical ritual. Although plotting a continental future, Henry was devoted to English saints. He called his sons after two of them, Edward and Edmund. His special concern was the building of the new shrine of Edward the Confessor. The king damned for corrupting his realm with aliens made being English respectable. Although kings of England held French ambitions for another three centuries, Henry III's reign marked the parting of the ways.

Henceforward, the kings of England were English rather than
Frenchmen or men of princely lineage for whom the kingdom
was just one part of their accidental but legitimate inheritance.
Before 1259, such a position would have been unthinkable, not
least to Henry himself.

Henry's final years witnessed increasing infirmity. Even in his
son's absence on crusade, Henry does not seem to have given the
lead. Seriously ill for much of the time, in April 1271 the council
emphasised his decline by restricting his access to his revenues to
6/8d a day pocket money. He was still trundled about to symbolise authority, but he played little active part in affairs. His death,
in November 1272, severed a link with a distant and now foreign
past. As a boy, Henry had been protected by William Marshal
who, when a child, had played games with King Stephen, grandson of the Conqueror. Almost as a requiem for an age, Henry
III's body went to Westminster Abbey, his new national shrine.
But his heart went to lie beside his mother, his uncle and his
grandfather, at Fontevrault, in Anjou.

D. Carpenter, 'The personal rule of Henry III', *Speculum*, 1985.
F. M. Powicke, *Henry III and the Lord Edward*, 1947.

GUALA BICCHIERI (*d*.1227), cardinal priest of St
Martin, was papal legate to England from May 1216 to November 1218, a period crucial for the survival of the Angevin
dynasty. One of Innocent III's inner circle of advisers, Guala was
effectively head of the church in England as the pope's agent. His
role became immeasurably more important on the death of King
John in October 1216 in the midst of civil war. Since 1213, John
had been a papal vassal, England a papal fief. With John dead,
Guala, whose name headed John's chosen executors, immediately presided over the coronation of the young Henry III
which was preceded by the young king's homage to the legate for
his kingdom. Although leaving routine administration to the
regent, William Marshal, and Peter des Roches, bishop of
Winchester, Guala, representating the king's temporal as well as
spiritual overlord, lent legitimacy and active support to the
regime, whose plight was further endangered by the invasion of
Louis of France. In the winter of 1216-17, with the approval of

the new pope, Honorius III, Guala turned the royalist cause into a crusade, allowing supporters of the king the same privileges and indulgences as those who fought the infidel. At the very least this boosted morale and gave waverers an incentive and a justification for throwing in their lot with the king's party. In the aftermath of the civil war, Guala, keeping out of factious politics, avoided vindictiveness, although he selectively disciplined certain clerical rebel sympathisers. Nonetheless, he found his influence over ecclesiastical patronage useful in rewarding members of his household, including a number of his nephews, while at the same time disapproving of indigenous pluralists. In 1218, however, the return of fellow cardinal Archbishop Stephen Langton compromised Guala's position and he was allowed to resign his legation. Guala's role in helping save Henry III was one of the clearest demonstrations of effective papal monarchy in the Middle Ages. His achievement was recalled with admiration fifty years later when in 1264 a successor, Cardinal Gui Foulquois, was trying to gain entry to a kingdom once more in the hands of rebels.

HUBERT DE BURGH (*d*.1243; Justiciar of England 1215-32) was one of the most powerful royal ministers of the thirteenth century, dominating government from 1219 until his fall in 1232, a period when, it was said by a contemporary chronicler, 'he lacked nothing of royal power save the dignity of a royal diadem'. Yet Hubert's career was founded on a series of paradoxes. One of the richest men in the kingdom by 1232, he failed to establish a solid dynastic base. A noted commander and brave warrior, he could also read. A public advocate of the *Magna Carta* principles of protection against arbitrary judgements and disseisins, he used his office as the king's *alter ego* to feather his nest. Built up (not without his own connivance) as a champion of England and Englishness, his advancement owed much to his service in the continental interests of his Angevin masters. One of the most authoritarian of justiciars, he lacked the legal training or experience of his predecessors. In his hands the power of his office had never been greater; after his fall, it rapidly disappeared from English government.

Hubert belonged to a Norfolk gentry family. His elder brother served Prince John in Ireland in 1185. In the mid-1190s, Hubert was himself attached to the prince's household, serving as chamberlain by 1198. After John's accession, Hubert continued as chamberlain to the king's household until 1205, amassing the fruits of royal service, including numerous sheriffdoms and the custody of castles, such as Windsor, Wallingford and Dunster. He was employed on diplomatic embassies to Portugal (1200) and Philip II of France (1203). Tangible proof of his standing is seen in 1201 when he received the wardenship of the Welsh Marches, three important castles in Gwent, the wardenship of the Cinque Ports and the custody of Dover castle. In 1202, he was transferred to helping John in France, becoming successively castellan of Falaise and Chinon. The famous story of Hubert's refusal to mutilate Arthur of Brittany, then in his keeping at Falaise, was certainly current in own lifetime, and may have been given to the chronicler Ralph of Coggeshall by Hubert himself, presumably to avoid implication in John's most notorious crime. The legend embodied in Shakespeare's *King John* was thus of contemporary manufacture. At Chinon, Hubert defended the castle heroically against the French months after the rest of Normandy and Anjou had been lost, his resistance ending with his being severely wounded and taken prisoner.

Hubert's captivity from 1205 to 1207 proved in the long term not to be as severe a setback as it appeared at the time. Although he lost most of what he had been granted since 1199, a lesson in royal gratitude and the fragility of his own fortune which was not lost on him, Hubert was equally not implicated in the worst excesses of John's rule. Even as sheriff of Lincolnshire from 1208, he operated through a deputy. Although by 1212 his holdings were assessed at fifty knights' fees, only in 1213 was he recalled to active royal service, as seneschal of Poitou, a potentially vital appointment in view of John's impending campaign in France. Whatever his administrative skills, it was as a soldier that Hubert was conspicuous. In the face of baronial opposition to the king in 1214-15, Hubert remained loyal. In some ways his position resembled that of William Marshal who had also been recalled to the colours in 1213: both were able to preserve a reputation for loyalty untarnished by association with tyranny. In Hubert's case this made him an acceptable compromise choice for king and barons as justiciar, which he was appointed at Runnymede at the same time as *Magna Carta* was sealed.

Hubert's justiciarship falls into distinct phases. During the civil war of 1215-17, the central administration, Exchequer and the exploitation of royal financial and judicial rights through sheriffs and eyres, over which the justiciar traditionally presided, ceased to function. Given wide authority in Kent, East Anglia and London, Hubert's role was primarily military. With the invasion of Louis of France, his defence of Dover was crucial, especially his refusal to surrender the castle on hearing of John's death. In May 1217, Hubert engineered the defeat of the relief French fleet off Sandwich, thereby convincing Louis to come to terms.

Between 1217 and 1219, Hubert's power was overshadowed by that of the regent, William Marshal, the papal legates, Guala and Pandulf, and his predecessor as justiciar and later fierce rival, the bishop of Winchester, Peter des Roches. Until the Marshal's death in 1219, Hubert was one of a group who acted to re-establish royal government through cooperation with the magnates according to the principles of *Magna Carta*, which was reissued, with Hubert's approval, in 1216 and 1217. To his rising eminence he probably owed his marriage in 1217 to Isabella, widow of Geoffrey de Mandeville, divorced first wife of King John and heiress of the earldom of Gloucester.

Hubert's ascent to political dominance began after the Marshal's death in 1219, when, as one of a triumvirate with the legate Pandulf and Peter des Roches, he assumed the day to day running of the government, symbolised by his custody of the Great Seal. This accretion of power was probably due to his perceived political moderation. Although conscious of having to restore royal rights, as justiciar he respected the need to proceed within limits acceptable to the majority of magnates. The gibe that this was government by the magnates for the magnates is not entirely misleading. He was quite prepared to repudiate the actions of John's government (in which, of course, Peter des Roches had figured prominently). Equally, as he still lacked a sizeable heritable patrimony, he had to conciliate to survive. Ironically, this insecurity which made him politcially acceptable to the baronial power-brokers also made Hubert socially suspect

in their eyes. Although originally coming from a background by
no means inferior to his predecessor but one, Geoffrey FitzPeter,
unlike him Hubert was regarded as a *novus homo*, a parvenu, a
man on the make. It was only in 1227 that he was created earl of
Kent and even then his estates barely survived his political fall
and his title died with him. It may also be the case that Hubert
was suspected because he was disliked. If the anecdotes about
him are remotely true, there may have been an unattractive edgi-
ness about his character which, combined with a degree of self-
righteousness and pride, leaves a rather unappealing impression.
Unfortunately, although personalities are the stuff of politics,
beyond outlines drawn by others they are irrecoverable.

The central task of the Minority administration was the
resumption of royal property and rights and the provision of
legal and political arbitration. As justiciar, Hubert was central
to these efforts. As his power grew, so that of the other triumvirs
declined until in 1221, with the support of Archbishop Langton
and the bishops, Hubert got Pandulf withdrawn by the pope and
Peter des Roches's guardianship of the young Henry III ended. A
final confrontation with former partisans of John, led by Falkes
de Bréauté, in 1223-4, culminating in the siege of Bedford, left
Hubert triumphant. He had also, in 1221, managed to net, as his
third and grandest wife, Margaret, eldest sister of Alexander II,
king of Scots.

Hubert's victory seemed complete. He had the ear of the
young king; eased Peter des Roches out of favour; and purged the
administration, Peter des Roches's son (or nephew) Peter des
Rivaux being sacked as senior clerk of the Wardobe. But the victory was won at a price. Although Bishop Peter spent most of
the next few years abroad, he had vowed revenge, a pursuit
which would attract the support of a number of other dissidents
of 1223-4, such as the earl of Chester. With the king's attainment
of majority in 1227, Hubert's political position became even
more narrowly based, a vulnerability tacitly acknowledged by
his appointment as justiciar for life in 1228.

The king's majority in 1227 shifted the priorities of government. Hitherto, the direction had been towards the restoration
of royal rights and income, but without a return to the authoritarian methods of John's reign. Politically, this had depended on

allowing baronial supporters of the regime much latitude, not least the justiciar himself. The effectiveness of Hubert's rule was haphazard, dependent upon shifting coalitions of self-interest and, as in 1221 and 1223-4, *ad hoc* victimisation of opponents. Financially, Hubert's rule was at least a partial success. From 1220, royal income accounted at the exchequer grew steadily, while expenditure remained more or less constant, at a modest level compared to the large amounts amassed and spent on the foreign and domestic wars of 1213-17. But in the 1220s, income was far less than it had been under John and did not allow for any expansive or aggressive policies which a new king might have in mind.

Politics and finance were inseparable. In 1225, in order to gain agreement to a fifteenth, Hubert consented to re-issuing *Magna Carta*. But such gestures could only work occasionally. More serious still for the justiciar was Henry III's own ambitions. Brought up by Peter des Roches with a clear sense of his continental inheritance and his lost legacy there, Henry was eager to attempt to win back his French lands. Hubert's administration had been unable to stop the conquest of Poitou in 1224. Worse the fiasco of the failed preparations for a Poitou campaign in 1229 were laid by the king squarely,and perhaps fairly, at Hubert's door. On top of the expense, Hubert, with the caution of the veteran of Chinon, who had seen war achieve little of benefit in a long career, may have thought the enterprise futile. The subsequent disastrous expedition to Brittany of 1230 did little for Hubert's reputation or his relations with the king. However, despite such problems, Hubert's fall was sudden and unexpected.

By 1232, with Peter des Roches back in England, Hubert lacked the depth of baronial or episcopal support that he had enjoyed a decade earlier. Langton had died in 1228 and some of the leading magnates — the earls of Chester, Cornwall and Pembroke — were either neutral or hostile. Politically his grip was loosening; his attempt to defeat the Welsh came to nothing and he failed to secure a subsidy at a great council in 1232. In the Spring of that year, the king appointed Peter des Rivaux treasurer of the household. Already there had been damaging attacks on Hubert's cherished marriage, on the grounds of consanguinity. But Hubert was an experienced player in the game of faction. In June and early July 1232 he seemed to have restored royal confidence in him, being appointed justiciar for Ireland and having the king confirm charters granted to him and his wife. But in July his enemies struck with accusations that Hubert was behind a series of coordinated attacks on papal tax collectors and Italian clergy in England. On 29 July, he was stripped of the justiciarship and, in the next few months, of his estates, title, treasure and liberty. Although the new government of Peter des Roches and Peter des Rivaux collapsed in 1234, for Hubert there was only the partial restoration of lands and title: office, favour and power were gone for ever.

Even in retirement, Hubert was occasionally harassed by the king, who was no doubt nervous of such an eminent political outcast. He might have been more nervous if he had known that, in a manner made familiar by twentieth century fallen ministers, Hubert had been telling his story, or parts of it, to the voracious consumer of anecdotes, Matthew Paris. Hubert cast himself in heroic mould, the defender of Dover and the victor of Sandwich. It is from Paris that comes an image of Hubert as a national hero, champion of 'England for the English'. There may have lain some truth behind this rehearsal of the chronicler's own prejudices. Foreign entanglements had almost cost Hubert his life in 1205; foreigners, Peter des Roches and Peter des Rivaux, had cost him his job in 1232. There may be substance to the allegations of incitement of the anti-Italian riots of 1231-2. But if Hubert was wary of 'aliens', it was for politics not sentiment. Factional rivalry and military conflict dictated Hubert's attitude. To see him as harbinger of nationalism is to view his career through a monocle of hindsight.

What is more certain is that Hubert's period in office revealed that the English political scene had changed significantly and, as it turned out, permanently. These changes led to greater insularity of attitude and personnel, but were hardly caused by them. The loss of Normandy, Anjou and Poitou severed the continental connection for all but the king's own relatives. This could lead to a dislocation of interests between an increasingly insular baronage and cosmopolitan kings. But this should not be exaggerated: Henry III, for all his continental longings, chose an

Anglo-Saxon saint as his patron and named his two surviving sons after Old English king-saints. More specificially, the consequent presence of the king more or less permanently in the realm had profound effects on politics and government. Simply put, the king was there to do his own business: there was less or no need for an *alter ego*. However, the justiciarship was decreasingly effective as an insititution anyway, because of the growing bureaucratic specialisation and departmental separation within the royal administration. Unlike in the twelfth century, it was inconceivable that one man could have the range of knowledge or time efficiently to oversee or control all the legal, financial and clerical activities of the king. The triumph of the written word and the keeping of records were causes and symptoms of these developments.

Hubert de Burgh transcended the changes because of the unique political circumstances of the long minority of Henry III. It would be harsh to condemn him as an anachronism. His personal behaviour may have included favouritism and peculation, although he failed to secure the dynastic patrimony he craved. But he seems to have recognised that the methods of Richard I and John were counterproductive for all except the narrow royalist interest. In his conduct of business, he appears to have taken seriously both the lessons of 1213-17 and the general principle which lay behind *Magna Carta*, that monarch and magnate, king and subject have to rule and be ruled by mutual interest, protection and security. Royal rights had to be asserted within a framework of consent and the support of the powerful. He proved as much after 1219; he learnt as much in 1232. *Magna Carta* of 1215 had been a failed expedient. By reissuing it three times, Hubert, the justiciar appointed at Runnymede, ensured the charter's permanence in English politics.

D. Carpenter, *The Minority of Henry III*, 1990.
D. Carpenter, 'The Fall of Hubert de Burgh', *Journal of British Studies*, xix, 1980.

PANDULF MASCA (*d*.1226) was an Italian papal official who, between 1219 and 1221, in the words of T. F. Tout, 'almost acted as king of England' and, unlike some who actually wore

the crown in this period, did so with considerable skill and success. A sub-deacon of the Roman church, Pandulf first came to
England in 1211 on an unsuccessful mission to negotiate an end
to the Interdict, earning notoriety and praise for apparently
resisting John's attempts at physical intimidation. Two years
later, in very different circumstances, Pandulf was back to
receive John's submission and cession of the kingdom to the
pope. From 1213 to 1215, Pandulf continued to act as a papal
agent in England, for some of the time under the Legate
Nicholas (1213-14). His reward, illustrating the new Angevin-
papal alliance, was his election to the see of Norwich in 1215. In
the same year he returned to Rome to attend the Lateran Council and resume work in the papal chamber. Although in the confidence of the new pope, Honorius III, with whom he may have
worked at the Curia, Pandulf never became a cardinal. When, in
1218, he was appointed to succeed the distinguished Cardinal
Guala as Legate to England, he had to rely on his personality,
ability and the full papal authority ('plenarium potestatem')
Honorius granted him in matters spiritual and temporal.

In the first few months as legate, Pandulf made such a good
impression that in April 1219 the dying regent, William Marshal,
commended the young Henry III to his guardianship, despite the
furious protestations of the king's tutor, Peter des Roches. After
the regent's death, a governing triumvirate emerged of the
legate, Peter des Roches and the justiciar, Hubert de Burgh.
Unlike Guala, Pandulf was an experienced administrator who
concerned himself closely in government. While consulting
meticulously with his colleagues, as legate and guardian of the
king he took the lead. It was his implementation of the papally
inspired policy of resumption of royal castles, lands and rights
and renewed control over local agents of the crown that gave the
Minority government its direction and objective. Under the slo-
gan Pandulf used to the justices of the bench in 1220 'royal
rights are to be preserved' and publically stated in repeated papal
bulls of 1219, 1220 and 1221, this policy provided the foundation upon which Angevin government could be rebuilt.

Pandulf was not shy in getting involved in specific cases, but
his activity was inevitably wide. He initiated talks leading to
peace with the Welsh and the 1220 truce with Scotland. To

underpin the campaign for restitution of the king's rights, he organised Henry III's second coronation in 1220 in a more orthodox ceremony than the hugger-mugger affair of 1216. Typical of his diplomatic treatment of colleagues, Pandulf allowed the sensitive Archbishop Langton to exercise his traditional right to crown the king. As legate, as well as controlling ecclesiastical patronage, Pandulf lent material support to the regime. Where lay taxation, such as the scutage of 1217 or the 1220 carucage, produced meagre sums, his profitable tax for the crusade allowed him to give loans to the government, thus, in D. Carpenter's words, becoming its paymaster as well as director.

By 1221, central authority was becoming more accepted; the policy of resumption was beginning to bear fruit and, especially important, royal income was at last rising substantially (the £8,000 raised in 1220 was £3,000 more than the previous year): and it never looked back. Politically, however, Pandulf's position in both church and state was becoming increasingly anomalous in the face of the growing authority of Langton and Hubert de Burgh, or so, at least, Langton on a visit to Rome seems to have persuaded the pope. On the archbishop's return to England in July 1221, Pandulf resigned, not to be replaced. Back in Rome in 1222, he was finally consecrated bishop of Norwich. His interest in English affairs remained to the end. In 1225, he was encouraging Hubert de Burgh in his handling of the rebels of 1223-4, urging him to ensure that 'the pride of the traitors does not ascend further than is expedient'. However, Pandulf did not meddle after his retirement. He was in no position to, as his authority had always been that of a representative, never wielded in his own right. He remained simply a bishop *in absentia*. In 1226 his body was brought to Norwich for burial in the cathedral he had never entered as bishop in life. Like so many of his contemporaries, Pandulf's career knew no nationalities. With his predecessor Guala, Pandulf, despite his relatively modest status, put into practice the rhetoric of papal monarchy as effectively as anyone in the Middle Ages. This may explain his relative neglect by champions of an insular reading of English history. It is ironic that so many of those who in these years stood between England and factional anarchy were not natives. But unlike many of the others, Pandulf earned the accolade of local praise: even Matthew Paris had a good word to say for him.

D. Carpenter, *The Minority of Henry III*, 1990.

ROGER OF WENDOVER (*d*.1236) was a monk of St. Alban's. He rose to be prior of the dependent cell at Belvoir but had to be removed in 1219 for financial mismanagement. Sometime after 1202, perhaps as late as 1231, he began writing a history from the Creation to his own day, the *Flores Historiarum (Flowers of History)*. Unoriginal to 1202, from then until he finished writing in 1234 Roger used no surviving chronicle. Unfortunately, he seemed to have relied heavily on his own imagination or gossip to fill the gap. The black reputation, almost gothic horror that surrounds the posthumous reputation of King John derives largely from Roger's account written a decade or so after the king's death. His anecdotes establishing the image of John as lecherous, idle and sadistic, as far as they can be checked, appear to have been invented. His picture of the young Henry III is more sympathetic, perhaps because royal policy was less destructive of church interests; perhaps because, in retrospect, anyone was better than John. Roger has Henry declare 'I prefer to be considered a stupid king rather than a cruel or tyrannical one'. Roger took his stand with the barons, and was virulent in opposition both to royal exactions and the intrusive authority of the pope (who had in 1215 supported the royalists). Roger's attitudes were partisan. His portrait of John, however, may accurately reflect what was said of the late king in the years after the civil war and the often uneasy minority of Henry III. Roger was, in fact, a dull storyteller, loading his tales with circumstantial evidence in a pedestrian literary style. His fame, and the currency of his stories, depend largely on his successor as chief historiographer at St. Alban's, Matthew Paris, who incorporated, edited and 'improved' Roger's account in his *Chronica majora*.

A. Gransden, *Historical Writing in England c.550-c.1307*, 1979.

EDMUND RICH OF ABINGDON (*c*.1170-1240; archbishop of Canterbury 1234-40; canonised 1246) provides an example of how the best men often made ineffective prelates, political failure nonetheless being a qualification for sainthood. Born near and educated at Oxford, Edmund's intense personal piety was fostered by his forceful mother, Mabel (his father having escaped into Eynsham Abbey). For the rest of his life Edmund wore a particularly painful hair-shirt. In 1192, Edmund went to Paris, whence he returned to teach the Quadrivium before turning to theology. At Oxford, Edmund gained a reputation as a popular preacher and teacher famed for the slickness of his expositions, some of which so defied logical explanation that they were ascribed to divine inspiration. Seemingly a model don, Edmund occasionally dozed off while teaching, a result, perhaps, of his inability to lie down to sleep at night because of his hair-shirt. In 1222, he abandoned lecturing on theology, allegedly because he found the fashionable disputation method of teaching and learning, by which pupils and masters orally exchanged competing arguments and texts in a combative search for truth, conducive to vanity. As canon and treasurer of Salisbury, Edmund displayed administrative skills. These, with his contacts with the royal family as a spiritual adviser to the king's sister, Eleanor and his achievements as a scholar recommended him as archbishop after Pope Gregory IX had rejected three other candidates. As a spiritual guide, Edmund set an impressive example; as a politician, he was handicapped by a tender conscience without the stomach for confrontation of his colleague Robert Grosseteste of Lincoln. After playing a pivotal eirenic role in the removal of Peter des Roches's government in 1234, Edmund suffered consistent disappointment and rebuff, both from the king and the pope. In 1236, he acquiesced in the decision of the council at Merton on bastardy although it ran counter to canon law; 1238 saw his impotent outrage at the marriage of Simon de Montfort to Princess Eleanor, in contradiction to her oath of chastity he had witnessed; the political crisis of 1238 exposed the loss of episcopal influence in the previous four years. Edmund resisted papal demands for taxation for the war against Frederick II and the scheme to reserve three hundred English benefices for papal appointment. This championing of the rights of the indigenous church won him the approval of Matthew Paris who composed a respectful biography of Edmund after his death. But Archbishop

Edmund ran aground on the shallows of detail. Unlike Grosseteste he failed to articulate clear principles and strategies. A sympathiser with the reforming attitudes of Langton, Edmund
lacked the skill to assert ecclesiastical interests in the secular
world or implement change within the church. In 1237, as a
recognition of his exposed weakness, a papal legate, Otto, was
appointed to pursue both papal interests and church reform.
Edmund's position was severely compromised. An unsuccessful
appeal to the papacy in 1237 over the rights of Canterbury was
followed by continued failure to resolve his conflict with the
monks of Canterbury over a clutch of vested interests, including
his foundation of a house of secular canons at Maidstone. In
1240, he withdrew again, ostensibly to visit the pope. Seeking
the shades of Becket and Langton at Pontigny, he died at nearby
Soissy In death, his personal qualities soon obscuring his public
failure, Edmund became an ideal subject for canonisation by a
papacy eager to claim martyrs for ecclesiastical rights. Miracles
of healing soon began to be ascribed to him, his tomb becoming
a place of veneration. In 1246 he became the last archbishop of
Canterbury to be canonised. His cult was immediately popular,
especially among Englishmen, including those who thwarted
him in life such as Henry III, who visited the shrine in 1254.
Richard of Cornwall, Edmund's ally in 1238, was especially
devoted, visiting Edmund's shrine in 1247 and naming his second
son after him. Such was the ubiquitous appeal of the dead archbishop that he was admired by royalists and rebels alike in the
1260s, including Simon de Montfort whose marriage Edmund
had so vigorously opposed. His shrine continued to attract English pilgrims, including Edward I in 1286. In England the cult
was maintained at Catesby, in Northamptonshire, a house reputedly founded by Edmund for his equally ascetic sisters. Edmund
conformed in aspiration to the academic reforming prelates of
the age of Innocent III, scholars, administrators, spiritual advisers and statesmen. Although failing to put these ideals into
effective practice, Edmund's personality left its mark on contemporaries. He combined scholarship with piety: the mystical *Mirror of the Holy Church* has been ascribed to him. He believed in
personal conversion and the supremacy of private conscience: an
unlikely archbishop and an unlikely saint. His most lasting

memorial is appropriately where he achieved most unalloyed renown, in the community of students and scholars named after him at Oxford, St. Edmund Hall.

C. H. Lawrence, *Edmund of Abingdon*, 1960.

ELIAS OF DEREHAM (*fl.*1188-*d.*1245) presided over the building of the new Salisbury Cathedral for the first twenty-five years of its construction, 1220-45. A secular clerk, later rector of Melton Mowbray and Harrow and canon of Salisbury and Wells, he seems to have begun his career in East Anglia as a protégé of Hubert Walter in the 1180s. This connection gave him his introduction to royal administration and the world of ecclesiastical and high politics. He was an executor of the wills of Hubert Walter himself (1205); Walter's successor as archbishop of Canterbury, Stephen Langton (1228); and Peter des Roches, bishop of Winchester and a former justiciar (1238). He acted as steward of the archiepiscopal estates under both Walter and Langton and may have acted as the archbishop's attorney in a suit in the king's courts in 1204. In 1215, he was present at the signing of *Magna Carta* at Runnymede, being appointed one of the commissioners to distribute copies of the charter. During the Interdict and later he was associated with Bishop Jocelyn of Bath (1206-42), mentioned as his steward in 1229. But his particular administrative skills lay, apparently, in art, architecture and design. His Canterbury connection was underlined in 1220 when he played a leading role ('by counsel and invention' says Matthew Paris) in the construction of a new shrine to receive the body of Thomas Becket and again in 1237 when he advised Archbishop Rich on a suitable site for his proposed college of secular canons. Elias seems to have been eclectic in his pursuits. Apart from supervising buildings for kings and bishops, in 1238 he was responsible for constructing a marble tomb for Henry III's sister, Joan, queen of Scotland and in 1244 he was given £20 by the king to make a hanging pyx for the High Altar at Salisbury. His main occupation in his later years, as far as his career has left traces in surviving records, was in connection with the King's Works and Salisbury Cathedral. In the 1230s, he was in charge of work for the king at Winchester and Clarendon. At

Salisbury, his position was unique in medieval England. The new cathedral was the only one to be built on a green field site, initially away even from a major settlement. Although it is unlikely that Elias was what would today be called an architect, it is possible that the theoretically satisfying but architecturally strained homogenous proportions of Salisbury were his contribution. In a cosmographical St. Alban's manuscript, his interest in theories of proportion is attested by a diagram of the world being labelled 'according to Master Eyas de Derham'. At Salisbury, he would have supervised the building of the Lady chapel (completed 1225) and the east arm of the church (completed by 1237). Presumably to be near his work, Elias built himself a house in the Close (known as Leadenhall). From what survives of his interests, he appears something of a dilettante, an amateur artist or decorator, a designer whose administrative skills allowed him to try his hand at architecture. Alternatively, he was simply another well-connected, intellectually alert civil servant who specialised in buildings and furnishing buildings not as a creator but as an administrator. Perhaps personal taste determined the projects he managed, but it may have been his efficiency and experience in organising men, materials and money not his taste, let alone genius, that secured him his position.

J. Harvey, *English Mediaeval Architects*, 1987.

RICHARD, EARL OF CORNWALL (1209-72; king of the Romans 1257-72) was the second son of King John and younger brother of Henry III. His career exemplifies the ambition and reality of Angevin rule in the mid-thirteenth century. Claimant to the county of Poitou (1225), the duchy of Gascony (1242-3) and the Holy Roman Empire (1257-72), and repeatedly refusing to accept the papally-proffered title of king of Sicily, by contrast Richard's material power rested on his estates in the Thames valley and East Anglia, his earldom of Cornwall, his control of the Cornish tin mining industry and his position in the English baronage and court. Angevin dreams remained international: Richard himself was an active crusader. Angevin authority, however, rested on control of England. Richard's failure to give

Richard of Cornwall agreeing a treaty
with Nazir Lord of Kerak
(From Matthew Paris's Chronica Majora)

substance to his foreign aspirations underlined this withdrawal
to insular, national preoccupations. Few individuals more neatly
illustrate how the rulers of England, in spite of themselves,
became English monarchs. Richard of Cornwall even notoriously spoke good English.

Richard was a tremendous swell, a lover of ceremonies, titles,
pomp, luxury, pretty women and fine clothes: even in prison he
insisted on wearing scarlet robes. But he lacked one essential element to complete the perfect image of what he spent his life
being, a king-in-waiting. A puny child, Richard's poor physique
denied him a proper training in arms. For all his pride and tenacity in defending or asserting his rights, Richard was a talker, not
a fighter. Never was this better displayed than on his crusade of
1240-1. No battles were fought, still less victories achieved. The
treaty Richard negotiated with the sultan of Cairo was less

realistic than that signed the year before with the sultan of Damascus by the count of Champagne. Yet Richard's reputation soared at what contemporaries saw as his success, hardly surprising as he handled his own publicity. The story of his triumphs depended on his own newsletter and carefully targeted reminiscences with well-placed chroniclers, such as Matthew Paris. The whole exercise was a masterpiece of self-promotion. There was another, equally characteristic side to Richard's crusade. He secured the release of French prisoners and the burial of Christian soldiers killed in a rout at Gaza in 1239. Gestures and diplomacy, rather than blood and iron, won for Richard the admiration of western chivalry, and more. At a very tricky moment at Taillebourg in 1242, Richard managed by negotiation to extricate his brother from an untenable military position because the French were grateful at his having secured the release of their compatriots the year before.

From 1215 until 1223, Richard was educated at Corfe Castle by an obscure royalist backwoodsman, Roger d'Acastre, under the aegis of the influential Poitevin Peter de Mauley. Roger may not have been the ideal gentleman scholar to act as Richard's tutor. Much of the tuition may have been unfashionably in English and Richard never developed an interest in any of the arts, apart from the sartorial, either directly or as a patron. His concern in the construction of his religious foundations, notably at Hailes in Gloucestershire, did not stretch beyond the financial and pious. The contrast with his brother Henry, the refined mastermind of Westminster Abbey, is plain. What Richard's education does seem to have provided — or at least not impeded — was an excellent head for finance and business acumen, what would now be called management skills, *i.e.* the ability to deal with people, to strike bargains, to achieve through negotiation and personal contact simultaneous public consensus and private advantage.

The position of the king's brother was rarely enviable. Although in the hundred and fifty years before Henry III's accession, two out of seven kings had succeeded brothers, the awkward, hand-to-mouth experiences of Henry I or John before ascending the throne were less than encouraging precedents. For more than twenty years, until 1239, Richard was the heir presumptive during which time his relations with the king were often strained. Ironically, after the birth of the future Edward I, Richard's position at court was increasingly important, his influence more consistent and significant. Before 1239, Richard could be seen by some as a potential leader of disaffected barons and, on more than one occasion, acted as such, in 1233 and 1238, for example. Thereafter, his role was that of a mediator in crises whose loyalties were hardly in doubt. Oddly, and perhaps typical of Henry III, the barometer of Richard's loyalty was the grants he received rather than the services he performed. His loyalty was purchased at a high price, which, however, for the king was worth it.

Richard's public career began in 1225 when he was knighted and sent as figurehead of a successful campaign to secure continued Angevin overlordship, if not much practical control, over Gascony. In 1225, Richard was granted Cornwall, a traditional holding for cadets of the royal line since the Conquest: William I's brother Robert of Mortain; Reginald, bastard son of Henry I; and King John in the 1190s all held Cornwall. Although created earl of Cornwall in 1227, Richard only received his lands in fee (*i.e.* with tenure rather than at the king's pleasure) on his marriage in 1231. His first marriage points to Richard's disaffection with his brother, whom he did not consult. Isabel Marshal (*d*.1240) was the sister of the leader of baronial opposition to the regime of Hubert de Burgh. Richard spent the next decade running with the foxes of magnate discontent opposition and hunting with the hounds of royal favourites. On three occasions, 1227, 1233 and 1238, he challenged his brother, only to be bought off with lavish grants. As Richard's biographer, Denholm-Young put it, 'Richard never quarrelled with Henry without coming away a richer man'.

The years around 1240 were pivotal in Richard's career. The death of his first wife in 1240 loosened ties with the traditional opponents to royal authority, while his crusade won him an international fame and cosmopolitan contacts, a position reinforced by his friendship with the Emperor Frederick II and his second marriage to Sanchia of Provence (*d*.1262), sister to Henry III's wife Eleanor. He was provided with an income granted by the pope, from the money paid by those who had taken the

Cross but had redeemed their vows for cash rather than actually going on crusade. In England, Richard's importance was increasing. Politically, his contacts with the higher nobility and his proximity and influence over the king made him a ubiquitous arbiter of potentially damaging disputes between nobles and with the crown. In this capacity Richard acted between Simon de Montfort and Gilbert Marshal, both his brothers-in-law, and the king in 1239; in 1244 he negotiated a treaty with Scotland and sat on the committee to investigate baronial grievances against the crown in 1244; in the 1250s he acted as ambassador to France and settled disputes between Londoners and Westminster Abbey. In 1252, he determined the amount of Simon de Montfort's expenses when lieutenant in Gascony; in 1260 he mediated between the earl of Gloucester and the Lord Edward and the king; and in 1267 and 1270 he handed down awards to resolve the grievances of the new earl of Gloucester, especially with the Lord Edward. As a troubleshooter, Richard clearly set great store by his ability. What evidence we have, for example on the 1270 award, suggests that others did not share his self-esteem, Earl Gilbert forcefully exposing Richard's award as one-sided and short-sighted. Given the repeated difficulties faced by the court during Henry's reign, Richard's political and legal skills may have been exaggerated, but at least they appeared better than Henry's.

Richard was almost a sort of vice-king. He fought for his brother in Brittany in 1230; in Poitou in 1242-3 and against the barons in 1263-4. He was regent in 1253-4, 1264 and, *de facto*, 1270-72. At other times, in the words of the royalist chronicler Thomas Wykes, 'on his nod hung all the business of the realm'. Richard had little consistent political philosophy, unlike his verbose brother who was forever lauding the power of kingship. Some saw Richard as a trickster, a man who would do anything for the right price. In March 1246, he was strongly opposed to papal demands on the English church. By July he had completely changed his mind, adopting a pro-papal stance. Between these dates he had received the papal grant of crusade vow redemptions. Nonetheless, Richard's influence lent an element of cohesion to English politics and it is perhaps significant that the two major disasters for Henry III's regime, the Sicilian Business and the Provisions of Oxford, did not involve Richard, the first because he opposed the scheme from the start; the latter because he was out of the country. His reaction to the papal invitation to conquer Sicily suggests a man of realism: 'You might as well say: I will sell or give you the moon; go up and take it'.

What set Richard apart from other magnates, besides his birth, was his great wealth and the financial role which that allowed him to play. In addition to his very extensive estates centred on Cornwall, Wallingford, Berkhampstead and Eye, he enjoyed the monopoly on Cornish tin (the Stannaries) which alone brought in between 1,000 and 3,000 marks a year, the cash redemption of crusade vows and tallages from the Jews. Such were his resources that he was able to retain many of his noble followers on crusade. Between 1240 and 1271, he lent the crown just under £40,000. In 1256-7, he spent 28,000 marks buying the votes of three German electors. Most spectacularly, in 1247, he undertook the farm of the royal Mint for twelve years, during which time coinage worth £1 million was produced, and organised the first complete recoinage since 1180. For a capital outlay of 10,000 marks, Richard made profits of perhaps £20,000. The recoinage was perhaps Richard's most constructive act in government. At times, it appeared that Richard's finances and those of the state were synonymous, recognised in 1271 when his own treasurer, Philip of Eye, became the king's Treasurer.

This Croesus had political ambitions. He wanted to become a king. So, in keeping with the grandeur of his brother's foreign policy, in 1257 Richard bought himself one, the crown of Germany. For a few years it seemed possible that he would be able to persuade the pope to crown him emperor as well. In the event, although crowned king of the Romans (*i.e.* emperor-designate) at Aachen in May 1257, he was never more than king of the Rhineland and even that was largely honorific, his four brief visits (1257-9; 1260; 1262-3; 1268-9) having more ceremonial than political significance. It was through his German connections that in 1269 he married his third wife, Beatrice of Falkenburg (*d.*1277), like the other two a noted beauty.

After 1260, Richard saw that his imperial longings were as chimeric as his brother's Sicilian hopes had been. During the baronial wars of the 1260s, Richard, although again acting as mediator in trying to increase magnate support for the royalists, was a consistent advocate of his brother's cause. By 1264, he pushed for a military solution, although himself no warrior. After the surprise defeat of the royalists at Lewes, he was captured in a nearby windmill attempting to make good his escape. From May 1264 until September 1265 he was held in comfortable captivity. Thereafter, while profiting from grants of land from the disinherited rebels, he worked for compromise, but power had shifted to the next generation, to the Lord Edward and Richard's own son Henry, surnamed 'of Almain' in deference to his father's German crown. Only when Edward and Henry departed on crusade in 1270, did Richard again emerge as a leading political figure, his brother by then having slid into the shadows of senility. Ironically, Richard predeceased his brother, dying in April 1272 four months after a debilitating stroke. His passing, followed in November by Henry III, marks an epoch in English political history. They were the last of the Angevins, whose ambitions were neither predominantly English nor British.

N. Denholm Young, *Richard of Cornwall*, 1947.

SIMON DE MONTFORT (*c*.1208-1265) is one of the most famous men in English history. Mistaken by Victorians as the founder of parliamentary government, Simon led the most concerted and radical attempt to control royal power and authority before the seventeenth century. For three months in 1263 and another fifteen in 1264-65, Simon ruled England ostensibly in the name of a programme of reform devised in 1258-9 which denied the free exercise of the royal prerogative, instead insisting on government by council, consent by parliament, accountable central and local administration, and justice equitable in recognising the interests and liberties of barons, knights, gentry, freemen and even peasants. Royalty was put into commission on behalf of the *communitas regni*, the community of the realm, led by barons but acting with regard to a wider political nation. Montfort's failure was personal, political and ideological. Later generations removed incompetent or malicious monarchs through deposition. His problem of limiting the authority of a sane, adult monarch was essentially the same faced by the Army and Parliament in 1648-9 when for the first time a solution was hit upon more revolutionary than that attempted by Simon de Montfort.

Simon was no plaster hero of liberty or constitutionalism. If, in Sir Maurice Powicke's words, he was a 'kind of saint', he was also 'a public nuisance'. Idealism was matched by avarice; conscience by harshness; piety by pride. He wore a hair-shirt, yet travelled in magnificence. By circumstance an adventurer and by instinct and ambition a ruler, he possessed adamantine principle and arrogant self-righteousness, a defender of liberties and a nepotist. Quick-witted, serious-minded, silver-tongued yet acerbic, his personality charmed, dazzled, confused, angered and frightened, his memory reviled by enemies and revered by pilgrims. For a generation after his arrival in England in 1230 a well-connected younger son with nothing to commend him but a famous name and a reputation as a good warrior, Simon scorched the political world of England and northern France in a career so dramatic, indeed improbable, that his violent and sordid end can almost appear classically tragic.

Simon de Montfort's father and namesake had a career every bit as remarkable as his son. The elder Simon (c.1170-1218), a cruel, pious man, had fought on the Fourth Crusade (1202-4) and in 1209 had assumed the leadership of the crusade against the Albigensians. With military command he ruled areas conquered from the heretics and their allies which he secured by a crushing victory at Muret (1213). Simon bore responsibility for the bestiality of the crusaders' treatment of opponents, heretics or Christians. In 1218, he met his death, crushed by a stone flung from a mangonel at the siege of Toulouse. Simon's connection with England was the part interest he had through his mother in the earldom of Leicester, a claim acknowledged in 1205/6 without any practical results. Such was Simon's fame that there were rumours that in 1210 or 1212 barons disaffected from King John thought of offering him the English crown. The younger Simon retained a keen and sometimes touchy loyalty to the memory of a father many of whose attitudes, abilities and ambitions he shared.

*Simon de Montfort's dismemberment
after the Battle of Evesham in 1265*
(From an early fourteenth century Rochester manuscript)

Young Simon's inheritance was crucial in forming his career. The third son of a famous father, he had close contacts throughout the highest reaches of the French nobility and church: both Louis IX and Eudes Rigaud, archbishop of Rouen were among his friends; but he had no patrimony of his own. His links with France and a ceaseless quest for patronage made Simon an unusual and often uncomfortable member of the English nobility. Unlike most mid-thirteenth century barons, Montfort could escape local political difficulties across the Channel and could, as with the county of Bigorre in the 1250s, seek estates outside England. In this international aspect, Simon and Henry III had more in common with each other than either had with the majority of the English baronage. However, until the last few years of his life, Simon never had the estates commensurate with his status and ambitions. Unmatched by financial stability, his political pretensions caused friction. The surprise is that, despite a consistent need for royal favour, Simon was able to be so much his own man. In that sense, Henry III only had himself to blame for creating and maintaining Montfort in power and influence, ultimately a fact not lost on the king. But, by skill and audacity, Simon forced himself into Henry's favour so far that he could not be removed without major disruption.

First arriving in England in 1230, Simon rapidly established himself as a prominent figure at Henry III's court. The young king, perhaps because of his experience with the litigious and dour native barons who ruled his youth, had a penchant for Frenchmen who shared his cosmopolitan outlook and whose political loyalties could be guaranteed. Successively he favoured Poitevin veterans of his father's reign, Savoyard relatives of his wife and his Lusignan half-brothers. Although Simon fitted this pattern, he retained his independence. Before joining Henry on the Breton campaign of 1230, he had earned fame as a soldier, possibly in Languedoc in 1228-9. Simon also sought his own alliances in the English nobility as claimant to the earldom of Leicester, to which end he attracted the patronage of the aged Ranulf of Chester, premier baron in England. Not the least of Simon's skills was that of impressing people.

In the 1230s, Montfort exerted powerful influence over King Henry, their relationship providing one of the most unusual political and personal confrontations in English history. Henry moved from affection to jealousy to suspicion to hatred, while Simon affected cooler emotions. Unafraid to exploit the king's friendship for gain, Simon frequently displayed open disdain and contempt for Henry, making their contacts increasingly uneasy. Yet they were yoked together by Simon's ambition and Henry's position as the man who could best further them. The final scene of their relationship, at Evesham in 1265, when Henry, captive and in borrowed armour, was forced into the field to see Simon butchered by the troops of his own son and Montfort's godson, Edward, is too dramatic for fiction.

Tangible rewards held Simon at the English court. In 1231, he was given the honour of Leicester. Rising in influence, by 1236-7 he was thought to be a dominant voice in royal counsels. In 1238, his prospects were transformed by his hasty marriage to the king's strong-minded sister, Eleanor (1215-75). She brought Simon lands (including her dowry from her first marriage to William Marshal (d.1231), loyalty and status. In 1239, Simon was invested with the earldom of Leicester. The marriage was a success. They had five sons and a daughter and Eleanor pursued their mutual interests with a vigour equalling her husband's. The liaison was not without scandal. Eleanor had taken vows of chastity after the death of her first husband and it was rumoured that Simon had seduced her before the wedding, which was conducted almost in secret.

By agreeing to the marriage, King Henry ensured his new brother-in-law a central role in English politics, an opportunity Simon grasped with enthusiasm. He fought alongside Henry in Poitou in 1242 and Wales in 1245. In 1248-52, he governed Gascony effectively if controversially. In 1253-4, he assisted the king in his successful campaign there. With his contacts at the French court, Simon was repeatedly used in diplomatic missions, especially in the negotiations preparatory to the Treaty of Paris (1259) in which his wife, as a child of King John, had a direct stake. In domestic politics, until the late 1250s, Simon tended to take the curial side: that was where the rewards in land, fees, pensions, wardships *etc.* came from. Out of self-interest, Montfort did not oppose Henry III's personal rule.

However, Simon's loyalty was neither without tension nor unconditional. In 1239, in a row over Simon's use of the king's name to borrow money, the king was only narrowly dissuaded from throwing him into the Tower. As it was the Montforts went into exile. In 1242, after the fiasco at Saintes, Simon's exasperation at Henry's amoebic military style, boiled over, telling the king he should be locked up, a gibe which Henry stored in bitterness for twenty years. In 1252, Simon was arraigned for being both too harsh and too extravagant in Gascony. Once again the dispute took a nasty personal turn, Henry accusing Montfort of being a traitor to which the earl replied by questioning the king's credentials as a Christian.

Another source of dispute which finally destroyed Simon's allegiance to Henry III was financial. As a parvenu with four healthy sons, Simon was desperate to establish a substantial patrimony of his own to endow his dynasty. Apart from Leicester, much of his property was not held in fee (i.e. heritable) and his wife's was primarily dower lands which would leave family control on her death. As the 1240s and 1250s progressed, Simon had three central grievances. First, the king owed him money; secondly, specifically, Eleanor was not receiving her due from her dower lands, in 1259 Simon claiming that the arrears amounted to over 36,000 marks; and thirdly the king refused to convert grants of money and tenancies into heritable lands. The importance of these considerations to Simon was demonstrated by the way Henry bought his support with grants and the manner in which Montfort exploited his political position in 1259-61 and 1263-5 to amass a vast patrimony. With Simon, private gain always walked beside public policy. The two combined to dictate resistance to the king in the late 1250s when Henry's concentration of patronage on the Lusignans aroused Simon's indignation. Ironically, in 1264-5, his concentration on his own nearest relatives lost him baronial support just as surely as Henry's identical policy had in 1258.

Away from England, Simon acquired a stature which suggests qualities beyond those of an adept featherer of his own nest. Like his father, he was a crusader, taking the cross twice, in 1236 and 1247, and visiting the Holy Land in 1240-1. One unexpected result was the request in June 1241 by the 'barons, knights and citizens' of the commune of Acre to the Emperor Frederick II to appoint Simon as governor of the kingdom of Jerusalem. In 1253, the French nobility offered Simon the stewardship of France in the continued absence of Louis IX in Palestine, ostensibly because of his father's reputation and the earl's own love of France and French blood. During the first five years of the so-called baronial reform movement, 1258-63, its supposed champion spent half his time across the Channel. This made his political choices easier, as he did not have to stay in England to cope with their consequences or compromise. It is equally significant that in the final two years of his life, he only visited the land of his birth for a few days.

Simon de Montfort's adherence to the baronial confederacy of April 1258 which led to the Provisions of Oxford and the oath to uphold them in June was a turning point in his life. Although he had been driven into opposition by largely selfish motives concerning patronage and the fear of a military coup by the Lusignans, and continued to milk the reform movement and the king for material gain, his commitment to the reform programme was sincere. He took oaths seriously; he saw himself as religiously obligated to abide by the terms agreed and sworn at Oxford. To this oath, while never missing an opportunity to gain secular advantage, he held firm. The combination of principle and self-interest aroused cynicism in observers and it is a measure of

Simon's own self-assurance that he was able to suppress in his own mind the inevitable contradictions. Just before the battle of Evesham, knowing he was doomed, he apparently turned on his son Henry: 'your presumption and the pride of your brothers has brought me to this end'. In fact, it was Simon's own presumption and pride that had permitted the excesses of his children.

The importance Simon attached to the oath of 1258 is of a part with his spiritual life. Simon was more than a mercenary bully with a sharp wit and ready sword. He numbered among his close friends and mentors Robert Grosseteste, one of the sternest moralists of the day, the Franciscan Adam Marsh, who was his spiritual counsellor, and the saintly Cantelupes, Walter and Thomas. Through them he was in touch both with the theology and learning of the nascent university of Oxford, but also the fresh religious emphasis on lay piety through confession and the practices of personal devotion. Central to both were conscience and asceticism. It was King Henry's lack of these that Simon hurled in his face in 1252. The language of his will of 1259 reveals a man acutely aware of the reality of sin. It is shot through with the remorse of a troubled conscience, the more convincing because private, hidden, like his hair-shirt. Simon was nothing if not thoughtful. He appreciated the importance of learning. He had his sons well educated: the eldest Henry actually wrote out the 1259 will; Amaury later composed a treatise on alchemy a copy of which, in his own handwriting, survives in the Bodleian Library, Oxford. Simon's academic concerns were tinged with morality. From Grosseteste, he learned of the Aristotelian distinction between just and tyrannical rule; but by Adam Marsh he was told how to apply conscience and faith to his daily life. At least two independent sources, although with the historical disadvantage of hindsight, comment on how the oath of 1258 intensified Simon's already extensive private devotions and self-denial, even to the point of abstinence from sexual intercourse with his wife.

For one so committed to the 1258 oath, Simon's role was less prominent in the initial implementation of the reform programme in 1259. This established control of royal actions by a standing council, which also determined appointments. Abuses by local officials, royal and baronial, were to be investigated by a new judicial eyre and grievances redressed. The key concept was justice and the recognisition of the liberties (*i.e.* customary legal rights) of subjects. The king should be governed and govern according to established laws, rather than by his own volition. Such ideas had the virtue of being academically up-to-date and coinciding with the practical desires of a political nation which, for almost the first time, was acknowledged as including more than the nobility. What had begun as a factional move against royal favourites became a root and branch reform of government and the constitution.

In the conduct of this revolution, Simon's role was sporadic and occasionally inconsistent. In the autumn of 1260, for example, by allying himself with the Lord Edward and the earl of Gloucester, Montfort was re-admitted to influence at the price of watering down the Provisions' commitment to investigate baronial officials. However, when, in 1261, Henry III skilfully engineered himself back into power, persuading the pope to repudiate his oath to the Provisions, Simon was energetic in organising armed resistance to this *revanche*, to little avail. In doing so, he signalled what was to become a lasting legacy of the movement when in September 1261 he summoned three knights from each shire to meet him at St. Alban's. This came to nothing, as the king trumped him by summoning a similar assembly at the same time, but it shows Simon's understanding of the importance of gaining the support of those outside the baronage, those who were increasingly assuming local power.

In 1262-3, the cause of reform faded, the king reviving charges against Simon, who was basking in the comfortable refuge of northern France. But a series of political accidents and a threat of war with Wales undermined Henry's position. Simon returned to England to take command of the disparate forces opposed to the king, including disaffected Marcher barons, the new earl of Gloucester, alienated followers of the Lord Edward as well as reformers. At no time were reformers a majority among the barons or shire knights. Perhaps only in the church, or at least the university educated elite and the friars, was the cause of reform given the transcendent moral aura which Simon himself attached to it. But from his return to England in April

1263 until his death at Evesham in August 1265, Simon placed the cause of reform at the centre of politics, backed up by his own military skill.

This briefly won for him power in the summer of 1263, when he ably exploited a wave of anti-alien feeling to impose himself on the king's council. But, ominously, he was unable to provide order which was imperative if effective reform, especially at local level, was to be implemented. By early 1264, following the condemnation of the Provisions by Louis IX at the Mise of Amiens (from which Simon, usually so persuasive on such occasions, was absent because of a broken leg), the reformers' plight was desperate. To identify his position with a just cause even more clearly, Simon's troops had begun to wear the white crosses of English crusaders to the Holy Land. But at Lewes in May 1264, whatever the element of divine intervention, it was generalship and luck that gave Simon victory over superior royalist forces. Soon he had negotiated (in the so-called Mise of Lewes) the surrender into his hands of the king, his sons and his brother, Richard of Cornwall. Now master of England, Montfort spent the next six months trying to gain popular support and raising an army large enough to deter a threatened invasion by royalists in France. His role in the summer of 1264 has been likened by his most recent and best biographer to that of Winston Churchill in 1940. Like Churchill, when the invasion scare was over, Simon reaped the political harvest, if only briefly.

The problem for Montfort's regime was its lack of legitimacy. Condemned by popes and the king of France, Simon lived the fiction that he was acting in the name of the king. Apart from the ineffectual title of Steward of England associated with his earldom he lacked formal office. To widen his appeal, as well as implement the Provisions' principles of consultation and justice, he summoned two parliaments in 1264-5, to the second of which, meeting in January, he requested the presence of burgesses from towns and knights from the shires. In the development of parliamentary institutions, this was but a small marker, not an epoch-making initiative. Formal assemblies of prelates and magnates to give advice and consent had been commonplace at least since the reign of King John. Knights had been consulted in national assemblies as early as 1213 and 1227.

Frequently, the main purpose of such assemblies had been to approve taxation, following the principles of *Magna Carta*. The name 'parliament' first appears in official records in 1237, thereafter inconsistently. In 1254, separate or joint assemblies of prelates, magnates and knights were convened, as they were in June 1264 by the Montfort government. The precedent of January 1265, the addition of burgesses, was not commonly repeated until Edward I's reign. For the first effective parliamentary scrutiny of fiscal policy, it is to the assemblies of the end of Henry's reign concerning money for Edward's crusade that the historian must turn. The Provisions of Oxford were clear that control of the executive was in the hands of a council chosen and run by the barons. The significance of the January parliament of 1265 was immediate and political, not visionary and constitutional. There was urgent business to discuss, namely the release of Edward, and the need to extend support for Montfort's narrow factional oligarchy to embrace as wide a section of the local communities as possible.

Simon de Montfort was not the father of parliamentary government, still less parliamentary democracy. However, by the nature of the cause, its clerical support and the lack of baronial sympathy, Simon was forced to become the first populist political leader in English history. He appealed to and won the adherence of freemen and peasants not previously used to the glare of active participation in national politics. Partly through the preaching of the clergy, especially the friars, who seemed more supportive than the laity, Simon's cause of restricting royal prerogative was transformed into a moral crusade for liberty, justice and virtue. Simon was aware of this and played to it.

Whatever his attempts to involve the people of England in a revivalist campaign for political renewal, the reality was increasingly grim. In 1265, Simon's position was gravely weakened by the defection of Gilbert of Clare, earl of Gloucester (March), the invasion of William of Valence, rebellion by the Marcher lords and the escape of Edward (May). Much of the blame for his predicament lay with Simon himself. His excessive patronage of his own sons made him no more palatable to the barons than Henry III. Their own loutish and rapacious behaviour ranked them as no better than the loathed Lusignans. Simon's regime was too narrowly based among the powerful of the realm to survive. Montfort's rule was too partisan and selfish to garner wider sympathy. The single-mindedness that had won him power destroyed him. Over-confident, over-ambitious, avaricious for self and family, unsuccessful in translating principles into policies, Simon did not, as R. F. Treharne believed, add 'greatness' to this period, merely extremism and exaggeration. Except in a few dons' cells, his position was as untenable ideologically as it was politically. Events of 1264-5 had made the compromises sought in earlier years impossible. There were even signs that Simon was toying with transferring the crown from the Angevins to the Montforts, a logical, if desperate recognition of the fundamental flaws in the Provisions of Oxford. In the end, the issue was not about justice but authority. On that score, Simon's pretensions were vapid.

The final act was, appropriately, military. Outmanoeuvred in ideas and politics, this most intellectual and politically adroit ruler was to be defeated by superior military skill and his own tactical blunders in the campaign to secure the Severn in the summer of 1265. His career had come full circle. He had first attracted notice as a commander. His military prowess had been proved from Wales to Syria: his fortifications at Kenilworth were so good that they withstood the longest siege in English history (six months in 1266). When he saw the speed and skill of the army of Edward and Clare springing the trap at Evesham, he exclaimed: 'By the arm of St. James, they come on well: they did not learn that for themselves but from me'. Humility was a virtue Simon de Montfort's spiritual advisers had been pressing on him for years.

Simon's defeat and death at Evesham was appropriate in another way. Through him, England experienced popular violence and civil war unknown for half a century and an aristocratic bloodbath not seen since Hastings. Simon's own harshness rebounded upon him. However civilised and devout, Montfort was eager to resort to war; he massacred Jews with contemporary eagerness; he cared little for the interests of others except on an almost metaphysical level. His Will talks of his regret at his treatment of the poor. Did he think of them when he grabbed for power and ruled through coercion? Or was his no doubt genuine remorse and self-doubt that of which confessions are made: spiritually uplifting personally but of little value to his victims? Like Thomas Becket, he identified his own desires completely with the interest of his cause, a dangerous arrogance, the mentality of the tyrant through the ages. Simon de Montfort was not a hypocrite or a charlatan, but in life he did as little to merit the prayers of those who sought his shrine at Evesham as he did the sordid indignities inflicted on his body. It is hard to avoid admiring the tenacity with which he espoused what he saw genuinely as his duty; it is also hard to ignore how his actions so debased political life that it was acceptable for his killers to send to Lady Mortimer his severed head, hands and testicles.

J. R. Maddicott, *Simon de Montfort*, 1994.

ELEANOR OF PROVENCE (*d*.1291; queen of England 1236-72) was the second daughter of Raymond Berengar IV, count of Provence and Beatrice of Savoy. In January 1236, she married Henry III of England as part of the king's attempts to outbid his rival, Louis IX of France, who had married Eleanor's eldest sister, Margaret. The prize was influence in the strategically vital territory controlled by her father. This straddled the routes from France and south-west Germany to Italy and, thus, to the papacy, for over half a century the cockpit of European conflict as Hohenstaufen, Capetian, Guelph and Ghibelline battled for control of the peninsula. The importance of Provence-Savoy was confirmed by the marriages of Eleanor's younger sisters to Richard of Cornwall and Charles of Anjou, who respectively became king of Germany and king of Naples. To England with Eleanor came her uncles, on whom Henry showered favour, in particular Boniface of Savoy, archbishop of Canterbury; William, bishop-elect of Valence and Peter, who became lord of Richmond. Although mainly recruited to help Henry's continental schemes, these Savoyards aroused the dislike and suspicion of native barons and chroniclers who feared their power and aggressive pursuit of rights. Their unpopularity attached itself to the queen. She managed the rare feat of being disliked both by her husband's Lusignan relatives and by the king's enemies, famously the Londoners who, in 1263, attacked her barge. In

France 1263-65, she apparently failed to raise mercenaries for her husband's cause, plunging heavily in debt, not for the first time apparently. In 1276, she took the veil at Amesbury, although retaining property and influence within her family. In 1290, her son Edward I convened a family conference at Amesbury at which he settled matters concerning the marriages of his children and the succession to the kingdom. Eleanor, although on occasion formally acting on her husband's behalf, played no independent political role, but received a poor press for all that.

ALEXANDER OF HALES (1170/80-1245) was prominent as a philosopher in the attempt to reconcile newly acquired texts of Aristotle to Christian revelation and as the earliest Franciscan professor of theology at the University of Paris. An Englishman by birth, he followed the conventional path of an ambitious clergyman whose interests went beyond the cure of souls. A prebendary of St. Paul's Cathedral and archdeacon of Coventry, he apparently acquired the wealth necessary to pursue his academic career. Although he remained, according to Roger Bacon, honest, it is unlikely that his ecclesiastical jobs occupied him fully, any more than similar positions engaged men like Geoffrey of Monmouth, Gerald of Wales, Walter Map or Peter of Blois to the exclusion of all else. By the 1220s he was lecturing successfully at Paris where he joined the new Mendicant Order of St. Francis. In about 1231 he helped found the Franciscan school at Paris, becoming its first professor. Although Alexander resigned his Chair in 1238, the establishment of the Franciscans within the University of Paris, then the leading centre of theological studies in northern Europe, was of great significance both for the study of theology and history of the Franciscan Order. Rapidly, the order which had begun as a reaction against the wealth, corruption and compromises of material life became embroiled in fierce academic debates and institutional rivalries both with the traditional university authorities and with the other mendicants, the Dominicans. The Franciscan Order, with its international network and internal discipline, attracted some of the most fertile intellects of the day working on philosophy and theology. Alexander's own most influential work was a *Commentary* on the *Sentences* of Peter Lombard (*d.*1160). The

Sentences were a compendium of questions drawn from the Bible and the Church Fathers each of which contained conflicting authoritative opinions about God, Creation, the Incarnation, Redemption and the Sacraments. Lombard resolved the contradictions through dialectic: the question was followed by two answers, one contrary to the other, in the discussion of which opposing statements a solution was reached. This process of inquiry, the so-called *quaestio* technique, became the basis of the scholastic method which dominated philosophical discourse for generations and marked the contributions of some of the most outstanding medieval theologians, notably the Dominican Thomas Aquinas (1226-74). Alexander's *Commentary* incorporated Aristotelian arguments within a rigidly syllogistic framework. Perhaps his greatest influence on thirteenth century thought was exercised through his pupils, outstanding among whom was St. Bonaventura (1221-74), the leading Franciscan theologian of his generation who, as head of the Order, redefined the ideals of St. Francis to accommodate the Order's new and active role in worldly affairs. Alexander's greatest intellectual legacy was the synthetical *Summa Theologica*, a work often, but wrongly, attributed to him, produced at papal request before 1250. The *Summa* reflects Alexander's arguments about God being the source of all ideas and images and, thus, that knowledge is derived not distinctly but from the intellect confronting such divine creations. The *Summa* was a massive work, designed as a sort of philosophical treasury for Franciscans but which, according to Friar Roger Bacon, was heavier than a horse, unusable and ultimately left to rot. Nevertheless, Alexander made a significant contribution to scholastic method and the invasion of Aristotelianism into Christian theology and its triumph over earlier Arabic glosses. This conquest dominated intellectual debate in general, and the study of philosophy and theology in particular, for more than two centuries. Alexander's own adoption of the life of a Mendicant Friar, combining intellectual sophistication with simplicity of living, points to a catalyst which was to produce much of the subtlest thought of the later middle ages. Alexander's achievement was not insular. Like Stephen Langton before him, he acquired his reputation in Paris and his influence embraced Western Christendom.

ROBERT GROSSETESTE (c.1170-1253; bishop of Lincoln 1235-1253), theologian, natural scientist and church reformer, was one of the most controversial figures in mid-thirteenth century England. Traditionally, it was thought he had studied at Paris and Oxford where he had been elected the first Chancellor of the University in 1214, already a theologian of substance. Recent research by R. W. Southern has shown that this picture is almost certainly false. Instead, a more unusual career emerges, of provincial obscurity and a much later flowering of talent and influence. Born at Stow Langtoft in Suffolk, Grosseteste probably received his early education in Lincoln and Cambridge. Described as *magister* before 1192, he met the chronicler Gerald of Wales c.1194/5 who was impressed by his knowledge of law, the liberal arts and medicine. For the next thirty years, Grosseteste was connected with the diocese of Hereford, much of it in the household of Hugh Foliot, archdeacon of Shropshire and later bishop of Hereford (1219-34). During this period, apart from administrative tasks, Grosseteste concentrated on mathematics, astronomy (*i.e.* astrology) and the natural sciences. He may also have done some peripatetic teaching. Lacking the financial support of a benefice, any more permanent academic position was not feasible. Possibly as a consequence of involvement in ecclesiastical attempts to emancipate the young Henry III from baronial control in 1221-3, even perhaps as a result of working for the king himself, Grosseteste, although still only in deacon's orders, received his first benefice, the lucrative rectorship of Abbotsley (Hunts.), in 1225.

This was the turning point of his life. At the age of c.fifty-five he now had the financial security to indulge his academic interests. He turned to theology and to teaching in Oxford. He was an instant success. By 1230, he had been elected Chancellor by the secular masters of the university, in the teeth of opposition from the bishop of Lincoln. He was archdeacon of Leicester (1229-32), as well as a prebend at Lincoln cathedral. In 1230 Grosseteste, like many other contemporary intellectuals, had some form of conversion experience which tempted him to join a Mendicant Order. Instead, he contented himself with becoming the theology lecturer for the Franciscans in Oxford. He retained influence in the university, however, in 1234 being entrusted with the hopeless task of expelling prostitutes from Oxford. At this time, he began to learn Greek in an attempt to synthesise Greek philosophy, science and theology with the Latin and Patristic inheritance. He had already come into contact with important secular figures, such as Simon de Montfort with whose expulsion of the Jews from Leicester in 1231 Grosseteste had been closely involved. Nevertheless, despite his long association with the diocese, his election in 1235 to the bishopric of Lincoln, covering, as it did, about one fifth of the population of England, was something of a surprise. If expectations had been of quiet rule by an aged don, they were severely disappointed.

Grosseteste proved himself a courageous and outspoken radical; scourge of lay encroachments and clerical backsliding; opponent alike of king and pope. At the heart of his ministry was a very extended interpretation of the pastoral role of a bishop embracing matters of sin, the welfare of souls, morality and administration: episcopal rights of visitation, pluralities, appointments to benefices, canon law etc. Within his diocese he attempted to impose the legatine decrees of 1237; he insisted on his authority to examine and, if necessary reject any candidate for a benefice; he maintained his right to visit (*i.e.* to investigate and reorganise) monasteries and his own cathedral chapter; he asserted his authority to dismiss and excommunicate errant clergy. On all fronts he made enemies: those patrons, including the king and the pope, whose candidates he rejected; the canons of his cathedral whose autonomy he challenged; the monks whose independence and control of churches he threatened; fellow clergy whose pluralities he condemned. His unorthodox career and his not belonging to the social elite which dominated the English episcopate gave him the freedom to attack many of the cozy habits, such as pluralism, which were accepted even by some contemporary reformers. On the other hand, if he was, in Matthew Paris's words, an 'indefatigable persecutor of monks', he was a patron of friars, notably his Oxford protégé Adam Marsh. He regarded friars as providing spiritual and moral purity lacking elsewhere in the clergy. But even here, he found criticisms as the Mendicants began to adapt their rules to suit their greater secular involvement.

Throughout the Middle Ages, Christian renewal tended to be of two kinds: spiritual revival or institutional reform. Grosseteste attempted both. His hopes for the creation of a truly Godly society were, however, over-ambitious. He wanted an authoritarian Church divorced from the habits of social authority. His policies were doomed to fail. As he grew older, the realisation of this prompted bitterness at his ecclesiastical superiors and an increasingly apocalyptic vision of Christendom's future. In 1250, he visited the pope at Lyons and delivered a blistering attack on the corruption of the church. Although previously a supporter of papal jurisdiction and taxation, the apparently increased venality of papal demands and its cynical exploitation of authority to manipulate the church to its own and its allies' secular advantage, convinced Grosseteste that the curia was the *causa, fons et origo*. The Lyons speech was typically audacious, courageous and fruitless. Increasingly disillusioned, on his deathbed in 1253, he prophesied the dissolution of Christendom. Others in the thirteenth century said much the same thing, but few went as far as the dying Grosseteste in identifying the pope himself as the Antichrist

His wider political influence can be assessed by his large surviving correspondence. He had contacts with the greatest in the land; opinions and advice on all the major issues of the day. His austere refusal to compromise on morality or faith cast him in the role of an Anselm rather than a Langton. He set standards that few were willing or able to meet: a moral arbiter and guide, not a factional leader. Yet, at least in the circle of the pious Simon de Montfort, his influence was great: radical, critical and self-righteous.

It is however as a scholar that he was most renowned. His early scientific interests were founded on the theoretical study of geometry and optics and his own experience and observation (*experimentum*) of the natural world. He extended these techniques of expounding general rules from specific examples when he turned to study Aristotelian philosophy and Scriptural theology in the 1220s. Although his approach was idiosyncratic in not following the usual Paris/Oxford models, his theology leaned heavily on the basic scholastic texts such as Peter Lombard's *Sentences*. Grosseteste, however, placed emphasis on the Bible rather than later glosses. This led to his appreciation of the need to study ancient languages. No less than his scholarly contemporaries, Grosseteste believed in the unity of creation and knowledge. In *De Luce* (*c*.1235-40), his study of optics and light is employed to discuss God's role as creator of the natural world. Experimental science he saw assisting the understanding of scripture and living a Christian life. The new weapon of theology, Greek was used to translate Aristotle's philosophical work *The Ethics*. Grosseteste also believed in addressing as wide an audience as possible: his *Château d'Amour*, a poem in French, provided an outline of Christian theology for a lay audience. Because his approach was so individual, so eclectic, and he himself such a maverick, Grosseteste founded no school. In his declaration of the primacy of the Bible and in his attacks on ecclesiastical corruption he later had a fan in John Wyclif. If he had a disciple, it was Roger Bacon, the troubled Oxford Franciscan: 'Lord Robert . . . was the only one above all men to know the sciences'. But for the rest of educated Christendom there was something rough-hewn, eccentric or, simply, unexpected about Grosseteste's thought. Its originality was, like its author, unsettling and challenging.

R. W. Southern, *Robert Grosseteste*, 1986.

ADAM MARSH (*d*. after 1259) was an early Franciscan scholar whose friendships with Robert Grosseteste and Simon de Montfort linked the new Order with innovative academic investigation, ecclesiastical reform and radical politics. His reputation relies chiefly on his surviving correspondence: very little of his academic work remains or has been identified. Marsh appears as a confidant and adviser, not a leader or shaper of the destinies of others. Preferment within the church may have been denied him by his own volition, by his Friar's vocation or by political suspicion of his purist views.

He had the credentials for a successful ecclesiastical career. A nephew of Richard Marsh, bishop of Durham (1217-27), after education at Oxford, where he became a leading Master of Arts, he sustained his position as a wealthy secular clerk and scholar by holding the living of Wearmouth. From this period dates his connection with Grosseteste who became a close friend. The original contact may have been when Grosseteste gathered around him a group of scholars, including Marsh, to translate the newly available Greek philosophical and scientific texts. Marsh possibly encountered the Franciscans in Oxford through Grosseteste who was their patron and regent of the Oxford Franciscans 1229-35. Seeking fresh ways of understanding the temporal world, Grosseteste's group was infected by the new way of religious life offered by the Mendicant Orders. Marsh's secretary abandoned the academic life for that of a missionary friar and this influence may have persuaded Marsh, already a famous teacher, to take the Franciscan habit c.1232.

Such a translation scarcely interrupted Marsh's career. At Oxford he continued to lecture and write on a range of subjects from Biblical commentaries and works on penance to mathematics, languages and natural philosophy (i.e. what passed in the thirteenth century for science). Between 1247 and 1249, he was regent of the friar's school at Oxford, the first of the Order to be so. Roger Bacon, an Oxford near-contemporary and fellow Franciscan, loyally coupled Marsh with Grosseteste as the two leading philosophers of his time. Within the Order, Marsh took a stand against excessive erosion of the original Franciscan ideal of poverty, although accepting the need for secular proctors to handle money for the necessities of life. There was inevitable compromise between St Francis's precepts and the realities of running an international organisation whose functions expanded beyond those of local charity or missionising. Whatever his theoretical position, Marsh's own career pointed up potential contradictions and tensions which were to split the Order in the early fourteenth century and lead to some so-called Spiritual Franciscans, who followed their founder's Rule with pristine severity, being condemned as heretics.

Away from Oxford, he moved freely in the greatest secular and ecclesiastical circles. An observer at the trial of Simon de Montfort for maladministration of Gascony in 1252, Marsh developed an intense admiration for him, acting almost as his secretary as well as spiritual and political adviser. Marsh was one of the earl's executors in 1259. He also facilitated contacts between Simon and Grosseteste, whom he assisted in the administration of the diocese of Lincoln up to 1253. Marsh's influence and abilities were recognised by the king who appointed him to an embassy to France in 1257 to discuss a possible settlement of outstanding territorial disputes. Although exerting much influence as a devout and rigorous friar, Marsh hardly conformed to the pattern of life followed by St Francis. Yet his career was a model of how the new Mendicant Orders could adapt and play a significant role in the wider life of the church and Christendom.

A. G. Little, *Franciscan Papers,* 1943.

HENRY DE REYNS (*d.c.*1253) was master of the king's masons and responsible for the rebuilding of Westminster Abbey for Henry III 1245-1253. It was once thought that the undoubted influence on the design of the new Abbey of contemporary northern French Gothic, including Rheims Cathedral, could be attributed to Henry's French origins, but there is no evidence that he was other than English. His name may have derived from the Essex village of Rayne. Alternatively, he may have travelled in France before entering royal service. Although the only direct evidence shows Henry as Keeper of the Works at Wetminster, in charge of paying the labourers and obtaining the materials, including marble and timber, it is probable that he had a hand in devising the architectural scheme. It has been noted that some of the moulding sections at Westminster are almost identical to those at the King's Chapel, Windsor, where Henry may have worked 1239-43. It is also possible that Henry supplied the designs for the abbey at Hailes (1246) built for the king's brother, Richard of Cornwall. From such slight evidence it has been surmised that Henry was the architect of Westminster Abbey. If so, he was a central figure in a project which occupied Henry III's ambitions and treasury for most of his reign as he sought to provide a suitable setting for the shrine of his patron saint, Edward the Confessor, and the relic of the Holy Blood which the king received into the Abbey, then half-demolished and half-built, in a lavish ceremony on the Confessor's Feast Day, 13 October 1247. Such was Henry's importance that he may have been afforded the honour of commemoration in the building he planned. In

the Abbey's eastern triforium there is a carved head of a craftsman in the meditative pose used to denote a designer. From the
date, it would seem to represent Henry de Reyns.

J. Harvey, *English Mediaeval Architects*, 1987.

MATTHEW PARIS (*c*.1200-1259) is one of the most distinguished English historians. Prolific, opinionated, erudite, his
chronicles have for centuries shaped views on his period, not
least because his prejudices — snobbish, conservative, xenophobic — mirrored those of so many of his successors as historians of thirteenth century England. In 1217, Matthew became a
monk at St Alban's, where, with the exception of visits to some
important ecclesiastical functions in England and a trip to Norway in 1248, he spent the rest of his life. Although cloistered,
Matthew was in no way isolated. St Alban's was a wealthy
monastery, conveniently situated on Watling Street within easy
reach of London, its guesthouse well-used by the great, the good
and the exotic: the abbey hosted Armenians in 1228 and 1252.
Among Matthew's informants, many of whom must have stayed
at the abbey, were Richard of Cornwall, the king's brother;
Hubert de Burgh, the justiciar; Peter des Roches; Robert Grosseteste; and royal officials such as John Mansel. Between 1216
and 1252, Henry III visited St Alban's nine times. In 1247,
Matthew attending the ceremonial reception of the Holy Blood
at Westminster Abbey, talked to the king who asked him to
record all that he had seen and invited him to dinner. On the
king's visit to St Alban's in 1257, Matthew hung around the royal
guest and dined at his table. The chronicler was obviously something of a celebrity, historiographer to the nobility as well as his
monastery.

Matthew's output was prodigious. On the abbey's history he
wrote the *Gesta Abbatum (Deeds of the Abbots)* covering the
period from the alleged foundation in 793 to 1255 and the *Vitae
Offarum (Lives of the Offas)* about Offa of Mercia, the supposed founder of the abbey, and his ancestor Offa of Angeln. For
these Matthew, an enthusiastic, if uncritical, believer in thorough documentation, plundered the abbey's archives. His
hagiography, which he composed both in Latin prose and, for a

lay audience, in French verse, reflected his historical interests, his subjects including St Alban, Edward the Confessor and, for Matthew, the politically correct Archbishops Becket, Langton and Rich, all opponents of royal authority. His masterpiece was the *Chronica majora (Greater Chronicle)*. Begun in 1240, it covered the period from the Creation to 1259. To 1236, Matthew was chiefly dependent on the *Flores Historiarum* of a fellow St Alban's monk Roger of Wendover which Matthew edited and expanded. For the last twenty-three years, however, Matthew was his own source, maintaining an original and almost contemporary account and commentary of events of a range and depth unparalleled in medieval England. His approach was encyclopaedic, cosmopolitan and judgemental. An artist of distinction, Matthew embellished his text with painted heraldic devices, maps (*e.g.* of Palestine; England, Scotland and the world) and numerous vivid marginal line drawings illustrating the narrative. The *Chronica* became bloated by his voracious appetite for information, so around 1250 he began writing shortened versions (the *Flores Historiarum* and *Abbreviatio Chronicarum*); a volume of extracts concerning English history (the *Historia Anglorum*); and a separate book of documents, the *Liber Additamentorum,* which he cross-referenced with the *Chronica majora*. Not only was this a massive historical enterprise, Matthew's original 1236-59 section alone comprising 300,000 words, but much of the actual writing and drawing was done by Matthew himself. On top of this, he found the time to illustrate the works of others.

What prevents this vast enterprise from sinking beneath its own weight is Matthew's readability. This not only turns on the marginal notes and the attractive, almost comic-strip drawings, but also on his style and what he has to say. Matthew's Latin is clear, his narrative easily followed. There are chapter headings, annual summaries of events and neat character sketches of leading figures. He was an early master of the succinct obituary and the telling epigram. Above all, he was an historian, not just a chronicler: he had a definite view on the events he described. His lack of objectivity forms his strength and weakness: it lends intellectual coherence to his work while seducing the reader into accepting his opinions as fact. Like many of his generation,

Matthew Paris on his deathbed in 1259
(From the postscript to his Chronica Majora)

surrounded by the seemingly endless conflicts of church, nobles
and king, Matthew had a deep suspicion of any central authority, royal or papal, which appeared to infringe the traditional
rights and habits of locally established hierarchies, noble, clerical or monastic. Although he came to moderate his vilification
of Henry III, perhaps as he got to know the king personally, his
antagonism to the court runs behind all his political analysis.
From Matthew, rather than the documents of government,
derives the familiar picture of Henry III as extravagant, petulant
and easily-led, especially by parasitic Savoyard and Poitevin relatives. As 1258-9 showed, this view was partly shared by some
baronial opponents of royal policy, but it cannot be accepted as
objective. Matthew's fulminations against the papal curia were,
unlike those of Robert Grosseteste, based on institutional self-
interest. Matthew feared papal power because of the possible

encroachments, through patronage of foreigners and taxation, on the freedom (*i.e.* usually, income) of the English church. It is no coincidence that the *Chronica majora* appealed to Elizabeth I's Protestant Archbishop Parker of Canterbury who collected two of Matthew's autograph copies, now at Corpus Christi College, Cambridge. But Matthew's vision of the English church in danger and his insinuation that there was widespread anti-papalism should be treated with caution. Matthew's cynicism at royal and papal motives may appear justified, but not because of Matthew's witness.

Matthew was a traditional Benedictine, proud of an Order somewhat left behind by the new Orders of monks and mendicant friars. The latter were a pet hate: new, ultramontane, and successful. Matthew's political and ecclesiastical model seems to have been that of a Benedictine abbey, autonomous, run by an abbot according to custom and the Rule, with established, immutably defined and mutually recognised obligations to superiors in church and state. This was a central theme of almost all his historical and hagiographical work. What catches the eye may be the descriptions of buffalo; the drawing of the elephant given to Henry III by Louis IX in 1255; the marginal cartoons; the interest in heraldry, art, architecture, and natural science; above all the sheer scale and bulk of the narrative. What cannot be denied is the nature of the literary achievement: the most original and, in the concept of the illustrated chronicle, innovative historical enterprise of its time. Matthew Paris was a historian on the grand scale, amongst Englishmen on a par with Bede, William of Malmesbury, Clarendon and Gibbon. When Matthew's continuator in 1259 claimed he was unworthy to undo the tie of Matthew's shoe, he said no more than the truth. After Matthew, monastic historiography in England, as elsewhere, began to decline. At St Alban's in the fourteenth century there was a revival with Thomas Walsingham, but he was a pale shadow of Matthew Paris.

R. Vaughan, *Matthew Paris,* 1958.

PETER DES RIVAUX (*c.*1190-1262) was the son of the powerful Peter des Roches, bishop of Winchester. Born in Normandy, he followed his father in making a career in the service of the Angevin kings of England. A cleric who ultimately held a clutch of lucrative benefices on both sides of the English Channel, Peter's official career centred upon royal finance. It is probably to Peter that the significant reforms of the Exchequer in the 1230s and 1240s should be attributed. Where his father never left the limelight, Peter operated largely away from the glare of political contest.

During the Minority, Peter worked in the royal household. He shared his father's loss of power in 1223 being dismissed as clerk of the Wardrobe. He returned to royal service in the early 1230s and in 1232 became the main instrument of his father's takeover of government. Between 1232 and 1234, Peter effectively controlled the entire financial affairs of the crown, both household and exchequer. Through his offices of treasurer of the household and the Exchequer; keeper of wardships, escheats and the king's small seal; controller of the Mint, ports and the Jews; and, briefly, nominal sheriff of twenty-on counties, Peter, as Matthew Paris put it, had the whole of England under his regulation.

The point of being this financial Poo-Bah was reform. After the civil was of 1215 17, the management of royal revenue had been haphazard. Despite administrative innovations by William of Ely a generation earlier, Exchequer procedures were too cumbersome to be effective. To restore control over raising customary revenue and to maximise its yield required changes at the centre and in the provinces. The political objective was the financial emancipation of the crown from the vested influences of the baronage. Secure and profitable ordinary income would reduce the tensions which had brought the Angevin dynasty to its knees. Magnates would not need to be harassed and the king would not feel exploited or cheated.

Although Peter des Rivaux's extraordinary authority was swept away with the fall of his father's government in 1234, and he himself briefly imprisoned, he was recalled as keeper of the Wardrobe in 1236 and thereafter served the king in numerous posts in the household and the Exchequer until dismissed in 1258 by the baronial reformers, even though many of them had indirectly benefited from the work of Peter and his colleagues over the previous quarter century. The changes had a double thrust. Sheriffs' fiscal role was severely reduced, with separate accounting systems and local agents becoming responsible for the royal demesne, wardships and escheats. Regular commissions investigated the extent of royal rights. At the centre, more intelligible and discrete methods of accounting and keeping records allowed for firmer royal scrutiny and control. Apart from increasing royal profits, the system which emerged during Henry III's personal rule meant the end of extortionate curial sheriffs and heavy-handed general eyres. Sheriffs became more local, their remit more judicial. Although royal rights were vigorously defended, magnates were allowed to enjoy what was theirs broadly unhindered. As the Crown was better able to exploit its own, it had less need to invade what belonged to others: the shires became increasingly what they were to remain, the preserves of the nobility, not the battle ground of royal agents. This highly significant development occurred not through great political upheaval, but partly through the careful and sustained service over decades of increasingly professional administrators of whom Peter des Rivaux, with his brief moment of glory, was one of the most prominent.

PETER OF SAVOY (*d*.1268; count of Savoy 1263-8) was one of the brothers of Henry III's mother-in-law. On his marriage in 1236 to Peter's niece, Eleanor of Provence, Henry eagerly employed her uncles to further his expansive international schemes and provide political ballast at home. Peter's elder brother, William, bishop-elect of Valence (*d*.1239), was briefly a dominant figure in royal councils 1236-7. His clerk, Peter d'Aigueblanche stayed in England to become one of Henry's most valued officials and diplomats, as well as bishop of Hereford (1240-68). Another brother, Boniface, became archbishop of Canterbury (1241-70). On Peter were lavished the largest secular rewards, including the honour of Richmond and the wardenship of the Cinque Ports. Knighted by Henry in 1241, Peter, while never abandoning his continental interests, became an influential English courtier and magnate. As such, he attracted the opprobrium of nationalist observers, such as Matthew Paris who invented scurrilous stories of Peter importing bevies of foreign ladies to corrupt English aristocrats. Henry found in Peter a diplomat, whose existing European experience was usefully employed on his behalf. It is a sign of how Henry mismanaged his affairs that Peter was one of the original seven nobles, led by another foreigner Simon de Montfort, who in April 1258 formed a sworn commune to reform English government. Although Peter soon abandoned the opposition, with the rest he had acted out of resentment at the favours given to the king's Lusignan relatives. Reconciled with Henry, Peter was active on his behalf before leaving England in 1262. The following year he succeeded his nephew as count of Savoy. Although resented by insular chroniclers and jealous rivals within the English nobility, Peter's energy, administrative proficiency, wide geographical range of action and military skill earned him the nickname of 'little Charlemagne'. The role that Peter and his Savoyard brothers played in English political life exposed a gulf which divided the cosmopolitan Angevin monarch from the majority of his English nobles. Of these relatives, Peter was possibly the ablest. Whether Henry was wise to promote him, especially in view of his actions in 1258, is less obvious.

HENRY OF BRACTON (or **BRATTON** *c*.1208-1268) was until recently considered the author of the greatest English law book of the thirteenth century, *De Legibus et Consuetudinibus Angliae* (*Concerning the Laws and Customs of England*). It now appears more probable that he may, at most, have compiled or transmitted an earlier text. A Devon man, Bracton owed his preferment as a royal clerk and justice to his fellow Devonian, the royal justice William Ralegh, who may also have drawn Bracton to the attention of Henry III's brother, Richard of Cornwall. Bracton was Ralegh's personal clerk in the mid 1230s. By 1240, he was in royal service in the *Coram Rege*, the central royal courts at Westminster. He was a justice-in-eyre, particularly in his native South West, from 1244, and a justice at the *Coram Rege* 1247-51 and 1253-7. Meanwhile, his ecclesiastical career developed profitably, with prebends at Exeter and Bosham, an archdeaconry at Barnstaple and the chancellorship of Exeter in 1264.

Bracton's relationship with *De Legibus* is unclear, although well established by the end of the Middle Ages. Modern research has demonstrated that the prototype of *De Legibus* was composed before 1236 by a connection of Martin Patteshull, a leading royal justice of the day. It was then revised by a clerk of William Ralegh who clearly had access to the records of Patteshull's cases. It is conceivable that this clerk was Bracton. There were further revisions until some time after 1256 the basis of the surviving, swollen work was produced. Even then, there was no single authoritative text; an epitome was produced in 1292, and two further summaries by the early fourteenth century, one of which, in Latin, was called, obscurely, the *Fleta*. The composition of *De Legibus* was, therefore, a process rather than a single creative event. Its origins, though, belong to a generation before Bracton, as the central role in the text of the cases of Patteshull and Ralegh indicate.

The *De Legibus* was the first attempt to describe English Common Law as it had developed since the procedural reforms of Henry II's reign, in particular the so-called possessory assizes. The task was made possible by the introduction, from the 1190s, of detailed records, kept on rolls, of cases heard before royal justices, either at Westminster or on tour. The formulae for settling civil disputes had begun to be collected from the early thirteenth century, the first law books. But *De Legibus* goes much further. Its intention was to delineate what English law and custom was and how it worked. Thus the bulk of the work comprises examples of actual cases organised by areas of law, such as possession, right, royal prerogative *etc.* General principles are adduced from extant case law. This makes the *De Legibus* unusual in western Europe at the time. Elsewhere, canonists were editing collections of Decretals, judicial decisions exposing general maxims, or compiling *Summa* of theological orthodoxy. Civil lawyers were either transcribing apparently immemorial customs (as, famously, Philippe de Beaumanoir's *Customary* of the Beauvaisis) or asserting ideal laws and prerogatives (such as the Emperor Frederick II's *Liber Augustalis*). The impact of Roman Law is evident in *De Legibus* but only in so far as the purpose of the work was to collate, systematize and state law as it existed. *De Legibus* was practical, not abstract, descriptive, not prescriptive. With its emphasis on case law, *De Legibus* mirrored what was to be one of the most distinctive features of English Common Law down to the twentieth century.

Henry de Bracton, *De Legibus et Consuetudinibus Angliae* ed. & trans E. S. Thorne, who established that Bracton was not the author, 1968-77.

JOHN MANSEL (*d.*1265) was one of Henry III's most accomplished and versatile servants, particularly expert in the conduct of foreign policy. From humble origins, educated at court, by 1234 he was employed in the Exchequer. For the next thirty years Mansel acted variously as royal secretary, councillor, keeper of the Great Seal, legal agent, diplomat and ambassador. His rewards were lavish. The clerical son of a cleric, he was a prodigious pluralist, his income from benefices allegedly running into thousands of marks a year. He wore his clerical garb lightly. Until a stone crushed his leg during the Gascon expedition in 1243, Mansel had made a name as a soldier, in Italy in 1238 and again on the 1242-3 French campaign. Unlike other contemporary bellicose clerics (*e.g.* Boniface of Savoy, archbishop of Canterbury), Mansel actually fought, on one occasion unhorsing his opponent, the seneschal of the count of Boulogne. After 1243, he had to content himself with administration and luxurious living. A member of the king's council from 1244, he held the Great Seal 1246-7 and 1248-9, but his main expertise was in foreign affairs. Here his achievement was remarkable, including the treaty and marriage alliance with Castile (1254); the Sicilian agreement with Innocent IV (1254); the election of Richard of Cornwall as King of the Romans (1257); the Treaty of Paris (1259); the papal absolution of the king's oath to support the Provisions of Oxford (1261); and the Mise of Amiens (1264). Mansel became an almost indispensible advisor to the king, reflected in his taking the Cross with his master in 1250 despite recurrent poor health. There were few issues concerning royal interests on which Mansel was not employed. One modern writer has called him 'almost the Wolsey of his age'. Unsurprisingly, he became a focus for the hostility of government critics, such as Matthew Paris and the baronial reformers of 1258-9. In 1263 he was forced into exile by Montfortian rebels, dying abroad two years later. How far he influenced or merely executed royal policy is obscure. Although his skill as a negotiator was, judged by results, exceptional, his own attitudes are hidden. It is intriguing that one of his friends and an executor to his will was Robert Tweng, a veteran nationalist, anti-papal terrorist directly opposed to most of the foreign policy initiatives so smoothly operated by Mansel himself. This alone suggests that there was more to the politics of Henry III's reign than met the eyes of royalist or baronial apologists.

JOHN OF GLOUCESTER (*fl.c*.1245-*d*.1260) was Henry III's master mason in the later 1250s. Already a successful mason in the 1240s, during the following decade he was particularly associated with Henry III's grandiose schemes at Westminster, both at the Abbey and the Palace. But his work for the king also included activity at Gloucester, Woodstock, Windsor, Guildford, Merton, Oxford and Old Sarum, largely on secular buildings. The value placed upon him is reflected in his rewards: he amassed property in Gloucester, Oxfordshire, Middlesex, Southwark, Northampton and Surrey. In 1255, he received from the king robes 'such as the knights of the Household receive'. His duties and presumably skills were many: the supervision of the large number of labourers at Westminster; designing the Queen's lodgings at Windsor; general maintenance of the stone fabric of royal dwellings; renewing the drains and sewers at the Palace of Westminster; even constructing lecterns for the king and the Westminster Chapter House. At Westminster, he worked closely with the king's chief carpenter, Alexander (*fl*.1239-*d.c*.1269). Together, they received patents in January 1257 as masters, respectively, of the king's masonry and carpentry. Their positions had earlier been recognised when, in November 1256, they had been ordered to take charge of all royal works in the kingdom because, significantly, the king 'had suffered much damage through causing his works to be carried on by sheriffs and other officers'. Either this can be seen as another encroachment on local power, part of a policy which so irritated the political nation that it led to overt opposition two years later; or Henry, desperately short of money but insistent on maintaining his regality in stones no less than in rhetoric and policy, was determined to avoid the peculation and financial mismanagement inevitable in a localised system of audit and accountability, a problem not unique to Henry III. Whatever the royal motive, John and Alexander set about their new responsibilities by touring the King's works south of the Trent in 1257, viewing not only buildings but the marble quarries at Purbeck. Like many other servants of Henry III, John found that his office was something of a poisoned chalice. The king was nearly bankrupt: in 1259 wages arrears to the Windsor workmen alone had reached £410. It may be that John was expected to cover any immediate shortfall. If so, it ruined him: at his death in 1260 he owed the king 80 marks and the income from his extensive lands was said to reach only two marks a year. This was the grim reality behind the soaring achievement of Westminster Abbey.

J. Harvey, *English Mediaeval Architects,* 1987.

SIMON STOCK (*d.*1265), an Englishman who became sixth Prior-General of the Carmelite Order of mendicants, embodies the twelfth century tradition of anchorites, eremitic holy men and women, with the thirteenth century's passion for corporate organisation. Unlike St Francis, however, his vocation was dictated by a physical as well as emotional return to Biblical precept. His life coincided with a brief moment when Western Christendom encompassed the Near East and whose horizons were set at a distance only imagined in the two subsequent centuries. Yet his career also exemplified the retreat from that Eastern dimension as the Order was transformed under his leadership.

Simon's origins are obscure. Possibly born as early as 1166, later legends attribute to him a noble lineage to compare, presumably deliberately, with the archetype of thirteenth century Christ-like holy men, Francis of Assisi. Hagiographic etymology relates his cognomen, 'Stock', to his having spent twenty years in a tree trunk. What is more certain is that at some time in the first half of the thirteenth century Simon went to Palestine and joined a congregation of hermits on Mt Carmel. There existed a long tradition of Christian hermits and monks on the Biblical site of Elijah's cell and his confrontation with the priests of Baal.

In the early thirteenth century, one group of Latin hermits organised themselves under a simple Rule, dedicated to the Virgin Mary. Originally designed for the holy men living on Mt Carmel itself, after the Crusade of Richard of Cornwall (1240-41) the Order was taken up by patrons in the West, not least in England where land grants to members of the Order began in the early 1240s. It was at one of these estates, Aylesford in Kent, that the first General Chapter of the Order was held in 1245 and where, at another Chapter two years later, Simon was elected prior.

As prior, Simon confirmed the translation of the Carmelites from a group of hermits wedded to their eremitic tradition in the Holy Land into an international Mendicant Order. Symbolic of the change was the substitution (only finally accepted in 1286-87) of a simple white habit for the original, somewhat bizarre multi-coloured habit, which, unsurprisingly, had caused some less than flattering comment. In 1248, Simon secured the approval of Pope Innocent IV for a new constitution for the Order and permission for brothers to settle in the West. Almost immediately, the nature and focus of the Carmelites shifted: they became extensive landowners in the West and significant members of the ecclesiastical community; and they began to attend the schools and universities at Oxford, Cambridge, Paris and Bologna. Such innovation met with resistance from traditionalists within the Order and from existing vested interests outside. But it conformed to similar developments in, for example, the Franciscans. To survive and to answer the demand of laymen for fresh outlets for religious patronage and spiritual vocations, simplicity, other-wordly idealism and intimacy with the sites of Holy Geography had to give way to more institutionalised and accessible temporal structures. This Simon's priorship largely set in motion.

WILLIAM LONGESPEE (*c*.1212-1250) rather unexpectedly became one of the most famous Englishmen of the thirteenth century. An unlikely candidate for immortality, William was the son of Ella, countess of Salisbury in her own right (*c*.1191-1261), founder and later abbess of Lacock abbey (Wiltshire) and William Longespee (*d*.1226), a bastard son of Henry II. Despite his lineage and the favour of his cousin Henry III, his achieve-ments were less than modest. He campaigned regularly with the king, sharing in the failures in Brittany (1230), Wales (1233) and Gascony (1242-3). He was unable to obtain recognition as earl of Salisbury after his mother took the veil (1237). A companion of his other cousin, Richard of Cornwall, on crusade in 1240, he briefly rose to prominence as leader of a substantial English con-tingent that joined Louis IX of France's crusade in 1249. Heavily subsidised from central funds for hiring knights and serjeants, William left England, we are told, his saddle-bags stuffed with cash. His availability to lead the English crusaders suggests that he was a very minor political player. The crusade was a disaster. He quarrelled with his French colleagues and was killed at the battle of Mansourah in the Nile Delta (February 1250). Yet whatever his insignificance in life, in death William found apoth-eosis as an English martyr. At the hands of myth-makers, includ-ing Matthew Paris, within two generations William had become a national hero, specifically manufactured to stand in contrast and indictment to the French who were portrayed as panic-stricken cowards. By the early fourteenth century a poem in French detailing William's self-sacrificing heroism was circulat-ing and he featured in the Middle English epic *Richard Coer de Lyon*. William became a symbol and a barometer of a growing literary fashion for nationalist anti-French feeling. William was a specifically English hero, signifying the beginnings of the devel-opment of a national consciousness which was to be such a feature of English history in the later middle ages.

S. Lloyd, 'William Longespee II: The Making of an English Cru-sading Hero', *Nottingham Medieval Studies*, xxxv, 1991.

WILLIAM, called of Valence after his birthplace in Poitou (after 1225-1296), the fourth son of Isabella of Angoulême, widow of King John and Hugh of Lusignan, count of La Marche, was the most prominent and disliked of Henry III's Poitevin half-brothers who had their fortunes made in England after their arrival in 1247. William's brothers Guy and Geoffrey were richly rewarded with estates and pensions, while another brother, Aymer, received the richest see in England, Winchester

(1250). For William himself was reserved the largest prize, a wealthy heiress, Joan of Munchesni, who brought with her property worth £700 a year, to which Henry added another £800 worth. For the next decade, William and his brothers continued to enjoy the king's largesse, despite the dwindling scope for royal patronage. By the mid-1250s, William was second only to Richard of Cornwall in preferment and prominence at court. This naturally caused resentment, especially among those like Simon de Montfort who thought they were insufficiently supported. Added insult was the king's explicit protection of his half-brothers from hostile legal action and their own rapacity and violence. They behaved, as indeed they were, above the law. One Norfolk chronicler wrote 'no Englishman could get his right or obtain a writ against them'. The Lusignans were not unique in this: in 1256, Henry included Richard of Cornwall, the earl of Gloucester and his wife's uncle Peter of Savoy in this privilege. However, the Lusignans, through their aggressive exploitation of the king's friendship and immunity, were especially hated. Their apparent monopoly of royal favour turned jealousy into serious political opposition. It is striking that two of those associated in the protection against writs of 1256, Gloucester and Peter of Savoy, were among the first to attack Henry and the Lusignans in 1258. Simon de Montfort's relations with William of Valance had been notoriously bad for years, the earl seeming to blame the Poitevin for much of his disappointment over patronage. However, the crisis of 1258-9 was lent its especially bitter edge by the collective vendetta against the Lusignan favourites who were the first casualties of their refusal to swear to the Provisions of Oxford, being forced into exile. The barons dressed up their factional rivalry by accusing the Lusignans of inciting the king to believe he was above the law. More significantly, the accident of their foreign birth allowed participants and observers alike to characterise the baronial reforms as in some sense a national reaction against malign alien influence. Thus, negatively, William and his brothers contributed to the emergence of national identity among the English political classes. Restored in 1261, William played a leading part in the royalist cause. Escaping after Lewes, he returned with an army in 1265 for the campaign which ended at Evesham. William's career remained attached to the monarchy. He went on crusade with the Lord Edward (1270-3) and continued assiduously to increase his landed holdings thereafter for the rest of his life. William, a lover of tournaments whose passion for his hobby extended to searching out the best horses in Europe, was vain and arrogant, with the love of those spoilt when young of throwing his weight about. That his power derived from no quality of his except the accident of birth was his blessing, but his patron's cross.

HUGH BIGOD (*d*.1266) was prominent in the imposition of the baronial programme of reform enshrined in the Provisions of Oxford (1258) and the Provisions of Westminster (1259), acting as justiciar of England from June 1258 to October 1260. His early career is obscure, although by 1258 he had amassed extensive landed interests in Yorkshire and Sussex; had accompanied the king on campaign in Wales in 1257; and served as a negotiator with the French in 1257-8, preparatory to the Peace of Paris (1259). In April 1258, he swore an oath of confederacy with six other magnates, including his brother, the earl of Norfolk, and Simon de Montfort. This group formed the nucleus of the baronial coalition which sought to limit and define royal prerogative in the wake of the financially disastrous Sicilian enterprise; royal manipulation of local justice and administration; and the growing power of the king's Lusignan half-brothers. These were no disinterested framers of a parliamentary constitution. Rather, they were intent on resisting encroachment on their rights and influence to the benefit of the Crown and royal favourites. They did not look forward to a constitutional monarchy but harked back to the days of consensual baronial government during Henry III's Minority (1216-27). At the parliament at Oxford in June 1258, Hugh Bigod was appointed justiciar, a revival of an office closely associated with the Minority, unfilled since 1234. Apart from assuming control of central administration, Hugh's chief and immediate function was to hear pleas and complaints against royal administration, much of his work being based upon the local enquiries ordered in 1258 and conducted over the following months by the knights of the shire. Hugh drew the plaudits of sympathetic observers as a fearless and efficient judge, impervious to the influence of 'powerful persons'. He also seems to have been impervious to procedural niceties, his itinerary through the south and Midlands in 1258-9 being marked by controversy over his favouring of complainants and his casual treatment of existing rights. Hugh's summary justice may have prompted the return to formal procedures of writs, appeals and recognition of existing liberties, rights and exemptions enshrined in the Provisions of Westminster (March 1259). Hugh's conduct may also suggest that he was not one of the growing number of semi-professional royal justices, his appointment as justiciar owing more to his noble connections and experience of court than to legal expertise: Hugh's role was and remained essentially political. Although partisan against the Lusignan faction, Hugh was not anti-royalist *per se*. In 1259-60, he was regent in Henry III's absence in France, in the spring of 1260 organising resistance to an imagined threat to the king from the Lord Edward. After resigning his office in 1260, Hugh continued as a royal ally except briefly in 1261 when his own territorial position was threatened by the royal resumption of castles. Soon reconciled to the king, thereafter he was loyal, fighting for the king in 1264 and suffering exile after Henry's defeat at Lewes. Hugh's brief career at the top of English politics demonstrates that the tensions of 1258-65 were as much personal and factional as ideological or constitutional. However, all sides had to cope with an expanding political nation, exemplified in the increasing role of the knights of the shire. The failure of baronial reform indicated that it was the crown, not the magnates, which was best able to adapt. The lasting legacy of Hugh's justicarship were the Provisions of Westminster, confirmed by the king in 1263 and forming the basis for the Statute of Marlborough of 1267, a significant episode in the creation of a common law of property, but one guaranteed by royal courts not baronial power.

WALTER CANTELUPE (*d*.1266; bishop of Worcester 1236-66) was a leading partisan of the movement against the rule of Henry III in the 1260s. A close friend and advisor of Simon de Montfort, he was a conservative who, in defence of his views, espoused radical solutions. As so many thirteenth century ecclesiastics, Cantelupe trod the increasingly precarious path of obedience to the universal authority of the papacy and faithfulness to the rights of provincial churches in matters secular as well as spiritual. Thirteenth century dons could — and did — talk in terms of abstract principles. Propagandists could — and did — talk in terms of absolutes. Cantelupe, on the other hand, a clerical man of affairs, was forced to take sides and adopt political positions which earned him defeat and obloquy. The contemporary royalist chronicler Thomas Wykes hit on a general truth when he commented that Cantelupe would have deserved canonisation if he had not supported Montfort. The prizes of this world and the next tend to go to the victors.

The key to unlock the conundrums of conflicting loyalties was the law. Cantelupe acted as a royal justice-in-eyre before becoming a bishop. Thereafter he vigorously implemented canonical instructions for reform, producing his own Constitutions in 1240 and regularly holding diocesan synods and visiting religious houses. As bishop, he was hostile to innovative taxation, papal as much as royal. Increasingly, he became a spokesman for provincial rights, which in the 1250s placed him against the papal taxation of the church in support of Henry III's Sicilian adventure.

In his early career as a bishop he was closely connected with Bishop Grosseteste of Lincoln, a man who suffered fools ill and pious intellectuals highly. Cantelupe's opinions were of significance because of his credentials as a courtier and aristocrat. From 1229 when he collected Archbishop Richard Grant's *pallium* from Rome to 1257 when he was admitted to the king's council, Cantelupe served two masters with skill and success. After 1258, he lent public and startling support to the cause of Montfort and the baronial reformers. In 1263, Cantelupe had been appointed by the pope to raise men and money for a new crusade, itself a recognition of his prominent status in the English church. He turned this authority to novel purpose when, at Lewes in 1264 and Evesham in 1265, he offered Montfort's supporters the sanction of the church. Before the battle of Lewes he granted absolution for their sins to the rebels, a direct echo of crusader privileges. For such partisan use of the consolations of the church and his anti-royalist behaviour, he was suspended after the baronial defeat at Evesham by the papal legate,

Ottobuono. He died shortly after, on 12 February 1266. Cantelupe was a political failure for the simple reason that he, unlike most of his episcopal colleagues, refused to trim. His legalistic views on legitimate rights of local and central powers led him to rebel, and even to espouse a doctrine of Christian resistance more associated with twentieth century Latin America than thirteenth century England. In this he was not the least remarkable English bishop of the period.

AARON OF YORK (*d*.1268) was a native of Lincoln who, in the first half of the thirteenth century, built up a substantial financial empire based on York. By 1241, he was one of the two richest Jews in England (the other being worth a relief of 7,000 marks three years later). In his heyday, from the 1220s to 1240s, Aaron was giving personal loans as large as £250; doing business with merchants from Florence, Siena and Bordeaux; leasing property in York to prominent citizens; and helping those with money, such as the Cistercian abbey of Rievaulx, to buy out smaller landowners in financial difficulty. R. B. Dobson has described Aaron in his prime as 'this Croesus of thirteenth century England'. However, by 1255, Aaron was exempted from the Jewish tallage 'his wealth having entirely evaporated'. His fall was a mirror of the fate of English Jewry in the thirteenth century, brought down by the attrition of constant royal tallages and an increasingly hostile social and legal environment. The year of Aaron's bankruptcy was pivotal: a new tallage; a new blood-libel at Lincoln; and Henry III's mortgaging of the whole community to his wealthy brother Richard of Cornwall. Aaron's family kept in business until the end, but suffered increasing financial deprivation and violent persecution. After the expulsion of 1290, the memory of such financial moguls as Aaron of York was preserved only in the names of where they lived and conducted business, as in York's Jewbury and Jubbergate.

R. B. Dobson, 'The Decline and Expulsion of the Medieval Jews of York', *Translation of the Jewish Historical Society of England*, xxvi, 1979.

BONIFACE OF SAVOY (*d*.1270; archbishop of Canterbury 1241-70) was the last non-English archbishop of Canterbury, the first since Theobald (1138-61). The eleventh child of Thomas I, count of Savoy, he was the uncle of Henry III's wife, Eleanor. A Carthusian — although hardly an advertisement for that strict and rigorous order — Boniface rose quickly, as well-connected clergy often do, becoming bishop of Belley in 1234. His relationship to Henry III secured his preferment to Canterbury in 1241, but he was consecrated by Innocent IV only in 1245 and not enthroned at Canterbury until 1249. His main concern in these years was as commander of the papal guard, a preference which did not go unnoticed in England. For services to the papacy he received the privilege of collecting all the first fruits(*i.e.* a tax on the revenue of new incumbents) in his province, which added to his unpopularity. When in England in 1249-50, he implemented the decree of the Council of Lyons (1245) instructing archbishops to visit all religious establishments in their provinces, regardless of the rights of their suffragan bishops. Predictably, this met with fierce institutional resistance. On one occasion, the archbishop was so exasperated by the recalcitrance of the canons of St Bartholomew's Priory in Smithfield in London that he personally mugged the subprior. His temperament was perhaps revealed in his wearing a coat of mail under his episcopal vestments during these visitations. He also tended to be accompanied by a gang of Provençal thugs who greatly facilitated collection of money. It was typical that he felt no compulsion to support King Henry in all things, arguing with him over church appointments and with the king's favoured half-brother, Aymer of Lusignan, bishop-elect of Winchester. Boniface's military career continued on the continent in-the 1250s, but from 1256 he began to concentrate on English affairs. In the face of growing hostility to the king's foreign advisors and favourites, Boniface inevitably supported the royalists in the civil conflicts of 1258-65, although he retired to France from 1262 to 1265. After the royalist victory at Evesham in 1265, he returned to England but his power was overshadowed by the Cardinal Legate Ottobuono. In 1270, accompanying the Lord Edward on crusade, Boniface died in his native Savoy.

His career illustrates some of the less edifying aspects of the development since the eleventh century of an international church under the universal authority of the papacy. Boniface owed his position to his birth, was a frequent absentee and treated his see much as a secular lord would a fief or principality: property to be exploited with rights to be protected. In some ways he resembled the forceful aristocratic prelates of the earlier Middle Ages. Yet his promotion was as a papal servant and his insistence on visitation rights mark him as an effective if tactless diocesan, in line with contemporary centralising tendencies at the papal curia. A century ago the historian Mandell Creighton (himself bishop of Peterborough then London) was dismissive: 'Archbishop Boniface did nothing that was important either for church or state in England'. In this he was following the hostile account of Boniface's career in England by the xenophobic Matthew Paris for whom the archbishop represented all that was threatening to the indigenous rights of the English church. Boniface's cosmopolitan interests and outlook would have made him unsympathetic to Paris (and to Bishop Creighton) regardless of what he actually did.

[Mandell Creighton contributed the *D.N.B.* article.]

THOMAS DOCKING (*fl.*1230-70), from Docking in Norfolk, was an influential Franciscan scholar and teacher at Oxford University whose career and interests shed light on the preoccupations of contemporary learned circles. He heard Grosseteste lecture to the Franciscans at Oxford in 1229/30, making him one of the earliest of the Mendicants to make an academic career in an English university. By the 1240s, his fellow Franciscan, Adam Marsh was singing Docking's praises as a leading light in the Order at Oxford. He rose to become the seventh Franciscan reader in Divinity at Oxford (1262-5) and a Doctor of Divinity. Active as a lecturer and writer throughout the 1250s and 1260s, Docking is last heard of in 1269. His main works were Commentaries on the Bible which show him to be a discursive exegete, with a then characteristically Oxonian knowledge of natural science and optics, and an interest in morality, theology and contemporary politics. His discussion of a responsible man assuming royal power for the public good may be a reference to Simon de Montfort in 1264-5. Among his lost works was a *Biblical Grammar.* Superficially intractable, Docking's scholarship had a contemporary relevance in its concern with the relationship of the contemplative and active life, one of the great themes of medieval thought. As a Mendicant engaged in the life of a growing university in a city in which national and local politics were never far away, Docking was in a good position to comment. A scholar and teacher whose influence was maintained as much by his pupils as by his writing, he, as much as any, helped confirm the position of the Friars in the forefront of English academic life, and he did so by basing his scholarship upon the Bible. For all the excitement of new discoveries of Aristotle and others, the Bible remained throughout the Middle Ages the great repository of ideas and focus for enquiry. Biblical study was by no means sterile of fresh insights, as was illustrated a century later by another Oxford lecturer on the Bible, John Wyclif.

J. Catto (ed.), *History of the University of Oxford*, vol. i, 1984.

ROGER BACON (*c.*1220-1292), nicknamed 'the Marvellous Doctor', was a polymath and encyclopaedist around whom a number of fanciful anecdotes have clustered, some, perhaps,of his own invention. He was suspected (wrongly) of necromancy; to him has been attributed (wrongly) the discovery of gunpowder and spectacles. He liked to see himself as an empirical scientist, but his observations and descriptions were, in keeping with the academic fashion of the time, entirely theoretical. By his own account, he was a prodigiously energetic researcher. Educated in the traditional Liberal Arts (the Trivium: grammar; rhetoric; and logic; and the Quadrivium: music; astronomy; geometry; arithmetic) at Paris in the early 1240s, he lectured on Aristotle before, on returning to Oxford, he began his scientific enquiries. Influenced, perhaps, by the Oxford tradition of Grosseteste, between 1247 and 1257 Bacon studied optics, languages, alchemy, astronomy and mathematics. His empiricism did not extend to experiments in the modern understanding of the term. Thus he described, but did not make, spectacles and, in 1252, provided exact directions for concocting gunpowder, but did not actually assemble the recipe. Like many other academics of the thirteenth century, Bacon, in mid-career, became a Mendicant Friar, joining the Franciscans in 1257. If he hoped the new Order would be open to new ideas, he was misled. Thereafter, he fought a running battle with superiors in his attempts to establish science on the university curriculum and in compiling an encyclopaedia of nature in order to further the cause of Christianity which, in Bacon's lifetime, seemed genuinely threatened by Moslems and Mongols. He managed to interest Pope Clement IV (1265-68) in his project and between 1266 and 1268 he produced three weighty volumes, the *Opus majus, Opus minus* and *Opus tertium*, in which he attempted to summarize all human knowledge. Yet he achieved this prodigious feat against the instructions of his Order and was punished for it. But he kept on writing: *c.*1268-72 came the *Communia naturalium* (on natural philosophy); the *Communia mathematica* (on general mathematical principles) and a *Compendium philosophiae*. By the late 1270s, the Order had run out of patience and Bacon was imprisoned for unorthodox teaching, alchemy and heresy. Even this failed to stem his output and he was still writing when he died in 1292. He was buried in the Franciscan church in Oxford. From his own works, Bacon emerges as a man whose erudition was matched only by his self-confidence. Like contemporary theologians, such as Aquinas, he believed that all knowledge could be unified and was, perhaps, rather unfastidious in what he acquired. The boundaries between science and magic, astronomy and astrology, speculation and heresy, empiricism and alchemy were too fluid for his work to escape suspicion. That he was not condemned further is probably explained by the sheer weight and volume of his work: few then or since could possibly have read even a fraction of it. But his personality left its mark in the legends of his learning and his discoveries.

THOMAS CANTELUPE (?1218-1282; bishop of Hereford 1275-82), the only Englishman to be canonised in the fourteenth century (1320), was an unlikely candidate for sanctity. Well connected (his uncle Walter was bishop of Worcester), an academic with anti-royalist views, litigious, a greedy pluralist, a misogonist and an anti-semite, Thomas was a fairly typical product of the socially superior and intellectually advanced clergy of the thirteenth century. A red-faced, ginger-haired man with a large nose, throughout his career Thomas's affluence and taste for preferment never interfered with his professional commitment to radical causes, reform in church and state or the friendship of the Mendicant Friars. As a student of canon law at Paris, he lived in style with his own household, apparently even entertaining Louis IX. In 1245, he was granted permission by Innocent IV to hold benefices in plurality. This allowed a secure income without the constraint of duties, a common ploy which sustained generations of civil servants, lawyers and scholars.

Thomas specialised in law. Before Paris, he had studied civil law at Orleans, and he went on to teach canon law at Oxford. In 1262 he became Chancellor of Oxford University. Thomas showed his political allegiances in 1263 when he refused the Lord Edward entry to Oxford, although his most onerous task as chancellor was quelling riots amongst the students and between them and the townspeople. His legal skill was soon employed by the partisans of Simon de Montfort as a baronial commissioner at the Mise of Amiens (1263-4) and, very briefly, chancellor of England in the first half of 1265. After Montfort's defeat at Evesham, Thomas withdrew to lecture on theology at Paris. But his ability, or contacts, saw him back in Oxford in the early 1270s, where he once more became chancellor. His appointment by Edward I as bishop of Hereford in 1275 marked his rehabilitation and was another sign of Edward's policy of partial reconciliation of former rebel sympathisers. His cultivation of Robert Kilwardby, archbishop of Canterbury, may have helped too. By now his benefices brought him an annual income reputed to be £1,000 a year. He was archdeacon of Stafford; a canon at York and London; a prebendary of Lichfield and rector of a clutch of parishes. Later encomiasts suggest that he visited his parishes and was generous with his money. As bishop, Thomas continued his lucrative pluralism, but he also worked hard to raise the standard of his diocesan clergy, although here too there is a whiff of hypocrisy. He dismissed the cathedral precentor for being a pluralist without papal permission: it may have been a coincidence that the precentor had been a rival candidate for the bishopric in 1275. Thomas was also eager in defence of his privileges. It was on the way to Rome to appeal aganist his excommunication by the inflexible Archbishop Pecham for defending his rights as a suffragan that he died at Orvieto on 25 August 1282.

His cult seems to have been started deliberately by his pupil and successor Richard Swinfield (bishop of Hereford 1282-1317) in 1287. A week before Swinfield's carefully prepared translation of Thomas's bones to a new shrine-like tomb, the late bishop performed his first miracle. It was the first of many in a curative cult which grew rapidly. Of all surviving English medieval miracle collections, only Becket's is larger.Swinfield no doubt had one eye on the profits of pilgrimage as well as, presumably, the other on the spiritual advantages of a fresh channel of Divine Grace. Thomas Cantelupe would have approved.

R. Finucane, *Miracles and Pilgrims*, 1977.

HENRY OF ALMAIN(E) (1235-1271) was the eldest son of Richard of Cornwall, younger brother of Henry III. He was closely associated in his father's ventures, particularly in the acceptance of the crown of Germany (*i.e.* Almain(e)) in 1257. Although he initially opposed the Provisions of Oxford (1258), like many younger nobles he flirted with the baronial critics of royal government. In 1263-4, however, he firmly supported the royalist cause and was captured after the battle of Lewes (1264). In France when Simon de Montfort was defeated at Evesham (1265), his independent political influence grew. He played an important part in organising the crusade with the Lord Edward (1268-70), whom he accompanied to Tunis. However, he did not go with Edward to Palestine, but returned to France, perhaps to protect his cousin's interests with the new king of France, Philip III. At Viterbo, when at prayer in church, he was assassinated by two of Simon de Montfort's sons, Guy and Simon, and his body mutilated in revenge, they claimed, for the death of their father at Evesham. Guy, who actually dealt the fatal blow, was excommunicated and outlawed but managed to survive off his wits with the assitance of various Italian patrons until dying in a Sicilian prison in 1292. Apart from the shock at the removal of a major figure of the new generation of political leaders, Henry of Almaine's murder without heirs made more possible the ultimate reversion of Richard of Cornwall's extremely valuable lands to the crown. This occured with the death of Henry's younger brother, also without heirs, in 1300.

GILBERT CLARE, EARL OF GLOUCESTER (1243-95) played a central and disruptive role in the civil wars of the 1260s. Inheriting vast estates in the west country, the Welsh Marches and Ireland after his father's death (1262), Gilbert initially was a strong partisan for the rebellion of Simon de Montfort in 1263-4. Earl Simon knighted Gilbert and his brother shortly before the battle of Lewes (May 1264) After Montfort, Gilbert was the most powerful man in the kingdom during the next year, but relations between the two deteriorated. Gilbert wished for more authority, a greater share of the spoils of victory, and an entirely free hand in policing and defending his lands. Gilbert posed as the defender of the Provisions of Oxford, of which his father had been an initiator, and implied that Montfort's dictatorship was betraying their principles. Here, it is difficult to disentangle selfless ideology from inflated self-importance. In May 1265, Gilbert broke with Montfort, allying with the newly escaped Lord Edward with whom he won the battle of Evesham. His perceived treachery led to bitterness with surviving Montfortians, but relations with the royalists were hardly less tense. A champion of disinherited rebel sympathisers, he protested at the failure to implement the Provisions of Oxford, not seeing that the royalist victory had made them redundant. Gilbert seems to have imagined that he could, under the guise of constitutional moderation and propiety, exercise an independent role in English politics. When his error became apparent, he took to arms in 1267, occupying London before his grievances were submitted to the arbitration of Richard of Cornwall. Although his discontent simmered, he was outwardly reconciled to the regime, taking the Cross in 1268 and promising to travel with the Lord Edward to the Holy Land in 1270 which in the event, despite a threatened forfeit of 20,000 marks, he did not. In 1271, he succeeded in getting agreement to the restoration of the lands of the Disinherited. Thereafter, his political independence emasculated by tight royal control, Gilbert remained loyal to Edward I. Having been divorced from his first wife (a niece of Henry III's, allegedly hypochondriac) in 1271, Gilbert married Edward I's sister Joan of Acre in 1290. This not only tied him more closely to the court, but the stipulation that inheritance of his vast estates was restricted to the descendents of this union, greatly increased the chance of them reverting to the crown (which they did in 1314). Even as late as 1292, Gilbert found himself on trial in a dispute about power in the Welsh Marches, only gaining release and restoration of his lands on agreement to pay of a fine of 10,000 marks. Gilbert, nicknamed the 'Red Earl' because of his colouring, tried to carve out an independent political position for himself from which to negotiate loyalty to the crown. Whatever his private views on the Provisions of Oxford, he used the civil war as a convenient way of extending his own interests, his policy being essentially factional not constitutional. His failure and subsequent humiliations were a function probably of his own political incompetence and certainly of the renewed royal strength after the baronial wars. Increasingly under Edward I, Earl Gilbert appeared something of an anachronism.

SELECT BIBLIOGRAPHY

This list is intended as suggestions for further general reading. The list is neither exhaustive nor prescriptive for an understanding of the period. Any serious student will wish to read primary sources, but even the casual observer may be inspired by visible relics — the castles, cathedrals, churches, city walls, houses, tombs *etc* — to investigate further. The following may assist.

Age of Chivalry, ed J. Alexander & P. Binski (1987).

F. Barlow, *William Rufus* (1983).

F. Barlow, *The English Church 1066-1154* (1979).

F. Barlow, *The Feudal Kingdom of England 1042-1216* (3rd edn 1972).

F. Barlow, *Thomas Becket* (1986).

D. Bates, *William the Conqueror* (1988).

D. Carpenter, *The Minority of Henry III* (1990).

M. Chibnall, *Anglo-Norman England* (1986).

M. T. Clanchy, *From Memory to Written Record: England 1066-1307* (1979).

M. T. Clanchy, *England and its Rulers* (1983).

H. M. Colvin ed, *The History of the King's Works,* vol i (1963).

D. Crouch, *William Marshal* (1990).

R. H. C. Davies, *King Stephen* (1967).

R. H. C. Davies, *The Normans and their Myth* (1976).

D. C. Douglas, *William the Conqueror* (1964).

English Historical Documents, Gen ed. D. C. Douglas, vol ii, (1981) & iii (1975).

English Romanesque Art 1066-1200, ed J. Drew *et al* (1984).

J. Gillingham, *Richard the Lionheart* (1978).

J. Gillingham, *The Angevin Empire* (1984).

A. Gransden, *Historical Writing in England 550-1307* (1974).

J. Green, *The Government of England under Henry I* (1986).

J. Harvey, *English Mediaeval Architects* (1987).

J. C. Holt, *King John* (Historical Association Pamphlet 1963).

J. C. Holt, *The Northerners* (1961).

J. C. Holt, *Magna Carta and Medieval Government* (1985).

J. C. Holt, ed., *Domesday Studies* (1987).

M. Keen, *Chivalry* (1984).

C. H. Knowles, *Simon de Montfort* (Historical Association Pamphlet 1965).

D. Knowles, *The Monastic Order in England* (1949; 2nd edn. 1963).

D. Knowles, *The Religious Orders in England,* vol i (1948).

J. Le Patourel, *The Norman Empire* (1976).

J. R. Maddicott, *Simon de Montfort* (1994).

E. Miller & J. Hatcher, *Medieval England: Rural Society and Economic Change 1086-1348* (1978).

F. M. Powicke, *King Henry III and the Lord Edward* (1947).

S. Reynolds, *Fiefs and Vassals* (1994).

O. Rackham, *The History of the Countryside* (1986).

R. W. Southern, *The Making of the Middle Ages* (1953).

R. W. Southern, *St Anselm and his Biographer* (1963).

R. W. Southern, *Robert Grosseteste* (1986).

C. J. Tyerman, *England and the Crusades 1095-1588* (1988).

W. L. Warren, *The Governance of Norman and Angevin England* (1987).

W. L. Warren, *Henry II* (1973).

W. L. Warren, *King John* (1961).

GLOSSARY

Aid. An extraordinary grant of tax to the king for which, from King John's reign, it was customary to have the assent of the lay and ecclesiastical magnates, later afforced by representatives of the knights of the shires and burgesses.

Amercement. A punishment, levied in money, imposed at the 'mercy', *i.e.* discretion of the king or his justices for minor infringements of regulations, especially fiscal or judicial, or minor offences.

Assize. Originally a rule, regulation or law imposed by the king, with the assent of the magnates, which changed or modified customary law (*e.g.* Assize of Arms 1181 on the military obligations of freemen). The term was applied, by extension, to legal procedures resulting from such alterations of the law (*e.g.* assizes of *mort d'ancestor* and *novel disseisin*). Later, the name was given to the courts and judges which heard such pleas. A **Grand Assize** was a procedure introduced in 1179 as an alternative to trial by combat of issues of right to freehold, the case being heard before a jury of twelve knights of the shire. This process was careful and slow. For more rapid solutions to matters of tenure of property, rather than absolute right, quicker procedures were instituted, known as **Petty Assizes,** including *mort d'ancestor* and *novel disseisin*.

Baron. A tenant-in-chief of the king, *i.e.* one who held land and titles directly from the king.

Benefice. In an ecclesiastical context, a position, office of profit or living; a cure of souls with an income attached. Originally a benefice was a grant of land by a lord to his vassal.

Carucate. From *caruca,* a plough, was a measurement of land which could be kept under the plough by a team of eight oxen in a year. This could vary from between sixty and a hundred acres. This formed the basis of a new land tax in 1194.

Chapter. In ecclesiastical terms, the governing body of a cathedral, comprising a prior and the priory monks in monastic cathedrals, such as Canterbury and a Dean and canons in cathedrals run by secular clerics, as at York. The name derives from the meetings of these bodies at which it was customary for chapters of the Bible to be read aloud.

Curialis. A courtier, hence curial officials, curial sheriffs *etc*, men based at or deriving their authority and influence from their position at the king's court.

Demesne. Land farmed directly by a lord or his villeins. The **Royal Demesne** was all land in the kingdom not in church or private hands and from which the king derived rent or other revenue.

Disseisin. Wrongful deprivation of possession of land held in freehold (seisin).

Escheat. Reversion of a fief to a lord in the absence of an heir or as a result of the holder being declared an outlaw.

Eyre. Derived from the Latin *itinere,* to journey. A visitation by the king or his justices, hence justices-in-eyre, to hear pleas. Usually organised on circuits of a number of counties, the system became regular from the 1160s and was an especial feature of the re-establishment of royal power after 1217.

Familiaris. A member of a household of a king or magnate, often implying special attachment or closeness without formal office.

Farm. Derived from the Anglo-Saxon *feorm* or food-rent. A fixed payment or rent, usually annual. **Sheriff's Farm:** an agreed sum payable annually in composition for the regular royal revenues from the sheriff's county. Anything the sheriff collected above his 'farm' he kept as profit.

Fealty. An oath of fidelity sworn, often on the Gospels or relics, to a lord. **Not** to be confused with **Homage.** Fealty could be sworn without any reciprocal undertaking or gift, such as land. Fealty was unilateral. In theory, fealty to the king took precedence over all other obligations, including homage to a lesser lord.

Fief. Property, usually a landed estate, occasionally money or rent, held from a lord in return for homage and the performance of services, often military. In England fiefs were normally heritable.

Fine. Not necessarily a monetary penalty. Usually in this period a sum paid to the Crown in return for a grant, privilege, concession or merely to avoid the king's displeasure.

Franchise. A privilege or right, often of jurisdiction, granted to an individual or group (a town or monastery) by a lord, in England prominently by the king.

Hide. An Anglo-Saxon measurement of land, originally calculated as that sufficient to support a household for a year but by the eleventh century a unit of assessment for the geld or land tax, similar in nature to the carucate.

Homage. The oath and associated ceremony by which a vassal bound himself to his lord by becoming his man (*homo*) and acknowledged the obligations of holding a fief. Homage implied a reciprocal agreement by the superior to be a good lord. The ceremony, classically, required the vassal to place his hands between those of his lord.

Honor or Honour. The estates or group of estates held by the greater tenants-in-chief of the Crown from which they derived their status, prestige and often titles. Within an honor there were often inferior lordships held of the greater lord.

Hundred. An administrative sub-division of a shire with its own court.

Interdict. Literally a prohibition. Specifically, that by Pope Innocent III in 1208 forbidding any priests in England from performing their priestly functions, including the administration of the sacraments. The only exceptions were the baptism of infants and the hearing the confessions of the dying, both of which were accepted as being matters which could legitimately be conducted by laymen. The Interdict was lifted in 1213.

Knight's Fee. An estate or fief technically owing the service and therefore providing for the maintenance of one knight. In practice a unit of assessment of taxes or services.

Manor. Ultimately derived from the latin *manere*, to stay, remain, hence to dwell. A unit of territorial and agricultural organisation, generally comprising the lord's demesne and the lands farmed by his tenants. Also a centre used for taxation purposes.

Mark. A sum of money equivalent to two-thirds of a pound sterling, *i.e.* 13s 4d.

Mort d'Ancestor. A legal procedure developed under Henry II to provide redress for plaintiffs who had been deprived of their rightful inheritance.

Novel Disseisin. A legal procedure developed under Henry II to provide redress for plaintiffs who had had their freehold unjustly taken from them.

Pipe Roll. The record of the annual audit of the accounts of the sheriffs and others with debts to the crown. The first surviving Pipe Roll is from 1130. From 1155, the series is more or less complete.

Pleas of the Crown. Serious crimes, breaches of the peace and certain specific offences which could only be tried by officers of the Crown.

Relief. From the latin *relevare,* to take up. A payment to a lord by a tenant on entry into possession of an inherited fief.

Scutage. Literally 'shield-money', payment in lieu of military service levied by the Crown on tenants-in-chief according to the number of knight's fees they held.

Seisin. The enjoyment of rights and revenues derived from possession of freehold land.

Serf. A legally unfree, servile peasant.

Sheriff. Originally the Anglo-Saxon shire-reeve, after the Conquest the sheriff was the officer appointed by the king responsible for administering the king's lands and justice in a shire. He was the key royal fiscal and judicial agent in the twelfth century. Thereafter, the sheriff's authority was supplemented or superseded by justices-in-eyre and local commissions established in the thirteenth century. Increasingly, the Exchequer exerted direct control of royal revenues in the localities, further weakening the power of the sheriff.

Writ. A written command of the king, after the Conquest both sealed and signed. From the twelfth century, an order to royal officials to initiate legal proceedings in the king's courts. From the 1170s, certain writs were formalized to expedite judicial proceedings under the **Petty Assizes.**

INDEX

Aaron of Lincoln, banker, 234-5; clients of, 224
Aaron of York, financier, 404
Abelard, theologian, 120, 179
Adam of Dryburgh, monk, whips Hubert Walter, 266
Adam of Eynsham, biographer of Hugh of Avalon, 269
Adela of Blois, daughter of William I, 67-8; family of, 122, 140
Adela of Louvain, second wife of Henry I, 82
Adelard of Bath, Arabist and astrologer, 117-18; attacks royal officials, 91; translates Euclid, 91; teaches at Laon, 91; Henry II's tutor, 183
Adelelm, royal treasurer, 93
Aelgifu, wife of Ranulf Flambard, 66
Aethelbald, king of Mercia, 28, 53
Aethelmar, bishop of Elmham, 46
Aethelric, bishop of Selsey, 9
Aethelwig, abbot of Evesham, 22
Aethelwine, bishop of Durham, 30
Ailnoth 'Ingeniator', 222-3
Ailred, abbot of Rievaulx, 163-7; friend of Walter Espec, 113, 114; literary tastes of, 153, 154; and the nun of Watton, 167-8; and Godric of Finchale, 167-70; and Gilbert Foliot, 198; plagiarised by Peter of Blois, 277
Aldred, archbishop of York, crowns William I, 6; pluralist, 22
Alexander II, king of Scots, 317, 351
Alexander II, pope, 5
Alexander III, pope, 170, 175, 207, 210, 232
Alexander VI, pope, 60
Alexander of Hales, theologian, 379-80
Alexander 'the Magnificent', bishop of Lincoln, 91, 93, 177; as patron, 114, 118, 152
Alexander, royal carpenter, 396
Alfonso VI, king of Castile, 82
Alfred, king of Wessex, 78, 165
Alfwen of Flamstead, hermit, 171, 172
Anastasius IV, pope, 161, 162, 242
Andrew of Champagne, author of The Art of Courtly Love, 197
Anselm, archbishop of Canterbury, 54-60; at Bec, 14, 174; at Harrow, 32; and friends, 44-5, 67, 101, 106; dispute with William II, 32, 44, 50-1, 52; in exile, 33; and sodomy, 52-3; and Ranulf Flambard, 64; and Henry I, 74, 77; and Robert of Meulan, 84-5; consecrates Roger of Salisbury, 89; friendship with Gilbert Crispin, 94-5; life recorded by Eadmer, 96-7; and John of Salisbury, 179; as archbishop, 241
Anselm of Laon, 91, 105, 177
Aquinas, Thomas, theologian, 274, 380, 408
Arnulf, count of Flanders, 29
Arnold of Lisieux, 210
Arthur of Brittany, 309-10; birth, 226; rival of John, 298, 299, 300, 301, 304; and succession, 252, 258, 333; captured at Mirebeau, 196, 311; murder of, 312, 349

Bacon, Roger, 407-8; on Grosseteste, 384; on Adam Marsh, 385; on Alexander of Hales, 379, 380
Baldwin II, king of Jerusalem, 82, 129
Baldwin of Ford, archbishop of Canterbury, 238-42;

education, 119; elected archbishop, 273; as secular clerk, 282; as archbishop, 193, 222, 277; preached cross in Wales, 279
Bartholomew, bishop of Exeter, 176, 238
Basset, Ralph, royal judge, 81
Beatrice of Falkenburg, third wife of Richard of Cornwall, 366
Beatrice of Savoy, 378
Beatrice of Say, wife of Geoffrey FitzPeter, 294
Becket, Gilbert, father of Thomas, 202
Becket, Thomas, archbishop of Canterbury, 202-11; early career, 175, 176; as chancellor, 176; as archbishop, 212, 241; unlike Anselm, 57; and Henry II, 62, 184-5, 186, 188, 190, 193, 276; circle of, 179, 221-2; and Canterbury monks, 273; and Roger of York, 215-17; and Godric of Finchale, 170; and Henry of Blois, 141, 143; and Gilbert Foliot, 199-201; and Gilbert of Sempringham, 115; arrogance of, 378; death of, 180, 222, 240; cult of, 230, 239, 255, 320, 324, 360; ideals of ignored, 224, 232
Bellebelle, mistress of Henry II, 219
Benedict of Peterborough, 209, 275
Ben Reuven, Jacob, refutes Christianity using work of Gilbert Crispin, 95
Berengar IV, Raymond, count of Provence, 378
Berengar of Tours, controversial theologian, 14
Berengaria of Navarre, wife of Richard I, 196, 258
Bernard, St., abbot of Clairvaux, 98, 116, 120, 125, 160, 161, 162, 164, 179, 204
Berold, Rouen butcher, sole survivor of White Ship, 102, 110
Bertrand of Born, troubadour, 257
Bicchieri, Guala, papal legate, 347-8; in England, 290, 328, 350; and coronation of Henry III, 323; leaves England, 355
Bigod, Hugh, earl of Norfolk, 219-20; ally of Stephen, 123; and Great Rebellion, 189, 233; and demolition of Framlingham Castle, 223
Bigod, Hugh, justiciar, 401-2
Bigod, Roger, progenitor of the earls of Norfolk, 45-6
Blanche of Castile, queen of France, 196
Bloet, Robert, chancellor and bishop of Lincoln, 62, 64, 114, 118
Blondel, minstrel, 254
Bonaventura, St., 380
Boniface of Savoy, archbishop of Canterbury, 405-6; and nepotism, 342, 378, 392; and war, 395
Boso, nephew of John of Salisbury, 158, 159
Bray, vicars of, 19-20
Brihtheah, bishop of Worcester, 21
Brown, Thomas, 220-1; career of, 228

Cade, William, financier, 227-8
Calixtus II, 107
Cantelupe, Thomas, bishop of Hereford, 408-10; and Simon de Montfort, 373
Cantelupe, Walter, bishop of Worcester, 402-4; friend of Simon de Montfort, 373; and nephew, Thomas, 408
Carlyle, Thomas, 281, 285
Carpenter, D., 356
Celestine II, pope, 161, 174

Celestine III, pope, 260
Champart of Jumièges, Robert, archbishop of Canterbury, 3
Charlemagne, 135
Charles I, 209
Charles of Anjou, 344, 378
Charles the Good, count of Flanders, 159
Chaucer, Geoffrey, 155
Christina of Markyate, née Theodora, 171-3; and attempted rape by Ranulf Flambard, 66; protected by Thurstan of York, 108
Churchill, Winston S., 44, 375
Clanchy, M.T., 185
Clare, Gilbert, earl of Gloucester, and Baronial Wars, 411-12, 374, 376-7; reconciled to Henry III, 365
Clement III, anti-pope, 56
Clement IV, pope, formerly Gui Foulquois, 348, 408
Clifford, Rosamund, 218-19; and Henry II, 192
Cnut, 3; laws of, 81; and the waves, 119
Coleswein of Lincoln, 8
Conan, Norman rebel murdered by Henry I, 77
Constance of Brittany, 226, 300, 309, 310, 333
Crispin, Gilbert, abbot of Westminster, 94-6; his Vita Herluini, 97
Cromwell, Thomas, 88
Cuthbert, St., 163, 169, 170

D'Abitot, Urse, 62
D'Acastre, Roger, tutor to Richard of Cornwall, 363
D'Aigueblanche, Peter, bishop of Hereford, 342, 392
Daniel of Morley, 274
Daniel, Walter, biographer of Ailred of Rievaulx, 166
Dante Alighieri, on Anselm, 60; on Henry III, 346
D'Athée, Gerard, mercenary, 160, 303
David I, king of Scots, 133-4; marriage of, 21; and English civil war, 123, 131, 135, 146-7, 165; knights Henry II, 183; court of, 163; and Ailred of Rievaulx, 163-4
David, earl of Huntingdon, 327
Davis, R. H. C., 150
De Beaumanoir, Philippe, jurist, 394
De Bréauté, Falkes, 317-19; serves John, 303, in Minority, 322, 324; rebels, 351; fall of, 315; and Bedford castle, 233
De Burgh, Hubert, king's justiciar and earl of Kent, 348-54; as justiciar, 214, 290, 315, 318, 322, 328-30, 334, 336, 356, 364; as chamberlain, 326; and death of Arthur of Brittany, 304; and Matthew Paris, 387; fall of, 343; personality, 335; social standing of, 84, 293
De Cignogné, Engelard, mercenary, 160, 303, 329
De Clinton, Geoffrey, 100-1; and Henry I, 73; accused of treason, 78; disgraced, 92
De Clinton, Roger, bishop of Coventry, 100
De Courson, Robert, cardinal, 320
De Forz, William, 304
De Gaugy, Richard, business partner of William Marshal, 291
De Glanvill, Hervey, 144-6; family of, 235
De La Barre, Luke, Norman rebel, driven to suicide by Henry I, 77
De Lacy, Hugh, viceroy in Ireland, 230
De Lucy, Godfrey, bishop of Winchester, 214
De Lucy, Richard, royal justiciar, 211-15; as

justiciar, 138, 188-9, 232; and Battle Abbey, 273; family of, 313
De Mandeville, Geoffrey, first earl of Essex, 149-51; arrested, 125-6; ravages East Anglia, 121; and civil war, 132
De Mandeville, Geoffrey, second earl of Essex, royal justice, 212
De Mandeville, Geoffrey, fifth earl of Essex, and the Gloucester inheritance, 304, 327
De Mandeville, William, succession to, 295
De Mauley, Peter, 303, 304, 328, 329, 341, 363
De Montfort, Amaury, Norman baron, 76
De Montfort, Amaury, son of Simon de Montfort, 373
De Montfort, Simon, earl of Leicester, 367-78; marriage, 338, 358; and Baronial Wars, 411; and Adam Marsh, 384-5; and Walter Cantelupe, 402; resents Lusignans, 400; and Henry III, 344-5, 393, 401; and Richard of Cornwall, 365; and Grosseteste, 382, 383; and shrine of Edmund Rich, 359; academic support for, 409; defeat of, 410; personality of, 335
De Montfort the elder, Simon, 368
De Moreville, Hugh, assassin of Becket, 209
De Percy, Alice, mistress of Hugh du Puiset, 244
De Quincy, Saer, 307
De Redvers, Baldwin, 131
De Redvers, Richard, 73; close friend of Henry I, 74
De Reyns, Henry, master mason, 386-7
Dermot, king of Leinster, 229
De Say, Geoffrey, 295, 327
D'Escures, Ralph, archbishop of Canterbury, 101-2; death of, 105
Des Rivaux, Peter, 390-2; and Hubert de Burgh, 351-3; as minister, 329, 330, 339
Des Roches, Peter, royal justiciar and bishop of Winchester, 324-31; and John, 294, 315; as justiciar, 214; in Minority, 290, 347, 350, 355; and Hubert de Burgh, 351-3; and coronation of Henry III, 323; in royal service, 303; arouses suspicion, 332; and Falkes de Bréauté, 318; on crusade, 318; guardian of Henry III, 351; and Henry III, 338-40; and Matthew Paris, 387; criticises Magna Carta, 336; personality, 335; father of Peter des Rivaux, 390; fall of, 358; his will, 360
Des Roches, William, seneschal of Anjou, 303
De Susa, Henry, known as Hostiensis, canonist, 342
De Tancarville, William, 287
De Tracey, William, assassin of Becket, 209
De Troyes, Chrétien, 154 197
De Valence, Aymer, bishop of Winchester, 342; 399-400; 405
De Vesci, Eustace, northern baron, 315-17; wife of, 395
Diceto, Ralph, chronicler, 275-6; quoted by Jocelin of Brakelond, 285
Dobson, R.B., 404
Docking, Thomas, 406-7
Domesday Book, 41-3
Donalbane, king of Scots, 12
Dunstan, St., archbishop of Canterbury, 12, 15, 111
Du Puiset, Hugh, bishop of Durham, 242-4; patron of Roger of Howden, 274-5; fall of, 259

Eadmer, chronicler, 96-7; on Harold II, 5; on Lanfranc, 15; on Hugh of Avranches, 45; on William II, 50, 52; and Anselm, 55, 57, 59

Eadmer the Lefthanded, 33
Edgar, king of England, 12
Edgar, king of Scots, 48
Edgar Aetheling, 11-12; claim to throne, 6; relatives of 75, 133
Edmund, St., king of the East Angles, 255, 285
Edmund Ironsides, 11, 75, 183
Edmund Crouchback, earl of Lancaster, 341
Edric the Wild, 28
Edward the Confessor, 3-5, 6, 19, 31, 163, 353-4; banishes Hereward the Wake, 29; death of, 5; relatives of, 11, 75; and Domesday Book, 41-2; and law courts, 79; laws of, 81; cult of, 22, 95, 167, 346, 386
Edward I, 194, 345, 346, 365, 370, 376, 374, 376, 377, 379, 405, 409, 410, 411-12; birth, 340, 364; and cult of Edmund Rich, 359; personality, 335; genetic deformity, 335; family of, 309; and reputation of Richard I, 248; and Jews, 235; and Geoffrey of Monmouth, 154
Edward II, 248, 254
Edward VII, 225
Edward VIII, 53, 225
Edward the Exile, 11
Edwin, earl of Mercia, 6
Edwin, king of Northumbria, 5
Eilaf, father of Ailred of Rievaulx, 163
Eleanor of Aquitaine, 194-8; a bluestocking, 134; wife of Henry II, 182, 187, 189, 197; and Rosamund Clifford, 218; supports Richard I, 254; as regent, 213; and William Marshal, 286, 287; at Mirebeau, 309; family of, 225, 226, 298; as patron, 277; burial, 311
Eleanor, daughter of John, wife of Simon de Montfort, 338, 358, 370-1, 373
Eleanor of Provence, wife of Henry III, 378-9; marriage, 341; family of, 392, 405; and cult of Edward the Confessor, 167
Elias of Dereham, building supervisor, 360-1
Elizabeth of Beaumont, seduced by Henry I, 136
Elizabeth I, 53
Ella, countess of Salisbury, 398
Elphege, St., archbishop of Canterbury, 15
Emma, queen of England, wife of Ethelred II and Cnut, 3
Engelram of Trie, jousts with Becket, 205
Ermengard of Béziers, 135
Ermengard of Narbonne, 135
Espec, Walter, lord of Helmsley, founder of Rievaulx, 113-14; education, 148; defeats Scots, 165; literary interests, 153; friend of Robert of Gloucester, 105
Ethelred II the Unready, 3, 11, 102, 123; nickname used by Walter Map, 293; family of, 133, 135, 163
Eudo, royal steward, 62
Eugenius III, pope, 99, 115, 125, 142, 157, 158, 161, 162, 174-5, 179
Eustace of Boulogne, son of King Stephen, 125, 127, 135, 162, 175, 183

Fabrizio, physician of Henry I; disappointed candidate for Canterbury, 101
Fantosme, Jordan, writer, 176
FitzAilwin, Henry, mayor of London, 272
FitzAlan, William, 304
FitzCount, Brian, 147-8; and Henry I, 71-3; audits Exchequer, 92; supports Empress Matilda, 93, 130, 131; and Wallingford Castle, 233

Fitzgerald, Maurice, Marcher lord, 229
FitzGilbert, Ralph, literary patron, 153
FitzGodwine, Robert, adventurer, 12
FitzHerbert, William, archbishop of York, 160-1; and York election, 142, 162, 164; nepotist, 242
FitzHubert, Robert, mercenary and bestial psychopath, 105
FitzJocelin, Reginald, bishop of Bath, 277
FitzNeal, Richard, bishop of London, 244-8; and Dialogue of the Exchequer, 178, 220-1; as hostage, 178; praises Roger of Salisbury, 88; and Ralph Diceto, 276; on Robert of Leicester, 137, 140; family of, 177
FitzOsbern, William, 28-9; serves William I, 8
FitzOsbert, William, London agitator, 270-2; and Hubert Walter, 268
FitzPeter, Geoffrey, king's justiciar, 293-6; protégé of Hubert Walter, 266; as justiciar, 214, 288, 303; and William Marshal, 287; death of, 327; social standing of, 84, 351
FitzRoy, Geoffrey, archbishop of York, 223-4; illegitimacy of, 201, 219; loyalty of, 192; and Lincoln, 269; arrest of, 261; as patron, 277
FitzStephen, Robert, Marcher lord, 229
FitzUrse, Reginald, assassin of Becket, 209
FitzWalter, Robert, lord of Dunmow, 313-15; opposes John, 307; plots, 294, 316
Flambard, Ranulf, bishop of Durham, 61 6; Bayeux origins, 25; as libertine, 32, 171, 173; as royal official, 38; and William II, 51; imprisonment of, 75; employs William of Corbeil, 105; friends of, 106; as patron, 107, 170
Florence of Worcester, chronicler, 22
Foliot, Gilbert, bishop of London, 198-201; friend of Ailred of Rievaulx, 165; as bishop of Hereford, 175; and Becket dispute, 207-8, 217; as patron, 276, 292
Foliot, Hugh, bishop of Hereford, 381
Francis, St., 379, 380, 385, 386, 397
Frederick I Barbarossa, emperor and king of Germany, 158, 205
Frederick II, emperor and king of Germany, 329, 331, 358, 364, 372, 394
Fulk V, count of Anjou, grandfather of Henry II, 76, 129, 182, 191

Gaimar, Geoffrey, poet, 30, 119, 153
Gelasius II, 107
Geoffrey, brother of Henry II, 82, 130, 182, 192
Geoffrey of Brittany, 226-7; and Brittany, 187, 225; rebels, 189; family of, 309; death of, 191
Geoffrey, bishop of Coutances, 26-7; serves William I, 8, 18; as justice, 9
Geoffrey the Goldsmith, of London, 271
Geoffrey of Lusignan, half-brother of Henry III, 342, 399
Geoffrey of Monmouth, chronicler, 151-4; lived in Oxford, 120; on Henry I, 80; and Robert of Gloucester, 103, 105; not believed, 112, 167; and Walter Espec, 114; as archdeacon, 379; influence of, 119, 310
Geoffrey, abbot of St. Alban's, 171-2, 211
George IV, 225
Gerald of Wales, 278-81; meets Grosseteste, 381; as archdeacon, 379; on Hugh of Avalon, 269; preaches cross in Wales, 240-1; on Richard of Clare, 229; attacks Geoffrey of Brittany, 226-7; on Henry II, 182, 191, 192

Gerard of Cremona, translator, 274
Gerold, clerk of Hugh of Avranches, 45
Gervase of Canterbury, chronicler, 230, 231, 239, 240
Gervase of Southampton, banker, 227
Giffard, William, chancellor, 62, 64, 75
Gilbert of Sempringham, 114-16; cult of, 265; and nun of Watton, 168
Gildas, chronicler, 152
Gillingham, J., 298
Glanvill, Ranulf, king's justiciar, 235-7; as justiciar, 214, 238; and Geoffrey FitzPeter, 293; dismissal of, 251; on crusade, 241, 262; family of, 144, 262; social standing of, 84
Godric of Finchale, hermit, 169-70; friend of Ranulf Flambard, 65; protected by Thurstan of York, 108; and Ailred of Rievaulx, 166; and eremitic life, 171-2
Godwin, invents cult of his nephew William of Norwich, 154-5
Gregory VII, pope, 14-15, 43
Gregory IX, 329, 330, 358
Grim, Edward, companion of Becket, 209
Grosseteste, Robert, bishop of Lincoln, 381-4; personality, 335; at Oxford, 406; academic influence of, 407; and science, 274; as bishop, 359; as politician, 358; friend of Adam Marsh, 384-5; and Matthew Paris, 387, 389; and Walter Cantelupe, 403; friend of Simon de Montfort, 373
Guerin of Corbeil, heretic, 320
Gundulf, bishop of Rochester, 32-4; death of, 101
Guthlac, St., 109
Guy of Etampes, 91
Guy of Lusignan, king of Jerusalem, 241
Guy of Lusignan, half-brother of Henry III, 342, 399
Guy, son of Simon de Montfort, 410

Hadrian I, pope, 158
Hadrian IV, pope, formerly Nicholas Brakespeare, 157-9; as pope, 179; as patron, 228; at curia, 119-20
Haimo, royal steward, 62
Harald Hadrada, king of Norway, 6
Harding, Stephen, 97-100
Harold II, 4-6, 11
Harthacnut, 335
Hemming of Worcester, his Cartulary, 23
Henry I, 69-84; as king, 45, 147, 148, 177, 300; patronage of, 46, 47, 120; early career of, 48, 299, 363; and death of William II, 69; accession, 32, 33, 50, 64; marriage of, 12, 53; and Anselm, 58-9; and justice, 63; laws of, 322; and Ranulf Flambard, 64-5; and Robert Curthose, 67; and Adela of Blois, 68; and Robert of Meulan, 84-6; and Roger of Salisbury, 88-93; and Geoffrey de Clinton, 100-1; and Henry of Blois, 140; and David I, 133; and Beaumont twins, 136, 138; and Stephen of Blois, 122; and succession, 102; and Thurstan of York, 107-8; death of, 119, 122, 220; family of, 128, 129, 182; and Henry II, 184; reputation of, 113
Henry II, 180-94; early career of, 121, 126, 127, 128, 130, 132-3, 134, 137, 146-7, 152, 165; as king, 133, 159, 178, 211-15, 219-20, 236-7, 243, 244, 245-7, 292; and church, 175-8, 198-201, 232, 238-9; and war, 6, 257, 301; and crusade, 251;

and rebellion, 219-20, 250; and Becket, 61, 204-10, 217; and justice, 63; as patron, 269-70; and taxation, 227; and Henry I, 70, 82; and law, 394; and Becket, 265, 298; and Robert of Leicester, 138-40; and William Marshal, 286, 287; and Ranulf of Chester, 334; and Henry of Blois, 143; and Samson of Bury, 284; and Hugh of Avalon, 270; and Gilbert of Sempringham, 115; and Christina of Markyate, 171; and Ireland, 158, 229-30; and London, 272; and Jews, 235; and building, 222-3, 233; and loyalty, 224; and wife, 195-7; and mistresses, 218-19; family of, 195, 223, 225, 226, 248, 298-9; his horoscope, 117-18; burial of, 196, 311; character of, 112, 276, 277, 280, 300
Henry III, 335-47; inheritance of, 187; Minority of, 286, 289-91, 308, 317-19, 322-3, 332, 347-8, 351, 352, 354, 401; coronation, 328, 356; as king, 302, 325, 328-31, 334, 392, 397; marriage, 299, 378-9; and Westminster Abbey, 386, 396; and Sicilian Business, 403; and family, 399-400; and Richard of Cornwall, 361, 363-7; and Grosseteste, 381; and Simon de Montfort, 369-78; and the Jews, 404; and Matthew Paris, 387, 389; and Adam Marsh, 386; and cult of Edmund Rich, 359; and nepotism, 399, 405-6; and family, 197, 310-11, 392, 393; and Baronial Wars, 402-3; imprisonment of, 254; and reputation of Richard I, 248; outlook of, 353-4; reputation of, 357; pet elephant, 390
Henry I, king of France, 3
Henry V, emperor and king of Germany, 79, 128
Henry VI, emperor and king of Germany, 196, 254, 255
Henry, the Young King, son of Henry II, 225-6; coronation of, 188, 201, 208, 211, 216; as regent, 213; and William Marshal, 286, 287; opposes Richard of Dover, 232; rebels, 189, 191; death, 187, 191
Henry of Almaine, 410-11; on crusade, 367
Henry of Blois, bishop of Winchester, 140-4; and Henry I, 68; and Stephen, 123-5; and Nigel of Ely, 178; rebuked by Brian FitzCount, 147-8; and civil war, 131-2, 135; and legateship, 125; rivalry with Archbishop Theobald, 174-5; nepotist, 242; as politician, 267; family of, 160-1
Henry of Bracton, 393-5
Henry of Huntingdon, chronicler, 118-19; on William II, 52; on Henry I, 69, 83, 84; damning verdict on William of Corbeil, 106; on Stephen's accession, 123; and Geoffrey of Monmouth, 153, 154
Henry, son of Simon de Montfort, 373
Henry, earl of Northumberland, son of David I of Scots, 134, 163
Henry of Warwick, Anglo-Norman baron, 78
Herbert of Bosham, 221-2; describes Henry II, 192
Hereward the Wake, 29-31; rebellion of, 7
Herfast, bishop of East Anglia, 24
Herleve, mother of William I, 1, 25
Herluin, founder of Bec, 25
Hodierna, Richard I's wetnurse, 248
Honorius II, pope, 108
Honorius III, 161, 323, 348, 355
Hugh of Avalon, bishop of Lincoln, 269-70; as bishop, 238, 244; and Rosamund Clifford, 218; and Henry II, 193

Hugh of Avranches, earl of Chester, 44-5
Hugh of Avranches, grammarian, tutor of Henry III, 338
Hugh of Buckland, sheriff, 91
Hugh the Chanter, of York, 35
Hugh III of Le Puiset, French gangster, 242
Hugh of Lincoln and blood-libel against Jews, 155
Hugh IX, count of Lusignan, 303, 310
Hugh X, count of Lusignan, 310-11; 342
Hugh of Nonant, bishop of Coventry, propagandist, 260-1
Hugh, earl of Shrewsbury, 86-7
Huitdeniers, Osbert, London merchant, 203

Innocent II, pope, 142, 160
Innocent III, pope, 265, 295, 307, 319-20, 321, 323, 324, 326, 347, 359
Innocent IV, pope, 383, 398, 405
Isabella of Angoulême, second wife of King John, 310-11; marriage, 301, 303; trusts Peter des Roches, 328; family of, 342, 399
Isabella, daughter of Richard of Clare, 287
Isabella, first wife of Richard of Cornwall, 364
Isabella of Gloucester, first wife of King John, 299; marries Hubert de Burgh as her third husband, 350
Isabel of Vermandois, wife of Robert of Meulan, 85
Ivo, bishop of Chartres, 67

James II, 125
James of St. George, castle-builder, 234
Joan, queen of Scotland, 360
Jocelin of Brakelond, monk and chronicler, 284-5; and Samson of Bury, 281-4
Jocelyn, bishop of Bath, 360
John, 296 309, early career, 243, 276, 258 260 264, 270, 283, 288, 311-13, 333, 363, 364; as king, 185, 196, 256, 264, 266, 268, 283, 325-8, 339, 349-50, 354; marriage, 310; household of, 349; and the church, 255, 320-2, 323-4, 355; loses lands, 341; and Richard I, 252, 254, 255, 258; and Hubert Walter, 262; and Geoffrey of York, 224; and Geoffrey Fitzpeter, 294-6; and Gerald of Wales, 279-80; and Hugh of Avalon, 270; and William Marshal, 286, 288-9; and Falkes de Bréauté, 318; and national assemblies, 375; plots against, 368; and Ireland, 187, 188; inheritance of, 187; opponents of, 313-17; and Arthur of Brittany, 309-310; failure of, 249; death and burial, 22, 347; reputation of, 332, 357; vindictiveness of, 312-13; friends of, 326; sexual appetite of, 76; family of, 361
John, son of Edward I, 309
John of Canterbury, bishop of Poitiers, 176
John of Ford, biographer of Wulfric of Haselbury, 155-6
John of Gloucester, master mason, 396-7
John of Pagham, bishop of Worcester, 176
John of Salisbury, 178-80; pupil of Robert Pullen, 119; at papal curia, 158; and Odo of battle, 273; his Policraticus, 137; in Theobald's household, 176; and slanderous story about Roger of York, 217-18; at Becket's murder, 209
John of Warenne, earl of Surrey, 36-7
John of Worcester, chronicler, 22; illustrations of Henry I from his chronicle, 72-3
Judith, wife of Earl Waltheof, 20

Kilwardby, Robert, archbishop of Canterbury, 409

Lanfranc, archbishop of Canterbury, 12-19; at Bec, 174; serves William I, 8; and Wulfstan of Worcester, 21, 22; rebukes Herfast of East Anglia, 31; and Gundulf of Rochester, 32; and Penenden Heath inquest, 9, 23, 27; and claims of York, 34-5; supports Waltheof, 20; and trial of bishop of Durham, 43, 51, 200; and William II, 48; and Anselm, 55; as patron, 94; as administrator, 240
Langton, Stephen, archbishop of Canterbury, 319-24; as an academic, 380; and John, 307; in exile, 312, 316; and reform, 359; as archbishop, 241, 360; suspended, 328; and papal legates, 348, 351, 356; as politician, 267, 315; death of, 352
Le Breton, Richard, assassin of Becket, 209
Le Frison, Robert, count of Flanders, 29, 159
Leopold, duke of Austria, 254
Llewelyn, prince of North Wales, 302, 330
Lombard, Peter, theologian, 204, 221, 379-80, 383
Longchamp, William, chancellor and bishop of Ely, 259-61; as chancellor, 243, 253, 264, 267, 270, 272, 288, 299; household of, 222; and Ralph Diceto, 276
Longespee, William, 398-9
Losinga, Herbert, bishop of Thetford/Norwich, 38, 63
Losinga, Robert, bishop of Hereford, 39-40; and the abacus, 91, 117
Lothar of Supplinberg, king of Germany, 128
Louis VI 'the Fat', king of France, 76, 85, 102
Louis VII, king of France, 133, 189, 190, 191, 192-5, 197, 208, 225, 226, 252
Louis VIII, king of France, 22, 289, 290, 303, 308, 315, 331, 332, 334, 347, 350
Louis IX, king of France, 329, 335, 198, 340, 369, 372, 375, 390, 399, 409
Lucius II, pope, 161

Mabel of Bellême, 37; brutal murder of, 87
Malcolm III Canmore, king of Scots, 7, 11, 75, 133, 135
Malcolm IV, king of Scots, 170
Maminot, Gilbert, bishop of Lisieux, royal physician and astrologer, 40
Mansel, John, 395-6; and Matthew Paris, 387
Map, Walter, 292-3; on Gilbert Foliot, 201, on Henry II, 190, 194; as archdeacon, 379
Margaret, St., queen of Scots, 11, 75, 133
Marie, countess of Champagne, daughter of Eleanor of Aquitaine, 197
Marsh, Adam, Franciscan, 384-6; friend of Simon de Montfort, 373; of Grosseteste, 383; praises Thomas Docking, 406
Marsh, Richard, bishop of Durham, 384
Marshal, Gilbert, earl of Pembroke, 229, 363
Marshal, John, 126, 286-7
Marshal, Richard, earl of Pembroke, 330, 341
Marshal, William, earl of Pembroke, 285-92; career, 221; played 'knights' with King Stephen, 126; loyalty of, 160, 349; and Henry II, 193; and Young King, 226; and John, 300, 304; as regent, 322, 333-4, 336, 347, 350; death, 355
Marshal the younger, William, earl of Pembroke, 370
Mary I, 298

Masca, Pandulf, papal legate, 354-7; in England, 350; suspends Langton, 322; and Henry III, 290; withdraws from England, 351

Matthew of Bristol, tutor to Henry II, 183

Matilda, Empress, 127-33; birth, 75; a bluestocking, 134; and succession, 76, 82, 92-3, 103, 106; as regent, 213; marriages, 79, 82, 90; and civil war, 104-5, 136, 142, 146, 147-50, 177, 183, 219; and King Stephen, 122-7; supported by David I, 134; advice to Henry II, 186; family of, 182

Matilda of Flanders, wife of William I, 3, 37, 67

Matilda/Edith, wife of Henry I, 12, 75, 90, 91, 102, 128, 133

Matilda of Boulogne, wife of King Stephen, 134-5; marriage, 122; rallies royalists, 124, 131-2; and civil war, 136

Matilda of Briouze, 312-13

Matilda of Ramsbury, mistress of Roger of Salisbury, 89

Maurice, royal chancellor and bishop of London, 31-2; and Ranulf Flambard, 61, 64; crowns Henry I, 74

Maurice, castle architect, 232-4

Melisende, queen of Jerusalem, 128, 129, 228

Mercadier, mercenary, 160, 196

Miles of Gloucester, 148-9; supports Matilda, 131; related to Gilbert Foliot, 198

Morkere, earl of Northumbria, 6, 30

Mowbray, William, bribes John, 305

Murdac, Henry, archbishop of York, 161-3; and York election, 161, 242

Nennius, British historian, 152

Nest, daughter of Rhys ap Tewdwr, mistress of Henry I, 76, 278

Nicholas, papal legate, 322, 355

Nigel, royal treasurer and bishop of Ely, 177-8; education of, 91; and nepotism, 93; defends Devizes against Stephen, 94; supports Matilda, 131; and Ranulf Glanvill, 235; retirement of, 212; and Exchequer privileges, 139; family of, 244

O'Connor, Rory, king of Connaught, 229-30

Odelerius, father of Orderic Vitalis, 37, 109

Odo, abbot of Battle, 272-3

Odo of Bayeux, 23-5; as bishop, 3; serves William I, 18; disloyalty of, 8, 17; and Robert of Mortain, 25-6; as viceroy, 28; as patron, 34, 41, 45, 46, 61; and Bayeux Tapestry, 4-5; at Penenden Heath inquest, 9, 16; opposes William II, 37, 26, 43, 48; as a royal justice, 63

Odo, prior of Canterbury, 232

Oger the Breton, did well out of the Conquest, 30

Osmund, chancellor and bishop of Salisbury, 40-1; and Ranulf Flambard, 64

Otto IV, king of Germany, 197

Otto, papal legate, 359

Ottobuono, papal legate, 405

Paris, Matthew, chronicler, 387-90; well-connected informants of, 353, 363; and nationalism, 332, 353; translator, 167; on John, 296; and Henry III, 339, 340, 346; on Geoffrey FitzPeter, 293; on William Marshal, 289; on Hubert Walter, 262; on Elias of Dereham, 360; and Edmund Rich, 358; on Peter des Roches' crusade, 329; on Grosseteste, 382; on Pandulf, 357; criticism of

Boniface of Savoy, 406; on John Mansel, 395; constructs myths, 399; on Peter des Rivaux, 391; critical of Peter of Savoy, 392; and Falkes de Bréauté, 318

Paschal II, pope, 58, 85, 107, 157

Passelew, Robert, royal justice, 330

Patteshull, Martin, royal justice, 394

Paulinus, St., shrine of at Rochester, 33

Pecham, John, archbishop of Canterbury, 410

Pedro Alfonso, Henry I's physician, 83, 117

Peter of Blois, 276-8; as archdeacon, 379; on Henry II, 190, 194

Peter of Savoy, uncle of Henry III's wife, 392-3; opposes Henry III, 345; at court, 342; and nepotism, 378; and Lusignans, 400

Philip I 'the Fat', king of France, 11, 49

Philip II, king of France, 190, 191, 196, 226, 236, 250, 253, 254, 255, 256, 258, 274, 288, 300, 303, 304, 309, 310, 313, 332, 333, 349

Philip III, king of France, 410

Philip of Eye, royal treasurer, 366

Philip of Alsace, count of Flanders, 189, 225

Plantagenet, Geoffrey, count of Anjou, father of Henry II, 76, 82, 92, 123, 125, 129-32, 182, 195

Pullen, Robert, 119-20; at papal curia, 157; reputation of, 179

Ralegh, William, royal justice, 393, 394

Ralph, bishop of Bethlehem, 228-9

Ralph, abbot of Coggeshall, chronicler, 331-2; verdict on John, 298; on murder of Arthur of Brittany, 349

Ralph of Laon, 177

Ralph the Timid, earl of Hereford, 3

Ralph IV of Tosny, 21

Ranulf I, earl of Chester, 146

Ranulf II, earl of Chester, 146-7; arrest by Stephen, 126, 132; treaty with Robert of Leicester, 126, 138

Ranulf III, earl of Chester, 333-5; and John, 304; and Hubert de Burgh, 351; and Minority, 289; patron of Simon de Montfort, 370

Raynald of Châtillon, 278

Raymond of Poitiers, prince of Antioch, 195

Regenbald, chancellor, 19-20; leaves office, 31

Reginald of Coldingham, biographer of Godric of Finchale, 166, 169

Reginald, earl of Cornwall, bastard of Henry I, 131, 364

Rich of Abingdon, Edmund, archbishop of Canterbury, 357-60; as archbishop, 360

Richard I, 248-59; and succession, 196, 299; and Aquitaine, 181, 187, 196, 225, 226; rebels against Henry II, 189, 191, 224; accession of, 83, 187, 237, 243; as king, 185, 194, 196, 224, 244, 264, 271, 325-6, 331, 354; and church, 240; and John, 299-301; and William Marshal, 286, 287-8, 292; and Hubert Walter, 262; and Hugh of Avalon, 270; rebellions against, 283; and crusade, 241, 259, 274; homage to Henry VI, 307; ransom of, 261, 271; reputation of, 332; death and burial of, 196, 270, 311; and family, 309

Richard, son of William I, 50, 69, 71

Richard of Anstey, petitioner to Henry II, 186

Richard, bishop of Bayeux, 34

Richard of Clare, lord of Strigoul, 229-30

Richard, earl of Cornwall, 361-7; marriages, 378; and Henry III, 340, 341, 343, 346; on crusade, 398, 399; as king of the Romans, 395; and Henry of Bracton, 393; and Matthew Paris, 387; founds Hailes Abbey, 386; and cult of Edmund Rich, 359; as arbitor, 411; imprisonment of, 375; and Jews, 404; family of, 410

Richard of Devizes, chronicler, on Ranulf Flambard, 237; verdict on John, 299

Richard of Dover, archbishop of Canterbury, 231-2; as archbishop, 217, 273; household of, 277

Richard, first abbot of Fountains, 116-17

Richard of Ilchester, bishop of Winchester, 198, 214, 244, 273

Richildis of Flanders, 28-9

Ridel, Geoffrey, bishop of Ely, 214

Rigaud, Eudes, archbishop of Rouen, 369

Robert of Bellême, earl of Shrewsbury, 87-8, 76, 78; life imprisonment of, 77; violent nature of, 101

Robert of Cricklade, writer, 176

Robert Curthose, duke of Normandy, 66-7; and disloyalty to William I, 8, 24, 26, 47-8; and Edgar Atheling, 11-12; and succession, 129; opposes William II, 36, 43, 46, 57, 87; supports William II, 48; on crusade, 25, 48, 50; marriage of, 53; and Ranulf Flambard, 64; and Henry I, 70-1, 74, 76-8, 86, 87; imprisonment of, 77, 82, 89-90, 92, 103, 254; failure of, 249; character of, 225

Robert the Devil, duke of Normandy, 1

Robert, earl of Gloucester, bastard of Henry I, 103-5; education of, 48; and his legacy, 71, 80; and the succession, 82, 129; gaoler of Robert Curthose, 92; audits Exchequer, 92; supports Empress Matilda, 93, 130-7; and Stephen, 123-6; and civil war, 132, 135, 136, 146, 148, 159, and literature, 113, 153

Robert, earl of Leicester, 137-40; and his brother, 136-7; and Henry I, 74, 82; treaty with Ranulf of Chester, 147; as justiciar, 84, 178, 188, 211-13; education of, 85; relations with Robert of Gloucester, 104-5; friend of Ailred of Rievaulx, 165

Roibert of Melun, bishop of Hereford, 200

Robert, lord of Meulan, 84-7; adviser to William II, 38; minister of Henry I, 74, 78; own exchequer, 247; family of, 136, 137

Robert of Mortain, 25-6, loyalty to William I, 8, in Bayeux Tapestry, 24; and Cornwall, 364

Robert, abbot of St. Stephen's, Caen, 268, 271

Robert of Torigni, chronicler, 119

Robin Hood, 31

Roger II, king of Sicily, 220, 228

Roger of Beaumont, Norman magnate, 8, 84

Roger, chancellor, son of Roger of Salisbury, 93-4

Roger, earl of Hereford, rebel, 20

Roger of Howden, chronicler, 274-5; on taxes, 264; on Richard I's venality, 251; attacks Geoffrey of Brittany, 226

Roger of Markyate, hermit, 171-2

Roger of Montgomery, earl of Shrewsbury, 37-8; family of, 87; as patron, 109

Roger of Pitres, 148

Roger of Pont l'Eveque, archbishop of York, 215-18; in Theobald's household, 176; and Becket, 204, 207, 208, 210; crowns Young King, 225

Roger, bishop of Salisbury, 88-94; rise of; 47, 73; compared with Ranulf Flambard, 62; and Henry of Blois, 144; as Henry I's justiciar, 79-80, 85,

189, 211, 213; recognises Stephen, 122, 123; fall of, 123-4, 136, 138, 141, 177; as patron, 105; reputation of, 246-7; family of, 177

Roger, earl of Warwick, 100

Roger of Wendover, chronicler, 357; influenced by Henry of Huntingdon, 119; and Magna Carta, 322; and Peter des Roches, 325; and Falkes de Bréauté, 318; and Matthew Paris, 388

Rollo, count of Normandy, 165

Saladin, sultan of Egypt and Damascus, 251, 253-4, 258, 278

Samson, abbot of Bury St. Edmund's, 281-4; as abbot, 285; as papal judge-delegate, 270

Samson, bishop of Worcester, 46-7; family of, 34

Sanchia of Provence, second wife of Richard of Cornwall, 364

Saxo Grammaticus, Danish historian, 157

Scotus, Marianus, chronologist, 39

Segrave, Stephen, 330

Simeon of Durham, chronicler, 106-7; on Ranulf Flambard, 66

Simon, son of Simon de Montfort, 410

Siward, earl of Northumbria, 20

Stephen, count of Blois, father of king Stephen, 67-8, 122, 140

Stephen, 120-7; family of, 67, 160, 242; and Henry I, 68, 74; and succession, 82, 148, 220; coronation of, 106; as king, 162, 211; and church, 174-5, 295; and wife, 134-5; and Roger of Salisbury, 88, 93-4; and civil war, 103-4, 112, 129-33, 146-8, 150-1, 152, 159-60, 199, 219, 244; and David I, 134; and Waleran of Meulan, 136, 137; and Robert of Leicester, 138; and Henry of Blois, 141-3; imprisonment of, 254; plays 'knights' with William Marshal, 286, 347; and Henry II, 182-4; failure of, 249, and Geoffrey of Monmouth, 153; compared with John, 298

Stigand, archbishop of Canterbury, 13, 31, 46, 205

Stock, Simon, leader of Carmelites, 397-8

Stuteville, Nicholas, 304

Suger, abbot of St. Denis, 52, 67, 68, 160, 204

Sweyn Esthrithson, king of Denmark, 30

Swift, Jonathan, 278

Swinfield, Richard, bishop of Hereford, 410

Theobald of Bec, archbishop of Canterbury, 174-7; as archbishop, 174, 136, 405; and civil war, 159; relations with papacy, 125, 158; as patron, 215-16, 231-2; and Becket, 188, 203-5, 206; covers up sex scandal, 217; and Henry of Huntingdon, 119; and Henry of Blois, 141, 143; contacts of, 179

Theobald IV, count of Blois, brother of King Stephen, 68, 82, 123

Theobald of Etampes, early teacher at Oxford, 120

Thomas of Bayeux, archbishop of York, 34-6; and Bayeux training, 25; relatives of, 47; misses Henry I's coronation

Thomas of Monmouth, manager of cult of William of Norwich, 155

Thomas II, archbishop of York, 25, 47, 85

Thorkell of Arden, 8

Thurstan, archbishop of York, 107-8; and Bayeux background, 25; relations with Canterbury, 85; patron of Christina of Markyate, 171; and Ailred of Rievaulx, 163-4; patron of Henry Murdac, 161; sponsor of Cistercians, 116

Tirel of Poix, Walter, 68-9; kills William II, 50
Tostig, earl of Northumbria, 6
Turbe, William, bishop of Norwich, 155
Turchil, author of treatise on the abacus, 91
Tweng, Robert, dissident, 396

Urban II, pope, 25, 56, 112
Urban III, pope, 241
Urraca, queen of Castile, 82, 128
Uhtred, earl of Northumbria, 21

Vacarius, canon lawyer, 176, 216
Victor IV, anti-pope, 175
Vitalis, Orderic, chronicler, 108-10; on William
    FitzOsbern, 28; flatters Roger of Montgomery,
    37; on William II, 50-1, 52, 69; on Ranulf
    Flambard, 62; on Adela of Blois, 68; and 'men
    raised from the dust', 78, 100; on Henry I, 80;
    records Robert of Meulan's political testament,
    86
Von Dassel, Rainald, archbishop of Cologne, 205

Wace, writer of romances, 28, 37
Walcher, prior of Malvern, author of astronomical
    treatises, 117
Waldef, monk and son of David I of Scots, 163-4
Waleran, lord of Meulan, 135-7; and Henry I, 74,
    82; imprisoned by Henry I, 78; education of, 85;
    and brother, 137-8; close adviser of Stephen, 93,
    123-4; rivalry with Robert of Gloucester, 104;
    and Archbishop Theobald, 174; and literature,
    153
Walkelin, archdeacon of Suffolk, 159
Walkelin, bishop of Winchester, 38-9; and William
    II, 51, 62
Walsingham of St. Alban's, Thomas, chronicler, 390
Walter of Albano, papal legate, 56
Walter of Coutances, archbishop of Rouen, as
    viceroy, 253, 254, 260, 276
Walter of Coutances, archdeacon of Oxford, 152
Walter, Hubert, king's justiciar and archbishop of
    Canterbury, 261-8; as justiciar, 214, 253, 254,
    259, 270, 293, 294; as chancellor, 288; as
    archbishop, 242; on crusade, 237, 241; opposes
    Gerald of Wales, 279; and Ralph Diceto, 276;
    and Peter of Blois, 277; and Richard I, 254; and
    John, 300, 303; opposition to, 271; death of, 320;
    vestments of, 326; as patron, 360; support for
    Arthur of Brittany, 309; and Geoffrey of York,
    224; family of, 235; and record keeping, 295
Walter, bishop of Rochester, brother of Archbishop
    Theobald, 176
Waltheof, earl of Huntingdon, 20-1; execution of,
    8; cult of, 109; daughter of, 133
Warenne, William, 36-7; elopes with Isabel of
    Vermandois, 85; marriage, 85-6
Watton, nun of, 167-9; scandal of, 115, 166
William I, 1-11; as duke of Normandy, 27, 37; and
    inheritance, 103; pacifies England, 20, 28-9, 30,
    36-8; and Lanfranc, 12-15, 17-18; and church,
    34-5; and church reform, 27; and Domesday
    Book, 41-3; as king, 19, 26-7, 38, 41, 56, 61, 63,
    69, 184, 194; death of, 43, 45, 48; and brothers,
    23-6; in Bayeux Tapestry, 24; relatives of, 44, 66,
    70, 82, 140, 242, 347; laws of, 81; employs
    Robert of Meulan, 84; as patron, 32, 87; and
    astrology, 39-40; and castles, 233; and Tower of
    London, 33

William II, 47-54; as king, 32, 43-6, 56, 75, 107; and
    Domesday Book, 41; rebellions against, 17, 24-5,
    26, 36; and Anselm, 55-8; and Ranulf Flambard
    61-4; and Robert Curthose, 12, 66-7; friendship
    with Walter Tirel, 69; and Henry I, 70-1, 74;
    and Robert of Meulan, 84-5; and Tower of
    London, 34; death of, 32; reputation of, 160
William I, king of Sicily, 220
William II, king of Sicily, 277
William the Lion, king of Scots, 189, 236, 301, 315
William, brother of Henry II, 192
William X, duke of Aquitaine, 194
William Atheling, son of Henry I, 102-3; birth, 75;
    baptism, 33; and succession, 76, 81-2; drowning
    of, 82, 92, 128-9
William of Boulogne, son of King Stephen, 211,
    235-6
William of Briouze, 311-12; and murder of Arthur
    of Brittany, 310; persecuted by John, 304
William of Canterbury, architect, 231
William Clito, son of Robert Curthose, 67, 76, 82,
    100, 129, 136
William of Corbeil, archbishop of Canterbury,
    105-6; in household of Ranulf Flambard, 65;
    crowns Stephen, 123
William of Ely, Exchequer official, 391
William, prior of the Holy Sepulchre, archbishop
    of Tyre, 228
William of Jumièges, Norman chronicler, 4
William Longsword, earl of Salisbury, bastard of
    Henry II, 219, 305, 398
William of Malmesbury, chronicler, 110-13;
    translates biography of Wulfstan of Worcester,
    22; on contemporaries, 40; on William I, 28;
    historian of the English, 390; on Samson of
    Worcester, 47; on William II, 52-3, 69; on Ranulf
    Flambard, 61; on Henry I, 70-1, 76; and Queen
    Matilda, 75; on vicious queens, 82; on Robert of
    Meulan, 86; on Roger of Salisbury, 89; and
    Robert of Gloucester, 103, 105; and Geoffrey of
    Monmouth, 153
William of Mortain, son of Robert of Mortain, 78;
    blinded and imprisoned by his first cousin,
    Henry I, 77
William of Newburgh, chronicler, 119, 154, 244,
    268, 298
William of Norwich, St., 154-5
William of Poitiers, Norman chronicler, 4, 53, 111
William, first abbot of Rievaulx, 114
William of St. Calais, bishop of Durham, 41-4;
    Bayeux background of, 25; possible author of
    Domesday Book, 41-4; trial of, 17-18, 51; and
    Anselm, 56; as royal minister, 62; and Durham
    Priory, 65; death of, 38
William of Sens, architect, 230-1
William, bishop-elect of Valence, 342, 378, 392
William of Valence, 399-401; marriage of, 342; and
    Baronial Wars, 376
William of Ypres, mercenary, 159-60; loyalty of,
    124; evil reputation of, 104
Wulfric of Haselbury, hermit, 155-7; and eremitic
    life, 171-2; and Baldwin of Ford, 238
Wulfstan, bishop of Worcester, 21-3; as bishop, 47;
    cult of, 265
Wyclif, John, 384, 407
Wykes, Thomas, chronicler, 365, 403

Ykenai, mistress of Henry II, 219, 223